A PRACTITIONER'S GUIDE TO STOCHASTIC FRONTIER ANALYSIS USING STATA

A Practitioner's Guide to Stochastic Frontier Analysis Using Stata provides practitioners in academia and industry with a step-by-step guide on how to conduct efficiency analysis using the stochastic frontier approach. The authors explain in detail how to estimate production, cost, and profit efficiency and introduce the basic theory of each model in an accessible way, using empirical examples that demonstrate the interpretation and application of models. This book also provides computer code, allowing users to apply the models in their own work, and incorporates the most recent stochastic frontier models developed in academic literature. Such recent developments include models of heteroscedasticity and exogenous determinants of inefficiency, scaling models, panel models with time-varying inefficiency, growth models, and panel models that separate firm effects and persistent and transient inefficiency. Immensely helpful to applied researchers, this book bridges the chasm between theory and practice, expanding the range of applications in which production frontier analysis may be implemented.

Subal C. Kumbhakar is a distinguished research professor at the State University of New York at Binghamton. He is coeditor of *Empirical Economics* and guest editor of special issues of the *Journal of Econometrics, Empirical Economics*, the *Journal of Productivity Analysis*, and the *Indian Economic Review*. He is associate editor and editorial board member of *Technological Forecasting and Social Change: An International Journal*, the *Journal of Productivity Analysis*, the *International Journal of Business and Economics*, and *Macroeconomics and Finance in Emerging Market Economies*. He is also the coauthor of *Stochastic Frontier Analysis* (Cambridge University Press, 2000).

Hung-Jen Wang is professor of economics at the National Taiwan University. He has published research papers in the *Journal of Econometrics*, the *Journal of Business and Economic Statistics, Econometric Review, Economic Inquiry*, the *Journal of Productivity Analysis*, and *Economics Letters*. He was a coeditor of *Pacific Economic Review* and is currently associate editor of *Empirical Economics* and the *Journal of Productivity Analysis*.

Alan P. Horncastle is a Partner at Oxera Consulting LLP. He has been a professional economist for more than twenty years and leads Oxera's work on performance assessment. He has published papers in the *Journal of the Operational Research Society*, the *Journal of Regulatory Economics*, the *Competition Law Journal*, and *Utilities Policy* and has contributed chapters to *Liberalization of the Postal and Delivery Sector* and *Emerging Issues in Competition, Collusion and Regulation of Network Industries*.

A Practitioner's Guide to Stochastic Frontier Analysis Using Stata

SUBAL C. KUMBHAKAR
Binghamton University, NY

HUNG-JEN WANG
National Taiwan University

ALAN P. HORNCASTLE
Oxera Consulting LLP, Oxford, UK

CAMBRIDGE
UNIVERSITY PRESS

CAMBRIDGE
UNIVERSITY PRESS

32 Avenue of the Americas, New York, NY 10013-2473, USA

Cambridge University Press is part of the University of Cambridge.

It furthers the University's mission by disseminating knowledge in the pursuit of education, learning, and research at the highest international levels of excellence.

www.cambridge.org
Information on this title: www.cambridge.org/9781107609464

First published 2015

A catalog record for this publication is available from the British Library.

Library of Congress Cataloging in Publication Data
Kumbhakar, Subal.
A practitioner's guide to stochastic frontier analysis using Stata / Subal C. Kumbhakar, Hung-Jen Wang, Alan P. Horncastle.
pages cm
ISBN 978-1-107-02951-4 (hardback)
1. Production (Economic theory) – Econometric models. 2. Stochastic analysis. 3. Econometrics. I. Title.
HB241.K847 2015
338.50285′555–dc23 2014023789

ISBN 978-1-107-02951-4 Hardback
ISBN 978-1-107-60946-4 Paperback

Additional resources for this publication at https://sites.google.com/site/sfbook2014/

To Damayanti Ghosh

SUBAL C. KUMBHAKAR

To Yi-Yi Chen

HUNG-JEN WANG

To Maria, Joan, and Victor

ALAN P. HORNCASTLE

Contents

Preface

This book deals with the estimation of productive efficiency using an econometric approach, which is popularly known as *stochastic frontier analysis.* The terminology relates to the fact that we are interested in the estimation of frontiers that envelop the data while maintaining the traditional econometric assumption of the presence of a random statistical noise. The frontiers we estimate are consistent with neoclassical microeconomic theory. Because, in reality, producers are not always efficient, the efficiency analysis can be viewed as an extension of the neoclassical theory. In this sense, the approach we consider in this book is based on sound neoclassical production theory and not purely an *ad hoc* empirical exercise.

Our primary goal in writing this book was to extend the everyday application of these tools beyond the expert practitioner or academic by making it relatively easy for the reader to carry out the complex computations necessary to both estimate and interpret these models. Our secondary goal was to ensure that the latest theoretical models can be implemented by practitioners, as many applications are limited by the software currently available.

As such, we aim at providing the reader with sufficient tools to apply many of the developed models to real data. In order to do this we have created a series of programs written for use in Stata, and they can be downloaded from the following website: https://sites.google.com/site/sfbook2014/. These commands are not part of the official Stata package, but instead are commands that we wrote ourselves in the form of Stata ado-files.

Thus, this book does not represent a comprehensive research monograph covering all areas of stochastic frontier models. Our focus is mostly on those models for which we have provided Stata codes and, as such, our list of references is limited to this purpose.

For a purely theoretical underpinning of stochastic frontier analysis the reader should consider first reading the book by Kumbhakar and Lovell (2000), *Stochastic Frontier Analysis* (Cambridge University Press). However, this is not essential as this book is intended to provide stand-alone reference materials for the reader to gain *both* a basic understanding of the theoretical underpinnings *and* a practical understanding of estimating production, profit, and cost efficiency.

As such, each chapter includes a theoretical introduction of the stochastic frontier model followed by worked examples of applying the theory to real data (examples include dairy farming, electricity generation, and airlines). These empirical examples are interwoven with the theory such that the reader can immediately apply the theory covered in the text. In order to follow these empirical examples, and thus to get the most benefit from this book, the reader must have Stata installed along with the programs provided with this book. Instructions on installation of the programs and explanations on the command syntax are provided in Appendix E, along with information on how to download the datasets and the empirical examples.

This book incorporates some of the most recent stochastic frontier models developed in the academic literature. Such recent developments include models of heteroscedasticity and exogenous determinants of inefficiency (Wang [2002]); scaling models (Wang and Schmidt [2002]); panel models with time-varying inefficiency (Kumbhakar [1990]); growth models (Kumbhakar and Wang [2005]); and the panel models of Greene (2005a), Wang and Ho (2010), Kumbhakar et al. (2014), and Chen et al. (2014). Other developments using semi- and nonparametric approaches are not included in this book.

We wish to express our gratitude to Knox Lovell, Peter Schmidt, Robin Sickles, Bill Greene, Leopold Simar, Mike Tsionas, Subhash Ray, and many others whose work and ideas have influenced our thinking in a major way. David Drukker of StataCorp was kind enough to provide comments on some chapters. We are thankful to him for this. We also thank Scott Parris, our ex-editor, and Karen Maloney, the current Senior Editor at Cambridge University Press, for their constant support. The excellent research assistance provided by Chun-Yen Wu is also gratefully acknowledged. We would also like to thank Oxera for its support to Alan. Last, but not least, we thank our family members, especially our wives (Damayanti Ghosh, Yi-Yi Chen, and Maria Horncastle), for their constant support and encouragement in finishing this project, which took several years.

Subal C. Kumbhakar, Hung-Jen Wang, and Alan P. Horncastle

PART I

GENERAL INFORMATION

1

Introduction

1.1 What This Book Is About

This is a book on stochastic frontier (SF) analysis, which uses econometric models to estimate production (or cost or profit) frontiers and efficiency relative to those frontiers. Production efficiency relates actual output to the maximum possible, and is defined as the ratio of the actual output to the maximum potential output. More generally, SF analysis can be applied to any problem where the observed outcome deviates from the potential outcome in one direction, that is, the observed outcome is either less or more than the potential outcome. In the context of production efficiency, the potential output, given inputs and technology, is the maximum possible output that defines the frontier and the actual output falls below the frontier due to technical inefficiency. For cost efficiency, the frontier is defined by the potential minimum cost, and the actual cost lies above the minimum frontier owing to inefficiency. Similarly, the profit frontier is defined in terms of the maximum possible profit and profit efficiency is defined as the ratio of actual to maximum possible profit (assuming that they are both positive or negative). Other examples include the observed wage offer being less than the potential maximum; the reported crime rate being less than the true crime because of underreporting; actual investment being less than the potential optimal because of borrowing constraints; and so on. The common denominator in all of these problems is that there is something called the potential maximum or minimum or optimal level, which defines the frontier. This frontier is unobserved. So the question is how to estimate the frontier function so that efficiency can be estimated. Another complicating factor is that the frontier is often viewed as stochastic and the problem is how to estimate efficiency relative to the stochastic frontier when we can estimate only the "deterministic" part of the frontier. This book deals with the issues related to estimating the stochastic frontier econometrically first, and then estimating efficiency relative to the stochastic frontier for each observation.

The best way to understand why this type of analysis is important is to consider the questions that the techniques introduced in this book can answer or, at least, help to answer. The list of questions below is somewhat long but, even then, it is far from exhaustive. Worldwide, efficiency improvement is often regarded as one of the most important goals behind many social and economic policies and reforms. Examples are numerous. For instance, opening up of markets to competition, the removal of trade barriers, and the privatization of state enterprises are all motivated, at least in part, by the potential for efficiency improvements. At a high level, many policies are well understood by economists, but when you consider the details and the specifics of individual industries within the economies, things are less clear.

For instance, how do we measure the improvement in efficiency? Does the efficiency come from the production side – producing more given the same input and technology – or the cost side – costing less to produce the same output? Which one is the appropriate metric? Why do some firms achieve greater efficiency gains than others? What are the determinants of the efficiency gain? Has privatization generally "worked" or is it the opening of the market to competition, rather than privatization per se, that has resulted in efficiency improvements? Has regulation or, for that matter, deregulation been successful? And, at an industry level, are some reforms more successful than others?

Even within a relatively competitive and/or mature industry, there may be public policy questions that could be considered to improve the operation of the market. For example, currently the U.K. government foregoes tax revenues via approved (or tax advantaged) employee share schemes, which are assumed to align employee and employer incentives and thus increase industry productivity and efficiency. But what is the evidence? That is, are companies with such schemes really more productive and efficient than those without such schemes?

Similar questions arise with respect to different forms of corporate ownership and the public-private interfaces within an economy. For instance, when we consider publicly owned corporations, public private partnerships, not-for-profit companies, family owned firms, private companies, or the recent influx of private equity investment, which forms of ownership turn out to be the most effective, and does this depend on the sector? Public-private partnership are frequently used in many parts of the world, but is such an approach really the most cost-effective route in all cases?

At a micro-level, within businesses, there are numerous critical questions that would benefit from the sort of analysis set out in this book. For example, a key strategic question may be whether or not a take-over or merger with a current competitor makes sense. Although there are multiple reasons for considering takeovers, one of the key questions to answer is whether it will result in cost efficiency improvements and/or cost savings through economies of scale and scope. A business may be interested in knowing whether a profit-sharing scheme would help boost employees' incentives and increase production efficiency. For these questions, the measure of efficiency and the effects of efficiency determinants are important.

Examples given here are in the context of production economics, which has traditionally been the main field of research for stochastic frontier analysis. However, recent development in the literature has found wider applications of the analysis in other fields of research in economics and finance. Examples include using the SF model to test the underpricing hypothesis of the initial public offerings and the convergence hypothesis of economic growth. The analysis is also applied to estimate the effects of search cost on observed wage rates, the impact of financing constraints on firms' capital investment, and wage discrimination in the labor market, to name just a few.

1.2 Who Should Read This Book?

The issues raised in the previous section represent some everyday questions that are asked by academics, policy makers, regulators, government advisors, companies, consulting firms, and the like. For them, this book provides practical guidelines to carry out the analysis and help them to answer the questions. Students of industrial organization, government policy, and other fields of economic and financial research will also find the modeling techniques introduced in the book useful.

The increasing demand of the SF analysis from academics and industry is evident from the increasing number of journal articles, conferences, and workshops on the associated topics. There are several journals (e.g., *Journal of Productivity Analysis, Journal of Econometrics, European Journal of Operational Research, Empirical Economics*) that publish efficiency-related papers (or more generally papers that use SF as a tool) on a regular basis. There are several well-established international conferences focusing on the development and applications of efficiency estimation, and they are also held on a regular basis. They include the North American Productivity Workshop, the European Workshop on Efficiency and Productivity Analysis, the Asia-Pacific Productivity Conference, the Helenic Efficiency and Productivity Workshop, and so on.

In terms of applied econometric modeling skills, some familiarity with Stata is assumed, although the reader is taken through the modeling examples step-by-step, so even a non-Stata user should be able to follow the examples.

Throughout the book, we provide Stata codes for estimating systems in both cross-sectional and panel models. We also provide Stata codes for many of the cross-sectional and panel (single equation) models that are not otherwise available. As such, users do not need to do any complex coding for estimating many of the models. The user can also practice running some of the models using the datasets and examples that are used in this book. Because the source codes (the Stata ado-files) are also provided, the more advanced Stata user can tailor the codes for their own models if further extensions are needed.

If the reader is not a Stata user and does not plan to use it, he or she can still benefit from reading the book. It is detailed enough so that one can understand the theory behind the models and follow the discussion of the results from various worked examples.

1.3 The Structure of This Book

Part I: General Information

This section of the book provides the general background material required before examining specific modeling of the subsequent chapters.

- **Chapter 1: Introduction**
  This chapter explains what this book is about, who would find this book of interest, and explains the structure of the rest of the book.
- **Chapter 2: Production, Distance, Cost, and Profit Functions**
  This chapter provides the reader with general background information on the production theory and terminology necessary to understand the remainder of the book. The aim is to provide the reader with a guide to the topics and reference materials for advanced discussions. This chapter is written in such a way that someone familiar with the production theory covered in intermediate microeconomics textbooks would understand the material.

Part II: Single Equation Approach with Cross-Sectional Data

- **Chapter 3: Estimation of Technical Efficiency in Production Frontier Models Using Cross-Sectional Data**

Many of the basic ideas in modeling and applying SF technique are explained in detail in this chapter. Some knowledge of statistics and econometrics is necessary to understand the technical details, although someone without such knowledge can still use, interpret and follow the practical examples. More specifically, this chapter introduces the estimation of a production frontier model as well as inefficiency and efficiency indexes using distribution-free and parametric approaches. For the parametric approach, models with various distributional assumptions including half-normal, truncated-normal, exponential, and so on are discussed and compared.

- **Chapter 4: Estimation of Technical Efficiency in Cost Frontier Models Using Cross-Sectional Data**
  This chapter extends the SF analysis from the production frontier to the cost frontier. It explains the different assumptions used in production and cost functions, and details the differences in the modeling, data requirements and the interpretation of results. Here the focus is on the technical inefficiency and assumes no allocative inefficiency (i.e., all the producers are assumed to be allocatively efficient). It shows how the technical inefficiency in a production frontier model is transmitted to the cost frontier model.
- **Chapter 5: Estimation of Technical Efficiency in Profit Frontier Models Using Cross-Sectional Data**
  This chapter discusses the relationship between production, cost, and profit functions. It also explains how technical inefficiency appears in the different models and explains how to interpret the models.

Part III: System Models with Cross-Sectional Data

- **Chapter 6: Estimation of Technical Efficiency in Cost Frontier Models Using Cost System Models with Cross-Sectional Data**
  This chapter introduces a cost system model that consists of the cost function and the cost share equations, derived from the first-order conditions of the cost minimization problem. It assumes that all the producers are allocatively efficient. The chapter also explains how different covariance structures of the error terms in the system can be used in estimating the model.
- **Chapter 7: Estimation of Technical Efficiency in Profit Frontier Models Using System Models with Cross-Sectional Data**
  This chapter introduces a profit system model that consists of the first-order conditions of profit maximization. An advantage of estimating a profit function using only the first-order conditions is that the profit variable is not directly used in the estimation. Because profit can be negative in real data and hence logarithms cannot be taken, this approach allows us to undertake the estimation using the Cobb-Douglas and/or translog functions without worrying about negative profit.

Part IV: The Primal System Approach

This section of the book examines the primal approach to SF modeling. The terminology "The Primal System Approach" might be confusing to readers because we are explicitly using the first-order conditions of cost minimization and profit maximization, which relate to prices. Here, by primal system approach, we refer to a system approach where the production function is used along with the first-order conditions from either cost minimization or profit maximization. Thus, we are separating the primal system approach from the single equation primal approach which is estimated without using any price information.

- **Chapter 8: Cost Minimization with Technical and Allocative Inefficiency: A Primal Approach**
  This chapter introduces allocative inefficiency and how it may be incorporated in a cost frontier model theoretically. Then it shows the difficulty in empirically estimating such a model. We then present the primal system approach, which estimates both technical and allocative inefficiency. These are introduced into the model via the first-order conditions of cost minimization.
- **Chapter 9: Profit Maximization with Technical and Allocative Inefficiency: A Primal Approach**
  This chapter extends ideas similar to the previous chapter to the case in which producers maximize profit and are allowed to be allocatively inefficient. We call this the primal profit system because we do not use the profit function in this analysis. Instead, we append allocative inefficiency in the first-order condition with respect to output to the cost system discussed in the previous chapter. The problem of using the profit function is that profit has to be positive which is not the case for many applications. The primal approach avoids this problem.

Part V: Single Equation Approach with Panel Data

- **Chapter 10: Single Equation Panel Model**
  This chapter explains the difference between panel data and cross-sectional data, and why the use of panel data may either help or complicate the estimation process. Then it shows how we may avoid such difficulties by adopting a certain modeling strategy. Estimation of some of the more recent formulations that separate time-varying technical inefficiency from fixed firm effects are also considered.
- **Chapter 11: Productivity and Profitability Decomposition**
  This examines how to estimate changes in productivity and profitability over time and decompose these changes into their constituent parts.

Part VI: Looking Ahead

- **Chapter 12: Looking Ahead**
  This chapter briefly sets out some of the topics that we have not covered in the the book.

Appendices

- **Appendix A: Deriving the Likelihood Functions of Single Equation Frontier Models**
  In this appendix, we derive the likelihood functions of the single equation frontier models.
- **Appendix B: Deriving the Efficiency Estimates**
  In this appendix, we derive the inefficiency index and the technical efficiency index.

- **Appendix C: Deriving the Confidence Intervals**
  In this appendix, we derive the confidence intervals for the inefficiency index and the technical efficiency index.
- **Appendix D: Bootstrapping Standard Errors of Marginal Effects on Inefficiency**
  This appendix shows an example of bootstrapping standard errors of variables' marginal effects on inefficiency.
- **Appendix E: Software**
  This appendix explains where to download dataset and Stata .do files used as empirical examples in the book. It also contains instructions on how to download and install the Stata commands written by authors of the book. Detailed explanations on the commands and the syntax are also provided in this appendix.

2

Production, Distance, Cost, and Profit Functions

2.1 Introduction

In Chapter 1, we introduced a series of questions that the tools discussed in this book are designed to help answer. In this chapter, we provide the reader with the necessary theoretical underpinnings in order to answer these questions and to understand the models that are developed in later chapters. This is important as it is necessary to understand which is the most appropriate tool to use in which circumstance and what the limitations are of the different approaches.

In some of the following sections the text is fairly technical, but these sections are useful as a general reference for the practitioner when modeling specific issues. For example, Section 2.5 on the functional forms of the production function provides the required formulae for some of the key economic issues discussed in many chapters.

The study of the production, cost, and profit functions has a long history and the practical applications of modeling these functions are extensive. In line with the questions introduced in Chapter 1, a summary of the major objectives for studying these functions may include the following:

(i) If a firm were to expand its operations by increasing its inputs by 10 percent, how much would output increase by? How much lower would its unit costs be (and thus how much lower could it reduce its prices by or increase its margins)?
(ii) If a firm were to invest in new IT equipment, how many fewer manual employees would be needed to produce the same level of output? How many more IT personnel would be needed?
(iii) Can we consider the use of certain inputs independently of others?
(iv) Compared to last year, how much more output can be produced for a given level of inputs?
(v) Compared to industry best practice, for a given input level, how much more output can an organization produce compared to its current output level?

From a theoretical perspective, these questions boil down to considering (i) scale economies, (ii) substitutability/complementarity of inputs, (iii) separability of inputs, (iv) technical change, and (v) technical efficiency. Economists are, in general, interested in examining some or all of these economic effects, whereas everyone can benefit from the insights that such studies can shed light on.

In what follows, we first consider the production function. We discuss measurements of the economic effects discussed here and also introduce a number of alternative functional forms that can be used for estimation purposes. We then consider situations in which we have multiple inputs and outputs. We finish the chapter by considering allocative efficiency and expenditure/finance constrained models (in which presence of constraints is manifested in the one-sided error term).

2.2 The Production Function and Technical Efficiency

All production processes represent a transformation of inputs (for example, labor, capital, and raw material) into outputs (which can be either in physical units or services). A production function simply describes this transformation relationship – a "black box" – which converts inputs into outputs. For example, if we consider the simple case of one input and one output, the production function shows the output level that can be produced for a given production technology and a given level of input. We will describe such an output level as the maximum output in the sense that the production technology is used at its full potential. By changing the input level, one can trace the graph of the production function relating the output with various input levels. That is, if we were to plot the maximum possible outputs for different levels of input, the line so produced would represent the firm's production function. Note that it is a technological relationship and does not say whether the input used or the output produced maximizes profit or minimizes cost. Once a particular behavior is assumed, it is possible to determine the optimal level of input and output consistent with profit maximization, cost minimization, or other economic behavior.

In order to examine the economic effects discussed here, we need a more formal definition of a production function. A *production function* is a mathematical representation of the technology that transforms inputs into output(s). If inputs and outputs are treated as two separate categories, the relationship between inputs and outputs can be expressed as $F(\boldsymbol{x}, \boldsymbol{y}) = 0$, where $\boldsymbol{x}$ is a J dimensional non-negative input vector and $\boldsymbol{y}$ is an M dimensional non-negative output vector. This formulation is very general and we will consider a much more restricted formulation, which for a single output case can be expressed as:

$$y = f(x_1, x_2, \ldots, x_J) \equiv f(\boldsymbol{x}), \tag{2.1}$$

where the function $f(\cdot)$ specifies the technology governing the input–output relationship, and is single valued. In this formulation, $f(\boldsymbol{x})$ is the production function, which gives the maximum possible output, for a given $\boldsymbol{x}$. Alternatively, given y and all other inputs, except x_j, this function gives the minimum value of x_j. A well-defined production function should satisfy the following regularity conditions (Chambers [1988], p. 9):

1. $f(\boldsymbol{x})$ is finite, non-negative, real-valued, and single-valued for all non-negative and finite $\boldsymbol{x}$;
2. $f(0) = 0$ meaning that no inputs implies no output;
3. $f(\boldsymbol{x}) \geq f(\boldsymbol{x}')$ for $\boldsymbol{x} \geq \boldsymbol{x}'$ (monotonicity);
4. $f(\boldsymbol{x})$ is continuous and twice-differentiable everywhere;
5. The input requirement set $V(y) = \{\boldsymbol{x} | f(\boldsymbol{x}) \geq y\}$ is a convex set, which implies quasi-concavity of $f(\boldsymbol{x})$;
6. The set $V(y)$ is closed and nonempty for any $y > 0$.

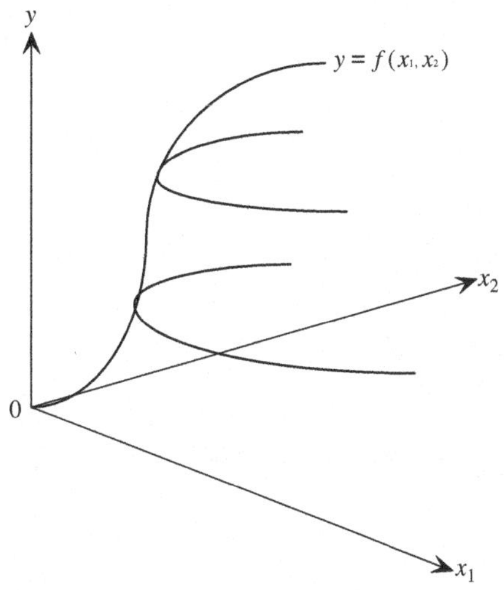

Figure 2.1. A Production Function with Two Inputs and One Output

Assumption 1 defines the production function and assumption 2 is self-explanatory. Assumption 3 simply says that more inputs lead to no lesser output, that is, the additional use of any input can never decrease the level of output. This, along with assumption 4, implies that marginal products are all non-negative. Assumption 4 is made largely for mathematical simplicity, especially for parametric models so that one can use calculus. It is not necessary to describe the technology. The definition of quasi-concavity, in assumption 5, states that the input requirement set is convex. This makes the production function quasi-concave and implies a diminishing marginal rate of technical substitution. Finally, assumption 6 means that it is always possible to produce positive output.

We now illustrate these properties using a production technology that uses two inputs, x_1 and x_2, to produce a single output y. The production function is illustrated in Figure 2.1.

Given the input bundle $\{x_1, x_2\}$, the maximum output attainable is indicated by the corresponding point on the *surface* of the corn-shape structure. If we slice the corn vertically at a given value of x_2, it reveals the relationship between values of x_1 and y given the value of x_2, as shown in Figure 2.2. The curve in the graph is often referred to as the *total product curve* of x_1. The total product curve of x_2 for a given x_1 can be obtained similarly by slicing the corn-shape structure vertically at a given value of x_1.

The slope of the total product curve of x_i, $\partial y/\partial x_i$, indicates the *marginal product* of x_i, that is, input x_i's marginal effect on output when all other inputs are held constant. It is usually assumed that $\partial y/\partial x_i \geq 0$ and that $\partial^2 y/\partial x_i^2 < 0$. The implication of the second inequality is referred to as the *law of diminishing marginal productivity* or *law of diminishing returns.* Together, the two inequalities imply that an increase in an input has a positive (or at least non-negative) effect on output, but the positive effect diminishes as we keep increasing the same input while holding other inputs unchanged.

The surface of the corn-shape structure of Figure 2.1 and the inside area of it together constitute the *feasible production set*, meaning that it contains all the input–output combinations feasible to producers under the given production technology. The production function *per se*, by contrast, depicts the *maximum* output achievable for given inputs under the production technology, and these input–output combinations are on the *surface* of the

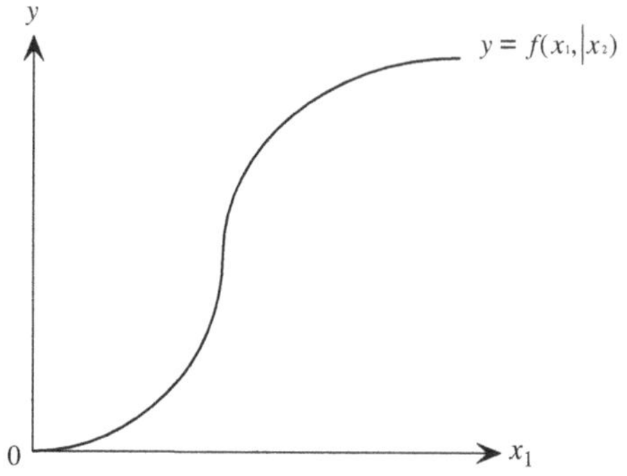

Figure 2.2. The Total Product Curve of x_1

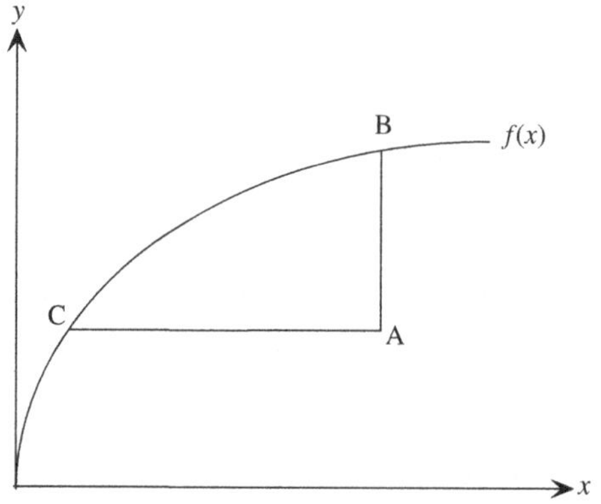

Figure 2.3. IO and OO Technical Inefficiency for the One-Input, One-Output Case

corn-shape structure. We may call the production function the *frontier* of the feasible production set. If actual output, given inputs, falls short of the maximum possible output level, then the production will not be on the frontier.

When modeling production behavior, standard production theory implicitly assumes that all production activities are on the frontier of the feasible production set (subject to random noise). The production efficiency literature relaxes this assumption and considers the possibility that producers may operate below the frontier due to technical inefficiency.

2.2.1 Input-Oriented and Output-Oriented Technical Inefficiency

A production plan is *technically inefficient* if a higher level of output is technically attainable for the given inputs (output-oriented measure), or that the observed output level can be produced using fewer inputs (input-oriented measure).

Graphically, the inefficient production plans are located below the production frontier. Figure 2.3 provides an example. In the figure, $f(\boldsymbol{x})$ is the production frontier, and point A is an inefficient production point. There are two ways to see why it is inefficient. The first way is to see that at the current level of input x, more output can be produced. The distance $\overline{AB}$ shows the output loss due to the technical inefficiency, and it forms the basis from which the *output-oriented* (OO) technical inefficiency is measured.

The other way to see why point A is inefficient is to recognize that the same level of output can be produced using less inputs, which means that the production can move to the frontier by using less of the input. The distance $\overline{AC}$ represents the amount by which the input can be reduced without reducing output. Because this move is associated with reducing inputs, the horizontal distance $\overline{AC}$ forms the basis to measure the *input-oriented* (IO) technical inefficiency.

It is clear from Figure 2.3 that estimates of inefficiency are conditional on the given technology (production frontier). An input–output combination may appear inefficient for one technology, but it could be efficient with respect to a different technology. The implication for empirical analysis is that, when estimating the technical inefficiencies of different producers, it is important that they are estimated with respect to the appropriate technology. For example, Japanese and Bangladeshi rice farmers may have very different production technology at their disposal. If we pool their data together to estimate a single production function, from which the technology efficiency is estimated, then the results would be difficult to justify. In other words, if a single, common production function is estimated, the data should contain only those who share the same production technology, unless the heterogeneous production technologies can be properly taken into account by the specification of the production function.

There are several approaches to take account of different production technologies. One approach is the *metafrontier* approach. Perhaps the most intuitive way to explain this approach is that, when modeling, units are first grouped by technology. Thus, in the example given earlier, we would have two subsets – farms in Japan and farms in Bangladesh. Their efficiency can then be estimated relative to their own group's overall production frontier. Each group's production frontier can then be compared to each other. This allows one to estimate the technical efficiency of a firm relative to the technology it uses as well as the technology gap that captures the difference between the technology it uses and the best practice technology (the metafrontier). For more detail on this approach, see Battese et al. (2004) and O'Donnell et al. (2008).

The metafrontier approach requires knowledge as to which group a unit should be placed. There might, however, be unobserved or unknown differences in technologies. In such circumstances, the differences in technologies might be inappropriately labeled as inefficient if such variations in technology are not taken into account. In circumstances where it is not straightforward to categorize units prior to modeling, a different approach is required to take into account the technological heterogeneity when estimating efficiency. One such an approach involves using the *latent class (finite mixture) model*. Latent classes are unobservable (or latent) subgroups of units that are homogeneous in certain criteria. Latent class modeling is a statistical method for identifying these subgroups of latent classes from multivariate categorical data. The results of the latent class modeling can also be used to classify units to their most likely latent class, as well as estimating each unit's efficiency with respect to the appropriate production technology. For more detail on this approach, see Orea and Kumbhakar (2004) and Greene (2005b).

Inefficient production can also be explained in terms of isoquants. If we slice the corn structure in Figure 2.1 horizontally at a given level of y (say, y_1), then we obtain a contour of the corn structure, which shows the *isoquant* of the production function as illustrated in Figure 2.4.

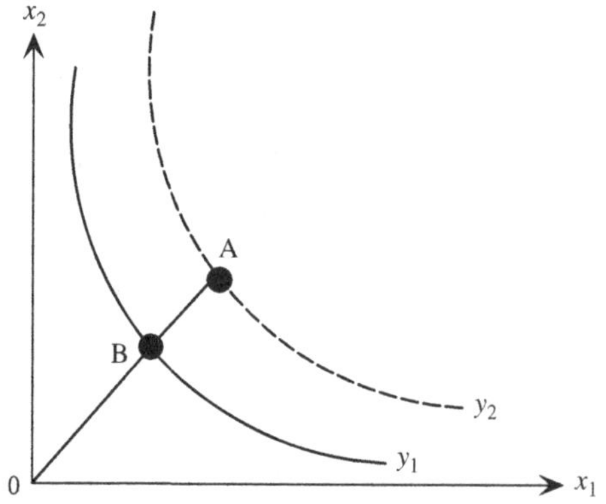

Figure 2.4. IO and OO Technical Inefficiency in a Two-Inputs One-Output Case

In Figure 2.4, point A is the observed input combination. If the production is technically efficient, the input combination at point A should produce output level y_2. In this instance, the isoquant passing through point A is on the contour of the production corn, and thus it represents the *frontier* output level (i.e., point A lies on the frontier on a plane above y_1 at $y = y_2$). However, with technical inefficiency, inputs at point A *only* produce observed output level y_1, where $y_1 < y_2$ (i.e., point A lies inside the frontier on a plane below y_2 at $y = y_1$).

The IO technical inefficiency can be measured by moving radially downward from point A to point B. The isoquant at point B has an output level equal to y_1. This move shows that the observed output (y_1) could be produced using less of both inputs. More precisely, input quantities can be reduced by the proportion $\overline{AB}/\overline{OA}$, which is the measure of IO technical inefficiency. By contrast, IO technical efficiency (which measures the inputs in efficiency units) is $1 - \overline{AB}/\overline{OA} = \overline{OB}/\overline{OA}$.

Mathematically, a production plan with IO technical inefficiency is written as:

$$y = f(\boldsymbol{x} \cdot \exp(-\eta)), \eta \geq 0, \tag{2.2}$$

where η measures IO *technical inefficiency* (TI), and $\exp(-\eta)$ measures IO *technical efficiency* (TE). For small η, $\exp(-\eta)$ can be approximated by $1-\eta$. Thus, we get the following familiar relationship, $TE = 1 - TI$, which is clear from Figure 2.4 ($\overline{OB}/\overline{OA} = 1 - \overline{AB}/\overline{OA}$).

We can also measure efficiency using the OO measure. The input quantities (given by point A) that is associated with output level y_1, can be used to produce a higher level of output as shown by the isoquant labeled y_2. Viewed this way, the inputs are not changed but a higher level of output is produced. So one can measure inefficiency in terms of the output differential. This is what we call OO technical inefficiency (TI) and it is measured by $(y_2 - y_1)/y_2$, and technical efficiency (TE) is measured by y_1/y_2.

A mathematical formulation of OO technical inefficiency is:

$$y = f(\boldsymbol{x}) \cdot \exp(-u), \; u \geq 0, \tag{2.3}$$

where u measures OO technical inefficiency. Again, for small u, we can approximate $\exp(-u)$ by $1 - u$, which gives us the familiar result, $TE = \exp(-u) = 1 - u = 1 - TI$.

2.2.2 Non-Neutral Technical Inefficiency

It is worth pointing out that the above mathematical formulation of OO technical inefficiency is *neutral*. That is, the impact of inefficiency on output does not depend on the level of input and output quantities. However, it is possible to have *non-neutral* technical inefficiency. Econometrically, this can be achieved by making u a function of input quantities.

In contrast, the specification of the IO technical inefficiency is not automatically neutral – it is only neutral if the production function is homogeneous (see Section 2.3.1 for a formal definition of a homogeneous function). Nevertheless, within an econometric model, it is also possible to make η a function of explanatory variables (z variables). In doing so, we can say two things. First, technical inefficiency is non-neutral. Second, we can interpret the z variables as *exogenous* determinants of technical inefficiency. By exogenous, we mean that these z variables are outside a firm's control (such factors might include, for example, regulation). It is also possible to think of situations in which η depends on the input quantities, x. If inputs are *endogenous*, then this formulation will make inefficiency endogenous.[1] That is, if inefficiency depends on the x variables (which are choice or decision variables), it can be argued that firms can adjust their efficiency level by adjusting input quantities.

2.3 Statistics from Production Functions

A few economic effects are often derived from the production technology. These are quite standard and discussed in many microeconomics textbook (e.g., Varian [2009]). In this section, we discuss some of these issues, with and without technical inefficiency, which are of particular interest to economists. We first define the economic effects in the standard model (i.e., without technical inefficiency). For a production function $f(x_1, \ldots, x_n)$, the following notations are used:

$$f_i = \frac{\partial f}{\partial x_i},$$
$$f_{ij} = \frac{\partial f_i}{\partial x_j}.$$

Here f_i is the marginal product of x_i and f_{ij} is the cross-partial that shows the change in the marginal product of x_i due to a change in x_j. Several important economic effects can now be quantified in terms of the first and second derivatives of the production function (Fuss et al. [1978] discuss some other statistics).

Economic effect	Formula	Number of distinct effects
Output level	$y = f(\boldsymbol{x})$	1
Returns to scale	$\mu = \left(\sum_{i=1}^{n} x_i f_i\right) \Big/ f$	1
Elasticity of substitution	$\sigma_{ij} = \frac{-f_{ii}/f_i^2 + 2(f_{ii}/f_i f_j) - f_{ii}/f_j^2}{1/x_i f_i + 1/x_j f_j}$	$\frac{n(n-1)}{2}$

[1] This is also true for the OO technical inefficiency models, as discussed earlier.

When time series or panel data are available, we can include a time trend as an additional regressor in the production function. This will help us to examine technical change as an additional economic effect of interest. The related economic effects of interest are listed here.

Economic effect	Formula	Number of distinct effects
Rate of technical change	$TC = (\partial \ln y/\partial t)$	1
Speed of technical change	$\partial TC/\partial t$	1

Now we examine the impact of IO and OO technical inefficiency on the economic effects mentioned in these tables.

2.3.1 Homogeneity and Returns to Scale

An important economic issue is the impact on output of increasing inputs. This issue is important when considering, for example, the impact on a public or private organization's cost base (and, thus, its demands on the public purse or its competitiveness) of responding to an increase or decrease in demand.

We start by considering what would happen to output if *all* inputs are changed by the same proportion. For instance, if we double all the inputs, does the output increase by more than double, exactly double, or less than double? A production function is *homogeneous* if it satisfies the following condition:

$$\lambda^{\gamma} y = f(\lambda x_1, \lambda x_2, \ldots, \lambda x_n). \tag{2.4}$$

That is, if all inputs are increased by a factor of λ and the output increases by a factor of λ^{γ}, then the function is *homogeneous of degree* γ in $\boldsymbol{x}$. If $\gamma = 1$, the output increases by the same proportion as all the inputs do, and this is the case of *constant returns to scale*, and the production function is also labeled as *linear homogeneous*. If $\gamma > 1$, then the proportional increase of output is more than the proportional increase in inputs, and this is the case of *increasing returns to scale*. Similarly, if $\gamma < 1$, we have *decreasing returns to scale*. Note that for homogeneous functions, returns to scale (RTS) is independent of x.

If the production function is not homogeneous, then RTS will depend on x. The general definition of RTS is $\text{RTS} = \partial \ln f(\lambda x)/\partial \ln \lambda|_{\lambda=1}$, which is γ for a homogeneous production function. RTS can be also expressed as the sum of input elasticities, that is,

$$\text{RTS} = \sum_j \frac{\partial \ln f(\lambda x)}{\partial \ln(\lambda x_j)}|_{\lambda=1} = \sum_j \epsilon_j(\boldsymbol{x}), \tag{2.5}$$

$$\text{where} \quad \epsilon_j(\boldsymbol{x}) = \frac{\partial \ln f(\cdot)}{\partial \ln x_j}.$$

This formulation assumes that producers are technically efficient. If we allow technical inefficiency and compute RTS using this formula, it is clear that the OO technical inefficiency does not affect RTS. This is because the technical inefficiency term (after taking logs of the production function) appears additively. This is, however, not the case with the IO measure of technical inefficiency because $\ln y = \ln f(\boldsymbol{x} \exp(-\eta))$, $\text{RTS} = \sum_i \frac{\partial \ln y}{\partial \ln x_i}$ will depend on η (unless the production function is homogeneous).

2.3.2 Substitutability

Another important economic issue is the degree to which one input can be replaced by another input without affecting the output level. Such an issue is important when considering, for example, whether or not investment in new equipment is beneficial and how much labor such an investment might save.

Economists call the degree to which a firm can substitute one input for another the *elasticity of substitution* (Allen [1938]). In the two input case this is defined as:

$$\sigma_{12} = d\ln(x_2/x_1)/d\ln(MRTS), \tag{2.6}$$

where $MRTS$ (the marginal rate of technical substitution) $= f_1/f_2$. The value of σ_{12} lies between zero and infinity for convex isoquants. If σ_{12} is infinity, the inputs x_1 and x_2 are *perfect substitutes*; if $\sigma_{12} = 0$, then x_1 and x_2 must be used in fixed proportions. For the Cobb-Douglas production function, the elasticity of substitution is unity, while, for the Constant Elasticity of Substitution (CES) production function, the elasticity of substitution is constant but not unity. The CES production function approaches to the CD function as $\sigma_{12} \to 0$. Details of these production functions are introduced in Section 2.5.

In the multifactor case the partial elasticity of substitution (σ_{ij}) for a pair of inputs (x_i and x_j) is defined as:

$$\sigma_{ij} = \sigma_{ji} = \frac{\sum_i x_i f_i}{x_i x_j} \frac{F_{ji}}{F}, \tag{2.7}$$

where:

$$F = \begin{bmatrix} 0 & f_1 & f_2 & \cdots & f_J \\ f_1 & f_{11} & f_{12} & \cdots & f_{1J} \\ f_2 & f_{12} & f_{22} & \cdots & f_{2J} \\ \cdots & \cdots & \cdots & \cdots & \cdots \\ f_J & f_{1J} & f_{2J} & \cdots & f_{JJ} \end{bmatrix}, \tag{2.8}$$

and F_{ji} is the cofactor associated with f_{ij}. For $J = 2$,

$$\sigma_{12} = \frac{-f_1 . f_2(x_1 f_1 + x_2 f_2)}{x_1 x_2 (f_{11} f_2^2 - 2 f_{12} f_1 f_2 + f_{22} f_1^2)}. \tag{2.9}$$

For the general case, σ_{ij} is negative when the inputs are *complements*, and it is positive when the inputs are *substitutes* (for details, see Allen [1938]).

From this formula and the definitions of IO and OO technical inefficiency, it is clear that OO technical inefficiency does not affect substitution elasticities, whereas the IO technical inefficiency might affect substitution elasticities (this can be examined by computing the own and cross-partial derivatives ($f_{ij}\ \forall\, i, j$)).

2.3.3 Separabilitiy

Although the production process is characterized by many inputs, in empirical analysis they are often aggregated into a small number of groups (e.g., capital, labor, materials). Some inputs can be aggregated into one intermediate input that is used in the final production process if the production process is *separable*. For example, coal, oil, natural gas, and electricity can be aggregated into a single input called energy. To address the aggregation issue, let's assume that the production function with three inputs can be written as:

$$y = f(x) = G(x_a, x_3), \tag{2.10}$$

where $x_a = g(x_1, x_2)$ and the functions $G(\cdot)$ and $f(\cdot)$ satisfy the properties of a production function. The $g(\cdot)$ is often called the *aggregator function* because it aggregates several inputs into one. This production function is separable in x_1 and x_2. An important feature of the separable production function is that the MRTS between x_1 and x_2 is independent of x_3. This means that:

$$\partial \text{MRTS}_{12}/\partial x_3 = \partial(f_1/f_2)/\partial x_3 = 0. \tag{2.11}$$

Thus, separability depends on how the marginal rate of technical substitution between two inputs responds to changes in another input. In the general case, inputs x_i and x_j are separable from input x_k if $\frac{\partial(f_i/f_j)}{\partial x_k} = 0$. If n inputs are divided into m groups, then the production function is weakly separable if the marginal rate of technical substitution between x_i and x_j, each of which belong to one group, is independent of all inputs that do not belong to the group in which x_i and x_j belong. If this is the case, then the production function can be written as:

$$f(x) = G(f^1(x^1), \ldots, f^m(x^m)), \tag{2.12}$$

where G is strictly increasing and quasi-concave and each of the subproduction functions are strictly monotonic and concave. If the production process is technically inefficient and one is willing to model it as output-oriented, then the u term can be appended to the function $f(x)$ in the same way as before. However, if inefficiency is input oriented, its impact on output will be affected by how the $f(\cdot)$ and $G(\cdot)$ functions are specified, that is, whether these functions are homogeneous or not. We do not discuss these issues in this book.

2.3.4 Technical Change

The final economic issue examined in this section is the rate of productivity improvement that occurs over time. Such an issue is often of central importance to governments when considering the country's international competitiveness but can be critical at the micro-level as well, especially when comparing across producers in the same region, producing the same output(s) and facing the same prices.

Technical change refers to a change in the production technology that can come from improved methods of using the existing inputs (disembodied technical change) or through changes in input quality (embodied technical change). Here, we focus on disembodied technical change only, and view technical change as a shift in the production function over time, as illustrated in Figure 2.5. In this case, the shift takes place because, for example, labor in effective units is increasing due to experience (learning by doing).

If we write the production function as $y = f(x, t)$, then the rate of technical change is defined as:

$$TC(x, t) = \frac{\partial \ln f(x, t)}{\partial t}. \tag{2.13}$$

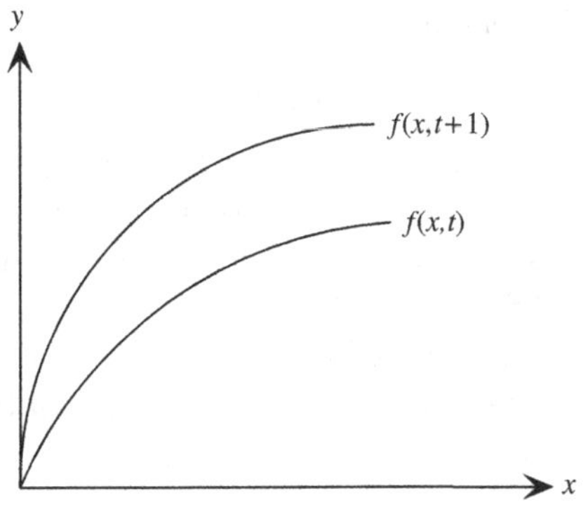

Figure 2.5. Technical Change

Technical change is said to be neutral if the shift is independent of x, that is, $TC(x, t) = TC(t)$. The most common form of neutral technical change is *Hicks neutral*, which occurs when

$$y = f(x, t) = A(t)f(x). \tag{2.14}$$

If $TC(x, t)$ depends on x then it is non-neutral.

If technical inefficiency is output-oriented and it varies over time (i.e., $y = A(t)f(x) \exp(-u(t))$), then the rate of change in output holding input quantities unchanged will be the sum of the rate of efficiency change and technical change. Furthermore, the rate of technical change will not be affected by inefficiency. By contrast, if technical inefficiency is input-oriented (IO) and is time-varying, such a decomposition is not always possible. To avoid this problem, one can define technical change (in the IO framework) as the shift in the production frontier using (2.13), that is,

$$TC(x, t) = \frac{\partial \ln f(x \cdot \exp(-\eta), t)}{\partial t}|_{\eta=0}. \tag{2.15}$$

Although not popular in the literature, one can talk about technical change via some special inputs such as R&D, management, and so on (say, z). In such a case TC is embodied in these inputs and one can define technical change cross-sectionally as

$$TC(x, z) = \frac{\partial \ln f(x, z)}{\partial z}. \tag{2.16}$$

The z variables can appear either neutrally or non-neutrally into the production function. It can also be factor augmenting (Kumbhakar [2002]). Again, these approaches can be used with technical inefficiency (Kumbhakar and Wang [2007]).

2.4 Transformation of Production Functions

A transform of a production function $f(x)$ is defined by

$$H(x) = \mathcal{F}(f(x)), \tag{2.17}$$

where $\mathcal{F}(.)$ is a twice differentiable, finite and nondecreasing function of $f(x)$. In the above formulation, $H(x)$ can be viewed as a production function and $f(x)$ as the aggregate of all inputs. Thus $\mathcal{F}(f(x))$ can be viewed as a single input production function. The curvature of the isoquants of $H(x)$ can be completely derived from that of $f(x)$.

A production function is *homothetic* if

$$y = f(x) = \mathcal{F}(f^*(x)) \Rightarrow f^*(x) = \mathcal{F}^{-1}(y) \equiv h(y), \tag{2.18}$$

where $f^*(x)$ is a linear homogeneous production function. In the above formulation, $h(y)$ is the output function which shows the amount of aggregate input, $f^*(x)$, needed to produce y. An example of this is the Generalized Production Function due to Zellner and Revankar (1969) (see Section 2.5.2).

There are two important properties of an homothetic production function. First, the MRTS is constant along any ray from the origin (meaning that the isoquants are parallel). Second, returns to scale for the homothetic production function can be expressed as (see Chambers [1988], p. 39)

$$RTS = \frac{h(y)}{h'(y)y}. \tag{2.19}$$

These concepts will be useful when we bring behavioral assumptions into the model explicitly.

2.5 Functional Forms of Production Functions

Some commonly used production functions (in terms of their parametric forms) include the Cobb-Douglas (CD), the generalized production function (GPF), the transcendental, and the translog. Each of these is discussed here.

2.5.1 The Cobb-Douglas (CD) Production Function

The Cobb-Douglas production function is given by

$$\begin{aligned} y = f(x) &= A\prod_{j=1}^{J} x_j^{\beta_j} \\ \Rightarrow \quad \ln y &= \beta_0 + \sum_j \beta_j \ln x_j, \\ \text{where} \quad \beta_0 &= \ln A. \end{aligned} \tag{2.20}$$

Strict concavity requires

$$\begin{aligned} 0 < \beta_j < 1 \;\; \forall j = 1, \ldots, J, \\ 0 < \sum_j \beta_j < 1, \\ A > 0. \end{aligned} \tag{2.21}$$

Quasi-concavity requires

$$\begin{aligned} \beta_j > 0 \, \forall j, \\ A > 0. \end{aligned} \tag{2.22}$$

The function is homogeneous of degree $r = \sum \beta_j$, as shown here:

$$f(\boldsymbol{x}.\lambda) = \lambda^{\sum \beta_j} f(\boldsymbol{x}) = \lambda^r f(\boldsymbol{x}).$$

The elasticity of output with respect to input x_j is given by

$$\varepsilon_j = \frac{\partial \ln y}{\partial \ln x_j} = \beta_j, \tag{2.23}$$

which is constant for all observations but varies across inputs.

Returns to scale is given by

$$RTS = \sum_{j=1}^{J} \varepsilon_j = \sum_j \beta_j = r. \tag{2.24}$$

Using (2.7), it is easily shown that, in the case of the CD production function, the elasticity of substitution is given by

$$\sigma_{ij} = 1. \tag{2.25}$$

The CD production function is separable. This is simple to check. Think of two groups and write the CD function as $\prod_{j=1}^{J} x_j^{\beta_j} = \prod_{j=1}^{m} x_j^{\beta_j} \times \prod_{j=m+1}^{J} x_j^{\beta_j} = G(f_1(x_1, \ldots, x_m), f_2(x_{m+1}, \ldots, x_J))$, where $G(\cdot)$ is a linear homogeneous function (i.e. $G(z) = z$), and f_1, f_2 are CD functions themselves.

With technical change, the CD production function can be specified as

$$\ln y = \beta_0 + \sum_j \beta_j \ln x_j + \beta_t t, \tag{2.26}$$

where the measure of technical change is $\frac{\partial \ln y}{\partial t} = \beta_t$. Thus the speed of technical change is zero.

The Cobb-Douglas Production Function with OO and IO Technical Inefficiency

Because the OO technical inefficiency enters the production function as the u term in the following expression:

$$y = f(x)e^{-u}, \tag{2.27}$$

the logarithm of the production function makes $-u$ an additive term to the corresponding neoclassical specification

$$\ln y = \ln f(x) - u. \tag{2.28}$$

With the IO technical inefficiency (η) in the production function

$$y = f\left(xe^{-\eta}\right), \tag{2.29}$$

which, in logarithmic form, becomes

$$\ln y = \beta_0 + \sum \beta_j \ln x_j - \left(\sum_j \beta_j\right)\eta. \tag{2.30}$$

Because the CD function is homegeneous, there is no essential difference between IO and OO technical inefficiency. So none of the economic measures discussed here are affected by the presence of inefficiency.

2.5.2 The Generalized Production Function (GPF)

The GPF function (Zellner and Revankar [1969]) is

$$\begin{aligned} ye^{\theta y} &= A\prod_j x_j^{\beta_j}, \\ \Rightarrow \quad \ln y + \theta y &= \beta_0 + \sum \beta_j \ln x_j, \\ \text{where} \quad \beta_0 &= \ln A. \end{aligned} \tag{2.31}$$

If $\theta = 0$, the GPF reduces to the CD function.

The input elasticities of the GPF can be derived as follows (Chambers [1988], p. 39):

$$\begin{aligned} &\ln y + \theta y = \beta_0 + \sum \beta_j \ln x_j \\ \Rightarrow \quad &\frac{\partial \ln y}{\partial \ln x_j}\left(1 + \theta y\right) = \beta_j \\ \Rightarrow \quad &\varepsilon_j = \frac{\beta_j}{1 + \theta y}. \end{aligned} \tag{2.32}$$

The returns to scale, which is the sum of input elasticities, is thus given by

$$RTS = \sum_j \varepsilon_j = \frac{\sum \beta_j}{1 + \theta y}, \tag{2.33}$$

which varies with y and is observation-specific. Thus, the main advantage of this function over the CD is that for a sample of data points one might observe all three returns to scale. That is, it is possible to observe some firms having scale economies ($RTS > 1$), others operating at constant returns to scale ($RTS = 1$), and others operating with decreasing returns to scale ($RTS < 1$), whereas the optimal level of output (corresponding to unitary returns to scale) at which other firms may be operating can also be determined.

The formula of other economic effects are the same as those of the CD functions.

The GPF with technical change can be specified as

$$\ln y + \theta y = \beta_0 + \sum_j \beta_j \ln x_j + \beta_t t, \tag{2.34}$$

where the measure of technical change is $\frac{\partial \ln y}{\partial t} = \beta_t/(1 + \theta y)$.

The Generalized Production Function with OO and IO Technical Inefficiency

Similar to the CD production function, the GPF with OO technical inefficiency adds $-u$ to the log of the production function (Kumbhakar [1988]).

With IO technical inefficiency η, the log of the GPF is

$$\ln y + \theta y = \beta_0 + \sum_j \beta_j \ln x_j - \left(\sum_j \beta_j\right)\eta. \tag{2.35}$$

2.5.3 The Transcendental Production Function

The transcendental production function (Halter [1957]) is given by

$$y = A\prod_j x_j^{\beta_j} e^{\sum_j \alpha_j x_j}$$
$$\Rightarrow \quad \ln y = \beta_0 + \sum_j \beta_j \ln x_j + \sum_j \alpha_j . x_j. \tag{2.36}$$

The elasticity of y with respect to x_j in the transcendental production function is given by

$$\varepsilon_j = \frac{\partial \ln y}{\partial \ln x_j} = \beta_j + \alpha_j x_j, \tag{2.37}$$

which means that RTS is given by

$$RTS = \sum_{j=1}^{J} \varepsilon_j = r + \sum_{j=1}^{J} \alpha_j x_j. \tag{2.38}$$

The elasticity of substitution, $\sigma_{ij} = \sigma_{ji}$, can be calculated using the formula in (2.7).

The requirement that $\varepsilon_j \geq 0$ imposes parameter restrictions on β_j and α_j. Note that RTS changes with input quantities. Thus, this function can exhibit all three returns to scale (increasing, constant, and decreasing) for a sample of observations.

With technical change, the transcendental production function can be specified as

$$\ln y = \beta_0 + \sum_j \beta_j \ln x_j + \sum_j \alpha_j x_j + \beta_t t, \tag{2.39}$$

where the measure of technical change is $\frac{\partial \ln y}{\partial t} = \beta_t$.

The Transcendental Production Function with OO and IO Technical Inefficiency

Again, the OO technical inefficiency adds the term $-u$ to the log of the transcendental production function. For the IO technical inefficiency, the function is expressed as

$$\begin{aligned} \ln y &= \beta_0 + \sum \beta_j \left(\ln x_j - \eta\right) + \sum \alpha_j x_j e^{-\eta}, \\ &= \beta_0 + \sum_j \beta_j \ln x_j + \sum \alpha_j x_j - \left(\sum \beta_j\right)\eta + \sum_j \alpha_j x_j \left(e^{-\eta} - 1\right). \end{aligned} \tag{2.40}$$

Using the approximation

$$e^{-\eta} \approx 1 - \eta, \tag{2.41}$$

we have

$$\ln y = \beta_0 + \sum_j \beta_j \ln x_j + \sum_j \alpha_j x_j - \left[\sum_j \left(\beta_j + \alpha_j x_j\right)\right]\eta. \tag{2.42}$$

Since the OO technical inefficiency affects output in a neutral fashion, none of the economic measures is affected by the presence of inefficiency. This is true irrespective of the functional form of the production technology. On the other hand, the economic measures are likely to be affected by the presence of IO technical inefficiency. For example, if a transcendental functional form is chosen, the input elasticities ε_j are

$$\varepsilon_j = \frac{\partial \ln y}{\partial \ln x_j} = \beta_j + \alpha_j x_j - \eta\, \alpha_j x_j, \tag{2.43}$$

and depend on η. This, in turn, means that

$$RTS = \sum_{j=1}^{J} \varepsilon_j = r + (1-\eta) \sum_{j=1}^{J} \alpha_j x_j, \tag{2.44}$$

also depends on IO technical inefficiency η. For details on the IO and OO inefficiency in the transcendental production function, see Kumbhakar and Tsionas (2008).

2.5.4 The Translog Production Function

The translog production function (Christensen, Jorgenson, and Lau [1971]) is

$$\ln y = \beta_0 + \sum_j \beta_j \ln x_j + \frac{1}{2} \sum_j \sum_k \beta_{jk} \ln x_j \ln x_k, \quad \beta_{jk} = \beta_{kj}. \tag{2.45}$$

The function is not homogeneous unless $\sum_k \beta_{jk} = 0\ \forall j$.

The input elasticity of x_j of the translog production function is given by

$$\varepsilon_j = \frac{\partial \ln y}{\partial \ln x_j} = \beta_j + \sum_k \beta_{jk} \ln x_k. \tag{2.46}$$

Returns to Scale is given by

$$RTS = \sum_j \varepsilon_j = \sum_j \left(\beta_j + \sum_k \beta_{jk} \ln x_k \right), \tag{2.47}$$

which is observation-specific. The elasticity of substitution, $\sigma_{ij} = \sigma_{ji}$, can be calculated using the formula in (2.7), which is quite cumbersome for the translog production function.

To accommodate technical change, the translog function can be specified as

$$\ln y = \beta_0 + \sum_j \beta_j \ln x_j + \frac{1}{2} \sum_j \sum_k \beta_{jk} \ln x_j \ln x_k + \beta_t\, t + \frac{1}{2} \beta_{tt}\, t^2 + \sum_j \beta_{jt} \ln x_j\, t, \tag{2.48}$$

where the measure of technical change is

$$TC = \beta_t + \beta_{tt}\, t + \sum_j \beta_{jt} \ln x_j. \tag{2.49}$$

If $\beta_{jt} = 0\ \forall j$, then technical change is neutral; otherwise, it is nonneutral. The speed of technical change $\frac{\partial TC}{\partial t} = \beta_{tt}$ is constant and it can be increasing or decreasing depending on the sign of β_{tt}.

The Translog Production Function with OO and IO Technical Inefficiency

The OO technical inefficiency simply adds $-u$ to the standard translog production function discussed earlier. Therefore, it does not affect the economic effects we are are interested in. For the IO technical inefficiency, the model is a little bit more complicated:

$$\begin{aligned}
\ln y &= \beta_0 + \sum_j \beta_j (\ln x_j - \eta) + \frac{1}{2}\sum_j\sum_k \beta_{jk} (\ln x_j - \eta)(\ln x_k - \eta) \\
&= \beta_0 + \sum_j \beta_j \ln x_j + \frac{1}{2}\sum_j\sum_k \beta_{jk} \ln x_j \ln x_k - \eta \sum_j \beta_j \\
&\quad + \frac{1}{2}\left(\sum_j\sum_k \beta_{jk}\right)\eta^2 - \left[\sum_j\left(\sum_k \beta_{jk}\ln x_k\right)\right]\eta \\
&= \beta_0 + \sum_j \beta_j \ln x_j + \frac{1}{2}\sum_j\sum_k \beta_{jk} \ln x_j \ln x_k \\
&\quad - \eta\left[\sum_j \beta_j + \sum_j\left(\sum_k \beta_{jk}\ln x_k\right)\right] + \frac{1}{2}\eta^2 \sum_j\sum_k \beta_{jk}.
\end{aligned} \tag{2.50}$$

If the production function is homogeneous, that is,

$$\sum_j \beta_{jk} = 0 \ \forall \text{k}, \tag{2.51}$$

then

$$\ln y = \beta_0 + \sum_j \beta_j \ln x_j + \frac{1}{2}\sum_j\sum_k \beta_{jk} \ln x_j \ln x_k - \eta \sum_j \beta_j. \tag{2.52}$$

With IO technical inefficiency both input elasticities and RTS are

$$\begin{aligned}
\varepsilon_j &= \frac{\partial \ln y}{\partial \ln x_j} = \beta_j + \sum_k \beta_{jk} \ln x_k + \beta_{j0}\,\eta, \\
RTS &= \sum_j \varepsilon_j = \sum_j \left(\beta_j + \sum_k \beta_{jk} \ln x_k + \beta_{j0}\,\eta\right),
\end{aligned} \tag{2.53}$$

where $\beta_{j0} = \sum_k \beta_{jk}$. Thus, input elasticities, as well as *RTS*, depend on IO technical inefficiency.

2.6 Multiple Output Production Technology (Distance Functions)

So far, our discussion has been based on a single output production function. A single output production function is useful if either a single output is in fact produced, or multiple outputs can be reasonably aggregated into a single output. Here we focus on multiproduct production functions in which one cannot distinguish what fraction of an input x_j is used in the production of output m and what fraction is used to produce output l (i.e., the input is nonallocable). This may not be the case in reality, but since detailed information on how much of each input goes into the production of which output is usually not available, we make this assumption and start with the function

$$F(\boldsymbol{y}, \boldsymbol{x}) = 0, \tag{2.54}$$

which is simply the transformation function where $\boldsymbol{y}$ is a vector of M outputs and $\boldsymbol{x}$ is a vector on J inputs. For a given $\boldsymbol{x}$, the above function specifies the *production possibility function* (PPF), which is assumed to be concave. This is analogous to an isoquant – the only difference is that it shows all possible output combinations that can be produced with a given $\boldsymbol{x}$. By changing $\boldsymbol{x}$ we can generate a family of product transformation curves. As mentioned earlier, the PPF expressed as $F(y, \boldsymbol{x}) = 0$ is quite general, and it does not mean that for a single output one can express y as a function of $\boldsymbol{x}$ from $F(y, \boldsymbol{x}) = 0$. If we make additional assumptions so that for a single output, y can be explicitly solved in terms of $\boldsymbol{x}$ from the PPF, then starting from the implicit production function $F(y, \boldsymbol{x}) = 0$ we get the familiar production function

$$y - f(\boldsymbol{x}) = 0. \tag{2.55}$$

We discuss these issues later in the context of specific functional forms of PPF while discussing distance functions.

To accommodate OO technical inefficiency, we write the PPF as

$$F(\boldsymbol{y} \cdot \exp(u), \boldsymbol{x}) = 0, u \geq 0, \tag{2.56}$$

where $\boldsymbol{y}$ is the vector of actual outputs, and u is a scalar representing output technical inefficiency. This specification suggests that an inefficient producer can increase all outputs (radially) by a factor of $\exp(u) \geq 1$. For a scalar output, this specification reduces to

$$y \cdot \exp(u) = f(\boldsymbol{x}), \tag{2.57}$$

or equivalently,

$$y = f(\boldsymbol{x}) \exp(-u), \tag{2.58}$$

which is the standard formulation of OO technical inefficiency.

In Figure 2.6, we show the PPF for the production plan indicated by point A that uses input quantities $\boldsymbol{x}$. Because A is an interior point, both outputs can be increased without

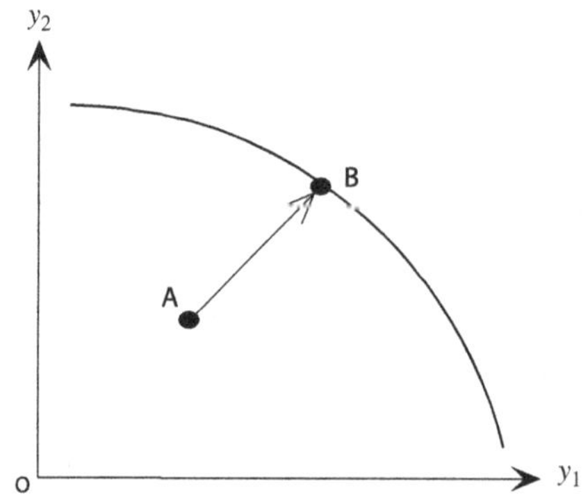

Figure 2.6. Production Possibility Curve with OO Technical Inefficiency

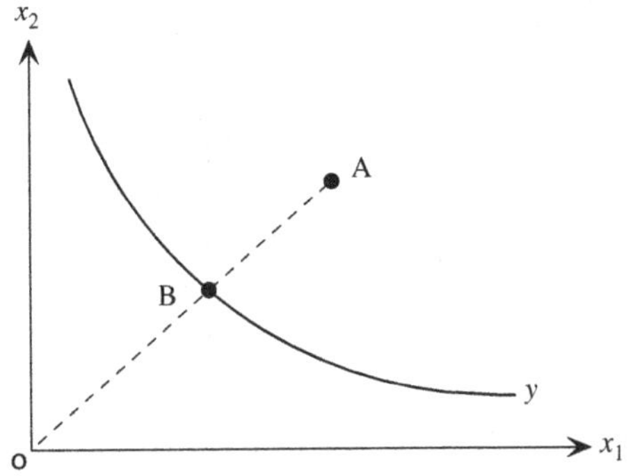

Figure 2.7. Isoquant with IO Technical Inefficiency

increasing $\boldsymbol{x}$. The radial expansion of output suggests that the efficient point is B, which can be attained by expanding outputs at the rate of $\overline{OB}/\overline{OA} = \exp(u) \geq 1$.

For IO technical inefficiency, we write the PPF as $F(\boldsymbol{y}, \boldsymbol{x}\exp(-\eta)) = 0$ where $\eta \geq 0$ is a scalar and it shows the rate at which all inputs can be reduced without reducing outputs. Alternatively, it can be viewed as the rate at which inputs are overused. For a scalar output (with the assumption that a solution of y is possible), this formulation would give the production function $y = f(\boldsymbol{x}\exp(-\eta))$ which is the standard formulation of the IO technical inefficiency. Alternatively, if there is a single input and one assumes that a solution of x is possible, the solution can be written as $x = g(\boldsymbol{y})\exp(\eta)$ where η is the rate at which the input x is over-used. This can be viewed as an *input requirement frontier function* (Diewert [1974], Kumbhakar and Hjalmarsson [1998]). In general, given $\boldsymbol{y}$, the PPF generates the isoquant. An inefficient producer uses input quantities $\boldsymbol{x}$ to produce $\boldsymbol{y}$ but an efficient producer can produce the same output vector using $\boldsymbol{x}\exp(-\eta) \leq \boldsymbol{x}$.

The radial contraction of inputs can be shown in the isoquant of Figure 2.7 as $\exp(-\eta) = \overline{OB}/\overline{OA}$.

2.6.1 Distance Functions

When there are many outputs, an alternative to the multiple output production function is provided by *the distance function*, which is simply the transformation function or the PPF. An advantage of using the distance function is that it does not require price data or explicit behavioral assumptions. This can be compared with another alternative approach where output prices and behavioral assumptions are used to estimate a multiple output production function by modeling both technical and allocative efficiency (see Section 2.8).

We use a single-output single-input example to explain the distance function. Although, in the case of a single output, the distance function is no different from the production function, we use the simple model to illustrate the distance function graphically, in Figure 2.8.

In Figure 2.8, the production frontier is the curve OT. Consider the observed point A, which is below the frontier. The observed output ($\overline{AR}$) could be produced by using only a fraction ($\overline{OS}/\overline{OR}$) of the observed input quantity ($\overline{OR}$). Thus, $\overline{OR}/\overline{OS}$ is the largest scalar by which we can divide the observed input quantity and still be able to produce the observed output. Thus, the input distance function (for a single output and multiple inputs) can be algebraically expressed as

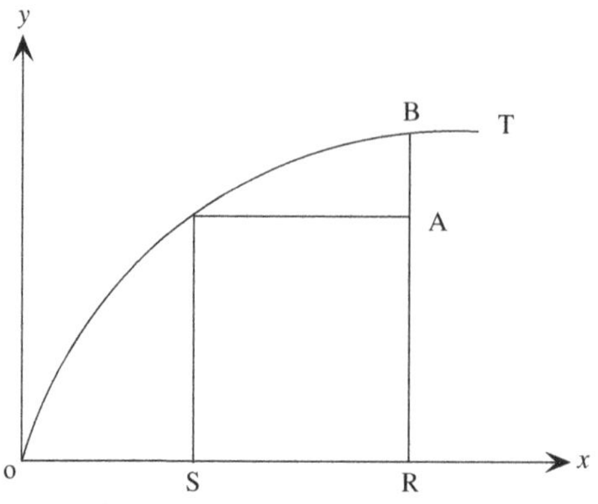

Figure 2.8. Distance Function with a Single Input and a Single Output

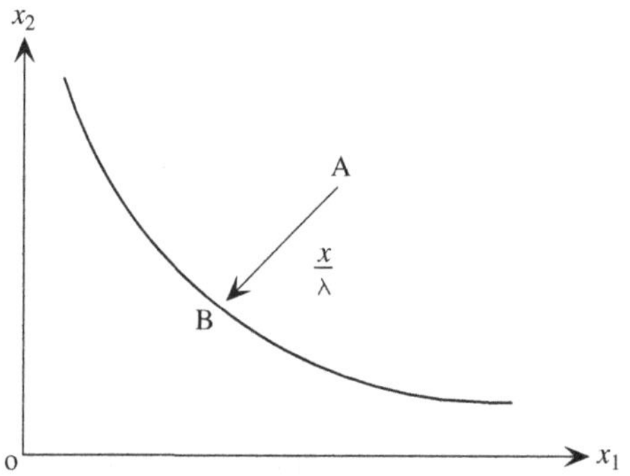

Figure 2.9. Input Distance Function: Two Inputs and a Single Output

$$D_I(y, \boldsymbol{x}) = \max_{\lambda}\{\lambda | f(\boldsymbol{x}/\lambda) \geq y\}. \tag{2.59}$$

It is clear that $D_I(.) \geq 1$. Furthermore, $D_I(y, \boldsymbol{x})$ is homogeneous of degree 1 in $\boldsymbol{x}$, and concave in $\boldsymbol{x}$.

If there are multiple outputs and multiple inputs the input distance function is defined as:

$$D_I(\boldsymbol{y}, \boldsymbol{x}) = \max_{\lambda}\{\lambda | (\boldsymbol{x}/\lambda) \in V(\boldsymbol{y})\}, \tag{2.60}$$

where $V(\boldsymbol{y})$ is the input requirement set introduced earlier.

The properties of $D_I(.)$ are as follows:

1. $D_I(\boldsymbol{y}, \boldsymbol{x})$ is decreasing in each output level;
2. $D_I(\boldsymbol{y}, \boldsymbol{x})$ is increasing in each input level;
3. $D_I(\boldsymbol{y}, \boldsymbol{x})$ is homogeneous of degree 1 in feasible input vector $\boldsymbol{x}$;
4. $D_I(\boldsymbol{y}, \boldsymbol{x})$ is concave in $\boldsymbol{x}$.

Figure 2.9 illustrates the case of two inputs and one output.

Another way to read Figure 2.8 is that, given the observed input quantity ($\overline{OR}$), the output ($\overline{AR}$) is below the maximum possible level. In fact, the maximum output level is $\overline{BR}/\overline{AR}$ times the observed output. Thus $\overline{AR}/\overline{BR}$ is the smallest scalar by which we can divide the actual

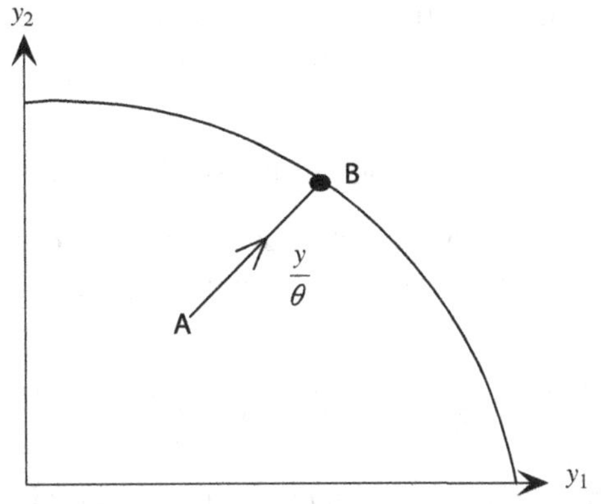

Figure 2.10. Output Distance Function: Single Input and Two Outputs

output and still be able to produce the implied output using the observed input quantity. Thus, the output distance function for a single output case can be algebraically defined as

$$D_O(y, \boldsymbol{x}) = \min_{\theta}\{\theta | (y/\theta) \leq f(\boldsymbol{x})\}. \tag{2.61}$$

It is clear that $D_O(.) \leq 1$.

For multiple outputs and multiple inputs the output distance function is defined as

$$D_O(\boldsymbol{y}, \boldsymbol{x}) = \min_{\theta}\{\theta | (\boldsymbol{y}/\theta) \in \mathcal{P}(\boldsymbol{x})\}, \tag{2.62}$$

where $\mathcal{P}(\boldsymbol{x})$ describes the sets of output vectors that are feasible for each input vector $\boldsymbol{x}$. $D_O(\boldsymbol{y}, \boldsymbol{x})$ is homogeneous of degree 1 in outputs, and is a convex function in $\boldsymbol{y}$. Figure 2.10 illustrates the case of a single input and two outputs.

The properties of $D_O(.)$ are as follows:

1. $D_O(\boldsymbol{y}, \boldsymbol{x})$ is decreasing in each input level;
2. $D_O(\boldsymbol{y}, \boldsymbol{x})$ is increasing in each output level;
3. $D_O(\boldsymbol{y}, \boldsymbol{x})$ is homogeneous of degree 1 in $\boldsymbol{y}$;
4. $D_O(\boldsymbol{y}, \boldsymbol{x})$ is concave in $\boldsymbol{y}$.

Because both the input and output distance functions are functions of $\boldsymbol{x}$ and $\boldsymbol{y}$, the only way to separate them is through the homogeneity restrictions. That is, when it comes to the parametric specification of input and output distance functions they are exactly the same to start with. Then we separate them through homogeneity restrictions. Thus, for example, $D = f(\boldsymbol{x}, \boldsymbol{y})$ is an input distance function if it is homogeneous of degree one in $\boldsymbol{x}$. This helps us to rewrite it as

$$\frac{D}{x_1} = f(\frac{x_2}{x_1}, \ldots, \frac{x_j}{x_1}, \boldsymbol{y}). \tag{2.63}$$

Once we impose linear homogeneity restrictions on D it becomes D_I. By contrast, if we impose linear homogeneity restrictions on $\boldsymbol{y}$ and write $D = f(\boldsymbol{x}, \boldsymbol{y})$ as

$$\frac{D}{y_1} = f(\boldsymbol{x}, \frac{y_2}{y_1}, \ldots, \frac{y_m}{y_1}), \tag{2.64}$$

the resulting function becomes an output distance function. So the homogeneity property is the key in separating the two distance functions.

2.6.2 The Translog Input Distance Function

With this background, we can now write the translog input distance function. For this, we first impose the linear homogeneity conditions and rewrite the distance function $D = f(\boldsymbol{x}, \boldsymbol{y})$ as

$$D_I x_1^{-1} = f(\tilde{x}, y) \quad \text{where} \quad \tilde{x} = \left(\frac{x_2}{x_1}, \ldots, \frac{x_J}{x_1}\right) \tag{2.65}$$

and then take log of both sides to obtain $\ln D_I - \ln x_1 = \ln f(\tilde{x}, y)$. Finally, we assume a translog form on $f(\tilde{x}, y)$ to obtain

$$\begin{aligned} \ln D_I - \ln x_1 &= \beta_0 + \sum_{j=2}^{J} \beta_j \ln \tilde{x}_j + \sum_{m=1}^{M} \gamma_m \ln y_m \\ &+ \frac{1}{2}\left[\sum_j \sum_k \beta_{jk} \ln \tilde{x}_j \ln \tilde{x}_k + \sum_m \sum_l \gamma_{ml} \ln y_m \ln y_l\right] \\ &+ \sum_j \sum_m \delta_{jm} \ln \tilde{x}_j \ln y_m. \end{aligned} \tag{2.66}$$

To make this distance function stochastic a random error term, v, is added. Furthermore, denoting $\ln D_I = u \geq 0$ and taking it to the right-hand side of the equation, we get an estimable equation in which the error term is $v - u$. Thus, one can use the standard stochastic production function approach to estimate this model. However, one has to impose symmetry restrictions in the above translog function, that is, $\beta_{jk} = \beta_{kj}$ and $\gamma_{ml} = \gamma_{lm}$.

2.6.3 The Translog Output Distance Function

We follow similar steps to those undertaken earlier in order to derive the translog output distance function, that is, first we impose the linear homogeneity conditions and rewrite the distance function $D = f(\boldsymbol{x}, \boldsymbol{y})$ as

$$D_O y_1^{-1} = f(x, \tilde{y}) \quad \text{where} \quad \tilde{y} = \left(\frac{y_2}{y_1}, \ldots, \frac{y_m}{y_1}\right) \tag{2.67}$$

and then take log of both sides to obtain $\ln D_O - \ln y_1 = \ln f(x, \tilde{y})$. Finally, we assume a translog form on $f(x, \tilde{y})$ to obtain

$$\begin{aligned} \ln D_O - \ln y_1 &= \beta_0 + \sum_j \beta_j \ln x_j + \sum_m \gamma_m \ln \tilde{y}_m \\ &+ \frac{1}{2}\left[\sum_j \sum_k \beta_{jk} \ln x_j \ln x_k + \sum_m \sum_l \gamma_{ml} \ln \tilde{y}_m \ln \tilde{y}_l\right] \\ &+ \sum_j \sum_m \delta_{jm} \ln x_j \ln \tilde{y}_m, \end{aligned} \tag{2.68}$$

where $\tilde{y}_m = y_m/y_1$. We need to impose symmetry restrictions in the translog function, i.e., $\beta_{jk} = \beta_{kj}$ and $\gamma_{ml} = \gamma_{lm}$. Like the input distance function, the translog output distance function can be made stochastic by adding a two-sided noise term v. Furthermore, denoting $\ln D_O \leq 0$ by $-u$ and moving it to the right-hand side, we get an estimable equation in which the error term is $v + u$. Because the output distance function satisfies these properties, it is desirable that the estimated function satisfies them as well.

2.7 The Transformation Function Formulation

In empirical research, the specification and estimation of the production function is important. In spite of many advances in the last eighty-plus years since the introduction of the Cobb-Douglas production function in 1928 some of the fundamental issues are still debated. The two main issues of concern are the specification and estimation of the underlying technology. The specification issue is important because there are many different ways in which one can specify the underlying technology. Although the alternative specifications are algebraically the same, they are not the same from an econometric estimation point of view. These specifications use different econometric assumptions, and their data requirements are often different. Needless to say, the empirical results differ and this creates an issue for applied researchers who want to know which approach is appropriate to use. The choice is often dictated by what is endogenous (i.e., the choice or decision variables) to producers, and what is the objective of producers. Here we address the specification issue without addressing endogeneity.

2.7.1 The Transformation Function with Inefficiency

To make the presentation more general, we start from a transformation function formulation and extend it to accommodate both input and output technical inefficiency, viz., $Af(\theta\boldsymbol{x}, \lambda\boldsymbol{y}) = 1$ where $\boldsymbol{x}$ is a vector of J inputs, $\boldsymbol{y}$ is a vector of M outputs, and the A term captures the impact of observed and unobserved factors that affect the transformation function neutrally. Input technical inefficiency is indicated by $\theta \leq 1$ and output technical inefficiency is captured by $\lambda \geq 1$ (both are scalars). Thus, $\theta\boldsymbol{x} \leq \boldsymbol{x}$ is the input vector in efficiency (effective) units so that, if $\theta = 0.9$, inputs are 90% efficient (i.e., the use of each input could be reduced by 10% without reducing outputs, if inefficiency is eliminated). Similarly, if $\lambda = 1.05$, each output could be increased by 5% without increasing any input, when inefficiency is eliminated. Because both θ and λ are not identified, we consider the following special cases. If $\theta = 1$ and $\lambda > 1$, then we have output-oriented technical inefficiency. Similarly, if $\lambda = 1$ and $\theta < 1$, then we have input-oriented technical inefficiency. Finally, if $\lambda \cdot \theta = 1$, technical inefficiency is said to be hyperbolic, which means that if the inputs are contracted by a constant proportion, outputs are expanded by the same proportion. That is, instead of moving to the frontier by either expanding outputs (keeping the inputs unchanged) or contracting inputs (holding outputs unchanged), the hyperbolic measure chooses a path to the frontier that leads to a simultaneous increase in outputs and a decrease in inputs by the same rate. We specify the technology in terms of the transformation function $f(\cdot)$ because it is much more general than the production, distance or input requirement function (Kumbhakar [2012]).

2.7.1.1 The Cobb-Douglas Transformation Function

We start from the case where the transformation function is separable (i.e., the output function is separable from the input function) so that $Af(\theta \boldsymbol{x}, \lambda \boldsymbol{y}) = 1$ can be rewritten as $Ag(\lambda \boldsymbol{y}) \cdot h(\theta \boldsymbol{x}) = 1$. Furthermore, if we assume that both $g(\cdot)$ and $h(\cdot)$ are Cobb-Douglas (to be relaxed later), the transformation function can be expressed as

$$\textbf{CD transformation function: } A \prod_m \{\lambda y_m\}^{\alpha_m} \prod_j \{\theta x_j\}^{\beta_j} = 1. \tag{2.69}$$

The α_m and β_j parameters are of opposite signs. That is, either $\alpha_m < 0 \ \forall m$ or $\beta_j > 0 \ \forall j$ and vice versa. This is implicit in all the formulations in Section 2.1. Note that there is one unidentifiable parameter in (2.69), meaning that the number of parameters (ignoring θ and λ) in A, α_m, and β_j are $M + J + 1$ but the regression function (2.69) can estimate $M + J$ parameters. Furthermore, both θ and λ cannot be identified, meaning that either one of them is set to unity or the product of them is set to unity. If we normalize $\alpha_1 = -1$ and $\theta = 1$, then we get the following specification:

$$\textbf{Production function: } y_1 = A \prod_{m=2} y_m^{\alpha_m} \prod_j x_j^{\beta_j} \lambda^{\sum_m \alpha_m}, \tag{2.70}$$

which can be viewed as a production function. Output-oriented technical efficiency in this model is $TE = \lambda^{\sum_m \alpha_m}$ and output-oriented technical inefficiency is $u = \ln TE = \{\sum_m \alpha_m\} \ln \lambda < 0$ since, in (2.70), $\ln \lambda > 0$ and $\alpha_m < 0 \ \forall \ m \Rightarrow \sum \alpha_m < 0$.

If we rewrite (2.69) as

$$A y_1^{\sum_m \alpha_m} \prod_{m=2} \{y_m / y_1\}^{\alpha_m} \prod_j x_j^{\beta_j} \theta^{\sum_j \beta_j} \lambda^{\sum_m \alpha_m} = 1, \tag{2.71}$$

and use the normalization $\sum_m \alpha_m = -1$ and $\theta = 1$, then we get the output distance function (ODF) formulation (Shephard [1953]), viz.,

$$\textbf{Output distance function: } y_1 = A \prod_{m=2} \{y_m / y_1\}^{\alpha_m} \prod_j x_j^{\beta_j} \lambda^{-1}, \tag{2.72}$$

where output-oriented technical inefficiency $u = -\ln \lambda < 0$. Technical inefficiency in models (2.70) and (2.72) are different because the output variables (as regressors) appear differently and different normalizations are used.

Similarly, we rewrite (2.69) as

$$A x_1^{\sum_j \beta_j} \prod_m y_m^{\alpha_m} \prod_{j=2} \{x_j / x_1\}^{\beta_j} \theta^{\sum_j \beta_j} \lambda^{\sum_m \alpha_m} = 1, \tag{2.73}$$

and use the normalization $\sum_j \beta_j = -1$ (note that now we are assuming $\beta_j < 0 \ \forall j$ and therefore $\alpha_m > 0 \ \forall \ m$) and $\lambda = 1$, to get the input distance function (IDF) formulation (Shephard [1953]), viz.,

$$\textbf{Input distance function: } x_1 = A \prod_m y_m^{\alpha_m} \prod_{j=2} \{x_j / x_1\}^{\beta_j} \theta^{-1}, \tag{2.74}$$

where input-oriented technical inefficiency is $u = -\ln \theta > 0$, which is the percentage overuse of inputs due to inefficiency.

Although IO and OO efficiency measures are popular, sometimes a hyperbolic measure of efficiency is used. In this measure, the product of λ and θ is unity, meaning that in this measure the approach to the frontier from an inefficient point takes the path of a parabola (all the inputs are decreased by k percent and the outputs are increased by $1/k$ percent). To get the hyperbolic measure from the IDF all we need to do is to use the normalization $\sum_j \beta_j = -1$ and $\lambda = \theta^{-1}$ in (2.73), which gives the **hyperbolic input distance function** (Färe et al. [1995], Cuesta and Zofio [2005]), viz.,

$$x_1 = A \prod_m y_m^{\alpha_m} \prod_{j=2} \{x_j/x_1\}^{\beta_j} \lambda^{\{1+\sum_m \alpha_m\}}. \tag{2.75}$$

Because (2.74) and (2.75) are identical algebraically, $-\ln\theta$ in (2.74) is the same as $(1 + \sum_m \alpha_m)\ln\lambda$ in (2.75), and one can get $\ln\lambda$ after estimating inefficiency from either of these two equations.

Finally, if we use the normalization $\beta_1 = -1, \lambda = 1$ in (2.69), it can be written as

$$\textbf{Input requirement function: } x_1 = A \prod_m y_m^{\alpha_m} \prod_{j=2} x_j^{\beta_j}\, \theta^{\sum_j \beta_j}, \tag{2.76}$$

which is the input requirement function (IRF) due to Diewert (1974) and Kumbhakar and Heshmati (1995). Input-oriented technical inefficiency in this model is $u = \{\sum_j \beta_j\}\ln\theta > 0$, since $\beta_j < 0$ and $\ln\theta < 0$.

Note that all these specifications are algebraically the same in the sense that if the technology is known inefficiency can be computed from any one of these specifications. It should be noted that, although we used α_m and β_j notations in all the specifications, these are not the same because of different normalizations. However, once a particular model is chosen, the estimated parameters from that model can be uniquely linked to those in the transformation function in (2.69).

2.7.1.2 The CET-CD Transformation Function

Because the CD output function does not satisfy the second-order (concavity) condition for profit maximization, we replace the CD output function by the constant elasticity of transformation (CET) output function (Powell and Gruen [1968]), viz., $g(\lambda y) = [\sum \delta_m(\lambda y_m)^c]^{1/c}$, $\delta_m \geq 0, \sum_m \delta_m = 1, c > 1$. For the CET function the elasticity of transformation between any two outputs is $1/(1-c)$. With this specification, the transformation function can be expressed as

$$\alpha_0 + (1/c)\ln\Big\{\sum_{m=1} \delta_m y_m^c\Big\} + \sum_j \beta_j \ln x_j + u = 0, \;\beta_j < 0, \tag{2.77}$$

where $u = \ln\lambda + (\sum_j \beta_j)\ln\theta$.

If we rewrite (2.77) as

$$-\ln y_1 = \alpha_0 + (1/c)\ln\left[\delta_1 + \sum_{m=2} \delta_m (y_m/y_1)^c\right] + \sum_j \beta_j \ln x_j + u, \tag{2.78}$$

then it can be viewed as an output distance function.[2] If we normalize $\theta = 1$, then the inefficiency terms becomes $u = \ln\lambda$.

By contrast, if we rewrite (2.77) as

$$-\ln x_1 = \{1/\sum_j \beta_j\}\{\alpha_0 + (1/c)\ln\left[\sum_{m=1} \delta_m y_m^c\right] + \sum_{j=2} \beta_j \ln(x_j/x_1)\} + u\{1/\sum_j \beta_j\}, \quad (2.79)$$

and normalize $\lambda = 1$, then it can be viewed as an input distance function in which the inefficiency term becomes $u = \ln\theta$.

Finally, if we normalize $\ln\lambda = -\ln\theta$ in (2.79), we get the hyperbolic input distance function formulation, viz.,

$$-\ln x_1 = \{1/\sum_j \beta_j\}\{\alpha_0 + (1/c)\ln\left[\sum_{m=1} \delta_m y_m^c\right] + \sum_{j=2} \beta_j \ln(x_j/x_1)\} + u_h, \quad (2.80)$$

where $u_h = \ln\lambda\{1 - (\sum_j \beta_j)\}/\{\sum_j \beta_j\}$. By contrast, using the normalization $\ln\lambda = -\ln\theta$ in (2.78), we get the hyperbolic output distance function formulation, viz.,

$$-\ln y_1 = \alpha_0 + (1/c)\ln\left[\delta_1 + \sum_{m=2} \delta_m (y_m/y_1)^c\right] + \sum_j \beta_j \ln x_j + u_{ho}, \quad (2.81)$$

where $u_{ho} = \ln\lambda(1 - \sum_j \beta_j)$. In the hyperbolic model we want to estimate either $\ln\lambda$ or $\ln\theta$. Thus, if either u_h or u_{ho} is estimated, one can get $\ln\lambda$ or $\ln\theta$.

We can also rewrite (2.77) as

$$\ln x_1 = -\{1/\beta_1\}\{\alpha_0 + (1/c)\ln\left\{\sum \delta_m y_m^c\right\} + \sum_j \beta_j \ln x_j\} + u, \quad (2.82)$$

where $u = -\{1/\beta_1\}(\ln\lambda + (\sum_j \beta_j)\ln\theta) = -\ln\theta\{\sum_j \beta_j\}/\beta_1$ after normalizing $\lambda = 1$. This can be viewed as the IRF.

Note that all the above formulations are derived from (2.77) and are therefore algebraically the same. Therefore, it is not necessary to estimate all of these models.[3] Estimated parameters and inefficiency from any of the above models can be used to obtain the corresponding parameters and inefficiency in other models. For example, if one estimates output-oriented inefficiency from (2.78), it can be easily converted to input-oriented and hyperbolic inefficiency. More specifically, u in (2.78) is $\ln\lambda > 0$ when it is viewed as output-oriented measure. We get the input-oriented measure $-\ln\theta > 0$ from $-u/\sum_j \beta_j$ and the hyperbolic measure $\ln\lambda = -\ln\theta$ from $u/(1 - \sum_j \beta_j)$. Note that, in the CET-CD case, RTS is $-\sum_j \beta_j$, so that all the above inefficiency measures are positive. Thus, the link among different inefficiency measures are made via RTS (which is constant in the CET-CD case).

To show whether these results also hold for more flexible functional forms, we now consider the translog functional form for the transformation function.

[2] Note that this can also be viewed as a production function. The functional form of $g(\cdot)$ is such that when one output is taken out of $g(\cdot)$ the other outputs are automatically expressed in ratio form. Thus, the ODF cannot be separated from the production function.

[3] In some of the specifications only a subset of regressors are endogenous while in others all the regressors are endogenous. We discuss estimation issues later.

2.7.1.3 The Translog Transformation Function

We write the transformation function as $Af(\boldsymbol{y}^*, \boldsymbol{x}^*) = 1$, where $\boldsymbol{y}^* = y\lambda$, $\boldsymbol{x}^* = x\theta$, and $f(\boldsymbol{y}^*, \boldsymbol{x}^*)$ is assumed to be translog (TL), that is,

$$\textbf{TL transformation function: } \ln f(\boldsymbol{y}^*, \boldsymbol{x}^*) = \sum_m \alpha_m \ln y_m^* + \frac{1}{2}\sum_m \sum_n \alpha_{mn} \ln y_m^* \ln y_n^* + \sum_j \beta_j \ln x_j^* + \frac{1}{2}\sum_j \sum_k \beta_{jk} \ln x_j^* \ln x_k^* + \sum_m \sum_j \delta_{mj} \ln y_m^* \ln x_j^*. \quad (2.83)$$

This function is assumed to satisfy the following symmetry restrictions: $\beta_{jk} = \beta_{kj}$ and $\alpha_{mn} = \alpha_{nm}$. As with the CD specification, some of the parameters in (2.83) are not identified. One can use the following (identifying restrictions) normalizations ($\alpha_1 = -1, \alpha_{1n} = 0, \forall\, n, \delta_{1j} = 0, \forall\, j, \theta = 1$) to obtain a pseudo production function, viz.,

$$\textbf{TL production function: } \ln y_1 = \alpha_0 + \sum_j \beta_j \ln x_j + \frac{1}{2}\sum_j \sum_k \beta_{jk} \ln x_j \ln x_k + \sum_{m=2} \alpha_m \ln y_m + \frac{1}{2}\sum_{m=2}\sum_{n=2} \alpha_{mn} \ln y_m \ln y_n + \sum_{m=2}\sum_j \delta_{mj} \ln y_m \ln x_j + u, \quad (2.84)$$

where

$$u = \ln\lambda\Big(-1 + \sum_{m=2} \alpha_m + \sum_{m=2}\sum_{n=2} \alpha_{mn} \ln y_n + \sum_{m=2}\sum_j \delta_{mj} \ln x_j\Big) + \frac{1}{2}\sum_{m=2}\sum_{n=2} \alpha_{mn} (\ln\lambda)^2. \quad (2.85)$$

If we rewrite (2.83) as

$$\ln f(\boldsymbol{y}^*, \boldsymbol{x}^*) = \sum_{m=2} \alpha_m \ln(y_m/y_1) + \frac{1}{2}\sum_{m=2}\sum_{n=2} \alpha_{mn} \ln(y_m/y_1)\ln(y_n/y_1) + \sum_j \beta_j \ln x_j^* + \frac{1}{2}\sum_j\sum_k \beta_{jk} \ln x_j^* \ln x_k^* + \sum_{m=2}\sum_j \delta_{mj} \ln x_j^* \ln(y_m/y_1) + \left[\sum_m \alpha_m\right] \ln y_1^* + \sum_m \left[\sum_n \alpha_{mn}\right] \ln y_m \ln y_1^* + \sum_j \left[\sum_m \delta_{mj}\right] \ln x_j^* \ln y_1^*, \quad (2.86)$$

and use a different set of identifying restrictions (normalizations), viz., $\sum_m \alpha_m = -1$, $\sum_n \alpha_{mn} = 0$, $\forall\, m$, $\sum_m \delta_{mj} = 0$, $\forall\, j$, $\theta = 1$, we obtain the output distance function representation,[4] viz.,

[4] Note that these identifying/normalizing constraints make the transformation function homogeneous of degree one in outputs. In the efficiency literature, one starts from a distance function (which is the transformation function with inefficiency built in) and imposes linear homogeneity (in outputs) constraints to get the ODF. Here we get the same end result without using the notion of a distance function to start with.

$$\textbf{TL ODF:}\ \ln y_1 = \alpha_0 + \sum_j \beta_j \ln x_j + \frac{1}{2}\sum_j\sum_k \beta_{jk} \ln x_j \ln x_k + \sum_{m=2} \alpha_m \ln \hat{y}_m + \frac{1}{2}\sum_{m=2}\sum_{n=2} \alpha_{mn} \ln \hat{y}_m \ln \hat{y}_n + \sum_j \sum_{m=2} \delta_{mj} \ln x_j \ln \hat{y}_m + u, \tag{2.87}$$

where $u = -\ln\lambda < 0, \hat{y}_m = y_m/y_1, m = 2, \ldots, M$.

Furthermore, if we rewrite (2.83) as

$$\ln f(\boldsymbol{y}^*, \boldsymbol{x}^*) = \sum_m \alpha_m \ln y_m^* + \frac{1}{2}\sum_m\sum_n \alpha_{mn} \ln y_m^* \ln y_n^* + \sum_{j=2} \beta_j \ln(x_j/x_1) + \frac{1}{2}\sum_{j=2}\sum_{k=2} \beta_{jk} \ln(x_j/x_1)\ln(x_k/x_1) + \sum_m\sum_{j=2} \delta_{mj} \ln(x_j/x_1) \ln y_m^* + \left[\sum_j \beta_j\right] \ln x_1^* + \sum_j \left[\sum_k \beta_{jk}\right] \ln x_j \ln x_1^* + \sum_m \left[\sum_j \delta_{mj}\right] \ln y_m^* \ln x_1^*, \tag{2.88}$$

and use a different set of identifying restrictions (normalizations), viz., $\sum_j \beta_j = -1$, $\sum_k \beta_{jk} = 0, \forall j$, $\sum_j \delta_{mj} = 0, \forall m$, $\lambda = 1$, we get the input distance function representation,[5] viz.,

$$\textbf{TL IDF:}\ \ln x_1 = \alpha_0 + \sum_{j=2} \beta_j \ln \hat{x}_j + \frac{1}{2}\sum_{j=2}\sum_{k=2} \beta_{jk} \ln \hat{x}_j \ln \hat{x}_k + \sum_m \alpha_m \ln y_m + \frac{1}{2}\sum_m\sum_n \alpha_{mn} \ln y_m \ln y_n + \sum_m\sum_{j=2} \delta_{mj} \ln \hat{x}_j \ln y_m + u, \tag{2.89}$$

where $u = -\ln\theta > 0, \hat{x}_j = x_j/x_1, j = 2, \ldots, J$.

To get to the hyperbolic specification in this IDF, we start from (2.88) and use the normalization $\ln\lambda = -\ln\theta$ in addition to $\sum_j \beta_j = -1$, $\sum_k \beta_{jk} = 0, \forall j$, $\sum_j \delta_{mj} = 0, \forall m$. This gives the **hyperbolic** IDF, viz.,

$$\ln x_1 = \alpha_0 + \sum_m \alpha_m \ln y_m + \frac{1}{2}\sum_m\sum_n \alpha_{mn} \ln y_m \ln y_n + \sum_{j=2} \beta_j \ln \hat{x}_j + \frac{1}{2}\sum_{j=2}\sum_{k=2} \beta_{jk} \ln \hat{x}_j \ln \hat{x}_k + \sum_m\sum_{j=2} \delta_{mj} \ln \hat{x}_j \ln y_m + u_h, \tag{2.90}$$

[5] Note that these identifying/normalizing constraints make the transformation function homogeneous of degree one in inputs. In the efficiency literature one defines the IDF as the distance (transformation) function which is homogeneous of degree one in inputs. Here we view the homogeneity property as identifying restrictions on the transformation function without using the notion of a distance function.

where

$$u_h = \ln\lambda\{1 + [\sum_m \alpha_m] + \sum_m [\sum_n \alpha_{mn}] \ln y_m + [\sum_j \delta_{mj}] \ln \hat{x}_j\} + \frac{1}{2}\sum_m \sum_n \alpha_{mn}\{\ln\lambda\}^2. \tag{2.91}$$

It is clear from this that u_h is related to $\ln\lambda$ in a highly nonlinear fashion. It is quite complicated to estimate $\ln\lambda$ from (2.90) starting from distributional assumption on $\ln\lambda$ unless RTS is unity.[6] However, because (2.89) and (2.90) are identical, their inefficiencies are also the same. That is, $u = -\ln\theta$ in (2.89) is the same as u_h in (2.90). Thus, the estimated values of input-oriented inefficiency $\ln\theta$ from (2.89) can be used to estimate hyperbolic inefficiency $\ln\lambda$ by solving the quadratic equation $-\ln\theta = \ln\lambda\{1+[\sum_m \alpha_m]+\sum_m [\sum_n \alpha_{mn}] \ln y_m + [\sum_j \delta_{mj}] \ln \hat{x}_j\} + \frac{1}{2}\sum_m \sum_n \alpha_{mn}\{\ln\lambda\}^2$.

Finally, if we use the following set of identifying restrictions (normalizations), $\beta_1 = -1$, $\beta_{1j} = 0, \forall j$, $\delta_{m1} = 0, \forall m$, $\lambda = 1$, the input requirement function is obtained, viz.,

$$\textbf{TL IRF:} \quad \ln x_1 = \alpha_0 + \sum_{j=2} \beta_j \ln x_j + \frac{1}{2}\sum_{j=2}\sum_{k=2} \beta_{jk} \ln x_j \ln x_k + \sum_m \alpha_m \ln y_m$$
$$+ \frac{1}{2}\sum_m \sum_n \alpha_{mn} \ln y_m \ln y_n + \sum_m \sum_{j=2} \delta_{mj} \ln x_j \ln y_m + u, \tag{2.92}$$

where

$$u = \ln\theta(-1 + \sum_{j=2} \beta_j + \frac{1}{2}\sum_{j=2}\sum_{k=2} \beta_{jk} \ln x_j + \sum_m \sum_{j=2} \delta_{mj} \ln y_m) + \frac{1}{2}\sum_{j=2}\sum_{k=2} \beta_{jk}(\ln\theta)^2. \tag{2.93}$$

It is clear from this that starting from the translog transformation function specification in (2.83) one can derive the production function, the output and input distance functions, and the input requirement function simply by using different normalizations. Furthermore, these formulations show how technical inefficiency transmits from one specification into another. As earlier, we warn the readers that the notations α, β, and δ are not the same across different specifications. However, starting from any one of them, it is possible to express the parameters in terms of those in the transformation function. Note that other than the input and output distance functions, technical inefficiency appears in a very complicated form. So although all these specifications are algebraically the same, the question that naturally arises is which formulation is easier to estimate, and whether a particular specification has fewer endogenous regressors and is preferred to other specifications.

2.8 Allocative Inefficiency

In the production function framework, inefficiency is discussed in the technical sense, viz., whether the inputs are fully utilized given the technology. It does not address the concern, however, of whether the observed *combination* of inputs is the best (in some sense). Recall that an isoquant depicts different input combinations that can all produce the same level

[6] This relationship is similar to the relationship between input- and output-oriented technical inefficiency, estimation of which is discussed in detail in Kumbhakar and Tsionas (2006).

of *frontier* output. The fact that different input combinations produce the same level of frontier output raises the question: How should the producer choose among different input combinations? Which one is the *best*?

Obviously, we need a criterion to judge what is the best, and the criterion should come from one that is relevant to the producers' production decisions. Two such behavioral criteria are often used, viz., cost minimization and profit maximization. In the next two sections, we discuss how the concept of allocative inefficiency can be accommodated under these two behavioral assumptions.

2.8.1 Cost Minimization and Allocative Inefficiency

The cost minimization criterion is most widely used in empirical applications. This behavioral assumption helps us determine the least-cost input combination for producing a given level of output. In this case, the production technology is characterized by inputs, output, and input prices. So now we ask what is the best that the producers can do to minimize the cost of producing a given level of output, and the answer provides standards against which the economic performance of producers can be estimated.

If firms minimize cost subject to the production function to produce a specific level of output, the first-order conditions of cost minimization state that the slope of the isoquant (the marginal rate of technical substitution) equals the ratio of input prices, viz.,

$$\frac{dx_2}{dx_1} = -\left.\frac{f_1}{f_2}\right|_{y=y_1} = \frac{w_1}{w_2}, \tag{2.94}$$

where w_i is the price of input x_i. If a firm fails to use inputs according to the above rule, then it is said to be *allocatively inefficient*. In such a case, the cost of producing the same level of output will be higher. In the example illustrated in Figure 2.11, the cost of producing y_1 using input combination given by point A (the point of tangency between the isoquant and the isocost line) is less than producing y_1 using any other input combinations that are on the y_1 isoquant.

To address the problem of allocative inefficiency, the production function alone does not suffice – the price information needs to be included in the econometric model. A natural choice is to estimate the model in a cost minimization framework in which a system of equations consisting of the cost function and the cost share equations are estimated. This

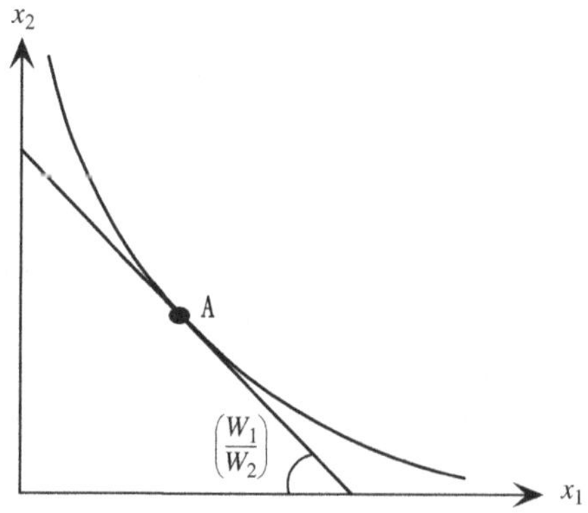

Figure 2.11. Optimal Input Allocation

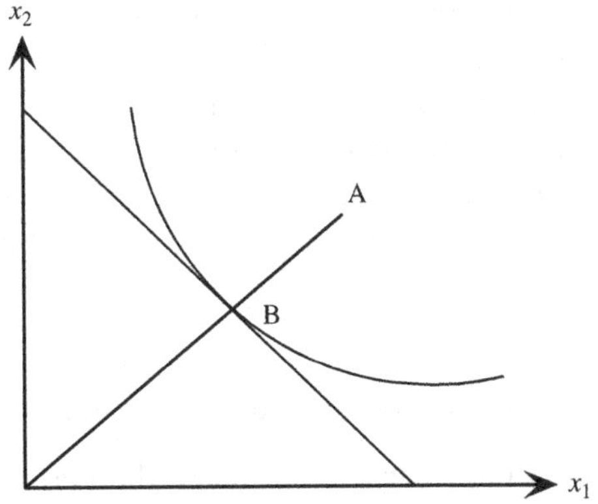

Figure 2.12. Technically Inefficient but Allocatively Efficient Allocation

approach is discussed in Chapter 6. Alternatively, we may also estimate a system consisting of the production function and the first-order conditions of cost minimization. We misuse the terminology a bit and call this the *primal approach*, although, in this approach, we use data on input prices (via the first-order conditions) along with information on input and output quantities. This approach is discussed in Chapter 8. Yet another alternative is to estimate a single equation cost function in which technical and allocative inefficiencies are lumped together. We discuss the implications of such a model and estimation results in Chapter 8.

If the firms are allocatively efficient, then the point of tangency between the isoquant and the isocost line (i.e., point B) gives the input combination that is optimal (the least cost input combination), as shown in Figure 2.12. Substituting these optimal input quantities, which are functions of output and input prices, in the definition of cost ($c^a = \boldsymbol{w}'\boldsymbol{x}$) gives the neoclassical cost frontier, $c^a = c(\boldsymbol{w}, y)$. If firms are inefficient (technically and/or allocatively), then actual cost will exceed the minimum cost. For example, point A represents a firm that is allocatively efficient but technically inefficient. If the production function ($f(\boldsymbol{x})$) is linear homogeneous and there is no allocative inefficiency, then the cost function can be expressed as

$$c^a = c(\boldsymbol{w}, y) \cdot \exp(u), \tag{2.95}$$

where $u \geq 0$ is OO technical inefficiency. If the production function is nonhomogeneous, then the cost function will be of the form $c(\boldsymbol{w}, y\exp(u)) \geq c(\boldsymbol{w}, y)$. We can then define cost efficiency as the ratio of $c(\boldsymbol{w}, y)$ and $c(\boldsymbol{w}, y\exp(u))$, which will be between 0 and 1, by construction. Thus, we use the cost frontier (not the production frontier) to judge the performance of producers relative to the best that can be achieved economically (while the production frontier describes the best that be achieved technically).

If technical inefficiency is input oriented and firms are fully efficient allocatively, the corresponding cost function (shown in detail in Chapter 4) will be of the form $c^a = c(\boldsymbol{w}, y)\exp(\eta)$, irrespective of whether the production function is homogeneous or nonhomogeneous. Thus, it is easy to work with the cost function under IO technical inefficiency because η appears additively in the log cost function. It is, however, more complicated if firms are both technically and allocatively inefficient. The formulation is very complex for both OO and IO technical inefficiency model. These issues will be discussed in Chapters 6 and 8.

Extension of the cost minimization problem for multiple outputs is relatively straightforward. The cost frontier in the multiple output case is $c(\mathbf{w}, \mathbf{y})$ where $\mathbf{y}$ is a vector of outputs. With IO technical inefficiency, the cost function can be written as $c^a = c(\mathbf{w}, \mathbf{y}) \cdot \exp(\eta)$, $\eta \geq 0$. If the production function is homogeneous, then $c^a = c(\mathbf{w}, \mathbf{y}) \cdot \exp(u/r)$, $u \geq 0$ under OO technical inefficiency. Thus, u/r in the above expression is OO technical inefficiency and η is IO technical inefficiency where r measures the degree of homogeneity (returns to scale).

2.8.2 Profit Maximization and Allocative Inefficiency

Earlier, we used cost minimization behavior to judge the performance of producers. A restriction of the cost minimization framework is that output quantity is assumed to be exogenously given. This may be the case for some firms (such as those in the electricity, water, telecommunications, postal sectors), but for others output is likely to be a choice variable. A more general framework that allows output and inputs to be endogenous can be analyzed under the assumption of profit maximization. So we now turn to the profit maximization behavior as the criterion in choosing optimal input and output quantities.

If firms maximize profit subject to the production function, the first-order conditions suggest that the value of marginal product should be equal to the input price (i.e., $p f_j(\cdot) = w_j$, where w_j and p are input and output prices). This is shown in Figure 2.13. These first-order conditions can be used to solve for optimal input quantities in terms of output and input prices. These are the *input demand functions*, that is, $x_i = x_i(\mathbf{w}, p)$. Substituting the input demand functions back into the production function then gives the optimal level of output to be produced, $y = y(\mathbf{w}, p)$, which is the *output supply function*. Finally, using the optimal levels of output and inputs in the definition of profit gives the profit function, $\pi^a = p \cdot y(\mathbf{w}, p) - \mathbf{w}'\mathbf{x}(\mathbf{w}, p) = \pi(\mathbf{w}, p)$, which is homogeneous of degree 1 in $\mathbf{w}$ and p.

The procedure described here is used to derive the profit function when firms are fully efficient. If firms are assumed to be technically inefficient but allocatively efficient, and the production function is homogeneous, then the profit function will be of the form

$$\pi^a = \pi(\mathbf{w}, p) \exp(-u/(1 - r)), \ u \geq 0, \tag{2.96}$$

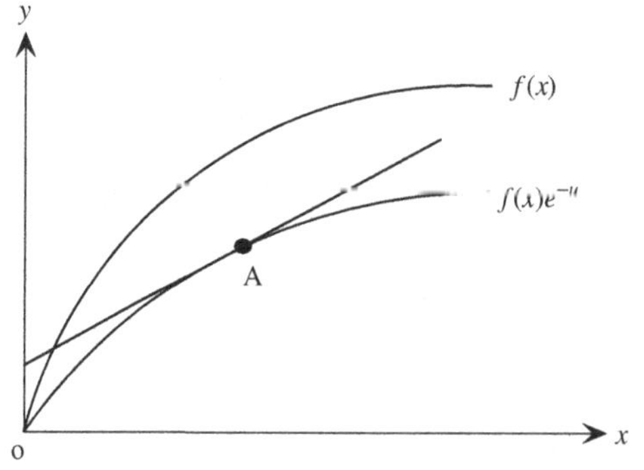

Figure 2.13. Technically Inefficient but Allocatively Efficient under Profit Maximization

where $r < 1$ is returns to scale and u is OO technical inefficiency (see Kumbhakar [2001]) for the derivation of the profit function when the production function is nonhomogeneous). We can define profit efficiency as the ratio of π^a and $\pi(\boldsymbol{w}, y)$, which will be between 0 and 1, by construction. A similar result is obtained when the production function is homogeneous but technical inefficiency is input-oriented. Thus, we can use the profit frontier to judge the performance of producers.

If we impose behavioral assumptions (cost minimization or profit maximization) on producers, then it is relatively easy to accommodate multiple outputs. However, we defer further discussion of multiple output cost and profit functions to later chapters.

2.9 The Indirect Production Function

In this subsection, we discuss an SF model that is formulated slightly differently. Producers (especially farmers) from developing countries often face a shortage of funds to purchase inputs. Both the cost minimization and profit maximization behaviors fail to capture the problem associated with the shortage of funds required for purchasing variable inputs. This can be true for both developed and developing countries. For example, Lee and Chambers (1986) found the expenditure constraint to be effective even in the case of U.S. agriculture. To accommodate this problem, output maximization subject to a specified expenditure on variable inputs is often used as the rational economic behavior. This calls for the use of an alternative dual approach, viz., the indirect production function (IPF) approach (Shephard [1974]).

2.9.1 Modeling

We start with the familiar production function relating inputs and output

$$y = f(\boldsymbol{x}, \boldsymbol{z}) \exp(-u), \tag{2.97}$$

where $\boldsymbol{z}$ denotes the quasi-fixed input vector, and, as usual, $u \geq 0$ represents technical inefficiency, which can be interpreted as the percent loss of potential output, given the quantities of $\boldsymbol{x}$ and $\boldsymbol{z}$. The resource (or budget) constraint faced by the producer can be written as

$$C = w'x \tag{2.98}$$

where $\boldsymbol{w}$ denotes the vector of prices of variable inputs and C represents the fund available for the purchase of variable inputs. The producer's objective is to maximize output, subject to the budget constraint and the production function in (2.97).[7] The Lagrangian for the problem can be written as

$$\mathcal{L} = f(\cdot) \exp(-u) + \Lambda(C - \boldsymbol{w}'\boldsymbol{x}), \tag{2.99}$$

where Λ denotes the Lagrange multiplier associated with the budget constraint. The exogenous variables are the elements in vectors $\boldsymbol{z}$, $\boldsymbol{w}$ and the total budget of the producer, C, while the input vector $\boldsymbol{x}$ is determined endogenously. Solving the first-order conditions for

[7] This problem is equivalent to profit maximization with a given output price in a single product case.

the problem, we get the solution of the endogenous variables in terms of the exogenous variables, viz.,

$$x_i = g_i(\mathbf{w}, C, \mathbf{z}) \; \forall\, i = 1, \ldots, n. \tag{2.100}$$

Substituting these optimal values of x_i in (2.97) we get the optimal value of the objective function,

$$y = \psi(\mathbf{w}, C, \mathbf{z}) \exp(-u), \tag{2.101}$$

which represents the indirect production function (henceforth IPF). It expresses the maximum attainable output for the producer as a function of the availability of funds, the prices of variable inputs, the amounts of fixed inputs, and technical inefficiency. After adding a random error term (v) in the logarithmic version of (2.101) we get the stochastic IPF which is econometrically identical to the stochastic production frontier. The difference is the arguments of the IPF.

Unfortunately, the preceding analysis does not provide a framework to analyze the effect of the borrowing constraint (which is different from the concept of the budget constraint). This situation is common in countries where the credit market is not competitive and, therefore, there is likely to be a gap between what the producers want to borrow and what they actually can borrow. To examine the effect of this type of constraint on output and profit, we assume that the desired budget for a particular producer is C^*, which by definition cannot be lower than the actual expenditure (C). That is, $y^* = \psi(\mathbf{w}, C^*, \mathbf{z})$, where the strict inequality means that the producer in question is credit (expenditure)-constrained. First, we assume that producers are fully efficient. The presence of this constraint means that the producer in question can only spend C and not C^*, and because $C^* \geq C$, output will be lower, as will be profit. That is, output associated with C^* (i.e., $y^* = \psi(\mathbf{w}, C^*, \mathbf{z})$) will be higher than output associated with the budget C.

Without loss of generality, we show this graphically in Figure 2.14 for a single input and single output. In this graph, the expression for profit ($\pi = py - wx$) is rewritten (in terms of output) as $y = \pi/p + (w/p)x$, where p is output price. Thus, the vertical intercept of the line measures (normalized) profit, π/p. Normalized profit without constraint is measured

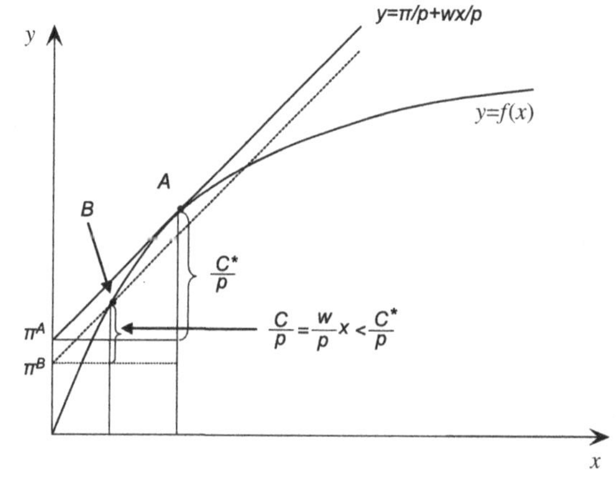

Figure 2.14. Output and Profit with and without Expenditure Constraints

by the intercept of the solid line (π^A) and profit associated with the expenditure constraint is measured by the intercept of the dotted line (π^B). It is clear from the figure that $\pi^A \geq \pi^B$, that is, profit is reduced due to the presence of expenditure constraints, all other things being equal.

If producers are technically inefficient, the IPF can still be expressed as (2.101) from which one can estimate the effect of technical inefficiency as well as the effect of the credit constraint on output (see Kumbhakar and Bokusheva [2009] for details). This idea can be explained in terms of the above graph which can be thought of as $y = f(x,z)e^{-u}$. Thus the above analysis in the graph is for a given level of inefficiency. That is, observed output $y = y^*e^{-u}$. To identify y^* we need C^*, which is the level of expenditure without credit-constraint, and can be obtained from the solution of C from the equation $\partial y/\partial C = 1$. This optimum value of C^* is then substituted into the IPF to get y^*, which is the unconstrained output level for a given level of inefficiency, (point A in the figure). If we denote the constrained output level as y^C (point B in the figure), then $y^C < y^*$, and therefore $\ln y^* - \ln y^C$ will be the percentage (when multiplied by 100) of output loss due to the credit constraint. The percentage of output loss due to technical inefficiency is $u \times 100$) (see Kumbhakar and Bokusheva [2009] for details).

There are non-production type constrained models in which SF model can be used in a straightforward manner. In the presence of financing constraints the observed investment-to-capital ratio (I/K) will be less than the efficient (optimal) investment-to-capital ratio which is specified as (Wang [2003])

$$\ln(I/K)^* = \beta_0 + \beta_1 \ln(\text{Tobin's } Q) + \beta_2 \ln(SALE/K) + v, \tag{2.102}$$

and $\ln(I/K) = \ln(I/K)^* - u$. Thus, the difference between the optimal investment-to-capital ratio and the observed investment-to-capital ratio will be attributed to financing constraint. The percentage difference can be represented by a non-negative term u. This is a straightforward application of the SF model, except for the difference in interpretation. In this formulation u times 100 can be viewed as the percentage shortfall of investment from its desired (frontier) level due to the presence of financial constraints. Thus, u can be labeled as investment inefficiency (which parallels the definition of technical inefficiency in production function models). It measures the shortfall of investment from its desired level as a result of the presence of financial constraints (just like technical inefficiency measures output shortfall, in percentage terms).

An advantage of the SF approach is that one can directly estimate the impact of firm characteristics (z) such as size and leverage on the degree of financial constraints, rather than estimate the impact of these characteristics on investment of the average firm and infer from it whether or not they contribute to financial constraints. This can be done by extending the basic model proposed above to accommodate the z variables. In the stylized literature, firm characteristics that impact on the financial constraint of firms include physical assets, cash flows, and financial fragility that is usually measured using the debt-to-equity ratio. In certain contexts, the financial constraint is also affected by membership of business groups, and the impact of business group membership on financial constraints can be time varying. These z variables can be used as determinants of financial constraints, from which one can compute the marginal effects of these z variables in easing investment constraints. More details on this model can be found in Wang (2003) and Bhaumik et al. (2012).

PART II

SINGLE EQUATION APPROACH: PRODUCTION, COST, AND PROFIT

3

Estimation of Technical Efficiency in Production Frontier Models Using Cross-Sectional Data

3.1 Introduction

In Chapter 1, we introduced a series of questions that the tools discussed in this book are designed to help answer. In this Chapter, we focus on the examination of technical inefficiency in the context of production frontier models using cross-sectional data. That is, based on observations across a number of units (be it countries, companies, schools, hospitals, bank branches, retail outlets, water treatment works, farms, etc.) for one given point in time, this chapter introduces tools to model a production frontier. In modeling the impact of technical inefficiency on production it is assumed, at least implicitly, that inputs are exogenously given and that the objective is to maximize output (i.e., output is the only choice variable). Only quantities are modeled (e.g., the number of staff or total hours employed, the amount of output produced) and no price information is included in the modeling, so only technical efficiency is measured and allocative efficiency and economic or cost efficiency cannot be considered (see Chapter 8). As such, the approaches set out in this chapter can answer questions such as those set out below.

Which schools, or which universities, are the best in terms of graduation rates, staff numbers per student graduated, and so on (controlling for characteristics such as the level of student educational attainment upon entry, etc.)? That is, given the quality of the students upon entry, the socioeconomic characteristics of the local catchment area, and/or the parents of the students and other characteristics, what is the maximum graduation rate per staff member (or minimum number of total staff per graduated student) that a given school should be expected to achieve and how far away from this maximum (minimum) is each school? The former might help the parents/students in deciding which college/university to attend, whereas the minimum number of total staff per graduated student is of more interest to budget holders.[1]

Given the characteristics of patients on admission, which hospitals are best at treating cancer patients (e.g., in terms of the percentage of patients with prostate cancer cured per staff member)? Thus, from a government's perspective, which hospitals should specialize in this type of treatment?

Which police forces are best at reducing crime in terms of residents' level of fear of local crime or the number of burglaries solved per year per police officer, given the socioeconomic

[1] In contrast, parents and students are more likely to view high ratios of *teaching* staff per student as a positive indicator.

characteristics of the area? By how much could crime be reduced if the worse performing police forces could replicate the performance of the best performing police forces? From a government's perspective, are there any lessons that we can learn from those police forces that, given the local community characteristics, enjoy relatively low crime levels in their neighborhood? Can we transfer these lessons across police forces?

Which of the supermarket's regional outlets are doing well and which are underachieving, and which of the regional managers seem to be achieving the greatest sales, given the outlets that they supervise and the local market characteristics? From the company's perspective, should we transfer these managers to the poorer performing areas to improve the performance of those outlets? At a more strategic level, are retails outlets characterized by economies of scale (i.e., if inputs are increased does output increase by more than the percentage increase in inputs?), or diseconomies of scale, or do economies of scale vary according some factor? That is, given the local market characteristics, what is the optimal size for a new store?

Which farms in the dairy industry are more productive and which are the least productive? If the farm were to operate at a more efficient level, how much more milk could be produced, given the amount of feed, cattle, land, and labor? Is their efficiency affected by the use of information technology, managers' education levels, or the type of ownership? Does investment in IT affect a farm's efficiency? And, if so, by how much does efficiency improve if a farmer were to increase investment in IT by 10 percent? It is this example that we use throughout this chapter as a way of illustrating the approaches introduced in this chapter.

Thus, this chapter explores the estimation of technical efficiency within a production frontier context using only cross-sectional data. The following two chapters examine the same issues within the context of cost frontier models and then profit frontier models. It is not until Chapter 8 that we generalize these models to incorporate allocative efficiency and it is not until Chapter 10 that we generalize these models to a panel data framework.

3.2 Output-Oriented Technical Efficiency

As discussed in Chapter 2, technical efficiency can be modeled as either output-oriented or input-oriented. In this section and the sections on estimation that follow, we discuss output-oriented technical efficiency for the production frontier model, which is widely used in the single equation stochastic production frontier literature. We discuss input-oriented technical efficiency for the production frontier model in Section 3.5.

A *stochastic production frontier model* with output-oriented technical inefficiency can be specified as

$$\ln y_i = \ln y_i^* - u_i, \quad u_i \geq 0, \tag{3.1}$$

$$\ln y_i^* = f(\boldsymbol{x}_i; \boldsymbol{\beta}) + v_i, \tag{3.2}$$

where the subscript i denotes observations (firms, individuals, etc.), y_i is a scalar of observed output, $\boldsymbol{x}_i$ is a $J\times 1$ vector of input variables, $\boldsymbol{\beta}$ is a $J\times 1$ vector of the corresponding coefficient vector, v_i is a zero-mean random error, and $u_i \geq 0$ is production inefficiency. Equation (3.2) defines the stochastic production frontier function. Given $\boldsymbol{x}$, the frontier gives the maximum possible level of output, and it is stochastic because of v_i. Given that $u_i \geq 0$, observed output (y_i) is bounded below the frontier output level (y_i^*).

It is sometimes convenient to write the model in the following form:

$$\ln y_i = f(\boldsymbol{x}_i; \boldsymbol{\beta}) + \epsilon_i, \tag{3.3}$$

$$\epsilon_i = v_i - u_i, \tag{3.4}$$

where ϵ_i is the error term which is often labeled as the *composed error term.*

The term u_i specified in (3.1) is the log difference between the maximum and the actual output (i.e., $u_i = \ln y_i^* - \ln y_i$), therefore $u_i \times 100\%$ is the percentage by which actual output can be increased using the same inputs if production is fully efficient. In other words, $u_i \times 100\%$ gives the percentage of output that is lost due to technical inefficiency. The estimated value of u_i is referred to as the output-oriented *(technical) inefficiency*, with a value close to 0 implying close to fully efficient.

Rearranging (3.1), we have

$$\exp(-u_i) = \frac{y_i}{y_i^*}. \tag{3.5}$$

Therefore, $\exp(-u_i)$ gives the ratio of actual output to the maximum possible output. The ratio is referred to as the *technical efficiency* of firm i. Because $u_i \geq 0$, the ratio is bounded between 0 and 1, with a value equal to 1 implying that the firm is fully efficient technically. The value of $\exp(-u_i) \times 100\%$ is the percentage of the maximum output that is produced by producer i. Thus, if $\exp(-u_i) \times 100\% = 95\%$, the producer is producing only 95% of the maximum possible (frontier) output.

The efficiency measure $\exp(-u_i)$ and the technical inefficiency measure u_i are central to the efficiency study. In the following sections, we will discuss how a statistic can be constructed to estimate these measures.

3.3 Estimation Methods: Distribution-Free Approaches

Our focus in this chapter is on parametric models in which a parametric functional form for the production frontier $f(x)$ will be assumed. The estimation of the model involves (i) estimating the parameters of the frontier function $f(x)$, and (ii) estimating inefficiency. Broadly speaking, various methods of estimating $f(x)$ are developed, and the choice of method may depend on whether distributional assumptions on the error components are made or not. One approach is not to make specific distributional assumptions on the error components and this approach is labeled as the *distribution-free approach* (this section). Another approach is to impose very specific distributional assumptions on the error components and apply the maximum likelihood (ML) method and this approach is labeled as the *parametric approach* (see Section 3.4). In both sections, a specific empirical example of dairy farming is used in order to demonstrate the approaches using Stata.

We first examine the distribution-free approaches. An obvious advantage of these approaches is that the estimation results do not depend on the distributional assumption on u_i. The drawback, however, is that the statistical properties of the estimator of u_i may not be readily available. (Further discussion on the costs and benefits of the approaches are provided in the relevant sections.) In the following sections, we present three approaches that do not make distributional assumptions on the error components.

3.3.1 Corrected OLS (COLS)

An early estimator for a production frontier model is the *corrected ordinary least square* (COLS) estimator proposed by Winsten (1957). The proposed model is a frontier model that is deterministic (i.e., the model is a simpler version of model (3.1) to (3.2) in that it excludes the statistical error v_i). Thus, the deterministic frontier production model is

$$\ln y_i = \ln y_i^* - u_i, \quad u_i \geq 0, \tag{3.6}$$
$$\ln y_i^* = f(\boldsymbol{x}_i; \boldsymbol{\beta}). \tag{3.7}$$

Compared to (3.1) to (3.2), the model does not allow any random error v_i and the frontier function (3.7) is therefore nonstochastic. Forsund and Hjalmarsson (1978) used this type of model extensively.

In what follows, we assume that the frontier function $f(\cdot)$ is either log-linear or linear in parameters, although this is not a requirement of the approach. We separate the intercept term from the rest of the function and write it as

$$\ln y_i = \beta_0 + \tilde{\boldsymbol{x}}_i'\tilde{\boldsymbol{\beta}} - u_i, \tag{3.8}$$

where $\tilde{\boldsymbol{x}}_i$ is a vector of inputs and other environmental variables. The variables may be in log (for a log linear function) and the vector may have cross-products terms (for a translog function specification).

The idea of COLS is straightforward. Because what is needed is to have the estimated frontier function bound observations ($\ln y_i$) from above, the estimation proceeds by first obtaining consistent estimates of the slope coefficients of the model, and then the estimated production function is shifted upward to the extent that the function after the adjustment bounds all the observations below. The following two-stage procedure explains how this is achieved.

1. At the first stage, we run an OLS regression of $\ln y$ on $\tilde{\boldsymbol{x}}$ and a constant of 1 and obtain

$$\ln y_i = \hat{\beta}_0 + \boldsymbol{x}_i'\hat{\tilde{\boldsymbol{\beta}}} + \hat{e}_i, \tag{3.9}$$

   where $\hat{e}_i$ are the OLS residuals. Because $\mathrm{E}(u_i) \neq 0$, the $\hat{\beta}_0$ obtained from (3.9) is a biased estimate of β_0 in (3.8). Nevertheless, $\hat{\tilde{\boldsymbol{\beta}}}$ is a consistent estimate of $\tilde{\boldsymbol{\beta}}$ in (3.8). That is, the OLS estimation of (3.8) produces consistent slope coefficients but a biased intercept. At this stage, we also obtain the zero-mean OLS regression residual $\hat{e}_i$ as

$$\hat{e}_i = \ln y_i - [\hat{\beta}_0 + \tilde{\boldsymbol{x}}_i'\hat{\tilde{\boldsymbol{\beta}}}]. \tag{3.10}$$

   The value of $\hat{e}_i$ can be greater than, equal to, or less than 0.
2. At the second stage, the OLS intercept is adjusted upward by the amount of $\max\{\hat{e}_i\}$, so that the adjusted function bounds observations from above. The residuals become

$$\hat{e}_i - \max\{\hat{e}_i\} = \ln y_i - \underbrace{\left\{\left[\hat{\beta}_0 + \max\{\hat{e}_i\}\right] + \tilde{\boldsymbol{x}}_i'\hat{\tilde{\boldsymbol{\beta}}}\right\}}_{\text{estimated frontier function}} \leq 0, \tag{3.11}$$

   and

$$\hat{u}_i \equiv -(\hat{e}_i - \max\{\hat{e}_i\}) \geq 0, \tag{3.12}$$

where $\hat{u}_i$ in (3.12) is the estimated inefficiency for model (3.8). Technical efficiency of each observation can then be calculated as $\widehat{TE}_i = \exp(-\hat{u}_i)$.

Example

The dataset, `dairy`, which contains data on 196 dairy farms, is used in this and all the subsequent empirical illustrations of this chapter. Appendix E provides information on how to download the dataset. In the basic model, the output, `ly`, is the log of the amount of milk production, and the inputs (all in logarithms) include labor hours (`llabor`), feed (`lfeed`), the number of cows (`lcattle`), and the land size of the farm (`lland`).

Before we start, we first store the variable names of $\boldsymbol{x}_i$ in Stata's global macro and name the macro `xvar`. This way, we may refer to the macro (for convenience) in places where the full list of the $\boldsymbol{x}_i$ variables is required.

```
. use dairy, clear
. global xvar  llabor lfeed lcattle lland
```

Model 1: OLS

We begin with a standard OLS estimation of the model.

```
. regress ly $xvar

      Source |       SS           df       MS         Number of obs =       196
-------------+------------------------------          F(  4,    191) =    337.37
       Model |  28.5612726         4  7.14031816      Prob > F      =    0.0000
    Residual |  4.04240268       191  .021164412      R-squared     =    0.8760
-------------+------------------------------          Adj R-squared =    0.8734
       Total |  32.6036753       195  .167198335      Root MSE      =    .14548

------------------------------------------------------------------------------
          ly |      Coef.   Std. Err.      t    P>|t|     [95% Conf. Interval]
-------------+----------------------------------------------------------------
      llabor |   .1254299   .0501422     2.50   0.013      .0265262    .2243336
       lfeed |   .1677741   .0433321     3.87   0.000      .0823031     .253245
     lcattle |   .7710345   .0664727    11.60   0.000      .6399196    .9021493
       lland |   .0193328   .0448032     0.43   0.667     -.0690398    .1077055
       _cons |   7.272442   .5551692    13.10   0.000      6.177392    8.367492
------------------------------------------------------------------------------
```

As we discussed earlier, the OLS coefficients of `llabor`, `lfeed`, `lcattle`, and `lland` are consistent for the production frontier model, whereas the estimated constant (intercept) is not. Although the coefficient on `lland` is not significant, we retain it in the model as it aligns with expectations and is found to be significant in subsequent models. This is also useful for comparison purposes. The result shows that the output elasticity of cattle is about 77 percent, and, setting the quasi-fixed production factor of land aside, the three variable inputs indicate a production technology close to constant returns to scale (i.e., the sum of the coefficients, 0.125 + 0.168 + 0.771, is close to 1). Note that in this model we cannot separate a variable input from a quasi-fixed input. All the x variables in this model are treated as exogenous (i.e., independent of both u and v).

Model 2: COLS

Following the OLS estimation, the code provided here obtains the efficiency measure of each observations via the COLS approach outlined in Section 3.3.1 and then saves the efficiency measure in `eff_cols`. (Note that the use of `double` is used for extra accuracy and is optional.)

```
. predict e, residual     /* save the OLS residuals in the variable e */
. quietly summarize e     /* obtain summary statistics without any output*/
. generate double u_star = - (e - r(max))  /* obtain the inefficiencies using equation (3.12) */
. generate double eff_cols = exp(-u_star)  /* the technical efficiency index */
. summarize eff_cols

    Variable |       Obs        Mean    Std. Dev.       Min        Max
-------------+--------------------------------------------------------
    eff_cols |       196    .7708748    .1060425   .4425342          1
```

The results show that, on average, the dairy farmers achieve 77 percent of the maximum potential output in their production. Notice that the maximum efficiency index is 1, which is true by construction. The least efficient farmer achieves only 44 percent of his/her maximum achievable output.

We plot the histogram of the efficiency index in Figure 3.1 (and save the chart for use later):

```
. histogram eff_cols, bin(100) `kden' saving(eff_cols)
```

As demonstrated, the COLS estimates of technical inefficiency are easy to compute, but the simplicity comes at a price. COLS assumes that the frontier function is *deterministic*, and the randomness of the model comes entirely from the variation in inefficiency. Therefore, deviations from the estimated frontier are entirely attributed to inefficiency, and there is no role for other randomness such as data errors, atypical events (e.g., unusually good weather not experienced by all farmers), or luck. One of the consequences is that the estimated inefficiency is highly sensitive to outliers (no matter what the cause). If a dataset has

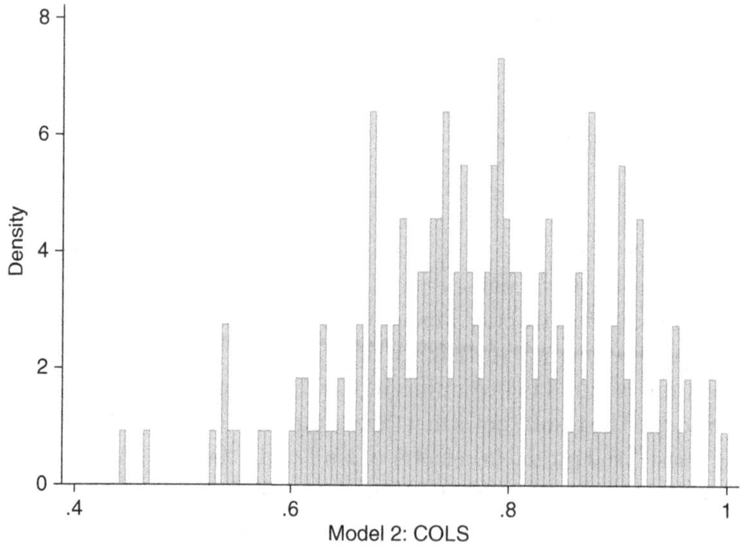

Figure 3.1. Histogram of COLS Efficiency

an unduly large value on one of the y_i observations, COLS would overestimate the efficient frontier, inadvertently making estimated technical inefficiencies larger than they otherwise would be.

3.3.2 Corrected Mean Absolute Deviation (CMAD)

The COLS estimates of technical efficiency are based on the OLS residuals. An alternative to the OLS regression is to use the mean (or median) absolute deviation (MAD) regression. We can thus estimate efficiency from the residuals of the median regression to compute the COLS-type efficiency index using the same procedure as for COLS (we will call this approach corrected MAD, or CMAD). The difference between OLS and MAD regression is that MAD regression passes through the median whereas the OLS regression passes through the mean of the data. In this sense, MAD is just another regression and therefore CMAD can be used as a robustness check.

Example

Model 3: CMAD

We first run the MAD regression on the dataset of 196 dairy farms and then provide the results.

```
. qreg ly $xvar

(iteration log omitted)

Median regression                                    Number of obs =        196
  Raw sum of deviations  63.7397 (about 12.649474)
  Min sum of deviations 21.55983                     Pseudo R2     =     0.6618

------------------------------------------------------------------------------
          ly |      Coef.   Std. Err.      t    P>|t|     [95% Conf. Interval]
-------------+----------------------------------------------------------------
      llabor |   .1214217   .0573883     2.12   0.036     .0082254     .234618
       lfeed |    .118011   .0489572     2.41   0.017     .0214448    .2145772
     lcattle |   .7649174   .0762851    10.03   0.000      .614448    .9153868
       lland |   .0551765   .0512162     1.08   0.283    -.0458456    .1561985
       _cons |   7.721349   .6323743    12.21   0.000     6.474015    8.968684
------------------------------------------------------------------------------
```

The coefficient estimates are quite similar to those of the OLS model, with slight differences for `lfeed` and `lland`. We calculate the efficiency estimates (in the same way as we did above for the COLS model) and compare them to the COLS estimates (which we saved before).

```
. predict e_cmad, residual
. quietly summarize e_cmad /* obtain summary statistics of the residual  */
. generate double eta_star_q = -(e_cmad - r(max)) /* obtain the inefficiencies */
. generate double eff_cmad = exp(-eta_star_q) /* the technical efficiency index */
. summarize eff_cols eff_cmad

    Variable |       Obs        Mean    Std. Dev.       Min        Max
-------------+--------------------------------------------------------
    eff_cols |       196    .7708748    .1060425   .4425342          1
    eff_cmad |       196    .7674637    .1058017   .4413492          1
```

The results are similar to that found in the COLS case.

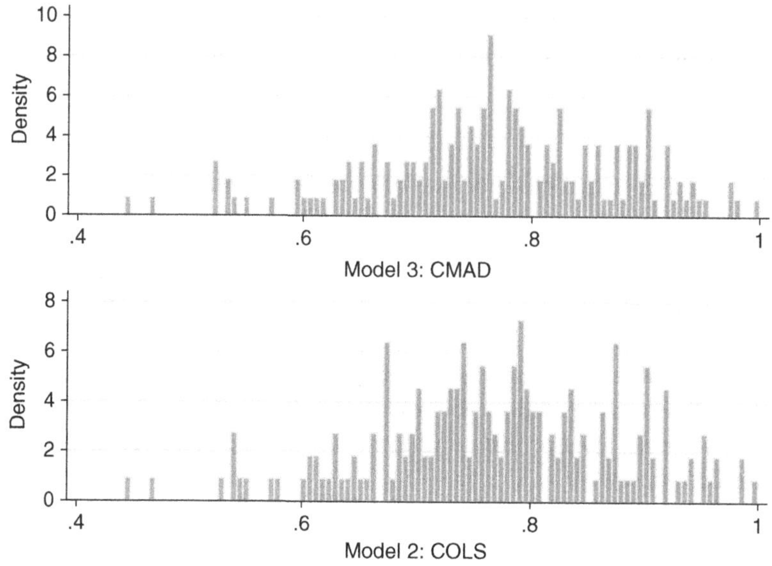

Figure 3.2. Histogram of CMAD Efficiency Compared to COLS Efficiency

The two histograms of the efficiency results from the two models are compared in Figure 3.2 and were created using the following code:

```
. label variable eff_cmad "Model 3: CMAD"
. histogram eff_cmad, bin(100) `kden' saving(eff_cmad)
. graph combine eff_cmad.gph eff_cols.gph, col(1) scale(1)
```

In both cases, there is a reasonable dispersion of efficiencies. However, although it is not the case in this example, the most efficient farm(s) may be a long way from the rest of the farms; that is, there may be a significant outlier(s). This could result in very high estimates of inefficiency. One possible way to mitigate this sensitivity would be to use an adjusted benchmark such as the upper quartile or top decile rather than the extreme value, but such an approach is somewhat *ad hoc.*

3.3.3 Thick Frontier Approach

Berger and Humphrey (1991) propose a distribution-free approach known as the *thick frontier approach* (TFA). It is most often applied within a cost frontier model estimation framework, although it may also be used within a production frontier model estimation framework.

The approach groups samples into four quartiles (or N quantiles) according to an observed efficiency indicator such as the average output or the average cost. In the context of production function estimation, firms in the first quartile have lower average output, and thus they are hypothesized to have lower-than-average production efficiency. Firms in the last quartile have a higher average output and are hypothesized to have a higher-than-average production efficiency. The production function is first estimated using data of the last sample quartile (the efficient group) and then estimated using data of the first sample quartile (the inefficient group). Differences between the two estimated production functions (evaluated at their respective mean values) are due to either market factors or inefficiency. Evaluating at the mean of the data is essential because it is supposed to purge the effect of the noise terms in each strata. TFA uses various methods to purge the market factor influence from the overall difference, obtaining a measure of production inefficiency between the most and the least efficient groups of firms.

The TFA is not geared toward econometric rigor, but it is aimed at drawing quick inference on the cost inefficiency that does not rely on particular distributional assumptions. Compared to COLS, TFA allows the existence of random errors within the quartiles, although the between-quartile variations are assumed to be due entirely to market factors and inefficiency. It is also worth noting that TFA generally requires a large dataset; otherwise stratifications of the data may make each sample too small to be useful. Another problem is how to stratify the data when there are multiple inputs. Stratifications based on the average product of labor and capital are unlikely to give similar results. In this respect, perhaps a classification based on profit or cost per unit of output would be a better approach, even if one uses a production function approach, simply because the classification will be unique.

Because most of the applications of TFA are in the cost minimization framework, we defer discussions of the estimation details and the empirical example demonstration until Section 4.3.3.

3.4 Estimation Methods: Maximum Likelihood Estimators

For a cross-sectional data model, a major drawback of the distribution-free approach discussed in the previous sections is that the statistical errors of the frontier function cannot be distinguished from the inefficiency effect of the model, and therefore it is impossible, in general, to allow for both inefficiency and statistical error in the model.[2]

Aigner et al. (1977) and Meeusen and van den Broeck (1977) were the first to estimate the model in (3.1)–(3.2), which has both v_i and u_i present in the model. The two random variables, v_i and u_i, are identified by imposing parametric distributions on them. Once the distributional assumptions are made, the log-likelihood function of the model is derived and numerical maximization procedures are used to obtain the ML estimates of the model parameters.

The choice of distributional assumption is at the center of the ML approach. The choice is often not an issue for the random error variable v_i for which a zero-mean normal distribution is widely accepted in this context. The choice of distributional assumption for the random variable u_i that represents inefficiency is more the issue at stake. The distribution must be in the nonnegative domain *and* its joint distribution with v_i would ideally have a closed form. The literature has identified several such distributions; we will discuss many of them in the ensuing subsections.

The other issue is the independence of u_i and v_i. This assumption is not too restrictive for the production models because v_i represents shocks outside the control of a firm and therefore it is unlikely to be related to inefficiency, u_i. One can, however, think of cases in which production risk is captured by the v_i term and risk-taking behavior might be reflected in the inefficiency term. There are approaches currently available to handle such nonindependence

[2] The issue of inseparability is mitigated if panel data is available (see Chapter 10).

issues,[3] but at the cost of making additional assumption on the correlation between v_i and u_i. Because this approach is still in development and the model is quite complex both in terms of the modeling aspect of it and its estimation, we decided not to discuss this approach in this book.

Regardless of the choice of distributions, the likelihood function of a stochastic frontier model is highly nonlinear and estimation can be difficult. Given this potential difficulty, it is desirable to have a simple test on the validity of the stochastic frontier specification prior to undertaking the more "expensive" ML estimation. If support for the particular stochastic frontier specification is unfounded, then time is better spent on considering alternative model specifications rather than on the numerical details of the maximization.

In the following section, we first introduce such a test. This is then followed in the subsequent sections by detailed discussions on ML estimation with various distributional assumptions on u_i.

3.4.1 A Skewness Test on OLS Residuals

Schmidt and Lin (1984) propose an OLS residual test to check for the validity of the model's stochastic frontier specification. Because the test statistic is easy to compute, it is ideal to serve as a pre-test of the model before the more expensive ML estimation is carried out.

The idea behind the test is that, for a production-type stochastic frontier model with the composed error $v_i - u_i$, $u_i \geq 0$ and v_i distributed symmetrically around zero, the residuals from the corresponding OLS estimation should skew to the left (i.e., negative skewness).[4] This is true regardless of the particular distributional function we may choose for u_i in the model estimation after the pretesting. Similarly, for a cost-type frontier model with the composed error $v_i + u_i$, the distribution of the OLS residuals should skew to the right (i.e., positive skewness). A test of the null hypothesis of no skewness as opposed to the alternative hypothesis can thus be constructed using the OLS residuals. If the estimated skewness has the expected sign, rejection of the null hypothesis provides support for the existence of the one-sided error.

Schmidt and Lin (1984) suggest a sample-moment based statistic for the skewness test. The statistic, which is commonly referred to as the $\sqrt{b_1}$ test, is

$$\sqrt{b_1} = \frac{m_3}{m_2\sqrt{m_2}}, \tag{3.13}$$

where m_2 and m_3 are the second and the third sample moments of the OLS residuals, respectively. The second sample moment of a random variable x is $\sum(x - \bar{x})^2/n$, and the third sample moment is $\sum(x - \bar{x})^3/n$. A result showing $\widehat{\sqrt{b_1}} < 0$ indicates that the OLS residuals are skewed to the left, while $\widehat{\sqrt{b_1}} > 0$ indicates that they are skewed to the right. Under the null hypothesis of no skewness, the statistic should be statistically indifferent from zero. The Stata command `sktest` performs this test. The distribution of $\sqrt{b_1}$ is nonstandard, and its critical values are tabulated in a number of studies including D'Agostino and Pearson (1973).

[3] See Smith (2008) and Bandyopadhyay and Das (2006), who use a copula approach.

[4] Note that, as we have discussed in Section 3.3.1, the slope coefficients of the OLS estimation are consistent estimates of those of the corresponding stochastic frontier model.

Coelli (1995) suggests a variant of this test. He notes that under the null hypothesis of no skewness, the third moment of the OLS residuals is asymptotically distributed as a normal random variable with mean 0 and variance $6m_2^3/N$. Thus, the statistic

$$\text{M3T} = m_3/\sqrt{6m_2^3/N} \tag{3.14}$$

has an asymptotic distribution of a standard normal random variable. The main advantage of this alternative test is that the critical values of the distribution are commonly available.

Example

Following the OLS estimation of the production function of dairy farms, we plot the histogram of the residuals compared to a normal density. This could be achieved using the following code.

```
. label variable e "Model 1: OLS"
. histogram e, bin(100) normal
```

However, in order to demonstrate the skewness of the OLS residuals more clearly, we instead used the following code.

```
. quietly summarize e /* obtain summary statistics without any output */
. local sd = r(sd) /* saves the standard deviation in `sd' */
. graph twoway histogram e, bin(100) `kden' xlabel(-.6(.2).6) ///
> xtitle("Model 1: OLS") || function normalden(x,0,`sd'),range(-.6 .6) ///
> saving(eff_ols, replace) legend(off)
```

The resulting chart is reproduced in Figure 3.3.

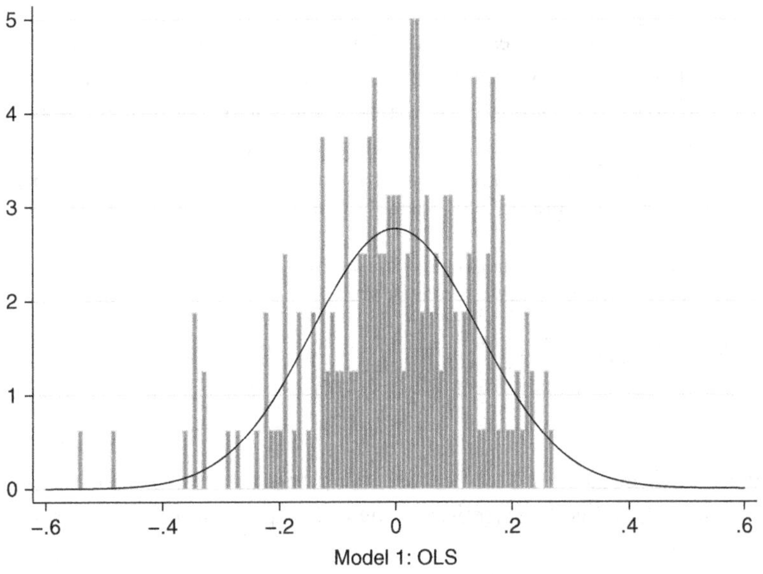

Figure 3.3. Histogram of OLS Residuals

There appears to be some evidence of a negative skew, although it is far from clear. To formally examine and test this, we use the skewness statistic. The point estimate of the statistic $\sqrt{b_1}$ is obtained from the summary statistic of the OLS residuals, e.

```
. summarize e, detail   /* The -detail- option shows the statistic */

                          Residuals
-------------------------------------------------------------
      Percentiles      Smallest
 1%    -.4861149      -.5450444
 5%    -.2731016      -.4861149
10%    -.1894513      -.3645601       Obs                 196
25%    -.0821035      -.3447073       Sum of Wgt.         196

50%     .0101231                      Mean          -3.86e-10
                        Largest       Std. Dev.      .1439801
75%     .0994077       .2340004
90%     .1711118       .2554969       Variance       .0207303
95%     .2116255       .2558538       Skewness      -.7377269
99%     .2558538       .2701932       Kurtosis        3.92576
```

The statistic is labeled "Skewness" in the table, and it has a value equal to -0.738. The negative sign indicates that the distribution of the residuals skews to the left which is consistent with a production frontier specification. To assess the statistical significance of the statistic, we use Stata's `sktest` command with the `noadj` option. The `noadj` option presents the unaltered test as described by D'Agostino, Belanger, and D'Agostino Jr. (1990). (See the Stata reference manual on `sktest` for more information on this command and the `noadj` option or type `help sktest` in Stata.)

```
. sktest e, noadj /* -noadj- option presents the unaltered test */

                    Skewness/Kurtosis tests for Normality
                                                      ------- joint ------
    Variable |      Obs   Pr(Skewness)   Pr(Kurtosis)     chi2(2)    Prob>chi2
-------------+----------------------------------------------------------------
           e |      196      0.0001         0.0258         20.62        0.0000
```

The test returns a p value that is less than 0.01 (the second column in the table); the null hypothesis of no skewness is confidently rejected. Therefore, we have found support for a left-skewed error distribution, and the skewness is statistically significant. As such, we can have some confidence that we do not, at this stage, need to revisit the specification of the model and can proceed to the next stage of estimating the stochastic frontier model.

The M3T statistic suggested by Coelli (1995) may be computed as follows:

```
. quietly summarize e      /* summarize the residuals to get some statistics */
. local e_mean = r(mean)   /* the mean of e */
. local N = r(N)           /* the number of observations */
. egen double m2 = mean((e - `e_mean')^2)
. egen double m3 = mean((e - `e_mean')^3)
. generate double M3T = m3/sqrt(6*((m2)^3)/`N')
. display M3T[1]
-4.2164605
```

The computed statistic equals -4.216. Because it has a normal distribution, the critical value is 1.96, so the result confirms the rejection of the null hypothesis of no skewness in the OLS residuals.

Now that we have found support for the stochastic frontier specification of the model, we may proceed to estimate the model with parametric distributional assumptions on v_i and u_i.

3.4.2 Parametric Distributional Assumptions

In the first estimation of the stochastic frontier model with parametric distributional assumption, Aigner et al. (1977) adopted a half-normal distribution assumption for u_i. The half-normal distribution has a single parameter and is thus relatively easy to estimate. The single-parameter distribution, however, is also less flexible. Subsequent developments in the literature have suggested more flexible distribution functions in an attempt to relax the rigidity.

In the following subsections, we discuss models with different distributions on u_i; the half-normal distribution (3.4.3), the truncated-normal distribution (3.4.4), the truncated-normal distribution with scaling properties (3.4.5), and the exponential distribution (3.4.6).[5] Readers are encouraged to read through the next section (on the half-normal distribution model) even if their interests lie in other models, because many of the discussions there are pertinent to the later sections but are not repeated.

3.4.3 Half-Normal Distribution

Based on (3.1) and (3.2), a production stochastic frontier model with a normal distribution on v_i and a half-normal distribution on u_i is represented as the following:

$$\ln y_i = \ln y_i^* - u_i, \tag{3.15}$$

$$\ln y_i^* = \boldsymbol{x}_i\boldsymbol{\beta} + v_i, \tag{3.16}$$

$$u_i \sim i.i.d. N^+(0, \sigma_u^2), \tag{3.17}$$

$$v_i \sim i.i.d. N(0, \sigma_v^2), \tag{3.18}$$

where v_i and u_i are distributed independent of each other. The $\boldsymbol{\beta}$, σ_u^2, and σ_v^2 are the parameters to be estimated.

3.4.3.1 Deriving Half-Normal Distributions from Truncated Normals and Folded Normals

Equation (3.17) assumes that the inefficiency effect follows a half-normal distribution. A half-normal distribution can be derived in two different ways.

The first approach is to treat it as the nonnegative truncation of a zero-mean normal distribution. We shall denote the distribution derived in this way as $N^+(0, \sigma_u^2)$, where σ_u^2 is the variance of the normal distribution before truncation. Suppose that a random variable Z has a normal distribution $z \sim N(\mu, \sigma_z^2)$ with the probability density function denoted by $g(z)$. If it is truncated from above at the point α so that $z \geq \alpha$, then the density function of z, $f(z)$, is

$$f(z) = \frac{g(z)}{1 - \Phi\left(\frac{\alpha-\mu}{\sigma_z}\right)} = \frac{\frac{1}{\sigma_z}\phi\left(\frac{z-\mu}{\sigma_z}\right)}{1 - \Phi\left(\frac{\alpha-\mu}{\sigma_z}\right)}, \qquad z \geq \alpha, \tag{3.19}$$

[5] Other distributions, such as the Gamma distribution, have also been suggested, but they are not commonly examined in the literature and so are not included in our discussion.

where $\phi(\cdot)$ and $\Phi(\cdot)$ are the probability density and probability distribution functions, respectively, for the standard normal variable.[6] The density function of u_i in (3.17) can then be obtained by setting $\mu = 0$ and $\alpha = 0$ in the above equation to give the following:

$$f(u_i) = \frac{\frac{1}{\sigma}\phi\left(\frac{u_i}{\sigma}\right)}{1-\Phi(0)} = \frac{2}{\sigma}\phi\left(\frac{u_i}{\sigma}\right) = 2\left(2\pi\sigma^2\right)^{-\frac{1}{2}}\exp\left(-\frac{u_i^2}{2\sigma^2}\right), \qquad u_i \geq 0. \tag{3.20}$$

A different way to derive the half-normal distribution is to treat it as a *folded* zero-mean normal distribution. A folded normal distribution is defined as the absolute value of a normal distribution. If W has a normal distribution, $w \sim N(\mu, \sigma_w^2)$, and Z has a folded normal defined as $Z = |W|$, then the density function is[7]

$$f(z) = \left(\frac{1}{\sigma_w}\right)\left[\phi\left(\frac{z-\mu}{\sigma_w}\right) + \phi\left(\frac{z+\mu}{\sigma_w}\right)\right], \qquad z \geq 0. \tag{3.21}$$

As one can see, if $\mu = 0$, the folded normal density function is the same as (3.20) for the random variable z.

In general, if $\mu \neq 0$, the folded normal and the truncated normal with the truncation point at 0 do not have the same distribution function. It is only when $\mu = 0$ that the two formulations are the same.

Although the half-normal distribution can be derived in either way, in this book we will use the notation $N^+(0, \sigma^2)$ instead of $|N(0, \sigma^2)|$. The reason is that the notion of truncation provides a smooth transition to later sections in which we discuss the case of the truncated normal distribution. We note that whether using the truncated distribution notation ($N^+(\cdot)$) or the folded normal notation ($|N(\cdot)|$) does not matter here, because both of them result in the same density function in the current case. The notations, however, make a difference in the case of truncated normal models that are discussed later.

Figure 3.4 illustrates the shapes of half-normal distributions with various parameter values. Although the half-normal distribution has just one parameter, it can show a variety of scenarios. For example, with low variance values (such as $\sigma^2 = 0.5$), the probability is high near the zero values of u, which means that the probability of firms or producers being close to fully efficient is high. This specification might be appropriate for firms operating in a competitive market. If the market is competitive inefficient firms will be forced out of the market in the long run. Thus, it is very likely that the surviving firms will have clustered around the fully efficient level. Similarly, if the industry is competitive and the sample of firms have been in business for a long time, these firms are likely to be more homogeneous in terms of their size because the scale economies/diseconomies will be exploited in the long run. Thus, survival in the long run in a competitive industry means that firms are likely to be similar in terms of their efficiency levels and their efficiency levels are also expected to be close to 100 percent.[8] This means that the tail area of the distribution will be small.

6 See Johnson et al. (1995).

7 See Johnson et al. (1995).

8 By contrast, if firms are from a regulated industry that has been regulated for a while, one would expect convergence in efficiency to have occurred, thereby meaning that their efficiency levels would be similar though, not necessarily, close to fully efficient. For example, if regulatory incentives are strong, including those for the more efficient companies, convergence should tend toward the frontier (again, suggesting that the half-normal model would be appropriate). While, if incentives are weak for the efficient companies to improve, convergence may occur but at a level below 100 percent. In this case the distribution may be more like a truncated normal distribution with a positive mean.

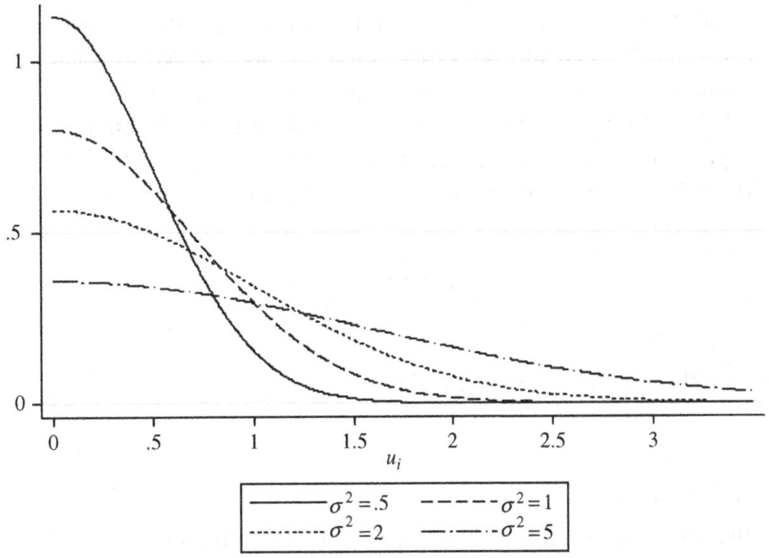

Figure 3.4. Density Plots of Half-normal Distributions

By contrast, with higher values of the variance parameter of the distribution (such as $\sigma^2 = 5$) performance is more varied. In this situation, one might find some firms that are highly inefficient thereby meaning that the tail of the distribution is long.

In the aforementioned scenarios, the half-normal distribution may be a good assumption,[9] although, in practice, the choice of which distribution to use can be aided though statistical testing.

3.4.3.2 The Log-Likelihood Function

The log likelihood function based on (3.15)–(3.18) for each observation i is[10]

$$L_i = -\ln\left(\frac{1}{2}\right) - \frac{1}{2}\ln(\sigma_v^2 + \sigma_u^2) + \ln\phi\left(\frac{\epsilon_i}{\sqrt{\sigma_v^2 + \sigma_u^2}}\right) + \ln\Phi\left(\frac{\mu_{*i}}{\sigma_*}\right), \tag{3.22}$$

where

$$\mu_{*i} = \frac{-\sigma_u^2 \epsilon_i}{\sigma_v^2 + \sigma_u^2}, \tag{3.23}$$

$$\sigma_*^2 = \frac{\sigma_v^2 \sigma_u^2}{\sigma_v^2 + \sigma_u^2}. \tag{3.24}$$

[9] The same argument can be used to justify the use of the exponential distribution. It is worth noting that the half-normal and the exponential distributions are quite close, and one might expect to see similar estimated efficiency levels from the two models.

[10] Azzalini (1985) showed that the distribution of ϵ_i is skew normal. He derived many properties of the skew normal distribution, some of which are directly applicable. Unfortunately, people in the SF literature (including us) became aware of his work only recently and consequently many of the skew normal distribution results were not used in the SF models. Instead these results, for example, $E(u_i|\epsilon_i), E(u_i^2|\epsilon_i)$, were derived from scratch. See Chen et al. (2014) for a recent application of the skew normal distribution on panel stochastic frontier models.

For detailed derivations, see Appendix A. The log-likelihood function is then the observational sum of (3.22), which can then be numerically maximized to obtain estimates of the model parameters. There is, however, a computational problem. The variance parameters, σ_u^2 and σ_v^2, have to be positive, but an unconstrained numerical maximization would not guarantee positive estimates. To ensure that the variance parameter estimates are positive, the following parameterization scheme can be used for the unconstrained numerical maximization:

$$\sigma_u^2 = \exp(w_u), \tag{3.25}$$

$$\sigma_v^2 = \exp(w_v), \tag{3.26}$$

where w_u and w_v are unrestricted constant parameters.

Example

Model 4: Half-Normal Model

In this and subsequent examples, we provide the Stata commands to estimate the model. We also introduce the author written Stata command sfmodel. We first set up the likelihood function by using the `sfmodel` command, and then estimate the model by using the `ml max` command.

```
. sfmodel ly, prod dist(h) frontier($xvar) usigmas() vsigmas()
. ml max, difficult gradient gtol(1e-5) nrtol(1e-5)
```

With the `sfmodel` command, the option `prod` indicates that this is a production frontier-type model, and `dist(h)` specifies the half-normal distribution. The line `ml max` starts the numerical maximization (see the Stata reference manual on `ml` for more information on the command). Here, we briefly explain the four options used in the example. The `difficult` option tells Stata that this is a difficult model so that Stata does extra work in searching for the optimal values. The `gradient` option asks for the gradients of the estimates to be printed in the Results Window. This sometimes provides valuable information particularly when the maximization encounters difficulty. It is recommended that the `gradient` option is specified at least in the exploration stage of your ML estimation. The other two options are the convergence criteria; it is our experience that the two options specified together prevents almost all cases of premature declaration of convergence.

The estimation results are provided here (we also show the computed gradients of the last two iterations).

```
------------------------------------------------------------------------------
Iteration 12:
                                                log likelihood =   110.46614
Gradient vector (length = .0219756):
     frontier:  frontier:  frontier:   frontier:  frontier:    usigmas:    vsigmas:
       llabor      lfeed     lcattle       lland      _cons       _cons       _cons
r1  -.0110148  -.0167347  -.0043226    -.007643  -.0014686    -.001421   -.0005236
------------------------------------------------------------------------------
Iteration 13:
                                                log likelihood =   110.46614
Gradient vector (length = 1.87e-07):
     frontier:  frontier:  frontier:   frontier:  frontier:    usigmas:    vsigmas:
       llabor      lfeed     lcattle       lland      _cons       _cons       _cons
r1  -1.00e-07  -1.38e-07  -3.58e-08   -6.46e-08  -1.16e-08   -5.95e-09    1.47e-08
```

```
------------------------------------------------------------------------------

                                                  Number of obs    =       196
                                                  Wald chi2(4)     =   1738.30
Log likelihood =  110.46614                       Prob > chi2      =    0.0000

------------------------------------------------------------------------------
          ly |      Coef.   Std. Err.      z    P>|z|     [95% Conf. Interval]
-------------+----------------------------------------------------------------
frontier     |
      llabor |    .102653   .0427101     2.40   0.016     .0189427    .1863632
       lfeed |    .155628   .0372683     4.18   0.000     .0825835    .2286725
     lcattle |   .7546799   .0574825    13.13   0.000     .6420163    .8673435
       lland |   .0360424   .0386583     0.93   0.351    -.0397265    .1118114
       _cons |   7.725265    .478893    16.13   0.000     6.786651    8.663878
-------------+----------------------------------------------------------------
usigmas      |
       _cons |  -3.133122   .2187722   -14.32   0.000    -3.561908   -2.704336
-------------+----------------------------------------------------------------
vsigmas      |
       _cons |  -5.336009   .4425821   -12.06   0.000    -6.203454   -4.468564
------------------------------------------------------------------------------
```

The iteration log shows that the estimation converged after thirteen iterations, and the gradient of each parameter is small enough (i.e., close to zero) to justify the convergence. The estimated coefficients on the frontier function are close to the OLS estimates (see page 51). This is no surprise because of the consistency of the OLS estimates (except for the intercept). The output elasticity of cattle is 75 percent, which is the largest among the inputs. As before, the elasticities of the three variable inputs add up close to 1, indicating a constant returns to scale production technology.

Note that the variance parameters are parameterized as an exponential function (see equations (3.25) and (3.26)). Therefore, the estimate of σ_v^2 is recovered by $\hat{\sigma}_v^2 = \exp(-5.336) = 0.0048$, and $\hat{\sigma}_u^2 = \exp(-3.133) = 0.044$. The process is automated by issuing the `sf_transform` command after the model is estimated. The command also reports the standard error (by the Delta method), z statistic, p value, and the confidence intervals. The code and results for our example is provided here:

```
. sf_transform

      sigma_u_sqr = exp(usigmas);
      sigma_v_sqr = exp(vsigmas).

   ---convert the parameters to natural metrics---

variable     |      Coef.   Std. Err.      t    P>|t|     [95% Conf. Interval]
-------------+----------------------------------------------------------------
 sigma_u_sqr |   .0435815   .0095344     4.57   0.000     .0283846    .0669147
 sigma_v_sqr |    .004815   .0021311     2.26   0.024     .0020224    .0114638
```

After the estimation, Stata saves key results internally, which may be retrieved and saved in other scalars or matrices of our choice for the later use. For instance, after the ML estimation, the model's log-likelihood value is saved by Stata in an internal macro `e(ll)`, and the model coefficients are saved in an internal matrix `e(b)`. We retrieve and save this information as they will be useful later (the log-likelihood value will be useful in conducting hypothesis testings, and the coefficients could be used as initial values for more complicated models). The required code is provided here:

```
. scalar ll_h = e(ll)                   /* the log-likelihood value */
. matrix b0 = e(b)                      /* the coefficient vector */
. matrix bf_h = b0[1,"frontier:"]       /* the slope coefficient vector */
. matrix bv_h = b0[1,"vsigmas:"]        /* vsigmas */
. matrix bu_h = b0[1,"usigmas:"]        /* usigmas */
```

We discuss how to use the coefficients as initial values in the next section (use of the log-likelihood value is covered in Section 3.4.3.4).

3.4.3.3 Supplying Initial Values

We should note at this point that we have estimated the model without providing initial values for the numerical maximization. Providing initial values is an option for Stata's ML estimation. If users do not provide initial values, Stata automatically searches for feasible values to start the maximization process. These initial values are *feasible* for getting the numerical process started, but there is no guarantee that these initial values are *good* (i.e., close to the optimizing values). Good initial values are always helpful in getting the estimation to converge to true values, and this is particularly true for numerically challenging models.

Although the current model we are considering is simple enough that choices of the initial values do not appear to matter much, we shall at this point discuss briefly how we may pick initial values for the stochastic frontier model as in subsequent more complex models this becomes more important. Given the assumption of a homoscedastic inefficiency distribution (that is, parameters of the inefficiency distributions are constant), the OLS estimates are consistent estimates of the slope coefficients $\boldsymbol{\beta}$, although the intercept (and the variance parameters) of the OLS model is not a consistent estimate of its counterpart. As such, the OLS estimates provide good starting values for the $\boldsymbol{\beta}$ parameters. The following example shows how the estimation can be undertaken using starting values from the estimated OLS model.

Example

We first estimate the OLS model (assuming we have not already done so) and then save the coefficient vector in the matrix `b_ols` for the later use.

```
. quietly regress ly $xvar /* estimate the OLS model silently */
. matrix b_ols = e(b) /* save the coefficient vector */
```

Let's take a look at the contents of the matrix.

```
. matrix list b_ols

b_ols[1,5]
        llabor       lfeed     lcattle       lland       _cons
y1  .12542989   .16777405   .77103446   .01933281   7.2724419
```

The `b_ols` is a 1×5 vector containing the slope coefficients but no variance estimates and `_cons` is Stata's default name for the intercept. We now use this vector as part of the initial values for the stochastic frontier model's parameters. The initial values for *all* of the model parameters need to be provided (i.e., it is not possible to provide initial values for only a subset of the parameters).

```
. sfmodel ly, prod dist(h) frontier($xvar)  usigmas() vsigmas()
. sf_init, frontier(b_ols) usigmas(0.1) vsigmas(0.1)
. ml max, difficult gtol(1e-5) nrtol(1e-5)
```

Here we use the command `sf_init` to set up initial values for the model; the command itself is a wrapper of Stata's `ml_init` command. Initial values for parameters in the frontier and variance equations are specified in their respective functions (`frontier()`, `usigmas()`, `vsigmas`, etc.). The order of the functions is irrelevant, but it is important that initial values are supplied for all of the parameters in the model.

This example used the OLS intercept as the initial value for the true model's intercept, and we arbitrarily chose 0.1 as the initial value for both of the variance parameters w_u and w_v. These three initial values are not consistent estimates of the true values, and so they may or may not work for every applications. Trial and errors may be needed. If finer initial values are sought, the command `sf_srch` is useful, as shown in the following example.

```
. sfmodel ly, prod dist(h) frontier($xvar)  usigmas() vsigmas()
. sf_init, frontier(b_ols) usigmas(0.1) vsigmas(0.1)
. sf_srch, frontier($xvar) usigmas() vsigmas() n(2)
. ml max, difficult gtol(1e-5) nrtol(1e-5)
```

The command `sf_srch` is a wrapper of Stata's `ml plot` command that helps to search for better initial values before starting the numerical maximization process. The search is undertaken for one parameter at a time given other parameter values. The option `n(#)` specifies the number of times the search is to be performed on the specified parameters. Thus, `n(2)` asks Stata to cycle through the parameters twice. Unlike `sf_init`, which requires a full specification of the model's parameters, the search of `sf_srch` can be performed on subsets of parameter values. By default, all constants of the model will be searched (i.e., the intercept and the two variance parameters (w_u, w_v) in the current model). Improving initial values for only the constants can thus be achieved by simply specifying `sf_srch, n(2)`.

3.4.3.4 A Likelihood Ratio Test of Inefficiency

As should now be clear, central to the stochastic frontier model is the one-sided error specification which represents technical inefficiency. It is therefore important to test the existence of the one-sided error for the model. If evidence for the one-sided error specification is not found, the model then reduces to a standard regression model for which a simple OLS estimation would suffice. This amounts to a test for the presence of u_i in the model, and a generalized likelihood ratio (LR) test for the null hypothesis of no one-sided error can be constructed based on the log-likelihood values of the OLS (restricted) and the SF (unrestricted) model.

Recall that the OLS-residual-based skewness test introduced in the earlier section also tests the validity of the one-sided error specification. This residual test is easy to perform since it requires only an OLS estimation of the model. Although useful as a screening device, the test does not use the information from the distribution functions of the random error. The LR test introduced here is more precise to the specific model we are estimating, but the disadvantage is that it can only be conducted after the ML estimation of the model has been undertaken.

The LR test statistic is

$$-2[\mathrm{L}(H_0) - \mathrm{L}(H_1)], \tag{3.27}$$

where $L(H_0)$ and $L(H_1)$ are log-likelihood values of the restricted model (OLS) and the unrestricted model (SF), respectively, and the degree of freedom equals the number of restrictions in the test.

For a half-normal model, the LR test amounts to testing the hypothesis that $\sigma_u^2 = 0$. The complication of the test is that the null hypothesis of $\sigma_u^2 = 0$ is on the boundary of the parameter value's permissible space, and therefore the LR test statistic does not have a standard chi-square distribution. Coelli (1995) shows that, in such cases, the test has a mixture of chi-square distributions. The critical values of the mixed distribution for hypothesis testing are tabulated in Table 1 of Kodde and Palm (1986).

Example

Computing the test statistic requires the log-likelihood values of the stochastic frontier model and the corresponding OLS model. We have saved the value of the stochastic frontier in the scalar `ll_h`. If we have not already done so, we may estimate the OLS model and save the log-likelihood value in a scalar (`ll_ols` in the example given here).

```
. quietly regress ly $xvar /* estimate the OLS model without any output */
. scalar ll_ols = e(ll)
```

The value of the test statistic can then be displayed using the following code:

```
. display -2*(ll_ols - ll_h)
  16.4262
```

This has a mix chi-square distribution with the degree of freedom equal to 1. The critical values of the distribution are obtained using the `sf_mixtable` command:

```
. sf_mixtable, dof(1)

        critical values of the mixed chi-square distribution
                                 significance level
 dof  |  0.25      0.1       0.05       0.025      0.01       0.005      0.001
-------------------------------------------------------------------------------
  1       0.455     1.642     2.705      3.841      5.412      6.635      9.500
source: Table 1, Kodde and Palm (1986, Econometrica).
```

Note that the degree of freedom of the statistic is 1 (i.e., `dof(1)`) because, in this instance, only one parameter (i.e., σ_u^2) is restricted in the test. This table shows that critical value of the statistic at the 1 percent significance level is 5.412. Given that the model's test statistic is 16.426, the result indicates an outright rejection of the null hypothesis of no technical inefficiency.

3.4.3.5 The Gamma Parameter

Another often-reported, but sometimes misused, statistic for a similar purpose is the gamma parameter, defined as

$$\gamma = \frac{\sigma_u^2}{\sigma_u^2 + \sigma_v^2}. \tag{3.28}$$

Battese and Corra (1977) used the gamma parameterization in formulating the likelihood function. The parameterization has an advantage in the numerical maximization process:

The ratio has a value between 0 and 1, and therefore searches of the maximizing value are conveniently restricted to this (tight) parameter space.

For a simple half-normal model, a hypothesis test of $\gamma = 0$ may also serve as a test of the existence of the one-sided error. The ratio, however, should not be interpreted as the share of total variation attributable to the inefficiency variation, because the variance of the one-sided error, $\text{var}(u)$, is not equal to σ_u^2 (as will be shown in (3.59)). In the case of a half-normal distribution, $\text{var}(u) = (1 - 2/\pi) \times \sigma_u^2 \approx 0.36338\,\sigma_u^2$.

For more complicated models, such as one that has a two-parameter inefficiency distribution (e.g., the truncated-normal) or one that parameterizes inefficiency by nonconstant variables, the gamma parameter does not convey useful information regarding the presence of the one-sided error (we will come back to this issue in subsequent sections). As such, our preference is to use the LR test discussed earlier.

3.4.3.6 Technical Efficiency

After the model parameters are estimated, we can proceed to estimate observation-specific efficiency, which is often the main interest of a stochastic frontier model. The estimated efficiency levels can be used to rank producers, identify under-performing producers, and those at, or close to, the efficiency frontier. This information is, in turn, useful in help designing public policy or subsidy programs aiming at, for example, improving the overall efficiency level of private and public sectors. For example, establishing which hospitals are best at treating certain ailments, which police forces are best at tackling certain types of crime, or which schools are best at improving students' education would enable government funding to be appropriately targeted. Alternatively, further investigation could reveal what it is that makes these establishments attain such high levels of performance. This could then be used to identify appropriate government policy implications and responses (e.g., further development of specialist hospitals, restrictions on school of class sizes) or identify processes and/or management practices that should be spread (or encouraged) across the less efficient, but otherwise similar, units. More directly, efficiency rankings are used in regulated industries such that regulators can set the more inefficient companies tougher future cost reduction targets, in order to ensure that customers do not pay for inefficiency.

Recall that in the earlier sections we have discussed estimating the inefficiency, u_i, and the efficiency, $\exp(-u_i)$. Although definitions of these two indices may seem intuitive, estimating the index *for each observation* is less straightforward. To see this, note that $u_i \sim N^+(0, \sigma_u^2)$. The maximum likelihood estimation of the model yields the estimated value of σ_u^2, which gives us information about the shape of the half-normal distribution on u_i. This information is all we need if the interest is in the average technical inefficiency of the sample. This measure is known as the *unconditional mean of* u_i. However, if the interest is in the technical efficiency of each observation, this information on σ_u^2 is not enough as it does not contain any individual-specific information.

The solution, first proposed by Jondrow et al. (1982), is to estimate u_i from the expected value of u_i conditional on the composed error of the model, $\epsilon_i \equiv v_i - u_i$. This *conditional mean of* u_i given ϵ_i gives a point estimate of u_i. The composed error contains individual-specific information, and so the conditional expectation yields the observation-specific value of the inefficiency. This is like extracting signal from noise.

Jondrow et al. (1982) show that the density function of $(u_i|\epsilon_i)$ is $N^+(\mu_{*i}, \sigma_*^2)$, based on which, the equation of $E(u_i|\epsilon_i)$ is (see Appendix B for the derivation):

$$E(u_i|\epsilon_i) = \frac{\sigma_* \phi(\frac{\mu_{*i}}{\sigma_*})}{\Phi\left(\frac{\mu_{*i}}{\sigma_*}\right)} + \mu_{*i}, \tag{3.29}$$

where μ_{*i} and σ_* are defined in (3.23) and (3.24).

Maximum likelihood estimates of the parameters are substituted into the equation to obtain the empirical estimate of inefficiency. The estimate has a value that is guaranteed to be nonnegative.

Jondrow et al. (1982) also suggested an alternative to the conditional mean estimator, viz., *the conditional mode of* $(u_i|\epsilon_i)$:

$$M(u_i|\epsilon_i) = \begin{cases} \mu_{*i} & \text{if } \mu_{*i} > 0, \\ 0 & \text{if} \mu_{*i} \leq 0. \end{cases}$$

This modal estimator can be viewed as the maximum likelihood estimator of u_i given ϵ_i. Note that ϵ_i is not known and we are replacing it by the estimated value from the model. Because by construction some of the ϵ_i will be positive (and therefore $\mu_{*i} < 0$), there will be some observations that are fully efficient (i.e., $M(u_i|\epsilon_i) = 0$). In contrast, none of the observations will be fully efficient if one uses the conditional mean estimator $(E(u_i|\epsilon_i))$. Consequently, average inefficiency for a sample of firms will be lower if one uses the modal estimator.

Because the conditional distribution of u is known, one can derive moments of any continuous function of $u|\epsilon$. That is, we can use the same technique to obtain observation-specific estimates of the efficiency index, $\exp(-u_i)$. Following Battese and Coelli (1988), it can be shown that

$$E\left[\exp(-u_i)|\epsilon_i\right] = \exp\left(-\mu_{*i} + \frac{1}{2}\sigma_*^2\right) \frac{\Phi\left(\frac{\mu_{*i}}{\sigma_*} - \sigma_*\right)}{\Phi\left(\frac{\mu_{*i}}{\sigma_*}\right)}, \tag{3.30}$$

where μ_{*i} and σ_* are defined in (3.23) and (3.24). Maximum likelihood estimates of the parameters are substituted into the equation to obtain point estimates of $\exp(-u_i)$. The estimate has a value between 0 and 1, with the value equal to 1 indicating full efficiency.

Before we provide an example that demonstrates how to calculate observation-specific estimates of technical efficiency, we first examine how to calculate the confidence intervals of technical efficiency.

3.4.3.7 Confidence Interval

The confidence interval of $E(u_i|\epsilon_i)$ is derived by Horrace and Schmidt (1996), Hjalmarsson et al. (1996) and Bera and Sharma (1999) based on the density function of $u_i|\epsilon_i$. The formulas for the lower bound (L_i) and the upper bound (U_i) of a $(1-\alpha)100\%$ confidence interval are

$$L_i = \mu_{*i} + \Phi^{-1}\left\{1 - \left(1 - \frac{\alpha}{2}\right)\left[1 - \Phi\left(-\frac{\mu_{*i}}{\sigma_*}\right)\right]\right\}\sigma_*, \tag{3.31}$$

$$U_i = \mu_{*i} + \Phi^{-1}\left\{1 - \frac{\alpha}{2}\left[1 - \Phi\left(-\frac{\mu_{*i}}{\sigma_*}\right)\right]\right\}\sigma_*, \tag{3.32}$$

where μ_{*i} and σ_* are defined in (3.23) and (3.24). See Appendix C for the derivation of this.

The lower and upper bounds of a $(1-\alpha)100\%$ confidence interval of $E(\exp(-u_i)|\epsilon_i)$ are, respectively,

$$\mathcal{L}_i = \exp(-U_i), \tag{3.33}$$

$$\mathcal{U}_i = \exp(-L_i). \tag{3.34}$$

The results followed because of the monotonicity of $\exp(-u_i)$ as a function of u_i.

It should be noted that the construction of this confidence interval assumed that the model parameters are known and given, while in fact they are estimated with uncertainty. The confidence interval does not take into account the parameter uncertainty. Alternatively, we may bootstrap the confidence interval (Simar and Wilson [2007]), which takes into account the estimation uncertainty.

Example

The command `sf_predict` is used to obtain the (in)efficiency index and the associated confidence intervals. The command has to be used following the maximum likelihood estimation of the model. For example,

```
. sf_predict, bc(bc_h) jlms(jlms_h) ci(95)
```

generates the variable `jlms_h` containing the estimated values of the inefficiency measure from $E(u_i|\epsilon_i)$ evaluated at $\hat{\epsilon}_i$ and the variable `bc_h` containing the estimated values of the efficiency index $E(\exp(-u_i)|\epsilon_i)$ evaluated at $\hat{\epsilon}_i$. The 95 percent confidence intervals associated with $E(u_i|\epsilon_i)$ and $E(\exp(-u_i)|\epsilon_i)$ are also calculated by the above code using the additional option of `ci(95)`. The upper and lower bounds of `jlms_h` are saved as `jlms_h_95U` and `jlms_h_95L`, respectively, and the upper and the lower bounds of `bc_h` are saved in `bc_h_95U` and `bc_h_95L`, respectively.

We now take a look at the summary statistics and the first ten observations of the created variables.

```
. summarize bc_h jlms_h

    Variable |       Obs        Mean    Std. Dev.       Min        Max
-------------+--------------------------------------------------------
        bc_h |       196    .8532533    .0887712     .52415    .969845
      jlms_h |       196    .1662996    .1123002   .0309775   .6481454

. list bc_h bc_h_95U bc_h_95L jlms_h jlms_h_95U jlms_h_95L in 1/10

     +---------------------------------------------------------------------+
     |      bc_h    bc_h_95U    bc_h_95L     jlms_h   jlms_~95U   jlms_~95L |
     |---------------------------------------------------------------------|
  1. | .93876928   .99702283   .84506772   .06418514   .16833851   .00298161 |
  2. |  .8432195   .95376099   .74013326   .17261617   .30092503   .04734218 |
  3. | .92286756   .99500665   .82270444   .08157006   .19515827   .00500586 |
  4. | .84007532   .95074147   .73728763   .17636186   .30477719   .05051311 |
  5. | .87381074    .9779158   .76871818   .13681458   .26303085    .0223317 |
     |---------------------------------------------------------------------|
  6. |  .8858463   .98432854   .78067592    .1230272   .24759516   .01579556 |
  7. | .70081616   .79563282   .61462812   .35767767   .48673788   .22861748 |
  8. | .88772599   .98517367     .782597   .12088817   .24513741   .01493734 |
  9. | .93843591   .99698965    .8445578     .064547    .1689421   .00301489 |
 10. | .52414999   .59506468   .45968877   .64814538    .7772056   .51908517 |
     +---------------------------------------------------------------------+
```

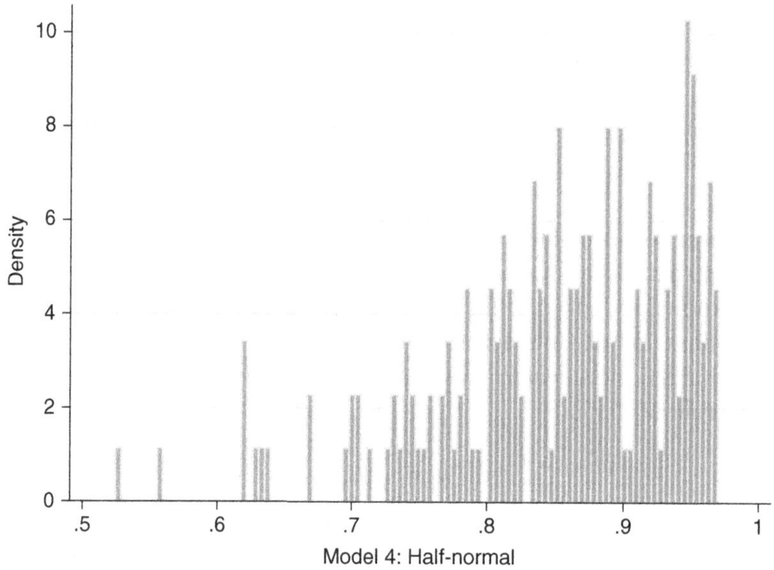

Figure 3.5. Histogram of Efficiency Index

The mean of bc_h equals 0.853, implying that, on average, the dairy farmers produce 85.3 percent of the maximum output, or about 15 percent of the potential output is lost due to technical inefficiency. By contrast, the mean of jlms_h equals 0.166, implying that, on average, the dairy farmers lost about 17 percent of their potential output due to technical inefficiency. The discrepancy between the two figures is due to the fact that $1 - e^{u} \approx u$ and the approximation is close when u is small.

We plot the histogram of the efficiency index in Figure 3.5. The code to produce this plot is provide here:

```
. label variable bc_h "Model 4: Half-normal"
. histogram bc_h, bin(100) `kden'
```

3.4.3.8 Heteroscedasticity, Exogenous Determinants, and Marginal Effects

Heteroscedasticity in v and u. The original half-normal model of Aigner et al. (1977) assumes that the v_i and the pretruncated u_i are homoscedastic, that is, both σ_v^2 and σ_u^2 parameters are constants. Caudill and Ford (1993), Caudill, Ford, and Gropper (1995), and Hadri (1999) consider models in which these random variables are heteroscedastic. Unlike a classical linear model in which heteroscedasticity affects only the efficiency of the estimators and not their consistency, ignoring heteroscedasticity in the stochastic frontier framework leads to inconsistent estimates (Wang and Schmidt [2002]).

Kumbhakar and Lovell (2000, Section 3.4) provide a detailed discussion on the consequences of ignoring the heteroscedasticity. The following is a summary of their discussion (assuming that v_i and u_i are heteroscedastic).

- Ignoring the heteroscedasticity of v_i still gives consistent estimates of the frontier function parameters ($\boldsymbol{\beta}$) except for the intercept, which is downward-biased. Estimates of the technical efficiency are biased.

- Ignoring the heteroscedasticity of u_i causes biased estimates of the frontier function's parameters as well as the estimates of technical efficiency.

Caudill and Ford (1993), Caudill, Ford, and Gropper (1995), and Hadri (1999) propose that the heteroscedasticity can be parameterized by a vector of observable variables and associated parameters. For instance, $\sigma^2_{u,i} = \exp(\boldsymbol{z}_{u,i}; \boldsymbol{w}_u)$, where $\boldsymbol{z}_{u,i}$ is a $m \times 1$ vector of variables including a constant of 1, and $\boldsymbol{w}_u$ is the $m \times 1$ corresponding parameter vector. The exponential function is used to ensure a positive estimate of the variance parameter. Therefore, the parameterizations are

$$\sigma^2_{u,i} = \exp(\boldsymbol{z}'_{u,i}\boldsymbol{w}_u), \tag{3.35}$$

$$\sigma^2_{v,i} = \exp(\boldsymbol{z}'_{v,i}\boldsymbol{w}_v). \tag{3.36}$$

The vectors $\boldsymbol{z}_{u,i}$ and $\boldsymbol{z}_{v,i}$ may or may not be the same vector, and they may also contain all or part of the $\boldsymbol{x}_i$ vector.

The log-likelihood function of the heteroscedastic model is the same as in (3.22), except that we now use (3.35) and (3.36) instead of (3.25) and (3.26) in place of σ^2_u and σ^2_v, respectively, in the log-likelihood function. All the parameters of the model are estimated at the same time via the maximum likelihood method. After the parameters are estimated, the technical (in)efficiency index can be computed using (3.29) and (3.30) with the appropriate equations of σ^2_u and σ^2_v substituted into the expressions.

Exogenous Determinants of Inefficiency. Although the models of Caudill and Ford (1993) and Caudill, Ford, and Gropper (1995) are motivated by the heteroscedasticity problem in the random variable u_i, their model can also be used to address a different issue, namely, exogenous determinants of the inefficiency. In this section, we briefly explain how the two issues are related (more discussion will be provided in Section 3.4.4.5).

For a stochastic frontier analysis, a researcher may not only want to know the levels of inefficiency for each producer, but also the factors that can explain inefficiency. For instance, in studying the efficiency level of the dairy industry, a researcher may want to know whether the inefficiency of a farm is affected by the use of information technology, the farmer's education, or the type of ownership. Similarly, the government might be interested in whether its "subsidization" of share schemes (via tax advantages) improves firms' performance. To answer these questions, we may want to estimate the relationship between the inefficiency measure and the possible determinants of inefficiency. The papers that first deal with this issue are (in chronological order): Kumbhakar, Ghosh, and McGuckin (1991); Reifschneider and Stevenson (1991); Huang and Liu (1994); and Battese and Coelli (1995). In one of their models, Reifschneider and Stevenson (1991) allow the variance of the inefficiency term to be a function of z variables, which they call *inefficiency explanatory variables.*

The early literature adopts a two-step procedure to investigate the relationship. The approach estimates the observation-specific inefficiency measure in the first step, and then regresses the index on a vector of exogenous variables $\boldsymbol{z}_i$ in the second step. A negative coefficient of the exogenous variable in the regression indicates that firms with larger values of the variables tend to have a lower level of inefficiency (i.e., they are more efficient).

The two-step procedure, however, has long been recognized as biased because the model estimated in the first step is mis-specified (Battese and Coelli [1995]). As explained in Wang and Schmidt (2002), if $\boldsymbol{x}_i$ and $\boldsymbol{z}_i$ are correlated then the first step of the two-step procedure is biased. Even when $\boldsymbol{x}_i$ and $\boldsymbol{z}_i$ are uncorrelated, ignoring the dependence of the inefficiency on $\boldsymbol{z}_i$ will cause the first-step technical efficiency index to be underdispersed, so that the results of the second-step regression are likely to be biased downward. Wang (2002) provides Monte Carlo evidence of the bias.

Given the undesirable statistical properties of the two-step procedure, the preferred approach to studying the exogenous influences on efficiency is the single-step procedure. This procedure estimates the parameters of the relationship between inefficiency and $\boldsymbol{z}_i$ together with all the other parameters of the model in the maximum likelihood method. Although the single-step procedure was first discussed in the context of truncated-normal models, the application to the half-normal model is straightforward.

The single-step procedure accounts for the exogenous influences on inefficiency by parameterizing the distribution function of u_i as a function of exogenous variables ($\boldsymbol{z}_i$) that are likely to affect inefficiency. If u_i follows a half-normal distribution, that is, $u_i \sim N^+(0, \sigma_u^2)$, then σ_u^2 is the (only) parameter to be parameterized by the $\boldsymbol{z}_i$ vector. The parameterization function of (3.35) is well suited for this purpose. Note that, given $u_i \sim N^+(0, \sigma_u^2)$, the mean of u_i is a function of σ_u^2 (instead of 0) because of the truncation. In particular,

$$\begin{aligned} \mathrm{E}(u_i) &= \sigma \left(\frac{\phi(0)}{\Phi(0)} \right) = \sqrt{2/\pi}\, \exp(\boldsymbol{z}_i'\boldsymbol{w}) \\ &= \exp\{\frac{1}{2} \ln(2/\pi) + (\boldsymbol{z}_i'\boldsymbol{w})\}. \end{aligned} \tag{3.37}$$

Note that the $\frac{1}{2}\ln(2/\pi)$ term can be absorbed by the constant term in $\boldsymbol{z}_i'\boldsymbol{w}$. Therefore, by parameterizing σ_u^2, we allow the $\boldsymbol{z}_i$ variables to affect the expected value of inefficiency.

Marginal Effects of the Exogenous Determinants. If the effects of the exogenous factors on efficiency are the key concern, the maximum likelihood estimates of $\boldsymbol{w}_u$ in the equation (3.35) may not be very informative. This is because the relationship between $E(u_i)$ and $\boldsymbol{z}_u$ is nonlinear, and so the slope coefficients $\boldsymbol{w}_u$ are *not* the marginal effects of $\boldsymbol{z}_u$. For instance, assume the kth variable in $\boldsymbol{z}_u$ has an estimated coefficient that is 0.5. This number itself tells us nothing about the magnitude of the kth variable's (marginal) effect on the inefficiency.

As such, the computation of the marginal effect of the z variables may be useful for empirical purposes. Given the half-normal assumption of u_i in (3.17) and the parameterization function of (3.35), the marginal effect of the kth variable of $\boldsymbol{z}_{u,i}$ on $E(u_i)$ can be computed as[11]

$$\frac{\partial E(u_i)}{\partial z[k]} = w[k] \frac{\sigma_{u,i}}{2} \left[\frac{\phi(0)}{\Phi(0)} \right] = w[k]\, \sigma_{u,i} \phi(0), \tag{3.38}$$

where $\phi(0)$ is approximately 0.3989.

Note that the equation also implies

$$\operatorname{sign}\left(\frac{\partial \mathrm{E}(u_i)}{\partial z[k]} \right) = \operatorname{sign}(w[k]). \tag{3.39}$$

11 Here marginal effects are based on the unconditional mean of u_i, although the JLMS formula uses the conditional mean, viz., $E(u_i|\epsilon_i)$ as a point estimate of u_i. Sun and Kumbhakar (2013) derive the formulae for computing marginal effects using the JLMS formula.

Therefore, the sign of the coefficient reveals the direction of impact of z_i on $E(u_i)$. So if we do not compute the exact marginal effect, we may still say something about the direction of the impact by the sign of the coefficient. This is a convenient property, but as we will see later, the property does not always hold in models with a more complicated setup.

Example

Model 5: Half-Normal Model with Heteroscedasticity

Returning to our example of dairy farming, we estimate a half-normal model with an exogenous determinant of inefficiency (IT expenditure as a percentage of total expenditure, `comp`). This is achieved by adding `usigmas(comp)` to the previous model, Model 4 (see page 62). In specifying `sf_init`, we need to provide two initial values in `usigmas()`; the first one is for the coefficient of `comp` and the second one is for the variance parameter w. We also save the efficiency index in `bc_h2`. The code is provided here:

```
. sfmodel ly, prod dist(h) frontier($xvar) usigmas(comp) vsigmas()
. sf_init, frontier(b_ols) usigmas(0.1 0.1) vsigmas(0.1)
. sf_srch, frontier($xvar) usigmas(comp) n(1) nograph fast
. ml max, difficult  gtol(1e-5) nrtol(1e-5)
. sf_predict, bc(bc_h2)
```

The estimation results are as follows:

```
Number of obs    =         196
                                                Wald chi2(4)      =     1739.84
Log likelihood =  110.59382                     Prob > chi2       =      0.0000
```

ly	Coef.	Std. Err.	z	P>|z|	[95% Conf.	Interval]
frontier						
llabor	.1011541	.0428404	2.36	0.018	.0171885	.1851197
lfeed	.155526	.0372888	4.17	0.000	.0824414	.2286106
lcattle	.756702	.0575811	13.14	0.000	.6438452	.8695588
lland	.0348882	.0387301	0.90	0.368	-.0410214	.1107978
_cons	7.736939	.4797281	16.13	0.000	6.796689	8.677189
usigmas						
comp	-.0298775	.0590676	-0.51	0.613	-.1456478	.0858929
_cons	-2.950646	.4180384	-7.06	0.000	-3.769986	-2.131306
vsigmas						
_cons	-5.308163	.4377181	-12.13	0.000	-6.166075	-4.450252

The estimated coefficients of the frontier function are very similar to those of Model 4. The log-likelihood value of the model is 110.594 which is not significantly different from Model 4's log-likelihood value of 110.466. The coefficient of `comp` is -0.030 with the p value equal to 0.613. These statistics imply that the inclusion of `comp` in this model is not supported by the data. As such, we do not examine the marginal effects of `comp` in this model.

3.4.4 Truncated-Normal Distribution

The one-parameter half-normal distribution discussed so far is inherently restrictive. For instance, Figure 3.4 of the half-normal distribution implies that most of the observations are clustered near full efficiency. However, it can be argued that the majority of the firms in some industries might exhibit a certain degree of inefficiency (e.g., operational units in the public sector or firms in a recently privatized industry), such that the appropriate distribution should have a nonzero mode. Which scenario is the most likely is, of course, an empirical question, but the inflexibility of the half-normal distribution limits the exploration of the alternatives.

Stevenson (1980) proposes a truncated-normal model which allows the inefficiency distribution to have a nonzero mode. As such, it can be seen as a way to address the above concern. A production frontier model with a truncated-normal distribution of u_i can be specified as

$$\ln y_i = \ln y_i^* - u_i, \tag{3.40}$$

$$\ln y_i^* = \boldsymbol{x}_i\boldsymbol{\beta} + v_i, \tag{3.41}$$

$$u_i \sim N^+(\mu, \sigma_u^2), \tag{3.42}$$

$$v_i \sim N(0, \sigma_v^2). \tag{3.43}$$

The notation $N^+(\mu, \sigma_u^2)$ indicates a truncation of the normal distribution $N(\mu, \sigma_u^2)$ at 0 from above. We may also write (3.40) and (3.41) as

$$\ln y_i = \boldsymbol{x}_i\boldsymbol{\beta} + \epsilon_i, \tag{3.44}$$

$$\epsilon_i = v_i - u_i. \tag{3.45}$$

Except for the μ parameter in equation (3.42), the model is the same as the half-normal model. If we let $\mu = 0$, it collapses to a half-normal model. The half-normal model is thus a special case of the truncated-normal model.

3.4.4.1 Deriving the Truncated Distribution

Suppose z_i has a truncated distribution obtained by truncating a normal distribution $N(\mu, \sigma^2)$ from above at point α so that $z_i \geq \alpha$. The density function of z_i, $f(z_i)$, is given in (3.19). If we let $\alpha = 0$ so that $z_i \geq 0$, the density function of z_i becomes

$$f(z_i) = \frac{\frac{1}{\sigma}\phi(z_i)}{1 - \Phi\left(\frac{-\mu}{\sigma}\right)} = \frac{1}{\sqrt{2\pi}\sigma\Phi\left(\frac{\mu}{\sigma}\right)} \exp\left\{-\frac{(z_i - \mu)^2}{2\sigma^2}\right\}, \quad z_i \geq 0. \tag{3.46}$$

Figure 3.6 illustrates the shapes of truncated-normal distributions with various parameter values of the mean, μ, and the variance, σ^2. It can be seen from the figure that the percentage of firms that are close to fully efficient depends on how far from zero the mean of the distribution is. Similarly, if the variance is large, some firms can be very inefficient. Since the half-normal is a special case of truncated normal, it is often preferred to estimate the model with the truncated normal assumption and test the hypothesis that the mean is zero.

Such a formulation might be appropriate, for example, in a recently privatized industry or in the public sector. Without the pressures of the competitive market, the public sector is often regarded as inefficient, with budget holders more interested in spending their budget before the end of the financial year than improving the efficiency of their department. This is one of the justifications of privatization; namely, by moving public sector corporations into the private sector, the hope is that market disciplines will improve the efficiency of those corporations, reduce the burden on the public sector purse, and improve the service to customers. As such, recently privatized industries might be expected to be inefficient for

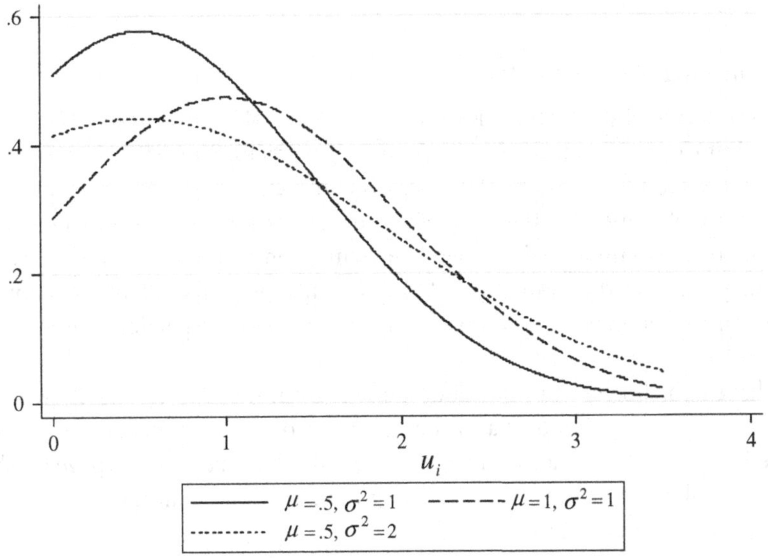

Figure 3.6. Density Plots of Truncated-Normal Distributions

a number of years before these inefficiencies are driven out. Even in the private sector such a formulation might be appropriate. For example, in the short run, before companies are able to respond to significant changes in market conditions, or if restrictions exist that interfere with the efficient operation of the market. For example, the presence of trade unions or regulations might result in more companies being inefficient than efficient.

3.4.4.2 The Log-Likelihood Function

Based on (3.40)–(3.43), the log-likelihood function for the ith observation can be derived as

$$L_i = -\frac{1}{2}\ln(\sigma_v^2 + \sigma_u^2) + \ln\phi\left(\frac{\mu + \epsilon_i}{\sqrt{\sigma_v^2 + \sigma_u^2}}\right) + \ln\Phi\left(\frac{\mu_{*i}}{\sigma_*}\right) - \ln\Phi\left(\frac{\mu}{\sigma_u}\right), \tag{3.47}$$

where

$$\mu_{*i} = \frac{\sigma_v^2\mu - \sigma_u^2\epsilon_i}{\sigma_v^2 + \sigma_u^2}, \tag{3.48}$$

$$\sigma_*^2 = \frac{\sigma_v^2\sigma_u^2}{\sigma_v^2 + \sigma_u^2}. \tag{3.49}$$

See Appendix A for the derivation. To ensure a positive estimation of the variance parameters, the following parameterization can be used in the likelihood function for unconstrained numerical maximization.

$$\sigma_u^2 = \exp(w_u), \tag{3.50}$$

$$\sigma_v^2 = \exp(w_v), \tag{3.51}$$

where w_u and w_v are unrestricted constant parameters.

Example

Model 6: Truncated-Normal Model

Compared to the model with a half-normal distribution of u_i, the model with a truncated-normal distribution requires estimating one more parameter (μ). The need to estimate this additional parameter adds substantial numerical complexity to the ML estimation. As such, the choice of initial values for the numerical maximization becomes particularly important in this case. Good initial values help the estimation to converge smoothly, whereas a bad choice may result in the estimation failing to converge. This statement is applicable, of course, to all numerical maximization problems, but the issue is particularly relevant for the current model.

Here we have two choices of initial values, one is from the OLS estimates (which is saved in the vector `b_ols`; see page 64), and the other is from the estimates of the half-normal model (saved in `bf_h`, `bv_h`, and `bu_h`; see page 64). The example on page 65 shows how initial values may be supplied by the user using the `sf_init` command. It also shows the use of `sf_srch` to refine the initial values.

The following commands estimate a truncated-normal model of Stevenson (1980).

```
. sfmodel ly, prod dist(t) frontier($xvar) mu() usigmas() vsigmas()
. sf_init, frontier(b_ols) mu(0.1) usigmas(0.1) vsigmas(0.1)
. sf_srch, frontier($xvar) mu() usigmas() vsigmas() n(2)
. ml max, difficult gtol(1e-5) nrtol(1e-5)
```

The uses of `sf_init` and `sf_srch` are optional. If we wish to use the results of the half-normal model as initial values, we may replace the second line by

```
. sf_init, frontier(bf_h) mu(0.1) usigmas(bu_h) vsigmas(bv_h)
```

The following is the estimation result (the results are identical regardless of which set of initial values are used or even, in this instance, if initial values are not provided, although convergence is much slower in this case).

```
Number of obs    =  196
                                                Wald chi2(4)      = 1678.14
Log likelihood =  110.85049                     Prob > chi2       = 0.0000

------------------------------------------------------------------------------
          ly |      Coef.   Std. Err.      z    P>|z|     [95% Conf. Interval]
-------------+----------------------------------------------------------------
frontier     |
      llabor |   .0977799   .0435682     2.24   0.025     .0123879     .183172
       lfeed |   .1491791   .0379532     3.93   0.000     .0747922    .2235659
     lcattle |   .7564538    .057729    13.10   0.000     .6433071    .8696005
       lland |   .0423259   .0391527     1.08   0.280    -.0344119    .1190637
       _cons |   7.756931   .4890218    15.86   0.000     6.798466    8.715396
-------------+----------------------------------------------------------------
mu           |
       _cons |  -1.212626   4.464969    -0.27   0.786    -9.963804    7.538552
-------------+----------------------------------------------------------------
usigmas      |
       _cons |  -1.743111   2.861989    -0.61   0.542    -7.352507    3.866284
-------------+----------------------------------------------------------------
vsigmas      |
       _cons |  -4.845751   .3533778   -13.71   0.000    -5.538359   -4.153144
------------------------------------------------------------------------------
```

We use `sf_transform` to obtain $\hat{\sigma}_u^2$ and $\hat{\sigma}_v^2$ from the log scales.

```
. sf_transform

      sigma_u_sqr = exp(usigmas);
      sigma_v_sqr = exp(vsigmas).

   ---convert the parameters to natural metrics---

variable      |      Coef.    Std. Err.       t     P>|t|      [95% Conf. Interval]
--------------+-------------------------------------------------------------------
  sigma_u_sqr |   .1749755   .5007798      0.35    0.727      .000641    47.76561
  sigma_v_sqr |   .0078617   .0027782      2.83    0.005      .003933    .0157149
```

The estimates on the frontier function are quite similar to those of the previous, half-normal model. The mu parameter is highly insignificant. Indeed, the log-likelihood value of the model (110.851) is only slightly larger than that of the half-normal model (110.466).

Although the model is not preferred in comparison to the half-normal model, the inefficiency specification is still supported by the data. This is shown using the LR test with the mixed chi-square distribution. The test has two degrees of freedom because the null hypothesis has two restrictions: $\sigma_u^2 = 0$ and $\mu = 0$. The value of the test and the relevant critical values are provided using the following code.

```
. scalar ll_t = e(ll)
. display -2*(ll_ols - ll_t) /* test against OLS model */
17.194892

. sf_mixtable, dof(2)

  critical values of the mixed chi-square distribution
                              significance level
  dof  | 0.25      0.1        0.05       0.025       0.01       0.005      0.001
----------------------------------------------------------------------------------
   2      2.090     3.808      5.138      6.483       8.273      9.634      12.810
source: Table 1, Kodde and Palm (1986, Econometrica).
```

The result indicates that the OLS model is rejected in favor of the truncated-normal frontier model.

3.4.4.3 Technical Efficiency

As we discussed in the section on the half-normal model, the (in)efficiency-related measures can be obtained for each observation using $E(u_i|\epsilon_i)$ or $E(\exp(-u_i)|\epsilon_i)$, with the former being the point estimate of u_i and approximating the technical inefficiency of production, and the later measuring technical efficiency. The formulas are the same as in (3.29) and (3.30), respectively, which are reproduced here for convenience (see also Appendix B):

$$E(u_i|\epsilon_i) = \frac{\sigma_* \phi(\frac{\mu_{*i}}{\sigma_*})}{\Phi\left(\frac{\mu_{*i}}{\sigma_*}\right)} + \mu_{*i},$$

$$E\left[\exp(-u_i)|\epsilon_i\right] = \exp\left(-\mu_{*i} + \frac{1}{2}\sigma_*^2\right) \frac{\Phi\left(\frac{\mu_{*i}}{\sigma_*} - \sigma_*\right)}{\Phi\left(\frac{\mu_{*i}}{\sigma_*}\right)},$$

where μ_{*i} and σ_* are as given in (3.48) and (3.49), respectively.

It should be noted that estimates of firm-specific inefficiency as well as efficiency assume that the model parameters are known and given, while in fact they are estimated with uncertainty (see page 69).

3.4.4.4 Confidence Interval

The lower and upper bounds of a $(1-\alpha)100\%$ confidence interval of $E(u_i|\epsilon_i)$ are, respectively,

$$L_i = \mu_{*i} + \Phi^{-1}\left\{1-\left(1-\frac{\alpha}{2}\right)\left[1-\Phi\left(-\frac{\mu_{*i}}{\sigma_*}\right)\right]\right\}\sigma_*, \tag{3.52}$$

$$U_i = \mu_{*i} + \Phi^{-1}\left\{1-\frac{\alpha}{2}\left[1-\Phi\left(-\frac{\mu_{*i}}{\sigma_*}\right)\right]\right\}\sigma_*, \tag{3.53}$$

where μ_{*i} and σ_* are defined in (3.48) and (3.49). (See also Appendix C.)

The lower and upper bounds of a $(1-\alpha)100\%$ confidence interval of $E(\exp(-u_i)|\epsilon_i)$ are, respectively,

$$\mathcal{L}_i = \exp(-U_i), \qquad \mathcal{U}_i = \exp(-L_i). \tag{3.54}$$

These formulas appear similar to those for the half-normal model, except for the definitions of μ_* and σ_* used in the equations. The similarity is not surprising, since in both cases the confidence intervals are constructed based on $(u_i|\epsilon_i) \sim N^+(\mu_{*i}, \sigma_*^2)$, with the differences being how μ_{*i} and σ_*^2 are defined in the two models.

Example

Following the estimation of the model, the (in)efficiency index and the associated confidence intervals can be obtained from the `sf_predict` command.

```
. sf_predict, jlms(jlms_t) bc(bc_t) ci(95)
```

The command creates variables `jlms_t` and `bc_t` for the inefficiency and efficiency index, respectively. The lower and upper bounds of the 95% confidence intervals are saved as `jlms_t_95L`, `jlms_t_95U`, `bc_t_95L`, and `bc_t_95U`.

We now take a look at the summary statistics and the first ten observations of the created variables.

```
. summarize bc_t jlms_t

    Variable |       Obs        Mean    Std. Dev.       Min        Max
-------------+--------------------------------------------------------
        bc_t |       196    .8910183    .0755853   .5535397   .9701945
      jlms_t |       196    .1214718    .0941693   .0306446   .5951837

. list bc_t bc_t_95U bc_t_95L jlms_t jlms_t_95U jlms_t_95L in 1/10

     +-----------------------------------------------------------------------+
     |      bc_t    bc_t_95U    bc_t_95L     jlms_t    jlms_t~U    jlms_t~L |
     |-----------------------------------------------------------------------|
  1. | .95091475   .99830991   .85477768   .05121048   .15691387   .00169152 |
  2. | .89334459   .99221582   .76496891   .11518983   .26792009   .00781464 |
  3. |  .9447952   .99797258   .84236956   .05783723   .17153645   .00202948 |
  4. | .89455152   .99244548   .76642116   .11381233   .26602344    .0075832 |
  5. | .91588239    .9955835   .79436012   .08971899   .23021837   .00442628 |
     |-----------------------------------------------------------------------|
```

```
  6. | .92137161   .99616611   .80239982    .0835963   .22014826   .00384125 |
  7. | .75475758   .89077333   .63447118   .28509607   .45496341   .11566529 |
  8. | .92450867   .99646717   .80718719   .08011162   .21419968   .00353908 |
  9. | .95094501   .99831147   .85484152   .05117783   .15683918   .00168995 |
 10. | .55353969    .6536533   .46524593   .59518366   .76518913   .42517819 |
     +---------------------------------------------------------------------+
```

The mean of `bc_t` equals 0.891, implying that, on average, the dairy farmers produce 89.1 percent of the maximum output, or that they lost about 11 percent of the potential output due to technical inefficiency (this compares to an estimate of 15 percent under the half-normal formulation). On the other hand, the mean of `jlms_t` equals 0.121, implying that, on average, the dairy farmers lost about 12 percent of the output due to technical inefficiency (this compares to an estimate of 17 percent under the half-normal formulation). Although, as discussed earlier, it is the half-normal model, in this instance, that provides the preferred formulation and thus the preferred estimates of inefficiency.

3.4.4.5 Heteroscedasticity, Exogenous Determinants, and Marginal Effects

Heteroscedasticity. As discussed for the half-normal case, heteroscedasticity may take place in either of the error components: v_i and u_i. If the data is heteroscedastic, the consequence of ignoring it is the same as we have discussed for the half-normal model (see Section 3.4.3.8 for more detail).

As in the case of a half-normal model, we can parameterize σ_u^2 and σ_v^2 to address the problem of heteroscedasticity. Again, we use an exponential function for the parameterization:

$$\sigma_{u,i}^2 = \exp(\mathbf{z}_{u,i}{}'\mathbf{w}_u), \tag{3.55}$$

$$\sigma_{v,i}^2 = \exp(\mathbf{z}_{v,i}{}'\mathbf{w}_v). \tag{3.56}$$

The vectors $\mathbf{z}_{u,i}$ and $\mathbf{z}_{v,i}$ may or may not be the same. The parameterization functions are substituted into the maximum likelihood function, and the parameters are estimated together with the other parameters in the model.

Exogenous Determinants of Efficiency. In Section 3.4.3.8, we discussed how the quest for understanding the attributes of inefficiency evolved from a two-step estimation procedure to a theoretically preferred one-step estimation method. This section explores the issue further.

The one-step estimation method of investigating exogenous effects on inefficiency was first introduced in the truncated-normal model by Kumbhakar, Ghosh, and McGuckin (1991) and Reifschneider and Stevenson (1991). The same modeling strategy was later followed by Huang and Liu (1994) and Battese and Coelli (1995), each with slightly different algebraic form for the pre-truncated mean function of u_i. These studies, which we label KGMHLBC, assume that the mean of the distribution of the pretruncated u_i is a linear function of the exogenous variables under investigation. That is, they abandon the constant-mean assumption on μ, and assume, instead, that the mean is a linear function of some exogenous variables, viz.,

$$\mu_i = \mathbf{z}_i'\boldsymbol{\delta}, \tag{3.57}$$

where $\mathbf{z}_i$ is the vector of exogenous variables of observation i, and $\boldsymbol{\delta}$ is the corresponding coefficient vector. The log-likelihood function is the same as (3.47), except that (3.57) is used in place of μ in the function. The maximum likelihood estimation can be carried out to obtain estimates of $\boldsymbol{\delta}$ and the other parameters.

In addition to being a sensible approach in investigating the exogenous influences on efficiencies, another appeal of the KGMHLBC model is that it makes the distributional shape of u_i even more flexible. It is more flexible because each observation now has an observation-specific mean of the pre-truncated distribution, with the mean determined by observation-specific variables. This is in contrast to the Stevenson (1980) model, where the mean of the pre-truncated distribution is identical for all the observations. In a literature where the distributional assumption of u_i is essential and yet potentially open to criticism, anything that introduces greater flexibility is always regarded as beneficial.

Recall that in Section 3.4.3.8, we showed that the half-normal heteroscedastic model proposed by Caudill and Ford (1993), Caudill, Ford, and Gropper (1995), and Hadri (1999) (CFCFGH hereafter), which parameterizes σ_u^2 by a function of $\mathbf{z}$, can also be used to address the issue of exogenous determinants of inefficiency. The same conclusion applies here as well. A natural question to ask then is: Which of the parameterization approaches, KGMHLBC or CFCFGH, is better in investigating exogenous influences on efficiency of a truncated-normal model? Wang (2002) argues that neither approach can be easily justified, and the better parameterization approach may come from combining both features of the models.

To explore this point further, note that the mean and the variance of inefficiency (u_i) are, respectively,

$$E(u_i) = f(\mu, \sigma_u) = \sigma_u \left[\frac{\mu}{\sigma_u} + \frac{\phi\left(\frac{\mu}{\sigma_u}\right)}{\Phi\left(\frac{\mu}{\sigma_u}\right)} \right], \tag{3.58}$$

$$V(u_i) = g(\mu, \sigma_u) = \sigma_u^2 \left[1 - \frac{\mu}{\sigma_u} \left[\frac{\phi\left(\frac{\mu}{\sigma_u}\right)}{\Phi\left(\frac{\mu}{\sigma_u}\right)} \right] - \left[\frac{\phi\left(\frac{\mu}{\sigma_u}\right)}{\Phi\left(\frac{\mu}{\sigma_u}\right)} \right]^2 \right], \tag{3.59}$$

where ϕ and Φ are the probability density and cumulative distribution functions of a standard normal variable, respectively. The equations indicate that both the mean and the variance of u_i are functions of μ *and* σ_u, and there is no justification of choosing one over the other in the parameterization.

It is from this moment-equation perspective that the boundary between KGMHLBC and CFCFGH is blurred: regardless which of μ and σ_u^2 is parameterized, both moments of u_i are observation-specific, and thus exogenous influences can be introduced either way. If the goal is to study how exogenous variables affect the inefficiency, there is no particular reason why $\mathbf{z}_i$ should be assumed to exert the influence through μ but not σ_u, or through σ_u but not μ. Without further information and assumptions, the decision of parameterizing only μ or σ_u would appear arbitrary.

The Wang (2002) model calls for parameterizing μ and σ_u^2 by the *same* vector of exogenous variables. The double parameterization is not only less ad hoc, but it also accommodates non-monotonic relationships between the inefficiency and its determinants. The latter can be of great importance to empirical research. The downside of this approach is that the model is more complex and, as a result, convergence might be a problem. More discussion on this issue is provided in the next section.

The double parameterization uses both (3.55) and (3.57). The log-likelihood function is the same as in (3.47), except that (3.55) and (3.57) are substituted into the equation in place of σ_u^2 and μ, respectively.

Example

Model 7: Truncated-Normal Model with Heteroscedasticity

As in Model 5, in this example we hypothesize that the dairy farmers' efficiency levels are affected by the farmer's investment in the IT equipment used in the production process. In this case, the variable comp (i.e., the farmer's IT expenditure as a ratio of total operating expenditure) is used to augment the truncated-normal model.

As discussed earlier, with the truncated-normal model, there are a number of ways to make the farmer's technical inefficiency a function of comp. The Battese and Coelli (1995) model would make μ (mu) a function of comp. Wang (2002) argues that making both μ and σ_u^2 (usigmas) functions of comp is less ad hoc in restricting how comp affects inefficiency.

The following code shows how to estimate the Battese and Coelli model. In this example, we do not provide initial values for the maximization problem, and Stata in this scenario will come up with a set of feasible initial values to start the numerical maximization process. Instead, we use the command sf_srch to further refine the initial values provided internally by Stata.

```
. sfmodel ly, prod dist(t) frontier($xvar) mu(comp) usigmas() vsigmas()
. sf_srch, frontier($xvar) mu(comp) usigmas() vsigmas() n(1)
. ml max, difficult gtol(1e-5) nrtol(1e-5)
```

Curiously, the model specified here does not converge in the estimation regardless of the initial values we have tried. A plausible explanation is that the model is mis-specified. The more flexible model of Wang (2002) does converge and is discussed next.

Model 8: Truncated-Normal Model with Exogenous Determinants in μ and σ_u^2

The following code estimates the Wang (2002) model with μ and σ_u^2 parameterized by the same vector of variables (here, comp).

```
. sfmodel ly, prod dist(t) frontier($xvar) mu(comp) usigmas(comp) vsigmas()
. sf_srch, n(1) frontier($xvar) mu(comp) usigmas(comp) nograph fast
. ml max, difficult gtol(1e-5) nrtol(1e-5)


(iteration log omitted)

                                                Number of obs    =       196
                                                Wald chi2(4)     =   1742.96
Log likelihood =  118.32646                     Prob > chi2      =
0.0000

------------------------------------------------------------------------------
          ly |      Coef.   Std. Err.      z    P>|z|     [95% Conf. Interval]
-------------+----------------------------------------------------------------
frontier     |
      llabor |   .1008781   .0422606     2.39   0.017     .0180489    .1837073
       lfeed |   .1453378   .0367848     3.95   0.000     .0732409    .2174348
    lcattle  |   .7412325   .0563299    13.16   0.000      .630828    .8516371
       lland |   .0533866   .0377931     1.41   0.158    -.0206865    .1274596
       _cons |   7.751977   .4748133    16.33   0.000      6.82136    8.682594
-------------+----------------------------------------------------------------
```

```
mu          |
       comp |  -1.68236   2.050301    -0.82   0.412    -5.700876    2.336156
      _cons |  7.536007   8.635172     0.87   0.383    -9.388619    24.46063
------------+----------------------------------------------------------------
usigmas     |
       comp |  .3708864   .0694269     5.34   0.000     .2348121    .5069607
      _cons | -3.578518   1.549023    -2.31   0.021    -6.614546   -.5424891
------------+----------------------------------------------------------------
vsigmas     |
      _cons | -4.778852   .2115916   -22.59   0.000    -5.193564    -4.36414
-----------------------------------------------------------------------------
```

Again, the estimated coefficients of the frontier function are very similar to those of Model 4. The log-likelihood value of the model is 118.326, which is higher than Model 4's log-likelihood value of 110.466. The LR test clearly supports the truncated-normal specification with determinants of inefficiency over the half-normal specification. The coefficient of `comp` for `usigmas` is 0.371 with the p value equal to 0.000 (the coefficient of `comp` for `mu`, in contrast, is insignificant at -1.682 with the p value equal to 0.412). These statistics imply that the inclusion of `comp` in this model is supported by the data.

In the code given here, we save the log-likelihood value of the estimated model in `ll_w` and the slope coefficient vector and the variance parameter in `b_wf` and `b_wv`, respectively (they will be used later):

```
matrix b0 = e(b)                  /* all the parameter estimates */
matrix b_wf = b0[1,"frontier:"]   /* the slope coefficient vector */
matrix b_wv = b0[1,"vsigmas:"]    /* the variance parameter */
scalar ll_w = e(ll)               /* the log-likelihood value */
```

The command `sf_transform` can be used to obtain $\hat{\sigma}_v^2$. It does not, however, return $\hat{\sigma}_u^2$, because σ_u^2 is now a function of variables.

```
. sf_transform

      sigma_u_sqr = exp(usigmas);
      sigma_v_sqr = exp(vsigmas).

   ---convert the parameters to natural metrics---

   sigma_u_sqr appears to be a function of variables.
   The transformation is done only if sigma_u_sqr is constant.

variable     |      Coef.   Std. Err.       t    P>|t|      [95% Conf. Interval]
-------------+------------------------------------------------------------------
 sigma_v_sqr |   .0084056   .0017786     4.73    0.000      .0055522    .0127256
```

An LR test against the null hypothesis of no technical inefficiency (OLS) would have four degrees of freedom, because there are two parameters in each of the `mu` and `usigmas` functions.

```
. display -2*(ll_ols - ll_w)
 32.146837

. sf_mixtable, dof(4)

critical values of the mixed chi-square distribution
                              significance level
 dof  | 0.25     0.1      0.05     0.025     0.01      0.005     0.001
--------------------------------------------------------------------------
  4      4.776    7.094    8.761    10.383    12.483    14.045    17.612
source: Table 1, Kodde and Palm (1986, Econometrica).
```

The LR statistic has a value equal to 32.147, and the critical value at the 1 percent significance level of the test is 12.483. It is evident that the null hypothesis of no technical inefficiency is clearly rejected.

Marginal Effects. Because the KGMHLBC and CFCFGH models are nested in the Wang (2002) model, we present the formulas for computing the marginal effects in the Wang model. The key parameterization equations (3.57) and (3.55) are reproduced here for ease of reference.

$$\mu_i = \boldsymbol{z}_i'\boldsymbol{\delta},$$
$$\sigma_{u,i}^2 = \exp(\boldsymbol{z}_i'\boldsymbol{w}).$$

For the Wang (2002) model, the marginal effect of the kth element of $\boldsymbol{z}_i$ on $E(u_i)$ and $V(u_i)$ are as follows:[12]

$$\frac{\partial \mathrm{E}(u_i)}{\partial z[k]} = \delta[k]\left[1 - \Lambda_i\left[\frac{\phi(\Lambda_i)}{\Phi(\Lambda_i)}\right] - \left[\frac{\phi(\Lambda_i)}{\Phi(\Lambda_i)}\right]^2\right] + w[k]\,\frac{\sigma_{u,i}}{2}\left[(1+\Lambda_i^2)\left[\frac{\phi(\Lambda_i)}{\Phi(\Lambda_i)}\right] + \Lambda_i\left[\frac{\phi(\Lambda_i)}{\Phi(\Lambda_i)}\right]^2\right], \tag{3.60}$$

$$\frac{\partial V(u_i)}{\partial z[k]} = \frac{\delta[k]}{\sigma_{u,i}}\left[\frac{\phi(\Lambda)}{\Phi(\Lambda)}\right](E(u_i)^2 - V(u_i)) + w[k]\sigma_{u,i}^2\left\{1 - \frac{1}{2}\left[\frac{\phi(\Lambda)}{\Phi(\Lambda)}\right]\left(\Lambda_i + \Lambda_i^3 + (2+3\Lambda_i^2)\left[\frac{\phi(\Lambda)}{\Phi(\Lambda)}\right] + 2\Lambda_i\left[\frac{\phi(\Lambda)}{\Phi(\Lambda)}\right]^2\right)\right\}, \tag{3.61}$$

where $\Lambda_i = \mu_i/\sigma_{u,i}$, and $\delta[k]$ and $w[k]$ are the corresponding coefficients in (3.57) and (3.55), and $E(u_i)$ and $V(u_i)$ are given in (3.58) and (3.59). For the KGMHLBC model, σ_u^2 is not parameterized, so the marginal effect formulas are the same as the above except that $w[k] = 0$ and $\sigma_{u,i} = \sigma_u$. For the CFCFG model, the marginal effect formula is obtained by setting $\delta[k] = 0$ and $\mu_i = 0$.

Wang (2002) shows that the marginal effect of a z variable on inefficiency of KGMHLBC is monotonic, implying that an exogenous variable would *either* increase the mean and/or the variance of inefficiency, *or* decrease the mean and/or the variance of the inefficiency. The direction of the impact is monotonic in the sample, and it is determined by the sign of the δ coefficient. By contrast, the marginal effect from the Wang model is nonmonotonic, implying that, depending on the values of exogenous variables, the impact on inefficiency can change directions in the sample.

Allowing for a nonmonotonic relationship between inefficiency and its determinants has important empirical implications. For instance, we may expect a younger farmer's technical efficiency to increase with age due to the accumulation of experience, whereas age may be a detrimental factor for a senior farmer due to deteriorated physical and mental capability. In this case, age and inefficiency has a nonmonotonic relationship. Starting from a lower value of age, an increase in age helps improve efficiency, whereas when the value of age is quite

[12] See Sun and Kumbhakar (2013) for formulas using $E(u_i|\epsilon_i)$ and $V(u_i|\epsilon_i)$.

high, an increase in age impairs efficiency. As this example illustrates, the accommodation of nonmonotonicity can be important in empirical work.

Although it may be reasonable to expect that adding square terms of variables in a KGMHLBC type model may also account for the nonlinearity, the empirical example of Wang (2002) indicates that the square-term approach does not perform well, in the sense that it fails to capture the nonlinearity in the data adequately. The Wang (2002) model begins with flexible parameterization of the exogenous determinants, and nonmonotonicity arises naturally as a result.

Example

Continuing the previous example, Model 8 (from page 81), we now investigate how technical inefficiency is affected by the farmer's expenditure on IT equipment, by showing how to obtain the marginal effects. As discussed earlier, for the Wang (2002) model, the estimated coefficients of `comp` on `mu` and `usigmas` are not directly interpretable, as they do not provide the marginal effects of the technical inefficiency due to the nonlinearity of the model; the marginal effects formulas are given in (3.60) and (3.61). Following the estimation of Model 8, we use the command `sf_predict` with the `marginal` option to obtain the marginal values.

```
. sf_predict, bc(bc_w) marginal

The following is the marginal effect on unconditional E(u).

The average marginal effect of comp on uncond E(u) is -.03604191 (see comp_M).

The following is the marginal effect on uncond V(u).

The average marginal effect of comp on uncond V(u) is -.0064839 (see comp_V).
```

The `marginal` option asks Stata to calculate the marginal effect of all the variables specified in parameterizing the one-sided distribution. In our example, `comp` is the only variable. The marginal effects on the unconditional expectation of u, $E(u)$, and the unconditional variance of u, $V(u)$, are calculated for every observation in the sample, and the results are saved as new variables under the name `comp_M` and `comp_V`, respectively, and the mean values for the entire sample are displayed.

The output shows that the mean of the marginal effects on both $E(u)$ and $V(u)$ are negative. Thus, increasing the expenditure share on the IT equipments reduces, on average, the level of technical inefficiency as well as the uncertainty of the technical inefficiency. In particular, the level of technical inefficiency is reduced, on average, by 3.6 percent for every 1 percentage increase in the IT expenditure share. We can also obtain the standard error of the mean marginal effect by bootstrapping; a bootstrap program is provided in Appendix D. The results show that both of the mean statistics are significant at the 1 percent level.

As discussed earlier, an advantage of the Wang (2002) model is the accommodation of nonmonotonic efficiency effects. In the current example, nonmonotonicity means that the marginal effect of `comp` on inefficiency does not need to be positive or negative for *all* observations. The sign can alternate, and this depends on the value of `comp` as well as on values of other variables. Whether the estimation result indeed implies nonmonotonic effects can be easily checked by tabulating values of `comp_M` and/or `comp_V` to see if both positive and

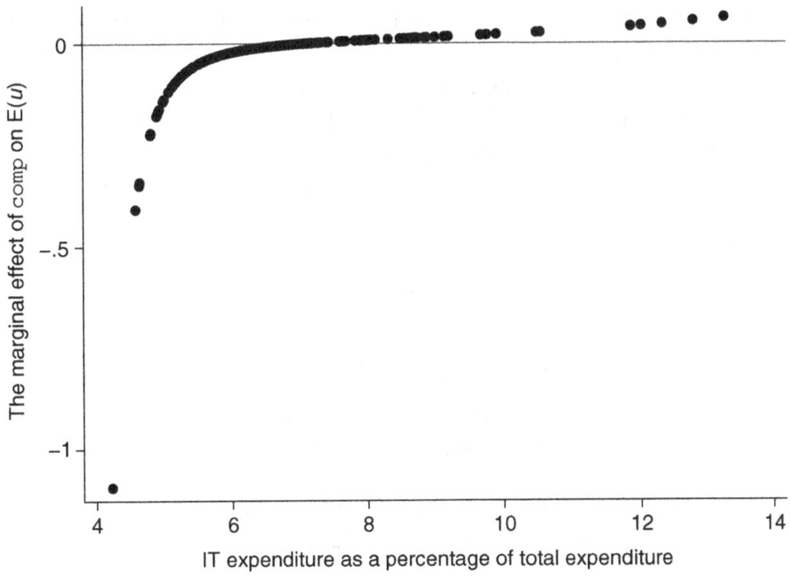

Figure 3.7. Marginal Effects of `comp` on Inefficiency

negative values exist. Alternatively, it is informative to draw a scatter plot of the marginal effects against values of `comp`. This can be achieved by running the following code:

```
. scatter comp_M comp, yline(0)
```

The resulting graph is shown in Figure 3.7.

The graph indicates that, for many observations, the marginal effect of the IT expenditure share is negative. A closer investigation reveals that about 70 percent of the observations have negative marginal effects of `comp` on inefficiency. The size of the negative effect is larger when the value of `comp` is smaller. The negative effect implies that technical inefficiency reduces as the expenditure share on IT equipment increases. When the expenditure share continues to rise, however, the marginal effect moves toward 0 and eventually becomes positive. This result indicates that there is an *optimal* share of IT expenditure to total expenditure with regard to technical efficiency improvement. By tabulating the data, it can be seen that the optimal share is about 7.1 percent. Expending more than this optimal share does not improve technical efficiency.

3.4.5 Truncated Distribution with the Scaling Property

In modeling determinants ($\boldsymbol{z}_i$) of inefficiency, the models discussed so far take the approach of parameterizing one or all of the distribution parameters as functions of $\boldsymbol{z}_i$. Wang and Schmidt (2002) proposed a different modeling strategy in which the random variable representing inefficiency has the following form:

$$u_i \sim h(\boldsymbol{z}_i, \boldsymbol{\delta})\, u^*, \tag{3.62}$$

where $h(\cdot) \geq 0$ is an observation-specific nonstochastic function of the exogenous variables, and $u^* \geq 0$ is a random variable, and a distributional assumption (such as half-normal or truncated-normal) can be imposed on u^*. Importantly, u^* does not depend on $\boldsymbol{z}_i$ and is common to all observations.

The model specified in (3.62) implies that the random variable u_i ($i = 1, 2, \ldots, N$) follows a common distribution given by u^*, but each is weighted by a different, observation-specific *scale* of $h(\boldsymbol{z}_i, \boldsymbol{\delta})$. Wang and Schmidt (2002) labeled $h(\cdot)$ the *scaling function*, and u^* the *basic distribution*. The u_i in (3.62) is then said to exhibit the *scaling property*. The fully specified model is

$$\ln y_i = \ln y_i^* - u_i, \tag{3.63}$$

$$\ln y_i^* = \boldsymbol{x}'\boldsymbol{\beta} + v_i, \tag{3.64}$$

$$\begin{aligned} u_i &\sim h(\boldsymbol{z}_i, \boldsymbol{\delta}) \cdot N^+(\tau, \sigma_u^2) \\ &\equiv \exp(\boldsymbol{z}_i'\boldsymbol{\delta}) \cdot N^+(\tau, \exp(c_u)), \end{aligned} \tag{3.65}$$

$$v_i \sim N(0, \sigma_v^2), \tag{3.66}$$

where τ and c_u are unconstrained constant parameters, and $\boldsymbol{z}_i$ is a variable vector which does *not* contain a constant. In this setup, the distribution of u_i is based on the basic distribution $N^+(\tau, \sigma_u^2)$ and the scale is stretched by the nonstochastic and nonnegative scaling function $\exp(\boldsymbol{z}_i'\boldsymbol{\delta})$.

An attractive feature of the model with a scaling property is that it captures the idea that the *shape* of the distribution of u_i is the same for all firms. The scaling function $h(\cdot)$ essentially stretches or shrinks the horizontal axis, so that the scale of the distribution of u_i changes but its underlying shape does not. In comparison, the KGMHLBC and Wang (2002) models have a different truncation point for every u_i, so that for some u_i the distribution is close to a normal (i.e., when the pretruncation mean is positive and large), while for some u_i the distribution is the extreme right tail of a normal with a mode of zero (i.e., when the pretruncation mean is negative and small). In comparison, for a model with the scaling property the mean and the standard deviation change with $\boldsymbol{z}_i$, but the truncation point is always the same number of standard deviations from zero, so the shape does not change.

Another advantage of the scaling property specification is the ease of interpretation on the $\boldsymbol{\delta}$ coefficients.

$$\frac{\partial \ln \mathrm{E}(u_i)}{\partial z[k]} = \delta[k]. \tag{3.67}$$

That is, $\delta[k]$ is the semi-elasticity of expected inefficiency with respect to $z[k]$. This type of interpretation is usually unavailable in other model specifications.

Some of the models introduced in the earlier sections can be seen as a special case of the scaling-property model; see Table 3.1.

Table 3.1. *Models with Scaling Properties*

	$h(\boldsymbol{z}_i; \boldsymbol{\delta})$	u^*
Aigner et al. (1977)	1	$N^+(0, \sigma_u^2)$
CFCFGH	$\exp(\boldsymbol{z}_i'\boldsymbol{\delta})$	$N^+(0, 1)$
Stevenson (1980)	1	$N^+(\mu, \sigma_u^2)$

There are also models, such as the model of KGMHLBC and Wang (2002), that do not have this scaling property.

3.4.5.1 The Log-Likelihood Function

The likelihood function of the scaling property model for the ith observation (see Appendix A for the derivation) is given by

$$L_i = -\frac{1}{2}\ln(\sigma_v^2 + \breve{\sigma}_{u,i}^2) + \ln\phi\left(\frac{\breve{\mu}_i + \epsilon_i}{\sqrt{\sigma_v^2 + \breve{\sigma}_{u,i}^2}}\right) + \ln\Phi\left(\frac{\mu_{*i}}{\sigma_{*i}}\right) - \ln\Phi\left(\frac{\breve{\mu}_i}{\breve{\sigma}_{*i}}\right), \quad (3.68)$$

where

$$\breve{\mu}_i = \tau\cdot\exp(z_i'\boldsymbol{\delta}), \quad (3.69)$$

$$\breve{\sigma}_{u,i}^2 = \exp(c_u + 2z_i'\boldsymbol{\delta}), \quad (3.70)$$

$$\mu_{*i} = \frac{\sigma_v^2\breve{\mu}_i - \breve{\sigma}_{u,i}^2\epsilon_i}{\sigma_v^2 + \breve{\sigma}_{u,i}^2}, \quad (3.71)$$

$$\sigma_{*i}^2 = \frac{\sigma_v^2\breve{\sigma}_{u,i}^2}{\sigma_v^2 + \breve{\sigma}_{u,i}^2}. \quad (3.72)$$

As usual, we parameterize $\sigma_v^2 = \exp(w_v)$, where w_v is a constant for estimation purposes. The log-likelihood function is the sum of (3.68) for all observations.

3.4.5.2 Technical Efficiency

Formulas of the two efficiency-related measures are obtained as earlier. They are similar to those we have seen in the previous sections, except that we now use the new notations μ_{*i} and σ_{*i} defined earlier (Appendix B shows the derivation).

$$E(u_i|\epsilon_i) = \frac{\sigma_{*i}\phi(\frac{\mu_{*i}}{\sigma_{*i}})}{\Phi\left(\frac{\mu_{*i}}{\sigma_{*i}}\right)} + \mu_{*i}, \quad (3.73)$$

$$E\left[\exp(-u_i)|\epsilon_i\right] = \exp\left(-\mu_{*i} + \frac{1}{2}\sigma_{*i}^2\right)\frac{\Phi\left(\frac{\mu_{*i}}{\sigma_{*i}} - \sigma_{*i}\right)}{\Phi\left(\frac{\mu_{*i}}{\sigma_{*i}}\right)}. \quad (3.74)$$

3.4.5.3 Confidence Interval

As we have seen several times already, the formulas of the upper and lower bounds of the confidence intervals *look* the same for all the models we have introduced, with the difference being how some of the variables are defined in each model. The lower and the upper bounds of the $(1-\alpha)100\%$ confidence intervals of $E(u_i|\epsilon_i)$ are, respectively,

$$L_i = \mu_{*i} + \Phi^{-1}\left\{1 - \left(1 - \frac{\alpha}{2}\right)\left[1 - \Phi\left(-\frac{\mu_{*i}}{\sigma_{*i}}\right)\right]\right\}\sigma_{*i}, \quad (3.75)$$

$$U_i = \mu_{*i} + \Phi^{-1}\left\{1 - \frac{\alpha}{2}\left[1 - \Phi\left(-\frac{\mu_{*i}}{\sigma_{*i}}\right)\right]\right\}\sigma_{*i}, \tag{3.76}$$

where μ_{*i} and σ_{*i} are defined in (3.71) and (3.72), respectively (see Appendix C for the derivation).

The lower and upper bounds of a $(1-\alpha)100\%$ confidence interval of $E(\exp(-u_i)|\epsilon_i)$ are, respectively,

$$\mathcal{L}_i = \exp(-U_i), \qquad \mathcal{U}_i = \exp(-L_i). \tag{3.77}$$

3.4.5.4 Heteroscedasticity, Exogenous Determinants, and Marginal Effects

Heteroscedasticity. With the scaling function being related to observation-specific variables $\mathbf{z}_i$ as shown in (3.65), the random variable u_i is heteroscedastic. If a heteroscedastic v_i is also desirable, we may parameterize the variance of v_i by

$$\sigma_{v,i}^2 = \exp(\mathbf{z}_{v,i}\mathbf{w}'). \tag{3.78}$$

The log-likelihood function of the heteroscedastic-consistent model is essentially the same as (3.68), with the obvious substitution of σ_v by $\sigma_{v,i}$ in (3.78).

Marginal effects. The marginal effect formula is particularly easy to derive for this model. From (3.65), we have

$$E(u_i) = \exp(\mathbf{z}_i'\boldsymbol{\delta}) \cdot E(u^*), \tag{3.79}$$

where,

$$u^* \sim N^+(\tau, \sigma_u^2), \tag{3.80}$$

so that,

$$\frac{\partial E(u_i)}{\partial z[k]} = \delta[k]\exp(\mathbf{z}_i'\boldsymbol{\delta}) \cdot E(u^*). \tag{3.81}$$

The $E(u^*)$ is a scalar, which can be calculated from

$$E(u^*) = \sigma_u\left[\frac{\tau}{\sigma_u} + \frac{\phi\left(\frac{\tau}{\sigma_u}\right)}{\Phi\left(\frac{\tau}{\sigma_u}\right)}\right]. \tag{3.82}$$

To obtain the estimated value, one can replace τ and σ_u in the above equation by $\hat{\tau}$ and $\exp(\frac{1}{2}\cdot\hat{c_u})$, respectively.

Similarly, for the marginal effect on the variance, we have

$$V(u_i) = \exp(2\cdot\mathbf{z}_i'\boldsymbol{\delta}) \cdot V(u^*), \tag{3.83}$$

so that

$$\frac{\partial V(u_i)}{\partial z[k]} = 2\delta[k]\cdot\exp(2\cdot\mathbf{z}_i'\boldsymbol{\delta}) \cdot V(u^*), \tag{3.84}$$

where $V(u^*)$ is a scalar that can be obtained from

$$V(u^*) = \sigma_u^2 \left[1 - \frac{\tau}{\sigma_u} \left[\frac{\phi\left(\frac{\tau}{\sigma_u}\right)}{\Phi\left(\frac{\tau}{\sigma_u}\right)} \right] - \left[\frac{\phi\left(\frac{\tau}{\sigma_u}\right)}{\Phi\left(\frac{\tau}{\sigma_u}\right)} \right]^2 \right]. \tag{3.85}$$

After the model is estimated, values of $\hat{\tau}$ and $\exp(\frac{1}{2} \cdot \hat{c}_u)$ can be substituted for τ and σ_u, respectively, in the formula to obtain the estimated value of $V(u^*)$.

Example

Model 9: Truncated-Normal Model with the Scaling Property

In this example, we estimate a scaling-property model with `comp` being the exogenous determinant of inefficiency by adding `scaling hscale(comp) tau cu` to the model. We use the results of the truncated-normal model (`b_wf`, `b_wv`), from Model 8 on page 82, as initial values for the slope coefficients and the variance parameter.

```
. sfmodel ly, prod dist(t) frontier($xvar)  scaling hscale(comp) tau cu vsigmas() show
. sf_init, frontier(b_wf) hscale(0.1) vsigmas(b_wv) tau(0.1) cu(0.1)
. sf_srch, n(1) frontier($xvar) hscale(comp) nograph fast
. ml max, difficult gtol(1e-5) nrtol(1e-5)
```

The result is the following:

```
                                                  Number of obs   =        196
                                                  Wald chi2(4)    =    1672.38
Log likelihood =  110.86797                       Prob > chi2     =     0.0000

------------------------------------------------------------------------------
          ly |      Coef.   Std. Err.      z    P>|z|     [95% Conf. Interval]
-------------+----------------------------------------------------------------
frontier     |
      llabor |   .0975554   .0436132     2.24   0.025     .0120751    .1830357
       lfeed |   .1494707    .038018     3.93   0.000     .0749567    .2239846
     lcattle |   .7573623    .057954    13.07   0.000     .6437746      .87095
       lland |   .0414283   .0394979     1.05   0.294    -.0359862    .1188429
       _cons |   7.758483   .4892531    15.86   0.000     6.799564    8.717401
-------------+----------------------------------------------------------------
hscale       |
        comp |  -.0087897   .0461323    -0.19   0.849    -.0992073    .0816278
-------------+----------------------------------------------------------------
tau          |
       _cons |  -1.001555   3.528355    -0.28   0.777    -7.917003    5.913894
-------------+----------------------------------------------------------------
cu           |
       _cons |  -1.822194   2.523573    -0.72   0.470    -6.768305    3.123918
-------------+----------------------------------------------------------------
vsigmas      |
       _cons |  -4.851521   .3724912   -13.02   0.000     -5.58159   -4.121451
------------------------------------------------------------------------------
```

Notice that the coefficient of `comp` in the scaling function (`hscale`) is very small in size and is clearly insignificance. Because the scaling function is parameterized as $\exp(\delta \cdot \text{comp})$ where δ is the coefficient, the estimated scaling function is essentially a constant of 1. As shown in (3.65), the result makes the model close to the truncated-normal model (Model 6) that we estimated earlier, which had a very similar log-likelihood value of 110.851. The insignificant

$\hat{\tau}$ also echoes the result of the truncated-normal model estimated earlier. The $\hat{\sigma}_v^2$ is obtained by `sf_transform`.

```
. sf_transform

        sigma_u_sqr = exp(usigmas);
        sigma_v_sqr = exp(vsigmas).

    ---convert the parameters to natural metrics---

    The transformation cannot be done for sigma_u^_sqr in the
    scaling-property model since it is a function of variables.
    The transformation is done only if sigma_u^_sqr is constant.

variable     |       Coef.   Std. Err.       t    P>|t|      [95% Conf. Interval]
-------------+----------------------------------------------------------------
 sigma_v_sqr |    .0078165    .0029116    2.68    0.007      .0037666     .016221
```

We now calculate the efficiency index and compute the marginal effect of `comp`. The efficiency index is saved in the variable `bc_s`.

```
. sf_predict, bc(bc_s) marginal

The following is the marginal effect on unconditional E(u).

The average marginal effect of comp on uncond E(u) is -.00107849 (see comp_M).

The following is the marginal effect on uncond V(u).

The average marginal effect of comp on uncond V(u) is -.00022596 (see comp_V).
```

The marginal effect indicates that, on average, IT expenditure reduces the expected value of inefficiency and the variance of inefficiency. Because it is a scaling function model, the effect on the variance is twice as big as the effect on the mean. The result shows that mean inefficiency is reduced by 0.11 percent for a 1 percent increase in the expenditure share on IT equipment. That is, efficiency increases as more is spent on IT.

3.4.6 The Exponential Distribution

The exponential distribution was proposed in the literature to model the distribution of u_i by Meeusen and van den Broeck (1977). Similar to the half-normal distribution, the exponential distribution is a one-parameter distribution. Denoting η to be a non-negative parameter, the density function of a random variable u_i with an exponential distribution is given by

$$f(u_i) = \frac{1}{\eta} \cdot \exp(-\frac{u_i}{\eta}), \qquad u_i \geq 0. \tag{3.86}$$

The random variable has a mean equal to $\eta > 0$ and a standard deviation equal to η^2.

Figure 3.8 illustrates the shapes of exponential distributions with various parameter values. As shown, the distributions have characteristics that are similar to those of a half-normal distribution. Among them, the mode of the distribution is at 0, implying that the majority of the producers cluster around the most efficient level.

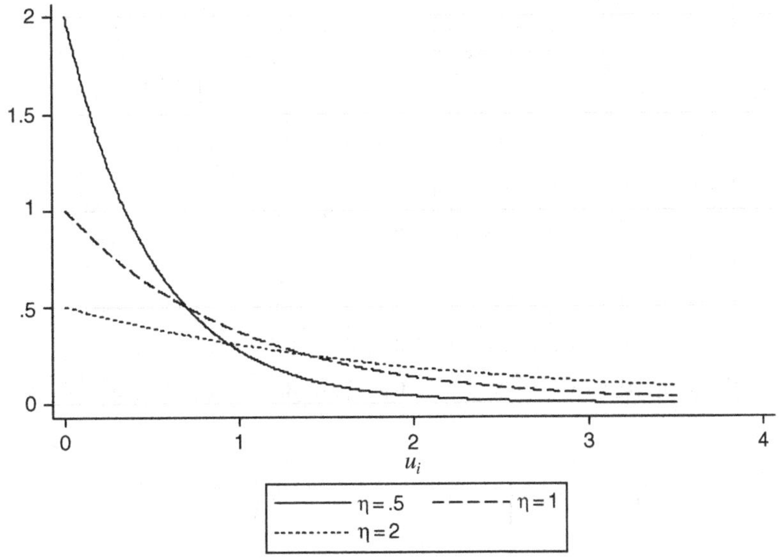

Figure 3.8. Density Plots of Exponential Distributions

3.4.6.1 The Log-likelihood Function

The model consists of (3.40), (3.41), and (3.43), and has an exponential distribution for u_i as in (3.86). The log-likelihood function of the ith observation (see Appendix A for the derivation) is given by

$$L_i = -\ln(\eta) + \ln\left[\Phi\left(-\frac{\epsilon_i}{\sigma_v} - \frac{\sigma_v}{\eta}\right)\right] + \frac{\epsilon_i}{\eta} + \frac{\sigma_v^2}{2\eta^2}. \tag{3.87}$$

The log-likelihood function of the model is the sum of L_i for all observations. To ensure positive estimates of η and σ_v, we substitute the following reparameterization into the model:

$$\eta^2 = \exp(w_\eta), \tag{3.88}$$

$$\sigma_v^2 = \exp(w_v), \tag{3.89}$$

where w_η and w_v are unconstrained constants.

We leave the illustration of the exponential model for the more complex model with heteroscedasticity.

3.4.6.2 Technical Efficiency

The observation-specific measure of technical efficiency, $E(\exp(-u_i)|\epsilon_i)$, and the observation-specific measure of inefficiency, $E(u_i|\epsilon_i)$, for this model are

$$E(u|\epsilon_i) = \frac{\sigma_v \phi(\frac{\mu_{*i}}{\sigma_v})}{\Phi\left(\frac{\mu_{*i}}{\sigma_v}\right)} + \mu_{*i}, \tag{3.90}$$

$$E\left[\exp(-u_i)|\epsilon_i\right] = \exp\left(-\mu_{*i} + \frac{1}{2}\sigma_v^2\right)\frac{\Phi\left(\frac{\mu_{*i}}{\sigma_v} - \sigma_v\right)}{\Phi\left(\frac{\mu_{*i}}{\sigma_v}\right)}, \tag{3.91}$$

where,

$$\mu_{*i} = -\epsilon_i - \frac{\sigma_v^2}{\eta}. \tag{3.92}$$

3.4.6.3 Confidence Interval

The lower and upper bounds of a $(1 - \alpha)100\%$ confidence interval of $E(u_i|\epsilon_i)$ are, respectively,

$$L_i = \mu_{*i} + \Phi^{-1}\left\{1 - \left(1 - \frac{\alpha}{2}\right)\left[1 - \Phi\left(-\frac{\mu_{*i}}{\sigma_v}\right)\right]\right\}\sigma_v, \tag{3.93}$$

$$U_i = \mu_{*i} + \Phi^{-1}\left\{1 - \frac{\alpha}{2}\left[1 - \Phi\left(-\frac{\mu_{*i}}{\sigma_v}\right)\right]\right\}\sigma_v, \tag{3.94}$$

where μ_{*i} is in (3.92).

The lower and upper bounds of a $(1 - \alpha)100\%$ confidence interval of $E(\exp(-u_i)|\epsilon_i)$ are, respectively,

$$\mathcal{L}_i = \exp(-U_i), \qquad \mathcal{U}_i = \exp(-L_i). \tag{3.95}$$

3.4.6.4 Heteroscedasticity, Exogenous Determinants, and Marginal Effects

Heteroscedasticity. The previous discussions on the pitfalls of ignoring heteroscedasticity of v_i and u_i apply here as well. In the case of the exponential distribution, Wang (2003) parameterized η^2 in order to account for the heteroscedasticity as

$$\eta_i^2 = \exp(\boldsymbol{z}_i\boldsymbol{\delta}). \tag{3.96}$$

Notice that we choose to parameterize η^2, which is also the variance of u, instead of η. The heteroscedasticity of v_i can also be accounted for by parameterizing its variance, such as

$$\sigma_{vi}^2 = \exp(\boldsymbol{z}_i\boldsymbol{w}). \tag{3.97}$$

The log-likelihood function of the heteroscedastic-consistent model is similar to (3.87), except that η and σ_v is substituted by η_i and σ_{vi} in these expressions.

Exogenous Determinants. Because the exponential distribution has only one parameter, the exogenous determinants of inefficiency u_i can be modeled only through the single parameter. In fact, the heteroscedastic-consistent parameterization of u_i in (3.96) also allows the exogenous determinants of inefficiency $(\boldsymbol{z}_i)$ to enter into the model.

Marginal Effects. If u_i is exponentially distributed with the density function of (3.86), the mean of u_i is η_i and the variance of u_i is η_i^2. Given the parameterization of $\eta_i^2 = \exp(\boldsymbol{z}_i\boldsymbol{\delta})$, the marginal effects on the mean and the variance of u_i are easily calculated.

$$\frac{\partial E(u_i)}{\partial z[k]} = \frac{1}{2}\delta[k] \cdot \exp\left(\frac{1}{2}z_i\delta\right), \tag{3.98}$$

$$\frac{\partial V(u_i)}{\partial z[k]} = \delta[k] \cdot \exp(z_i\delta). \tag{3.99}$$

Example

Model 10: Exponential Model with Heteroscedasticity

The following lines of code estimate the model with an exponential distribution on u_i, and we investigate whether IT expenditure affects inefficiency by parameterizing η by the variable `comp` by adding `etas(comp)` to the model.

```
. sfmodel ly, prod dist(e) frontier($xvar) etas(comp) vsigmas()
. sf_srch, n(1) frontier($xvar) etas(comp) nograph fast
. ml max, difficult gtol(1e-5) nrtol(1e-5)
. sf_predict, bc(bc_e) marginal

(iteration log omitted)

                                                Number of obs    =        196
                                                Wald chi2(4)     =    1655.50
Log likelihood =  110.77906                     Prob > chi2      =     0.0000

------------------------------------------------------------------------------
          ly |      Coef.   Std. Err.      z    P>|z|     [95% Conf. Interval]
-------------+----------------------------------------------------------------
frontier     |
      llabor |   .0965515   .0436428     2.21   0.027     .0110131    .1820898
       lfeed |   .1486927   .0380662     3.91   0.000     .0740844     .223301
     lcattle |   .7558717   .0578597    13.06   0.000     .6424688    .8692747
       lland |   .0437683   .0389383     1.12   0.261    -.0325494    .1200859
       _cons |   7.757096   .4914832    15.78   0.000     6.793807    8.720386
-------------+----------------------------------------------------------------
etas         |
        comp |  -.0050543   .1027064    -0.05   0.961    -.2063553    .1962466
       _cons |    -4.3485   .6672375    -6.52   0.000    -5.656261   -3.040739
-------------+----------------------------------------------------------------
vsigmas      |
       _cons |  -4.761202    .242812   -19.61   0.000    -5.237105     -4.2853
------------------------------------------------------------------------------
```

We now calculate the efficiency index and compute the marginal effect of `comp`. The efficiency index is saved in the variable `bc_e`.

```
. sf_predict, bc(bc_e) marginal

The following is the marginal effect on unconditional E(u).
The average marginal effect of comp on uncond E(u) is -.00028252 (see comp_M).
The following is the marginal effect on uncond V(u).
The average marginal effect of comp on uncond V(u) is -.00006317 (see comp_V).
```

Thus, inefficiency, on average, is reduced by 0.028 percent for 1 percentage increase in the expenditure share on IT equipment, although, as is clear from the model estimation results, this impact is clearly insignificant.

Because σ_v^2 is estimated by the exponential function, we use `sf_transform` to obtain $\hat{\sigma}_v^2$.

```
. sf_transform

       sigma_u_sqr = exp(usigmas);
       sigma_v_sqr = exp(vsigmas).

   ---convert the parameters to natural metrics---

   sigma_u_sqr appears to be a function of variables.
   The transformation is done only if sigma_u_sqr is constant.

variable     |       Coef.   Std. Err.       t    P>|t|      [95% Conf. Interval]
-------------+----------------------------------------------------------------
 sigma_v_sqr |    .0085553   .0020773     4.12   0.000      .0053156    .0137695
```

A Comparison across Models. In Figure 3.3 we plot the histograms of the efficiency index from the various output-oriented models that have been presented in this chapter. Note that the results from Models 4–10 are from models where distribution assumptions are imposed on the inefficiency term. In fact, the plots of the efficiency scores from these models are not too different (although the later models show a somewhat greater clustering near the frontier). The results from Models 2 and 3 are also similar to each other and, in each case, the best firm has an efficiency score of 1. (Remember, these models do not make distribution assumptions and hence cannot separate inefficiency from noise – the way we did in Models 4–10.) The efficiency estimates are relative and therefore these are directly affected by how close together the residuals are.

The consistency between the different models can be further examined by looking at the summary statistics and correlations. The distribution-free models result in estimated technical efficiency of around 77 percent, while the stochastic frontier models estimate technical efficiency of around 85 to 90 percent.

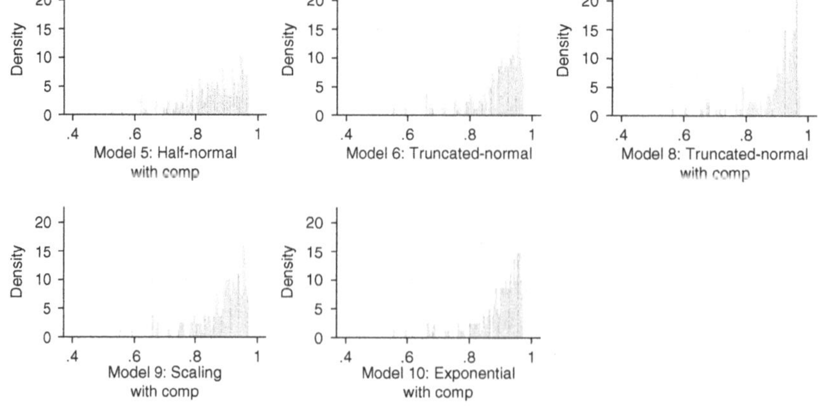

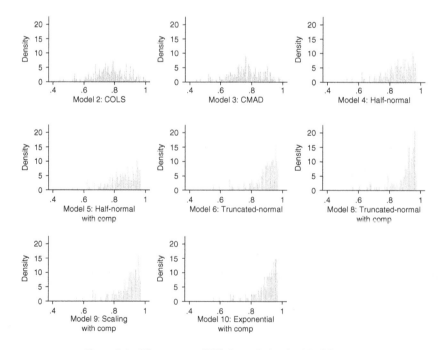

Figure 3.9. Histograms of Efficiency Index for Models 2–10

```
. summarize eff_cols eff_cmad bc_h bc_h2 bc_t bc_w bc_s bc_e

    Variable |       Obs        Mean    Std. Dev.       Min        Max
-------------+--------------------------------------------------------
    eff_cols |       196    .7708748    .1060425   .4425342          1
    eff_cmad |       196    .7674637    .1058017   .4413492          1
        bc_h |       196    .8532533    .0887712     .52415    .969845
       bc_h2 |       196    .8545238    .0880955   .5248041   .9694997
        bc_t |       196    .8910183    .0755853   .5535397   .9701945
-------------+--------------------------------------------------------
        bc_w |       196    .9019902    .0750691   .5610273   .9722008
        bc_s |       196    .8899826    .0757229   .5534238   .9699198
        bc_e |       196    .8993694    .0726473   .5561522   .9708368

. correlate eff_cols eff_cmad bc_h bc_h2 bc_t bc_w bc_s bc_e
(obs=196)

             | eff_cols eff_cmad     bc_h    bc_h2     bc_t     bc_w     bc_s     bc_e
-------------+------------------------------------------------------------------------
    eff_cols |   1.0000
    eff_cmad |   0.9918   1.0000
        bc_h |   0.9752   0.9772   1.0000
       bc_h2 |   0.9740   0.9758   0.9999   1.0000
        bc_t |   0.9289   0.9355   0.9832   0.9845   1.0000
        bc_w |   0.8906   0.9022   0.9580   0.9597   0.9891   1.0000
        bc_s |   0.9305   0.9367   0.9839   0.9853   1.0000   0.9885   1.0000
        bc_e |   0.9117   0.9194   0.9725   0.9743   0.9986   0.9914   0.9983   1.0000
```

The correlations are high. This consistency between the results is confirmed by examining Kendall's rank correlation coefficients (not reported).

3.5 Input-Oriented Technical Inefficiency

So far, our analysis has focused exclusively on output-oriented technical inefficiency. Because technical inefficiency can be viewed in terms of input usage as well, we briefly introduce input-oriented technical inefficiency in this section and demonstrate its similarity with its cousin – the output-oriented measure. Due to the close resemblance of the two measures (as will be clear from the discussion that follows), we do not repeat the analysis provided above using this alternative approach. Instead, we demonstrate its similarity and provide two modeling examples.

In the IO approach the production function is written as

$$y = f(\mathbf{x}e^{-\eta}). \tag{3.100}$$

For ease of comparison, the OO approach is provided here:

$$y = f(\mathbf{x})e^{-u}. \tag{3.101}$$

For a Cobb-Douglas formulation, the IO model can be expressed as

$$\ln y = \beta_0 + \sum \beta_j \ln x_j - \left(\sum_j \beta_j\right)\eta, \tag{3.102}$$

which is essentially the same as the OO model with the reparameterization $u = \eta \sum_j \beta_j$. Thus, it is not necessary to have separate sections on the estimation of η. Once u is estimated from the models discussed extensively in this chapter, one can easily obtain η from the relationship $u = \eta \sum_j \beta_j$.

This is quite intuitive. Think of a single y and single x. Because the relationship between $\ln y$ and $\ln x$ is linear, geometrically speaking, the vertical distance from a point below the line (an inefficient point) which measures OO inefficiency, u, is the product of the horizontal distance (IO inefficiency, η) times the slope (β), that is, $u = \eta\,\beta$. For the general case, the relationship is $u = \eta \sum_j \beta_j$.

Example

Model 11: Input-Oriented Half-Normal Model

Having estimated the half-normal model above (Model 4), we need to calculate the sum of the estimated coefficients (excluding the constant) and then divide the previous estimated (in)efficiencies by this scalar to get the IO measure of inefficiency. This is undertaken here:

```
. scalar r = [frontier]_b[llabor] + [frontier]_b[lfeed] + [frontier]_b[lcattle] + [frontier]_b[lland]
. display r
1.0490032

. generate double jlms_h_IO = jlms_h/r
. summarize jlms_h_IO jlms_h

    Variable |        Obs        Mean    Std. Dev.       Min        Max
-------------+---------------------------------------------------------
   jlms_h_IO |        196    .1585311    .1070542    .0295304   .6178679
      jlms_h |        196    .1662996    .1123002    .0309775   .6481454
```

The mean of `jlms_h_IO` equals 0.159, implying that, on average, the dairy farmers used about 16 percent more input than necessary due to technical inefficiency (this compares to an estimate of a 17 percent loss of output under the output-oriented formulation). This similarity is due to the estimate of returns to scale, at 1.049, being very close to 1.

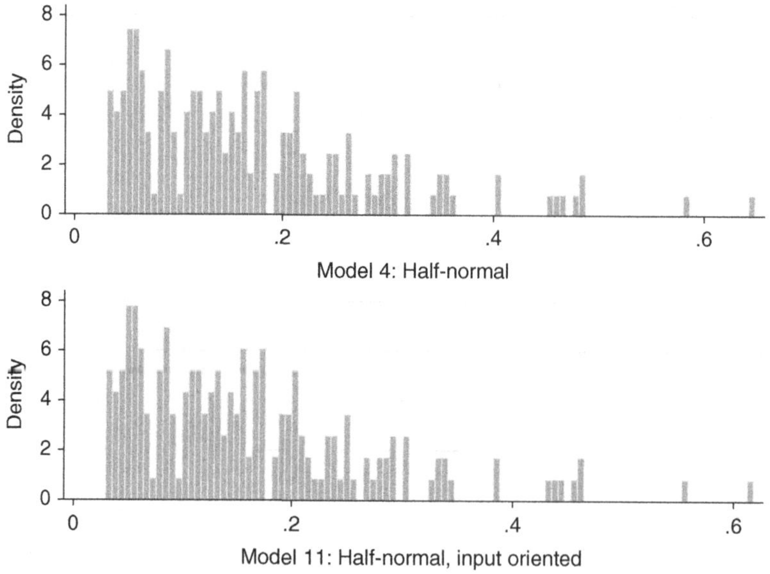

Figure 3.10. Histogram of Input-Oriented Compared to Output-Oriented Efficiencies for the Half-Normal Model

The similarity is also clearly noticeable in the comparison of the two histograms (shown in Figure 3.10) – under the Cobb-Dogulas model, each farm is ranked similarly in terms of (in)efficiency, but the estimated (in)efficiency is scaled by the inverse of the estimated returns to scale (here, close to 1).

```
. histogram jlms_h, bin(100) `kden´ saving(jlms_h, replace)
. histogram jlms_h_IO, bin(100) `kden´ saving(jlms_h_IO, replace)
. graph combine jlms_h.gph jlms_h_IO.gph, col(1) scale(1)
```

By contrast, if the production function is specified as a translog it can be expressed as

$$\begin{aligned}
\ln y &= \beta_0 + \sum_j \beta_j \left(\ln x_j - \eta\right) + \frac{1}{2}\sum_j\sum_k \beta_{jk}\left(\ln x_j - \eta\right)\left(\ln x_k - \eta\right) \\
&= \beta_0 + \sum_j \beta_j \ln x_j + \frac{1}{2}\sum_j\sum_k \beta_{jk}\ln x_j \ln x_k - \eta\sum_j \beta_j \\
&\quad + \frac{1}{2}\left(\sum_j\sum_k \beta_{jk}\right)\eta^2 - \left[\sum_j\left(\sum_k \beta_{jk}\ln x_k\right)\right]\eta \qquad (3.103) \\
&= \beta_0 + \sum_j \beta_j \ln x_j + \frac{1}{2}\sum_j\sum_k \beta_{jk}\ln x_j \ln x_k \\
&\quad - \eta\left[\sum_j \beta_j + \sum_j\left(\sum_k \beta_{jk}\ln x_k\right)\right] + \frac{1}{2}\eta^2\sum_j\sum_k \beta_{jk}.
\end{aligned}$$

Equating this with the OO specification, we get the following relationship between u and η:

$$u = \eta\left[\sum_j \beta_j + \sum_j\left(\sum_k \beta_{jk}\ln x_k\right)\right] + \frac{1}{2}\eta^2\sum_j\sum_k \beta_{jk}. \qquad (3.104)$$

This is a quadratic equation in η. Given an estimate of u from the OO translog model, one can obtain estimates of η by solving this quadratic equation for each observation. Being a quadratic equation, one might encounter situations with either no real roots or the roots being negative. This problem might be related to the violation of theoretical economic properties, such as positive input elasticities. That is, the input elasticities $\beta_j + \sum_k \beta_{jk}\ln x_k$ have to be positive for all j. However, this may not be true for some observations. Thus, if this condition is violated for some observations there is no point in using those observations to compute η. Similarly, no inefficiency can be computed for the observations for which no roots are real. If both roots are positive, one should consider the smaller one.

Given the complexity of estimating the IO model, one might estimate the OO model first and get estimates of IO inefficiency (if so desired) from the relationship between them.

3.6 Endogeneity and Input and Output Distance Functions

Note that in estimating IO and OO inefficiency we have not addressed the issue of whether the inputs and output are endogenous. (So far in this chapter, we have assumed that inputs are exogenously given.) To address the endogeneity of inputs (and outputs), from both an economic and econometric perspective, one has to develop a system approach. For example, see chapters 4 and 5 of Kumbhakar and Lovell (2000) for details on some of these models and Kumbhakar and Wang (2006), in which a model that addresses the endogeneity of inputs using a cost minimization setup is considered. The system models that can address the endogeneity of either inputs or both inputs and output (and, therefore, accommodate both technical and allocative inefficiency) are not addressed in this chapter but are examined in subsequent chapters, in which we examine cost and profit frontier models.

There are issues to be considered when choosing between the IO and OO measures. If the technology is known (i.e., not to be estimated), then the issue is purely mathematical and involves deriving u from η and vice versa using the relationship $y = f(x\exp(-\eta)) = f(x)\exp(-u)$. The problem can be trivial for some functional forms, such as the Cobb-Douglas, while it can be quite complicated for other functional forms, such as the translog or Trancendental. If the technology is not known (which is the case in reality) and it has to be estimated econometrically, then the issue of endogeneity cannot be avoided.

In estimating a production frontier, the usual assumption is that inputs are exogenously given (we will consider alternative assumptions in subsequent chapters). Thus, OO inefficiency is natural and one should estimate OO inefficiency using either a production function or an output distance function (ODF). In such a framework output(s) is(are) endogenous. Although one can use the estimated technology and estimated u to compute IO inefficiency, it may not be meaningful to do so because the objective is not to reduce input usage.

By contrast, if output(s) is(are) exogenously given, and the objective is to minimize input cost, then the natural choice is to use an input distance function (IDF) and estimate η. Note that, in an IDF, inputs are endogenous. Again, in such a case, it is not meaningful to re-estimate u using the estimated technology and estimated values of η. Because the endogenous variable(s) in a production function (ODF) and IDF is(are) not the same, the econometrically estimated technology will not be the same. The issue is similar to regressing y on x and x on y in which case the estimated slope coefficients are not reciprocals.

If both y and x are endogenous, then the SF estimates from both IDF and ODF are inconsistent (Kumbhakar [2012]).

Example

Model 12: Input Distance Function Model

Because the dairy farm example, used so far in this chapter, has only one output, the production function (in Model 4) and the ODF are the same.

We now illustrate the IDF using this dataset. For this, we write the production function as

$$\ln \mathtt{y}_j = \beta_0 + \beta_1 \ln \mathtt{labor}_j + \beta_2 \ln \mathtt{feed}_j + \beta_3 \ln \mathtt{cattle}_j + \beta_4 \ln \mathtt{land}_j + v_j - u_j, \tag{3.105}$$

which can be rewritten as

$$\begin{aligned} \ln \mathtt{y}_j = \beta_0 &+ (\beta_1 + \beta_2 + \beta_3 + \beta_4) \ln \mathtt{labor}_j + \beta_2(\ln \mathtt{feed}_j - \ln \mathtt{labor}_j) + \\ &\beta_3(\ln \mathtt{cattle}_j - \ln \mathtt{labor}_j) + \beta_4(\ln \mathtt{land}_j - \ln \mathtt{labor}_j) + v_j - u_j. \end{aligned} \tag{3.106}$$

Rearranging with the input, `labor`, on the left-hand side gives the input distance function

$$\begin{aligned}\ln \mathtt{labor}_j &= (1/r)[\beta_0 - \ln \mathtt{y}_j + \beta_2(\ln \mathtt{feed}_j - \ln \mathtt{labor}_j) + \beta_3(\ln \mathtt{cattle}_j \\ &\quad - \ln \mathtt{labor}_j) + \beta_4(\ln \mathtt{land}_j - \ln \mathtt{labor}_j) + v_j - u_j], \\ \Rightarrow \ln \mathtt{labor}_j &= \tilde{\beta}_0 + \tilde{\beta}_1 \ln \mathtt{y}_j + \tilde{\beta}_2(\mathtt{nlfeed}_j) + \tilde{\beta}_3(\mathtt{nlcattle}_j) \\ &\quad + \tilde{\beta}_4(\mathtt{nlland}_j) + v_j^\star - u_j^\star,\end{aligned} \tag{3.107}$$

where $r = (\beta_1 + \beta_2 + \beta_3 + \beta_4)$, $v^\star = v/r$, $u^\star = u/r$, and $\tilde{\beta}_j = \beta_j/r$ for $j = 0, 1, 2, 3, 4$.

To use this IDF, we start by normalizing the data. We chose labor as the numeraire and define the other variables.

```
. generate nllabor = - llabor
. generate nlfeed = lfeed - llabor
. generate nlcattle = lcattle - llabor
. generate nlland = lland - llabor
```

Using the above variables, we can estimate the IDF model in (3.107) using the following code.

```
. global xvar_idf ly nlfeed nlcattle nlland

. sfmodel nllabor, prod dist(h) frontier($xvar_idf) usigmas() vsigmas() show
. sf_srch, n(1) frontier($xvar_idf) usigmas(comp) nograph fast
. ml max, difficult  gtol(1e-5) nrtol(1e-5)

. sf_transform
. sf_predict, jlms(jlms_star) marginal
```

Note that u^* is η, which is IO inefficiency. So the interpretation of inefficiency from this model is IO and we can recover u from u^* multiplied by r. We compare the result to that from Model 4:

```
. scalar r_idf = - 1/[frontier]_b[ly]
. generate jlms_h_idf = jlms_star * r_idf
. summarize jlms_h jlms_h_idf
```

Variable	Obs	Mean	Std. Dev.	Min	Max
jlms_h	196	.1662996	.1123002	.0309775	.6481454
jlms_h_idf	196	.1334878	.0665528	.0373672	.4470965

The IDF model shows that input-oriented inefficiency is 13 percent, compared to the 17 percent we estimated under the output-orientated model.

4

Estimation of Technical Efficiency in Cost Frontier Models Using Cross-Sectional Data

4.1 Introduction

In Chapter 1, we introduced a series of questions that the tools discussed in this book are designed to help answer. The production function is the first tool we introduced to answer some of the questions. Although helpful, the production function approach, which focuses only on the input–output relationship, cannot answer some of the important questions for entrepreneurs and policy makers. Note that the production function is merely a technological relationship and there is no economic behavior embedded in it. This is also true of distance functions. Thus, neither of these can be used to help answer economic questions. For instance, whether (and by how much) a firm is able to reduce costs, while maintaining the same level of output/service, is often an important question. This is especially true for firms that are operating in a competitive or regulated environment, where outputs are demand determined, set by governments/regulators (e.g., quality of service), and/or cannot be stored (for example, electricity utilities, telecommunciations companies, transportation services, hospitals, and fire and police services). In this chapter, we introduce the *cost frontier model*, where the choice variables are the inputs in the production process and the objective is to minimize costs, given the required outputs. This model may help us to answer questions relating to the cost of production such as those outlined here.

By comparing hospitals, can we identify which hospitals can still treat the same number of patients for the same level of care but for lower cost? And, if so, by how much lower could costs be and what are the key drivers of these, currently, higher costs?

Does a takeover or merger with a current competitor makes sense? Among other things, will it result in cost savings through economies of scale and scope? Can the purchaser learn from the takeover target and improve its own cost efficiency or vice versa; that is, is the takeover target worthwhile?

Has privatization, regulation, or deregulation of an industry been "successful"? For example, in the United States, the electricity sector is regulated in different ways depending on the particular state the company is in. Such differences across states provide useful comparisons for analysis. Thus, we can examine, for example, whether and by how much electricity power generation plants are more or less cost efficient as a result of the particular form of regulation in the state. It is this example that we use throughout this chapter as a way of illustrating the approaches introduced in this chapter.

Before we continue, we wish to point out that there are two different sources of extra cost that may be reduced in order to minimize cost for a given level of output. If the production process exhibits *technical inefficiency*, the firm may improve its efficiency thereby obtaining the same level of output using fewer inputs. If, by contrast, the same level of output can be produced by different *combinations* of inputs, then the firm may also reduce the cost by improving *allocative inefficiency*; that is, choosing the "correct" input combination which cost the least. The least cost combination depends not only on the technology but also on the relative price ratios of inputs. Obviously, both technical inefficiency and allocative inefficiency increase cost.

In this chapter, we derive the cost frontier model by showing how technical inefficiency is transmitted from the production function to the cost function. That is, we want to examine the extent to which cost is increased if the production plan is inefficient. Note that in this chapter we are explicitly using economic behavior, that is, cost minimization, while estimating the technology. In this chapter, our focus is on the examination of cost frontier models using cross-sectional data. We also restrict our attention to examining only technical inefficiency and we assume that producers are fully efficient allocatively. Cost frontier models with both technical and allocative inefficiencies will be considered in Chapter 8.

In what follows, we start with the input-oriented technical inefficiency (Farrell [1957]), since this specification is often assumed in the cost frontier literature. The IO inefficiency is natural because in a cost minimization case the focus is on input use, given outputs. That is, it is assumed that output is given and inputs are the choice variables (i.e., the goal is to minimize cost for a given level of output). The discussion on output-oriented technical inefficiency will be discussed later in this chapter.

4.2 Input-Oriented Technical Inefficiency

Here we focus on firms for whom the objective is to produce a given level of output with the minimum possible cost. We also assume that the firm is technically inefficient; that is, it either produces less than the maximum possible output or uses more inputs than is necessary to produce a given level of output. In the context of cost minimization, the input-oriented measure which focuses on input overuse is intuitive and appropriate. For an inefficient firm in this setup, the additional cost must be due to the overuse of inputs, and cost savings (from eliminating inefficiency) will come from eliminating the excess usage of inputs. Farrell (1957) used a radial measure of inefficiency, thereby assuming that the technically efficient point in the production iso-quant can be obtained by reducing usage of all the variable inputs by the same proportion.

The cost minimization problem for producer i under input-oriented technical inefficiency specification is (the producer/observation subscript i is omitted):

$$\min \ \boldsymbol{w}'\boldsymbol{x} \quad \text{s.t.} \quad y = f(\boldsymbol{x}e^{-\eta}), \tag{4.1}$$

$$\text{first-order conditions:} \qquad \frac{f_j(\boldsymbol{x}e^{-\eta})}{f_1(\boldsymbol{x}e^{-\eta})} = \frac{w_j}{w_1}, \quad j = 2, \ldots, J, \tag{4.2}$$

where $\eta \geq 0$ is the input-oriented technical inefficiency that measures the percentage by which all the inputs are overused in producing output level y. Alternatively, one can interpret $\eta \geq 0$ as the percentage by which the usage of all the inputs can be reduced without reducing the output level y. It is also possible to view $e^{-\eta} \leq 1$ as the efficiency factor. Thus, although an inefficient firm uses x_j amounts of input, effectively it is worth only $x_j^e \equiv x_j e^{-\eta} \leq x_j$.

The marginal product of $x_je^{-\eta}$ is $f_j(\cdot)$, which is the partial derivative of $f(\cdot)$ with respect to the input $x_je^{-\eta}$, and this also depends on how effectively the input is used. The second set of equations $(J-1)$ represent the first-order conditions of the cost minimization problem.

The $(J-1)$ FOCs in (4.2) with the production function in (4.1) can be used to solve for the J input demand functions. In fact, because $x_je^{-\eta}$ appears everywhere in (4.2), it is easier to solve for x_j, $j=1,\ldots,J$, in their effective units which are simply x_j adjusted for technical inefficiency $(x_je^{-\eta})$. These input demand functions can be expressed as $x_je^{-\eta} = \psi_j(\boldsymbol{w}, y)$, $j = 1,\ldots,J$. We use them to define the cost function C^* as

$$C^*(\boldsymbol{w}, y) = \sum_j w_jx_je^{-\eta}, \tag{4.3}$$

which can be viewed as the minimum cost function for the following problem:

$$\min_{\{x_je^{-\eta}\}} \boldsymbol{w}'\boldsymbol{x}e^{-\eta} \quad \text{s.t.} \quad y = f(\boldsymbol{x}e^{-\eta}). \tag{4.4}$$

The $C^*(\cdot)$ function is the *frontier* cost function, which gives the minimum cost given the vector of input prices $\boldsymbol{w}$ and the observed level of output y. Note that this cost function measures the cost of producing y when inputs are adjusted for their efficiency (i.e., the cost of effective units of inputs). Thus, the minimum cost $\boldsymbol{w}'\boldsymbol{x}e^{-\eta}$ would be less than the actual cost $\boldsymbol{w}'\boldsymbol{x}$. Although $C^*(\cdot)$ is not observed, it can be used to derive the input demand functions and we can also relate it to actual (observed) cost.

To relate actual cost C^a with the unobserved minimum cost C^*, first, we make use of Shephard's lemma to (4.3), which is

$$\frac{\partial C^*}{\partial w_j} = x_je^{-\eta}, \tag{4.5}$$

$$\Longrightarrow \quad \frac{\partial \ln C^*}{\partial \ln w_j} = \frac{w_jx_je^{-\eta}}{C^*} = \frac{w_jx_j}{w'x} \equiv S_j. \tag{4.6}$$

$$\text{Therefore,} \quad w_jx_je^{-\eta} = C^* \cdot S_j, \tag{4.7}$$

$$\text{or,} \quad x_je^{-\eta} = \frac{C^* \cdot S_j}{w_j}. \tag{4.8}$$

Then we write actual cost as

$$C^a = \sum_j w_jx_j = C^* \exp(\eta), \tag{4.9}$$

$$\Rightarrow \quad \ln C^a = \ln C^*(\boldsymbol{w}, y) + \eta. \tag{4.10}$$

The relationship in (4.10) shows that log actual cost is increased by η because all the inputs are overused by η.

For the efficiency index of a producer, we take the ratio of the minimum to actual cost, which from (4.9) is

$$\exp(-\eta) = \frac{C^*}{C^a}. \tag{4.11}$$

By definition, the ratio is bounded between 0 and 1, and in the estimation it is numerically guaranteed by imposing $\eta \geq 0$ so that $\exp(-\eta)$ is between 0 and 1. Although this efficiency index has an intuitive interpretation, viz., the higher values indicating higher level of efficiency, one may also be interested in knowing the percentage increase in cost due to inefficiency, which may be obtained based on the approximation

$$\frac{C^a}{C^*} - 1 = \exp(\eta) - 1 \approx \eta. \tag{4.12}$$

Alternatively,

$$\eta = \ln C^a - \ln C^*(\boldsymbol{w}, y), \tag{4.13}$$

$$\Rightarrow \quad \eta = \ln\left(\frac{C^a}{C^*(\boldsymbol{w}, y)}\right). \tag{4.14}$$

Thus $100 \times \eta$ (when η is small) is the percentage by which actual cost exceeds the minimum cost due to technical inefficiency. Note that this interpretation of η is consistent with input-oriented technical inefficiency. Because the inputs are overused by $100 \times \eta$ percent and we are assuming no allocative inefficiency in this chapter, cost is increased by the same percentage. This is true irrespective of the functional form chosen to represent the underlying production technology.

When estimating the model in (4.10), a noise term, v, is usually appended to the equation to capture modelling errors. Unlike the production function, the v term does not have a natural interpretation. It is quite ad hoc and added to the cost function to make it stochastic.[1]

In the following, we add a subscript to represent producer i, and use the translog specification on $\ln C^*(\boldsymbol{w}_i, y_i)$, viz.,

$$\begin{aligned} \ln C_i^a &= \ln C^*(\boldsymbol{w}_i, y_i) + v_i + \eta_i \\ &= \beta_0 + \sum_j \beta_j \ln w_{j,i} + \beta_y \ln y_i + \frac{1}{2}\sum_j \sum_k \beta_{jk} \ln w_{j,i} \ln w_{k,i} + \frac{1}{2}\beta_{yy} \ln y_i \ln y_i \\ &\quad + \sum_j \beta_{jy} \ln w_{j,i} \ln y_i + v_i + \eta_i. \end{aligned} \tag{4.15}$$

4.2.1 Price Homogeneity

Symmetric restrictions require $\beta_{jk} = \beta_{kj}$. Because the cost function is homogeneous of degree 1 in the input prices (i.e., $w_{1,i}, \ldots, w_{J,i}$), it has to satisfy the following additional parameter restrictions:

$$\sum_j \beta_j = 1, \qquad \sum_j \beta_{jk} = 0 \;\forall k, \qquad \sum_j \beta_{jy} = 0. \tag{4.16}$$

An easier way to impose the price homogeneity condition is to use $w_{j,i}$ for an arbitrary choice of j and normalize C_i^a and other input prices by it. To see how this works, consider a simple model with $J = 2$.

[1] This is not a problem specific to stochastic frontier analysis. It applies to the neoclassical cost function as well where a noise term is appended before estimation.

$$\ln C_i^a = \beta_0 + \beta_y \ln y_i + \beta_1 \ln w_{1,i} + \beta_2 \ln w_{2,i} + \frac{1}{2}\beta_{yy}(\ln y_i)^2 + \frac{1}{2}\beta_{11}(\ln w_{1,i})^2 + \frac{1}{2}\beta_{22}(\ln w_{2,i})^2 + \beta_{12} \ln w_{1,i} \ln w_{2,i} + \beta_{1y} \ln w_{1,i} \ln y_i + \beta_{2y} \ln w_{2,i} \ln y_i + v_i + \eta_i. \tag{4.17}$$

Price homogeneity requires that $\beta_1 + \beta_2 = 1$; $\beta_{11} + \beta_{12} = 0$, $\beta_{22} + \beta_{12} = 0$; and $\beta_{1y} + \beta_{2y} = 0$. Equivalently, the constraints are $\beta_1 = 1 - \beta_2$, $\beta_{12} = -\beta_{22}$, $\beta_{11} = -\beta_{12} = \beta_{22}$, and $\beta_{1y} = -\beta_{2y}$. If we substitute these constraints into the cost function, the price homogeneity restrictions will be built into the model. After the substitutions and straightforward manipulation, we get

$$\ln\left(\frac{C_i^a}{w_{1,i}}\right) = \beta_0 + \beta_y \ln y_i + \beta_2 \ln\left(\frac{w_{2,i}}{w_{1,i}}\right) + \frac{1}{2}\beta_{yy}(\ln y_i)^2 + \frac{1}{2}\beta_{22} \ln\left(\frac{w_{2,i}}{w_{1,i}}\right)^2 + \beta_{2y} \ln\left(\frac{w_{2,i}}{w_{1,i}}\right) \ln y_i + v_i + \eta_i. \tag{4.18}$$

The above equation is equivalent to the one obtained by dividing C_i^a and other input prices ($w_{2,i}$ in this case) by $w_{1,i}$. We may also choose to express β_2, β_{12}, and β_{22} as functions of β_1 and β_{11} based on the price homogeneity conditions, and derive a similar model that has $w_{2,i}$ appearing as the normalizing price. That is, price homogeneity can be built into the model by an arbitrary choice of $w_{1,i}$ and $w_{2,i}$ as the normalizing price.

We now illustrate how to set up a cost frontier model, taking into account this homogeneity condition.

Example

In order to show how to empirically estimate a cost frontier model, here and throughout this chapter, we demonstrate the estimation using data on fossil fuel fired steam electric power generation plants in the United States as provided in the dataset, `utility`. It is a panel dataset, but, for illustration purposes, we assume that the observations are from a cross section.

The data contains the following variables: The output (`y`), which is net steam electric power generation in megawatt-hours; three inputs, which are labor and maintenance (`lab`), fuel (`fue`), and capital stock (`k`); and the corresponding input prices, `wl`, `wf`, and `wk`. The total cost (`tc`) is then defined as the sum of the costs of the three inputs.

We consider a cost frontier model with input-oriented technical efficiency, and a translog specification of the cost function, viz.,

$$\begin{aligned} \ln\left(\frac{tc}{wf}\right)_i &= \beta_0 + \beta_y \ln y_i + \beta_l \ln\left(\frac{wl}{wf}\right)_i + \beta_k \ln\left(\frac{wk}{wf}\right)_i \\ &+ \frac{1}{2}\beta_{yy} \ln y_i \ln y_i + \frac{1}{2}\beta_{ll} \ln\left(\frac{wl}{wf}\right)_i \ln\left(\frac{wl}{wf}\right)_i \\ &+ \frac{1}{2}\beta_{kk} \ln\left(\frac{wk}{wf}\right)_i \ln\left(\frac{wk}{wf}\right)_i + \beta_{lk} \ln\left(\frac{wl}{wf}\right)_i \ln\left(\frac{wk}{wf}\right)_i \\ &+ \beta_{ly} \ln y_i \ln\left(\frac{wl}{wf}\right)_i + \beta_{ky} \ln y_i \ln\left(\frac{wk}{wf}\right)_i + \eta_i + v_i. \end{aligned} \tag{4.19}$$

We generate the variables, in the ratio form, for this translog model. The regression variables are then placed in the macro list `xvar`.

```
. use utility, clear

. foreach X of varlist y tc wl wk wf  /* generate the log variables */
  2.  generate double l`X' = ln(`X')
  3.

. foreach X of varlist tc wl wk  /* divide cost and price by wf and take logs */
  2.  generate double l`X'D = ln(`X'/wf)
  3.

. generate double ly = ln(y)
. generate double ly2 = 0.5*(ly)^2
. generate double lwlD2 = 0.5*(lwlD)^2
. generate double lwkD2 = 0.5*(lwkD)^2
. generate double lwlkD = lwlD* lwkD
. generate double lylwlD = ly*lwlD
. generate double lylwkD = ly*lwkD

. global xvar ly ly2 lwlD lwkD lwlD2 lwkD2 lwlkD lylwlD lylwkD
```

We can now estimate the model.

Model 1: OLS

The following is the result of the OLS estimation.

```
. regress ltcD $xvar

      Source |       SS       df       MS              Number of obs =     791
-------------+------------------------------           F(  9,   781) = 1035.77
       Model |  617.658267     9  68.6286964           Prob > F      =  0.0000
    Residual |   51.748185   781  .06625888            R-squared     =  0.9227
-------------+------------------------------           Adj R-squared =  0.9218
       Total |  669.406452   790  .84734994            Root MSE      =  .25741

------------------------------------------------------------------------------
        ltcD |      Coef.   Std. Err.      t    P>|t|     [95% Conf. Interval]
-------------+----------------------------------------------------------------
          ly |  -.1837754   .3363095    -0.55   0.585    -.8439531    .4764022
         ly2 |   .0655263   .0173857     3.77   0.000      .031398    .0996546
        lwlD |   .8929707   1.326377     0.67   0.501    -1.710715    3.496656
        lwkD |   2.374389   1.912694     1.24   0.215    -1.380241    6.129019
       lwlD2 |  -.0869149   .2490054    -0.35   0.727    -.5757141    .4018843
       lwkD2 |   .9245507   .4644409     1.99   0.047     .0128504    1.836251
       lwlkD |   .3586179   .2832849     1.27   0.206    -.1974721     .914708
      lylwlD |   .0279913    .042102     0.66   0.506    -.0546553    .1106378
      lylwkD |  -.0078886    .061159    -0.13   0.897     -.127944    .1121669
       _cons |   8.466802   5.196454     1.63   0.104    -1.733869    18.66747
------------------------------------------------------------------------------
```

By construction this model satisfies the price homogeneity condition. However, there are other conditions that we will need to check.

4.2.2 Monotonicity and Concavity

Production theory requires a cost function to be monotonic and concave in input prices and output. The monotonicity condition requires cost to be nondecreasing in input prices and output: $C_i^*(\mathbf{w}_i^1, y_i) \geq C_i^*(\mathbf{w}_i^0, y_i)$ if $\mathbf{w}_i^1 \geq \mathbf{w}_i^0$ and $C_i^*(\mathbf{w}_i, y_i^1) \geq C_i^*(\mathbf{w}_i, y_i^0)$ if $y_i^1 \geq y_i^0$. Given that

$$\frac{\partial C_i^*}{\partial w_{j,i}} = \frac{\partial \ln C_i^*}{\partial \ln w_{j,i}} \times \frac{C_i^*}{w_{j,i}}, \tag{4.20}$$

and both C_i^* and $w_{j,i}$ are positive, then,

$$\text{sign}\left(\frac{\partial C_i^*}{\partial w_{j,i}}\right) = \text{sign}\left(\frac{\partial \ln C_i^*}{\partial \ln w_{j,i}}\right). \tag{4.21}$$

Note that the partial derivative on the right-hand side of (4.21) is simply input j's cost share. Thus, the monotonicity condition on input prices can be checked from the positivity of the estimated cost shares. Similarly, we can also check the sign of $\partial \ln C_i^*/\partial \ln y_i$ for the monotonicity condition of output. Returning to (4.15), the partial derivatives (i.e., the input shares) are the following:

$$\frac{\partial \ln C_i}{\partial \ln w_{s,i}} = \beta_s + \sum_j \beta_{sj} \ln w_{j,i} + \beta_{sy} \ln y_i, \qquad s = 1, \ldots, J, \tag{4.22}$$

$$\frac{\partial \ln C_i}{\partial \ln y_i} = \beta_y + \beta_{yy} \ln y_i + \sum_j \beta_{jy} \ln w_{j,i}. \tag{4.23}$$

As the shares are functions of $\ln y_i$ and $\ln w_{j,i}$, $j = 1, \ldots, J$, the partial derivatives are observation-specific.

The concavity condition requires that the following Hessian matrix with respect to input prices is negative semidefinite (Diewert and Wales [1987]):

$$\frac{\partial^2 C_i^*}{\partial \boldsymbol{w}_i \partial \boldsymbol{w}_i'} = \frac{\partial^2 \ln C_i^*}{\partial \ln \boldsymbol{w}_i \partial \ln \boldsymbol{w}_i'} - \text{diag}(\boldsymbol{S}_i) + \boldsymbol{S}_i \boldsymbol{S}_i', \tag{4.24}$$

where $\boldsymbol{S}_i$ is the vector of input shares defined as

$$\boldsymbol{S}_i = \frac{\partial \ln C_i^*}{\partial \ln \boldsymbol{w}_i}. \tag{4.25}$$

A matrix is negative semidefinite if all the eigenvalues are less than or equal to zero. Notice that for a translog model, the first matrix on the right-hand side of (4.24) contains only the coefficients – but not data – of the model and hence is observation invariant. However, each of the share equations in the $\boldsymbol{S}_i$ vector is a function of the data. Thus, the Hessian matrix of (4.24) is observation-specific. Therefore, like monotonicity, concavity conditions cannot be imposed by restricting the parameters alone. Ideally, monotonicity and the concavity conditions should be satisfied for each observation.[2]

Example

Checking the Monotonicity Conditions

We continue with the previous example and check the monotonicity conditions of the cost model; the computations are based on (4.22) and (4.23). The first three commands compute the partial derivatives with respect to input prices of labor (`wl`), capital (`wk`), and fuel (`wf`). The fourth command computes the partial derivative with respect to output. Recall that Stata returns the coefficient of the variable `lwlD`, for example, as `_b[lwlD]`.

[2] Ryan and Wales (2000) suggested normalizing the data at a point in such a way that the number of concavity violations is minimum. That is, they were in favor of imposing monotonicity and concavity conditions locally. By contrast, Terrell (1996) suggested a procedure to impose monotonicity and concavity conditions globally. These procedures are often quite demanding to apply in practice.

```
. quietly generate double mono_wl = _b[lwlD] + _b[lwlD2]*lwl + _b[lwlkD]*lwk ///
                                    + (-_b[lwlD2]-_b[lwlkD])*lwf + _b[lylwlD]*ly
. quietly generate double mono_wk = _b[lwkD] + _b[lwlkD]*lwl + _b[lwkD2]*lwk ///
                                    + (-_b[lwlkD]-_b[lwkD2])*lwf + _b[lylwkD]*ly
. quietly generate double mono_wf = (1-_b[lwlD]- _b[lwkD]) + (-_b[lwlD2] -_b[lwlkD])*lwl ///
                                    + (-_b[lwlkD]-_b[lwkD2])*lwk + (_b[lwlD2]+2*_b[lwlkD] ///
                                    +_b[lwkD2])*lwf + (-_b[lylwlD]-_b[lylwkD])*ly
. quietly generate double mono_y  = _b[ly] + _b[ly2]*ly + _b[lylwlD]*lwl + _b[lylwkD]*lwk ///
                                    + (-_b[lylwlD] -_b[lylwkD])*lwf
```

Before estimation, we used the input price `wf` to divide the total cost and other input prices in order to impose the price homogeneity condition. As shown in (4.19), the resulting model then does not have coefficients related to `wf`, which are needed here in order to compute the partial derivatives. In the codes shown earlier, these coefficients are recovered using the conditions in (4.16). For instance, given that `_b[lwlD2]` and `_b[lwlkD]` are $\hat{\beta}_{ll}$ and $\hat{\beta}_{lk}$ (see (4.19)), respectively, the coefficient β_{lf} is estimated by `(-_b[lwlD2]-_b[lwlkD])` because $\beta_{ll} + \beta_{lk} + \beta_{lf} = 0$. The result is used in the second line in the computation of `mono_wl`.

The monotonicity condition requires `mono_wl`, `mono_wk`, `mono_wf`, and `mono_y` to be positive for all the observations. Let us look at the summary statistics of these variables.

```
. summarize mono_wl mono_wk mono_wf mono_y

    Variable |       Obs        Mean    Std. Dev.       Min        Max
-------------+--------------------------------------------------------
     mono_wl |       791    .1609071    .0627451  -.0300165   .3565643
     mono_wk |       791    .6470175     .228109  -.3361181   1.421158
     mono_wf |       791    .1920754    .2742896  -.7193091   1.366135
      mono_y |       791    .9579812     .061839   .7706173   1.100025
```

It shows that some observations have negative values on `mono_wl`, `mono_wk`, and `mono_wf`. We may list the observations with violations using the command such as `list if mono_wl <0` to see the number of observations violating `wl`'s monotonicity condition and to investigate the likely cause. Our preliminary investigation shows that only 6 out of the 791 observations violate the monotonicity condition for the price of labor and maintenance (`wl`) and only 2 observations do not satisfy the monotonicity condition for the price of capital stock (`wk`). However, 208 out of the 791 observations violate the monotonicity condition for the price of fuel (`wf`). Such a large number of violations warrants further investigation. A number of factors may lead to such violations. Imposing more structure in the estimation process (such as using share equations) could make the results align more with the theory. We will examine how to including share equations in the estimation process in Chapter 6. For now, we will ignore these violations.

Checking the Concavity Condition

For the concavity condition, we compute the Hessian matrix of (4.24) and check if it is negative semidefinite. The following codes illustrate how this may be done in Stata.

```
. matrix C = (_b[lwlD2], _b[lwlkD], (-_b[lwlD2]-_b[lwlkD])  ///
>            _b[lwlkD], _b[lwkD2], (-_b[lwlkD]-_b[lwkD2])  ///
>            (-_b[lwlD2] -_b[lwlkD]), (-_b[lwlkD]-_b[lwkD2]), (_b[lwlD2]+2*_b[lwlkD]+_b[lwkD2]))

. forvalues i = 1/`nofobs' {  /* loop over each observation */
  2.    matrix S = (mono_wl[`i'], mono_wk[`i'], mono_wf[`i'])'
  3.    matrix A = C - diag(S) + S*S'   /* the Hessian matrix */
  4.    matrix symeigen x v = A   /* v contains the eigenvalues of A */
  5.      scalar docheck = 1
```

```
    forvalues j = 1/3 {   /*loop over three eigen values */
      if v[1, `j']>0.0001 & docheck ==1 { /* check if any of the eigenvalues >0*/
        scalar violation = violation + 1  /* record the number of violations */
          scalar docheck = 0 /* ensures a maximum of 1 violation per observation is recorded */
        }
      }
    }

. display violation
791
```

Note that number of violations is a count of the number of violations for each power plant. Thus, for example, if the violation occurs for all three inputs for a firm, it will only be counted as 1 violation. The results of the concavity test for this particular application are not very good: All 791 observations have a violation. Further investigation reveals that there are 791 violations for one input, 434 for another and 0 for the final one. As stated earlier, we will see, in Chapter 6, that including share equations in the estimation can reduce the number of violations in some cases. The implication is that imposing more structure in the estimation process (as the share equations do) can make the results align more with the theory.

One should take these violations seriously. Quite often we focus on the estimates of cost efficiency and tend to ignore whether or not the estimated cost frontier function (which is the basis of estimated efficiency) satisfies the theoretical properties. The estimated efficiencies might not be particularly meaningful if the cost frontier fail to satisfy the properties. Note that here we are viewing the cost frontier as the minimum cost function derived from explicit optimization (i.e., cost minimizing behavior of producers). If one takes the view that the estimated relationship is just a regression in which the objective is to explain costs in terms of explanatory variables (cost drivers) then it may *not* be necessary for the estimated cost function to satisfy the concavity conditions (although it is desirable to satisfy monotonocity conditions).

Having set up the model and checked whether the model is consistent with theory, we can now turn to estimating efficiency.

4.3 Estimation Methods: Distribution-Free Approaches

This section and the next section discuss estimation methods for the cost frontier model. The methods are, not surprisingly, very similar to those of the production frontier model discussed in Chapter 3, and they are broadly classified into distribution-free approaches (this section) and maximum likelihood (ML) approaches (Section 4.4). Due to the similarity, we will not repeat many of the modeling details that are already provided in Chapter 3, but, instead, provide a few empirical examples in order to illustrate the practical differences. The exception is the "thick frontier" method, which was not fully discussed in Section 3.3.3, so details of this method are given below (the choice of focus reflects the fact that the thick frontier approach is mainly used for cost frontier estimation in the literature).

First, we examine the distribution-free approaches. As discussed in the previous chapter, *distribution free* reflects the fact that we do not need to impose distribution assumption on η in (4.10) to estimate the inefficiency effect.

4.3.1 Corrected OLS

The COLS approach, discussed in the production function context in Section 3.3.1, can be applied here with some modifications. For a cost minimization model, we first obtain consistent estimates of the slope coefficients via OLS, and then we shift the entire function *downward*, rather than upward as was the case for a production function, so that the adjusted function bounds observations above.[3]

In particular, suppose the OLS residual is

$$\hat{e} = \ln C^a - \ln \hat{C}^*(\boldsymbol{w}, y) \gtreqless 0. \tag{4.26}$$

We then adjust the OLS intercept downward by the amount of $\min\{\hat{e}\}$, so that the adjusted function bounds observations from below:

$$\hat{e} - \min\{\hat{e}\} = \ln C^a - \underbrace{\left\{\ln \hat{C}^*(\boldsymbol{w}, y) + \min\{\hat{e}\}\right\}}_{\text{estimated frontier function}} \geq 0, \tag{4.27}$$

and that

$$\hat{e}^* \equiv \hat{e} - \min\{\hat{e}\} \geq 0, \tag{4.28}$$

where $\hat{e}^*$ is the estimated inefficiency measure in (4.10). The technical efficiency of each observation can then be calculated as

$$\widehat{TE} = \exp(-\hat{e}^*). \tag{4.29}$$

The pitfalls of the COLS that we discussed in Section 3.3.1 apply here as well. The most important point is that deviations from the estimated frontier are attributed entirely to efficiency, and so there is no role for random error in the model. This makes COLS estimates vulnerable to extreme values in the data.

Example

Model 2: COLS

The OLS residuals are used to obtained the efficiency index as shown in (4.29). The mean of the efficiency index indicates that, on average, the minimum cost is about 62 percent of the actual cost. Or, roughly speaking, the actual cost exceeds the minimum cost by about 38 percent. Notice that the maximum efficiency index from COLS is unity, which is true by construction.

```
. quietly summarize epsilon
. generate double eta_star = (epsilon - r(min))
. generate double eff_cols = exp(-eta_star)
. summarize eff_cols

    Variable |       Obs        Mean    Std. Dev.       Min        Max
-------------+--------------------------------------------------------
    eff_cols |       791    .6199466    .1443679    .215253          1
```

[3] The COLS shifts the mean regression downward. It is also possible to shift the median regression downward by first estimating a quantile regression at the median (rather than mean) of the data.

4.3.2 Cases with No or Little Variation in Input Prices

There are often cases where input prices do not vary very much (such a situation could be consistent, for example, with a competitive market). In such a case the coefficients on input price variables are not identified and are subsumed by the intercept term. The translog cost function in such a situation becomes

$$\ln C_i^a = \beta_0 + \beta_y \ln y_i + \frac{1}{2}\beta_{yy}(\ln y_i)^2 + v_i + \eta_i. \tag{4.30}$$

Note that because input prices do not appear in the above cost function, we do not have to deal with the linear homogeneity (in input prices) condition.

Example

We now illustrate this case by estimating model (4.30) using the same example of electric power generation plants. Notice that in this case we do not have to normalize the total cost by one of the input prices since the price is constant in this case. Doing so only affects the intercept but not the slope coefficients.

```
. generate double ltc = ln(tc) /* generate log of total cost without input price normalization */

. regress ltc ly ly2

      Source |       SS       df       MS              Number of obs =     791
-------------+------------------------------           F(  2,    788) = 4260.45
       Model |  621.700803     2  310.850402           Prob > F      =  0.0000
    Residual |   57.493976   788  .072961898           R-squared     =  0.9153
-------------+------------------------------           Adj R-squared =  0.9151
       Total |  679.194779   790  .859740227           Root MSE      =  .27011

------------------------------------------------------------------------------
         ltc |      Coef.   Std. Err.      t    P>|t|     [95% Conf. Interval]
-------------+----------------------------------------------------------------
          ly |  -.0126262   .2757014    -0.05   0.963    -.5538221    .5285698
         ly2 |   .0609035   .0173925     3.50   0.000     .0267623    .0950446
       _cons |   4.963457   2.180545     2.28   0.023     .6830929    9.243822
------------------------------------------------------------------------------
```

We may also conduct the skewness test on the residual and calculate the technical efficiency index for this model. Although not shown here, the results are consistent with the fully specified cost model. For instance, the skewness statistic is 0.693 and is significant at the 1 percent level. The sample mean of the technical efficiency is 0.588 (compared to 0.620 in the fully specified model).

4.3.3 Thick Frontier Approach

Berger and Humphrey (1991) proposed the TFA, which is also distribution free. The idea of TFA is that, instead of measuring the "frontier" itself, TFA estimates mean regressions on the most efficient *group* of firms – those which constitute a *thick frontier* – and also the least efficient *group* of firms. It then compares the best group (defined in some way) with the worst and attributes the difference due to efficiency and market activities.

Thus, it is not an approach that is designed for measuring observation- (or firm-) specific efficiency, but focuses mainly on the efficiency differences *between the groups*, rather than the differences between firms.

The steps required for this estimation method are summarized below.

1. The data of firms is sorted by scale-adjusted costs, such as average cost (AC), from small to large, and the sorted sample divided into several quantiles. Firms in the first quantile of the sample are assumed to form the most efficient group of firms, and firms in the last quantile form the least efficient group. (In the case of production or profit frontier estimations where output, profit, or asset is used to sort the observations, then the first quantile would be the least efficient group of firms while the last quantile would be the most efficient group of firms.) Note that this is an assumption and differences in average costs between the top and bottom quartiles show both differences in technology and technical efficiency.
2. Model (4.10), without the inefficiency term, is then separately estimated using OLS for the first and the last quantiles. This gives us the estimated coefficient vectors $\hat{\beta}^L$ and $\hat{\beta}^H$, where the L and H superscripts indicate the low cost and the high cost firms, respectively.
3. Deviations of an observation from the sample mean within the group are considered to be random error, while differences in average costs between groups are attributed to market factors (or cost drivers) and inefficiency.

We denote $\hat{c}^L = C^*(\bar{y}^L, \bar{\boldsymbol{x}}^L; \hat{\beta}^L)/\bar{y}^L$ as the predicted average cost measured at the sample mean of the group of low-cost firms, and $\hat{c}^H = C^*(\bar{y}^H, \bar{\boldsymbol{x}}^H; \hat{\beta}^H)/\bar{y}^H$ as the predicted average cost of the high-cost firms (the variable with a bar indicates the sample mean of the variable). Furthermore, we define $\hat{c}^{H*} = C^*(\bar{y}^H, \bar{\boldsymbol{x}}^H; \hat{\beta}^L)/\bar{y}^H$ as the predicted cost of the high-cost firms using the low-cost technology. This measures the would-be cost of the high-cost firms had the low-cost technology been adopted by those firms. We can now decompose the difference in the average cost between the high- and low-cost firms into two factors, one is that of the efficiency difference and the other is the market effect. The decomposition is

$$\frac{\hat{c}^H - \hat{c}^L}{\hat{c}^L} = \frac{\hat{c}^H - \hat{c}^{H*}}{\hat{c}^L} + \frac{\hat{c}^{H*} - \hat{c}^L}{\hat{c}^L}. \tag{4.31}$$

The left-hand side of the expression is the percentage difference of the average cost between the high- and low-cost firms. The first term on the right-hand side measures the difference between high-cost firms' excess of average cost as a percentage of the low-cost firms's average cost. Because the excess cost is measured relative to the best available technology, it therefore measures the cost difference attributable to cost inefficiency between the two groups. In the second term, the technology is the same for the two groups of firms, and so the cost difference is due to market factors (i.e., differences in the cost drivers).

Compared to COLS, which is also distribution-free, TFA is less prone to extreme values in the data. The TFA also accommodates random errors *within* the stratified groups.

However, there are a number limitations of TFA that are well known in the literature, including the following:

1. TFA confounds differences in technology with differences in inefficiency. That is, the term $\frac{\hat{c}^H - \hat{c}^{H*}}{\hat{c}^L}$ on the right-hand side of (4.31) is not just inefficiency; in fact it represents technological differences between two groups of firms.
2. The heterogeneous technology assumption may also make the AC comparison problematic. Because a single technology can exhibit a U-shaped average cost curve, firms

with the lowest AC will be those that are scale-efficient (operating near constant AC, i.e., unitary returns to scale). Thus, low (high) AC is not a necessary condition for high- (low-) cost efficiency.

3. The cost functions are estimated using only subsets of the available data in TFA. If the efficient and the inefficient groups are defined by the first and the last quarter of the samples, and the regressions are conducted only in these two quarters of the samples, then only half of the total available observations are used. This can be a serious constraint for studies based on smaller datasets.
4. The number of quantiles used to separate samples is arbitrary, and it is clear that the measured cost inefficiency would increase with the number of quantiles chosen to separate the samples.

These limitations should be borne in mind when using the TFA. We illustrate how to apply the approach.

Example

Model 3: Thick Frontier Approach (TFA)

Using the thick frontier approach, we first separate the sample into a number of quantiles on the basis of average cost (here, we separate the sample into quantiles). The quantile group number for each observation is saved in the variable `gindex` (i.e., `gindex` contains the numbers 1, 2, 3, or 4, depending on to which quantile the observation belongs). Firms in the first quantile (i.e., `gindex` = 1) have the lowest average cost and thus form the most cost-efficient group. Firms in the last quantile (i.e., `gindex` = 4) have the highest average cost and thus form the most cost inefficient group.

```
. generate double avgc = tc/y
. xtile gindex = avgc, nquantile(4) /* mark the sample into 4 quartiles */
```

Next, we calculate the sample means for each variable from the two quantiles.

```
* the variables' mean of group 1 and group 4
. generate double lwf = ln(wf)
. foreach X in y $xvar lwf
  2.   quietly sum `X' if gindex == 1
  3.   scalar M1`X' = r(mean)
  4.   quietly sum `X' if gindex == 4
  5.   scalar M4`X' = r(mean)
  6.
```

An OLS regression is run on the first quantile sample (the most efficient group), and the coefficients represent the most cost-efficient technology.

```
. quietly regress ltcD $xvar if gindex == 1     /* the low cost, high efficiency group */
```

Using the technology estimated for the first quantile, we then calculate the predicted cost for the firms in the first as well as the last quantiles. The predicted cost is measured at the sample mean of the quantile and therefore is a scalar.

```
* average cost of group 1
. scalar C1 = M1lwf + _b[_cons] + _b[ly]*M1ly + _b[ly2]*M1ly2  ///
>     + _b[lwlD]*M1lwlD + _b[lwkD]*M1lwkD + _b[lwlD2]*M1lwlD2 ///
>     + _b[lwkD2]*M1lwkD2 + _b[lwlkD]*M1lwlkD  ///
>     + _b[lylwlD]*M1lylwlD + _b[lylwkD]*M1lylwkD
```

```
. scalar cL = exp(C1)/M1y

* average cost of group 4 using group 1 technology
. scalar C4 = M4lwf + _b[_cons] + _b[ly]*M4ly + _b[ly2]*M4ly2  ///
>      + _b[lwlD]*M4lwlD + _b[lwkD]*M4lwkD + _b[lwlD2]*M4lwlD2 ///
>      + _b[lwkD2]*M4lwkD2 + _b[lwlkD]*M4lwlkD ///
>      + _b[lylwlD]*M4lylwlD + _b[lylwkD]*M4lylwkD

. scalar cH_star = exp(C4)/M4y
```

The M1x is the variable x's mean in the first quantile, and M4x is the variable's mean in the fourth (last) quantile. In calculating `C1` and `C4`, we add the term `M1lwf` (which is the the mean of $\ln wf$ in the first quantile) and `M4lwf` (which is the the mean of $\ln wf$ in the fourth quantile), respectively, to the equations, to account for the fact that $\ln wf$ has been subtracted from the equations in the equation. The `C1` and `C4` are thus the predicted values of $\ln tc$ (instead of $\ln(tc/w_f)$) of the quantiles. The scalar `cL` is the predicted average cost of the low cost group, and `cH_star` is the predict average cost of the high-cost group using the better, low-cost technology.

Finally, we compute the predicted cost of the fourth quantile using its technology and compute the average inefficiency of the high-cost group of firms.

```
* average cost group 4
. quietly regress ltcD $xvar if gindex == 4 /* the high cost, low efficiency group */

. scalar C4a = M4lwf + _b[_cons] + _b[ly]*M4ly + _b[ly2]*M4ly2  ///
>      + _b[lwlD]*M4lwlD + _b[lwkD]*M4lwkD + _b[lwlD2]*M4lwlD2 ///
>      + _b[lwkD2]*M4lwkD2 + _b[lwlkD]*M4lwlkD ///
>      + _b[lylwlD]*M4lylwlD + _b[lylwkD]*M4lylwkD

. scalar cH = exp(C4a)/M4y
. display (cH - cH_star)/cL
.81286768
```

The result indicates that the average cost of the inefficient group is about 81 percent of the efficient group's average cost.

4.3.4 Quantile-Regression-Based TFA

To mitigate the disadvantage of TFA mentioned earlier, Wang et al. (2008) proposed an alternative estimation strategy of the thick frontiers. The alternative strategy is based on the quantile regression of Koenker and Bassett (1982). Readers are encouraged to acquire a basic understanding of quantile regression before reading the following section (see also Section 3.3.2).

The regression line in OLS passes through the mean of the data. By contrast, mean absolute deviation regression (based on minimizing absolute sum of errors) passes through the median values of the data (meaning that half of the residuals are positive and the other half negative). Instead of running these two regressions, one can think of running a whole set of regressions passing through different quantiles of the data. A quantile regression estimates *the response function* of the sample's $n\%$ quantile defined by values of the dependent variable. Thus, the quantile regression generates a whole spectrum of lines and gives a much broader picture, especially for checking the robustness of the estimated coefficients (i.e., the marginal effects). Therefore, similar to the TF in the previous section, the group of efficient observations can be defined as the one estimated in a higher (or lower) quantile of the sample, while an inefficient cost function is the one on the lower (or higher) quantile. Note that estimated technologies are likely to differ depending on the choice of top (75% vs. 85%) and bottom (25% vs. 15%) quantiles. Also, unlike the TF in which the regression only uses observations from subsamples, the quantile regression uses *all* the available data in estimation. Each regression line uses all the data but puts different weights based on the choice of the quantiles. For example, a 25 percent (75%) quantile regression fits the line in such a way that 25 percent (75%) of the residuals are positive (negative). Thus, this regression is likely to differ from the median regression, for example. Because each of these regressions use all the data, information in the data is not lost. Another advantage of the quantile regression approach is that it can compare differences in efficiency of firms at arbitrary chosen quantiles without losing observations in the estimation.

The estimation procedure is similar to that of TFA. We first transform the cost function so that the independent variable is expressed as the (log of) average cost. In the case of a single output model, the independent variable can be constructed as $\ln(C/y)$ which is the average cost, and we add the term $-\ln y$ on the right-hand side of the equation (*the response function*). As with the TFA approach, if the model has multiple outputs, we can use assets to adjust the total cost, that is, $\ln(C/A)$, and then add $-\ln A$ (instead of $-\ln y$) to the response function. We then conduct the quantile regression estimation at the top quantile of average cost, which is assumed to represent the most efficient firms' cost function. Regressions at lower quantiles of average cost are then estimated, and the results are compared to the most efficient quantile. The comparison is undertaken in a similar way as in the TFA approach, except that we have to remember to transform the expected average cost back to the expected level of cost.

As in the case of TFA, the quantile regression approach is not geared toward econometric rigor. Instead, the aim of the quantile regression approach is to gain reliable inference of the cost inefficiency that does not rely on particular distributional assumptions. One shortcoming of this method is that the cost differences between quantiles are entirely attributed to the market factors and inefficiency and there is no room to allow for random errors. Therefore, the individual inefficiency is not estimated as precisely as in the stochastic frontier models based on ML methods.

Example

Model 4: Quantile Regression Approach

In order to subdivide the sample into quantiles that are related to cost efficiency, the independent variable in the quantile regression approach to cost frontier estimation is the log of the average cost. Because we have a single output model, we use the inverse of output (y) to scale the cost before taking log on the variable. This amounts to subtracting $\ln y$ from both sides of equation (4.19). The coefficient of $\ln y$ is thus $\beta_y - 1$.

For the purpose of comparison to TFA, we also divide the sample into four quartiles based on the distribution of the independent variable. (Other subdivisions could, of course, be used.) Our objective is to compare the cost differences for firms in the first quartile (most cost-efficient) and the last quartile (least cost-efficient). Average cost is defined in terms of the normalized cost (tc/wf), i.e., $tc/wf * y$. The quantile information of each observation is saved in `qindex2`.

```
. generate double lavgcD = ln(tc/(wf*y))
. xtile gindex2 = lavgcD, nquantile(4)
```

For the first quartile, which comprises 25 percent of the sample, we estimate the quantile regression at the 12.5 percent quantile of the entire sample. The point chosen is the median of the first quartile sample, and we choose this point only for the purpose of comparing the result with the TFA (in practice, any point could be chosen). The coefficients from this estimation are taken to represent the best cost technology. After the estimation, we compute the predicted cost of *all* the observations in the data using the estimated coefficients (the best technology). The estimated values is thus the minimum cost of the observations.

```
. quietly qreg lavgcD $xvar, q(0.125)
. predict c_q1, xb
. generate double CC_best = exp(c_q1 + ln(y) + ln(wf))
```

The last line generates `CC_best`, which is the predicted minimum cost level. Note that `c_q1` is the predicted value of $\ln(tc/(wf * y)$, so $\ln(y)$ and $\ln(wf)$ are added back to obtain the predicted value of $\ln tc$.[4]

For the fourth quartile sample, which is presumed to comprised of least efficient firms, we conduct the quantile regression at the 87.5 percent quantile of the entire sample, and we take the estimation result as representative to firms in the fourth quartile. The predicted cost on the fourth quartile firms are calculated, and the results are compared to `CC_best`.

```
. quietly qreg lavgcD $xvar, q(0.875)
. predict c_q4 if gindex2 == 4, xb
(594 missing values generated)

. quietly generate double CC_q4 = exp(c_q4 + ln(y) + lwf) if gindex2 == 4
. quietly generate double c_ratio = CC_best/CC_q4 if gindex2 == 4

. summarize c_ratio

    Variable |       Obs        Mean    Std. Dev.       Min        Max
-------------+--------------------------------------------------------
     c_ratio |       197    .5259947    .0920458   .2895925   .7416512
```

The result indicates that for the least efficient group, the minimum cost is about 53 percent of the actual cost.

The advantage of the quantile regression approach is in its ability to increase the number of quantiles in the estimation to the effect that the efficiency profile can be built across the average cost distribution. For example, we may divide samples into N quantiles and compute the minimum to actual cost ratio on all the quantile samples. If N is sufficiently large, we effectively trace out the efficiency profile on the distribution. The TFA, by contrast, is not amenable to having a large number of quantiles: As N increases, the number of observations in each quantile decreases.

4.4 Estimation Methods: Maximum Likelihood Estimators

We now go back to the cost model with IO technical inefficiency and noise, viz.,

$$\ln C^a = \ln C^*(\boldsymbol{w}, y) + \eta + v. \tag{4.32}$$

[4] Unlike in the TFA, here we calculate the predicted cost for each observation instead of at the quartile mean. This should not make a substantial difference.

To estimate such a model, we impose distributional assumptions on v and η, based on which the likelihood function can be derived and the parameters estimated for any parametric cost frontier.

The ML approach to estimate the cost frontier estimation is very similar to the ML approach that we used to estimate the production frontier in Section 3.4. The only difference is that the variable $-u$ in Section 3.4 is replaced by η. Thus, the same modeling strategies can be applied to the cost model. In fact, if v is normally distributed (so that theoretically one can replace $-v$ with $+v$ without altering anything) one can multiply both sides of (4.32) by -1 to get the same structure of the composed error used in Section 3.4. In doing so one can use the same likelihood function, the same codes, and so on, to estimate the cost frontier.

There is, nevertheless, a direct way of handling the problem. With the same distribution assumption on u and η, the log-likelihood functions are very similar for the production and the cost functions, with only one important difference in the sign in front of the inefficiency term. Namely, ϵ is now $v + \eta$ whereas it was $v - u$ before, and so in practice we need to only replace ϵ by $-\epsilon$ to get the likelihood function for the cost frontier model. All of the statistical/economic properties of the models discussed in Section 3.4 are applicable to the cost frontier models once the sign difference is taken into account.

Because of the close relationship with the production frontier models, we will use only a simple example (a half-normal model) to show the similarity and the difference between production and cost frontier functions in the ML approach, and we shall refrain from other repetitions in this section. (See Section 3.4 for a detailed discussion on the ML approach.)

4.4.1 Skewness Test on OLS Residuals

First, we check the skewness of the residuals. Methods to conduct hypothesis testing of a cost frontier model are essentially the same as those of a production frontier model. See Section 3.4.1 for a detailed discussion. The only notable difference occurs in testing the skewness of the OLS residuals. For a cost frontier model, we expect the distribution of the OLS residuals to skew to the right (because the composed error is $v_i + \eta_i$ with $\eta_i \geq 0$), which implies a positive (rather than negative) skewness estimate from, for example, $\sqrt{b_1}$.

Example

The statistic of the skewness of the OLS residuals and the significance test are obtained from Stata as follows:

```
. quietly regress ltcD $xvar
. scalar ll_ols = e(ll)
. predict epsilon, resid
. summarize epsilon, detail

                         Residuals
-------------------------------------------------------------
      Percentiles      Smallest
 1%    -.4723418       -.508484
 5%     -.340547      -.5012135
10%     -.274575      -.4930392       Obs                 791
25%    -.1774009      -.4903636       Sum of Wgt.         791

50%    -.0347847                      Mean          -1.93e-10
                        Largest       Std. Dev.      .2559376
```

```
75%       .1226456          .8588427
90%       .3484637          .8897481          Variance          .065504
95%       .5268195          .9149475          Skewness          .9072631
99%       .7548438          1.027457          Kurtosis          4.006568

. sktest epsilon, noadj

                    Skewness/Kurtosis tests for Normality
                                                          ------- joint ------
    Variable |      Obs    Pr(Skewness)    Pr(Kurtosis)      chi2(2)     Prob>chi2
-------------+-----------------------------------------------------------------
     epsilon |      791      0.0000          0.0000           99.79        0.0000
```

The estimated skewness of the OLS residuals is 0.907. The positive value of the statistic indicates that the residual is skewed to the right, which is consistent with the assumption of a cost frontier model. The skewness test is significant, providing support for the cost frontier specification of the model. We turn to this next.

4.4.2 The Half-Normal Distribution

A stylized cost frontier model is (observation subscript i omitted)

$$\ln C^a = \ln C^*(\mathbf{w}, y) + \eta + v \tag{4.33}$$

$$= \ln C^*(\mathbf{w}, y) + \epsilon, \tag{4.34}$$

$$\eta \sim N^+(0, \sigma_u^2), \tag{4.35}$$

$$v \sim N(0, \sigma_v^2), \tag{4.36}$$

where $\epsilon \equiv v + \eta$ is the composed error of the model.

The corresponding log-likelihood function for observation i is

$$L = -\ln\left(\frac{1}{2}\right) - \frac{1}{2}\ln(\sigma_v^2 + \sigma_u^2) + \ln\phi\left(\frac{-\epsilon}{\sqrt{\sigma_v^2 + \sigma_u^2}}\right) + \ln\Phi\left(\frac{\mu_*}{\sigma_*}\right), \tag{4.37}$$

where,

$$\mu_* = \frac{\sigma_u^2\,\epsilon}{\sigma_v^2 + \sigma_u^2}, \tag{4.38}$$

$$\sigma_*^2 = \frac{\sigma_v^2\sigma_u^2}{\sigma_v^2 + \sigma_u^2}. \tag{4.39}$$

The log-likelihood function of the model is the sum of this function for all observations. Maximizing the log-likelihood function gives the ML estimates of model parameters.

As mentioned earlier, the above log-likelihood function can be obtained from the production frontier model's log-likelihood function by simply replacing ϵ with $-\epsilon$. In fact, by replacing ϵ with $-\epsilon$ in the functions of Section 3.4, all the results therein are readily extended to the cost frontier model. This is true for models with alternative distribution assumptions. This is also true for the model statistics such as $E(u|\epsilon)$, $E(e^{-u}|\epsilon)$, the associated confidence intervals, and the marginal effects. Discussions on heteroscedasticity, exogenous determinants, and other statistical properties of the model are also similar to those of the production frontier model (see Section 3.4).

One of the advantages of the parametric likelihood approach is that, unlike COLS, TFA, or quantile-based estimation, determinants of inefficiency can be included in the model and all the parameters estimated in one step. In the current example of power plants, we want to know whether technical efficiency is affected if regulation is adopted in the state in which the plant operates. The dummy variable `regu` takes a value equal to 1 if the power plant is in a state which enacted legislation or issued a regulatory order to implement retail access during the sample period, and a value equal to 0 otherwise.

Example

The same estimation commands introduced for estimating a production frontier model (see page 62) can be used in a similar way to estimate a cost frontier model. The only difference is that the option `cost` should be specified when using `sfmodel`, instead of `production`, for estimating cost frontier models.

Model 5: Translog Half-Normal Model with Heteroscedasticity

We first consider a half-normal model in which the parameter of the inefficiency, σ_u^2, is a function of `regu`. The log-likelihood function is (4.37) and we use the price of fuel (`wf`) to divide the cost and other prices in the translog model before estimation (see (4.19)). The model is estimated by the following commands.

```
. sfmodel ltcD, cost dist(h) frontier($xvar) usigmas(regu) vsigmas()
. sf_init, frontier(b0) usigmas(0 0) vsigmas(0)
. ml max, difficult gtol(1e-5) nrtol(1e-5)
```

The results are summarized in Tables 4.1 and 4.2.

Right after estimating the model, we save the value of the log-likelihood function of the model and the coefficient vectors for later use.

```
. matrix b0 = e(b)
. matrix bf_h = b0[1, "frontier:"]
. scalar ll_h = e(ll)
```

The LR test (which follows a mixed Chi-square distribution) can be used to test the distribution assumption of the inefficiency term. If the electricity generation plants are fully efficient (i.e., $\eta_i = 0$), the model reduces to an OLS. The hypothesis of no inefficiency $\eta_i = 0$ can therefore be tested by comparing the log-likelihood of the OLS model to that of the half-normal model. Given that there are two parameters in the η_i function (γ_0 and γ_1), the LR test has two degrees of freedom.

```
. display -2*(ll_ols - ll_h)
235.50261

. sf_mixtable, dof(2)

critical values of the mixed chi-square distribution

                          significance level
 dof |  0.25     0.1      0.05      0.025     0.01      0.005     0.001
-----------------------------------------------------------------------
  2     2.090    3.808    5.138     6.483     8.273     9.634     12.810
source: Table 1, Kodde and Palm (1986, Econometrica).
```

Thus, the LR test rejects the null hypothesis of no technical inefficiency.

Table 4.1. *Estimation Results of Cost Frontier Models: Part 1*

		Model 1 OLS	Model 5 Half-normal	Model 6 Truncated-normal	Model 7 Scaling	Model 8 Exponential
frontier	ly	−0.184	0.318	0.322	0.376	0.407*
		(0.336)	(0.240)	(0.233)	(0.236)	(0.236)
	ly2	0.066***	0.024*	0.019	0.018	0.015
		(0.017)	(0.013)	(0.013)	(0.013)	(0.013)
	lwlD	0.893	0.686	0.306	0.558	0.507
		(1.326)	(0.898)	(0.855)	(0.861)	(0.849)
	lwkD	2.374	2.196*	2.127*	1.805	1.573
		(1.913)	(1.222)	(1.217)	(1.229)	(1.240)
	lwlD2	−0.087	−0.053	0.018	−0.002	0.024
		(0.249)	(0.186)	(0.174)	(0.176)	(0.173)
	lwkD2	0.925**	0.614**	0.449	0.451	0.362
		(0.464)	(0.277)	(0.284)	(0.292)	(0.299)
	lwlkD	0.359	0.494***	0.484***	0.533***	0.553***
		(0.283)	(0.178)	(0.176)	(0.179)	(0.181)
	lylwlD	0.028	0.048	0.058**	0.054*	0.057*
		(0.042)	(0.030)	(0.029)	(0.030)	(0.030)
	lylwkD	−0.008	−0.067	−0.088**	−0.075*	−0.078*
		(0.061)	(0.042)	(0.042)	(0.043)	(0.044)
	constant	8.467	4.083	4.511	3.326	2.866
		(5.196)	(3.553)	(3.460)	(3.496)	(3.493)

Note: Significance: ***: 1% level, **: 5% level, *: 10% level.

Regarding the regulation effect, the result shows that the coefficient of `regu` is 1.053 and is highly significant (see Table 4.2). The coefficient, however, is not the marginal effect. We use `sf_predict` with the option `marginal` to calculate the marginal effect of `regu` on the mean and the variance of inefficiency. The same command also computes the efficiency index of each observation (using the Battese and Coelli [1988] formula) and saves the result in the variable `bc_h`.

```
. sf_predict, bc(bc_h) marginal

The following is the marginal effect on unconditional E(u).

The average marginal effect of regu on uncond E(u) is .16255587 (see regu_M).

The following is the marginal effect on uncond V(u).

The average marginal effect of regu on uncond V(u) is .06045897 (see regu_V).
```

A note on the notation: To be precise, the notations of $E(u)$ and $V(u)$ in the above printout should be $E(\eta)$ and $V(\eta)$, respectively. We use u instead of η in the notation, nevertheless, for simplicity. The positive marginal effect of `regu` on $E(u)$ implies that regulation causes an overuse of inputs, which in turn increases costs. The regulated plants, on average, overuse inputs by 16 percent. That is, on average, the cost of regulated plants, all other things being equal, is increased by 16 percent. The positive marginal effect on $V(u)$ implies that regulation also increases the variance of technical efficiency. More specifically, the variance of inefficiency, on average, is increased by 0.06. If required, the

Table 4.2. *Estimation Results of Cost Frontier Models: Part 2*

		Model 1 OLS	Model 5 Half-normal	Model 6 Truncated-normal	Model 7 Scaling	Model 8 Exponential
σ_v^2	constant		−5.215***	−4.989***	−4.888***	−4.712***
			(0.216)	(0.193)	(0.200)	(0.164)
σ_u^2	regu		1.053***			
			(0.117)			
	constant		−2.617***	−1.254***		
			(0.111)	(0.303)		
μ	regu			1.042***		
				(0.322)		
	constant			−1.318**		
				(0.572)		
hscale	regu				0.625***	
					(0.082)	
τ	constant				−0.788	
					(0.646)	
c_u	constant				−1.658***	
					(0.528)	
η^2	regu					1.427***
						(0.169)
	constant					−3.775***
						(0.166)
marginal effect of `regu` on E(u)			0.163	0.208	0.167	0.178
marginal effect of `regu` on E(u)			0.060	0.065	0.077	0.097
log likelihood		−44.126	73.863	85.152	79.684	77.920

Note: Significance: ***: 1% level, **: 5% level, *: 10% level.

standard errors of the marginal effects can be computed by bootstrapping the model (see Appendix D).

4.4.3 The Truncated-Normal, Scaling, and Exponential Models

We can also estimate the cost frontier model with different distributional assumptions on inefficiency. We consider three alternative assumptions: truncated-normal, truncated-normal with the scaling property, and the exponential. The distributions are parameterized by the regulation variable `regu`. The estimation commands are provided here. The results are summarized in Tables 4.1 and 4.2.

Example

Model 6: The Truncated-Normal Model

```
. sfmodel ltcD, cost dist(t) frontier($xvar) mu(regu) usigmas() vsigmas()
. sf_srch, n(2) frontier($xvar) mu(regu) fast
. ml max, difficult gradient  gtol(1e-5) nrtol(1e-5)
. sf_predict, bc(bc_t) marginal
```

Model 7: The Truncated-Normal Model with Scaling Property

```
. sfmodel ltcD, cost dist(t) scaling frontier($xvar) tau cu hscale(regu) vsigmas()
. sf_init, frontier(bf_t) tau(0) cu(0) hscale(0) vsigmas(0)
. sf_srch, n(2) frontier($xvar) hscale(regu) fast
. ml max, difficult gradient  gtol(1e-5) nrtol(1e-5)
. sf_predict, bc(bc_s) marginal
```

Model 8: The Exponential Model

```
. sfmodel ltcD, cost dist(e) frontier($xvar) etas(regu) vsigmas()
. sf_srch, n(2) frontier($xvar) eta(regu) fast
. ml max, difficult gtol(1e-5) nrtol(1e-5)
. sf_predict, bc(bc_e) marginal
```

These commands save the efficiency index of the three models in bc_t, bc_s, and bc_e.

As shown in Tables 4.1 and 4.2, the estimates of frontier parameters are pretty consistent across the models except for the OLS. The OLS has a larger intercept than other models have, which is true almost by construction. The marginal effects of regu on $E(u)$ and $V(u)$ are positive in all the models, and, therefore, the finding that regulations decrease power plants' technical efficiency is robust.

Summary statistics of the efficiency index from the various models including the COLS model are provided below.

```
. summarize eff_cols bc_h bc_t bc_s bc_e

    Variable |       Obs        Mean    Std. Dev.       Min        Max
-------------+--------------------------------------------------------
    eff_cols |       791    .6199466    .1443679    .215253          1
        bc_h |       791    .7581451    .1585842   .2733148   .9741473
        bc_t |       791    .7793189    .1588967   .2809368   .9749294
        bc_s |       791    .7862034    .1577054   .2803196   .9737757
        bc_e |       791    .8002938    .1559949   .2840678   .9735941
```

Except for COLS, the average efficiency index from the parametric models are similar to each other. On average, the minimum cost is about 76 to 80 percent of the actual cost. In contrast, COLS shows a much lower average efficiency index.

Table 4.3 shows the Kendall's rank correlation coefficient (τ) between the efficiency index The null hypothesis of independence between the index is rejected at the 1 percent level in every case.

Table 4.3. *Kendall's Correlation Coefficients (τ)*

	Model 5 Half-normal bc_h	Model 6 Truncated-normal bc_t	Model 7 Scaling bc_s	Model 8 Exponential bc_e
Model 2: COLS, eff_cols	0.837***	0.826***	0.828***	0.825***
Model 5: Half-normal, bc_h		0.968***	0.977***	0.960***
Model 6: Truncated-normal, bc_t			0.985***	0.986***
Model 7: Scaling, bc_s				0.983***

Note: Significance: ***: 1% level, **: 5% level, *: 10% level.

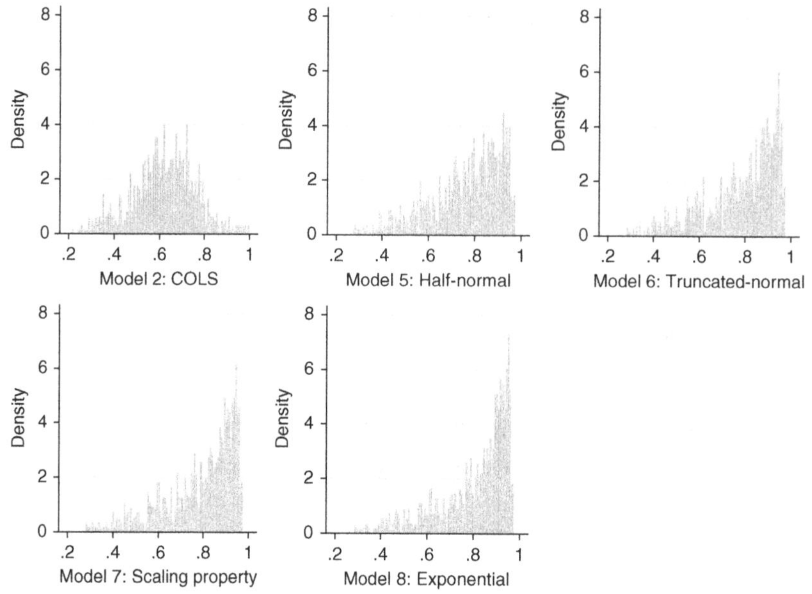

Figure 4.1. Histograms of Efficiency Index

Figure 4.1 shows the histograms of the efficiency index from the various models. These were created using the following code:

```
. label variable eff_cols "Model 2: COLS"
. histogram eff_cols, bin(100) `kden´ saving(eff_cols, replace)
. label variable bc_h "Model 5: Half-normal"
. histogram bc_h, bin(100) `kden´ saving(bc_h, replace)
. label variable bc_t "Model 6: Truncated-normal"
. histogram bc_t, bin(100) `kden´ saving(bc_t, replace)
. label variable bc_s "Model 7: Scaling Property"
. histogram bc_s, bin(100) `kden´ saving(bc_s, replace)
. label variable bc_e "Model 8: Exponential"
. histogram bc_e, bin(100) `kden´ saving(bc_e, replace)

. graph combine  eff_cols.gph  bc_h.gph bc_t.gph bc_s.gph bc_e.gph, col(3) ///
> scale(1) xcommon ycommon
. graph export sing_cost_alleff.eps, replace
```

The graphs indicate that the efficiency index distribution from COLS is visibly different from the other models. Kendall τ also indicates that COLS's efficiency ranking is less consistent with the rankings from the other models. The probability that a randomly chosen pair of observations have opposite rankings from COLS's and from any of the other model's is in the order of 8 percent.

4.5 Output-Oriented Technical Inefficiency

In this section, we derive the stochastic cost frontier model with output-oriented technical inefficiency. Recall that the input-oriented measure of inefficiency starts from the fact that, if a producer is not efficient, then he/she is not able to use the inputs effectively. That is, there are slacks in the inputs and it is possible to reduce input-usage without reducing output. Consequently, the input-oriented measure is practical and intuitive when output is exogenously given (demand determined) and the objective is to minimize cost (or maximize the proportional reduction in input usage) without reducing output. By contrast, output-oriented technical inefficiency measures the potential increase in output without increasing the input quantities. Alternatively, it can be viewed as a measure of output loss resulting from failure to produce the maximum possible output permitted by the technology. Thus, the output-oriented measure is intuitive when the inputs are exogenously given to the manager and the objective is to produce as much output as possible.

Although inefficient production can be viewed from either input- or output-oriented angles, it is shown below that without additional restrictions on the underlying production function, a stochastic cost frontier model with output-oriented technical inefficiency is difficult to estimate (Kumbhakar and Wang [2006]). Imposing the assumption of a homogeneous production function makes the estimation easier.

The cost minimization problem with output-oriented technical inefficiency is as follows (observation subscripts omitted):

$$\min \quad \boldsymbol{w}'\boldsymbol{x} \quad \text{s.t.} \quad y = f(\boldsymbol{x})e^{-u}, \tag{4.40}$$

where $u \geq 0$ is the output-oriented technical inefficiency. Multiplying e^{-u} on both sides of the production function, we rewrite the minimization problem and the associated FOCs as:

$$\min \quad \boldsymbol{w}'\boldsymbol{x} \quad \text{s.t.} \quad ye^{u} = f(\boldsymbol{x}), \tag{4.41}$$

$$\text{FOCs:} \quad \frac{f_j(\boldsymbol{x})}{f_1(\boldsymbol{x})} = \frac{w_j}{w_1}, \quad j = 2, \ldots, J, \tag{4.42}$$

where $f_j(\cdot)$ is the marginal product of x_j (the partial derivative of $f(\cdot)$ with respect to x_j). The $J-1$ FOCs and the production function in (4.41) can be used to solve for the input demand functions of the J inputs. The solution of x_j is $x_j = x_j(\boldsymbol{w}, ye^u)$. Therefore, the minimum cost of producing ye^u given the input prices, $\boldsymbol{w}$, is $C^* = C^*(\boldsymbol{w}, ye^u) = \sum_j \boldsymbol{w}'\boldsymbol{x}$. Because $\boldsymbol{w}'\boldsymbol{x}$ is also the *actual* cost (C^a) of producing output level y when the production is technically inefficient, we have

$$C^a = C^*(\boldsymbol{w}, ye^u). \tag{4.43}$$

To estimate the above relationship, we add a producer (observation) subscript i and assume that $C_i^*(\cdot)$ has a flexible functional form such as the translog. We also add a random error v_i for estimation purposes. With these, we write the translog model as

$$\begin{aligned} \ln C_i^a = {} & \beta_0 + \sum_j \beta_j \ln w_{j,i} + \beta_y \ln(y_i e^u) \\ & + \frac{1}{2} \sum_k \sum_j \beta_{jk} \ln w_{j,i} \ln w_{k,i} + \frac{1}{2} \beta_{yy} \ln(y_i e^u)^2 \\ & + \sum_j \beta_{jy} \ln w_{j,i} \ln(y_i e^u) + v_i. \end{aligned} \tag{4.44}$$

It is straightforward to show that, on expanding $\ln(y_i e^u)$ into $\ln y_i + u_i$, the model will have three stochastic components: u_i, u_i^2, and v_i. The presence of the u_i^2 term makes the derivation of the likelihood function in closed form impossible, and so the standard maximum likelihood approach of this model is not feasible.[5]

Imposing the homogeneity assumption on the production technology simplifies the problem. If the production technology is homogenous of degree r, then our translog model will have the following parametric restrictions (Christensen and Greene [1976]): $\beta_{yy} = 0$ and $\beta_{jy} = 0 \; \forall \, j$, and that $\beta_y = 1/r$ where r is the degree of homogeneity (which is the same as returns to scale). The simplification leads to the following estimation equation:

$$\begin{aligned}
\ln C_i^a &= \beta_0 + \sum_j \beta_j \ln w_{j,i} + \beta_y \ln(y_i e^u) + \frac{1}{2}\sum_k \sum_j \beta_{jk} \ln w_{j,i} \ln w_{k,i} + v_i \\
&= \beta_0 + \sum_j \beta_j \ln w_{j,i} + \beta_y \ln y_i + \frac{1}{2}\sum_k \sum_j \beta_{jk} \ln w_{j,i} \ln w_{k,i} + u_i/r + v_i. \qquad (4.45)
\end{aligned}$$

If one reparameterizes $\tilde{u}_i = u_i/r$, then the model (4.45) looks exactly like the cost frontier model with input-oriented inefficiency and it can be estimated using the standard maximum likelihood method.

The above example shows how the assumption of homogenous technology helps to simplify the model when the cost function has a translog specification. In fact, the simplification applies to other specifications as well (not just the translog function). In general, with a homogenous of degree r production technology, we have (see also Section 2.3.1):

$$C_i^*(\mathbf{w}_i, y_i \exp(-u_i)) = (y_i \exp(-u_i))^{\frac{1}{r}} \cdot C_i^*(\mathbf{w}_i), \qquad (4.46)$$

$$\text{or} \qquad \ln C_i^*(\mathbf{w}_i, y_i \exp(-u_i)) = \frac{1}{r} \ln y_i + \ln C_i^*(\mathbf{w}_i) + \frac{u_i}{r}. \qquad (4.47)$$

Alternative specifications of $\ln C_i^*(\mathbf{w}_i)$ do not make the model more difficult than (4.45).

Equation (4.45) can be derived in an alternative way. If the production function $f(\cdot)$ is homogeneous of degree r, then the production function in (4.40) is $y_i = f(\mathbf{x}_i)\exp(-u_i) = f(\mathbf{x}_i \cdot \exp(-u_i/r))$. With reference to (4.1), we have $\eta_i = u_i/r$. That is, *under the assumption of a homogeneous production function*, the output-oriented technical inefficiency (u_i) equals the input-oriented technical inefficiency (η_i) multiplied by a constant which is the returns to scale parameter (r). Because of the similarity, we can use the result from (4.10) and write the current model as

$$\ln C_i^a = \ln C_i^*(\mathbf{w}_i, y_i) + u_i/r + v_i. \qquad (4.48)$$

Aside from the apparent u_i/r versus η_i, there is an important difference between (4.48) and (4.10) concerning the specification of $\ln C_i^*(\mathbf{w}_i, y_i)$. For (4.10), a full, unrestrictive translog specification on $\ln C_i^*(\mathbf{w}_i, y_i)$ may be used for empirical estimations, which includes all the interaction terms between $x_{j,i}$ and y_i and the square term of y_i. In deriving (4.48), the technology is assumed to be homogeneous. In the translog specification of $\ln C_i^*(\mathbf{w}_i, y_i)$, this assumption imposes the following coefficient restrictions: $\beta_{yy} = 0$ and $\beta_{jy} = 0 \; \forall \, j$. Indeed, imposing the restrictions on the translog specification of $\ln C_i^*(\mathbf{w}_i, y_i)$ in (4.48) leads to the identical estimation model of (4.45).

[5] Simulated maximum likelihood proposed in Kumbhakar and Tsionas (2006) and Greene (2003) can be used to estimate these types of models for which the log-likelihood function cannot be expressed in a closed form.

4.5.1 Quasi-Fixed Inputs

In a cost minimization problem, the output level and the input prices are given, and a producer minimizes input cost by choosing an appropriate combination of inputs. Implicit in this minimization problem is the assumption that the inputs are *variable*; that is, the quantity of inputs used in production can be adjusted in the short run in response to changes in input prices. Some inputs, however, are adjustable only in the long run and it is difficult to immediately respond to short run price fluctuations. Land is a typical example of such an input. We call such inputs *quasi-fixed*.

Unlike variable inputs, the quasi-fixed inputs enter the cost function as exogenous variables because they are "fixed" in the short run. It is easy to include them in the model. Denote $\boldsymbol{q}_i$ as the vector of quasi-fixed inputs, the model in (4.48) can then be modified to

$$\ln C_i^a = \ln C_i^*(\boldsymbol{w}_i, \boldsymbol{q}_i, y_i) + u_i/r + v_i. \tag{4.49}$$

4.5.2 Estimation Methods

This section discusses the estimation method for the model in which the homogeneity assumption on the technology is imposed. Our focus is on the ML estimation. By defining

$$\tilde{u}_i = \frac{1}{r} u_i, \tag{4.50}$$

where r measures returns to scale, we write the model as

$$\begin{aligned} \ln C_i^a(\boldsymbol{w}_i, y_i) &= \ln C_i^*(\boldsymbol{w}_i, y_i) + u_i/r + v_i \\ &= \beta_y \ln y_i + \ln C_i^*(\boldsymbol{w}_i) + \tilde{u}_i + v_i. \end{aligned} \tag{4.51}$$

The second equality sign follows from (4.46). Note that $\beta_y = 1/r$ under the homogenous technology assumption. $\ln C_i^*(\boldsymbol{w}_i)$ can be assumed to take any functional form. The likelihood function can be derived after imposing distributional assumptions on $\tilde{u}_i$ and v_i, such as

$$\tilde{u}_i \sim N^+(\tilde{\mu}, \tilde{\sigma}_u^2), \tag{4.52}$$

$$v_i \sim N(0, \sigma_v^2). \tag{4.53}$$

In fact, the estimation methods introduced in Sections 4.3 and 4.4 for the cost frontiers with input-oriented technical inefficiency are equally applicable here.

Care should be taken, however, in interpreting the efficiency estimate of the model. For example, by directly applying the Jondrow et al. (1982) inefficiency formula to the model, we get $E(\tilde{u}_i|\epsilon_i)$ (ϵ_i is the composed error of the model) instead of $E(u_i|\epsilon_i)$. The interpretation of $100{*}E(\tilde{u}_i|\epsilon_i)$ is the percentage increase in cost due to input overuse. This is an *input-oriented* interpretation of inefficiency.

If one is interested in *output-oriented* measure of inefficiency, the parameters of the distribution of u_i can be easily recovered after the model is estimated. Take, for example, a truncated-normal distribution of u_i,

$$\begin{aligned} & u_i \sim N^+(\mu, \sigma_u^2), \\ & \Rightarrow \tilde{u}_i = \frac{1}{r} \cdot u_i \sim N^+(\mu/r, \sigma_u^2/r^2) \equiv N^+(\tilde{\mu}, \tilde{\sigma}_u^2), \end{aligned} \tag{4.54}$$

$$\text{therefore,} \qquad \hat{\mu} = \hat{r} \cdot \hat{\tilde{\mu}}, \quad \hat{\sigma}_u^2 = \hat{r}^2 \cdot \hat{\tilde{\sigma}}_u^2.$$

The standard errors of $\hat{\mu}$ and $\hat{\sigma}_u^2$ can be obtained using the Delta method together with the variances and covariance of $\hat{\tilde{\mu}}$ and $\hat{\tilde{\sigma}}_u^2$. The above computation requires an estimate of the returns to scale (r). In the simple case of a single output homogeneous function, r is simply the inverse of the output coefficient: $r = 1/\beta_y$. These estimated parameters can then be used to obtain point estimates of u as well as the confidence intervals.

Example

Model 9: The Truncated-Normal Model with Output-Oriented Technical Inefficiency

In this section, we continue with the empirical example of the previous section, and estimate the cost frontier function of the electric power plants with OO technical inefficiency. Section 4.5 shows that without imposing the homogeneity assumption on the production function, the cost frontier model with OO technical inefficiency is difficult to estimate. In this section the homogeneity assumption is imposed to make the estimation simple.

We estimated a cost frontier model with the translog specification in the previous section; see (4.19). The homogeneity assumption on the underlying production function imposes the constraint $\beta_{yy} = 0$ on (4.19), and it implies that $\beta_y = 1/r$ where r is the degree of homogeneity (returns to scale). The estimation model is (see (4.45)):

$$\begin{aligned}\ln\left(\frac{tc}{wf}\right) &= \beta_0 + \beta_y \ln y + \beta_l \ln\left(\frac{wl}{wf}\right) + \beta_k \ln\left(\frac{wk}{wf}\right) + \frac{1}{2}\beta_{ll} \ln\left(\frac{wl}{wf}\right)^2 \\ &\quad + \frac{1}{2}\beta_{kk} \ln\left(\frac{wk}{wf}\right)^2 + \beta_{lk} \ln\left(\frac{wl}{wf}\right) \ln\left(\frac{wk}{wf}\right) + u/r + v,\end{aligned} \tag{4.55}$$

where u is the OO technical inefficiency. Reparameterizing $\tilde{u} = u/r$, the model is estimated based on the distributions of $\tilde{u}$ and v. We assume that $\tilde{u}$ has a truncated-normal distribution. The model is estimated by the following commands, in which the OLS estimates are used as initial values of the model.

```
. global xvarOO ly lwlD lwkD lwlD2 lwkD2 lwlkD      /* see equation (4.55) */
. quietly regress ltcD $xvarOO
. matrix b0 = e(b)
. sfmodel ltcD, cost dist(t) frontier($xvarOO) mu(regu) usigmas() vsigmas()
. sf_init, frontier(b0) mu(0 0) usigmas(0) vsigmas(0)
. ml max, difficult  gtol(1e-5) nrtol(1e-5)
```

```
Number of obs    =         791
                                                  Wald chi2(6)     =    17785.54
Log likelihood =   80.657808                      Prob > chi2      =      0.0000

------------------------------------------------------------------------------
        ltcD |      Coef.   Std. Err.      z    P>|z|     [95% Conf. Interval]
-------------+----------------------------------------------------------------
frontier     |
          ly |   .9985249   .0078098   127.86   0.000     .9832179    1.013832
        lwlD |   1.271522   .7894127     1.61   0.107    -.2756987    2.818742
        lwkD |    .602258   1.050799     0.57   0.567     -1.45727    2.661786
       lwlD2 |   .0762499   .1761891     0.43   0.665    -.2690743    .4215742
       lwkD2 |   .4587336   .2869879     1.60   0.110    -.1037523     1.02122
       lwlkD |   .5414782   .1735625     3.12   0.002     .2013018    .8816545
       _cons |  -4.164497   2.188935    -1.90   0.057    -8.454731    .1257358
-------------+----------------------------------------------------------------
```

```
mu           |
        regu |   1.108019   .3670536     3.02   0.003     .388607    1.827431
       _cons |  -1.456988   .6629586    -2.20   0.028   -2.756363   -.1576132
-------------+----------------------------------------------------------------
usigmas      |
       _cons |    -1.1814   .3248781    -3.64   0.000    -1.81815   -.5446507
-------------+----------------------------------------------------------------
vsigmas      |
       _cons |  -4.913221   .1970107   -24.94   0.000   -5.299355   -4.527087
------------------------------------------------------------------------------
```

The estimates of mu and usigmas functions are those of $\tilde{u} = u/r$. We also calculate the efficiency index, $E(\exp(-\hat{\tilde{u}})|\hat{\epsilon})$ and the inefficiency index, $E(\hat{\tilde{u}}|\hat{\epsilon})$, and the marginal effects of regu.

```
. sf_predict, bc(bc_t_OO) jlms(jlms_t_OO) marginal

The following is the marginal effect on unconditional E(u).

The average marginal effect of regu on uncond E(u) is .20653678 (see regu_M).

The following is the marginal effect on uncond V(u).

The average marginal effect of regu on uncond V(u) is .06644109 (see regu_V).

. summarize bc_t_OO jlms_t_OO

    Variable |       Obs        Mean    Std. Dev.       Min        Max
-------------+--------------------------------------------------------
     bc_t_OO |       791    .7813426    .1577626   .2685034   .9750373
   jlms_t_OO |       791    .2749617    .2408788   .0255595    1.31848
```

The estimated efficiency index indicates that the minimum cost is about 78 percent of the actual cost. Alternatively, actual cost can be reduced by $1/0.78 - 1 \approx 28\%$ without reducing output. The latter figure is close to the estimated inefficiency, which is not surprising as $1/\exp(-\tilde{u}) - 1 = \exp(\tilde{u}) - 1 \approx \tilde{u}$.

5

Estimation of Technical Efficiency in Profit Frontier Models Using Cross-Sectional Data

5.1 Introduction

In modeling and estimating the impact of technical inefficiency on production it is assumed, at least implicitly, that inputs are exogenously given and the scalar output is a response to the inputs. By contrast, in modeling and estimating the impact of technical inefficiency on costs, it is assumed that output is given and inputs are the choice variables (i.e., the goal is to minimize cost for a given level of output). However, if the objective of producers is to maximize profit, *both* inputs and output are choice variables. That is, inputs and outputs are chosen by the producers in such a way that profit is maximized.

In this chapter, we derive the stochastic profit frontier model when both inputs and output are endogenous. In deriving the model, we assume that producers are maximizing their profit. However, although they may not be fully efficient technically, we assume, in this chapter, that they are allocatively efficient. Models with both technical and allocative inefficiency will be discussed in Chapter 9.

In the long run, profits are zero[1] for producers operating in a competitive market and producers with negative profits exit the industry. Similarly, if there are positive profits, then new firms will enter the market, which will drive profits down to zero. In this chapter, we do not take such a long-term perspective. The long run can be viewed as a sequence of short runs, in which firms can operate with positive as well as negative profit. Our focus here is to model profit efficiency (in particular, profit loss due to technical inefficiency). We consider profit maximization in the short run and argue that differences in profits are due to *quasi-fixed inputs* (i.e., inputs that are not chosen optimally in the short run) and technical inefficiency. However, the existence of quasi-fixed inputs is not necessary for modeling technical inefficiency in a profit maximizing framework.

The critical assumption in the preceding discussion of zero profits in the long run is that markets are competitive. There are clearly situations where markets are far from perfectly competitive and have only a few, or even only one, supplier, or the market may have many suppliers but there may exist legislation, regulation and other factors that interfere with the efficient operation of the market. One way of handling market imperfection is to use the shadow price approach (see Kumbhakar and Lovell [2000], chapter 6; Kumbhakar and

[1] An economist's definition of zero profits differs from an accountant's, in that, for the former, zero profits include a reasonable rate of return on owner's time and investments.

Lozano-Vivas [2005], and the references cited in that paper). In this chapter, we do not model noncompetitive markets.

In either of the two model settings discussed below we can examine a number of the questions first raised in Chapter 1. For example, in many cases analysts want to examine the impact of regulation. To do so, one can add regulation variable(s) in the model to examine whether changing regulations systematically affect profit. Such variables can be included as profit drivers as well as determinants of profit inefficiency. The profit function in this framework might not be the dual profit function, but an ad hoc regression in which profit is being explained by some covariates.

Even outside such market investigations, producers might be interested in knowing the key drivers of profitability and how their business compares to that of comparators. At the company-wide level understanding the key drivers would assist in resolving issues in order to increase margins if they are currently below normal. For example, an airline may currently be unprofitable because it may not have enough aircraft or raw materials given its current demand level and patterns. It may also be unprofitable due to poor management that fails to make the best use of its available aircraft and material inputs. Profit differences in the presence of quasi-fixed inputs (the cost of which are not included in the definition of profit) will be due to both inefficiency and the level of quasi-fixed inputs. (The example of airlines is used as the empirical illustration in this chapter.)

Profit inefficiency can be modeled in two ways. One way is to make the intuitive and commonsense argument that, if a producer is inefficient, his/her profit will be lower, everything else being the same. Thus, one can specify a model in which actual (observed) profit is a function of some observed covariates (profit drivers) and unobserved inefficiency. In this sense, the model is similar to a production function model. The error term in such a model is v-u where v is noise and u is inefficiency.

If the objective is to study profitability and examine whether firms are operating below the maximum possible profit (i.e., the profit frontier) and if so by how much, one can examine this without going through a formal analysis of the profit function. For example, if profitability is measured as the rate of return (ROR)[2] and ROR can be explained in terms of some variables (i.e., profit drivers), then one can simply use the production frontier type analysis (as set out in Chapter 3).[3] If a producer is not able to achieve the maximum ROR, then one can attach a one-sided inefficiency term with a negative sign in the ROR regression and estimate the ROR frontier using the ML method (again, in a similar way to estimating the production frontier). Inefficiency (i.e., deviations from the maximum ROR) can then be estimated in the same way we measured production inefficiency. If firms are regulated and the degree of regulatory tightness differs across firms located in different regions, then such a variable can be included in the analysis as a driver of profitability.

The other approach, and the one used in this chapter is to model profit efficiency in a formal way. Similar to the cost-minimizing model in Chapter 4, we make explicit use of the duality results. That is, derive a profit function allowing production inefficiency (IO or OO). Because profit maximization behavior is widely used in neoclassical production theory, we provide a framework to analyze inefficiency under profit maximizing behavior. This is in

[2] Measured either by the rate of return on assets (ROA) or the rate of return on equity (ROE).

[3] While maximizing ROR may be a valid criterion, it should be noted that, in standard economics textbooks, firms are assumed to be maximizing the *level* of profit, rather than the *rate* of return on assets or equity.

contrast to the ad hoc approach discussed above, in which one can simply use profit as the dependent variable and use some exogenous variables as profit drivers. Note that in this ad hoc approach the explicit profit maximization objective is not used, and hence, although we are explaining profit in terms of some covariates, it is not a profit function in the sense that it is used in production theory (i.e., the duality approach). If this ad hoc approach is used, one can write actual profit as the product of frontier profit and profit efficiency in the same way we expressed actual output as the product of frontier output and technical inefficiency. Consequently, when expressed in logs, the profit frontier model will look exactly the same as the production frontier model. Thus, there is no need to discuss the estimation methods for these types of models in this chapter given that we devoted so much attention to modeling and estimating production frontier models in Chapter 3. Instead, in this chapter, our focus will be on the profit frontier that is derived explicitly from the profit maximizing behavior of producers. In doing so we will start with the output-oriented technical inefficiency followed by input-oriented technical inefficiency.

5.2 Output-Oriented Technical Inefficiency

The profit maximization problem with output-oriented technical inefficiency is

$$\max_{y,\boldsymbol{x}} py - \boldsymbol{w}'\boldsymbol{x} \qquad \text{s.t. } y = f(\boldsymbol{x}, \boldsymbol{q})e^{-u}. \tag{5.1}$$

The first-order conditions are

$$p f_j(\boldsymbol{x}, \boldsymbol{q})e^{-u} = w_j, \qquad j = 1, 2, \dots J, \tag{5.2}$$

$$f_j(\boldsymbol{x}, \boldsymbol{q}) = \frac{w_j}{p \cdot e^{-u}}, \qquad j = 1, 2, \dots J, \tag{5.3}$$

where $\boldsymbol{x}$ and $\boldsymbol{q}$ are vectors of variable and quasi-fixed inputs, respectively; $u \geq 0$ is the output-oriented technical inefficiency, and $f_j(\boldsymbol{x}, \boldsymbol{q}) = \partial f(\boldsymbol{x}, \boldsymbol{q})/\partial x_j$ is the marginal product of variable input j.

Note that if we substitute $p \cdot e^{-u}$ by $\tilde{p}$ and $y \cdot e^{u}$ by $\tilde{y}$, then we can write this profit maximization problem using $\tilde{p}$ and $\tilde{y}$, and the standard neoclassical analytics can be applied. Consequently, the profit function for our problem can simply be written as $\pi(\boldsymbol{w}, \boldsymbol{q}, \tilde{p})$, which comes from the following standard neoclassical maximization problem:

$$\max_{\tilde{y},\boldsymbol{x}} \tilde{p}\tilde{y} - \boldsymbol{w}'\boldsymbol{x}, \qquad \text{s.t.} \qquad \tilde{y} = f(\boldsymbol{x}, \boldsymbol{q}). \tag{5.4}$$

Solutions of the input demand and the output supply functions of the above optimization problem will be functions of $\boldsymbol{w}$, $\boldsymbol{q}$, and $\tilde{p}$. Substituting these input demand and output supply functions in to the objective function, we obtain the *profit function*, $\pi(\boldsymbol{w}, \boldsymbol{q}, pe^{-u})$, which is

$$\pi(\boldsymbol{w}, \boldsymbol{q}, pe^{-u}) = pe^{-u} f(\boldsymbol{x}(\cdot), \boldsymbol{q}) - \boldsymbol{w}'\boldsymbol{x}(\cdot), \tag{5.5}$$

where $\boldsymbol{x}(\cdot) = \boldsymbol{x}(\boldsymbol{w}, \boldsymbol{q}, pe^{-u})$ is the *input demand function*. Note that actual profit π^a is

$$\begin{aligned}\pi^a &= py(\boldsymbol{w}, \boldsymbol{q}, pe^{-u}) - \boldsymbol{w}'\boldsymbol{x}(\boldsymbol{w}, \boldsymbol{q}, pe^{-u}) \\ &= pe^{-u} f(\boldsymbol{x}(\cdot), \boldsymbol{q}) - \boldsymbol{w}'\boldsymbol{x}(\cdot) \\ &= \pi(\boldsymbol{w}, \boldsymbol{q}, pe^{-u}).\end{aligned} \tag{5.6}$$

If we define the *profit frontier* as

$$\pi(\boldsymbol{w}, p, \boldsymbol{q}) = \pi(\boldsymbol{w}, \boldsymbol{q}, pe^{-u})\,|_{u=0}, \tag{5.7}$$

then the following relationship can be established

$$\pi^a = \pi(\boldsymbol{w}, \boldsymbol{q}, pe^{-u}) = \pi(\boldsymbol{w}, \boldsymbol{q}, p) \cdot h(\boldsymbol{w}, \boldsymbol{q}, p, u), \tag{5.8}$$

or,

$$\ln \pi^a = \ln \pi(\boldsymbol{w}, \boldsymbol{q}, pe^{-u}) = \ln \pi(\boldsymbol{w}, \boldsymbol{q}, p) + \ln h(\boldsymbol{w}, \boldsymbol{q}, p, u), \tag{5.9}$$

where $h(\cdot) = \pi(\boldsymbol{w}, \boldsymbol{q}, pe^{-u})/\pi(\boldsymbol{w}, \boldsymbol{q}, p) \leq 1$ and therefore $\ln h(\cdot) \leq 0$. This result follows from the monotonicity property of profit function, i.e., since $pe^{-u} \leq p$, $\pi(\boldsymbol{w}, \boldsymbol{q}, pe^{-u}) \leq \pi(\boldsymbol{w}, \boldsymbol{q}, p)$.

This equation shows that the log of actual profit, $\ln \pi^a$, can be decomposed into a profit frontier component, $\ln \pi(\boldsymbol{w}, \boldsymbol{q}, p)$, and an inefficiency component, $\ln h(\boldsymbol{w}, \boldsymbol{q}, p, u) \leq 0$. In the following, we show that the equation can be simplified by: (i) making the assumption of a homogeneous production technology; and (ii) utilizing the property of price homogeneity of a profit function.[4]

Following Lau's theorem (1978, p. 151), it can be shown that if the underlying production function is homogeneous of degree r ($r < 1$), then the corresponding profit function is

$$\begin{aligned} \ln \pi^a &= \ln \pi(\boldsymbol{w}, \boldsymbol{q}, pe^{-u}) = \ln \pi(\boldsymbol{w}, \boldsymbol{q}, p) + \ln h(\boldsymbol{w}, \boldsymbol{q}, p, u) \\ &= \frac{1}{1-r} \ln p + \ln G(\boldsymbol{w}, \boldsymbol{q}) - \frac{1}{1-r} u, \end{aligned} \tag{5.10}$$

where $G(\boldsymbol{w}, \boldsymbol{q})$ is a homogeneous function of degree $-r/(1-r)$ in $\boldsymbol{w}$. Now, let us consider the property that a profit function is homogeneous of degree 1 in prices (i.e., in $\boldsymbol{w}$ and pe^{-u}). The price homogeneity property can be built into the profit function by normalizing the profit and the input/output prices by one of the prices. Using p to normalize the equation, we have

$$\ln(\pi^a/p) = \ln G(\boldsymbol{w}/p, \boldsymbol{q}) - \frac{1}{1-r} u, \tag{5.11}$$

which imposes the linear homogeneity restrictions automatically.

Now, let us further simplify the equation by exploring the property that $G(\boldsymbol{w}, \boldsymbol{q})$ is homogeneous of degree $-r/(1-r)$. Recall that $f(x)$ is a homogeneous function of degree μ if $f(x) = \lambda^{-\mu} f(x\lambda)$ where $\lambda \geq 1$. In the present case $\mu = -r/(1-r)$. If we choose $\lambda = 1/(w_1/p)$ and define $\tilde{w}_j = (w_j/p)/(w_1/p)$, then the profit function in (5.11) can be expressed as

$$\begin{aligned} \ln(\pi^a/p) &= -\frac{-r}{1-r} \ln \lambda + \ln G((\boldsymbol{w}/p)\lambda, \boldsymbol{q}) - \frac{1}{1-r} u \\ &= \frac{-r}{1-r} \ln(w_1/p) + \ln G(\tilde{\boldsymbol{w}}, \boldsymbol{q}) - \frac{1}{1-r} u. \end{aligned} \tag{5.12}$$

[4] Note the distinction between the profit function being homogeneous of degree one – a theoretical property that follows from the definition – and the production function being homogeneous of degree one – which is a restriction on the technology and, therefore, not necessary to impose. The homogeneity of the production function can be empirically tested, whereas the homogeneity (in prices) of profit function is definitional and, therefore, not something to be tested.

To get a better feel for this, we start by assuming a translog form of $\pi(\boldsymbol{w}, \boldsymbol{q}, pe^{-u})$, viz.,

$$\begin{aligned}\ln \pi^a &= \ln \pi(\boldsymbol{w}, \boldsymbol{q}, pe^{-u})\\ &= \beta_0 + \sum \beta_j \ln w_j + \sum \gamma_q \ln q_q + \beta_p \ln(pe^{-u})\\ &+ \frac{1}{2}\Big[\sum_j \sum_k \beta_{jk} \ln w_j \ln w_k + \sum_q \sum_s \gamma_{qs} \ln q_q \ln q_s + \beta_{pp} \ln(pe^{-u}) \ln(pe^{-u})\Big]\\ &+ \sum_j \beta_{jp} \ln w_j \ln(pe^{-u}) + \sum_j \sum_q \delta_{jq} \ln w_j \ln q_q + \sum_q \gamma_{qp} \ln q_q \ln(pe^{-u}).\end{aligned} \tag{5.13}$$

The symmetry restrictions are $\beta_{jk} = \beta_{kj}$ and $\gamma_{qs} = \gamma_{sq}$. Expressing (5.13) in the normalized form (to impose the price homogeneity property of a profit function) and after a few algebraic manipulations, we have

$$\begin{aligned}\ln\left(\frac{\pi^a}{p}\right) &= \ln \pi(\boldsymbol{w}/pe^{-u}, \boldsymbol{q}) = \beta_0 + \sum_j \beta_j \ln\left(\frac{w_j}{p}\right) + \sum_q \beta_q \ln q_q\\ &+ \frac{1}{2}\sum_j \sum_k \beta_{jk} \ln\left(\frac{w_j}{p}\right) \ln\left(\frac{w_k}{p}\right)\\ &+ \frac{1}{2}\sum_q \sum_s \gamma_{qs} \ln q_q \ln q_s + \sum_j \sum_q \delta_{jq} \ln\left(\frac{w_j}{p}\right) \ln q_q\\ &+ \left[-1 + \sum_j \beta_j + \sum_j \sum_q \delta_{jq} \ln q_q + \sum_j \sum_k \beta_{jk} \ln\left(\frac{w_j}{p}\right)\right] u\\ &+ \left[\frac{1}{2}\sum_j \sum_k \beta_{jk}\right] u^2\\ &\equiv \ln \pi(\boldsymbol{w}/p, \boldsymbol{q}) + \ln h(\boldsymbol{w}/p, \boldsymbol{q}, u).\end{aligned} \tag{5.14}$$

Note that the penultimate line in (5.14), involving u and u^2, is the $\ln h(\cdot)$ function in (5.9) that represents profit inefficiency.[5] Thus, profit inefficiency depends not only on u but also on prices and quasi-fixed inputs. Consequently, profit inefficiency cannot be assumed to have a constant mean and variance (irrespective of its distribution).

Without further assumptions, this model is difficult to estimate, because of the presence of the u^2 term. If we make the assumption that the underlying production function is homogenous, then additional parameter restrictions apply, viz.,

$$\begin{aligned}\sum_k \beta_{jk} &= 0, \quad \forall j,\\ \sum_j \delta_{jq} &= 0, \quad \forall q.\end{aligned} \tag{5.15}$$

[5] See Kumbhakar (2001) for further details on the properties of profit functions with both technical and allocative inefficiency.

These restrictions simplify the profit function of (5.14) substantially. The last line becomes $\ln h(\mathbf{w}/p, \mathbf{q}, u) = -\left[1 - \sum_j \beta_j\right] u$. In addition, the restrictions also simplify the deterministic part of the profit function of (5.14) (i.e., the first three lines). The end result is

$$\begin{aligned}
\ln\left(\frac{\pi^a}{p}\right) &= \beta_0 + \frac{-r}{1-r}\ln(w_1/p) + \sum_j \beta_j \ln \tilde{w}_j + \sum_q \beta_q \ln q_q + \frac{1}{2}\sum_j\sum_k \beta_{jk}\ln\tilde{w}_j \ln\tilde{w}_k \\
&\quad + \frac{1}{2}\sum_q\sum_s \gamma_{qs}\ln q_q \ln q_s + \sum_j\sum_q \delta_{jq}\ln\tilde{w}_j \ln q_q - \tilde{u}, \qquad j,k = 2,\ldots,J, \\
&= \frac{-r}{1-r}\ln(w_1/p) + \ln G(\tilde{\mathbf{w}}, \mathbf{q}) - \tilde{u} \\
&\equiv \beta_0 + \alpha_1 \ln(w_1/p) + \sum_j \beta_j \ln(w_j/p) + \sum_q \beta_q \ln q_q + \frac{1}{2}\sum_j\sum_k \beta_{jk}\ln\tilde{w}_j \ln\tilde{w}_k \\
&\quad + \frac{1}{2}\sum_q\sum_s \gamma_{qs}\ln q_q \ln q_s + \sum_j\sum_q \delta_{jq}\ln\tilde{w}_j \ln q_q - \tilde{u}, \qquad j,k = 2,\ldots,J.
\end{aligned} \tag{5.16}$$

where $\alpha_1 = -r/(1-r) - \sum_j \beta_j$, $\ln\tilde{w}_j = \ln(w_j/p) - \ln(w_1/p)$, $j,k = 2,\ldots,J$, and

$$\tilde{u} = u\left[1 - \sum_j \beta_j\right] \geq 0. \tag{5.17}$$

As expected, we get Lau's result starting from the translog cost function and imposing homogeneity restrictions on the underlying production function.

For profit maximizing firms operating in a competitive market, returns to scale (r) is less than unity. From the homogeneity of $G(w)$ we get $\sum_j \beta_j = -r/(1-r)$. This implies that $1 - \sum_j \beta_j = (1 + r/(1-r)) = 1/(1-r) > 0$ (because $r < 1$). Because $\tilde{u}$ measures the difference of the log of maximum profit and the log of the actual profit, $100 \times \tilde{u}$ is the percentage by which the profit is foregone due to technical inefficiency. It is worth noting that since $\tilde{u} \neq u$, a 1 percent increase in output-oriented technical efficiency does not translate into a 1 percent increase profit (i.e., $\partial \ln \pi / \partial \ln\{e^{-u}\} \neq 1$). For a marginal change in u, the profit is increased by $\left[1 - \sum_j \beta_j\right] = -\partial \ln \pi / \partial u = 1/(1-r) > 1$ percent. Thus, the higher the value of r, the greater is the potential for profit to be increased from increased efficiency.

One can also measure profit efficiency directly from

$$e^{-\tilde{u}} = \frac{\pi^a}{\pi(\mathbf{w}/p, \mathbf{q})}, \qquad \tilde{u} \geq 0, \tag{5.18}$$

which measures the ratio of actual profit to maximum profit, and has a value between 0 and 1. Assuming π^a is positive, the exact percentage loss of profit can be computed as $\{1 - e^{-\tilde{u}}\} \times 100$. Furthermore, once u is computed from $\tilde{u}$, which is easily done for a homogeneous function, one can compute both profit inefficiency (profit loss) and technical inefficiency (output loss). That is, one can switch from profit loss to output loss and vice versa. However, this may not be that easy once we deal with nonhomogeneous production technologies.

5.3 Estimation Methods: Distribution-Free Approaches

The distribution-free approaches (COLS, thick frontier, etc.) introduced in Sections 3.3 and 4.3 can be applied here with minimal modification, provided that the underlying production function is homogeneous. If not, the profit inefficiency term cannot be assumed to be independent of the data, irrespective of distributional assumption. In this section, we provide an example of the distribution-free approach under the homogeneity assumption.

Example

We estimate a profit frontier function using the dataset `air` that has 274 airline-year observations. This is a subset of the data used in Kumbhakar (1992). The dataset has the following variables: output (`Y`), fuel (`F`), labor (`L`), materials (`MAT`), price of output (`P`), price of fuel (`WF`), price of labor (`WL`), the average stage length (`STAGE`, i.e., the average distance flown per aircraft departure), and the number of points (or destinations) served by an airline (`POINTS`). Note that this is a panel data but in this example we are treating it as a cross section.

The `F` and `L` are variable inputs of the model, and `MAT` is the quasi-fixed input. We assume a translog functional form for the profit function and that the underlying production technology is homogeneous. Following (5.16), the empirical model is

$$\begin{aligned}\ln\left(\frac{PFT}{P}\right) &= \beta_0 + \alpha_1 \ln\left(\frac{WL}{P}\right) + \beta_2 \ln\left(\frac{WF}{P}\right) + \beta_3 \ln(MAT) \\ &\quad + \frac{1}{2}\beta_{22}\left\{\ln\left(\frac{WL}{P}\right) - \ln\left(\frac{WF}{P}\right)\right\}^2 + \frac{1}{2}\gamma_{33}\ln(MAT)^2 \\ &\quad + \delta_{11}\ln(MAT)\left\{\ln\left(\frac{WL}{P}\right) - \ln\left(\frac{WF}{P}\right)\right\} - \tilde{u},\end{aligned} \tag{5.19}$$

where $PFT = P \cdot Y - WL \cdot L - WF \cdot F$ is the profit, and $\tilde{u}$ is the profit loss due to output-oriented technical inefficiency, as defined in (5.17). We use lower-case variables to denote the normalized profit and price variables (i.e., $wl \equiv \ln\left(\frac{WL}{P}\right)$). In addition, `mat` $= \ln($`MAT`$)$, `mat2` $= \frac{1}{2} \times \{\ln(\texttt{MAT})\}^2$, `wl_wk2` $= \frac{1}{2} \times \{\ln(\texttt{WL/WF})\}^2 = \frac{1}{2} \times \{\ln(\texttt{WL/P}) - \ln(\texttt{WF/P})\}^2$, `matwl_wk` $= \ln(\texttt{MAT})\ln(\texttt{WL/WF}) = \ln(\texttt{MAT}) \times \{\ln(\texttt{WL/P}) - \ln(\texttt{WF/P})\}$, `stage` $= \ln(\texttt{STAGE})$, and `points` $= \ln(\texttt{POINTS})$. Note that $\ln(\texttt{WL/WF}) = \ln(\texttt{WL/P}) - \ln(\texttt{WF/P})$. In the example below we do not use `points` or `stage`.

Model 1: OLS

We first estimate the model using OLS and compute the OLS residuals as `e`. The residual may be used to test whether it has the required skewness for a profit frontier model specification.

```
. use air, clear

. global xvar wl wf mat wl_wf2 mat2 matwl_wf
. regress pft $xvar

      Source |       SS       df       MS              Number of obs =     274
-------------+------------------------------           F(  6,   267) = 2541.21
       Model |  428.500462     6  71.4167437           Prob > F      =  0.0000
    Residual |  7.50361247   267  .028103418           R-squared     =  0.9828
-------------+------------------------------           Adj R-squared =  0.9824
       Total |  436.004075   273  1.59708452           Root MSE      =  .16764
```

```
-----------------------------------------------------------------------------
         pft |      Coef.   Std. Err.      t    P>|t|     [95% Conf. Interval]
-------------+---------------------------------------------------------------
          wl |   .6509269   .0820649     7.93   0.000     .4893503    .8125035
          wf |  -.0026366   .0648718    -0.04   0.968    -.1303619    .1250887
         mat |    .860173   .0264289    32.55   0.000     .8081374    .9122086
      wl_wf2 |   .3793603   .0863916     4.39   0.000      .209265    .5494557
        mat2 |  -.0432294   .0191686    -2.26   0.025    -.0809703   -.0054884
    matwl_wf |   .1339831   .0205521     6.52   0.000     .0935182     .174448
       _cons |  -.5365082   .0491742   -10.91   0.000    -.6333268   -.4396896
-----------------------------------------------------------------------------

. predict e, residual
. summarize e, detail

                          Residuals
-------------------------------------------------------------
      Percentiles      Smallest
 1%    -.4038865      -.5495467
 5%    -.2429653      -.5005071
10%    -.2104805      -.4038865       Obs                 274
25%     -.104915      -.3319948       Sum of Wgt.         274

50%    -.0086028                      Mean          -4.80e-11
                        Largest       Std. Dev.      .1657883
75%     .1017255       .3930083
90%     .2176956       .4010837       Variance       .0274858
95%     .2885235       .4213455       Skewness       .0851129
99%     .4010837       .4676737       Kurtosis       3.266128

. sktest e, noadj

                 Skewness/Kurtosis tests for Normality
                                                    ------- joint ------
    Variable |    Obs   Pr(Skewness)   Pr(Kurtosis)    chi2(2)    Prob>chi2
-------------+-------------------------------------------------------------
           e |    274      0.5559         0.2988         1.43        0.4901
```

The skewness measure, $\sqrt{b_1}$, of the OLS residuals is of the wrong sign, as it is positive (+0.0851), but it is not significant. Thus, this result is inconclusive with regard to the presumption of left-skewed residuals of a profit frontier function.

Finally, we save the OLS coefficients in a vector `b0` and the model's log-likelihood value in a scalar `ll_ols`.

```
. matrix b0 = e(b)
. scalar ll_ols = e(ll)
```

Model 2: COLS

The procedure of estimating the model via COLS is similar to that introduced in Sections 3.3 and 4.3. In the code that follows, we calculate the inefficiency measure via the COLS approach, save the results in `eff_cols` and then examine their summary statistics and histogram.

```
. quietly summarize e
. generate double u_star = -(e - r(max))
. generate double eff_cols = exp(-u_star)
. summarize eff_cols

    Variable |       Obs        Mean    Std. Dev.       Min        Max
-------------+--------------------------------------------------------
    eff_cols |       274    .6351402    .1069331   .3615987          1

. label variable eff_cols "Model 2: COLS"
. hist eff_cols, bin(80) saving(eff_cols_pft, replace)
. graph export sing_pft_eff_cols.eps, replace
```

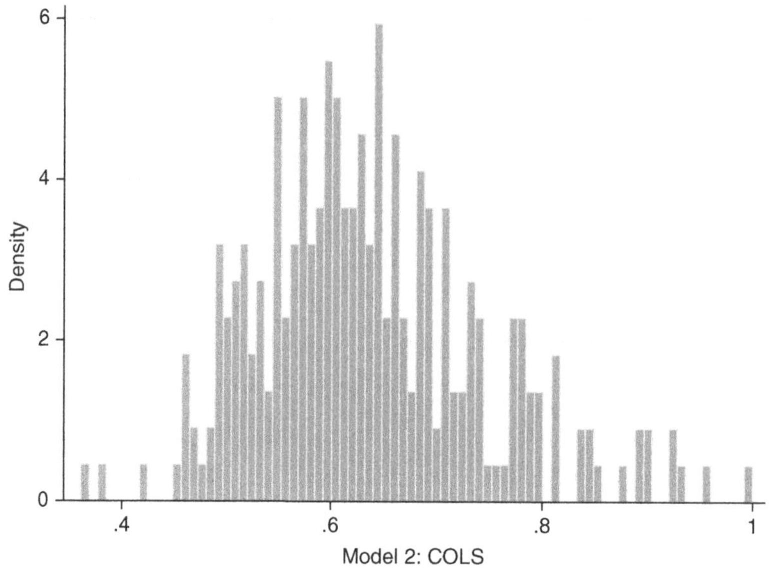

Figure 5.1. Histogram of Inefficiency Index

The results show that, on average, the airlines achieve 63.5 percent of their maximum potential profit. As previously discussed, COLS is highly sensitive to outliers. This does appear to be an issue, though no an extreme one, in this case, as is clear when we plot the estimated inefficiencies in the histogram in Figure 5.1.

5.4 Estimation Methods: Maximum Likelihood Estimators

We may also adopt the parametric approach to estimate the profit frontier model. The approach makes the assumption that u in (5.12) is a random variable of technical inefficiency and adds another random variable (v) to the model for statistical errors. More specifically, the parametric approach estimates the following model:

$$\ln(\pi^a/p) = \frac{-r}{1-r}\ln(w_1/p) + \ln G(\tilde{\boldsymbol{w}}, \boldsymbol{q}) - \frac{1}{1-r}u + v. \tag{5.20}$$

After assuming a parametric functional form on $\ln G(\tilde{\boldsymbol{w}}, \boldsymbol{q})$ and imposing distributional assumptions on u and v, the log-likelihood function of the model may be derived and the parameters are estimated using the maximum likelihood method.

Similarly, the example in (5.16) is easily extended for the parametric estimation by adding v to the model:

$$\ln\left(\frac{\pi^a}{p}\right) = \beta_0 + \alpha_1 \ln(w_1/p) + \sum_j \beta_j \ln(w_j/p) + \sum_q \beta_q \ln q_q + \frac{1}{2}\sum_j\sum_k \beta_{jk} \ln \tilde{w}_j \ln \tilde{w}_k$$
$$+\frac{1}{2}\sum_q\sum_s \gamma_{qs} \ln q_q \ln q_s + \sum_j\sum_q \delta_{jq} \ln \tilde{w}_j \ln q_q - \tilde{u} + v, \qquad j,k = 2,\ldots,J. \tag{5.21}$$

Note that $\ln \tilde{w}_j = \ln(w_j/p) - \ln(w_1/p)$, $j = 1, \ldots, J$. For ease of estimation, we may make distributional assumption on $\tilde{u}$ instead of u. If necessary, values of u may be recovered from estimated values of $\tilde{u}$ after the model is estimated.

Example

Continuing the example of airlines, the translog profit model with the homogeneous production function is

$$\begin{aligned}\ln\left(\frac{PFT}{P}\right) &= \beta_0 + \alpha_1 \ln\left(\frac{WL}{P}\right) + \beta_2 \ln\left(\frac{WF}{P}\right) + \beta_3 \ln(MAT) \\ &+ \frac{1}{2}\beta_{22}\left\{\ln\left(\frac{WL}{P}\right) - \ln\left(\frac{WF}{P}\right)\right\}^2 + \frac{1}{2}\gamma_{33}\ln(MAT)^2 \\ &+ \delta_{11}\ln(MAT)\left\{\ln\left(\frac{WL}{P}\right) - \ln\left(\frac{WF}{P}\right)\right\} - \tilde{u} + v.\end{aligned} \tag{5.22}$$

This is the same as (5.19) except that the random variable v is added and that both of the $\tilde{u}$ and v are assumed to be random variables.

The software introduced for estimating a production frontier model is applicable for estimating profit frontier models. For the `sfmodel` command, the option of `production` should be specified. Recall from page 62, the option `production` tells Stata that the error structure is in the form of $v - u$, $u \geq 0$, while the alternative option of `cost` indicates that the error structure is $v + u$, $u \geq 0$.

Model 3: Half-Normal Model with Heteroscedasticity

Here, we assume $\tilde{u}$ follows a half-normal distribution. We also assume that an airline's inefficiency level is related to the number of points served, `points`, and the average stage length, `stage`. Therefore, the variables `points` and `stage` are included in the model as an exogenous determinants of inefficiency. The following estimation commands use both `sf_init` to supply the initial values, where `b0` is the OLS coefficient vector saved earlier, and `sf_srch` to refine these initial values.

```
. sfmodel pft, prod dist(h) frontier($xvar) usigmas(stage points) vsigmas(stage points)
. sf_init, frontier(b0) usigmas(0 0 0 ) vsigmas(0 0 0)
. sf_srch, n(2) frontier($xvar) usigmas(stage) fast nograph
. ml max, difficult gtol(1e-5) nrtol(1e-5)

(iteration log omitted)
                                                Number of obs    =         274
                                                Wald chi2(6)     =     7650.01
Log likelihood =   119.98513                    Prob > chi2      =      0.0000

------------------------------------------------------------------------------
         pft |      Coef.   Std. Err.      z    P>|z|     [95% Conf. Interval]
-------------+----------------------------------------------------------------
frontier     |
          wl |   .6632369   .0855226     7.76   0.000     .4956157    .8308581
          wf |  -.1098485   .0681971    -1.61   0.107    -.2435124    .0238154
         mat |   .9180782   .0261559    35.10   0.000     .8668136    .9693428
      wl_wf2 |   .1825904    .096936     1.88   0.060    -.0074007    .3725816
        mat2 |   -.026437   .0206071    -1.28   0.200    -.0668261    .0139522
    matwl_wf |   .1096967   .0202139     5.43   0.000     .0700781    .1493153
       _cons |  -.5559805    .069133    -8.04   0.000    -.6914788   -.4204822
-------------+----------------------------------------------------------------
```

```
usigmas      |
       stage |  -.7845427   .6388747    -1.23   0.219    -2.036714    .4676287
      points |    1.53678    .659513     2.33   0.020     .2441586    2.829402
       _cons |  -6.344162   3.514511    -1.81   0.071    -13.23248    .5441542
-------------+----------------------------------------------------------------
vsigmas      |
       stage |   .7174997    .251337     2.85   0.004     .2248883    1.210111
      points |  -1.150832   .2518244    -4.57   0.000    -1.644399   -.6572654
       _cons |  -3.590334   1.469437    -2.44   0.015    -6.470377   -.7102903
------------------------------------------------------------------------------
```

For the variance of u, the estimated function is $\hat{\sigma}_u^2 = \exp(-0.785 \times$ `stage` $+ 1.537 \times$ `points` $- 6.344)$. Similarly, for the variance of v, the estimated function is $\hat{\sigma}_v^2 = \exp(0.717 \times$ `stage` $- 1.151 \times$ `points` $- 3.590)$. Neither of these are easily interpretable, but the marginal effect of `stage` and `points` on $E(\tilde{u})$ and $E(\tilde{v})$ can be computed using `sf_predict`.[6]

```
. sf_predict, bc(bc_h) marginal

The following is the marginal effect on unconditional E(u).

The average marginal effect of stage on uncond E(u) is -.03114806 (see stage_M).
The average marginal effect of points on uncond E(u) is .06101354 (see points_M).

The following is the marginal effect on uncond V(u).

The average marginal effect of stage on uncond V(u) is -.00321511 (see stage_V).
The average marginal effect of points on uncond V(u) is .00629784 (see points_V).
```

The average marginal effect of stage length on the mean of inefficiency is negative (−0.031), implying that increasing the stage length helps reduce profit inefficiency, while the marginal effect of points on the mean of profit inefficiency is positive (0.061), implying that the number of points served increases profit inefficiency. The standard error of the statistic can be bootstrapped (see Appendix D).

The log-likelihood value of the model is saved in the scalar `ll_h`, which is then used in the test against the OLS model. If there is no inefficiency-induced profit loss, the profit frontier model reduces to an OLS model. Therefore, a LR test can provide justification of the frontier approach. The LR test statistics has a mixed chi-square distribution with five degrees of freedom.

```
. scalar ll_h = e(ll)
. display -2*(ll_ols - ll_h)
31.766853

. sf_mixtable, dof(5)
critical values of the mixed chi-square distribution

                        significance level
 dof  |  0.25      0.1       0.05      0.025      0.01      0.005      0.001
---------------------------------------------------------------------------
  5      6.031     8.574     10.371    12.103     14.325    15.968     19.696
source: Table 1, Kodde and Palm (1986, Econometrica).
```

6 A note on the notation: To be precise, the output should use the notation of $E(\tilde{u})$ and $V(\tilde{u})$ instead of $E(u)$ and $V(u)$, respectively, but, because the output is in plain ASCII text, the tilde cannot be shown.

The value of the test statistic is 31.767, which is larger than 19.696 (the 0.1% critical value). Thus, the null hypothesis of an OLS specification is rejected at the 0.1 percent significance level.

We provide a histogram of the estimated profit inefficiencies in Figure 5.2:

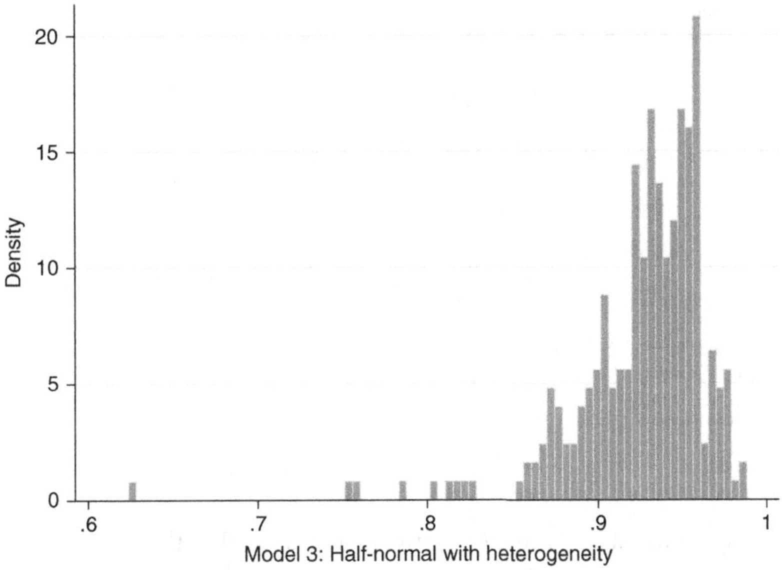

Figure 5.2. Histogram of Inefficiency Index

Model 4: Truncated-Normal Model with Heteroscedasticity

Here, we estimate a heteroscedastic model with `stage` and `points` in μ, σ_u^2, and σ_v^2 of a truncated-normal distribution (Wang [2002]).

```
. sfmodel pft, prod dist(t) frontier($xvar) mu(stage points) usigmas(stage points) vsigmas(stage points)
. sf_init, frontier(b0) mu(0 0 0) usigmas(0 0 0) vsigmas(0 0 0)
. sf_srch, n(2) frontier($xvar) mu(stage points) usigmas(stage points) fast nograph
. ml max, difficult gtol(1e-5) nrtol(1e-5)

(iteration log omitted)

                                                  Number of obs   =        274
                                                  Wald chi2(6)    =    4884.85
Log likelihood =  126.69674                       Prob > chi2     =     0.0000

------------------------------------------------------------------------------
         pft |      Coef.   Std. Err.      z    P>|z|     [95% Conf. Interval]
-------------+----------------------------------------------------------------
frontier     |
          wl |   .6961891   .0847503     8.21   0.000     .5300816    .8622966
          wf |  -.0978201   .0668505    -1.46   0.143    -.2288446    .0332044
         mat |   .9711937    .031272    31.06   0.000     .9099018    1.032486
      wl_wf2 |   .1974914    .093541     2.11   0.035     .0141544    .3808284
        mat2 |   .0031318   .0236771     0.13   0.895    -.0432744    .0495379
    matwl_wf |   .0994359   .0196917     5.05   0.000     .0608409    .1380309
       _cons |  -.4595309   .0809115    -5.68   0.000    -.6181145   -.3009474
```

```
-------------+----------------------------------------------------------------
mu           |
       stage |   .1786889   .0728287     2.45   0.014     .0359473    .3214304
      points |    .070945   .0594494     1.19   0.233    -.0455737    .1874636
       _cons |  -1.356602   .4185356    -3.24   0.001    -2.176916   -.5362871
-------------+----------------------------------------------------------------
usigmas      |
       stage |  -1.729625   .5082548    -3.40   0.001    -2.725786   -.7334637
      points |   1.278886   .7282282     1.76   0.079    -.1484147    2.706187
       _cons |   .2395027   3.035194     0.08   0.937    -5.709368    6.188373
-------------+----------------------------------------------------------------
vsigmas      |
       stage |   .6891896   .2314049     2.98   0.003     .2356444    1.142735
      points |  -1.275533    .257438    -4.95   0.000    -1.780102   -.7709639
       _cons |    -2.9945   1.432217    -2.09   0.037    -5.801594   -.1874056
------------------------------------------------------------------------------

. sf_predict, bc(bc_t) marginal

The following is the marginal effect on unconditional E(u).

The average marginal effect of stage on uncond E(u) is .04236584 (see stage_M).
The average marginal effect of points on uncond E(u) is .07828609 (see points_M).

The following is the marginal effect on uncond V(u).

The average marginal effect of stage on uncond V(u) is -.00509797 (see stage_V).
The average marginal effect of points on uncond V(u) is .00710243 (see points_V).
```

The value of the log-likelihood function of the model is saved in the scalar `ll_t`, which is then used in the test against the OLS model. As in the case of the half-normal model, if there is no inefficiency-induced profit loss, the profit frontier model reduces to an OLS model. Therefore, an LR test can provide justification of the frontier approach. The LR test has a mixed chi-square distribution with eight degrees of freedom.

```
scalar ll_t = e(ll)
display -2*(ll_ols - ll_t)
45.190069

sf_mixtable, dof(8)

critical values of the mixed chi-square distribution

                          significance level
 dof  |  0.25      0.1       0.05      0.025     0.01      0.005     0.001
-----------------------------------------------------------------------------
  8      9.648    12.737    14.853    16.856    19.384    21.232    25.370

source: Table 1, Kodde and Palm (1986, Econometrica).
```

The test statistic is 45.190 which is larger than the 0.1 percent critical value of 25.370. Thus, the null hypothesis of an OLS specification is rejected at the 0.1 percent significance level.

What about the two stochastic models, which is preferred, the truncated or the half-normal model? In this empirical illustration, the half-normal model is nested within the truncated-normal model, so we can test between the two specifications, again, using the likelihood ratio test (here, with three degrees of freedom).

```
display -2*(ll_h - ll_t)
13.423216

sf_mixtable, dof(3)
```

```
critical values of the mixed chi-square distribution

                              significance level
  dof |  0.25      0.1       0.05      0.025      0.01      0.005      0.001
-----------------------------------------------------------------------------
   3     3.475     5.528     7.045     8.542     10.501    11.971     15.357

source: Table 1, Kodde and Palm (1986, Econometrica).
```

The test statistic is 13.423, which is larger than the 0.5 percent critical value of 11.971. Thus, the null hypothesis of a half-normal specification is rejected at the 0.5 percent significance level.

The average marginal effect of `points` on $E(u)$ is positive, indicating that an increase in the number of points served increases inefficiency-induced profit loss. The marginal effects are also uniformly positive across the observations as shown here:

```
summarize points_M, detail

            the marginal effect of points on E(u)
-------------------------------------------------------------
      Percentiles      Smallest
 1%    .0148346        .0112009
 5%    .0255524        .0129852
10%    .0607995        .0148346       Obs                 274
25%    .0703253        .0159213       Sum of Wgt.         274

50%    .0730734                       Mean           .0782861
                       Largest        Std. Dev.      .0252178
75%    .0852483        .1481321
90%    .1098283        .1482311       Variance       .0006359
95%    .1313682        .1483304       Skewness       .2984924
99%    .1482311        .1511858       Kurtosis       4.712624
```

The average marginal effect of `stage` on $E(u)$ is also positive, indicating that an increase in the average stage length increases inefficiency-induced profit loss. The marginal effects, however, are not uniformly positive across the observations as shown here:

```
summarize stage_M, detail

            the marginal effect of stage on E(u)
-------------------------------------------------------------
      Percentiles      Smallest
 1%    -.133952       -.1362383
 5%   -.0995678       -.1348846
10%   -.0833787        -.133952       Obs                 274
25%   -.0380206       -.1335369       Sum of Wgt.         274

50%    .0418403                       Mean           .0423658
                        Largest       Std. Dev.       .095409
75%    .1330438        .1786889
90%    .1774543        .1786889       Variance       .0091029
95%    .1786515        .1786889       Skewness      -.0279528
99%    .1786889        .1786889       Kurtosis       1.759966
```

The relationship between average stage length and profit inefficiency is thus *nonmonotonic*. This is demonstrated clearly in Figure 5.3.

As initially illustrated, increasing the stage length improves profit efficiency, above a certain level further increases in stage length seem to increase the profit inefficiency. However, further increases in stage length changes the profit inefficiency very little.

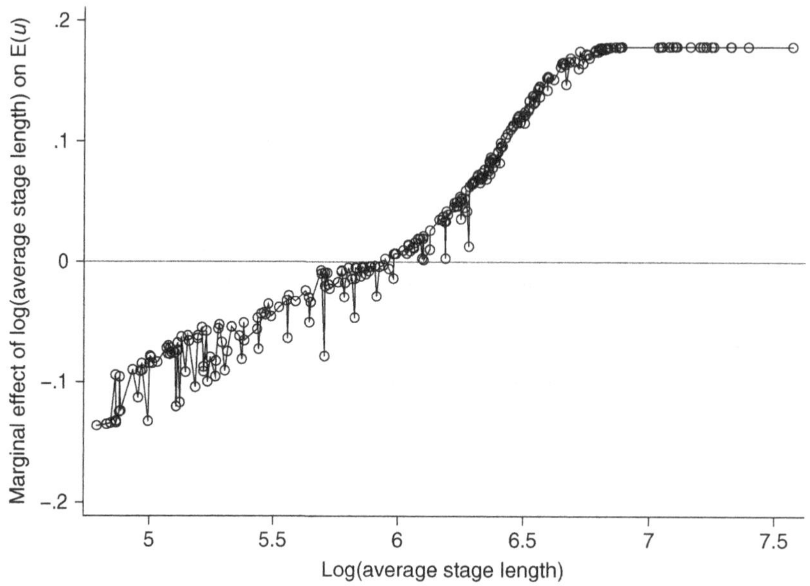

Figure 5.3. Marginal Effects of Stage Length

Models with other specifications on the inefficiency term, such as the KGMHLBC model or the model with the exponential distribution, can also be used for the profit inefficiency estimation. Because the way these models are estimated is essentially the same as that in the previous chapters, we do not provide any further empirical examples here.

We now compare the inefficiency measure computed from the models estimated earlier. The summary statistics are provided here:

```
summarize eff_cols bc_h bc_t

    Variable |       Obs        Mean    Std. Dev.       Min        Max
-------------+--------------------------------------------------------
    eff_cols |       274    .6351402    .1069331   .3615987          1
        bc_h |       274    .9262968    .0405448   .6235358   .9881969
        bc_t |       274    .899420     .0592185   .6058256   .9933191
```

The mean inefficiency is much lower for the COLS model, and the mean efficiency of the truncated-normal model is slightly lower than the half-normal model by about three percentage points.

Kendall's rank correlation coefficients between the indexes and histograms of the efficiency indexes are presented in Table 5.1 and Figure 5.4, respectively. Surprisingly, the correlation coefficients indicate that the *rankings* of the indexes show substantial differences.[7] In addition, the plots show a distinct distribution of COLS's inefficiency measure. The COLS model appears to be affected by an outlier(s) (this may explain both the much lower efficiency estimate and the low correlation).

7 Rankings are usually similar across models.

Table 5.1. *Kendall's Rank Correlation Coefficients* (τ)

	Model 3: Half-normal bc_h	Model 4: Truncated-normal bc_t
Model 2: COLS, eff_cols	0.508	0.393
Model 3: Half-normal, bc_h		0.529

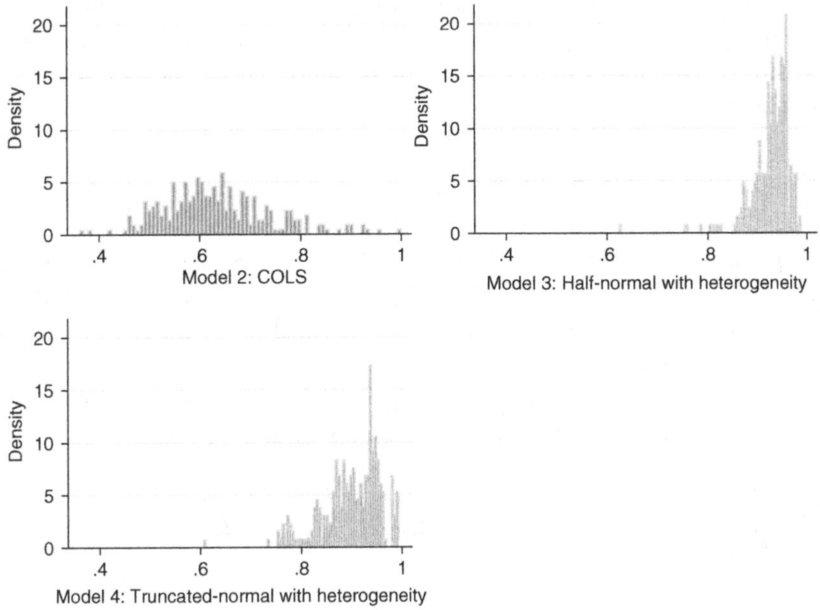

Figure 5.4. Histograms of Efficiency Index

5.5 Input-Oriented Technical Inefficiency

Now we consider profit maximization behavior with input-oriented representation of technical inefficiency, viz.,

$$\max_{y,x} \quad py - \boldsymbol{w}'\boldsymbol{x} \qquad \text{s.t.} \quad y = f(\boldsymbol{x}e^{-\eta}, \boldsymbol{q}), \tag{5.23}$$

for which the FOCs are

$$p \cdot f_j(\boldsymbol{x}e^{-\eta}, \boldsymbol{q})e^{-\eta} = w_j, \tag{5.24}$$

$$f_j(\boldsymbol{x}e^{-\eta}, \boldsymbol{q}) = \frac{w_j e^{\eta}}{p}, \tag{5.25}$$

where $\eta \geq 0$ is the input-oriented technical inefficiency, $\boldsymbol{q}$ is a vector of quasi-fixed inputs, and $f_j(\cdot)$ is the marginal product of x_j (partial derivative of $f(\cdot)$ with respect to x_j).

Note that if we replace $xe^{-\eta}$ by $\tilde{x}$ and we^{η} by $\tilde{w}$, then we are back to the familiar neoclassical framework, that is,

$$\max_{y,\tilde{x}} \quad py - \tilde{\boldsymbol{w}}'\tilde{\boldsymbol{x}} \qquad \text{s.t.} \quad y = f(\tilde{\boldsymbol{x}}, \boldsymbol{q}). \tag{5.26}$$

Solving the system, the input demand of $\tilde{x}_j$ and the output supply of y will both be functions of $\tilde{\boldsymbol{w}}$, p, and $\boldsymbol{q}$. Therefore, the profit function is $\pi(\boldsymbol{w}e^{\eta}, \boldsymbol{q}, p)$, which is also the actual profit, π^a. That is:

$$\pi^a = \pi(\boldsymbol{w}e^{\eta}, \boldsymbol{q}, p) = \pi(\boldsymbol{w}, \boldsymbol{q}, p) \cdot g(\boldsymbol{w}, \boldsymbol{q}, p, \eta), \tag{5.27}$$

$$\Longrightarrow \quad \ln \pi^a = \ln \pi(\boldsymbol{w}, \boldsymbol{q}, p) + \ln g(\boldsymbol{w}, \boldsymbol{q}, p, \eta), \tag{5.28}$$

where $\pi(\boldsymbol{w}, \boldsymbol{q}, p) \equiv \pi(\boldsymbol{w}e^{\eta}, \boldsymbol{q}, p) \mid_{\eta=0}$ is the profit frontier in the absence of technical inefficiency, and $g(\cdot) = \pi(\boldsymbol{w}e^{\eta}, \boldsymbol{q}, p)/\pi(\boldsymbol{w}, \boldsymbol{q}, p) \leq 1$ is profit efficiency.

It can be shown that if the production function is homogeneous, the corresponding profit function can be expressed as

$$\ln \pi^a = \ln \pi(\boldsymbol{w}, \boldsymbol{q}, p) + \ln G(\boldsymbol{w}, \boldsymbol{q}, p, \eta) = \frac{1}{1-r} \ln p + \ln G(\boldsymbol{w}) - \frac{r}{1-r}\eta, \tag{5.29}$$

where $G(\boldsymbol{w}, \boldsymbol{q}, p, \eta)$ is homogeneous of degree $-r/(1-r)$. A comparison of (5.10) and (5.29) shows that $u = r \cdot \eta$. That is, under the assumption of a homogeneous production function, the output-oriented technical inefficiency (u) is equal to the input-oriented technical inefficiency (η) multiplied by returns to scale (r).

Now we consider a translog form on $\pi(\boldsymbol{w}e^{\eta}, \boldsymbol{q}, p)$, and we impose the price homogeneity assumption by normalizing the profit and the price variables by p. The result is

$$\begin{aligned}
\ln\left(\frac{\pi^a}{p}\right) = \ln \pi(\boldsymbol{w}e^{\eta}/p, \boldsymbol{q}) &= \beta_0 + \sum_j \beta_j \ln\left(\frac{w_j}{p}\right) + \sum_q \beta_q \ln q_q \\
&+ \frac{1}{2}\sum_j \sum_k \beta_{jk} \ln\left(\frac{w_j}{p}\right) \ln\left(\frac{w_k}{p}\right) \\
&+ \frac{1}{2}\sum_q \sum_s \gamma_{qs} \ln q_q \ln q_s + \sum_j \sum_q \delta_{jq} \ln\left(\frac{w_j}{p}\right) \ln q_q \\
&+ \left[\sum_j \beta_j + \sum_j \sum_q \delta_{jq} \ln q_q + \sum_j \sum_k \beta_{jk} \ln\left(\frac{w_j}{p}\right)\right] \eta \\
&+ \left[\frac{1}{2}\sum_j \sum_k \beta_{jk}\right] \eta^2.
\end{aligned} \tag{5.30}$$

Without further assumptions, this model is difficult to estimate because both η and η^2 are in the model. If we assume that the underlying production function is homogenous, then additional parameter restrictions apply, viz., $\sum_k \beta_{jk} = 0 \ \forall j$, and $\sum_q \delta_{jq} = 0 \ \forall j$. These restrictions simplify the profit function in (5.30) substantially. The last two lines reduce to $\left[\sum_j \beta_j\right] \eta$. The assumption of homogeneous production function thus simplifies the profit frontier model as follows:

$$\ln\left(\frac{\pi^a}{p}\right) = \ln \pi(\boldsymbol{w}/p, \boldsymbol{q}) - \tilde{\eta}, \tag{5.31}$$

where

$$\tilde{\eta} = -\eta \sum_j \beta_j = \frac{r}{1-r}\eta \geq 0, \tag{5.32}$$

$$\begin{aligned} \ln \pi(\boldsymbol{w}/p, \boldsymbol{q}) &= \beta_0 + \sum_j \beta_j \ln\left(\frac{w_j}{p}\right) + \sum_q \beta_q \ln q_q \\ &+ \frac{1}{2}\sum_j \sum_k \beta_{jk} \ln(\omega_j)\ln(\omega_k) + \frac{1}{2}\sum_q \sum_s \gamma_{qs} \ln q_q \ln q_s. \end{aligned} \tag{5.33}$$

In the above expression $\omega_j = \frac{w_j/p}{w_J/p} = \frac{w_j}{w_J}$ and $\omega_k = \frac{w_k/p}{w_J/p} = \frac{w_k}{w_J}$.

As shown in (5.11) and (5.31), the profit functions associated with OO and IO technical inefficiency are observationally equivalent. Note that $\ln G(\boldsymbol{w}/p, \boldsymbol{q})$ in (5.11) is the same as $\ln \pi(\boldsymbol{w}/p, \boldsymbol{q})$ in (5.31).

The effect of IO technical inefficiency on profit can be measured using $\tilde{\eta}$ and $\exp(-\tilde{\eta})$, as we have seen in other cases. That is, $100 \times \tilde{\eta}$ gives the percentage of profit loss due to the technical inefficiency. Again, because $\tilde{\eta} \neq \eta$, a 1 percent decrease in input-oriented technical inefficiency does not translate into 1 percent increase in profit (i.e., $\partial \ln \pi / \partial \ln\{(\eta)\} \neq 1$). The percentage increase in profit is $r/(1-r) \gtreqless 1$ depending on the value of the returns to scale parameter, r. Instead of measuring inefficiency, one can measure of profit efficiency from $\exp(-\tilde{\eta})$, which is the ratio of actual to maximum profit.

We have noted the difference (in interpretation) between input- and output-oriented measures of technical inefficiency. Similar differences are observed if one examines their impact on profit. However, it is important to remind the reader that it does not matter whether one uses the input or the output-oriented measure. The estimation is exactly the same regardless of the inefficiency orientation. Furthermore, one can switch from u to η and vice versa. This will not be so simple once we move from the homogeneous to nonhomogeneous production technology. We deal with these issues in Section 7.6.

5.6 Estimation Methods: Distribution-Free Approaches

As shown earlier, the profit frontier models of output-oriented technical inefficiency and the input-oriented technical inefficiency are observationally equivalent. As such, we do not present any further examples beyond those provided in the previous section.

5.7 Estimation Methods: Maximum Likelihood Estimators

For the distributional-based MLE approach, we (i) assume the production function is homogeneous, (ii) normalize the profit and prices by p, and (iii) append a statistical error term v to the model. The result is

$$\ln\left(\frac{\pi^a}{p}\right) = \ln \pi(\boldsymbol{w}/p, \boldsymbol{q}) - \tilde{\eta} + v, \tag{5.34}$$

where $\tilde{\eta}$ and $\ln \pi(\boldsymbol{w}/p, \boldsymbol{q})$ are defined in (5.32) and (5.33).

After imposing distributional assumptions on $\tilde{\eta}$ and v, the likelihood function of the model can be derived. The estimation methods introduced for the production frontier models are suitable for estimating this model. Parameters of η can be recovered from parameters of $\tilde{\eta}$ after the model is estimated.

Again, given the observational equivalence, we do not present any further examples beyond those provide in the previous section.

PART III

SYSTEM MODELS WITH CROSS-SECTIONAL DATA

6

Estimation of Technical Efficiency in Cost Frontier Models Using System Models with Cross-Sectional Data

6.1 Introduction

In this chapter, we consider cases where outputs are exogenously given to a firm. Recall that, in Chapter 4, we introduced the cost frontier, which gives the minimum cost of producing any exogenously given level of output. A cost-minimizing firm chooses the levels of inputs in order to produce the given level of output with the lowest possible cost. When output and input prices are exogenously given to a firm, cost minimization is equivalent to profit maximization. Because inputs are endogenous in the cost minimization framework, input-oriented (as opposed to output-oriented) technical inefficiency is usually chosen as the preferred approach to model technical inefficiency.

In the standard neoclassical context, Christensen and Greene (1976) proposed using a system approach, consisting of the cost function and the cost share equations, to estimate the cost function parameters. Here we consider a similar system, but we allow producers to be technically inefficient. That is, compared to the cost function introduced in Chapter 4, which consists of only the cost function adjusted for technical inefficiency (see, for example, equation (4.15)), here we include the cost share equations and form a system to estimate the cost function parameters. The use of these share equations does not require any additional assumption, and the share equations do not contain any new parameter that is not in the cost function (other than the parameters associated with the errors in the cost share equations). Thus, the additional information provided by these share equations helps in estimating the parameters more precisely. (As such, this chapter does not provide new tools to answer additional questions; the questions that can be answered are the same as those set out at the start of Chapter 4. However, we use a different empirical example in this chapter: the examples used throughout this chapter examine U.S. commercial airlines.)

In addition to the efficiency gain in the parameter estimates, the inclusion of the share equations in the estimation has one important advantage in the current context: Residuals of the share equations may be interpreted as allocative inefficiency (or functions of them). This issue will be discussed in Chapter 8.

6.2 Single Output, Input-Oriented Technical Inefficiency

The derivation of the model is very similar to that given in Chapter 4 where we provide the details on the derivations. Here we only sketch the derivation while emphasizing the differences.

Following the common notation convention, a producer's cost minimization problem with input-oriented technical inefficiency is

$$\min_{\boldsymbol{x}} \ \boldsymbol{w}'\boldsymbol{x} \quad \text{s.t.} \quad y = f(\boldsymbol{x}e^{-\eta}), \tag{6.1}$$

which gives the following first-order conditions (FOCs):

$$\text{FOCs:} \qquad \frac{f_j(\boldsymbol{x}e^{-\eta})}{f_1(\boldsymbol{x}e^{-\eta})} = \frac{w_j}{w_1}, \quad j = 2, \ldots, J, \tag{6.2}$$

where $\eta \geq 0$ is the input-oriented technical inefficiency, and $f_j(\cdot)$ is the partial derivative of $f(\cdot)$ with respect to x_j.

The $J - 1$ FOCs in (6.2) with the production function in (6.1) can be used to solve for J input demand functions in the form $x_j e^{-\eta}, j = 1, \ldots, J$. That is, $x_j e^{-\eta}$ becomes a function of $\boldsymbol{w}$ and y, viz., $x_j e^{-\eta} = \psi_j(\boldsymbol{w}, y)$. We can use these to define the pseudo cost function given $\boldsymbol{w}$ and y as

$$C^*(\boldsymbol{w}, y) = \sum_j w_j x_j e^{-\eta}, \tag{6.3}$$

which can be viewed as the minimum cost function for the following problem:

$$\min_{\boldsymbol{x}e^{-\eta}} \ \boldsymbol{w}'\boldsymbol{x}e^{-\eta} \quad \text{s.t.} \quad y = f(\boldsymbol{x}e^{-\eta}). \tag{6.4}$$

The $C^*(\cdot)$ function is also the *frontier cost function*, which gives the minimum cost to produce the observed level of output, y, given the input prices, $\boldsymbol{w}$. Due to technical inefficiency, the observed input use ($\boldsymbol{x}$) is *too high*, in the sense that a fully efficient producer can produce the same level of output with less inputs. The efficient input use would be $\boldsymbol{x}e^{-\eta}$, which is less than the observed input $\boldsymbol{x}$ (since $0 \leq e^{-\eta} \leq 1$), and the efficient minimum cost would be $\boldsymbol{w}'\boldsymbol{x}e^{-\eta}$, which is less than the actual cost $\boldsymbol{w}'\boldsymbol{x}$.

We apply Shephard's lemma to (6.3), that is,

$$\frac{\partial C^*}{\partial w_j} = x_j e^{-\eta}, \tag{6.5}$$

$$\Longrightarrow \qquad \frac{\partial \ln C^*}{\partial \ln w_j} = \frac{w_j x_j e^{-\eta}}{C^*}. \tag{6.6}$$

Because the actual cost is $C^a = \sum_j w_j x_j = e^{\eta} \sum_j w_j x_j e^{-\eta} = C^* e^{\eta}$, we have

$$\ln C^a(\boldsymbol{w}, y, \eta) = \ln C^*(\boldsymbol{w}, y) + \eta, \tag{6.7}$$

and the actual cost share S_j of input j is

$$S_j = \frac{w_j x_j}{C^a} = \frac{w_j x_j}{C^* e^{\eta}} = \frac{\partial \ln C^*}{\partial \ln w_j}, \quad j = 1, \ldots, J. \tag{6.8}$$

In Chapter 4, the cost frontier model is based on (6.7) alone. For the purpose of estimating model parameters, a system of equations is formed consisting of (6.7) and the $J - 1$ share equations from (6.8). We drop one of the share equations (it does not matter which one) and include only $J - 1$ of them because $\sum_j S_j = 1$ by construction. A random statistical error, ζ_j, is also added to the jth share equation $j = 2, \ldots, J$ for estimation purposes. The system of equations is thus

$$\ln C^a(\boldsymbol{w}, y, \eta) = \ln C^*(\boldsymbol{w}, y) + \eta, \tag{6.9}$$

$$S_j = \frac{\partial \ln C^*}{\partial w_j} + \zeta_j, \qquad j = 2, \ldots, J. \tag{6.10}$$

It is worth pointing out here that we do not give ζ_j a structural interpretation except that it is a statistical error. In Chapter 8, we will show that ζ_j can be interpreted as a function of allocative inefficiency . For now, we assume that every producer is allocatively efficient.

Because the cost function is homogeneous of degree 1 in input prices, the parameters in (6.9) and (6.10) need to satisfy the homogeneity property. In addition, because the derivative of $\ln C^*(\boldsymbol{w}, y)$ appears on the right-hand side of (6.10) and thus the parameters of $\ln C^*(\boldsymbol{w}, y)$ also appear in (6.10), cross-equation constraints on the parameters of (6.9) and (6.10) have to be imposed in the estimation process.

Notice that the share equations in (6.10) introduce no new parameter to the model except those associated with ζ_i's which are *usually* not of interest. If only technical inefficiency is considered, the advantage of estimating the system of equations in (6.9) and (6.10), as opposed to the single equation in (6.9), is the gain in efficiency (i.e., more precise parameter estimates). The gain, however, comes at a cost which involves the estimation of a complicated system. By contrast, if both technical and allocative inefficiency are considered in the model and one wants to decompose technical and allocative inefficiency, it is necessary to use the system equation approach. We will discuss the cost frontier model with both technical and allocative inefficiency in Chapter 8.

An Illustration

Consider a model in which some inputs are quasi-fixed ($\boldsymbol{q}$), so that the cost function is $C^*(\boldsymbol{w}, \boldsymbol{q}, y)$. Assuming a translog specification, the cost system consists of the following equations:

$$\begin{aligned}
\ln C^a &= \ln C^*(\boldsymbol{w}, \boldsymbol{q}, y) + \eta \\
&= \beta_0 + \sum_j \beta_j \ln w_j + \sum_r \gamma_r \ln q_r + \beta_y \ln y \\
&\quad + \frac{1}{2}\left[\sum_j \sum_k \beta_{jk} \ln w_j \ln w_k + \sum_r \sum_s \gamma_{rs} \ln q_r \ln q_s + \beta_{yy} \ln y \ln y\right] \\
&\quad + \sum_j \sum_r \delta_{jr} \ln w_j \ln q_r + \sum_j \beta_{jy} \ln w_j \ln y + \sum_r \gamma_{ry} \ln q_r \ln y + \eta,
\end{aligned} \tag{6.11}$$

$$S_j = \beta_j + \sum_k \beta_{jk} \ln w_k + \sum_r \delta_{jr} \ln q_r + \beta_{jy} \ln y + \zeta_j, \qquad j = 2, \ldots, J. \tag{6.12}$$

The symmetry property require that $\beta_{jk} = \beta_{kj}$, and $\gamma_{rs} = \gamma_{sr}$. The cost function is homogeneous of degree 1 in input prices (i.e., $w_1, \ldots, w_J$), and so the following restrictions apply:

$$\sum_j \beta_j = 1, \qquad \sum_j \beta_{jk} = 0, \ \forall\, k, \qquad \sum_j \beta_{jy} = 0. \tag{6.13}$$

These constraints can be substituted into the model so that the homogeneity conditions are automatically satisfied. This procedure amounts to using one of the input prices to normalize cost and other input prices. Using w_1 as our normalizing price, we obtain

$$
\begin{aligned}
\ln\left(\frac{C^a}{w_1}\right) &= \ln C^*\left(\frac{\boldsymbol{w}}{w_1}, \boldsymbol{q}, y\right) + \eta \\
&= \beta_0 + \sum_{j=2} \beta_j \ln\left(\frac{w_j}{w_1}\right) + \sum_r \gamma_r \ln q_r + \beta_y \ln y \\
&\quad + \frac{1}{2}\left[\sum_{j=2}\sum_{k=2} \beta_{jk} \ln\left(\frac{w_j}{w_1}\right) \ln\left(\frac{w_k}{w_1}\right) + \sum_r\sum_s \gamma_{rs} \ln q_r \ln q_s + \beta_{yy} \ln y \ln y\right] \\
&\quad + \sum_{j=2}\sum_r \delta_{jr} \ln\left(\frac{w_j}{w_1}\right) \ln q_r + \sum_{j=2} \beta_{jy} \ln\left(\frac{w_j}{w_1}\right) \ln y + \sum_r \gamma_{ry} \ln q_r \ln y + \eta,
\end{aligned} \tag{6.14}
$$

$$
S_j = \beta_j + \sum_{k=2} \beta_{jk} \ln\left(\frac{w_k}{w_1}\right) + \sum_r \delta_{jr} \ln q_r + \beta_{jy} \ln y + \zeta_j, \qquad j = 2, \ldots, J, \tag{6.15}
$$

where S_j is computed from data as $(w_j x_j)/C^a$. Notice that there are no new parameters in (6.15). The parameters β_j, β_{jk}'s, δ_{jr}'s, and β_{jy} have already appeared in (6.14).

Three Variable Inputs and One Quasi-Fixed Input

The system of equations with three variable inputs and one quasi-fixed input is as follows.

$$
\begin{aligned}
\ln\left(\frac{C^a}{w_1}\right) &= \beta_0 + \beta_2 \ln\left(\frac{w_2}{w_1}\right) + \beta_3 \ln\left(\frac{w_3}{w_1}\right) + \gamma_q \ln q + \beta_y \ln y \\
&\quad + \frac{1}{2}\left[\beta_{22} \ln\left(\frac{w_2}{w_1}\right)^2 + \beta_{33} \ln\left(\frac{w_3}{w_1}\right)^2 + \gamma_{qq} \ln q^2 + \beta_{yy} \ln y^2\right] \\
&\quad + \beta_{23} \ln\left(\frac{w_2}{w_1}\right) \ln\left(\frac{w_3}{w_1}\right) + \delta_{2q} \ln\left(\frac{w_2}{w_1}\right) \ln q + \beta_{2y} \ln\left(\frac{w_2}{w_1}\right) \ln y \\
&\quad + \delta_{3q} \ln\left(\frac{w_3}{w_1}\right) \ln q + \beta_{3y} \ln\left(\frac{w_3}{w_1}\right) \ln y + \gamma_{qy} \ln q \ln y + \eta,
\end{aligned} \tag{6.16}
$$

$$
S_2 = \beta_2 + \beta_{22} \ln\left(\frac{w_2}{w_1}\right) + \beta_{23} \ln\left(\frac{w_3}{w_1}\right) + \delta_{2q} \ln q + \beta_{2y} \ln y + \zeta_2, \tag{6.17}
$$

$$
S_3 = \beta_3 + \beta_{23} \ln\left(\frac{w_2}{w_1}\right) + \beta_{33} \ln\left(\frac{w_3}{w_1}\right) + \delta_{3q} \ln q + \beta_{3y} \ln y + \zeta_3, \tag{6.18}
$$

where $S_2 = (w_2 x_2)/C^a$ and $S_3 = (w_3 x_3)/C^a$.

6.3 Estimation Methods: Distribution-Free Approach

To estimate the system in (6.9) and (6.10), we choose a functional form of $\ln C^*(\cdot)$ and impose the price homogeneity conditions on it. In the case of a translog function, the system consists of (6.14) and (6.15).

The distribution-free approach does not impose any distributional assumptions on η and ζ_j's. In Chapter 4 where the cost frontier model is estimated based on the single cost function, the COLS method amounts to estimating the equation by OLS and then adjusting the OLS residuals to obtain the inefficiency index. Here, one can estimate the system consisting of (6.9) and (6.10) (treating η as the zero-mean random error in the equation) using the seemingly unrelated regression equations (SURE) approach and adjust $\hat{\eta}$ afterward to obtain the inefficiency index.

The method of adjustment used to obtain the inefficiency index is essentially the same as the one we introduced in Chapter 4. In particular, suppose that, after the SURE estimation, the residual corresponding to the cost function is (the observation subscript i is dropped)

$$\hat{\eta} = \ln C^a - \ln \hat{C}^*(\mathbf{w}, y) \gtreqless 0. \tag{6.19}$$

We then adjust the intercept downward by the amount of $\min\{\hat{\eta}\}$, so that the adjusted function bounds observations from below:

$$\hat{\eta} - \min\{\hat{\eta}\} = \ln C^a - \underbrace{\left\{\ln \hat{C}^*(\mathbf{w}, y) + \min\{\hat{\eta}\}\right\}}_{\text{estimated frontier function}} \geq 0, \tag{6.20}$$

and that

$$\hat{\eta}^* \equiv \hat{\eta} - \min\{\hat{\eta}\} \geq 0, \tag{6.21}$$

where $\hat{\eta}^*$ is the estimated inefficiency. Technical efficiency of each observation can then be calculated as

$$\widehat{TE} = \exp(-\hat{\eta}^*). \tag{6.22}$$

Note that, by construction, estimated inefficiency will be 0 for one observation (namely, the best firm) and thus the efficiency of the best firm is 1.

Example

We consider a cost frontier model of U.S. commercial airlines. (Note that this is a different dataset to the one used in Chapter 5.) The model has three variable inputs: labor, fuel, and capital, and the output is an index of passengers and cargo. The cost is the sum of the costs of three inputs.

The dataset used is `airline`, which has the following variables: `TC` represents total cost; `Y` represents output; `PL`, `PF`, and `PK` represent the price of labor, fuel, and capital, respectively; and `sl`, `sf`, and `sk` represent the cost shares of labor, fuel, and capital, respectively. Again, while this is a panel dataset, in this example we are treating it as a cross section of 232 observations.

A translog specification of the cost function is used, and the price of fuel is used to normalize `TC`, `PK`, and `PL` so that the input price homogeneity restrictions are automatically imposed. After loading the data, we define lower-case variables as the log of the normalized upper-case (level) variables.

```
. use airline

. generate double tc     =     ln(TC/PF)
. generate double pl     =     ln(PL/PF)
. generate double pk     =     ln(PK/PF)
. generate double y      =     ln(Y)
. generate double plpl2  =     0.5*pl*pl
. generate double pkpk2  =     0.5*pk*pk
. generate double yy2    =     0.5*y*y
. generate double plpk   =     pl*pk
. generate double ply    =     pl*y
. generate double pky    =     pk*y
```

Using these defined variables, the model to be estimated is

$$\begin{aligned} tc = \beta_0 + \beta_1 pl + \beta_2 pk + \beta_y y + \left[\beta_{11} plpl2 + \beta_{22} pkpk2 + \beta_{yy} yy2\right] \\ + \beta_{12} plpk + \beta_{1y} ply + \beta_{2y} pky + \eta, \end{aligned} \quad (6.23)$$

$$sl = \beta_1 + \beta_{11} pl + \beta_{12} pk + \beta_{1y} y + \zeta_1, \quad (6.24)$$

$$sk = \beta_2 + \beta_{12} pl + \beta_{22} pk + \beta_{2y} y + \zeta_2. \quad (6.25)$$

Notice that the beta coefficients in (6.24) and (6.25) also appear in (6.23), and so cross-equation constraints on the parameters need to be imposed in the estimation process.

For convenience, we put the regression variables in macros.

```
. global xvar pl pk y plpl2 pkpk2 yy2 plpk ply pky  /* frontier variables */
. global svar pl pk y  /* share equation variables */
```

Model 1: SURE

Assuming η to be a zero-mean random variable, the model is a standard SURE system and can be estimated by the SURE approach. The results from it can be used as a benchmark against which the presence of inefficiency can be tested. Estimates from SURE also provide good initial values for the ML estimation.

We first make a list of the cross-equation parameter constraints implied by (6.23) to (6.25).

```
. constraint define 1 [share1]_b[_cons] =  [frontier]_b[pl]
. constraint define 2 [share1]_b[y]     =  [frontier]_b[ply]
. constraint define 3 [share1]_b[pk]    =  [frontier]_b[plpk]
. constraint define 4 [share1]_b[pl]    =  [frontier]_b[plpl2]

. constraint define 5 [share2]_b[_cons] =  [frontier]_b[pk]
. constraint define 6 [share2]_b[y]     =  [frontier]_b[pky]
. constraint define 7 [share2]_b[pk]    =  [frontier]_b[pkpk2]
. constraint define 8 [share2]_b[pl]    =  [frontier]_b[plpk]
```

We used `frontier` to refer to (6.23), `share1` for the share equation (6.24), and `share2` for the share equation (6.25).

We now run the SURE model.

```
. sureg (frontier: tc=$xvar) (share1: sl=$svar) (share2: sk=$svar), isure constraints(1-8)

(iteration log omitted)

Seemingly unrelated regression, iterated

Constraints:
 ( 1) - [frontier]pl + [share1]_cons = 0
 ( 2) - [frontier]ply + [share1]y = 0
 ( 3) - [frontier]plpk + [share1]pk = 0
 ( 4) - [frontier]plpl2 + [share1]pl = 0
 ( 5) - [frontier]pk + [share2]_cons = 0
 ( 6) - [frontier]pky + [share2]y = 0
 ( 7) - [frontier]pkpk2 + [share2]pk = 0
 ( 8) - [frontier]plpk + [share2]pl = 0
----------------------------------------------------------------------
Equation          Obs  Parms        RMSE    "R-sq"       chi2        P
----------------------------------------------------------------------
frontier          232      9    .8771019    0.5869  428681.31   0.0000
share1            232      3    .0413892    0.3452     106.58   0.0000
share2            232      3    .0356767    0.1328     435.46   0.0000
----------------------------------------------------------------------
```

```
------------------------------------------------------------------------------
             |      Coef.   Std. Err.      z    P>|z|     [95% Conf. Interval]
-------------+----------------------------------------------------------------
frontier     |
          pl |   .3207771   .0043647    73.49   0.000     .3122224    .3293319
          pk |   .4164399   .0045285    91.96   0.000     .4075642    .4253156
           y |   .8719786   .1191187     7.32   0.000     .6385103    1.105447
       plpl2 |   .0375639   .0085774     4.38   0.000     .0207525    .0543753
       pkpk2 |   .0885465   .0084757    10.45   0.000     .0719344    .1051586
         yy2 |    .042563   .0868079     0.49   0.624    -.1275774    .2127034
        plpk |  -.0095344   .0076771    -1.24   0.214    -.0245812    .0055124
         ply |  -.0143988   .0021987    -6.55   0.000    -.0187082   -.0100894
         pky |   .0060598   .0019424     3.12   0.002     .0022527    .0098669
       _cons |   2.370457   .0746263    31.76   0.000     2.224193    2.516722
-------------+----------------------------------------------------------------
share1       |
          pl |   .0375639   .0085774     4.38   0.000     .0207525    .0543753
          pk |  -.0095344   .0076771    -1.24   0.214    -.0245812    .0055124
           y |  -.0143988   .0021987    -6.55   0.000    -.0187082   -.0100894
       _cons |   .3207771   .0043647    73.49   0.000     .3122224    .3293319
-------------+----------------------------------------------------------------
share2       |
          pl |  -.0095344   .0076771    -1.24   0.214    -.0245812    .0055124
          pk |   .0885465   .0084757    10.45   0.000     .0719344    .1051586
           y |   .0060598   .0019424     3.12   0.002     .0022527    .0098669
       _cons |   .4164399   .0045285    91.96   0.000     .4075642    .4253156
------------------------------------------------------------------------------
```

As in the case of a single equation model, the skewness of the residuals from the main equation is informative in revealing the existence of inefficiency without actually estimating an inefficiency model. If cost inefficiency is present in the data, the distribution of residuals from the main equation should skew to the right with statistical significance. The test is a straightforward application of the result from Schmidt and Lin (1984).

```
. predict e, residual equation(frontier)
. summarize e, detail
                     Residuals: frontier
-------------------------------------------------------------
      Percentiles      Smallest
 1%    -1.369487      -1.501989
 5%    -1.190056      -1.401386
10%    -1.078746      -1.369487       Obs                 232
25%    -.6927396       -1.36263       Sum of Wgt.         232

50%    -.1322182                      Mean            .000084
                        Largest       Std. Dev.      .8789984
75%     .6240617       2.272367
90%     1.190318       2.500227       Variance       .7726381
95%     1.599636       2.555193       Skewness       .5579464
99%     2.500227       2.606183       Kurtosis       2.767634

. sktest, noadj

                   Skewness/Kurtosis tests for Normality
                                                     ------- joint ------
    Variable |    Obs   Pr(Skewness)   Pr(Kurtosis) adj chi2(2)    Prob>chi2
-------------+---------------------------------------------------------------
           e |    232      0.0008         0.5375        11.67         0.0029
```

The skewness (a value of 0.5579) is statistically significant, thereby supporting the presence of inefficiency. Before we proceed further, we save the log-likelihood value of the model, and also extract the coefficient vectors for later use.

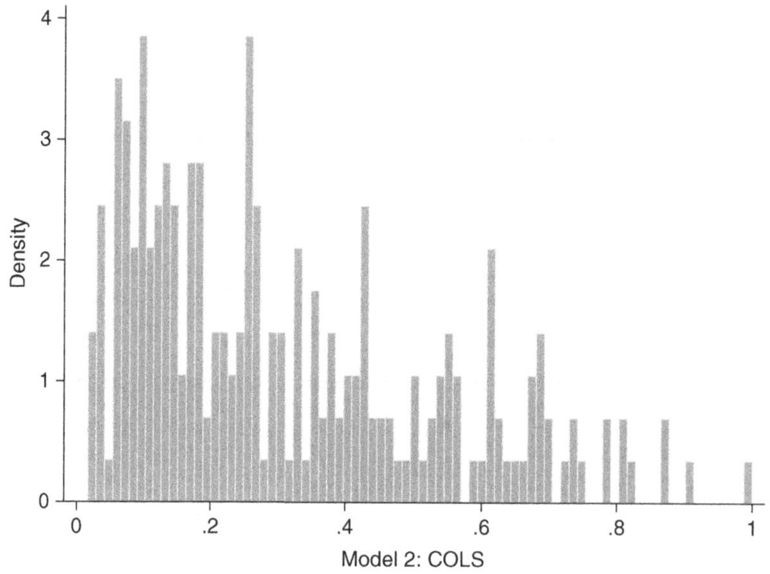

Figure 6.1. Histogram of Inefficiency Index

```
. scalar ll_sure = e(ll)
. matrix b0 = e(b)
. matrix b0_f = b0[1, "frontier:"]
. matrix b0_s1 = b0[1, "share1:"]
. matrix b0_s2 = b0[1, "share2:"]
```

Model 2: COLS

Following the SURE estimation, the code below obtains the efficiency of each observation via the COLS approach and then saves the efficiency index in `eff_cols`.

```
. quietly summarize e          /* obtain summary statistics of the residual */
. generate double eta_stat = (e - r(min))  /* double is used for extra accuracy */
. generate double eff_cols = exp(-eta_stat) /* the efficiency index */
. summarize eff_cols

    Variable |       Obs        Mean    Std. Dev.       Min        Max
-------------+--------------------------------------------------------
    eff_cols |       232    .3069178    .2232586   .0164378          1
```

We plot the histogram of the inefficiency index from this model in Figure 6.1.

6.4 Estimation Methods: Maximum Likelihood Estimators

In estimating this cost function using OLS, we treated technical inefficiency (η) as the noise term. Now we separate it from the noise terms, v, which is added to the (log) cost frontier function. The two error components are identified by imposing distributional assumptions on them. The likelihood function can be derived based on the distributional assumptions, and model parameters are then estimated numerically by maximizing the log-likelihood function. Following this approach, the system of equations is

$$\ln C^a = \ln C^*(\boldsymbol{w}, y) + \eta + v, \tag{6.26}$$

$$S_j = \frac{\partial \ln C^*}{\partial \ln w_j} + \zeta_j, \qquad j = 2, \ldots, J. \tag{6.27}$$

If the translog specification is adopted, then the system of equations become

$$\begin{aligned}
\ln\left(\frac{C^a}{w_1}\right) &= \ln C^*(\boldsymbol{w}/w_1, \boldsymbol{q}, y) + \eta + v \\
&= \beta_0 + \sum_{j=2} \beta_j \ln\left(\frac{w_j}{w_1}\right) + \sum_r \gamma_r \ln q_r + \beta_y \ln y \\
&\quad + \frac{1}{2}\left[\sum_{j=2}\sum_{k=2} \beta_{jk} \ln\left(\frac{w_j}{w_1}\right)\ln\left(\frac{w_k}{w_1}\right) + \sum_r\sum_s \gamma_{rs} \ln q_r \ln q_s + \beta_{yy} \ln y \ln y\right] \\
&\quad + \sum_{j=2}\sum_r \delta_{jr} \ln\left(\frac{w_j}{w_1}\right)\ln q_r + \sum_{j=2} \beta_{jy} \ln\left(\frac{w_j}{w_1}\right)\ln y + \sum_r \gamma_{ry} \ln q_r \ln y + \eta + v,
\end{aligned} \tag{6.28}$$

$$S_j = \beta_j + \sum_{k=2} \beta_{jk} \ln\left(\frac{w_k}{w_1}\right) + \sum_r \delta_{jr} \ln q_r + \beta_{jy} \ln y + \zeta_j, \qquad j = 2, \ldots, J. \tag{6.29}$$

This system is similar to (6.14) and (6.15). The difference is in the added v term.

We use the following distribution assumptions on the noise and inefficiency terms:

$$\begin{aligned}
\eta &\sim N^+(0, \sigma_u^2), \\
\boldsymbol{\xi} &\sim N(\boldsymbol{0}, \Omega),
\end{aligned} \tag{6.30}$$

where $N^+(\cdot)$ indicates the positive truncation of the underlying normal distribution and Ω is the $J \times J$ covariance matrix of $\boldsymbol{\xi} = (v, \zeta_2, \ldots, \zeta_J)'$. The elements of ξ are assumed to be independent of η.

Denote $Z = d\eta + \boldsymbol{\xi}$ where $d = (1, 0, \ldots, 0)'$, which is a column vector of $J \times 1$. Based on the above distributional assumptions on η and $\boldsymbol{\xi}$, the log-likelihood function for a sample of N firms can then be written as (Kumbhakar [2001])

$$\begin{aligned}
\mathcal{L} &= N \ln 2 - NJ/2 \ln(2\pi) - N/2 \ln|\Omega| + N \ln \sigma + \sum_i \Phi(Z_i'\Omega^{-1} d\sigma) \\
&\quad - N \ln \sigma_u ?(1/2) \sum_i a_i,
\end{aligned} \tag{6.31}$$

where i is a firm subscript, $\sigma^2 = (1/\sigma_u^2 + d'\Omega^{-1}d)^{-1}, a_i = Z_i'\Omega^{-1}Z_i - \sigma^2(Z_i'\Omega^{-1}d)^2$, and $\Phi(\cdot)$ is the cumulative distribution function of a standard normal variable.

Derivation of this log-likelihood function follows the usual procedure. Because both η and $\boldsymbol{\xi}$ are *i.i.d.* across firms, we drop the firm subscript in the following derivation. The pdf of Z, $f(Z)$, can be expressed as

$$f(Z) = \int_0^\infty f(Z, \eta) d\eta = \int_0^\infty f(Z|\eta) h(\eta) d\eta, \tag{6.32}$$

where $f(Z, \eta)$ is the joint pdf of Z and η, and $h(\eta)$ is the pdf of η. Using the distributional assumptions on η and $\boldsymbol{\xi}$, the above integral can be expressed as

$$f(Z) = \frac{2}{(2\pi)^{(J+1)/2}|\Omega|^{1/2}\sigma_u} \int_0^{\infty} \exp\left\{-\frac{1}{2}[(Z - d\eta)'\Omega^{-1}(Z - d\eta) + \eta^2/\sigma_u^2]\right\} d\eta$$

$$= \frac{2\sigma \exp(-a/2)}{(2\pi)^{(J/2)}|\Omega|^{1/2}\sigma_u} \Phi(Z'\Omega^{-1}d\sigma). \tag{6.33}$$

The log-likelihood function in (6.31) is the sum (over N firms) of $\ln f(Z)$. This likelihood function is derived allowing arbitrary correlations among all the error terms, that is, v and ξ_j are freely correlated. We consider some special cases of this by imposing constrains on Ω. For example, if

$$\Omega = \begin{pmatrix} \sigma_v^2 & \mathbf{0} \\ \mathbf{0}' & \Sigma \end{pmatrix}, \tag{6.34}$$

then the error in the cost function is uncorrelated with the errors in the cost share equations $\boldsymbol{\zeta}$ for which the variance covariance matrix is Σ. Furthermore, if Σ is diagonal then all the errors are independent of each other.

Maximization of the log likelihood in (6.31) gives consistent estimates of the parameters in the cost function as well as those in Ω and σ_u^2. The estimated parameters can be used to estimate η. Since the conditional mean of η given Z is $N(Z'\Omega^{-1}d\sigma^2, \sigma^2)$ truncated at zero from below ($\eta \geq 0$), we can use the Jondrow et al. (1982) type formula to estimate η, which is

$$\hat{\eta} = E(\eta|Z) = \tilde{\mu} + \sigma \frac{\phi(\tilde{\mu}/\sigma)}{\Phi(\tilde{\mu}/\sigma)}, \tag{6.35}$$

where $\tilde{\mu} = Z'\Omega^{-1}d\sigma^2$.

Alternatively, one can estimate technical efficiency from

$$\widehat{TE} = E(\exp(-\eta|Z)) = \frac{1 - \Phi[\sigma - (\tilde{\mu}/\sigma)]}{\Phi(\tilde{\mu}/\sigma)} \exp(-\tilde{\mu} + .5\sigma^2). \tag{6.36}$$

Example

Model 3: Half-Normal Model

For this example, we introduce the author written Stata command sfsystem. Following the previous example, we estimate the system of the cost frontier model with the simplest specification, that is, a half-normal distribution on η with no correlations among v, ζ_2, and ζ_3. The variance parameter of η is estimated from its reparameterization

$$\sigma_u^2 = \exp(\texttt{usigmas}), \tag{6.37}$$

and the variance-covariance matrix of v and the ζ's is (6.34) where Σ is a 2×2 diagonal matrix. To estimate (6.34), we use the Cholesky decomposition giving $\Omega = LL'$ where L is a lower triangular matrix and is parameterized as follows:

$$L = \begin{pmatrix} \exp(\texttt{s11}) & \mathbf{0} \\ \mathbf{0}' & \begin{pmatrix} \exp(\texttt{s22}) & 0 \\ 0 & \exp(\texttt{s33}) \end{pmatrix} \end{pmatrix}. \tag{6.38}$$

The `s11`, `s22`, and `s33` are parameters to be estimated without restrictions, and the exponential function is used to ensure that the estimates of the variance parameters are positive. Note that we have $\sigma_v^2 = \exp(2 \cdot s_{11})$. Once the parameters in L are estimated, it is trivial to get the parameters of Ω using the `sf_transform` command.

The model is estimated by using the following commands. Note that users do not need to specify the parameters of `usigmas`, `s11`, and so on, in the `sfsystem` command; they are automatically taken care of by the program. However, they would be needed in `sf_init` if users want to supply initial values.

```
. sfsystem tc, cost distribution(h) corr(no) frontier($xvar) share1(sl=$svar) ///
>               share2(sk=$svar) constraints(1-8)
. sf_init, frontier(b0_f) share1(b0_s1) share2(b0_s2) usigmas(0.1) s11(0.1) s22(0.1) s33(0.1)
. sf_srch, frontier($xvar) share1($svar) share2($svar) n(3) fast
. ml max, diff gtol(1e-2) nrtol(1e-2)
```

We use the results from the SURE model as part of the initial values, and we arbitrarily choose 0.1 as the initial value for other variables. This strategy seems to work well for this simple model. For more complicated models, we may need an "educated guess" for initial values of `s11`, `s22`, and so on, which may not seem straightforward given that these parameters are for the L matrix. We will show in the next example how to use `showini` to help obtain the initial values in such cases.

Output from running these commands is as follows:

```
Number of obs    =          232
                                                    Wald chi2(2)      =        630.39
Log likelihood =    606.6248                        Prob > chi2       =        0.0000

 ( 1)  - [frontier]pl + [share1]_cons = 0
 ( 2)  - [frontier]ply + [share1]y = 0
 ( 3)  - [frontier]plpk + [share1]pk = 0
 ( 4)  - [frontier]plpl2 + [share1]pl = 0
 ( 5)  - [frontier]pk + [share2]_cons = 0
 ( 6)  - [frontier]pky + [share2]y = 0
 ( 7)  - [frontier]pkpk2 + [share2]pk = 0
 ( 8)  - [frontier]plpk + [share2]pl = 0
------------------------------------------------------------------------------
             |      Coef.   Std. Err.      z    P>|z|     [95% Conf. Interval]
-------------+----------------------------------------------------------------
frontier     |
          pl |   .3011275   .0046653    64.55   0.000     .2919838    .3102713
          pk |   .4462863   .0049306    90.51   0.000     .4366226      .45595
           y |   .8590904   .0658606    13.04   0.000     .7300059    .9881748
       plpl2 |   .0447571   .0063092     7.09   0.000     .0323914    .0571229
       pkpk2 |   .0329783   .0079527     4.15   0.000     .0173913    .0485653
         yy2 |   .0514886   .0446101     1.15   0.248    -.0359456    .1389228
        plpk |   .0131531    .006169     2.13   0.033     .0010621    .0252442
         ply |  -.0120476   .0020077    -6.00   0.000    -.0159826   -.0081126
         pky |   .0015606    .001836     0.85   0.395    -.0020378     .005159
       _cons |   1.068436   .0842781    12.68   0.000     .9032534    1.233618
-------------+----------------------------------------------------------------
share1       |
          pl |   .0447571   .0063092     7.09   0.000     .0323914    .0571229
          pk |   .0131531    .006169     2.13   0.033     .0010621    .0252442
           y |  -.0120476   .0020077    -6.00   0.000    -.0159826   -.0081126
       _cons |   .3011275   .0046653    64.55   0.000     .2919838    .3102713
-------------+----------------------------------------------------------------
share2       |
          pl |   .0131531    .006169     2.13   0.033     .0010621    .0252442
          pk |   .0329783   .0079527     4.15   0.000     .0173913    .0485653
           y |   .0015606    .001836     0.85   0.395    -.0020378     .005159
       _cons |   .4462863   .0049306    90.51   0.000     .4366226      .45595
-------------+----------------------------------------------------------------
```

```
usigmas      |
       _cons |   .8587701    .118082     7.27   0.000     .6273335    1.090207
-------------+----------------------------------------------------------------
s11          |
       _cons |  -2.038613   .4652968    -4.38   0.000    -2.950578   -1.126648
-------------+----------------------------------------------------------------
s22          |
       _cons |   -3.27598    .047822   -68.50   0.000    -3.369709   -3.182251
-------------+----------------------------------------------------------------
s33          |
       _cons |  -3.398046   .0478265   -71.05   0.000    -3.491784   -3.304308
------------------------------------------------------------------------------
```

Because the translog parameters do not have a straightforward interpretation, one can use them (along with the data) to estimate cost elasticities with respect to input prices and output. The former are the cost shares (which follow from Shephard's lemma) and the latter is related to returns to scale (RTS) (RTS is the reciprocal of cost elasticity with respect to output).

We check the fitted values of share1 and share2 using equation (6.29).

```
. generate s1 = [share1]_b[_cons] + [share1]_b[y]*y + [share1]_b[pk]*pk + [share1]_b[pl]*pl
. generate s2 = [share2]_b[_cons] + [share2]_b[y]*y + [share2]_b[pk]*pk + [share2]_b[pl]*pl

. summarize s1 s2

    Variable |       Obs        Mean    Std. Dev.       Min        Max
-------------+--------------------------------------------------------
          s1 |       232    .3463499    .0334721   .2713747   .4259402
          s2 |       232    .4781218    .0201488   .4380272   .5192097
```

This shows that, on average, the labor cost share is 35 percent, the capital cost share is 48 percent, and the fuel cost share is 17 percent (i.e., 100% – 35% – 48%).

We compute the returns to scale. First, we calculate $ECY = \partial \ln C/\partial \ln y = \beta_y + \beta_{yy}y + \beta_{1y}pl + \beta_{2y}pk$ and then $RTS = 1/ECY$.

```
. generate ECY = [frontier]_b[y] + [frontier]_b[yy2]*y + [frontier]_b[ply]*pl + [frontier]_b[pky]*pk
. generate RTS = 1/ECY
. summarize RTS

    Variable |       Obs        Mean    Std. Dev.       Min        Max
-------------+--------------------------------------------------------
         RTS |       232    1.257905     .108159   1.108857   1.533604
```

Thus, we find economies of scale (increasing returns to scale). The estimates of RTS appear reasonable, in the sense that the estimates are neither too high nor too low. This provides additional confidence in the robustness of the model.

From the estimate of the variance parameters (`usigmas`, `s11`, etc.), we can get back the original parameters using the `sf_transform` command.

```
. sf_transform

      sigma_u_sqr = exp(usigmas), the estiamted variance of u.
      sigma_v_sqr, the estiamted variance of v.
      sigma_i_sqr, the estimated variance of the ith share equation.
      sigma_iv: covariance of the ith share and the v.
      sigma_ij: covariance of the ith and the jth share equation.
```

```
---convert the parameters to the original form---

variable     |      Coef.   Std. Err.       t    P>|t|      [95% Conf. Interval]
-------------+----------------------------------------------------------------
 sigma_u_sqr |   2.360256   .2787038      8.47   0.000      1.872611    2.974889
 sigma_v_sqr |   .0169544   .0157777      1.07   0.283      .0027363    .1050523
 sigma_1_sqr |   .0014273   .0001365     10.46   0.000      .0011833    .0017216
 sigma_2_sqr |   .0011181    .000107     10.45   0.000       .000927    .0013487
```

The program `sf_transform` also returns local macros of the estimated parameter values; type `return list` for a complete list of the returned macros.

Observation-specific efficiency index are calculated from $\exp(-u|Z)$ in (6.36) using the following command:

```
. sf_predict, bc(bc_mod3) jlms(jlms_mod3)

. summarize bc_mod3 jlms_mod3

    Variable |       Obs        Mean    Std. Dev.       Min        Max
-------------+--------------------------------------------------------
     bc_mod3 |       232    .8790631    .1702647   .4200552   .9935221
   jlms_mod3 |       232    .1549694    .2337283     .00652   .8757858
```

We plot the histogram of the inefficiency index from this model in Figure 6.2.

Model 4: Half-Normal Model with Partial Correlation

Here, we consider the case in which the error terms of the share equations are freely correlated, but there is no correlation between the error term of the cost frontier (v) and the error terms of the share equations. That is, the off-diagonal elements of Σ in (6.34) are nonzero. The L matrix from the Cholesky decomposition on Ω $(= LL')$ is parameterized as:

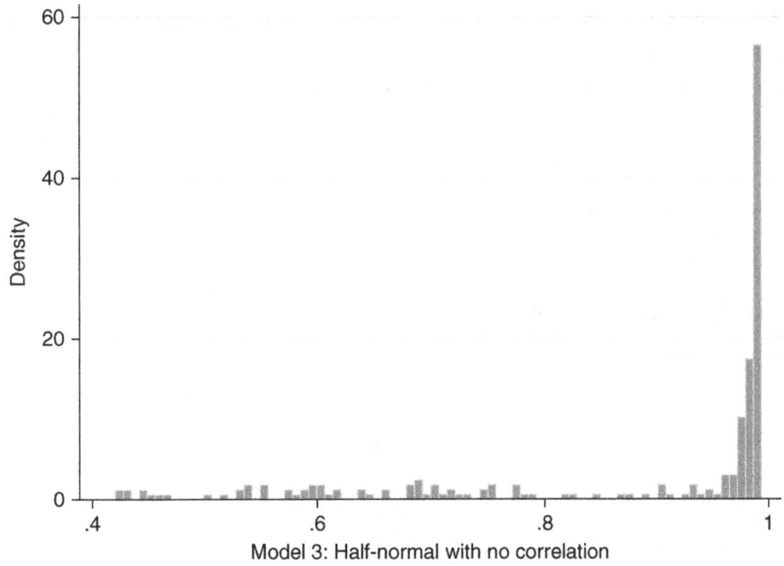

Figure 6.2. Histogram of Inefficiency Index

$$L = \begin{pmatrix} \exp(s11) & 0 & 0 \\ 0 & \exp(s22) & 0 \\ 0 & s32 & \exp(s33) \end{pmatrix}, \tag{6.39}$$

where `s11`, `s22`, and so on, are (unrestricted) parameters to be estimated, and the elements of Ω can be recovered using `sf_transform` after the model is estimated.

This parameterization of the matrix may make supplying initial values less intuitive. Here `showini` can help to make the task easier. Suppose that we want to use the following values as the initial values:

$$\Omega = \begin{pmatrix} 0.5 & 0 & 0 \\ 0 & 0.2 & -0.1 \\ 0 & -0.1 & 0.3 \end{pmatrix}, \tag{6.40}$$

then we can use the following command to obtain the corresponding values for the L matrix.

```
. showini, cov(0.5, 0, 0 \ 0, 0.2, -0.1 \0, -0.1, 0.3)

s11ini = -.34657359
s22ini = -.80471896
s33ini = -.69314718
s21ini = 0
s31ini = 0
s32ini = -.2236068
```

The command also generates macros `r(s11ini)`, `r(s22ini)`, and so on, which again can be saved in local macros to be used later.

```
. local s11_ini = r(s11ini)
. local s22_ini = r(s22ini)
. local s33_ini = r(s33ini)
. local s32_ini = r(s32ini)
```

We do not have to put `r(s21ini)` and `r(s31ini)` in local macros because, if we add the option `corr(partial)`, then the elements of the covariance matrix are automatically set to 0 and are not estimated.

We estimate the model using the following commands:

```
. sfsystem tc, cost corr(partial) distribution(h) frontier($xvar) ///
> share1(sl=$svar) share2(sk=$svar)  usigmas  constraints(1-8)
. sf_init, frontier(b0_f) share1(b0_s1) share2(b0_s2) usigmas(0.1) ///
> s11(`s11_ini') s22(`s22_ini') s33(`s33_ini') s32(`s32_ini')
. sf_srch, frontier($xvar) share1($svar) share2($svar) n(4) fast
. ml max, diff gtol(1e-5) nrtol(1e-5)
```

This produces the following output:

```
(iteration log omitted)


                                                Number of obs    =       232
                                                Wald chi2(2)     =    626.20
Log likelihood =   735.04311                    Prob > chi2      =    0.0000

 ( 1)   - [frontier]pl + [share1]_cons = 0
 ( 2)   - [frontier]ply + [share1]y = 0
 ( 3)   - [frontier]plpk + [share1]pk = 0
 ( 4)   - [frontier]plpl2 + [share1]pl = 0
 ( 5)   - [frontier]pk + [share2]_cons = 0
 ( 6)   - [frontier]pky + [share2]y = 0
```

```
( 7)  - [frontier]pkpk2 + [share2]pk = 0
( 8)  - [frontier]plpk + [share2]pl = 0
------------------------------------------------------------------------------
             |      Coef.   Std. Err.      z    P>|z|     [95% Conf. Interval]
-------------+----------------------------------------------------------------
frontier     |
          pl |   .3204209   .0045614    70.25   0.000     .3114807     .329361
          pk |   .4167845    .004915    84.80   0.000     .4071513    .4264176
           y |   .8575861   .0661896    12.96   0.000     .7278568    .9873154
       plpl2 |     .03669   .0089457     4.10   0.000     .0191567    .0542233
       pkpk2 |   .0877102   .0092121     9.52   0.000     .0696548    .1057655
         yy2 |    .052151   .0448884     1.16   0.245    -.0358286    .1401307
        plpk |  -.0086736   .0081438    -1.07   0.287    -.0246352    .0072879
         ply |  -.0143711   .0022063    -6.51   0.000    -.0186954   -.0100469
         pky |   .0060405    .001964     3.08   0.002     .0021912    .0098897
       _cons |   1.076698   .0840945    12.80   0.000     .9118762    1.241521
-------------+----------------------------------------------------------------
share1       |
          pl |     .03669   .0089457     4.10   0.000     .0191567    .0542233
          pk |  -.0086736   .0081438    -1.07   0.287    -.0246352    .0072879
           y |  -.0143711   .0022063    -6.51   0.000    -.0186954   -.0100469
       _cons |   .3204209   .0045614    70.25   0.000     .3114807     .329361
-------------+----------------------------------------------------------------
share2       |
          pl |  -.0086736   .0081438    -1.07   0.287    -.0246352    .0072879
          pk |   .0877102   .0092121     9.52   0.000     .0696548    .1057655
           y |   .0060405    .001964     3.08   0.002     .0021912    .0098897
       _cons |   .4167845    .004915    84.80   0.000     .4071513    .4264176
-------------+----------------------------------------------------------------
usigmas      |
       _cons |   .8565035    .118097     7.25   0.000     .6250376    1.087969
-------------+----------------------------------------------------------------
s11          |
       _cons |  -2.022447   .4561865    -4.43   0.000    -2.916556   -1.128338
-------------+----------------------------------------------------------------
s22          |
       _cons |   -3.18571   .0496965   -64.10   0.000    -3.283114   -3.088307
-------------+----------------------------------------------------------------
s33          |
       _cons |   -4.04193   .0497024   -81.32   0.000    -4.139345   -3.944515
-------------+----------------------------------------------------------------
s32          |
       _cons |  -.0310566   .0021021   -14.77   0.000    -.0351767   -.0269365
------------------------------------------------------------------------------
```

Because this model with the present data is relatively easy to estimate, we do not necessarily need to use the initial values for the `s` parameters and could, instead, have used the code shown here:

```
. sfsystem tc, cost corr(partial) distribution(h) frontier($xvar) ///
>     share1(sl=$svar) share2(sk=$svar)  usigmas  constraints(1-8)
. sf_srch, frontier($xvar) share1($svar) share2($svar) n(3) fast
. ml max, diff gtol(1e-5) nrtol(1e-5)
```

As in the previous example, we check the fitted values of `share1` and `share2` using equation (6.29) and RTS (see page 160 for details): At two decimal places, the results are the same as before (and, thus, not shown).

We again use `sf_transform` to obtain estimates of the variance parameters.

```
. sf_transform

     sigma_u_sqr = exp(usigmas), the estiamted variance of u.
     sigma_v_sqr, the estiamted variance of v.
```

```
sigma_i_sqr, the estimated variance of the ith share equation.
sigma_iv: covariance of the ith share and the v.
sigma_ij: covariance of the ith and the jth share equation.

 ---convert the parameters to the original form---
```

variable	Coef.	Std. Err.	t	P>|t|	[95% Conf.	Interval]
sigma_u_sqr	2.354912	.278108	8.47	0.000	1.868316	2.96824
sigma_v_sqr	.0175116	.0159771	1.10	0.273	.0029289	.1046978
sigma_1_sqr	.0017097	.0001699	10.06	0.000	.0014071	.0020775
sigma_2_sqr	.001273	.0001305	9.76	0.000	.0010173	.0015287
sigma_21	-.0012842	.0001417	-9.06	0.000	-.0015618	-.0010065

The estimates are saved in local macros by `sf_transform` and they can be used as initial values for other models. For example, the local macro `usigmas_ini`, defined here, provides a good initial value for the parameter `usigmas` in the next model we estimate.

```
. local usigmas_ini = ln(`r(sigma_u_sqr)')
```

The logarithm is taken because `usigmas` comes from the equation $\sigma_u^2 = \exp(\texttt{usigmas})$.

Finally, we compute the observation-specific efficiency index and save the results in `bc_mod4`.

```
. sf_predict, bc(bc_mod4) jlms(jlms_mod4)
. summarize bc_mod4 jlms_mod4
```

Variable	Obs	Mean	Std. Dev.	Min	Max
bc_mod4	232	.8789004	.1698625	.419686	.9933202
jlms_mod4	232	.1551312	.2333316	.0067246	.8769396

We plot the histogram of the inefficiency index from this model in Figure 6.3.

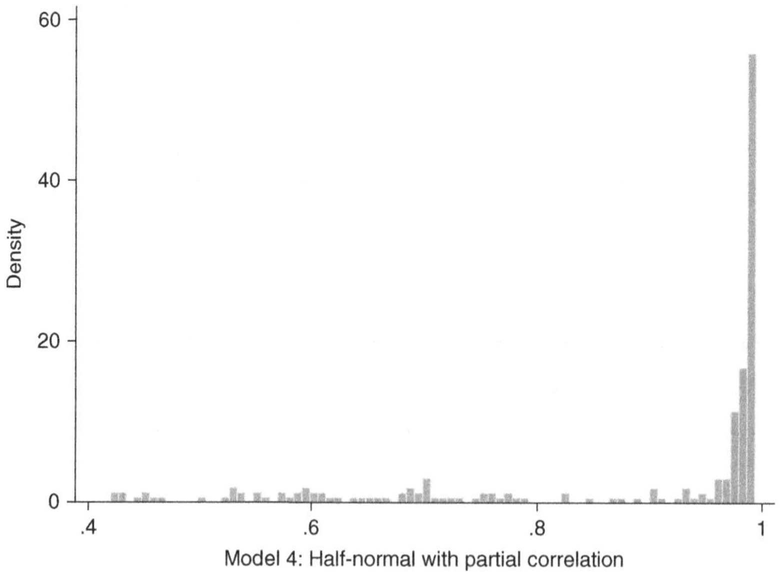

Figure 6.3. Histogram of Inefficiency Index

Before we proceed, we save coefficient vectors of this model; they will be used as initial values for the following models:

```
. matrix b4 = e(b)
. matrix b4_f = b4[1, "frontier:"]
. matrix b4_s1 = b4[1, "share1:"]
. matrix b4_s2 = b4[1, "share2:"]
. matrix b4_usigmas = b4[1, "usigmas:"]
. matrix b4_s11 = b4[1, "s11:"]
. matrix b4_s22 = b4[1, "s22:"]
. matrix b4_s32 = b4[1, "s32:"]
. matrix b4_s33 = b4[1, "s33:"]
```

Model 5: Half-Normal Model with Full Correlation

We now consider the case in which the error terms of the cost frontier and the share equations are all correlated. As such, we do not impose zero restrictions on the elements of Ω to allow for arbitrary correlations between v and ζ's. Given $\Omega = LL'$ where L is from the Cholesky decomposition, we estimate:

$$L = \begin{pmatrix} \exp(s_{11}) & 0 & 0 \\ s_{21} & \exp(s_{22}) & 0 \\ s_{31} & s_{32} & \exp(s_{33}) \end{pmatrix}, \tag{6.41}$$

where $s_{11}, s_{21}, \ldots, s_{33}$ are (unrestricted) parameters to be estimated. The elements of Ω can be recovered using `sf_transform` after the model is estimated.

The model is estimated using the following commands:

```
. sfsystem tc, cost corr(full) distribution(h) frontier($xvar) share1(sl=$svar) ///
>               share2(sk=$svar) usigmas constraints(1-8)
. sf_init, frontier(b4_f) share1(b4_s1) share2(b4_s2) usigmas(b4_usigmas)   ///
> s11(-0.1) s22(b4_s22) s33(b4_s33) s21(0) s31(0) s32(b4_s32)
. sf_srch, n(3) frontier($xvar)  share1($svar) share2($svar) fast
. ml max, diff gtol(1e-2) nrtol(1e-2)
```

This produces the following output:

```
(iteration log omitted)

                                                  Number of obs    =        232
                                                  Wald chi2(2)     =     717.75
Log likelihood =  736.15836                       Prob > chi2      =     0.0000

 ( 1)  - [frontier]pl + [share1]_cons = 0
 ( 2)  - [frontier]ply + [share1]y = 0
 ( 3)  - [frontier]plpk + [share1]pk = 0
 ( 4)  - [frontier]plpl2 + [share1]pl = 0
 ( 5)  - [frontier]pk + [share2]_cons = 0
 ( 6)  - [frontier]pky + [share2]y = 0
 ( 7)  - [frontier]pkpk2 + [share2]pk = 0
 ( 8)  - [frontier]plpk + [share2]pl = 0
------------------------------------------------------------------------------
             |      Coef.   Std. Err.      z    P>|z|     [95% Conf. Interval]
-------------+----------------------------------------------------------------
frontier     |
          pl |   .3201009   .0045858    69.80   0.000     .3111129    .3290888
          pk |   .4175628   .0049645    84.11   0.000     .4078325     .427293
           y |   .8307587   .0687713    12.08   0.000     .6959694    .9655479
       plpl2 |   .0382192    .009054     4.22   0.000     .0204737    .0559647
       pkpk2 |   .0869877   .0094221     9.23   0.000     .0685206    .1054547
```

```
         yy2 |   .0305021   .0498443     0.61   0.541    -.0671908    .1281951
        plpk |  -.0092196   .0082886    -1.11   0.266    -.0254649    .0070257
         ply |  -.0144166   .0022037    -6.54   0.000    -.0187357   -.0100975
         pky |   .0059828    .001959     3.05   0.002     .0021432    .0098224
       _cons |   1.076467   .0704945    15.27   0.000     .9383004    1.214634
-------------+----------------------------------------------------------------
share1       |
          pl |   .0382192    .009054     4.22   0.000     .0204737    .0559647
          pk |  -.0092196   .0082886    -1.11   0.266    -.0254649    .0070257
           y |  -.0144166   .0022037    -6.54   0.000    -.0187357   -.0100975
       _cons |   .3201009   .0045858    69.80   0.000     .3111129    .3290888
-------------+----------------------------------------------------------------
share2       |
          pl |  -.0092196   .0082886    -1.11   0.266    -.0254649    .0070257
          pk |   .0869877   .0094221     9.23   0.000     .0685206    .1054547
           y |   .0059828    .001959     3.05   0.002     .0021432    .0098224
       _cons |   .4175628   .0049645    84.11   0.000     .4078325     .427293
-------------+----------------------------------------------------------------
usigmas      |
       _cons |   .8590483   .1099113     7.82   0.000     .6436262     1.07447
-------------+----------------------------------------------------------------
s11          |
       _cons |  -2.010944   .3494912    -5.75   0.000    -2.695935   -1.325954
-------------+----------------------------------------------------------------
s22          |
       _cons |  -3.232561   .1020464   -31.68   0.000    -3.432568   -3.032553
-------------+----------------------------------------------------------------
s33          |
       _cons |  -4.102338   .1042814   -39.34   0.000    -4.306725    -3.89795
-------------+----------------------------------------------------------------
s32          |
       _cons |  -.0312221   .0023441   -13.32   0.000    -.0358165   -.0266278
-------------+----------------------------------------------------------------
s21          |
       _cons |   .0119831   .0121057     0.99   0.322    -.0117437    .0357099
-------------+----------------------------------------------------------------
s31          |
       _cons |   -.003133   .0092872    -0.34   0.736    -.0213355    .0150695
------------------------------------------------------------------------------
```

As in the previous example, we check the fitted values of `share1` and `share2` using equation (6.29) and RTS (see page 160 for details): Again, at two decimal places, the results are the same as before (and, thus, not shown).

Estimated values of the variance parameters can be obtained using `sf_transform`.

```
. sf_transform

    sigma_u_sqr = exp(usigmas), the estiamted variance of u.
    sigma_v_sqr, the estiamted variance of v.
    sigma_i_sqr, the estimated variance of the ith share equation.
    sigma_iv: covariance of the ith share and the v.
    sigma_ij: covariance of the ith and the jth share equation.

     ---convert the parameters to the original form---

variable     |      Coef.   Std. Err.      t    P>|t|     [95% Conf. Interval]
-------------+----------------------------------------------------------------
 sigma_u_sqr |   2.360912   .2594907     9.10   0.000      1.90337    2.928441
 sigma_v_sqr |   .0179191   .0125251     1.43   0.153     .0045535    .0705165
 sigma_1_sqr |   .0017004   .0001692    10.05   0.000     .0013688     .002032
    sigma_1v |   .0016041   .0016749     0.96   0.338    -.0016786    .0048867
 sigma_2_sqr |    .001258   .0001286     9.78   0.000      .001006      .00151
    sigma_2v |  -.0004194   .0012496    -0.34   0.737    -.0028685    .0020297
    sigma_21 |  -.0012695   .0001404    -9.04   0.000    -.0015447   -.0009942
```

Note that σ_v^2 = `sigma_v_sqr`, and the variances of the two share equations are, respectively, `sigma_1_sqr` and `sigma_2_sqr`.

This model allows correlations between all the equations, just as the SURE does. The only difference between SURE and this model is that the latter includes inefficiency and makes distributional assumptions on the error components. If there is no inefficiency, the model reduces to the one estimated by the SURE with the normality assumption on the error vector. This result enables us to conduct a likelihood ratio test on the existence of inefficiency. The degree of freedom of the test is 1 because the only constraint is $\sigma_u^2 = 0$. After saving the log-likelihood value of the model in scalar `ll_h_full`, the test is undertaken as follows.

```
. scalar ll_h_full = e(ll)

. display -2*(ll_sure - ll_h_full)
32.330203

. sf_mixtable, dof(1)

critical values of the mixed chi-square distribution

                              significance level
 dof  |  0.25      0.1      0.05      0.025      0.01      0.005      0.001
---------------------------------------------------------------------------
  1      0.455    1.642    2.705     3.841      5.412     6.635      9.500

source: Table 1, Kodde and Palm (1986, Econometrica).
```

Evidently, the null hypothesis of no inefficiency is overwhelmingly rejected.

In Figure 6.4, we plot the histogram of the efficiency index from all the models used in this chapter so far.

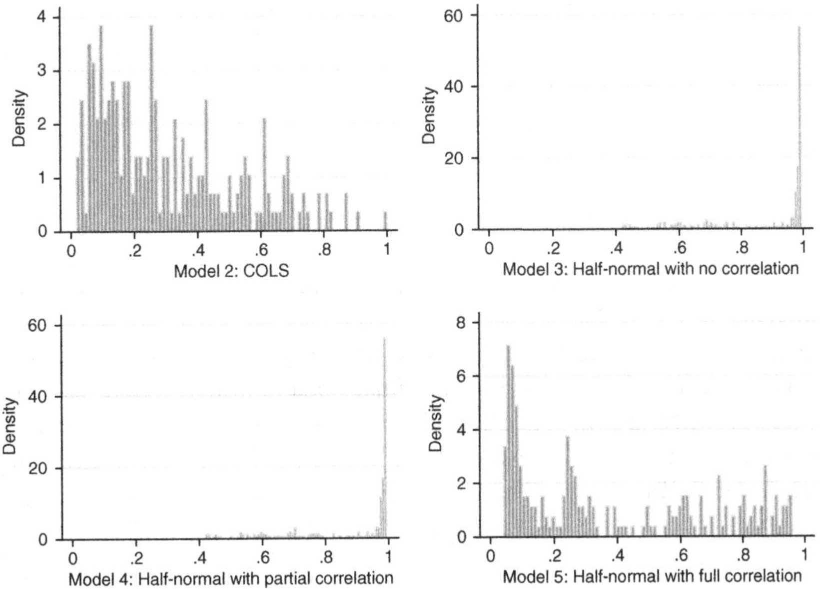

Figure 6.4. Histogram of Efficiency Index

6.4.1 Heteroscedasticity, Marginal Effects, Efficiency Index, and Confidence Intervals

To allow for determinants of inefficiency via the mean of η, we generalize the model, that is,

$$\begin{aligned} \eta &\sim N^{+}(\mu, \sigma_u^2), \\ \boldsymbol{\xi} &\sim N(\mathbf{0}, \Omega). \end{aligned} \tag{6.42}$$

To derive the log-likelihood function of this model, we define Z as before and derive the pdf of $Z, f(Z)$, as

$$f(Z) = \int_0^\infty f(Z, \eta) d\eta = \int_0^\infty f(Z|\eta) h(\eta) d\eta, \tag{6.43}$$

where $f(Z, \eta)$ is the joint pdf of Z and η, and $h(\eta)$ is the pdf of η. Using the distributional assumptions on η and $\boldsymbol{\xi}$, this integral can be expressed as

$$\begin{aligned} f(Z) &= \frac{1}{(2\pi)^{(J+1)/2}|\Omega|^{1/2}\sigma_u \, \Phi(\mu/\sigma_u)} \int_0^\infty \exp\Big\{-\frac{1}{2}[(Z - d\eta)'\Omega^{-1}(Z - d\eta) \\ &\quad + (\eta - \mu)^2/\sigma_u^2]\Big\} d\eta \\ &= \frac{\sigma \, \exp(-a/2)}{(2\pi)^{(J/2)}|\Omega|^{1/2}\sigma_u} \frac{\Phi([Z'\Omega^{-1}d + \mu/\sigma_u^2]\,\sigma)}{\Phi(\mu/\sigma_u)}, \end{aligned} \tag{6.44}$$

where $\sigma^2 = (1/\sigma_u^2 + d'\Omega^{-1}d)^{-1}$, $a = Z'\Omega^{-1}Z + \mu^2/\sigma_u^2 - \sigma^2(Z'\Omega^{-1}d + \mu/\sigma_u^2)^2$, and $\Phi(\cdot)$ is the cumulative distribution function of a standard normal variable. Note that this $f(Z)$ differs from the one in (6.33) and reduces to the one in (6.33) when $\mu = 0$. The log-likelihood function for a single observation is simply $\ln f(Z)$ in (6.44), which can be maximized to get consistent estimates of all the parameters.

To estimate technical inefficiency one can use

$$\hat{\eta} = E(\eta|Z) = \tilde{\mu} + \sigma \frac{\phi(\tilde{\mu}/\sigma)}{\Phi(\tilde{\mu}/\sigma)}, \tag{6.45}$$

where $\tilde{\mu} = [Z'\Omega^{-1}d + \mu/\sigma_u^2]\sigma^2$.

Alternatively, one can estimate technical efficiency from

$$\widehat{TE} = E(\exp(-\eta|Z)) = \frac{1 - \Phi[\sigma - (\tilde{\mu}/\sigma)]}{\Phi(\tilde{\mu}/\sigma)} \exp\left(-\tilde{\mu} + \frac{1}{2}\sigma^2\right). \tag{6.46}$$

Note that these formulas look exactly the same as those in (6.35) and (6.36) but the definition of $\tilde{\mu}$ is different.

Computations of the confidence intervals on the two measures can be obtained following the same procedure that we used in the single equation model. Here, we provide the formulas for constructing confidence bounds for the technical efficiency index. The lower and upper bounds of a $(1 - \alpha)$ 100% confidence interval for technical efficiency, modeled as $\exp(-\eta|\,Z)$, are given by

$$L_i = \exp(-\tilde{\mu} - z_L\sigma), \tag{6.47}$$

and

$$U_i = \exp(-\tilde{\mu} - z_U\sigma). \tag{6.48}$$

For a standard normal variable z,

$$Pr\,(z > z_L) = \frac{\alpha}{2}\left[1 - \Phi\left(\frac{\tilde{\mu}}{\sigma}\right)\right],$$

and

$$Pr\,(z > z_U) = \left(1 - \frac{\alpha}{2}\right)\left[1 - \Phi\left(\frac{\tilde{\mu}}{\sigma}\right)\right].$$

Hence,

$$z_L = \Phi^{-1}\left(1 - \frac{\alpha}{2}\left[1 - \Phi\left(\frac{\tilde{\mu}}{\sigma}\right)\right]\right), \tag{6.49}$$

and

$$z_U = \Phi^{-1}\left(1 - \left(1 - \frac{\alpha}{2}\right)\left[1 - \Phi\left(\frac{\tilde{\mu}}{\sigma}\right)\right]\right). \tag{6.50}$$

Like the single-equation cost frontier model, we can parameterize inefficiency (η) so that it is a function of exogenous variables. The parameterization enables researchers to investigate how inefficiency changes with changes in the values of exogenous variables. Although, in theory, we can have μ, σ_u^2, and even σ_v^2 parameterized by vectors of variables, which is what we have done for the single equation models, the complexity of the current model makes full-fledged parameterizations difficult to estimate. The Stata routines that we provide allows μ to be parameterized by a vector of exogenous variables ($\boldsymbol{z}$): $\mu = \boldsymbol{z}'\boldsymbol{\delta}$. However, both σ_u^2 and σ_v^2 remain constant in the model. Given the similarity with the earlier modeling, we do not provide an empirical example of this model.

6.5 Multiple Outputs, Input-Oriented Technical Inefficiency

The model in the previous section assumes that there is a single output in the production. In reality, firms often produce multiple outputs. If these multiple outputs are not taken into account then clearly the estimated inefficiency may be biased. Thus, in this section we examine how to empirically model multiple outputs.

The cost minimization problem of a firm with multiple outputs is

$$\min_{\boldsymbol{x}} : \boldsymbol{w}'\boldsymbol{x} \qquad \text{s.t.} \qquad F(\boldsymbol{y}, \boldsymbol{x}e^{-\eta}) = 0. \tag{6.51}$$

Note that we define the production possibility function as $F(\boldsymbol{y}, \boldsymbol{x}e^{-\eta}) = 0$. In the single output case this representation is simply $y - f(\boldsymbol{x}e^{-\eta}) = 0$. Thus, the technology specification is different from the single output model. The rest of the derivation is straightforward and similar to the derivation of a single output model.

The first-order condition of the above minimization problem is

$$FOCs: \quad \frac{w_j}{w_1} = \frac{\frac{\partial F}{\partial x_j e^{-\eta}}}{\frac{\partial F}{\partial x_1 e^{-\eta}}}, \qquad j = 2, \ldots, J. \tag{6.52}$$

The (inefficiency adjusted) input demand functions are $x_j^* = x_j e^{-\eta} = \phi(\boldsymbol{w}, \boldsymbol{y})$. If we define the pseudo-cost function as

$$C^*(\boldsymbol{w}, \boldsymbol{y}) = \sum_j w_j x_j e^{-\eta}, \tag{6.53}$$

then it can be viewed as the minimum cost of the following problem:

$$\min_{\boldsymbol{x}e^{-\eta}} \boldsymbol{w}'\boldsymbol{x}e^{-\eta} \quad \text{s.t.} \quad F(\boldsymbol{y}, \boldsymbol{x}e^{-\eta}) = 0. \tag{6.54}$$

Also note that $C^*(\boldsymbol{w}, \boldsymbol{y})$ is the cost frontier because it gives the minimum cost of producing $\boldsymbol{y}$ with input price $\boldsymbol{w}$.

Applying Shephard's lemma, and after some manipulation, we have

$$S_j = \frac{w_j x_j}{C^a} = \frac{w_j x_j}{C^* e^{\eta}} = \frac{\partial \ln C^*}{\partial \ln w_j}, \quad j = 1, \ldots, J, \tag{6.55}$$

which is exactly the same as in the single output case.

Because the actual cost is $C^a = \sum_j w_j x_j = C^* e^{\eta}$, we have

$$\ln C^a = \ln C^*(\boldsymbol{w}, \boldsymbol{y}) + \eta. \tag{6.56}$$

After imposing a functional form on $\ln C^*(\boldsymbol{w}, \boldsymbol{y})$, this equation can be estimated to obtain parameters of the cost function and the inefficiency index. This is similar to the single equation cost frontier estimation introduced in Chapter 4. We can also use the share equation in estimation. To do so, we append random errors to the share equations in (6.55) and obtain

$$S_j = \frac{\partial \ln C^*}{\partial \ln w_j} + \zeta_j, \qquad j = 2, \ldots, J. \tag{6.57}$$

We may use the system of equations consisting (6.56) and (6.57) to estimate the parameters in the model.

Now we consider an example in which $\ln C^*(\boldsymbol{w}, \boldsymbol{y})$ is translog and there are quasi-fixed inputs, $\boldsymbol{q}$, in the production process. The model is

$$\begin{aligned} \ln C^a &= \ln C^*(\boldsymbol{w}, \boldsymbol{q}, \boldsymbol{y}) + \eta \\ &= \beta_0 + \sum_j \beta_j \ln w_j + \sum_r \gamma_r \ln q_r + \sum_m \theta_m \ln y_m \\ &\quad + \frac{1}{2}\left[\sum_j \sum_k \beta_{jk} \ln w_j \ln w_k + \sum_r \sum_s \gamma_{rs} \ln q_r \ln q_s + \sum_m \sum_n \theta_{mn} \ln y_m \ln y_n\right] \\ &\quad + \sum_j \sum_r \delta_{jr} \ln w_j \ln q_r + \sum_j \sum_m \phi_{jm} \ln w_j \ln y_m + \sum_r \sum_m \gamma_{rm} \ln q_r \ln y_m + \eta, \end{aligned} \tag{6.58}$$

$$S_j = \beta_j + \sum_{k=1} \beta_{jk} \ln w_k + \sum_r \delta_{jr} \ln q_r + \sum_m \phi_{jm} \ln y_m + \zeta_j, \qquad j = 2, \ldots, J. \tag{6.59}$$

6.6 Estimation Methods

When it comes to estimation, the multiple output model is no different from the single output model. Note that a stochastic noise component, v, has to be added to (6.58). If the model is estimated by the single cost function such as (6.58), readers are referred to Chapter 4 for details. If the model is estimated using the system of equations in (6.58) and (6.59), then Section 6.2 contains the details. As such, no additional empirical example is provided in this section.

6.7 Multiple Outputs, Output-Oriented Technical Inefficiency

Now we consider the model with multiple outputs and output-oriented technical inefficiency. The cost minimization problem and the first-order conditions are

$$\min_{\boldsymbol{x}} : \boldsymbol{w}'\boldsymbol{x} \qquad \text{s.t.} \qquad F(\boldsymbol{y}e^{u}, \boldsymbol{x}) = 0, \tag{6.60}$$

$$\text{FOCs}: \qquad \frac{w_j}{w_1} = \frac{\partial F}{\partial x_j} \Big/ \frac{\partial F}{\partial x_1}, \qquad j = 2, \ldots, J. \tag{6.61}$$

The input demands are $x_j = x_j(\boldsymbol{w}, \boldsymbol{y}e^{u})$. The minimum cost is

$$C^* = \sum_j w_j x_j(\boldsymbol{w}, \boldsymbol{y}e^{u}) = C^*(\boldsymbol{w}, \boldsymbol{y}e^{u}), \tag{6.62}$$

which can be viewed as the minimum cost of the following problem:

$$\min_{\boldsymbol{x}} \ \boldsymbol{w}'\boldsymbol{x} \quad \text{s.t.} \quad F(\boldsymbol{y}e^{u}, \boldsymbol{x}) = 0. \tag{6.63}$$

Applying Shephard's lemma, and after some manipulations, we have

$$S_j = \frac{w_j x_j}{C^* e^{\eta}} = \frac{w_j x_j}{C^a} = \frac{\partial \ln C^*}{\partial \ln w_j}, \quad j = 1, \ldots, J, \tag{6.64}$$

which is exactly the same as in the single output case.

The system of equations is represented by

$$\ln C^a(\boldsymbol{w}, \boldsymbol{y}, u) = \ln C^*(\boldsymbol{w}, \boldsymbol{y}e^{u}), \tag{6.65}$$

$$S_j = \frac{\partial \ln C^*}{\partial \ln w_j} + \zeta_j, \qquad j = 2, \ldots, J, \tag{6.66}$$

where ζ_j is the random variable of statistical error appended to the jth share equation.

Consider an example where $\ln C^*(\boldsymbol{w}, \boldsymbol{y}e^{u})$ is translog. The system of equations for it is

$$\begin{aligned}
\ln C^a &= \ln C^*(\boldsymbol{w}, \boldsymbol{q}, \boldsymbol{y}e^{u}) \\
&= \beta_0 + \sum_j \beta_j \ln w_j + \sum_r \gamma_r \ln q_r + \sum_m \theta_m(\ln y_m + u) \\
&\quad + \frac{1}{2}\left[\sum_j \sum_k \beta_{jk} \ln w_j \ln w_k + \sum_r \sum_s \gamma_{rs} \ln q_r \ln q_s + \sum_m \sum_n \theta_{mn}(\ln y_m + u)(\ln y_n + u)\right] \\
&\quad + \sum_j \sum_r \delta_{jr} \ln w_j \ln q_r + \sum_j \sum_m \phi_{jm} \ln w_j(\ln y_m + u) + \sum_r \sum_m \gamma_{rm} \ln q_r(\ln y_m + u),
\end{aligned} \tag{6.67}$$

$$S_j = \beta_j + \sum_{k=1} \beta_{jk} \ln w_k + \sum_r \delta_{jr} \ln q_r + \sum_m \phi_{jm}(\ln y_m + u) + \zeta_j, \qquad j = 2, \ldots, J. \tag{6.68}$$

It is clear that this system is quite complicated. First, the inefficiency u appears nonlinearly (it involves u^2). Second, inefficiency also appears in the cost share equations. Derivation of the likelihood function for this model would be quite complex. In fact, it is not possible to get a closed form expression for the likelihood function.

If we assume that the underlying production function is homogeneous (in outputs), then the above cost function will satisfy the following parametric restrictions: $\sum_m \theta_{mn} = 0$, $\sum_m \phi_{jm} = 0$, $\sum_m \gamma_{rm} = 0$. With these restrictions, the inefficiency component is $u \sum \theta_m$. By denoting $\tilde{u} = u \sum \theta_m$, the cost system associated with the input and output-oriented inefficiency are identical (i.e., η simply needs to replaced by $\hat{u} = u \sum \theta_m$ in the previously derived equations). Thus, no additional empirical example is provided in this section.

7

Estimation of Technical Efficiency in Profit Frontier Models Using System Models with Cross-Sectional Data

7.1 Introduction

In Chapter 5, we presented a profit frontier model in which producers are assumed to maximize profit under competitive input and output markets. As explained previously, compared to the production and cost models, a profit model allows input and output variables to be endogenous (i.e., to be decision variables), which is arguably a more realistic assumption for a majority of industries and firms.

The profit model introduced in Chapter 5 was estimated from the profit function alone. In this chapter, we consider the estimation of a profit model that uses a system of equations consisting of the profit function and the profit share equations. Similar to the cost system (Chapter 6), share equations add information in estimating parameters and yield more efficient parameter estimates. As such, this chapter does not provide new tools to answer additional questions; the questions that can be answered are the same as those set out at the start of Chapter 5. Indeed, we also use the same empirical example of airlines from that chapter.

In what follows, we first derive the profit system and then provide the estimation methods and empirical examples. A large part of the derivation is the same as in Chapter 5. Therefore, we will focus on the differences and readers are referred to the earlier chapter for further details.

7.2 Single Output, Output-Oriented Technical Inefficiency

We assume that the input and output markets are competitive and that all firms are fully efficient allocatively. The assumption of full allocative efficiency is relaxed in Chapter 9. The first-order conditions of profit maximization that we use in this chapter are conditional on technical inefficiency. Because the long run profit is zero for producers operating in a competitive market and producers with negative profit exit the industry in the long run, it is perhaps better to focus on the short run and argue that differences in profits are due to quasi-fixed inputs and technical inefficiency. The assumption that some of the inputs are quasi-fixed (the costs of which are not subtracted to define profit) is likely to make variable profit (defined as total revenue minus cost of variable inputs) positive for all firms. Positive profit is essential in order to be able to use a Cobb-Douglas or translog profit function because in these functions profit appears in logarithmic form.

Here we follow the approach used in Kumbhakar (2001). Given the above assumptions, the profit maximization problem for a typical producer with output-oriented technical inefficiency is (we drop the producer subscript i for simplicity)

$$\max_{y,x} py - w'x \qquad \text{s.t. } y = f(x,q)\exp(-u), \tag{7.1}$$

$$\Longrightarrow \quad p \cdot f_j(x,q)\exp(-u) = w_j, \qquad j = 1,2,\ldots J, \tag{7.2}$$

$$\text{or,} \quad f_j(x,q) = \frac{w_j}{p \cdot \exp(-u)}, \qquad j = 1,2,\ldots J, \tag{7.3}$$

where x and q are vectors of variable and quasi-fixed inputs, respectively; $u \geq 0$ is the output-oriented technical inefficiency, and $f_j(x,q)$ is defined as $\partial f(x,q)/\partial x_j$. If we substitute $p \cdot \exp(-u)$ by $\tilde{p}$ and $y \cdot \exp(u)$ by $\tilde{y}$, then this maximization problem can be rewritten as

$$\max_{\tilde{y},x} \tilde{p}\tilde{y} - w'x, \qquad \text{s.t.} \qquad \tilde{y} = f(x,q). \tag{7.4}$$

This problem is no different from the standard textbook problem of profit maximization and therefore the profit function can be written as $\pi(w,q,\tilde{p})$.

To show that actual profit (π^a) is simply $\pi(w,q,\tilde{p})$, we start from the definition of π^a, viz.,

$$\begin{aligned} \pi^a &= p \cdot y(w,q,pe^{-u}) - w' \cdot x(w,q,pe^{-u}) \\ &= pe^{-u} f(x(\cdot),q) - w' \cdot x(\cdot) \\ &= \pi(w,q,pe^{-u}). \end{aligned} \tag{7.5}$$

If we define the *profit frontier* as

$$\pi(w,q,p) = \pi(w,q,pe^{-u})\,|_{u=0}, \tag{7.6}$$

then the following relationship can be established:

$$\pi^a = \pi(w,q,pe^{-u}) = \pi(w,q,p) \cdot h(w,q,p,u), \tag{7.7}$$

$$\text{or,} \quad \ln \pi^a = \ln \pi(w,q,pe^{-u}) = \ln \pi(w,q,p) + \ln h(w,q,p,u), \tag{7.8}$$

where $h(\cdot) = \pi(w,q,pe^{-u})/\pi(w,q,p) \leq 1$ and therefore $\ln h(\cdot) \leq 0$. This result follows from the fact that since $pe^{-u} \leq p$, $\pi(w,q,pe^{-u}) \leq \pi(w,q,p)$.

This model can be simplified by: (i) imposing restrictions that the underlying production function is homogeneous; and (ii) exploring the homogeneity property (in prices) of the profit function. If the underlying production function is homogeneous of degree r ($r < 1$), then following the theorem in Lau (1978), the profit function becomes

$$\begin{aligned} \ln \pi^a &= \ln \pi(w,q,pe^{-u}) = \ln \pi(w,q,p) + \ln h(w,q,p,u) \\ &= \frac{1}{1-r}\ln p + \ln G(w,q) - \frac{1}{1-r}u, \end{aligned} \tag{7.9}$$

where $G(w)$ is a homogeneous function of degree $-r/(1-r)$ in w. Because the profit function is homogeneous of degree 1 in prices (i.e., in w and pe^{-u}), the price homogeneity is built into the profit function by normalizing the profit and the input/output prices by one of the prices:

$$\ln(\pi^a/p) = \ln G(w/p,q) - \frac{1}{1-r}u. \tag{7.10}$$

An Illustration: The Translog Model

Consider a translog form of $\pi(\boldsymbol{w}, \boldsymbol{q}, pe^{-u})$, viz.,

$$\begin{aligned}\ln \pi^a &= \ln \pi(\boldsymbol{w}, \boldsymbol{q}, pe^{-u})\\ &= \beta_0 + \sum \beta_j \ln w_j + \sum \gamma_q \ln q_q + \beta_p \ln(pe^{-u})\\ &\quad + \frac{1}{2}\Big[\sum_j \sum_k \beta_{jk} \ln w_j \ln w_k + \sum_q \sum_s \gamma_{qs} \ln q_q \ln q_s + \beta_{pp} \ln(pe^{-u}) \ln(pe^{-u})\Big]\\ &\quad + \sum_j \beta_{jp} \ln w_j \ln(pe^{-u}) + \sum_j \sum_q \delta_{jq} \ln w_j \ln q_q + \sum_q \gamma_{qp} \ln q_q \ln(pe^{-u}).\end{aligned} \tag{7.11}$$

The symmetry restrictions are $\beta_{jk} = \beta_{kj}$ and $\gamma_{qs} = \gamma_{sq}$. We impose the homogeneity property (in prices) by expressing (7.11) in the normalized form. After a few algebraic manipulations, we have

$$\begin{aligned}\ln\left(\frac{\pi^a}{p}\right) &= \ln \pi(\boldsymbol{w}/pe^{-u}, \boldsymbol{q}) = \beta_0 + \sum_j \beta_j \ln\left(\frac{w_j}{p}\right) + \sum_q \beta_q \ln q_q\\ &\quad + \frac{1}{2}\sum_j \sum_k \beta_{jk} \ln\left(\frac{w_j}{p}\right) \ln\left(\frac{w_k}{p}\right)\\ &\quad + \frac{1}{2}\sum_q \sum_s \gamma_{qs} \ln q_q \ln q_s + \sum_j \sum_q \delta_{jq} \ln\left(\frac{w_j}{p}\right) \ln q_q\\ &\quad + \left[-1 + \sum_j \beta_j + \sum_j \sum_q \delta_{jq} \ln q_q + \sum_j \sum_k \beta_{jk} \ln\left(\frac{w_j}{p}\right)\right] u + \left[\frac{1}{2}\sum_j \sum_k \beta_{jk}\right] u^2.\end{aligned} \tag{7.12}$$

The profit frontier, $\ln \pi(\boldsymbol{w}/p, q)$, consists of the first three lines of (7.12), and the logarithm of the profit loss function, $\ln h(\boldsymbol{w}/p, u, q)$, consists of the last line.

Applying Hotelling's lemma to (7.12), we obtain the J profit share equations of the variable inputs as:

$$S_j^a = -\left[\beta_j + \sum_q \delta_{jq} \ln q_q + \sum_k \beta_{jk} \ln(w_k/p)\right] - \left[\sum_k \beta_{jk}\right] u, \qquad j = 1, \ldots, J, \tag{7.13}$$

where $S_j^a = (w_j x_j)/\pi^a$ is the cost share of variable input j to actual profit.

The complete system of the profit maximization problem consists of the profit function in (7.12) and the profit share equations in (7.13). Note that the profit share equations in (7.13) do not add any new parameters other than those already in (7.12). Two important features of the profit system are worth noting. First, technical inefficiency does not appear linearly in the profit function (meaning that, contrary to conventional wisdom, the log of actual profit is not just the log of the frontier profit minus technical inefficiency). Second, technical inefficiency is transmitted from the production function to the profit share equations as well, which is a property not present in the frontier cost system. Both of these issues have important implications in estimating technical inefficiency. Note that if a Cobb-Douglas function is used then: (i) u appears in a linear additive form (i.e., no u^2 and cross-products terms with u); and (ii) the share equations do not contain u.

7.3 Estimation Methods: Distribution-Free Approaches

The model introduced earlier may be estimated using the system consisting of (7.12) and (7.13), which is a complicated model because of the nonlinearity of u. The difficulty arises whether or not distribution assumptions are imposed on the stochastic terms.

To work around the problem, we show in this section and in Section 7.4 that a feasible approach is to base the estimation on only the share equations in (7.13). The estimation can be undertaken using either distribution-free approaches or parametric approaches (i.e., imposing distribution assumptions on the stochastic terms of the model). By estimating the share system we obtain consistent estimates of all the model parameters *except* the coefficients related to the quasi-fixed inputs (i.e., β_q and γ_{qs}), and the intercept β_0. Thus, if there are no quasi-fixed (q) variables in the profit function, all the parameters (except β_0) would be estimated in this step including the parameters of u and the inefficiency index. As such, it may not be necessary to estimate the profit frontier function itself.

If, however, there are quasi-fixed inputs, then values of β_q and γ_{qs} are part of the model but are not estimated when using only the share equations in estimation. If obtaining estimates of β_q and γ_{qs} are desired, a second step may be used in which one can construct the pseudo residual $\tilde{\varepsilon}$ from the first stage (see (7.25)) and regress it on the quasi-fixed inputs (e.g., $\ln q_q$ and $\ln q_q \times \ln q_s$, $\forall\, q, s$) to recover the remaining parameters.

An alternative approach to estimate the profit system model, which is discussed in greater detail in Section 7.5, is to impose the linear homogeneity assumption on the underlying production technology to simplify the model. The result leads to a simplified system consisting of (7.12) and (7.13) which can be estimated jointly. A system with a Cobb-Douglas specification on the production technology can also be estimated in this framework.

We first examine the distribution-free approaches (this section), before examining the the maximum likelihood (ML) approaches (Sections 7.4 and 7.5). Here, our focus is on estimating the model with inefficiency and we ignore the quasi-fixed input for the moment. If quasi-fixed inputs are of importance, one may still use the distribution-free estimation procedure below to obtain most of the model parameters (including the inefficiency index), and then follow the method outlined in Model 4 (on page 185) to recover the parameters related to the quasi-fixed inputs.

To proceed, we add zero-mean error terms (ζ_j) to each of the j share equation in (7.13) so that the composed error becomes $\zeta_j - a_j u$, where $a_j = \sum_k \beta_{jk}$. Note that, because $\mathrm{E}(u) \neq 0$ (i.e., that the error term does not have the mean equal to 0), the SURE estimate of β_j (the intercept) is inconsistent, although estimates of β_{jk} (the slope coefficients) are still consistent. We center the residual and rewrite the zero-mean composed error term as

$$\varepsilon_j = \zeta_j - a_j(u - \mu), \tag{7.14}$$

where $\mu = E(u)$. Note that now the intercept is $\beta_j^* = \beta_j - a_j\mu$ and so $\hat{\beta}_j^*$ is an inconsistent estimator of β_j.

The errors of the share equations, ε_j, can be summed up over J for each observation to define

$$\varepsilon = \sum_j \varepsilon_j = \sum_j (\zeta_j - a_j(u - \mu)) = \zeta - a(u - \mu) \equiv \zeta - u^* + b, \qquad (7.15)$$

where $u^* = a\,u$, $b = a\mu = \mu \sum_j a_j$, and $a = \sum_j a_j = \sum_j \sum_k \beta_{jk}$.

We may treat this equation as a stochastic frontier model where ε is the dependent variable (which in practice may be constructed from the results of a SURE estimation), b is a single constant (intercept), ζ is the model residual, and u^* is the inefficiency term. If the estimated $\hat{a} = \sum_j \sum_k \hat{\beta}_{jk}$ is positive, then $u^* \geq 0$ and a production frontier specification on (7.15) is appropriate. If $\hat{a} < 0$, define $u^{**} = -a\,u$, which is positive and we replace the term $-u^*$ in (7.15) by $+u^{**}$ and use a cost frontier estimation command to estimate it. From the estimates of u^* (or u^{**}), we can recover the estimated value of u as $\hat{u} = \hat{u}^*/\hat{a}$ if $\hat{a} > 0$ or $\hat{u} = \hat{u}^{**}/(-\hat{a})$ if otherwise.

Because $\beta_j^* = \beta_j - a_j\mu$, to get consistent estimators of β_j we need to get an estimate of $a_j\,\mu$. We already know $\hat{a}_j = \sum_k \hat{\beta}_{jk}$, so here we only need an estimate of μ. Note that $b = a\,\mu$ which, in turn, gives an estimate of $\mu = b/a$. Thus, the correction factor $a_j\,\mu$ can be estimated, which is then used to recover the original coefficients β_j from $\hat{\beta}_j = \hat{\beta}_j^* + \hat{a}_j\,\hat{\mu}$.

Example

Here and throughout this chapter, we consider a profit frontier model for U.S. airlines, which is the same example used in the earlier single equation profit chapter (Chapter 5). The dataset used is `air` and has 274 observations. Although it is a panel data we are again treating it as cross-sectional; the panel nature of the data is not exploited here. The dataset has the following variables (in logs): `y`, `l`, `f` and `mat` represents the quantity of output, labor, fuel, and materials respectively; `pl`, `pf`, and `pm` represent the price of labor, fuel, and materials, respectively. Materials, for illustration purposes, are considered as the quasi-fixed input.

Model 1: Classical Model with No Inefficiency and No Quasi-Fixed Inputs

In this first example, we introduce the author written Stata command sfsystem_profitshares, though for now we ignore the inefficiency term and the quasi-fixed input and consider only labor and fuel. As such, this is a classical profit system model without inefficiency (and, therefore, does not require distributional assumptions regarding u), and, as we show later, the estimation results are the same as those from SURE. We show this example mainly to illustrate the estimation command `sfsystem_profitshares` which will be used extensively in other models. This command is based on the log-likelihood function of (7.13) and it nests the model without inefficiency as a special case. Derivations of the log-likelihood function will be discussed in detail in Section 7.4.

The `sfsystem_profitshares` command only requires one to define the output, inputs, input prices, and output prices using `output(y)`, `inputs(l, f)`, `prices(pl, pf)`, and `yprice(py)`, respectively, and the log-likelihood function is constructed accordingly. The option `classical` is used in this first model so that the estimated model does not include an inefficiency term. As such, the option `distribution()` does not have to be specified. As before, `ml max` is then used to estimate the model.

```
. use air, clear

. sfsystem_profitshares, output(y) inputs(l f) prices(pl pf) ///
     yprice(py) noask classical
. sf_srch, n(3) inputs(l f) fast
. ml max, difficult

------------- Confirmation Message ----------------

(1) This model estimates the profit maximization behavior
    using share equations based on Kumbhakar (2001).

(2) The variable inputs' log prices are
    pl pf,
    with the corresponding log quantities being
    l f;
    the log of quasi-fixed inputs (if any) are
    ,
    and the price of output is
    py.

(3) The full variable specification of the profit function
    contains the following variables:
    pl pf plpl pfpf plpf.
    These are also the variables included in the share equations.
(4) You specified the -classical- option, so the model does not
    include the inefficiency effect.

(iteration log omitted)

                                          Number of obs   =        274
                                          Wald chi2(0)    =          .
Log likelihood =  329.19026               Prob > chi2     =          .

------------------------------------------------------------------------------
           y |      Coef.   Std. Err.      z    P>|z|     [95% Conf. Interval]
-------------+----------------------------------------------------------------
pl           |
       _cons |  -.9637256   .0420254   -22.93   0.000    -1.046094   -.8813574
-------------+----------------------------------------------------------------
pf           |
       _cons |  -.9967285   .0249109   -40.01   0.000    -1.045553    -.947904
-------------+----------------------------------------------------------------
plpl         |
       _cons |  -.2435163   .0273514    -8.90   0.000    -.2971241   -.1899085
-------------+----------------------------------------------------------------
pfpf         |
       _cons |   -.358049   .0091415   -39.17   0.000     -.375966   -.3401321
-------------+----------------------------------------------------------------
plpf         |
       _cons |   .0812943   .0136045     5.98   0.000       .05463    .1079587
-------------+----------------------------------------------------------------
s11          |
       _cons |  -1.587981   .0427263   -37.17   0.000    -1.671723   -1.504239
-------------+----------------------------------------------------------------
s22          |
       _cons |  -2.451321   .0427263   -57.37   0.000    -2.535063   -2.367578
-------------+----------------------------------------------------------------
s21          |
       _cons |   .0901845   .0064773    13.92   0.000     .0774892    .1028798
------------------------------------------------------------------------------
```

The `s11`, `s22`, and `s21` are parameterized factors of the variance parameters as discussed in Chapter 6. The original metrics can be recovered via `sf_transform` as follows:

```
. sf_transform

  ---convert the parameters to the original form---

variable     |      Coef.   Std. Err.       t    P>|t|      [95% Conf. Interval]
-------------+------------------------------------------------------------------
 sigma_1_sqr |   .0417539    .003568    11.70   0.000      .0353151    .0493668
 sigma_2_sqr |   .0155602   .0013296    11.70   0.000      .0129542    .0181662
    sigma_21 |   .0184281   .0019002     9.70   0.000      .0147037    .0221525
```

Alternatively, as this model does not include an inefficiency term, it can also be estimated using SURE. This is illustrated in the following code. Before estimating the model using the `sureg` command, the cost shares and normalized prices are generated.

```
. quietly generate double s_lab = WL*L/PFT
. quietly generate double s_fue = WF*F/PFT
. quietly generate double lwp_lab = -(pl-py)
. quietly generate double lwp_fue = -(pf-py)

. constraint define 1 [eq_lab]lwp_fue = [eq_fue]lwp_lab

. sureg (eq_lab: s_lab lwp_lab lwp_fue) (eq_fue: s_fue lwp_lab lwp_fue), isure constraint(1)

(iteration log omitted)

Seemingly unrelated regression, iterated

Constraints:
 ( 1)  [eq_lab]lwp_fue - [eq_fue]lwp_lab = 0
----------------------------------------------------------------------
Equation          Obs  Parms        RMSE    "R-sq"       chi2        P
----------------------------------------------------------------------
eq_lab            274      2    .2043378    0.1054     119.25   0.0000
eq_fue            274      2    .1247405    0.7486    1660.65   0.0000
----------------------------------------------------------------------

------------------------------------------------------------------------------
             |      Coef.   Std. Err.      z    P>|z|     [95% Conf. Interval]
-------------+----------------------------------------------------------------
eq_lab       |
     lwp_lab |  -.2435163   .0273459    -8.91   0.000    -.2971133   -.1899193
     lwp_fue |   .0812943   .0135988     5.98   0.000     .0546411    .1079475
       _cons |   .9637256   .0420248    22.93   0.000     .8813586    1.046093
-------------+----------------------------------------------------------------
eq_fue       |
     lwp_lab |   .0812943   .0135988     5.98   0.000     .0546411    .1079475
     lwp_fue |   -.358049   .0091403   -39.17   0.000    -.3759637   -.3401343
       _cons |   .9967285   .0249097    40.01   0.000     .9479063    1.045551
------------------------------------------------------------------------------
```

Except for the intercept, the estimated coefficients from SURE are the same as those estimated from the `sfsystem_profitshares` command. The intercepts have exactly the opposite signs because with SURE the estimated intercept is actually $-\hat{\beta}_j$.

Model 2: Distribution-Free Model with Technical Inefficiency and No Quasi-Fixed Input

Following the SURE estimation, we can now estimate inefficiency. First, we obtain the estimated errors from the SURE results and sum them up to obtain `res` (viz., ε).

```
. predict res_lab, resid equation(eq_lab)
. predict res_fue, resid equation(eq_fue)
. quietly generate res = res_lab + res_fue
```

```
. scalar beta_lab_star = -[eq_lab]:_cons   /* the constant beta_j; to be used later */
. scalar beta_fue_star = -[eq_fue]:_cons
```

Second, we obtain the a parameter as `a_para` from

```
. scalar a_para_lab = [eq_lab]:lwp_lab + [eq_lab]:lwp_fue
. scalar a_para_fue = [eq_fue]:lwp_lab + [eq_fue]:lwp_fue
. scalar a_para =  a_para_lab + a_para_fue

. display a_para
-.43897671
```

Because $\hat{a}$ is negative, we apply a *cost* frontier model with `res` as the dependent variable, by using `sfmodel` with the `cost` option. A constant, `cons`, is needed to force `sfmodel` to run, and we use `nocons` to instruct Stata not to append another constant. (We may also use a COLS model here to make the entire estimation procedure distribution free, if so desired.)

```
. quietly generate cons = 1

. sfmodel res, frontier(cons, nocons) dist(h) cost
. ml max, difficult

(iteration log omitted)
                                                  Number of obs    =        274
                                                  Wald chi2(1)     =      16.54
Log likelihood = -63.919927                       Prob > chi2      =     0.0000

------------------------------------------------------------------------------
         res |      Coef.   Std. Err.      z    P>|z|     [95% Conf. Interval]
-------------+----------------------------------------------------------------
frontier     |
        cons |  -.2203921   .0541962    -4.07   0.000    -.3266147   -.1141696
-------------+----------------------------------------------------------------
usigmas      |
       _cons |  -2.566081   .4744907    -5.41   0.000    -3.496066   -1.636096
-------------+----------------------------------------------------------------
vsigmas      |
       _cons |  -2.719512    .201725   -13.48   0.000    -3.114886   -2.324138
------------------------------------------------------------------------------
```

Third, we obtain estimates of inefficiency using

```
. sf_predict, jlms(u_2stars)
. quietly generate u = u_2stars/(-a_para)   /* the estimated inefficiency */
. summarize u

    Variable |       Obs        Mean    Std. Dev.       Min        Max
-------------+--------------------------------------------------------
           u |       274    .5020588    .2203295   .1626592   1.946268
```

Finally, we obtain the intercept from

```
. scalar b_para = [frontier]:cons
. quietly generate mu = b_para/a_para

. scalar beta_lab = beta_lab_star + a_para_lab*mu
. scalar beta_fue = beta_fue_star + a_para_fue*mu

. display beta_lab
-1.0451706

. display beta_fue
-1.1356756
```

We plot the estimated in Figure 7.1.

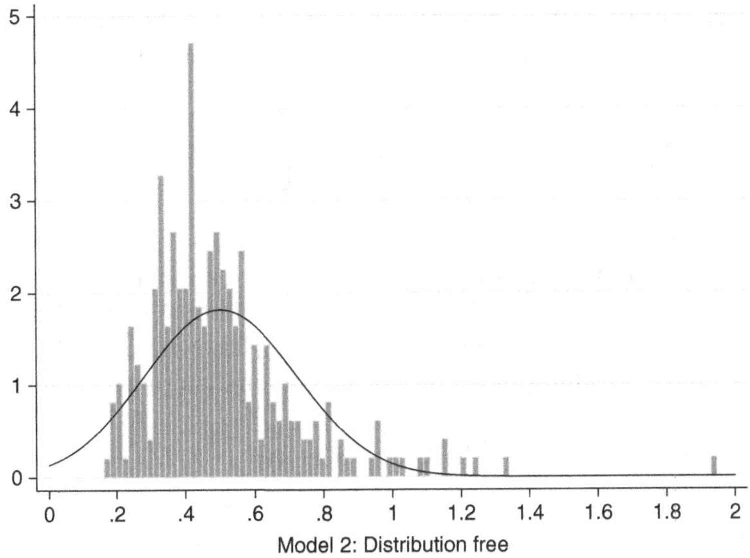

Figure 7.1. Estimated Efficiency from Distribution-Free Model

7.4 Estimation Methods: System of Share Equations, Maximum Likelihood Estimators

Here, we make distributional assumptions on the stochastic terms based on which the likelihood function of the model is derived. Model parameters are then estimated by numerically maximizing the log-likelihood function. As discussed earlier, estimating the profit system of (7.12) and (7.13) together is difficult due to the way the random variable u enters the model. Although it may still be estimated using the simulated maximum likelihood approach or the MCMC approach in a Bayesian framework (Kumbhakar and Tsionas [2005]), the conventional ML approach, that requires a closed form expression of the likelihood function, is either too difficult or perhaps infeasible. In this section, we show that feasible estimation may be achieved by estimating only the share equations of the system.

We start by considering a translog profit function with quasi-fixed inputs, that is, the system described in (7.12) and to (7.13). We add a zero-mean statistical error v to (7.12) and ζ to (7.13), and rewrite the system for ease of reference:

$$\begin{aligned}
\ln\left(\frac{\pi^a}{p}\right) = {} & \beta_0 + \sum_j \beta_j \ln\left(\frac{w_j}{p}\right) + \sum_q \beta_q \ln q_q \\
& + \frac{1}{2}\sum_j\sum_k \beta_{jk} \ln\left(\frac{w_j}{p}\right)\ln\left(\frac{w_k}{p}\right) \\
& + \frac{1}{2}\sum_q\sum_s \gamma_{qs}\ln q_q \ln q_s + \sum_j\sum_q \delta_{jq}\ln\left(\frac{w_j}{p}\right)\ln q_q \\
& + \left[-1 + \sum_j \beta_j + \sum_j\sum_q \delta_{jq}\ln q_q + \sum_j\sum_k \beta_{jk}\ln\left(\frac{w_j}{p}\right)\right] u \\
& + \left[\frac{1}{2}\sum_j\sum_k \beta_{jk}\right] u^2 + v,
\end{aligned} \tag{7.16}$$

The profit frontier consists of the first three lines of (7.16) and the logarithm of the profit loss function is in the last two lines, barring the v term. The share equations are:

$$S_j^a = -\left[\beta_j + \sum_q \delta_{jq} \ln q_q + \sum_k \beta_{jk} \ln(w_k/p)\right] - \left[\sum_k \beta_{jk}\right] u + \zeta_j, \qquad j = 1, \ldots, J, \tag{7.17}$$

where $S_j^a = (w_j x_j)/\pi^a$ is the cost share of variable input j to actual profit.

The log-likelihood function based on the system in (7.16) and (7.17) is infeasible, as previously stated. The log-likelihood function based on (7.17), however, can be derived as shown in Kumbhakar (2001). The function for the ith observation (ignoring the constant) is:

$$L_i = \ln \sigma - \frac{\boldsymbol{a}_i}{2} - \frac{1}{2} \ln |\boldsymbol{\Sigma}| - \ln \sigma_u + \ln \Phi\left(-\boldsymbol{Z}_i' \boldsymbol{\Sigma}^{-1} \boldsymbol{b} \sigma\right), \tag{7.18}$$

where

$$\sigma^2 = [1/\sigma_u^2 + \boldsymbol{b}' \boldsymbol{\Sigma}^{-1} \boldsymbol{b}]^{-1}, \tag{7.19}$$

$$\boldsymbol{a}_i = \boldsymbol{Z}_i' \boldsymbol{\Sigma}^{-1} \boldsymbol{Z}_i - \sigma^2 \left(\boldsymbol{Z}_i' \boldsymbol{\Sigma}^{-1} \boldsymbol{b}\right)^2, \tag{7.20}$$

$$\boldsymbol{b} = \begin{bmatrix} \beta_{10} \\ \beta_{20} \\ \vdots \\ \beta_{J0} \end{bmatrix} = \begin{bmatrix} \beta_{11} + \beta_{12} + \cdots + \beta_{1J} \\ \beta_{21} + \beta_{22} + \cdots + \beta_{2J} \\ \vdots \\ \beta_{J1} + \beta_{J2} + \cdots + \beta_{JJ} \end{bmatrix}, \tag{7.21}$$

$$\boldsymbol{Z}_i = (-\boldsymbol{b} u_i + \zeta_i) = \begin{bmatrix} -\beta_{10} u_i + \zeta_{i1} \\ -\beta_{20} u_i + \zeta_{i2} \\ \vdots \\ -\beta_{J0} u_i + \zeta_{iJ} \end{bmatrix}. \tag{7.22}$$

The command `sfsystem_profitshares` implements the maximum-likelihood estimation of the model. After the parameters are estimated, technical inefficiency can be obtained based on the formula of Kumbhakar (1987, 2001), which is a generalization of the Jondrow et al. (1982) result to a simultaneous equation system. The formula is based on the conditional mean of u_i given $\boldsymbol{Z}_i$. Since $u_i|\boldsymbol{Z}_i \sim N^+(\tilde{\mu}_i, \sigma^2)$, $u_i \geq 0$, the Jondrow et al. (1982) type estimator of u_i is

$$\hat{u}_i = E(u_i|\boldsymbol{Z}_i) = \tilde{\mu}_i + \sigma \frac{\phi(\tilde{\mu}/\sigma)}{\Phi(\tilde{\mu}_i/\sigma)}, \tag{7.23}$$

where $\tilde{\mu}_i = -\boldsymbol{Z}_i' \boldsymbol{\Sigma}^{-1} \boldsymbol{b} \sigma^2$.

Alternatively, one can estimate technical efficiency from

$$\widehat{TE}_i = E(\exp(-u_i|\boldsymbol{Z}_i)) = \frac{1 - \Phi[\sigma - (\tilde{\mu}_i/\sigma)]}{\Phi(\tilde{\mu}_i/\sigma)} \exp(-\tilde{\mu}_i + .5\sigma^2). \tag{7.24}$$

As indicated in (7.17), the share equations do not contain the coefficients of quasi-fixed inputs, β_q and γ_{qs}, and therefore the share-based estimation of (7.18) does not yield the estimates of these parameters. If desired, they can be recovered in the second step by regressing the following pseudo residual, $\tilde{\varepsilon}$, on the quasi-fixed inputs, $\ln q_q$ and $\ln q_q \times \ln q_s$, $\forall\, q, s$:

$$\tilde{\varepsilon} = \ln\left(\frac{\pi^a}{p}\right) - \sum_j \hat{\beta}_j \ln(\tilde{w}_j) - \frac{1}{2}\sum\sum \hat{\beta}_{jk} \ln(\tilde{w}_j)\ln(\tilde{w}_k) - \sum_q\sum \hat{\delta}_{jq}\ln(\tilde{w}_j)\ln q_q$$
$$- \left[-1 + \sum \hat{\beta}_j + \sum\sum \hat{\beta}_{jk}\ln(\tilde{w}_j)\right]\hat{u} - \left[\frac{1}{2}\sum\sum \hat{\beta}_{jk}\right]\hat{u}^2, \tag{7.25}$$

where $\tilde{w}_j = (w_j/p)$ and all the estimated β-coefficients and $\hat{u}$ are from the first stage.

In the following examples, we assume two variable inputs and at most one quasi-fixed input in the model. To facilitate the discussion, we write down the equation for this case as follows:

$$\begin{aligned}
\ln\left(\frac{\pi^a}{p}\right) &= \beta_0 + \beta_1 \ln\left(\frac{w_1}{p}\right) + \beta_2 \ln\left(\frac{w_2}{p}\right) + \beta_3 \ln q \\
&\quad + \frac{1}{2}\beta_{11} \ln\left(\frac{w_1}{p}\right)^2 + \frac{1}{2}\beta_{22} \ln\left(\frac{w_2}{p}\right)^2 + \frac{1}{2}\beta_{33} \ln q^2 \\
&\quad + \beta_{12} \ln\left(\frac{w_1}{p}\right)\ln\left(\frac{w_2}{p}\right) + \beta_{13} \ln\left(\frac{w_1}{p}\right)\ln q + \beta_{23} \ln\left(\frac{w_2}{p}\right)\ln q \\
&\quad + \Big[-1 + \beta_1 + \beta_2 + \beta_{11}\ln\left(\frac{w_1}{p}\right) + \beta_{22}\ln\left(\frac{w_2}{p}\right) + \beta_{12}\ln\left(\frac{w_1}{p}\right) \\
&\quad + \beta_{12}\ln\left(\frac{w_2}{p}\right) + \beta_{13}\ln q + \beta_{23}\ln q\Big]u + \left[\frac{1}{2}\beta_{11} + \frac{1}{2}\beta_{22} + \beta_{12}\right]u^2 + v.
\end{aligned} \tag{7.26}$$

The profit share equations of the model are

$$S_1^a = -\left[\beta_1 + \beta_{11}\ln\left(\frac{w_1}{p}\right) + \beta_{12}\ln\left(\frac{w_2}{p}\right) + \beta_{13}\ln q\right] + (\beta_{11} + \beta_{12})u + \zeta_1, \tag{7.27}$$

$$S_2^a = -\left[\beta_2 + \beta_{12}\ln\left(\frac{w_1}{p}\right) + \beta_{22}\ln\left(\frac{w_2}{p}\right) + \beta_{23}\ln q\right] + (\beta_{12} + \beta_{22})u + \zeta_2. \tag{7.28}$$

Example

Model 3: Half-Normal Model with No Quasi-Fixed Input (Share-Based Estimation)

Here we assume that there is no quasi-fixed input, which means β_3, β_{33}, β_{13}, β_{23}, β_{13}, β_{23} are equal to 0 in (7.26) to (7.28). We again use the `sfsystem_profitshares` command to estimate the model in (7.27) and (7.28). Because there is no quasi-fixed input, all the parameters in the frontier function (7.26) are contained in the share equations (7.27) and (7.28) (except for β_0), and so, `sfsystem_profitshares` is sufficient for the purpose of obtaining the model parameters and there is no need for a second step estimation.

The command `sfsystem_profitshares` was previously introduced for Model 1 on page 177. Here, we follow that example but drop the `classical` option and add the distribution option `dist()` for u. We assume u follows a half-normal distribution.

```
. sfsystem_profitshares, output(y) yprice(py) inputs(l f) ///
      prices(pl pf) noask dist(h)
. sf_srch, n(1) inputs(l f) fast
. ml max, difficult

------------- Confirmation Message ----------------

(1) This model estimates the profit maximization behavior
    using share equations based on Kumbhakar (2001, AJAE).

(2) The variable inputs' log prices are
    pl pf,
    with the corresponding log quantities being
    l f;
    the log of quasi-fixed inputs (if any) are
    ,
    and the price of output is
    py.

(3) The full variable specification of the profit function
    contains the following variables:
    pl pf plpl pfpf plpf.
    These are also the variables included in the share equations.

(iteration log omitted)

                                                  Number of obs   =        274
                                                  Wald chi2(0)    =          .
Log likelihood =  356.51047                       Prob > chi2     =          .

------------------------------------------------------------------------------
           y |      Coef.   Std. Err.      z    P>|z|     [95% Conf. Interval]
-------------+----------------------------------------------------------------
pl           |
       _cons |   -.865778    .022993   -37.65   0.000    -.9108433   -.8207126
-------------+----------------------------------------------------------------
pf           |
       _cons |  -.8133176   .0205868   -39.51   0.000     -.853667   -.7729683
-------------+----------------------------------------------------------------
plpl         |
       _cons |  -.2064043   .0199864   -10.33   0.000    -.2455768   -.1672317
-------------+----------------------------------------------------------------
pfpf         |
       _cons |  -.3190737   .0093938   -33.97   0.000    -.3374853   -.3006621
-------------+----------------------------------------------------------------
plpf         |
       _cons |   .0743484    .011456     6.49   0.000     .0518951    .0968017
-------------+----------------------------------------------------------------
s11          |
       _cons |  -1.628222   .0455572   -35.74   0.000    -1.717512   -1.538931
-------------+----------------------------------------------------------------
s22          |
       _cons |  -3.468005   .1596276   -21.73   0.000    -3.780869   -3.155141
-------------+----------------------------------------------------------------
s21          |
       _cons |   .0624739   .0065814     9.49   0.000     .0495746    .0753732
-------------+----------------------------------------------------------------
usigmas      |
       _cons |  -.8170173    .165268    -4.94   0.000    -1.140937   -.4930979
------------------------------------------------------------------------------
```

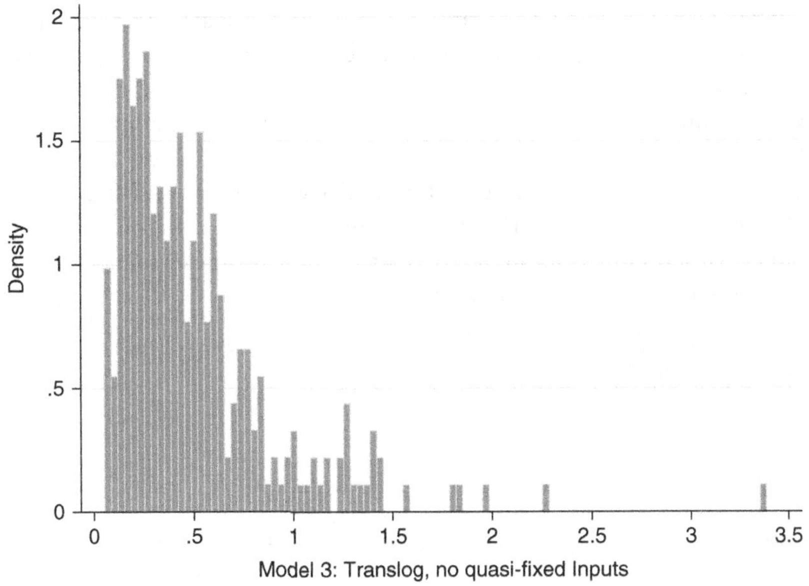

Figure 7.2. Estimated Inefficiency from Model 3

As explained in the previous example, the `s11` and other similar parameters cannot be directly interpreted. We use `sf_transform` to obtain estimated elements of the matrix in their original metrics.

```
. sf_transform

      sigma_u_sqr = exp(usigmas);

   ---convert the parameters to the original form---

variable     |      Coef.    Std. Err.       t    P>|t|      [95% Conf. Interval]
-------------+-------------------------------------------------------------------
 sigma_u_sqr |   .4417473   .0730067      6.05   0.000      .3195196     .6107315
 sigma_1_sqr |   .0385252   .0035102     10.98   0.000      .0322246     .0460576
 sigma_2_sqr |   .0048751   .0008661      5.63   0.000      .0031776     .0065726
    sigma_21 |   .0122623   .0017173      7.14   0.000      .0088965     .0156281
```

The resulting estimates of inefficiency are summarized here:

```
. sf_predict, jlms(jlms_mod3) bc(bc_mod3)
. summarize jlms_mod3 bc_mod3

    Variable |       Obs        Mean    Std. Dev.       Min        Max
-------------+--------------------------------------------------------
   jlms_mod3 |       274    .5069744    .4081912   .0529028   3.383694
     bc_mod3 |       274    .6475033    .1904346   .0343011   .9495509
```

A plot of the estimated inefficiency is provided in Figure 7.2.

Model 4: Half-Normal Model with One Quasi-Fixed Input (Share-Based Estimation)

In this model, we assume there is one quasi-fixed input in addition to two variable inputs, which is exactly the model in (7.26) to (7.28). The command `sfsystem_profitshares` would estimate most of the model's parameters based on the share equations, including β_1, β_2, β_{11}, β_{12}, β_{13} β_{22}, β_{23}, σ_u^2, and the covariance matrix of the two equations (i.e., $\mathbf{\Sigma}$). Technical inefficiency is then computed from (7.23). If estimates of β_3 and β_{33} are also desired, one can run a simple regression of the pseudo residual as defined in (7.25) on $\ln q$ and $(\ln q)^2$.

To use `sfsystem_profitshares` for this model, we add the quasi-fixed input `mat` as a third input in the `inputs()` option but leave out its price in the `prices()` option. Leaving out an input's corresponding price in the `prices()` informs `sfsystem_profitshares` that the input should be treated as quasi-fixed.

```
. sfsystem_profitshares, output(y) inputs(l f mat) prices(pl pf) ///
        yprice(py) noask dist(h)
. sf_srch, n(2) inputs(l f mat) usigmas() fast nograph
. ml max, difficult


------------- Confirmation Message ---------------

(1) This model estimates the profit maximization behavior
    using share equations based on Kumbhakar (2001, AJAE).

(2) The variable inputs' log prices are
    pl pf,
    with the corresponding log quantities being
    l f;
    the log of quasi-fixed inputs (if any) are
    mat,
    and the price of output is
    py.

(3) The full variable specification of the profit function
    contains the following variables:
    pl pf mat plpl pfpf matmat plpf plmat pfmat.
    However, the FOC-based system profit model only estiamtes
    coefficients of the following variables:
    pl pf plpl pfpf plpf plmat pfmat.
    That is, coefficients of the quasi-fiexed inputs (mat)
    and their square terms (if a translog model) are not estimated
    in this FOC-based system model, although they may be recovered
    after the estimation.


(iteration log omitted)


                                                Number of obs    =        274
                                                Wald chi2(0)     =          .
Log likelihood =  108.60236                     Prob > chi2      =          .

------------------------------------------------------------------------------
           y |      Coef.   Std. Err.      z    P>|z|     [95% Conf. Interval]
-------------+----------------------------------------------------------------
pl           |
       _cons |  -.8583542   .0229419   -37.41   0.000    -.9033195   -.8133889
-------------+----------------------------------------------------------------
pf           |
       _cons |   -.794397   .0236931   -33.53   0.000    -.8408345   -.7479594
-------------+----------------------------------------------------------------
plpl         |
       _cons |  -.2004629   .0232012    -8.64   0.000    -.2459364   -.1549894
-------------+----------------------------------------------------------------
```

```
pfpf         |
       _cons |  -.3104649   .0098267   -31.59   0.000     -.3297249    -.291205
-------------+----------------------------------------------------------------
plpf         |
       _cons |    .091956   .0143331     6.42   0.000      .0638637    .1200484
-------------+----------------------------------------------------------------
plmat        |
       _cons |  -.0278026   .0122324    -2.27   0.023     -.0517778   -.0038275
-------------+----------------------------------------------------------------
pfmat        |
       _cons |  -.0193269   .0070707    -2.73   0.006     -.0331851   -.0054686
-------------+----------------------------------------------------------------
s11          |
       _cons |  -1.638569   .0457005   -35.85   0.000      -1.72814   -1.548998
-------------+----------------------------------------------------------------
s22          |
       _cons |  -3.605193   .1877771   -19.20   0.000      -3.97323   -3.237157
-------------+----------------------------------------------------------------
s21          |
       _cons |    .060999   .0069866     8.73   0.000      .0473056    .0746925
-------------+----------------------------------------------------------------
usigmas      |
       _cons |  -.5715312   .2275136    -2.51   0.012      -1.01745   -.1256128
------------------------------------------------------------------------------
```

Again, we use `sf_transform` to obtain estimated elements of the matrix in their original form.

```
. sf_transform

     sigma_u_sqr = exp(usigmas);

   ---convert the parameters to the original form---

variable     |       Coef.   Std. Err.      t    P>|t|      [95% Conf. Interval]
-------------+----------------------------------------------------------------
 sigma_u_sqr |   .5646602   .1284679     4.40   0.000      .3615158    .8819563
 sigma_1_sqr |   .0377361   .0034491    10.94   0.000      .0315469    .0451396
 sigma_2_sqr |   .0044598   .0009106     4.90   0.000      .0026751    .0062444
    sigma_21 |   .0118495   .0017641     6.72   0.000      .0083921     .015307
```

The resulting inefficiency estimates are summarized here:

```
. sf_predict, jlms(jlms_mod4) bc(bc_mod4)
. summarize jlms_mod4 bc_mod4

    Variable |       Obs        Mean    Std. Dev.       Min        Max
-------------+--------------------------------------------------------
   jlms_mod4 |       274    .5727516    .4684256   .0569236   3.872403
     bc_mod4 |       274    .6171346    .2040352   .0210256   .9458697
```

A plot of the estimated inefficiency is provided in Figure 7.3.

If estimates of β_3 and β_{33} are desired, then we may construct the pseudo residual using (7.25) and regress the residual on relevant terms. For the current example, the pseudo residual is

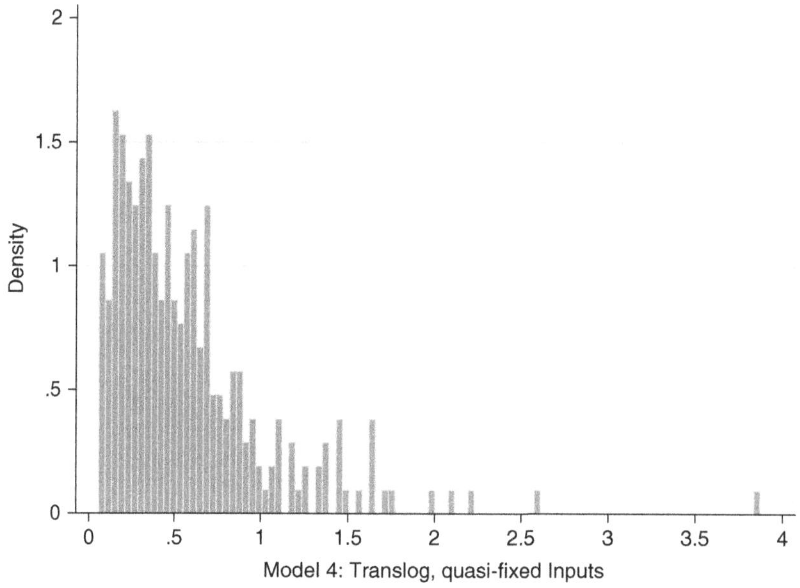

Figure 7.3. Estimated Inefficiency from Model 4

$$\begin{aligned}\tilde{\varepsilon} = \ln\left(\frac{\pi^a}{p}\right) - \hat{\beta}_1 \ln\left(\frac{w_1}{p}\right) - \hat{\beta}_2 \ln\left(\frac{w_2}{p}\right) \\ - \frac{1}{2}\hat{\beta}_{11} \ln\left(\frac{w_1}{p}\right)^2 - \frac{1}{2}\hat{\beta}_{22} \ln\left(\frac{w_2}{p}\right)^2 \\ - \hat{\beta}_{12} \ln\left(\frac{w_1}{p}\right) \ln\left(\frac{w_2}{p}\right) - \hat{\beta}_{13} \ln\left(\frac{w_1}{p}\right) \ln q - \hat{\beta}_{23} \ln\left(\frac{w_2}{p}\right) \ln q \\ - \Big[-1 + \hat{\beta}_1 + \hat{\beta}_2 + \hat{\beta}_{11} \ln\left(\frac{w_1}{p}\right) + \hat{\beta}_{22} \ln\left(\frac{w_2}{p}\right) + \hat{\beta}_{12} \ln\left(\frac{w_1}{p}\right) \\ + \hat{\beta}_{12} \ln\left(\frac{w_2}{p}\right) + \hat{\beta}_{13} \ln q + \hat{\beta}_{23} \ln q \Big] \hat{u} - \left[\frac{1}{2}\hat{\beta}_{11} + \frac{1}{2}\hat{\beta}_{22} + \hat{\beta}_{12}\right] \hat{u}^2,\end{aligned} \tag{7.29}$$

where all the estimated β-coefficients and $\hat{u}$ are from the first stage of the estimation. By regressing $\tilde{\varepsilon}$ on a constant, $\ln$ mat, and $\frac{1}{2} \ln \text{mat}^2$, the estimated coefficients of the later two variables yield $\hat{\beta}_3$ and $\hat{\beta}_{33}$. Note that, sfsystem_profitshares creates new variables (w_c1, w_c2, etc.) as the new input price variables, where w_ci is the normalized input price by output price (in logs).

```
. generate double resid_1 = _pft1a - (-0.85835*$w_c1 - 0.7944*$w_c2 - 0.5*0.20046*$w_c1*$w_c1 ///
>                 - 0.5*0.31046*$w_c2*$w_c2 + 0.09196*$w_c1*$w_c2 ///
>                 - 0.02780*$w_c1*mat - 0.019327*$w_c2*mat ///
>                 + jlms_mod4*(-1 - 0.85835 - 0.7944 ///
>                     -0.20046*$w_c1 -0.31046*$w_c1 + 0.09196*$w_c2 -0.31046*$w_c2) ///
>                 + (((jlms_mod4)^2)*0.5*(-0.20046+0.09196+0.09196-0.31046)))

. regress resid_1 mat mat2
```

```
      Source |       SS       df       MS              Number of obs =       274
-------------+------------------------------           F(  2,   271) =     22.22
       Model |  76.8612575     2  38.4306287           Prob > F      =    0.0000
    Residual |   468.77298   271   1.7297896           R-squared     =    0.1409
-------------+------------------------------           Adj R-squared =    0.1345
       Total |  545.634238   273  1.99866021           Root MSE      =    1.3152

------------------------------------------------------------------------------
     resid_1 |      Coef.   Std. Err.      t    P>|t|     [95% Conf. Interval]
-------------+----------------------------------------------------------------
         mat |   .5961112   .1579581     3.77   0.000     .2851302    .9070922
        mat2 |   .1199548    .142757     0.84   0.401    -.1610989    .4010085
       _cons |  -.0749105   .1043296    -0.72   0.473    -.2803101     .130489
------------------------------------------------------------------------------
```

Thus, $\beta_3 = 0.596$, and $\beta_{33} = 0.120$.

Model 5: Half-Normal Model with Quasi-Fixed Inputs and Heteroscedasticity (Share-Based Estimation)

We may also introduce determinants of inefficiency ($\boldsymbol{z}$) into the model by reparameterizing $\sigma_u^2(\boldsymbol{z}) = \exp(\gamma_0 + \boldsymbol{\gamma}'\boldsymbol{z})$. Replacing σ_u^2 by the parameterized function in (7.18), we can estimate the log-likelihood function and obtain model parameters including γ_0 and $\boldsymbol{\gamma}$.

Suppose that LOAD is used as the determinant of inefficiency in the current model. The following commands estimate the model:

```
. sfsystem_profitshares, output(y) inputs(l f mat) prices(pl pf) ///
>       yprice(py)  noask dist(h) usigmas(LOAD)
. sf_srch, n(2) inputs(l f mat) usigmas(LOAD) fast nograph
. ml max, difficult
```

Because LOAD appears to be insignificant in the model, we skip reporting the results.

7.5 Estimation Methods: Imposing Homogeneity Assumptions, Maximum Likelihood Estimators

In the previous section, the ML estimation is based on the share equations of the profit system. In this section, we show that the estimation of a full system consisting of the frontier and the share equations is possible if the homogeneity assumption is imposed on the underlying technology to simplify the model.

The homogeneity assumption on the translog profit system in (7.12) and (7.13) implies the following restrictions: $\sum_k \beta_{jk} = 0\,\forall j$, and $\sum_j \delta_{jq} = 0\,\forall\, q$. With these restrictions, the last line of (7.12) reduces to $\ln h(\boldsymbol{w}/p, \boldsymbol{q}, u) = -\left[1 - \sum_j \beta_j\right] u \equiv -\tilde{u}$. The profit function in (7.12) can then be rewritten as

$$\begin{aligned}\ln\left(\frac{\pi^a}{p}\right) &= \beta_0 + \sum_j \beta_j \ln\left(\frac{w_j}{p}\right) + \sum_q \beta_q \ln q_q + \frac{1}{2}\sum_{j=2}\sum_{k=2} \beta_{jk} \ln(\tilde{w}_j) \ln(\tilde{w}_k) \\ &+ \frac{1}{2}\sum_q\sum_s \gamma_{qs} \ln q_q \ln q_s + \sum_{j=2}\sum_q \delta_{jq} \ln(\tilde{w}_j) \ln q_q - \tilde{u},\end{aligned} \tag{7.30}$$

where $\tilde{w}_j = \frac{w_j/p}{w_1/p} = w_j/w_1$.

In addition, under the homogeneity assumption the u term drops out from the share equations in (7.13), and so the profit share equations are

$$
\begin{aligned}
S_1^a &= -\left[\beta_1 + \sum_q \delta_{1q} \ln q_q + \sum_k \beta_{1k} \ln(\tilde{w}_k)\right], \\
S_j^a &= -\left[\beta_j + \sum_q \delta_{jq} \ln q_q + \sum_k \beta_{jk} \ln(\tilde{w}_k)\right], \qquad j, k, q = 2, \ldots, J.
\end{aligned}
\tag{7.31}
$$

where $\delta_{1q} = -\sum_{j=2} \delta_{jq}$ and $\beta_{1k} = -\sum_{j=2} \beta_{jk}$.

This simplification implies that: (i) $\ln h(\cdot) = -\left(1 - \sum_j \beta_j\right) u \equiv -\tilde{u}$; and (ii) the share equations are independent of u. Consequently, the conventional wisdom holds in the sense that the log difference between the actual and the frontier profit is captured by an inefficiency term, and it is a scaled output-oriented technical inefficiency.

The homogeneity assumption helps us to estimate (7.30) and (7.31) jointly. For this, we add zero-mean random error variables v to (7.30) and ζ_j to (7.31), and assume $u_i \sim N^+(0, \sigma_u^2)$ and $\Xi_i = (v, \boldsymbol{\zeta}')' \sim N(0, \Sigma)$. Further more, define the following notations:

$$
\boldsymbol{b} = (1, 0, \ldots, 0)', \tag{7.32}
$$

$$
Z_i = \Xi_i - \boldsymbol{b} u_i. \tag{7.33}
$$

The log-likelihood function can be derived from the probability density function of Z_i. For the ith observation, the log-likelihood function (omitting the constant) is

$$
L_i = \ln \boldsymbol{\sigma} - \frac{\boldsymbol{a}_i}{2} - \frac{1}{2} \ln |\Sigma| - \ln \sigma_u + \ln \Phi\left(-Z_i' \Sigma^{-1} \boldsymbol{b} \boldsymbol{\sigma}\right), \tag{7.34}
$$

where

$$
\boldsymbol{\sigma}^2 = [1/\sigma_u^2 + \boldsymbol{b}' \Sigma^{-1} \boldsymbol{b}]^{-1}, \tag{7.35}
$$

$$
\boldsymbol{a}_i = Z_i' \Sigma^{-1} Z_i - \boldsymbol{\sigma}^2 \left(Z_i' \Sigma^{-1} \boldsymbol{b}\right)^2. \tag{7.36}
$$

Note that, although (7.35) and (7.36) look the same as (7.19) and (7.20), the definitions of Z_i and $\boldsymbol{b}$ are different. This model allows correlations or independence between v and $\boldsymbol{\zeta}$ through assumptions imposed on the variance-covariance matrix Σ.

After the parameters of the model are estimated, technical (in)efficiency can be estimated using the Jondrow et al. (1982) or the Battese-Coelli formula. The formulae are the same as the ones in (7.23) and (7.24).

In the case of two variable and one quasi-fixed inputs, the homogeneity assumption imposes the restrictions that $\beta_{11} + \beta_{12} = 0$, $\beta_{12} + \beta_{22} = 0$, and $\beta_{13} + \beta_{23} = 0$. These restrictions simplify the profit function substantially. It can be seen that the last line of (7.26) reduces to $[-1 + \beta_1 + \beta_2]\, u$, and that the u terms disappear from (7.27) and (7.28). Rewriting the system, we have

$$\ln\left(\frac{\pi^a}{p}\right) = \beta_0 + \beta_1 \ln\left(\frac{w_1}{p}\right) + \beta_2 \ln\left(\frac{w_2}{p}\right) + \beta_3 \ln q$$
$$+ \frac{1}{2}\beta_{22} \ln\left(\frac{w_2}{w_1}\right) \ln\left(\frac{w_2}{w_1}\right) + \frac{1}{2}\gamma_{11} \ln q^2 + \delta_{21} \ln\left(\frac{w_2}{w_1}\right) \ln q \tag{7.37}$$
$$- [1 - \beta_1 - \beta_2]\, u + v,$$

$$S_1^a = -\left[\beta_1 - \beta_{22} \ln\left(\frac{w_2}{w_1}\right) - \delta_{21} \ln q\right] + \zeta_1, \tag{7.38}$$

$$S_2^a = -\left[\beta_2 + \beta_{22} \ln\left(\frac{w_2}{w_1}\right) + \delta_{21} \ln q\right] + \zeta_2. \tag{7.39}$$

Because $[1 - \beta_1 - \beta_2]$ is a constant, we can define $\tilde{u} \equiv [1 - \beta_1 - \beta_2]u$ and substitute $\tilde{u}$ into (7.37) without loss of generality. Note that estimating only the share equations in this case is not of much value because these equations do not contain u.

Example

Model 6: Homogeneous Production Function

Here we estimate equations (7.37)–(7.39) by SURE and use the results as the initial values for the ML estimation on (7.34).

```
. quietly generate double wl = ln(WL/P)
. quietly generate double wf = ln(WF/P)
. quietly generate double wl_wf2 = 0.5*(wl-wf)^2
. quietly generate double mat2 = 0.5*mat^2
. quietly generate double matwl_wf = mat*(wl-wf)

. global xvar wl wf mat wl_wf2 mat2 matwl_wf   /* frontier variables */
. global svar wl_wf mat    /* share equation variables */

. constraint define 1 -[share1]_b[_cons] =  [frontier]_b[wf]
. constraint define 2 [share1]_b[wl_wf] =  [frontier]_b[wl_wf2]
. constraint define 3 [share1]_b[mat]      =  [frontier]_b[matwl_wf]

. constraint define 4 -[share2]_b[_cons] =  [frontier]_b[wl]
. constraint define 5 -[share2]_b[wl_wf] =  [frontier]_b[wl_wf2]
. constraint define 6 -[share2]_b[mat]     =  [frontier]_b[matwl_wf]


. sureg (frontier: pft=$xvar) (share1: s_fue=$svar) (share2: s_lab=$svar), isure constraints(1-6)

(iteration log omitted)

Seemingly unrelated regression, iterated

Constraints:
 ( 1)  - [frontier]wf - [share1]_cons = 0
 ( 2)  - [frontier]wl_wf2 + [share1]wl_wf = 0
 ( 3)  - [frontier]matwl_wf + [share1]mat = 0
 ( 4)  - [frontier]wl - [share2]_cons = 0
 ( 5)  - [frontier]wl_wf2 - [share2]wl_wf = 0
 ( 6)  - [frontier]matwl_wf - [share2]mat = 0
----------------------------------------------------------------------
Equation          Obs  Parms        RMSE    "R-sq"       chi2        P
----------------------------------------------------------------------
frontier          274      6    .5578031    0.8045    6485.34   0.0000
share1            274      2    .1761376    0.4987     993.97   0.0000
share2            274      2     .235723   -0.1905     993.97   0.0000
----------------------------------------------------------------------

------------------------------------------------------------------------------
             |      Coef.   Std. Err.      z    P>|z|     [95% Conf. Interval]
-------------+----------------------------------------------------------------
```

```
frontier     |
          wl |  -.6340367   .0152831   -41.49   0.000    -.6639911   -.6040823
          wf |  -.5763888   .0110372   -52.22   0.000    -.5980213   -.5547563
         mat |   1.376989   .0553375    24.88   0.000      1.26853    1.485449
      wl_wf2 |  -.2147463   .0068449   -31.37   0.000    -.2281621   -.2013306
        mat2 |   .0086261   .0481147     0.18   0.858    -.0856769    .1029291
   matwl_wf  |   .0214421   .0037351     5.74   0.000     .0141214    .0287628
       _cons |  -2.523882   .0457299   -55.19   0.000    -2.613511   -2.434253
-------------+----------------------------------------------------------------
share1       |
       wl_wf |  -.2147463   .0068449   -31.37   0.000    -.2281621   -.2013306
         mat |   .0214421   .0037351     5.74   0.000     .0141214    .0287628
       _cons |   .5763888   .0110372    52.22   0.000     .5547563    .5980213
-------------+----------------------------------------------------------------
share2       |
       wl_wf |   .2147463   .0068449    31.37   0.000     .2013306    .2281621
         mat |  -.0214421   .0037351    -5.74   0.000    -.0287628   -.0141214
       _cons |   .6340367   .0152831    41.49   0.000     .6040823    .6639911
------------------------------------------------------------------------------
```

The coefficients from this model are then saved using

```
. matrix b0 = e(b)
. matrix b0_f = b0[1, "frontier:"]
. matrix b0_s1 = b0[1, "share1:"]
. matrix b0_s2 = b0[1, "share2:"]
```

Now the stochastic frontier model in (7.34) can be estimated by `sfsystem` using these starting values.

```
. sfsystem pft, profit distribution(h) corr(no) frontier($xvar) share1(s_fue=$svar) ///
>              share2(s_lab=$svar) gamma sigmauv s11 s22 constraints(1-6) show
. sf_init, frontier(b0_f) share1(b0_s1) share2(b0_s2) gamma(0.1) sigmauv(0.1) s11(0.1) s22(0.1)
. sf_srch, frontier($xvar) share1($svar) share2($svar) n(3) fast
. ml max, diff gtol(1e-5) nrtol(1e-5)
```

This produces the following output:

```
(iteration log omitted)
                                                  Number of obs   =        274
                                                  Wald chi2(2)    =    1914.83
Log likelihood = -116.17867                       Prob > chi2     =     0.0000

 ( 1)  - [frontier]wf - [share1]_cons = 0
 ( 2)  - [frontier]wl_wf2 + [share1]wl_wf = 0
 ( 3)  - [frontier]matwl_wf + [share1]mat = 0
 ( 4)  - [frontier]wl - [share2]_cons = 0
 ( 5)  - [frontier]wl_wf2 - [share2]wl_wf = 0
 ( 6)  - [frontier]matwl_wf - [share2]mat = 0
------------------------------------------------------------------------------
             |      Coef.   Std. Err.      z    P>|z|     [95% Conf. Interval]
-------------+----------------------------------------------------------------
frontier     |
          wl |  -.5703957   .0221768   -25.72   0.000    -.6138614   -.5269299
          wf |  -.6807285   .0174537   -39.00   0.000    -.7149371   -.6465199
         mat |    1.35715   .0683863    19.85   0.000     1.223115    1.491185
      wl_wf2 |  -.3195134    .018149   -17.61   0.000    -.3550847    -.283942
        mat2 |  -.0323378   .0614966    -0.53   0.599     -.152869    .0881933
    matwl_wf |   .0506371   .0077678     6.52   0.000     .0354125    .0658618
       _cons |  -2.526308   .1574179   -16.05   0.000    -2.834842   -2.217775
-------------+----------------------------------------------------------------
share1       |
       wl_wf |  -.3195134    .018149   -17.61   0.000    -.3550847    -.283942
         mat |   .0506371   .0077678     6.52   0.000     .0354125    .0658618
       _cons |   .6807285   .0174537    39.00   0.000     .6465199    .7149371
-------------+----------------------------------------------------------------
share2       |
       wl_wf |   .3195134    .018149    17.61   0.000      .283942    .3550847
```

```
         mat |  -.0506371   .0077678    -6.52   0.000    -.0658618   -.0354125
       _cons |   .5703957   .0221768    25.72   0.000     .5269299    .6138614
-------------+----------------------------------------------------------------
usigmas      |
       _cons |  -15.63817   915.2975    -0.02   0.986    -1809.588    1778.312
-------------+----------------------------------------------------------------
s11          |
       _cons |  -.5688137   .0439113   -12.95   0.000    -.6548784   -.4827491
-------------+----------------------------------------------------------------
s22          |
       _cons |  -1.930609   .0488748   -39.50   0.000    -2.026402   -1.834816
-------------+----------------------------------------------------------------
s33          |
       _cons |  -1.333383    .048859   -27.29   0.000    -1.429145   -1.237621
------------------------------------------------------------------------------

. sf_transform

      sigma_u_sqr = exp(usigmas), the estiamted variance of u.
      sigma_v_sqr, the estiamted variance of v.
      sigma_i_sqr, the estimated variance of the ith share equation.
      sigma_iv: covariance of the ith share and the v.
      sigma_ij: covariance of the ith and the jth share equation.

   ---convert the parameters to the original form---

variable     |      Coef.   Std. Err.       t     P>|t|      [95% Conf. Interval]
-------------+----------------------------------------------------------------
 sigma_u_sqr |   1.62e-07   .0001479     0.00    0.999            0           .
 sigma_v_sqr |   .3205787   .0281541    11.39    0.000     .2698857    .3807934
 sigma_1_sqr |   .0210423   .0020569    10.23    0.000     .0173736    .0254858
 sigma_2_sqr |   .0694766   .0067891    10.23    0.000     .0573668    .0841426

. sf_predict, jlms(jlms_mod6) bc(bc_mod6)

. summarize jlms_mod6 bc_mod6

    Variable |       Obs        Mean    Std. Dev.       Min        Max
-------------+--------------------------------------------------------
   jlms_mod6 |       274    .0003204    2.39e-07    .0003195    .0003208
     bc_mod6 |       274    .9996797    2.39e-07    .9996793    .9996806
```

The inefficiency estimates are too low because $\sigma_u^2 \simeq 0$ and is insignificant.

Model 7: Cobb-Douglas Profit Function

The Cobb-Douglas profit frontier system is obtained by imposing the restrictions $\beta_{jk} = 0, \forall j, k$ on the translog system of (7.12) and (7.13). For the case of two variable and one quasi-fixed inputs, the system is

$$\ln\left(\frac{\pi^a}{p}\right) = \beta_0 + \beta_1 \ln\left(\frac{w_1}{p}\right) + \beta_2 \ln\left(\frac{w_2}{p}\right) + \beta_3 \ln q - [1 - \beta_1 - \beta_2]\, u + v, \tag{7.40}$$

$$S_1^a = -\beta_1 + \zeta_1, \tag{7.41}$$

$$S_2^a = -\beta_2 + \zeta_2. \tag{7.42}$$

Similar to Model 6, the share-equation-based estimation strategy does not have much value here as far as estimating inefficiency is concerned. This is because the Cobb-Douglas assumption eliminates u from the share equations.

Similar to the case in Model 6, a SURE estimation on (7.40)–(7.42) is conducted first and the results are used as initial values for the ML estimation on the system of equations.

```
. global xvarcd wl wf mat
. constraint define 1 -[share1]_b[_cons] =  [frontier]_b[wf]
. constraint define 2 -[share2]_b[_cons] =  [frontier]_b[wl]

. sureg (frontier: pft=$xvarcd) (share1: s_fue=mat) (share2: s_lab=mat), isure constraints(1-2)

(iteration log omitted)

Seemingly unrelated regression, iterated

Constraints:
 ( 1)  - [frontier]wf - [share1]_cons = 0
 ( 2)  - [frontier]wl - [share2]_cons = 0
----------------------------------------------------------------------
Equation          Obs  Parms        RMSE    "R-sq"       chi2        P
----------------------------------------------------------------------
frontier          274      3    .5862595    0.7840    4983.13   0.0000
share1            274      1    .2429655    0.0461       8.66   0.0033
share2            274      1     .208928    0.0648      11.99   0.0005
----------------------------------------------------------------------

------------------------------------------------------------------------------
             |      Coef.   Std. Err.      z    P>|z|     [95% Conf. Interval]
-------------+----------------------------------------------------------------
frontier     |
          wl |  -.8320258   .0158467   -52.50   0.000    -.8630848   -.8009669
          wf |  -.4741487   .0168478   -28.14   0.000    -.5071698   -.4411276
         mat |   1.423006   .0328056    43.38   0.000     1.358709    1.487304
       _cons |  -2.580786   .0470502   -54.85   0.000    -2.673003    -2.48857
-------------+----------------------------------------------------------------
share1       |
         mat |   .0375765   .0127689     2.94   0.003     .0125499     .062603
       _cons |   .4741487   .0168478    28.14   0.000     .4411276    .5071698
-------------+----------------------------------------------------------------
share2       |
         mat |   .0392887   .0113479     3.46   0.001     .0170471    .0615302
       _cons |   .8320258   .0158467    52.50   0.000     .8009669    .8630848
------------------------------------------------------------------------------
```

The coefficients from this model are then saved using

```
. matrix b0cd = e(b)
. matrix b0cd_f = b0cd[1, "frontier:"]
. matrix b0cd_s1 = b0cd[1, "share1:"]
. matrix b0cd_s2 = b0cd[1, "share2:"]
```

Now the stochastic frontier model is estimated using these starting values.

```
. sfsystem pft, profit distribution(h) corr(no) frontier($xvarcd) share1(s_fue=mat) ///
>            share2(s_lab=mat) gamma sigmauv s11 s22 constraints(1-2) show
. sf_init, frontier(b1cd_f) share1(b0cd_s1) share2(b0cd_s1) gamma(0.1) sigmauv(0) s11(0) s22(0)
. sf_srch, frontier($xvar) share1($svar) share2($svar) n(5) fast
. ml max, diff gtol(1e-5) nrtol(1e-5)
```

This produces the following output:

```
(iteration log omitted)
                                              Number of obs     =        274
                                              Wald chi2(1)      =    2022.29
Log likelihood = -200.62155                   Prob > chi2       =     0.0000

 ( 1)  - [frontier]wf - [share1]_cons = 0
 ( 2)  - [frontier]wl - [share2]_cons = 0
------------------------------------------------------------------------------
             |      Coef.   Std. Err.      z    P>|z|     [95% Conf. Interval]
-------------+----------------------------------------------------------------
frontier     |
          wl |  -.8497805    .016411   -51.78   0.000    -.8819455   -.8176155
```

```
         wf |  -.4335318   .0220666   -19.65   0.000    -.4767816   -.3902821
        mat |   1.434041   .0318889    44.97   0.000      1.37154    1.496543
      _cons |  -2.500439   .1521346   -16.44   0.000    -2.798617   -2.202261
-------------+----------------------------------------------------------------
share1       |
        mat |   .0194475   .0144813     1.34   0.179    -.0089354    .0478303
      _cons |   .4335318   .0220666    19.65   0.000     .3902821    .4767816
-------------+----------------------------------------------------------------
share2       |
        mat |   .0472133   .0114454     4.13   0.000     .0247807    .0696459
      _cons |   .8497805    .016411    51.78   0.000     .8176155    .8819455
-------------+----------------------------------------------------------------
usigmas      |
      _cons |  -15.15122   672.7134    -0.02   0.982    -1333.645    1303.343
-------------+----------------------------------------------------------------
s11          |
      _cons |  -.5649546    .047466   -11.90   0.000    -.6579863    -.471923
-------------+----------------------------------------------------------------
s22          |
      _cons |  -1.385602   .0470421   -29.45   0.000    -1.477803   -1.293402
-------------+----------------------------------------------------------------
s33          |
      _cons |  -1.574063   .0430976   -36.52   0.000    -1.658533   -1.489594
------------------------------------------------------------------------------

. sf_predict, jlms(jlms_mod7) bc(bc_mod7)

. summarize jlms_mod7 bc_mod7

    Variable |       Obs        Mean    Std. Dev.       Min        Max
-------------+--------------------------------------------------------
   jlms_mod7 |       274    .0004086    3.87e-07   .0004072   .0004092
     bc_mod7 |       274    .9995916    3.86e-07   .9995909   .9995929
```

Similar to Model 6, for this dataset the inefficiency estimates are too low because $\sigma_u^2 \simeq 0$ and is insignificant.

7.6 Single Output, Input-Oriented Technical Inefficiency

In Chapter 5, we derived the profit function with IO technical inefficiency. The translog profit function is

$$
\begin{aligned}
\ln\left(\frac{\pi^a}{p}\right) = \ln \pi(\boldsymbol{w}e^{\eta}/p, \boldsymbol{q}) &= \beta_0 + \sum_j \beta_j \ln\left(\frac{w_j}{p}\right) + \sum_q \beta_q \ln q_q \\
&+ \frac{1}{2}\sum_j\sum_k \beta_{jk} \ln\left(\frac{w_j}{p}\right)\ln\left(\frac{w_k}{p}\right) \\
&+ \frac{1}{2}\sum_q\sum_s \gamma_{qs} \ln q_q \ln q_s + \sum_j\sum_q \delta_{jq} \ln\left(\frac{w_j}{p}\right)\ln q_q \\
&+ \left[\sum_j \beta_j + \sum_j\sum_q \delta_{jq}\ln q_q + \sum_j\sum_k \beta_{jk}\ln\left(\frac{w_j}{p}\right)\right]\eta \\
&+ \left[\frac{1}{2}\sum_j\sum_k \beta_{jk}\right]\eta^2.
\end{aligned} \tag{7.43}
$$

Applying Hotelling's lemma to (7.43), we obtain the J profit share equations of the variable inputs as:

$$S_j^a = -\left[\beta_j + \sum_q \delta_{jq} \ln q_q + \sum_k \beta_{jk} \ln(w_k/p)\right] - \left[\sum_k \beta_{jk}\right]\eta, \qquad j = 1,\ldots,J, \quad (7.44)$$

where $S_j^a = (w_j x_j)/\pi^a$ is the cost share of variable input j to actual profit.

The complete system of the profit maximization problem with IO technical inefficiency consists of the profit function in (7.43) and the profit share equations in (7.44). Note that this system is not different from the one in (7.12) and (7.13), except for the -1 term in the last line of (7.12). Because of this similarity, we do not provide a separate empirical example of the IO profit system.

7.7 Multiple Output Technology

Most of the models in the efficiency literatures assume a single output. However, in reality most of the firms produce more than one output. One can justify the use of a single output model by aggregating all the outputs. For example, in the case of airlines, passenger and cargo outputs can be aggregated into a single output, such as revenue, which is not a physical measure of output. However, this might cause other problems associated with aggregation and prices. Furthermore, a single output model cannot capture substitutability between outputs. In some other cases production of an intended output (such as electricity) also produces an unintended output (pollution) and it does not make much sense to aggregate intended and unintended outputs because they have different properties. Intended output can be freely disposed but the unintended outputs cannot. Ignoring unintended outputs from the model is likely to give incorrect estimates of inefficiency. Similarly, in the case of airlines, if one models only passenger output, efficiency estimates are likely to be incorrect because the omitted output cargo will cause omitted variable bias. In this section we examine how to estimate a model with multiple outputs.

7.7.1 Output-Oriented Technical Inefficiency

We specify an multiple-output production technolgy with output-oriented technical inefficiency as

$$F(\boldsymbol{y}e^u, \boldsymbol{x}, \boldsymbol{z}) = 0, \qquad u \geq 0. \quad (7.45)$$

The corresponding profit maximization problem and the FOCs are

$$\max_{y,x} \pi = \boldsymbol{p}'\boldsymbol{y} - \boldsymbol{w}'\boldsymbol{x} \qquad \text{s.t.} \quad F(\boldsymbol{y}e^u, \boldsymbol{x}, \boldsymbol{z}) = 0 \quad (7.46)$$

$$\text{FOCs:} \qquad p_m = \lambda \frac{\partial F}{\partial(y_m e^u)} \cdot e^u, \qquad m = 1,\ldots,M; \quad (7.47)$$

$$-w_j = \lambda \frac{\partial F}{\partial x_j}, \qquad j = 1,\ldots,J. \quad (7.48)$$

$$\Longrightarrow \qquad \frac{w_j}{p_m^*} = -\frac{\partial F/\partial x_j}{\partial F/\partial y_m^*}. \quad (7.49)$$

where M is the number of outputs, J in the number of inputs, $p_m^* \equiv e^{-u}p_m$, and $y_m^* \equiv y_m e^u$.

These equations along with $F(\boldsymbol{y}^*, \boldsymbol{x}, \boldsymbol{z}) = 0$ can be solved for the efficiency adjusted output supply functions, $\boldsymbol{y}^*$, and the input demand function, $\boldsymbol{x}$, which are functions of $\boldsymbol{w}$, $\boldsymbol{p}^*$, and $\boldsymbol{z}$; i.e., $x_j = x_j(\boldsymbol{w}, \boldsymbol{p}e^{-u}), \boldsymbol{z}$, and $y_m e^u = y_m(\boldsymbol{w}, \boldsymbol{p}e^{-u}, \boldsymbol{z})$. Thus, the profit function is

$$\pi(\boldsymbol{w}, \boldsymbol{p}\exp(-u), \boldsymbol{z}) = \sum_m p_m \exp(-u) y_m e^u - \sum_j w_j x_j = \sum_m p_m y_m - \sum_j w_j x_j = \pi^a, \tag{7.50}$$

$$\Longrightarrow \qquad \ln \pi^a = \ln \pi(\boldsymbol{w}, \boldsymbol{p}\exp(-u), \boldsymbol{z}). \tag{7.51}$$

Note that $\pi(\boldsymbol{w}, \boldsymbol{p}\exp(-u), \boldsymbol{z})$ is homogeneous of degree 1 in $\boldsymbol{w}$ and $\boldsymbol{p}\exp(-u)$.

An Illustration: The Translog Case

Consider the translog form of the profit function $\pi(\boldsymbol{w}, \boldsymbol{p}\exp(-u), \boldsymbol{z})$. In order to avoid notational clutter and messy algebraic expressions, we do not include quasi-fixed variables in the following derivation. Adding quasi-fixed variables is a straightforward extension as seen in the previous section on single output.

$$\begin{aligned} \ln \pi^a = \beta_0 &+ \sum_j \beta_j \ln w_j + \sum_m \gamma_m \ln(p_m \exp(-u)) \\ &+ \frac{1}{2}\sum_j \sum_k \beta_{jk} \ln w_j \ln w_k + \frac{1}{2}\sum_m \sum_r \gamma_{mr} \ln(p_m \exp(-u)) \ln(p_r \exp(-u)) \\ &+ \sum_j \sum_m \delta_{jm} \ln w_j \ln(p_m \exp(-u)). \end{aligned} \tag{7.52}$$

The symmetry restriction requires that $\beta_{jk} = \beta_{kj}\ \forall\, jk$, and $\gamma_{mr} = \gamma_{rm}\ \forall\, rm$. The homogeneity property (degree 1 in prices) can be achieved by imposing the following restrictions:

$$\sum_j \beta_j + \sum_m \gamma_m = 1, \tag{7.53}$$

$$\sum_k \beta_{jk} + \sum_m \delta_{jm} = 0, \quad \forall\, j, \tag{7.54}$$

$$\sum_r \gamma_{rm} + \sum_j \delta_{jm} = 0, \quad \forall\, m. \tag{7.55}$$

As in the single-output model, the price homogeneity can be built in to the profit function by normalizing profit and prices by any one of the price variable. Here we choose $p_1 \exp(-u)$ as the normalizing price. The resulting normalized profit function is

$$\begin{aligned} \ln\left(\frac{\pi^a}{p_1}\right) = \beta_0 &+ \sum_j \beta_j \ln\left(\frac{w_j}{p_1}\right) + \sum_{m=2} \gamma_m \ln\left(\frac{p_m}{p_1}\right) \\ &+ \frac{1}{2}\sum_j \sum_k \beta_{jk} \ln\left(\frac{w_j}{p_1}\right) \ln\left(\frac{w_k}{p}\right) + \frac{1}{2}\sum_{m=2} \sum_r \gamma_{mr} \ln\left(\frac{p_m}{p_1}\right) \ln\left(\frac{p_r}{p_1}\right) \end{aligned}$$

$$+\sum_{j}\sum_{m=2}\delta_{jm}\ln\left(\frac{w_j}{p_1}\right)\ln\left(\frac{p_m}{p_1}\right) \tag{7.56}$$

$$+\left[-1+\sum_{j}\beta_j+\sum_{j}\sum_{m=2}\delta_{jm}\ln\left(\frac{p_m}{p_1}\right)+\sum_{j}\sum_{k}\beta_{jk}\ln\left(\frac{w_j}{p_1}\right)\right]u$$

$$+\left[\frac{1}{2}\sum_{j}\sum_{k}\beta_{jk}\right]u^2.$$

The first three lines represent the frontier profit, and the last two lines are the profit loss. Note that profit loss due to technical inefficiency is a quadratic function of output-oriented technical inefficiency.

Applying Hotelling's lemma to the above profit function, we have:

$$\frac{\partial\ln(\pi^a/p_1)}{\partial\ln(w_j/p_1)}\equiv -S_j^a,\qquad j=1,\ldots,J, \tag{7.57}$$

$$\frac{\partial\ln(\pi^a/p_1)}{\partial\ln\left(p_m/p_1\right)}\equiv R_m^a,\qquad m=2,\ldots,M. \tag{7.58}$$

Thus,

$$-S_j^a=\beta_j+\sum_{k}\beta_{jk}\ln\left(\frac{w_k}{p_1}\right)+\sum_{m=2}\delta_{jm}\ln\left(\frac{p_m}{p_1}\right)-\left(\sum_{k}\beta_{jk}\right)u,\qquad j=1,\ldots,J, \tag{7.59}$$

$$R_m^a=\gamma_m+\sum_{r}\gamma_{mr}\ln\left(\frac{p_r}{p_1}\right)+\sum_{j}\delta_{jm}\ln\left(\frac{w_j}{p_1}\right)-\left(\sum_{j}\delta_{jm}\right)u,\qquad m=2,\ldots,M. \tag{7.60}$$

We refer to (7.59) as *cost share equations* and (7.60) as *revenue share equations* and also introduce two new notations, viz.,

$$\beta_{j0}=\sum_{k}\beta_{jk},\quad\text{and}\quad \delta_{0m}=\sum_{j}\delta_{jm}. \tag{7.61}$$

7.7.2 Estimation Methods

Without further assumptions, estimation involving the log profit function in (7.56) is difficult, because the equation has both u and u^2, which are stochastic. The same problem appeared in the single output profit frontier model discussed in the previous sections, and the solution is also similar: We estimate the model in two steps. In the first step, we estimate the system of cost and revenue share equations (after appending random statistical errors to each of the equations) in (7.59) and (7.60) and obtain estimates of those parameters contained in these share equations. In the second step, we use the residuals from the first stage in a regression to recover remaining parameters in the profit frontier equation (7.56). If there are no quasi-fixed variables in the model, all the parameters (except the intercept) can be consistently estimated from the share equations (from the first stage).

Adding optimization errors $\boldsymbol{\zeta} \sim N(\boldsymbol{0}, \boldsymbol{\Sigma})$ to (7.59) and (7.60), the vector of random variables in the share equation system in (7.59) and (7.60) becomes

$$-\boldsymbol{b}u + \boldsymbol{\zeta}, \quad \text{where} \quad \boldsymbol{b} = (\beta_{10}, \ldots, \beta_{J0}, \delta_{02}, \ldots, \delta_{0M})'. \tag{7.62}$$

The likelihood function is essentially the same as the one for the single output case (see (7.18)), except that the revenue share equations are added.

The difficulty in estimating this model can be substantially reduced if the underlying production function is assumed to be homogenous. In this case, the restrictions $\sum_k \beta_{jk} = 0, \ \forall j$, and $\sum_j \delta_{jm} = 0, \ m = 2, \ldots, M$ apply, which simplifies the model. The simplification is the same as that in the single output case: The u^2 term will drop from the log profit frontier function, and the u term will drop from all the cost and revenue share equations. With this simplification, the estimation can be undertaken either by maximizing the log-likelihood function associated with the frontier function alone, or by maximizing the log-likelihood function associated with the entire system, consisting of the log profit frontier and the cost and revenue share equations. Again, the model is essentially the same as the one in the single output case discussed in the previous sections except that the revenue share equations are added to the system.

PART IV

THE PRIMAL APPROACH

8

Estimation of Technical and Allocative Efficiency in Cost Frontier Models Using System Models with Cross-Sectional Data: A Primal System Approach

8.1 Introduction

Until now, we have assumed that firms only incur technical inefficiency in the production of output, and the allocation of inputs is either at the most efficient level or inputs are exogenously given. If inputs are exogenously given, one may not address allocative inefficiency simply because the input allocation problem is assumed away. By contrast, if inputs are endogenous, then allocation decisions using some economic behavior have to be made. Such decisions may or may not be optimal. If the allocation is nonoptimal, then the producer is allocatively inefficient. In either case, endogeneity of inputs has to be taken into account in the model.

In a cost minimizing framework, input allocation is optimal if producers allocate inputs in such a way that input price ratios equal the ratio of their marginal products. In such a case, actual cost differs from the optimal cost (barring the noise term) due to technical inefficiency. On the other hand, if input allocation is nonoptimal, cost will be higher because of both technical and allocative inefficiency. In this chapter, we examine the impact of both technical and allocative inefficiency on costs, assuming that output and input prices are exogenous and the level of inputs are the choice variables (i.e., the goal is to use inputs to minimize cost for a given level of output and input prices).

In this setting, we are able to extend the questions we first set out in Chapter 4. In addition to examining whether, and by how much, a firm can reduce its costs, we are also able to identify how much of this cost reduction can be achieved through improvements in technical efficiency and how much can be achieved through an optimal mix of inputs.

For instance, we can reconsider the health care questions first asked in Chapter 4, namely, how much lower could the cost of treatment be at certain hospitals while still treating the same number of patients for the same level of care and how can this be achieved? Previously, we considered whether this could be achieved through improvements in technical efficiency. We can now extend this to examine whether costs can be reduced through better allocation of inputs. This could, for example, involve changing the mix of specialist physicians, general physicians, residents, nurses, nonmedical and support staff, and active beds.

While examining the cost efficiency of electricity power generation plants associated with a particular form of regulation in the state in which the plant operates, we ignored the issue of allocative efficiency. However, there is a well-known hypothesis in the literature, known as the Averch-Johnson effect which suggests that, under certain conditions, there may be an overuse of capital. It is this example, first used in Chapter 4, that we use throughout this chapter as a way of illustrating the new framework. We also directly examine the question as to whether or not there is evidence of an overuse of capital.

Estimation that accounts for both technical and allocative inefficiency is not straightforward with the widely adopted dual approach (which consists of a cost function and the first-order conditions). This is particularly the case when a flexible functional form, such as the translog, is assumed for the underlying production technology. In the case of a translog cost function, the specification as well as estimation issues are still debated (it is known as the Greene problem, following Greene [1980]).

Instead of the dual approach, Schmidt and Lovell (1979) show that the cost frontier problem can be reformulated as a primal problem that enables the estimation of the model parameters including both technical and allocative inefficiency and their costs. This is especially true when the production function is Cobb-Douglas. Kumbhakar and Wang (2006) used the same approach but used a flexible functional form for the production technology (namely, the translog). Although the estimation of the technology parameters, as well as technical and allocative inefficiency, are somewhat straightforward, the computation of the cost of technical and allocative inefficiency is nontrivial. Thus, there is no easy solution to the estimation of the cost of technical and allocative inefficiency when it comes to a flexible functional form for the underlying technology, no matter whether a primal or a dual approach is used.

In this chapter, we first describe how to formulate a cost minimization model with both technical and allocative inefficiency using the dual approach, and then discuss the issues with estimating this model. This is followed by a description of the primal system approach. We then show how this system can be estimated using empirical illustrations.

8.2 Cost System Approach with Both Technical and Allocative Inefficiency

The cost minimization problem for a producer is

$$\min \ \boldsymbol{w}'\boldsymbol{x} \quad \text{s.t.} \quad y = f(\boldsymbol{x})e^{v-u}, \tag{8.1}$$

where $\boldsymbol{w}$ is the vector of input prices, $\boldsymbol{x}$ is the vector of inputs, y is the output, v is the random error, and u captures the output-oriented inefficiency.[1] The first-order conditions of the above problem can be expressed as

$$\frac{f_j}{f_1} = \frac{w_j}{w_1}e^{\xi_j} = \frac{w_j^s}{w_1}, j = 2, \dots, J, \tag{8.2}$$

where $w_j^s = w_j e^{\xi_j}$ and $\xi_j \neq 0$ is **allocative inefficiency** for the input pair $(j, 1)$. That is, a producer is allocatively inefficient when it fails to allocate inputs in a way that equates the marginal rate of technical substitution (MRTS) with the ratio of the respective input prices.

The above minimization problem can be written as a standard neoclassical cost minimization problem, viz.,

$$\min \ \boldsymbol{w}^s\boldsymbol{x} \ \text{ s.t. } ye^{u-v} = f(x), \tag{8.3}$$

where the first-order conditions (given y, v, u and ξ_j) are exactly the same as earlier. The advantage of setting out the problem in the above format is that stochastic noise, technical

[1] Here we follow the formulation used by Hoch (1958, 1962), Mundlak and Hoch (1965), and Schmidt and Lovell (1979, 1980) and assume that the firm minimizes cost conditional on u and v.

and allocative inefficiency are already built-in to this optimization problem, and there is no need to append any extra terms in an ad hoc fashion at the estimation stage. Moreover, all the standard duality results hold, although the model we consider here allows the presence of statistical noise, technical and allocative inefficiency. For example, the solution for x_j (the conditional input demand functions) is $x_j = x_j(\mathbf{w}^s, ye^{u-v})$, $j = 1, \ldots, J$. Furthermore, the cost function, defined as $c^s(\cdot) = \mathbf{w}^s\mathbf{x}(\cdot)$, is

$$c^s(\cdot) = c(\mathbf{w}^s, ye^{u-v}). \tag{8.4}$$

Note that $c^s(\cdot)$ is neither the actual cost nor the minimum cost function. The former is the cost of inputs used at the observed prices, whereas the latter is the cost of producing a given level of output without any inefficiency. The cost function $c^s(\cdot)$ is an artificial construct that is useful for duality results. Because $c^s(\cdot)$ is derived from the neoclassical optimization problem in which the relevant input prices are w^s and output is ye^{v-u}, it can be viewed as the cost function when prices are $\mathbf{w}^s$ and output is ye^{v-u}. Thus, if one starts from the $c^s(\cdot)$ function, Shephard's lemma can be used to obtain the conditional input demand functions (i.e., $\frac{\partial c^s(\cdot)}{\partial w_j^s} = x_j$). Equivalently,

$$\begin{gathered}\frac{\partial \ln c^s(\cdot)}{\partial \ln w_j^s} = \frac{w_j^s x_j}{c^s(\cdot)} \Rightarrow x_j = \frac{c^s(\cdot)}{w_j^s} s_j^s(\cdot),\\ \text{where } s_j^s(\cdot) = \frac{\partial \ln c^s(\cdot)}{\partial \ln w_j^s}.\end{gathered} \tag{8.5}$$

Now, actual cost, c^a, is

$$\begin{aligned}c^a &= \sum_j w_j x_j = \sum_j w_j^s x_j \left(w_j/w_j^s\right) = c^s(\cdot)\sum_j s_j^s(\cdot)\left(w_j/w_j^s\right)\\ &\Rightarrow \ln c^a = \ln c^s(\cdot) + \ln\left[\sum_j s_j^s(\cdot)e^{-\xi_j}\right]\end{aligned} \tag{8.6}$$

This equation relates actual/observed cost with the unobserved cost function $c^s(\cdot)$, and the formulation is complete once a functional form on $c^s(\cdot)$ is chosen. For example, if $c^s(\cdot)$ is assumed to be Cobb-Douglas then this relationship becomes (Schmidt and Lovell [1979])

$$\begin{aligned}\ln c^a &= \alpha_0 + \sum_j \alpha_j \ln w_j^s + \alpha_y \ln\left(ye^{u-v}\right) + \ln\left(\sum_{j=1}^J \alpha_j e^{-\xi_j}\right)\\ &= \alpha_0 + \sum_{j=1}^J \alpha_j \ln w_j + \alpha_y \ln y + \alpha_y (u-v) + \sum_{j=2}^J \alpha_j \xi_j + \ln\left[\sum_{j=1}^J \alpha_j e^{-\xi_j}\right],\end{aligned} \tag{8.7}$$

and the actual cost share equations are

$$\begin{aligned}s_j^a &= \frac{w_j x_j}{c^a} = \frac{c^s(\cdot)}{e^{\xi_j}}\frac{\alpha_j}{c^a} = \alpha_j e^{-\xi_j}\left\{\sum_{k=1}^J \alpha_k e^{-\xi_k}\right\}^{-1}\\ &= \alpha_j + \left\{\alpha_j\left[\frac{e^{-\xi_j}}{\sum_{k=1}^J \alpha_k e^{-\xi_k}} - 1\right]\right\}\\ &\Rightarrow s_j^a \equiv \alpha_j + \eta_j(\boldsymbol{\xi}), j = 2, \ldots, J,\end{aligned} \tag{8.8}$$

where the cost share errors (η_j) are functions of allocative errors ($\boldsymbol{\xi}$). This relationship can also be directly derived from the Cobb-Douglas production function along with the first-order conditions of cost minimization.

The cost function in (8.7) can be written as

$$\ln c^a = \ln c^0(\cdot) + \ln c_u + \ln c_v + \ln c_\xi, \tag{8.9}$$

where $\ln c^0 = \alpha_0 + \ln\left[\sum_{j=1}^J \alpha_j\right] + \sum_{j=1}^J \alpha_j \ln w_j + \alpha_y \ln y$ is the minimum (neoclassical) cost function (frontier). The percentage increase in cost due to technical inefficiency, $\ln c_u$ (when multiplied by 100), is $\ln c_u = (\ln c^a - \ln c^a|_{u=0}) = \alpha_y u \geq 0$. Similarly, the percentage increase in cost due to input allocative inefficiency ($\ln c_\xi = \ln c^a - \ln c^a|_{\xi_j=0\ \forall\ j}$), when multiplied by 100, is $\sum_{j=2}^{J} \alpha_j \xi_j + \ln\left[\alpha_1 + \sum_{j=2}^{J} \alpha_j e^{-\xi_j}\right] - \ln\left[\sum_{j=1}^J \alpha_j\right]$. Production uncertainty can either increase or decrease cost since $\ln c_v = \ln c^a - \ln c^a|_{v=0} = -\alpha_y v \gtrless 0$, depending on $v \lessgtr 0$.

It is clear from equations (8.7) and (8.8) that the error components in the above system are quite complex. The input allocative inefficiency term (ξ_j) appears in a highly nonlinear fashion in both the cost function and cost share equations. Consequently, estimation of the model (the cost function and the cost share equations specified earlier) based on distributional assumptions on ξ_j, u, and v is quite difficult. The main problem in deriving the likelihood function is that the elements of $\boldsymbol{\xi}$ appear in the above system in a highly nonlinear fashion. Alternatively, if one makes a distributional assumption on the cost share errors, η_j, which are also nonlinear functions of the elements of $\boldsymbol{\xi}$, then, to derive the likelihood function one has to express ξ_j in terms of $\boldsymbol{\eta}$, because ξ_js appear in the cost function. Thus, even if one starts from a Cobb-Douglas production function, the estimation of the cost system is difficult (a closed-form expression of the likelihood function is not possible). Another potential problem with using the dual approach is solving ξ_j from $\eta_j(\boldsymbol{\xi})$, as this might have multiple solutions of ξ_j.

A similar result is obtained if one uses a translog function for $\ln c^s(\cdot)$. The actual cost function is

$$\ln c^a = \ln c^s(\cdot) + \sum_j s_j^s(\cdot)\, e^{-\xi_j}, \tag{8.10}$$

where

$$\ln c^s(\cdot) = \alpha_0 + \sum \alpha_j \ln w_j^s + \alpha_y \ln\left(ye^{u-v}\right) + \frac{1}{2}\sum_j\sum_k \alpha_{jk} \ln w_j^s \ln w_k^s + \frac{1}{2}\alpha_{yy}\left\{\ln\left(ye^{u-v}\right)\right\}^2$$
$$+ \sum_j \alpha_{jy} \ln w_j^s \ln\left(ye^{u-v}\right), \tag{8.11}$$

and

$$s_j^s(\cdot) = \alpha_j + \sum_k \alpha_{jk} \ln w_k^s + \alpha_{jy} \ln\left(ye^{u-v}\right). \tag{8.12}$$

The cost function in (8.10) can also be written as

$$\ln c^a = \ln c^0 + \sum \alpha_j\xi_j + \alpha_y (u-v) + \sum_j\sum_k \alpha_{jk} \ln w_j \xi_k + \frac{1}{2}\sum_j\sum_k \alpha_{jk}\,\xi_j\xi_k + \sum_j \alpha_{jy}\,\xi_j \ln y$$
$$+ \sum_j \alpha_{jy}\,\xi_j(u-v) + \alpha_{yy}\ln y(u-v) + \frac{1}{2}\alpha_{yy}(u-v)^2 + \sum_j s_j^s(\cdot)e^{-\xi_j}, \tag{8.13}$$

where the frontier (minimum) cost function, $c^0(\cdot)$, is given by

$$\ln c^0(\cdot) = \alpha_0 + \sum \alpha_j \ln w_j + \alpha_y \ln y + \frac{1}{2}\sum_j\sum_k \alpha_{jk} \ln w_j \ln w_k + \frac{1}{2}\alpha_{yy} \ln y^2$$
$$+ \sum_j \alpha_{jy} \ln w_j \ln y. \tag{8.14}$$

Finally, the actual cost share equations are

$$s_j^a = \frac{w_j x_j}{c^a} = \frac{c^s(\cdot)}{e^{\xi_j}}\frac{s_j^s(\cdot)}{c^a} = \frac{s_j^s(\cdot)e^{-\xi_j}}{\sum_{k=1}^{J} s_k^s(\cdot)e^{-\xi_k}} \equiv s_j^0(\cdot) + \left[\frac{s_j^s(\cdot)e^{-\xi_j}}{\sum_{k=1}^{J} s_k^s(\cdot)e^{-\xi_k}} - s_j^0(\cdot)\right] \tag{8.15}$$

$$= s_j^0(\cdot) + \eta_j\,(\xi, u, v, \text{ and data}), \tag{8.16}$$

where $s_j^s(\cdot)$ is written as

$$s_j^s(\cdot) = s_j^0 + \sum_k \alpha_{jk}\xi_k + \alpha_{jy}(u-v), \tag{8.17}$$

and

$$s_j^0(\cdot) = \alpha_j + \sum_k \alpha_{jk} \ln w_k + \alpha_{jy} \ln y. \tag{8.18}$$

It is clear from this algebraic expression that the translog cost function *cannot* be expressed as

$$\ln c^a = \ln c^0(\cdot) + \ln c_u + \ln c_v + \ln c_\xi, \tag{8.19}$$

which decomposes (in logarithmic form) the actual cost into the minimum (frontier) cost, $\ln c^0(\cdot)$, the increase in cost due to technical inefficiency, $\ln c_u$, the increase/decrease in cost due to production uncertainty, In v, and the increase in cost due to allocative inefficiency, In c_ξ. The u, v, and ξ_j terms interact among themselves, which makes it impossible to decompose log cost into the above four components. In other words, increases in costs due to technical (allocative) inefficiency will depend on allocative (technical) inefficiency and the noise components.

Thus, the translog cost function is more problematic than the Cobb-Douglas function in terms of estimation because the technical inefficiency, u, and the noise term, (v), are squared and they also interact with allocative inefficiency, ξ_j, as well as output and input prices. Thus, it is impossible to estimate the translog cost system starting from distributional assumption on u, v, and ξ_j.

Restricting the technology to be homogeneous does not fully solve the estimation problem either. If the underlying production technology is homogenous, then the parameters in the translog function satisfy the following restrictions:

$$\alpha_{yy} = 0, \alpha_{jy} = 0 \;\; \forall\, j. \tag{8.20}$$

Consequently, the cost function is linear in u and v, as in the Cobb-Douglas case, but the nonlinearity in ξ is not eliminated. Therefore, the observed cost can be expressed as $\ln c^a = \ln c^0(\cdot) + \ln c_u + \ln c_v + \ln c_\xi$. That is, the cost function (in logs) can be expressed as the sum of frontier cost plus the percentage change in costs (when multiplied by 100) due to technical and allocative inefficiency and production uncertainty. However, estimation of the model is still difficult, if not impossible, because of the nonlinearities in ξ. Unless the parameters of the cost system are estimated consistently, the cost impact of technical and allocative inefficiency cannot be computed (although algebraic expressions for the increase in cost due to technical and allocative inefficiency are known). In other words, the cost system formulation has the advantage of obtaining analytical solutions of $\ln c_u, \ln c_v, \ln c_\xi$, but econometric estimation of the model is too difficult.

Thus, an alternative approach is required for estimation purposes. We turn to this alternative next.

8.3 The Primal System Approach with Technical and Allocative Inefficiency

In this section we consider the alternative modeling strategy, viz., the primal approach that is easier to estimate than the dual approach. However, for many production functions, no analytical expressions for $\ln c_u, \ln c_v, \ln c_\xi$ will be available. In such instances, we compute them numerically by solving a system of nonlinear equations for each observation.

It is possible to avoid the estimation problem discussed in the preceding section if one starts from the production function and uses a system consisting of the production function and the first-order conditions of cost minimization. This system is algebraically equivalent to the cost system for self-dual production functions. The only difference is that one starts from a parametric production function, instead of a cost function. We start from the production function (Cobb-Douglas or translog),

$$\ln y = \ln f(x) + v - u \tag{8.21}$$

and write down the first-order conditions of cost minimization, viz.,

$$\begin{aligned} &\frac{f_j}{f_1} = \frac{w_j}{w_1} e^{\xi_j} \Rightarrow \frac{\partial \ln f}{\partial \ln x_j} \div \frac{\partial \ln f}{\partial \ln x_1} \equiv \frac{s_j}{s_1} = \frac{w_j x_j}{w_1 x_1} e^{\xi_j} \\ &\Rightarrow \ln s_j - \ln s_1 - \ln(w_j x_j) + \ln(w_1 x_1) = \xi_j, j = 2, ..J. \end{aligned} \tag{8.22}$$

Here we interpret $\xi_j (\gtreqless 0)$ as allocative inefficiency for the input pair $(j, 1)$.[2] The sign of ξ_j shows whether input j is over- or underused relative to input 1. Thus, for example, if $\xi_2 < 0$, then $w_2 e_2^{\xi} < w_2$ and input x_2 is overused relative to input x_1 (the numeraire), while if $\xi_3 > 0$, then input 3 is underused relative to input 1. However, other than that, ξ_j lacks interpretation, as the *extent* of overuse (or underuse) of inputs cannot be inferred from the

[2] It is worth noting that the estimation result are unaffected by the choice of the input used as the numeraire in equation (8.22).

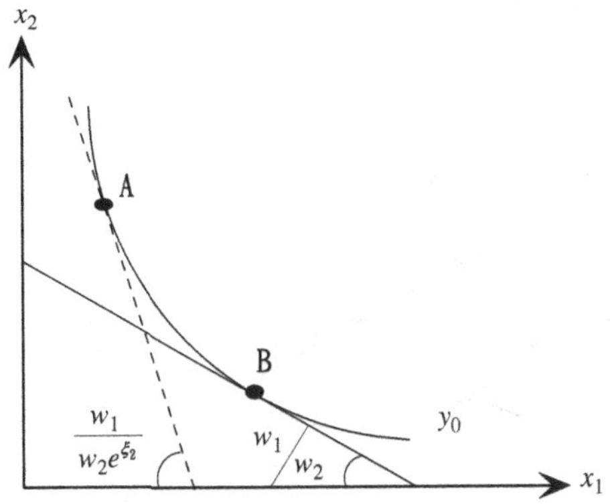

Figure 8.1. Allocative Inefficiency

values of ξ_j alone. For this we need to derive the input demand function. This is possible analytically for some functions, such as the Cobb-Douglas production function. However, it is not possible (analytically) for most production functions, including the translog. For such functions, one can compute the extent of the overuse (or underuse) of inputs numerically by solving systems of equations. These numerical solutions can then be used to compute the impact of technical and allocative inefficiency on cost. We return to this point in subsequent sections.

Figure 8.1 demonstrates allocative inefficiency graphically for two inputs (we assume in this figure that there is no technical inefficiency).

The input quantities given by point A is used to produce output level y_0. However, the optimal input quantities are given by point B which is the tangency point between the isoquant and the isocost line $\frac{f_1}{f_2} = \frac{w_1}{w_2}$. At point A the equality $\frac{f_1}{f_2} = \frac{w_1}{w_2}$ is not satisfied. The dotted isocost line is tangent to the observed input combination (point A). That is, the observed input quantities are optimal with respect to input price ratio $\frac{w_1}{w_2 e^{\xi_2}}$. Departure from the optimality condition is measured by the difference in slopes of the dotted and the solid isocost line. Failure on the part of the producer to allocate inputs optimally (given by point B) is viewed as **allocative inefficiency**. It is worth mentioning that such failure may not be a mistake, especially if producers face other constraints in input allocations (e.g., regulatory constraints).

We now assume that the producer is technically inefficient, i.e., $y = f(x)e^{-u}$ (ignoring the stochastic noise component). We can write this as $ye^u = f(x)$, which shows a neutral shift of the y_0 isoquant to y_0e^u. Allocative inefficiency can then be defined in terms of the new isoquant, y_0e^u. Figure 8.2 illustrates this graphically for two inputs.

Given the prices, the allocatively efficient input combination is given by the point B, whereas, the actual point is A (which is made technically efficient by shifting the isoquant). Allocative inefficiency is represented by the difference in the slope of the y_0e^u isoquant between points A and B.

Because technical inefficiency shifts the production function neutrally, the slope of the isoquant will be unchanged. Thus, one can define allocative inefficiency with respect to the y_0 isoquant by dropping down radially from point A to A' and B to B'. Allocative inefficiency is then represented by the difference in slope of the y_0 isoquant between point A' and B'.[3]

[3] Note that the slopes of the isoquants at A and A' (B and B') are the same.

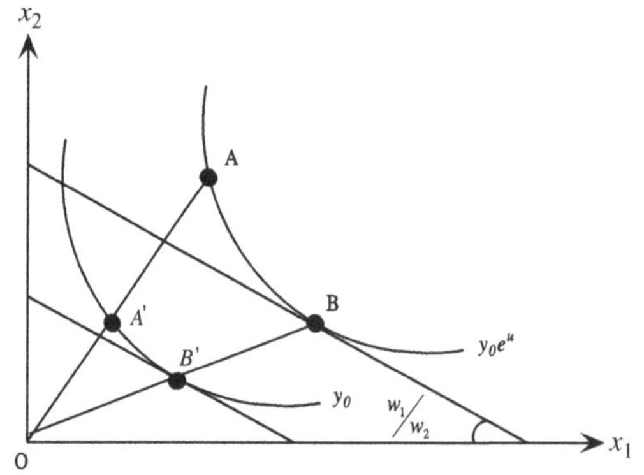

Figure 8.2. Technical and Allocative Inefficiency

It is worth noting that nothing in this model is ad hoc. None of the error terms are added in an ad hoc fashion (u, v and ξ_j are all introduced into the model in a theoretically consistent manner).

We now illustrate this model in the case of the Cobb-Douglas production function (and subsequently the generalized production function), where it is possible to derive the input demand functions analytically, before illustrating the case of the translog production function, where it is necessary to compute the impact numerically.

8.4 Estimation Methods When Algebraic Formula Can Be Derived

Although, *in general*, no algebraic formula can be derived for the input demand and cost functions, there are two cases where the algebraic formula can be derived – the Cobb-Douglas production function and the generalized production function. We examine these two cases next, with an empirical example to illustrate the former.

8.4.1 The Cobb-Douglas Production Function

The production function and the first-order conditions for the Cobb-Douglas model are:

$$\ln y = \alpha_0 + \sum_j \alpha_j \ln x_j + v - u$$
$$\ln\left({}^{\alpha_j}/_{\alpha_1}\right) - \ln\left({}^{w_j}/_{w_1}\right) - \ln x_j + \ln x_1 = \xi_j, j = 2, \ldots, J. \tag{8.23}$$

In order to estimate this system using the ML method, it is necessary to make distributional assumptions on the error components. Here, we make the following assumptions:

$$v \sim N(0, \sigma_v^2), \tag{8.24}$$
$$u \sim N^+(0, \sigma_u^2), \tag{8.25}$$
$$\boldsymbol{\xi} \sim MVN(0, \Sigma), \tag{8.26}$$
$$\xi_j \text{ are independent of } v \text{ and } u. \tag{8.27}$$

Some of these assumptions (for example, not allowing for systematic allocative inefficiency, i.e., $E(\xi_j) = 0\,\forall j$) are relaxed later. The joint distribution of $v - u$ and $\boldsymbol{\xi}$ is

$$f(v - u, \boldsymbol{\xi}) = g(v - u) \cdot h(\boldsymbol{\xi}), \tag{8.28}$$

where

$$g(v-u) = \frac{2}{\sigma}\phi\left\{\frac{(v-u)}{\sigma}\right\}\Phi\left\{\frac{-(v-u)\sigma_u}{\sigma_v\sigma}\right\}, \tag{8.29}$$

and $\phi(.)$ and $\Phi(.)$ are the pdf and cdf of a standard normal variable, respectively, and $\sigma = \sqrt{\sigma_u^2+\sigma_v^2}$, and the multivariate pdf for $\boldsymbol{\xi}$ is given by $h(\boldsymbol{\xi})$, and the likelihood function is

$$L = g(v-u)\cdot h(\boldsymbol{\xi})\cdot |J|, \tag{8.30}$$

where $|J|$ is the determinant of the Jacobian matrix:

$$|J| = \left|\frac{\partial(v-u,\xi_2,\xi_3,\ldots,\xi_J)}{\partial(\ln x_1,\ln x_2,\ldots,\ln x_J)}\right|. \tag{8.31}$$

The parameters of this model can be estimated by ML. After estimating the parameters, observation-specific estimates of the impact of technical inefficiency on output, u, can be estimated using the Jondrow et al. (1982) formula.

Allocative inefficiency, ξ_j, for the input pair $(j,1)$ can be obtained from the residuals of the FOCs (8.23). As discussed earlier, the sign of $\hat{\xi}_j$ shows whether input j is over- or underused relative to input 1.

Example

For the empirical illustrations in this chapter, we use the same dataset as first introduced in Chapter 4, namely, data on (investor-owned) fossil fuel fired steam electric power generation plants in the United States. This is a panel dataset of seventy-two electric power generation plants over eleven years (1986–1996). However, in this chapter, as before, we treat this dataset as a cross-sectional dataset (i.e., as if there are 791 separate electric power generation plants).

The output (`y`) is net steam electric power generation in megawatt-hours. The variable inputs (in logs) are: fuel (`lfuel`); labor and maintenance (`llabor`); and capital (`lk`). Associated prices (in logs) are: the price of fuel (`lw1`); the price of labor and maintenance (`lw2`); and the price of capital (`lw3`).

We start off with the standard OLS estimation of the production function and the COLS estimation of technical inefficiency of this model, as well as the standard stochastic frontier production model. (At this stage, we are simply following the approach set out in Chapter 3.)

Model 1: OLS

The following is the code for the OLS estimation of a Cobb-Douglas production model. We suppress the results from this model. (As usual, we save the estimated parameters for later use):

```
. use utility, clear

. global xlist llabor lfuel lk
. quietly regress lny $xlist
. matrix b0 = e(b)
```

Model 2: COLS

The OLS residuals are then used to obtain the efficiency index. The code and output is provided here:

```
. predict e, residual
. quietly summarize e
. generate double u_star = -(e - r(max))
. generate double eff_cols = exp(-u_star)
. summarize eff_cols

    Variable |       Obs        Mean    Std. Dev.       Min        Max
-------------+--------------------------------------------------------
    eff_cols |       791    .4987872    .1207305   .1563241          1
```

The mean of the efficiency index indicates that, on average, output is about 50 percent of the maximum potential level.

Model 3: Half-Normal Production Frontier Model

We now estimate a stochastic frontier production model, using the estimated parameters from the OLS model as starting values. Here, we use a half-normal model. As with previous applications, the coefficient estimates may be useful as starting values for the subsequent more complex primal models.

```
. sfmodel lny, frontier($xlist) usigmas() vsigmas() prod dist(h)
. ml init b0 0 0, copy
. sf_srch, n(2) frontier($xlist) usigmas() vsigmas() fast
. ml max, diff gradient
```

The coefficient estimates and inefficiencies are then saved as here:

```
. matrix b1 = e(b)
. sf_predict, bc(eff3) jlms(ineff3)
. summarize eff3 ineff3

    Variable |       Obs        Mean    Std. Dev.       Min        Max
-------------+--------------------------------------------------------
        eff3 |       791    .7521155    .1456502   .2637096   .9704736
      ineff3 |       791    .3118214     .224224   .0303695   1.338502
```

This indicates that, on average, output is about 25 percent to 31 percent of the maximum potential level.

Model 4: Primal Half-Normal Model with No Systematic Error

We now move on to the primal system approach, including allocative inefficiency in the model. As such, we introduce a new command.

The author-written Stata command `sfprim` is used in this instance. Because of the complexity of the model, `sfprim` can only handle models with up to five input variables. Among the input variables, at least one has to be a variable input (which has the price information) and the rest can be quasi-fixed input (for which price information is not needed).

As with the earlier commands, we first set up the model and then use the `ml max` to estimate the model.

```
. global plist lw2 lw1 lw3     /* the input prices */
. sfprim lny, inputs($xlist) prices($plist) dist(h) cd cost
. ml init b1, copy /* use the coefficients from Model 3 as initial values */
. sf_srch, n(3) inputs($xlist) fast /* search for better initial values */
. ml max, difficult gradient
```

Here, `sfprim` defines the model to be estimated: `inputs($xlist)` defines the inputs in the model with the first named input used as the numeraire; `prices($plist)` defines the associated input prices in the model, which should be listed in the same order as the corresponding input variables in `inputs($xlist)`; `dist(h)` sets the distributional assumption of technical inefficiency to be a half-normal; `cd` determines that model has a Cobb-Douglas production function; and `cost` determines that it is a primal cost system model that we are estimating. The default option is that there is no systematic error in the allocative inefficiency (i.e., $\xi_j = 0 \ \forall \ j$), while if `syserror` is specified then the model is estimated with systematic error in the allocative inefficiency (i.e., the FOC's error term is allowed to have a nonzero mean).

Note that if there are quasi-fixed inputs in the model (for instance, a time trend), then they should also be listed in `inputs()` *following* the list of variable inputs. For instance, suppose we have two variable inputs, `x1` and `x2`, with corresponding prices `xp1` and `xp2`, and two quasi-fixed inputs `q1` and `q2`, which have no corresponding prices. Then, we should specify `inputs(x1 x2 q1 q2)` and `prices(xp1 xp2)`. The program would count the number of prices ('N') listed in `prices()` and match that with the first N instances in `inputs()` and take those as variable inputs. The rest are treated as quasi-fixed inputs. Therefore, the order of variables listed in `inputs()` and `prices()` is important.

The estimation results are provided here:

```
-------------- Confirmation Message ----------------

(1) This model estimates the cost minimization behavior
    using production function systems based on duality.

(2) The production frontier has the specification of
    llabor lfuel lk .

(3) The variable inputs are
    llabor lfuel lk,
    with the corresponding prices being
    lw2 lw1 lw3.
(4) The system model consists of a production function
    and 2 FOCs of inputs.
(5) The technical inefficiency has a halfnormal distribution.
(6) There is no systematic error in the allocative inefficiency.

(iteration log omitted)

                                                  Number of obs   =        791
                                                  Wald chi2(0)    =          .
Log likelihood = -237.52672                       Prob > chi2     =          .

------------------------------------------------------------------------------
         lny |      Coef.   Std. Err.      z    P>|z|     [95% Conf. Interval]
-------------+----------------------------------------------------------------
llabor       |
       _cons |   .1689209   .0029037    58.17   0.000     .1632297    .1746121
-------------+----------------------------------------------------------------
lfuel        |
       _cons |   .5784661   .0068996    83.84   0.000     .5649432    .5919891
-------------+----------------------------------------------------------------
```

```
lk           |
       _cons |   .2726187   .0040559    67.22   0.000     .2646693    .2805681
-------------+----------------------------------------------------------------
linear       |
       _cons |   4.848494   .1204767    40.24   0.000     4.612364    5.084624
-------------+----------------------------------------------------------------
usigmas      |
       _cons |  -1.934312   .0920763   -21.01   0.000    -2.114778   -1.753846
-------------+----------------------------------------------------------------
vsigmas      |
       _cons |  -3.910929    .161022   -24.29   0.000    -4.226526   -3.595331
------------------------------------------------------------------------------
```

The inefficiencies are then saved as here:

```
. sf_predict, bc(eff4) jlms(ineff4)
. summarize eff4 ineff4

    Variable |        Obs        Mean    Std. Dev.       Min        Max
-------------+---------------------------------------------------------
        eff4 |        791    .7595995    .1336301   .3308068   .9641275
      ineff4 |        791    .2999439    .2034955   .0371283   1.115014
```

The results show that, on average, the electric power generation plants produce around 24 percent to 30 percent less than their maximum potential output due to the technical inefficiency. These are illustrated in Figure 8.3 (using the following code):

```
. label variable ineff4 "Model 4: Primal Cobb-Douglas, no systematic error"
. histogram ineff4, bin(100) `kden´ saving(sfprim_cost_ineff_mod4, replace)
. graph export sfprim_cost_ineff_mod4.eps, replace
```

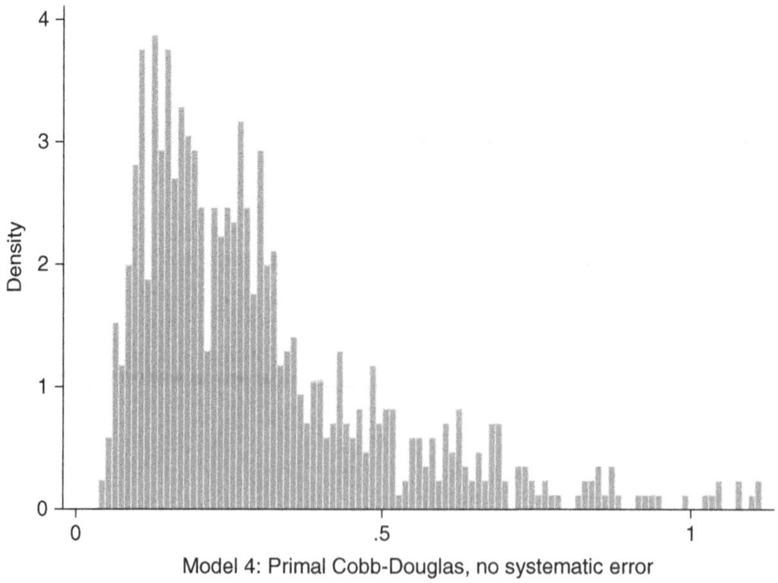

Figure 8.3. Estimated Inefficiency from Model 4 (Primal, Cobb-Douglas Function)

We next examine input allocative inefficiency, ξ, for fuel and capital (relative to labor). Using the FOCs from equation (8.23), $\hat{\xi}_j$ is generated using the code given here:

```
. scalar aa0 = [linear]_b[_cons]
. scalar aa1 = [llabor]_b[_cons]
. scalar aa2 = [lfuel]_b[_cons]
. scalar aa3 = [lk]_b[_cons]

. quietly generate double shr1 = aa1
. quietly generate double shr2 = aa2
. quietly generate double shr3 = aa3

. quietly generate double shr21 = (shr2)/(shr1)
. quietly generate double shr31 = (shr3)/(shr1)

. quietly generate double epsi1a = ln((shr21)) - ln(exp(lwfue)*fuel) + ln(exp(lwlab)*labor)
. quietly generate double epsi2a = ln((shr31)) - ln(exp(lwk)*k) + ln(exp(lwlab)*labor)

. summarize epsi1a epsi2a

    Variable |       Obs        Mean    Std. Dev.       Min        Max
-------------+--------------------------------------------------------
      epsi1a |       791   -.0046271    .5042984  -1.484423   2.189805
      epsi2a |       791   -.0086802    .5082674   -1.61742   1.998869
```

Because the mean values of $\hat{\xi}_F$ and $\hat{\xi}_K$ are negative (-0.005 and -0.009, respectively), this means that $\exp(\xi_F) < 1$ and $\exp(\xi_K) < 1$, and that labor/fuel and labor/capital ratios are on average lower than the cost minimizing ratios. This result shows that both fuel and capital are overused relative to labor. In addition, this result shows that capital is overused relative to both labor and fuel (the Averch–Johnson hypothesis). An overuse of capital relative to fuel (as well as labor) follows from the fact that $(w_K/w_F)\exp(\xi_K)/\exp(\xi_F) < w_K/w_F$ when evaluated at the mean values of ξ_F and ξ_K.

Based on the observation-specific values, we find that about 50 percent of the firms overused capital relative to both labor and fuel (as shown here):

```
. generate count = 0
. replace count = 1 if epsi1a > epsi2a
(386 real changes made)

. summarize count

    Variable |       Obs        Mean    Std. Dev.       Min        Max
-------------+--------------------------------------------------------
       count |       791    .4879899     .500172          0          1
```

However, this result is not surprising, because the estimated model does not allow for systematic allocative inefficiency, that is, $E(\xi_j) = 0 \; \forall \, j$ (we relax this assumption in the next example).

Although the estimates of output technical inefficiencies and input allocative inefficiencies (in terms of the relative over- or underuse of inputs) are useful economically, one is probably more interested in computing the effect of these inefficiencies on cost. This is because what matters most to cost-minimizing producers is knowing by how much their costs are increased due to inefficiency. However, as mentioned in Section 8.3, the estimates of ξ for each pair of inputs only tell us whether an input is relatively overused (or underused), and the *degree* of overuse (or underuse) cannot be inferred from the estimates of ξ. To address this issue, first, we compute the impact of u and ξ on $\ln x_j$. These results are then used to compute the impact of u and ξ_j on cost.

We examine how to calculate these next in the case of the Cobb-Douglas production function.

8.4.1.1 Technical and Allocative Inefficiency Effect on Input Demand

To quantify the effect of technical and allocative inefficiency on input demand, we derive the input demand function. This system of equations for the Cobb-Douglas production function (8.23) can be solved for $\ln x_j$, providing the input demand function,

$$\ln x_j = a_j + \frac{1}{r}\sum_{i=1}^{J} \alpha_i \ln w_i - \ln w_j + \frac{1}{r}\ln y + \frac{1}{r}\sum_{i=2}^{J} \alpha_i \xi_i - \xi_j - \frac{1}{r}(v-u), j = 2, \ldots, J,$$

$$\ln x_1 = a_1 + \frac{1}{r}\sum_{i=1}^{J} \alpha_i \ln w_i - \ln w_1 + \frac{1}{r}\ln y + \frac{1}{r}\sum_{i=2}^{J} \alpha_i \xi_i - \frac{1}{r}(v-u),$$

where $r = \sum_{i=1}^{J} \alpha_i$ is returns to scale (degree of homogeneity), and

$$a_j = \ln \alpha_j - \frac{1}{r}\left[\alpha_0 + \sum_{i=1}^{J} \alpha_i \ln \alpha_i\right]. \tag{8.32}$$

The input demand function in (8.32) has four parts:

1. the part not dependent on u, ξ, and v (often labeled as the neoclassical input demand functions);
2. the part dependent on input allocative inefficiency ξ, which is $1/r\sum_{i=2}^{J} \alpha_i \xi_i - \xi_j$ for $j = 2, \ldots, J$, while for input x_1 it is $1/r\sum_{i=2}^{J} \alpha_i \xi_i$;
3. the part dependent on OO technical inefficiency u (i.e., u/r);
4. the part dependent on v (i.e., $-v/r$).

Given everything else being equal, a higher value of r means lower values for each of the above components.

To examine the effect of technical inefficiency on input demand, we first note that $u/r = \eta$. Therefore, the effect of OO technical inefficiencies on input demand is obtained from $\left[\ln x_j|_{u=\hat{u}}\right] - \left[\ln x_j|_{u=0}\right] = (1/r)\hat{u} = \left[\ln x_j|_{\eta=\hat{\eta}}\right] - \left[\ln x_j|_{\eta=0}\right] = \hat{\eta} \geq 0$ for $j = 2, ..., J$. Thus, demand for each input is increased by $(1/r)\hat{u} = \hat{\eta}$ percent due to OO technical inefficiency.

In addition, we can see from this equation that, due to input allocative inefficiency, demand for x_j is changed by $\left[\ln x_j|_{\xi=\hat{\xi}}\right] - \left[\ln x_j|_{\xi=0}\right] = 1/r\sum_{i=2}^{J} \alpha_i \hat{\xi}_i - \hat{\xi}_j$ percent for $j = 2, \ldots, J$, while for input x_1 it is changed by $1/r\sum_{i=2}^{J} \alpha_i \hat{\xi}_i$ percent. Because $\hat{\xi}_j$ can be positive or negative, the presence of input allocative inefficiency can either increase or decrease demand for an input. Note that ξ_j are the residuals of the FOCs in (8.23).

Example

Calculating Technical and Allocative Inefficiency on Input Demand

Here, we continue with the the previous example (Model 4) and calculate technical and allocative inefficiency. Both technical and allocative efficiency can be calculated through the use of author-written commands. However, the program has not been generalized to be readily applied to cases with any number of inputs, because of the complexity in computing the cost of allocative inefficiency. As such, for greater flexibility, we first outline the procedures required for estimating technical and allocative inefficiency in this setting without recourse to the additional Stata commands.

We calculate the predicted value of $v - u$.

```
. quietly generate double v_u = lny - aa0 - aa1*llabor - aa2*lfuel - aa3*lk
```

We then calculate returns to scale (and find that the model predicts constant returns to scale).

```
. scalar rts = aa1 + aa2 + aa3
. display rts
1.0200058
```

We can now calculate the impact of technical inefficiency and allocative inefficiency on input demand (this will subsequently be used to calculate the impact of technical inefficiency and allocative inefficiency on cost).

First, we calculate the neoclassical input demand functions, $\ln x_j$, as given by equation (8.32), with $u = 0$, $\xi = 0$, and $v = 0$.

```
. quietly generate double optx1 = ln(aa1) - (aa0 + aa1*ln(aa1) + aa2*ln(aa2)  ///
>                      + aa3*ln(aa3))/scalar(r) - lwlab + lny/scalar(r) ///
>                      + (aa1*lwlab+aa2*lwfue+aa3*lwk)/scalar(r)
. quietly generate double optx2 = ln(aa2) - (aa0 + aa1*ln(aa1) + aa2*ln(aa2) ///
>                      + aa3*ln(aa3))/scalar(r) - lwfue + lny/scalar(r) ///
>                      + (aa1*lwlab+aa2*lwfue+aa3*lwk)/scalar(r)
. quietly generate double optx3 = ln(aa3) - (aa0 + aa1*ln(aa1) + aa2*ln(aa2) ///
>                      + aa3*ln(aa3))/scalar(r) - lwk + lny/scalar(r) ///
>                      + (aa1*lwlab+aa2*lwfue+aa3*lwk)/scalar(r)
```

Second, we calculate the the input demand functions, $\ln x_j$, as given by equation (8.32), with technical inefficiency, $u = \hat{u}$, and $\xi = 0$ and $v = 0$.

```
. scalar r = rts
. quietly generate double resid = - ineff4

. quietly generate double tex1 = ln(aa1) - (aa0 + aa1*ln(aa1) + aa2*ln(aa2) ///
>                      + aa3*ln(aa3))/scalar(r) - lwlab + lny/scalar(r) ///
>                      + (aa1*lwlab+aa2*lwfue+aa3*lwk)/scalar(r) - resid/scalar(r)
. quietly generate double tex2 = ln(aa2) - (aa0 + aa1*ln(aa1) + aa2*ln(aa2) ///
>                      + aa3*ln(aa3))/scalar(r) - lwfue + lny/scalar(r) ///
>                      + (aa1*lwlab+aa2*lwfue+aa3*lwk)/scalar(r) - resid/scalar(r)
. quietly generate double tex3 = ln(aa3) - (aa0 + aa1*ln(aa1) + aa2*ln(aa2) ///
>                      + aa3*ln(aa3))/scalar(r) - lwk + lny/scalar(r) ///
>                      + (aa1*lwlab+aa2*lwfue+aa3*lwk)/scalar(r) - resid/scalar(r)
```

Finally, we calculate the the input demand functions, $\ln x_j$, as given by equation (8.32), with allocative inefficiency, $\xi = \hat{\xi}$, and $u = 0$ and $v = 0$.

```
. quietly generate double allocx1 = ln(aa1) - (aa0 + aa1*ln(aa1) + aa2*ln(aa2) ///
>                      + aa3*ln(aa3))/scalar(r) - lwlab + lny/scalar(r) ///
>                      + (aa1*lwlab+aa2*lwfue+aa3*lwk)/scalar(r) ///
>                      + (aa2*epsi1b + aa3*epsi2b)/scalar(r)
. quietly generate double allocx2 = ln(aa2) - (aa0 + aa1*ln(aa1) + aa2*ln(aa2) ///
>                      + aa3*ln(aa3))/scalar(r) - lwfue + lny/scalar(r) ///
>                      + (aa1*lwlab+aa2*lwfue+aa3*lwk)/scalar(r) ///
>                      + (aa2*epsi1b + aa3*epsi2b)/scalar(r) - epsi1b
. quietly generate double allocx3 = ln(aa3) - (aa0 + aa1*ln(aa1) + aa2*ln(aa2) ///
>                      + aa3*ln(aa3))/scalar(r) - lwk + lny/scalar(r) ///
>                      + (aa1*lwlab+aa2*lwfue+aa3*lwk)/scalar(r) ///
>                      + (aa2*epsi1a + aa3*epsi2a)/scalar(r) - epsi2b
```

Having estimated the impact of technical and allocative inefficiency on input demand we can now estimate the impact of interest, namely the impact on costs.

8.4.1.2 Technical and Allocative Inefficiency Effect on Costs

The impact of both technical and input allocative inefficiencies on cost can be obtained by comparing the cost function with and without inefficiency. Because the cost function has an analytical solution for the Cobb-Douglas model, it is possible to get analytical solutions for the cost of technical inefficiency ($\ln c_u$) and the cost of input allocative inefficiency ($\ln c_\xi$). To examine the impact of technical and allocative inefficiency on cost, we derive the expression for $\ln c^a$:

$$\ln c^a = a_0 + \frac{1}{r}\ln y + \frac{1}{r}\sum_{i=1}^{J}\alpha_i \ln w_i - \frac{1}{r}(v-u) + (E - \ln r)$$

$$\text{where } a_0 = \ln r - \frac{\alpha_0}{r} - \frac{1}{r}\left(\sum_i \alpha_i \ln \alpha_i\right), \tag{8.33}$$

$$E = \frac{1}{r}\sum_{j=2}^{J}\alpha_j \xi_j + \ln\left[\alpha_1 + \sum_{j=2}^{J}\alpha_j e^{-\xi_j}\right] - \ln r.$$

As with the input demand functions in (8.32), the cost function in (8.33) has four parts:

1. the part not dependent on u, ξ, and v (often labeled as the neoclassical cost function);
2. the part dependent on input allocative inefficiency ξ, which is $(E - \ln r) \geq 0$;
3. the part dependent on technical inefficiency u (i.e., u/r);
4. the part dependent on v (i.e., $-v/r$).

Thus, it is clear that technical inefficiency increases cost by $\frac{1}{r}u.100\%$, whereas allocative inefficiency increases cost by $100(E - \ln r)\%$. Note that an increase in cost due to technical and allocative inefficiencies is inversely related to r.

We now return to our example to estimate the impact of on costs.

Example

Calculating the Impact of Technical and Allocative Inefficiency on Costs

We continue with the previous example (Model 4). Here, we show how to calculate the impact of technical and allocative inefficiency on costs, following the procedure discussed above. First, we calculate the cost of technical inefficiency by comparing costs with and without technical inefficiency.

```
. quietly generate double C_o = exp(lwlab)*exp(optx1) + exp(lwfue)*exp(optx2) + exp(lwk)*exp(optx3)
. quietly generate double C_te = exp(lwlab)*exp(tex1) + exp(lwfue)*exp(tex2) + exp(lwk)*exp(tex3)

. quietly generate double C_ratio_te = C_te/C_o -1
. summarize C_ratio_te, detail

                        C_ratio_te
-------------------------------------------------------------
      Percentiles      Smallest
 1%     .0592949       .0370707
 5%     .0876379       .0467718
```

```
10%       .108402       .0482145       Obs                  791
25%       .160832       .0552333       Sum of Wgt.          791

50%       .2741112                     Mean            .3716554
                         Largest       Std. Dev.       .3211126
75%       .4537015      1.881248
90%       .8039463      1.947933       Variance        .1031133
95%       1.033842      1.969742       Skewness        2.161312
99%       1.759265      1.983641       Kurtosis        8.617442
```

These results show that, on average, costs are increased by 37.2 percent, due to technical inefficiency.

Finally, the impact of allocative inefficiency on costs is calculated here:

```
. quietly generate double C_a = exp(lwlab)*exp(allocx1) + exp(lwfue)*exp(allocx2) ///
                            + exp(lwk)*exp(allocx3)
. quietly generate double C_ratio_a = C_a/C_o -1
. summarize C_ratio_a, detail

                          C_ratio_a
-------------------------------------------------------------
      Percentiles      Smallest
 1%     .0001686       8.04e-06
 5%     .0007982        .000012
10%     .0017524       .0000479       Obs                 791
25%     .0059623       .0000817       Sum of Wgt.         791

50%     .0160645                      Mean            .035308
                        Largest       Std. Dev.      .0692939
75%     .0345123         .45878
90%     .0746488       .6519368       Variance       .0048016
95%     .1411747       .6850843       Skewness       5.942713
99%      .326475       .8718511       Kurtosis       52.50924
```

Instead of this coding, it is possible to use the author-written command `sf_cst_compare`, which has to be issued after `sfprim` estimation, to do the computation automatically. However, this command only works in cases where the production function is Cobb-Douglas.

```
. sf_cst_compare, jlms(ineff4) error(tech) cd
```

Here, `jlms(ineff4)` identifies the JLMS technical inefficiency (i.e., $E(u|v-u)$) estimated from the primal model. The option `error(tech)` indicates that we are evaluating the impact of technical inefficiency on cost. The option `cd` is included to remind users that this command is only valid if the model has a Cobb-Douglas production function (i.e., `sfprim` has been executed with the `cd` option). The output from this command is a summary table of technical inefficiency, with average inefficiency of 37.2 percent, as set out earlier.

```
The following is the summary statistics of excess cost as a ratio
of optimal cost. Excess cost is defined as the difference between
the cost with technical inefficiency and the optimal (minimum)
cost. The optimal cost is the cost without technical and
allocative inefficiency.

                           C_ratio
-------------------------------------------------------------
      Percentiles      Smallest
 1%     .0592949       .0370707
 5%     .0876379       .0467718
10%      .108402       .0482145       Obs                 791
25%      .160832       .0552333       Sum of Wgt.         791

50%     .2741112                      Mean           .3716554
```

		Largest	Std. Dev.	.3211126
75%	.4537015	1.881248		
90%	.8039463	1.947933	Variance	.1031133
95%	1.033842	1.969742	Skewness	2.161312
99%	1.759265	1.983641	Kurtosis	8.617442

Alternatively, we may specify `error(alloc)` or `error(both)` in the command. The former evaluates the cost impact of allocative inefficiency, while the latter evaluates the cost impact when both technical and allocative inefficiency are assumed to exist. For instance, the following command produces summary statistics of the cost impact from the combined effect of technical and allocative inefficiency.

```
. sf_cst_compare, jlms(ineff4) error(both) cd

The following is the summary statistics of excess cost as a ratio
of optimal cost. Excess cost is defined as the difference between
the cost with technical and allocative inefficiency and the optimal (minimum)
cost. The optimal cost is the cost without technical and
allocative inefficiency.
```

C_ratio

	Percentiles	Smallest		
1%	.0722212	.0634868		
5%	.1119498	.0634925		
10%	.1382542	.065528	Obs	791
25%	.1921965	.0655625	Sum of Wgt.	791
50%	.3144844		Mean	.4213687
		Largest	Std. Dev.	.3579374
75%	.5032268	2.244875		
90%	.8673104	2.323046	Variance	.1281192
95%	1.115633	2.344513	Skewness	2.38414
99%	1.923718	2.6592	Kurtosis	10.41613

These results are summarized in the charts in Figure 8.4.

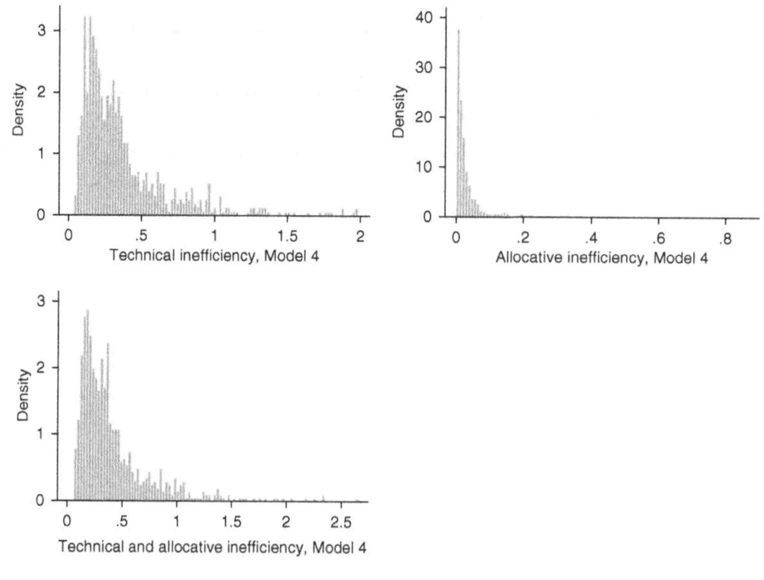

Figure 8.4. Technical and Allocative Inefficiency, Model 4

Model 5: Primal Half-Normal Model with Systematic Error

Given that the U.S. electric power generation plants are subject to rate of return regulation, which can potentially lead to a systematic overutilization of capital relative to any other input (the Averch-Johnson hypothesis), we now allow nonzero means for allocative inefficiency (ξ). The basic model is the same as given in equations (8.23) to (8.27), except that $\xi \sim MVN(\rho, \Sigma)$. We estimate this model by extending Model 4 with the additional option `syserror`.

```
. sfprim lny, inputs($xlist) prices(lw2 lw1 lw3) dist(h) cd noask syserror cost
. ml init b2, copy      /* use the coefficients from Model 4 as initial values */
. ml max, difficult gradient
```

Here the `noask` option prints the Confirmation Message without requiring the user to press `q` and return to continue. The estimation results are provided here:

```
------------- Confirmation Message ----------------

(1) This model estimates the cost minimization behavior
    using production function systems based on duality.

(2) The production frontier has the spcification of
    llabor lfuel lk .

(3) The variable inputs are
    llabor lfuel lk,
    with the corresponding prices being
    lw2 lw1 lw3.
(4) The system model consists of a production function
    and 2 FOCs of inputs.
(5) The technical inefficiency has a halfnormal distribution.
(6) There is systematic error in the allocative inefficiency.

(iteration log omitted)


                                                  Number of obs    =        791
                                                  Wald chi2(0)     =          .
Log likelihood = -227.63368                       Prob > chi2      =          .

------------------------------------------------------------------------------
         lny |      Coef.   Std. Err.      z    P>|z|     [95% Conf. Interval]
-------------+----------------------------------------------------------------
llabor       |
       _cons |   .2371233   .0187984    12.61   0.000     .2002791    .2739674
-------------+----------------------------------------------------------------
lfuel        |
       _cons |   .5982962   .0259084    23.09   0.000     .5475167    .6490758
-------------+----------------------------------------------------------------
lk           |
       _cons |   .1887179   .0244868     7.71   0.000     .1407247    .2367111
-------------+----------------------------------------------------------------
linear       |
       _cons |   5.226529   .1377733    37.94   0.000     4.956498    5.496559
-------------+----------------------------------------------------------------
usigmas      |
       _cons |  -1.876604   .0876133   -21.42   0.000    -2.048323   -1.704885
-------------+----------------------------------------------------------------
vsigmas      |
       _cons |  -4.083305   .1701026   -24.00   0.000      -4.4167    -3.74991
------------------------------------------------------------------------------
```

The inefficiencies are then saved as shown here (and found to be similar to those estimated from Model 4):

```
. sf_predict, bc(eff5) jlms(ineff5)
. summarize eff5 ineff5

    Variable |       Obs        Mean    Std. Dev.       Min        Max
-------------+--------------------------------------------------------
        eff5 |       791    .7542384    .1398341   .3013502   .9630922
      ineff5 |       791    .3084779    .2150393   .0382242   1.207073
```

In this model, we introduced systematic error in allocative efficiency in order to examine the Averch-Johnson effect. Based on the observation-specific values, we find that about 87 percent of the firms overused capital relative to both labor and fuel (as shown here):

```
. generate count = 0
. replace count = 1 if epsi1a > epsi2a
(688 real changes made)

. summarize count

    Variable |       Obs        Mean    Std. Dev.       Min        Max
-------------+--------------------------------------------------------
       count |       791    .8697851    .3367527          0          1
```

Calculation of technical and allocative inefficiency on costs is undertaken in the same way as in the previous example, so the coding is not replicated here, but the resultant charts summarizing technical and allocative inefficiency are provided in Figure 8.5 (the increased allocative inefficiency compared to Model 4 is clearly visible).

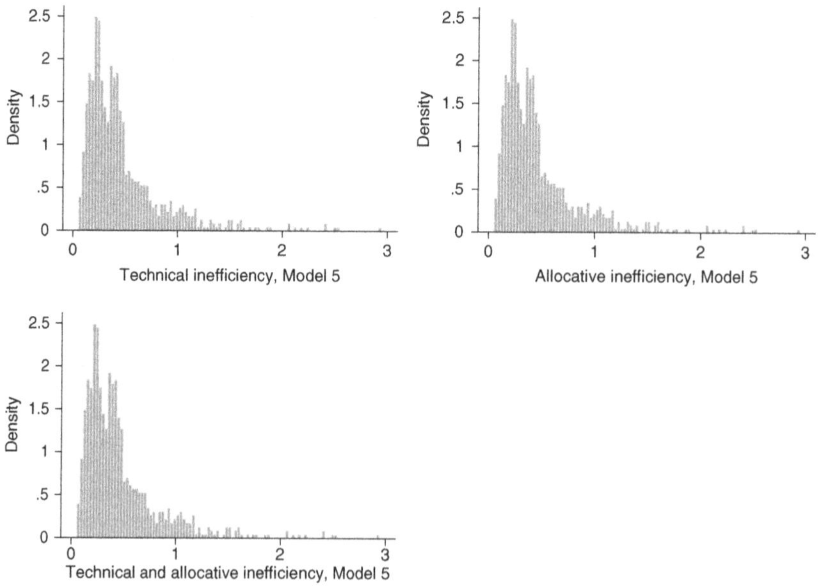

Figure 8.5. Technical and Allocative Inefficiency, Model 5

8.4.2 The Generalized Production Function

Another production function that is slightly more general in terms of returns to scale, for which costs of technical and allocative inefficiency can be derived algebraically is the Generalized Production Function (GPF), introduced by Zellner and Revankar (1969). This function is of the form

$$\ln y + \theta y = \alpha_0 + \sum_j \alpha_j \ln x_j + v - u \tag{8.34}$$

Here, u can be given an input-oriented (IO) technical inefficiency interpretation by rewriting the production function as

$$\ln y + \theta y = \alpha_0 + \sum_j \alpha_j \ln \left(x_j e^{-\eta}\right) + v \tag{8.35}$$

Thus,

$$u = \left(\sum_j \alpha_j\right)\eta = r\eta \tag{8.36}$$

where η is IO technical inefficiency. The input demand functions for the GPF are

$$\begin{aligned} \ln x_1 &= a_1 + \frac{1}{r}\sum_{i=1}^{J} \alpha_i \ln w_i - \ln w_1 + \frac{1}{r}\left[\ln y + \theta y\right] + \frac{1}{r}\sum_{i=2}^{J} \alpha_i \xi_i - \frac{1}{r}(v-u) \\ \ln x_j &= a_j + \frac{1}{r}\sum_{i=1} \alpha_i \ln w_i - \ln w_j + \frac{1}{r}\left[\ln y + \theta y\right] + \frac{1}{r}\sum_{i=2}^{J} \alpha_i \xi_i - \xi_j - \frac{1}{r}(v-u) \\ &\text{for } j = 2, \ldots, J \end{aligned} \tag{8.37}$$

As such, as in the Cobb-Douglas production case, technical inefficiency increases demand for all inputs by $\frac{1}{r}u$. The impact of allocative inefficiency ξ on demand for a particular input can be positive or negative.

Finally, the cost function is

$$\ln c^a = a_0 + \frac{1}{r}\left[\ln y + \theta y\right] + \frac{1}{r}\sum_{i=1}^{J} \alpha_i \ln w_i - \frac{1}{r}(v-u) + E - \ln r \tag{8.38}$$

$$RTS = \left\{\frac{\partial \ln c}{\partial \ln y}\right\}^{-1} = \left\{\frac{1}{r}(1+\theta y)\right\}^{-1} = \frac{r}{1+\theta y} \tag{8.39}$$

Again, technical inefficiency increases cost by $\frac{1}{r}u.100\%$ while allocative inefficiency increases cost by $100(E - \ln r)\%$.

The command `sfprim` supports the estimation of models with Cobb-Douglas and translog production functions, but it currently does not estimate a GPF model. The strategy of estimation, nevertheless, is similar.

8.5 Estimation Methods When Algebraic Formula Cannot Be Derived

The main reason for deriving $\ln x_j$ and $\ln c^a$ is that we want to quantify the impact of technical and allocative inefficiency on input demand and cost. However, there are not many production functions for which the input demand and cost functions can be derived algebraically. For example, for the translog production function, it is not possible to obtain algebraic expressions for $\ln x_j$ or $\ln c^a$.

We can, however, obtain these numerically without deriving the input demand and cost functions algebraically. The primal system can be used to obtain the necessary information to compute the effect of technical and allocative inefficiency on input demand and cost. This is discussed in Section 8.5.1 in the context of estimating a model with a translog production function.

8.5.1 Translog Production Function

Introducing the firm subscript, i, the translog production function can be expressed as

$$\ln y_i = \alpha_0 + \sum_j \alpha_j \ln x_{ji} + \frac{1}{2}\left[\sum_{jk} \alpha_{jk} \ln x_{ji} \ln x_{ki}\right] + v_i - u_i, \tag{8.40}$$

$$j = \text{labor, fuel, and capital.}$$

The corresponding first-order conditions (using labor as the numeraire) are

$$\ln s_{ji} - \ln s_{1i} - \ln(w_{ji}x_{ji}) + \ln(w_{1i}x_{1i}) = \xi_{ji}, \tag{8.41}$$

where

$$s_{ji} = \alpha_j + \sum_k a_{jk} \ln x_{ki}, \quad j = \text{fuel and capital.}$$

In order to estimate the above system using the ML method, we make the following assumptions (some of which are relaxed later).

$$v \sim N(0, \sigma_v^2), \tag{8.42}$$

$$u \sim N^+(0, \sigma_u^2), \quad \text{(nonnegative truncation)} \tag{8.43}$$

$$\boldsymbol{\xi} \sim MVN(0, \Sigma), \tag{8.44}$$

$$\xi_j \text{ are independent of } v \text{ and } u. \tag{8.45}$$

The joint distribution of $v - u$ and $\boldsymbol{\xi}$ is

$$f(v - u, \boldsymbol{\xi}) = g(v - u) \cdot h(\boldsymbol{\xi}), \tag{8.46}$$

and the likelihood function is

$$L = g(v - u) \cdot h(\boldsymbol{\xi}) \cdot |J|, \tag{8.47}$$

where $|J|$ is the determinant of the Jacobian matrix:

$$|J| = \left|\frac{\partial(v - u, \xi_2, \xi_3, \ldots, \xi_J)}{\partial(\ln x_1, \ln x_2, \ldots, \ln x_J)}\right|. \tag{8.48}$$

Extensions to the assumptions (8.42) to (8.45) include:

- u is truncated-normal instead of half-normal: $u \sim N^+(\mu, \sigma_u^2)$;
- u is heteroscedastic: $u = \boldsymbol{z}'\boldsymbol{\delta}$, and/or $\sigma_u^2 = \exp(\boldsymbol{z}'\boldsymbol{\theta})$;
- ξ_j is nonzero mean; that is, systematic allocative error: $\boldsymbol{\xi} \sim MVN(\boldsymbol{\rho}, \Sigma)$, $\boldsymbol{\rho} \neq 0$.

The parameters of this model can be estimated by ML. After estimating the parameters, technical inefficiency $\hat{u}$ can be estimated using the Jondrow et al. (1982) formula, while allocative inefficiency $\hat{\xi}_j$ can be obtained from the residuals of the FOCs (8.22). The extent of overuse (or underuse) of inputs can be computed numerically (discussed in Section 8.5.1.1). The effect of these inefficiencies on cost is derived by computing (numerically) the impact of $\hat{u}$ and $\hat{\xi}$ on $\ln x_j$ and then computing the impact of $\hat{u}$ and $\hat{\xi}_j$ on cost. We examine this next.

8.5.1.1 Technical and Allocative Inefficiency Effect on Input Demand

Because the input demand function cannot be derived analytically for a translog production function, numerical solutions have to be used to compute the effects of OO technical and input allocative inefficiencies. Using such an approach, we can follow the same steps as per the analytical approach earlier (see Section 8.4.1.1). That is, given the ML estimates $\hat{\alpha}_j$, $\hat{u}$, and $\hat{\xi}_j$, we solve for three different sets of input demand functions, $\ln x_j$, from the production function and the FOCs in (8.40) and (8.41):

1. The efficient input use, $\ln x_j^o$ (i.e., point B' in Figure 8.2). That is, the solution of $\ln x_j$ assuming $u = 0$, and $\xi_j = 0$;
2. The input use under technical inefficiency, $\ln \tilde{x}_j$ (i.e., point B in Figure 8.2). That is, the solution of $\ln x_j$ assuming $u = \hat{u}$, and $\xi_j = 0$;
3. The input use under allocative inefficiency, $\ln \check{x}_j$ (i.e., point A' in Figure 8.2). That is, the solution of $\ln x_j$ assuming $u = 0$, and $\xi_j = \hat{\xi}_j$.

Using these solutions of $\ln x$, the effect of technical inefficiency on the demand for x_j is simply η, which can be obtained from $\ln \tilde{x}_j - \ln x_j^0$ for $j = 1, \ldots, J$. Similarly, the impact of input allocative inefficiency on x_j is computed from $\ln \check{x}_j - \ln x_j^0$ for $j = 1, \ldots, J$.

Example

We now return to the empirical example of U.S. electricity generating plants, extending the model to a translog production function. As before, we first estimate the straight production function to obtain starting values for the primal model.

Model 6: Half-Normal Translog Production Frontier Model

First, we set up the translog model, by defining some new variables. Then, the standard production frontier model is estimated and the coefficients saved for subsequent use as potential starting values using the code given here (the results are omitted):

```
. quietly generate double llabor2 = 0.5*(llabor^2)
. quietly generate double lfuel2 = 0.5*(lfuel^2)
. quietly generate double lk2 = 0.5*(lk^2)
. quietly generate double labfue2 = llabor*lfuel
. quietly generate double labk2 = llabor*lk
. quietly generate double fuek2 = lfuel*lk
```

```
. global xlist_trans llabor lfuel lk llabor2 lfuel2 lk2 labfue2 labk2 fuek2

. sfmodel lny, frontier($xlist_trans) usigmas() vsigmas() prod dist(h)
. sf_srch, n(2) frontier($xlist_trans) usigmas() vsigmas() mu(regu) fast
. ml max, diff gradient
. matrix b3 = e(b)
```

Model 7: Primal Translog Model with No Systematic Error

The primal model with a translog production function is now estimated. Here, we use `sfprim` with the option `translog`, as this automatically sets up the translog model for us, based on the three inputs. That is, unlike the estimation using `sfmodel` where the full set of interaction terms needs to be supplied, `sfprim` only requires a list of the individual inputs and it will create the interaction terms automatically. In this instance, the OLS coefficients provide better starting values and so are used below. This highlights the importance of the initial values, especially with complex ML problems. Better initial values, such as those obtained by using `sf_srch`, really help in highly nonlinear models like the stochastic frontier model. As such, we would advise readers to try different initial values and utilize `sf_srch` when they get convergence problems.

```
. sfprim lny, inputs($xlist) prices($plist) dist(h) translog noask cost mltrick
. ml init b3, copy
. sf_srch, n(4) inputs(llabor lfuel lk) fast
. ml max, difficult gradient gtol(1e-5) nrtol(1e-5)
```

The `mltrick` option in `sfprim` is added here in order to perform a few numerical tricks which are sometimes useful for models that are otherwise difficult to get to achieve numerical convergence. It is rarely used. The estimation results are provided here:

```
------------- Confirmation Message ----------------

(1) This model estimates the cost minimization behavior
    using production function systems based on duality.

(2) The production frontier has the specification of
    llabor lfuel lk llaborllabor lfuellfuel lklk llaborlfuel llaborlk lfuellk .

(3) The variable inputs are
    llabor lfuel lk,
    with the corresponding prices being
    lw2 lw1 lw3.
(4) The system model consists of a production function
    and 2 FOCs of inputs.
(5) The technical inefficiency has a halfnormal distribution.
(6) There is no systematic error in the allocative inefficiency.

(iteration log omitted)

                                                  Number of obs    =        791
                                                  Wald chi2(0)     =          .
Log likelihood = -1834.3291                       Prob > chi2      =          .

------------------------------------------------------------------------------
         lny |      Coef.   Std. Err.      z    P>|z|     [95% Conf. Interval]
-------------+----------------------------------------------------------------
llabor       |
       _cons |   1.082622   .0240498    45.02   0.000     1.035485    1.129759
-------------+----------------------------------------------------------------
lfuel        |
       _cons |   .7490115   .0966228     7.75   0.000     .5596343    .9383887
-------------+----------------------------------------------------------------
```

```
lk           |
       _cons |  -.2374335   .0203991   -11.64   0.000    -.2774151   -.1974519
-------------+----------------------------------------------------------------
llaborllabor |
       _cons |   .1253195   .0028858    43.43   0.000     .1196635    .1309755
-------------+----------------------------------------------------------------
lfuellfuel   |
       _cons |  -.0175464   .0097343    -1.80   0.071    -.0366252    .0015324
-------------+----------------------------------------------------------------
lklk         |
       _cons |   .1492339   .0037613    39.68   0.000     .1418619    .1566059
-------------+----------------------------------------------------------------
llaborlfuel  |
       _cons |   .0303654   .0029195    10.40   0.000     .0246432    .0360876
-------------+----------------------------------------------------------------
llaborlk     |
       _cons |  -.1664992   .0029581   -56.29   0.000     -.172297   -.1607014
-------------+----------------------------------------------------------------
lfuellk      |
       _cons |  -.0168088   .0052853    -3.18   0.001    -.0271677   -.0064499
-------------+----------------------------------------------------------------
linear       |
       _cons |   3.817676    .595026     6.42   0.000     2.651446    4.983905
-------------+----------------------------------------------------------------
usigmas      |
       _cons |  -1.937697    .091722   -21.13   0.000    -2.117469   -1.757926
-------------+----------------------------------------------------------------
vsigmas      |
       _cons |  -4.043273    .181312   -22.30   0.000    -4.398638   -3.687908
------------------------------------------------------------------------------
```

We can now estimate the impact of technical inefficiency on output.

```
. sf_predict, bc(eff7) jlms(ineff7)
. summarize eff7 ineff7

    Variable |       Obs        Mean    Std. Dev.       Min        Max
-------------+--------------------------------------------------------
        eff7 |       791    .7594018     .135453   .3133237   .9599829
      ineff7 |       791    .3000394    .2054987   .0415572   1.168336
```

As with the Cobb-Douglas production function model, the results show that, on average, the electric power generation plants produce around 24 percent to 30 percent less than their maximum potential output due to the technical inefficiency.

We now turn to the impact of allocative inefficiency. First, we examine input allocative inefficiency ξ for fuel and capital (relative to labor). Using the FOCs from equation (8.41), $\hat{\xi}_j$ is generated using the code given here:

```
. scalar aa0 = [linear]_b[_cons]
. scalar aa1 = [llabor]_b[_cons]
. scalar aa2 = [lfuel]_b[_cons]
. scalar aa3 = [lk]_b[_cons]
. scalar aa11 = [llaborllabor]_b[_cons]
. scalar aa22 = [lfuellfuel]_b[_cons]
. scalar aa33 = [lklk]_b[_cons]
. scalar aa12 = [llaborlfuel]_b[_cons]
. scalar aa13 = [llaborlk]_b[_cons]
. scalar aa23 = [lfuellk]_b[_cons]

. quietly generate double shr1 = aa1 + aa11*llabor + aa12*lfuel + aa13*lk
. quietly generate double shr2 = aa2 + aa12*llabor + aa22*lfuel + aa23*lk
. quietly generate double shr3 = aa3 + aa13*llabor + aa23*lfuel + aa33*lk

. quietly generate double shr21 = (shr2)/(shr1)
. quietly generate double shr31 = (shr3)/(shr1)
```

```
. quietly generate double epsi1a = ln((shr21)) - ln(exp(lwfue)*fuel) + ln(exp(lwlab)*labor)
. quietly generate double epsi2a = ln((shr31)) - ln(exp(lwk)*k) + ln(exp(lwlab)*labor)

. summarize epsi1a epsi2a

    Variable |       Obs        Mean    Std. Dev.       Min        Max
-------------+--------------------------------------------------------
      epsi1a |       791    .0469235    .5501272  -1.677029   2.829902
      epsi2a |       791    .0570317    .5271161  -8.130948     2.1016
```

The estimates of ξ for each pair of inputs tell us whether an input is relatively overused (or underused). Because the mean values of $\hat{\xi}_F$ and $\hat{\xi}_K$ are positive (0.047 and 0.067, respectively), then $\exp(\xi_F) > 1$ and $\exp(\xi_K) > 1$, and that labor/fuel and labor/capital ratios are on average higher than the cost minimizing ratios. This result shows that both fuel and capital are underused relative to labor.

We next examine how to calculate the *degree* of overuse (or underuse) of inputs. As in the Cobb-Douglas case, we first calculate the predicted value of `v_u`.

```
. capture drop v_u
. quietly generate double v_u = lny - aa0 - aa1*llabor - aa2*lfuel - aa3*lk - ///
>         -0.5*aa11*(llabor)^2 -0.5*aa22*(lfuel)^2 - 0.5*aa33*(lk)^2 -  ///
>         -aa12*(llabor)*(lfuel) -aa13*(llabor)*(lk) ///
>         -aa23*(lfuel)*(lk)
```

We then calculate returns to scale.

```
. generate double RTS2 = aa1 + aa11*llabor + aa12*lfuel + aa13*lk  ///
>                  + aa2 + aa12*llabor + aa22*lfuel + aa23*lk  ///
>                  + aa3 + aa13*llabor + aa23*lfuel + aa33*lk

. summarize RTS2

    Variable |       Obs        Mean    Std. Dev.       Min        Max
-------------+--------------------------------------------------------
        RTS2 |       791    1.012706    .0453248   .9166126   1.124343
```

However, at this point, our approach has to differ to the Cobb-Douglas production function model because an analytical solution of $\ln x_j$ from the system of equations (8.40) and (8.41) is not possible. As such, we compute the effects of OO technical and input allocative inefficiencies on input demand numerically.

To do this, we solve the equations (8.40) and (8.41) in order to obtain the solutions of the $\ln x_j$ for each observation.[4] This involves solving nonlinear equations. To do so, we can use Stata's `nl` (nonlinear estimation) routine, with the original values as the initial values of the inputs for the `nl` least-squares estimation.[5] As discussed earlier, we solve for the $\ln x_j$ values three times. First, we solve for $\ln x_j$ from the production function and the FOCs in (8.40) and (8.41) using the estimated parameters and setting both $u = 0$ and $\xi_j = 0 \; \forall j$. Then, we solve the system again, but this time we allow allocative inefficiency only by setting $u = 0$ and $\xi_j = \hat{\xi}_j$. Finally, we solve the system again to capture the effect of only technical inefficiency by setting u $= \hat{u}_j$ and $\xi_j = 0, \forall j$. An automated estimation routine has not been provided yet.

[4] With labor, fuel, and capital inputs in the model, we have three unknowns ($\ln x_1$, $\ln x_2$, and $\ln x_3$), and three equations.

[5] See the Stata reference manuals for further guidance on `nl`.

8.5.1.2 Technical and Allocative Inefficiency Effect on Costs

We use the numerical solutions of $\ln x$ with and without inefficiency to compute the impact on costs. The cost of technical inefficiency of each observation is then given by:

$$C^{\text{tech}} = (\boldsymbol{w}'\tilde{\boldsymbol{x}})/(\boldsymbol{w}'\boldsymbol{x}^o) - 1. \tag{8.49}$$

The cost of allocative inefficiency of each observation is then given by:

$$C^{\text{allo}} = (\boldsymbol{w}'\check{\boldsymbol{x}})/(\boldsymbol{w}'\boldsymbol{x}^o) - 1. \tag{8.50}$$

The terms $w'x^o$, $w'\tilde{x}$, and $w'\check{x}$ correspond to the budget lines passing through B', B, and A' of Figure 8.2, respectively.

Because a routine to compute $\check{\boldsymbol{x}}$ for general models is not available yet, we omit the empirical example.

9

Estimation of Technical and Allocative Efficiency in Profit Frontier Models Using System Models with Cross-Sectional Data: A Primal System Approach

9.1 Introduction

In the previous chapter, we introduced "allocative inefficiency" into the analysis under the assumption that firms minimize cost. In the cost minimization framework, output is taken as exogenous. This may be reasonable in some situations. For example, in a regulated industry outputs may be determined by government policy and/or quality regulators. However, in many situations, this is *a very strong assumption*. If output is endogenous, then the estimation of cost frontier results are inconsistent.

If output is not exogenous, then firms need to make a decision on the optimum amount of output to be produced. This optimality has to be defined in terms of some economic behavior. In this chapter, we assume that firms maximize profit in making their decision on input use and the production of output. That is, now one can consider nonoptimal allocation of inputs and output (i.e., allocative inefficiency in inputs and output), in the presence of technical inefficiency. In this case, we measure the effect of inefficiency in terms of foregone profit.

In this setting, we are able to extend the questions we first set out in Chapters 1 and 5. That is, in addition to examining whether, and by how much, a firm can increase its profitability, we are also able to identify how much of this profit increase can be achieved through improvements in technical efficiency and how much can be achieved through an optimal mix of inputs.

For instance, we can reconsider what is the impact of different forms of corporate ownership. As a first step, we might consider state-owned organizations versus private companies and other forms of ownership, and ask, which are more profitable? In the setting of this chapter, we can then dig deeper than this and investigate what drives these differences. That is, overall, what drives this profit loss, is it primarily technical inefficiency or primarily allocative efficiency, does one form of ownership result in an under or overuse of capital? It is this example, and in particular, the Romanian mining industry, that we use throughout this chapter as a way of illustrating the new framework.

As with the cost framework of the previous chapter, estimation that accounts for both technical and allocative inefficiency is not straightforward with the profit function approach. This is particularly the case when a flexible functional form is assumed to represent the underlying technology. However, instead of the profit function approach, one can reformulate the problem in a primal setting, which enables us to estimate the production technology as well as both technical and allocative inefficiency.

In this chapter, we first describe how to formulate a profit maximization model with both technical and allocative inefficiency using the profit function approach, and briefly discuss the issues with estimating this model. We then describe how to formulate the problem using the primal approach and how this can be estimated. We also provide empirical illustrations.

9.2 The Profit Function Approach

With only technical inefficiency the profit function can be expressed as (Kumbhakar [2001])

$$\ln \pi_i = \ln f(\boldsymbol{w}_i, \boldsymbol{p}_i e^{u_i}) + v_i. \tag{9.1}$$

It is worth comparing this to the profit function that is often used empirically (as in Chapter 5), viz.,

$$\ln \pi_i = \ln f(\boldsymbol{w}_i, \boldsymbol{p}_i) + v_i - \tilde{u}_i. \tag{9.2}$$

The specification in (9.2) is based on the intuition that, if there is inefficiency, then actual profit will be less than optimal profit. Thus, a one-sided error is added to the (log) profit model to represent the profit loss due to either technical inefficiency or both technical and allocative inefficiency. This intuition works for some technologies such as the Cobb-Douglas but does not work with more flexible production technologies.[1]

The formulations in (9.2) and (9.1) suffer from a number of problems. First, the "profit inefficiency," $\tilde{u}_i$, in (9.2) is added in a somewhat ad hoc way, and it cannot be derived from (9.1) unless it is log-linear (which corresponds to a CD production technology). This means that the profit loss due to inefficiency estimated from the two models, using the same data, is likely to differ. Second, when $\pi_i \leq 0$, $\ln \pi_i$ is undefined and, therefore, none of the models can be used. Finally, the estimation of both models requires (large) variations in the price variables in order to get precise parameter estimates, which may not occur in practice.

The profit function with both technical and allocative inefficiency is more complex, especially from an estimation point of view. Details on the model and estimation issues are discussed in Kumbhakar (2001). We skip this here because we are not estimating a translog profit function with both technical and allocative inefficiency. It is too complicated to use the ML method. Thus, an alternative approach is required for estimation purposes. We turn to this alternative next.

9.3 The Primal Approach of Profit Maximization with Both Technical and Allocative Inefficiency

Now we consider the alternative modeling strategy, viz., the primal system approach that is easier to estimate. It is possible to avoid the estimation problem discussed in the preceding section if one focuses on the production function and uses a system consisting of the production function (instead of the profit function) and the first-order conditions of the

[1] See Kumbhakar (2001) for details.

profit maximization problem. This system is algebraically equivalent to the profit system for self-dual production functions.

We start by considering the profit maximization problem for a producer, namely,

$$\max_{y,\boldsymbol{x}} \ \Pi = py - \boldsymbol{w}'\boldsymbol{x} \quad \text{s.t.} \quad y = f(\boldsymbol{x})\exp(v-u), \quad u \geq 0 \tag{9.3}$$

$$\Longrightarrow \quad \max_{\boldsymbol{x}} \ \Pi = pf(\boldsymbol{x})\exp(v-u) - \boldsymbol{w}'\boldsymbol{x}, \tag{9.4}$$

$$\Longrightarrow \quad \max_{\boldsymbol{x}} \ \Pi = pf^*(\boldsymbol{x}) - \boldsymbol{w}'\boldsymbol{x}, \tag{9.5}$$

where $\boldsymbol{p}$ is the vector of output prices, y is the output, $\boldsymbol{w}$ is the vector of input prices, $\boldsymbol{x}$ is the vector of inputs, v is the random error of production, and u captures the output-oriented inefficiency.

The FOCs of this problem can be expressed as

$$pf_j^* = w_j \exp(\eta_j), \quad \eta_j \gtreqless 0, \quad j = 1, \ldots, J. \tag{9.6}$$

The FOCs can be expressed as

$$\frac{f_j^*}{f_1^*} = \frac{w_j}{w_1}\exp(\xi_j), \quad j = 2, 3, \ldots, J, \tag{9.7}$$

$$pf_1^* = w_1 \exp(\eta_1), \tag{9.8}$$

$$\text{where,} \quad \xi_j = \eta_j - \eta_1. \tag{9.9}$$

Using the result $s_j \equiv \partial \ln f^* / \partial \ln x_j = (\partial f^* / \partial x_j)(x_j / f^*)$, we have

$$\frac{s_j}{s_1} = \frac{w_j}{w_1}\frac{x_j}{x_1}\exp(\xi_j), \quad j = 2, 3, \ldots, J, \tag{9.10}$$

$$ps_1 \frac{y}{x_1} = w_1 \exp(\eta_1). \tag{9.11}$$

Finally, taking logarithms of these equations, the primal system to be estimated is

$$\begin{aligned} \ln y &= \ln f(\boldsymbol{x}) + v - u, \\ \ln s_j - \ln s_1 &= \ln(w_j/w_1) + \ln(x_j/x_1) + \xi_j, \quad j = 2, \ldots, J, \\ \ln p + \ln s_1 + \ln y - \ln x_1 - \ln w_1 &= \eta_1. \end{aligned} \tag{9.12}$$

There are a number of advantages to this primal system approach. First, as the model is based on the production function, there is no need to take log of profit, which could be an issue when profit is negative for some observations. Second, allocative inefficiency is accounted for in the model in a non *ad hoc* way, with "profit inefficiency" attributed to technical and/or allocative inefficiency. Finally, estimation does not rely on (large) variations in prices, which may not occur in practice (which would cause estimation issues otherwise).

We now examine how this system can be estimated.

9.4 Estimation Methods: Maximum Likelihood Estimators

Consider a translog production function, the primal system discussed earlier becomes

$$\begin{aligned}
&\ln y = a_0 + \sum_j a_j \ln x_j + \frac{1}{2}\sum_j \sum_k a_{jk} \ln x_j \ln x_k + v - u, \\
&\ln s_j - \ln s_1 - \ln(w_j/w_1) - \ln(x_j/x_1) = \xi_j,\ j = 2, 3, \ldots, J \qquad (9.13)\\
&\ln s_1 = \ln(w_1/p) + \ln x_1 - \ln y + \eta_1, \\
\text{where,}\ & s_j = a_j + \sum_k a_{jk} \ln x_k.
\end{aligned}$$

For estimation purposes, we add the following distribution assumptions:

$$v \sim N(0, \sigma_v^2), \qquad (9.14)$$

$$u \sim N^+(0, \sigma_u^2), \qquad (9.15)$$

$$(\boldsymbol{\xi}', \eta_1)' \sim MV\,N(0, \Sigma), \qquad (9.16)$$

η_j are independent of v and u.

The likelihood function is

$$L = f(v-u) \cdot g(\boldsymbol{\xi}', \eta_1) \cdot |J|, \qquad (9.17)$$

where $|J|$ is the determinant of the Jacobian matrix:

$$|J| = \left| \frac{\partial(v-u, \xi_2, \xi_3, \ldots, \xi_J, \eta_1)}{\partial(\ln y, \ln x_1, \ln x_2, \ldots, \ln x_J)} \right|. \qquad (9.18)$$

The production parameters of the above model, a_j, can be obtained by maximizing the above log-likelihood function. After estimation, technical inefficiency, u, can be estimated using the Jondrow et al. (1982) formula, that is, $\hat{u} = E(u|v-u)$, while allocative inefficiency, ξ_j, can be obtained from the residuals of the FOCs in (9.13).

Example

This example follows Kumbhakar and Wang (2006), and uses a primal profit system model with a translog production function and flexible technical inefficiency. The data is based on the Romanian mining industry (coal, oil and gas, radioactive materials, non–iron ore, and others) and consists of a panel of 102 firms over the period 1995–2002. However, in this chapter, as before, we treat this dataset as a cross section (of 459 observations).

The output (`y`) is the value of finished goods (in logs). The model contains three inputs (in logs): the variable input (`x1`) is the value of raw materials, the variable input (`x2`) is the number of employees, and the quasi-fixed input (`z1`) is capital. Other variables in the dataset include ownership dummies (`odum`$_n$), with `n=1` for domestic private ownership, `n=2` for state-owned, and `n=3` for others (mixed private, state, and foreign ownership), and `indum`$_k$ are industry dummies, with `k=1,2,...,5`. For the dummy variables, we drop the first dummy as the numeraire in each case.

Model 1: OLS

Estimating the production function using OLS provides the starting values for a single equation frontier model and/or the primal model. These estimated parameters are stored in the matrix `b0`.

```
. quietly generate double x1x1 = 0.5*(x1)^2
. quietly generate double x2x2 = 0.5*(x2)^2
. quietly generate double x1x2 = x1*x2

. global tllist x1 x2 x1x1 x2x2 x1x2
. global linear z1 indum* odum*
. regress y $tllist $linear
. matrix b0 = e(b)
```

For comparison purposes with the primal model, we now run a single equation frontier model using `sfmodel`. Again, we save the estimated parameters. We also examine the inefficiencies and marginal effects for comparison with the primal model.

Model 2: SFA Single Frontier

```
. global muvar odum*

. sfmodel y, frontier($tllist $linear) dist(t) mu($muvar)  usigmas() vsigmas() prod
. sf_init, frontier(b0) mu(0.1 0.1 0.1) usigmas(-0.1) vsigmas(-0.1)
. sf_srch, n(1) frontier($tllist $linear) mu($muvar) fast
. ml max, difficult gradient nrtol(0.0001) gtol(0.0001)

. matrix b_tl = e(b)

. sf_predict, bc(eff2) marginal

The following is the marginal effect on unconditional E(u).

The average marginal effect of odum2 on uncond E(u) is .5724467 (see odum2_M).
The average marginal effect of odum3 on uncond E(u) is -.12293452 (see odum3_M).

The following is the marginal effect on uncond V(u).

The average marginal effect of odum2 on uncond V(u) is .61181454 (see odum2_V).
The average marginal effect of odum3 on uncond V(u) is -.13138887 (see odum3_V).
```

These results indicate that, relative to private domestic ownership, state ownership increases technical inefficiency (and its variance), whereas other forms of ownership (mixed state, private, and foreign ownership) reduce inefficiency.

Model 3: SFA Primal System

We now run the primal system model, using the author-written command `sfprim` with `profit` as an option. We estimate the primal model using the estimated parameters from the single equation frontier model (i.e., Model 2) as starting values (the parameter values from the single equation frontier model were saved in the matrix `b_tl`).

```
. global tllist2 x1 x2

. sfprim y, profit yprice(p) inputs($tllist2) prices(w1 w2) ///
  > linear($linear) usigmas() dist(t) mu($muvar) mltrick translog noask
. ml init  b_tl, copy
. sf_srch, n(1) inputs($inputs) linear($linear) fast
. ml max, difficult nrtol(1e-4) gtol(1e-4) gradient
```

Note that even though we are employing a translog specification, in `inputs()` we only need to supply the individual input variables (namely, `x1` and `x2`). The cross-product terms will be automatically generated by `sfprim`. The results are provided here:

```
-------------- Confirmation Message ----------------

(1) This model estimates the profit maximization behavior
    using production function systems based on duality.

(2) The production frontier has the specification of
    x1 x2 x1x1 x2x2 x1x2 z1 indum* odum*.

(3) The variable inputs are
    x1 x2,
    with the corresponding prices being
    w1 w2,
    and the output price is
    p.
(4) The system model consists of a production function
    and 2 FOCs of inputs.
(5) The technical inefficiency has a truncated distribution.
    For a truncated distribution, the estimate of the mean will show up in mu.
(6) There is no systematic error in the allocative inefficiency.

(iteration log omitted)

                                                  Number of obs   =        459
                                                  Wald chi2(0)    =          .
Log likelihood =   -1561.52                       Prob > chi2     =          .

------------------------------------------------------------------------------
           y |      Coef.   Std. Err.      z    P>|z|     [95% Conf. Interval]
-------------+----------------------------------------------------------------
x1           |
       _cons |   .3191846   .0127843    24.97   0.000     .2941278    .3442415
-------------+----------------------------------------------------------------
x2           |
       _cons |   .1615667   .0111125    14.54   0.000     .1397867    .1833468
-------------+----------------------------------------------------------------
x1x1         |
       _cons |   -.038853   .0050813    -7.65   0.000     -.048812   -.0288939
-------------+----------------------------------------------------------------
x2x2         |
       _cons |  -.0621351    .005615   -11.07   0.000    -.0731403   -.0511298
-------------+----------------------------------------------------------------
x1x2         |
       _cons |    .041219   .0044576     9.25   0.000     .0324823    .0499557
-------------+----------------------------------------------------------------
linear       |
          z1 |   .1899457   .0250448     7.58   0.000     .1408587    .2390327
      indum2 |   .2921983   .2842697     1.03   0.304      -.26496    .8493566
      indum3 |    2.93508   .5200203     5.64   0.000     1.915859    3.954301
      indum4 |   .3138815   .3825265     0.82   0.412    -.4358566     1.06362
      indum5 |   .5964567   .2591594     2.30   0.021     .0885137      1.1044
       odum2 |   2.521826   .7016201     3.59   0.000     1.146676    3.896976
       odum3 |  -.2135215   .1984499    -1.08   0.282    -.6024762    .1754333
       _cons |    .156025    .347469     0.45   0.653    -.5250018    .8370518
-------------+----------------------------------------------------------------
```

```
mu           |
       odum2 |   3.632547   .8325505     4.36   0.000     2.000778    5.264316
       odum3 |  -.1822667   .5977757    -0.30   0.760    -1.353886    .9893521
       _cons |   .0602941   .6003432     0.10   0.920    -1.116357    1.236945
-------------+----------------------------------------------------------------
usigmas      |
       _cons |   .9854971   .1687456     5.84   0.000     .6547618    1.316232
-------------+----------------------------------------------------------------
vsigmas      |
       _cons |  -.9946555   .2912492    -3.42   0.001    -1.565493   -.4238176
------------------------------------------------------------------------------
```

We then calculate returns to scale.

```
. generate double ret = [x1]_cons + [x1x1]_cons*x1 + [x1x2]_cons*x2 ///
                  +[x2]_cons + [x2x2]_cons*x2 + [x1x2]_cons*x1

. summarize ret

    Variable |       Obs        Mean    Std. Dev.       Min        Max
-------------+--------------------------------------------------------
         ret |       459    .5098172    .0343962   .4065757   .5718983
```

Returns to scale are estimated to be 0.5. We then calculate output technical inefficiency. (Note that the marginal effects calculation is not supported for models with a system of equations, so are not reported here.)

```
. sf_predict, jlms(ineff3) bc(eff3)

. summarize ineff3 eff3

    Variable |       Obs        Mean    Std. Dev.       Min        Max
-------------+--------------------------------------------------------
      ineff3 |       459    1.990879     1.53377    .195649    6.91608
        eff3 |       459    .3024145    .2395464   .0011667   .8344726
```

Efficiency is estimated to be around 30 percent, i.e., the output loss due to technical inefficiency is 70 percent, and inefficiency estimates using the JLMS formula around 199 percent. The above results also indicate that, relative to private domestic ownership, state ownership increases technical inefficiency (and its variance), whereas other forms of ownership (mixed state, private, and foreign ownership) reduce inefficiency.

9.4.1 Technical and Allocative Inefficiency Effect on Profit

Profit loss due to technical inefficiency and allocative inefficiency can now be estimated. A procedure similar to the one used for the translog production function in Chapter 8 is followed. That is, given $\hat{a}_k$, $\hat{u}$, and $\hat{\xi}_j$, we numerically solve for three different sets of ($\ln y$, $\ln \boldsymbol{x}_j$) from the system (9.13) under different assumptions regarding inefficiency.

1. efficient output and use of inputs $(y^o, x_j^o | a_k = \hat{a}_k)$: that is, solutions assuming $u = 0$, and $\xi_j = 0$;
2. output and use of inputs under technical inefficiency $(\tilde{y}, \tilde{x}_j | a_k = \hat{a}_k)$: that is, solutions assuming $u = \hat{u}$, and $\xi_j = 0$;
3. output and use of inputs under allocative inefficiency $(\check{y}, \check{x}_j | a_k = \hat{a}_k)$: that is, solutions assuming $u = 0$, and $\xi_j = \hat{\xi}_j$.

The profit loss due to technical inefficiency is then given by

$$\pi^{\text{tech}} = 1 - (p\tilde{y} - \boldsymbol{w}'\tilde{\boldsymbol{x}})/(py^{o} - \boldsymbol{w}'\boldsymbol{x}^{o}), \tag{9.19}$$

and the profit loss due to allocative inefficiency is given by

$$\pi^{\text{allo}} = 1 - (p\check{y} - \boldsymbol{w}'\check{\boldsymbol{x}})/(py^{o} - \boldsymbol{w}'\boldsymbol{x}^{o}). \tag{9.20}$$

Example

Calculating the Impact of Technical and Allocative Inefficiency on Profit

We continue with the previous example (Model 3). The author-written command `sf_pft_compare` is the profit primal system equivalent of `sf_cst_compare` and computes the output and inputs from the profit system of equations (9.13) and reports summary statistics of the profit loss due to inefficiency.

As with `sf_cst_compare`, when using `sf_pft_compare`, we use `jlms()` to indicate the name of the variable of the JLMS inefficiency index, $E(u|v-u)$, that was created by `sf_predict` following `sfprim`. We then specify the option of evaluating the inefficiency's impact on profit, where the inefficiency could be either: technical, `error(tech)`; allocative, `error(alloc)`; or both, `error(both)`. The following is an example.

```
. sf_pft_compare, jlms(ineff3) error(tech)

The following is the summary statistics of profit loss as a ratio
of optimal profit. Profit loss is defined as the difference between
the optimal profit and the profit with technical
inefficiency. The optimal profit is the profit without technical and
allocative inefficiency.

        percentage of profit loss due to inefficiency
-------------------------------------------------------------
      Percentiles      Smallest
 1%    .4718269        .3637438
 5%    .5685482        .4090784
10%    .6549663        .4238549       Obs                 459
25%    .7969597        .4438398       Sum of Wgt.         459

50%    .9385552                       Mean           .8779061
                        Largest       Std. Dev.      .1430183
75%    .9962086        .9999813
90%     .999521        .9999846       Variance       .0204542
95%    .9998779        .9999854       Skewness      -1.213397
99%    .9999812        .9999891       Kurtosis       3.643803
```

This shows that 87.8 percent of potential profit is lost due to technical inefficiency. Note that after executing `sf_pft_compare`, several variables are created. These include the optimal (i.e., no inefficiency) output and inputs, the suboptimal (i.e., with inefficiency) output and inputs, and the profit–loss variable (for which the summary statistics are shown above).

The impact of allocative inefficiency on profit can be obtained in a similar way using

```
. sf_pft_compare, jlms(ineff3) error(alloc)
```

and the impact of both technical and allocative inefficiency can be obtained from the following command.

```
. sf_pft_compare, jlms(ineff3) error(both)
```

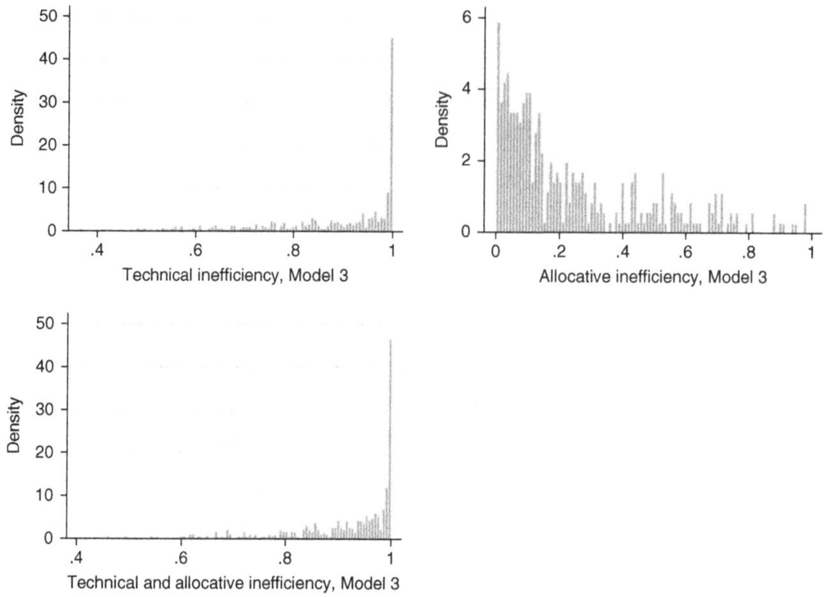

Figure 9.1. Technical and Allocative Inefficiency, Model 3

These results are summarized in the charts in Figure 9.1.

PART V

SINGLE EQUATION APPROACH WITH PANEL DATA

10

Estimation of Technical Efficiency in Single Equation Panel Models

10.1 Introduction

The models introduced in the previous chapters are for cross-sectional data, that is, data in which every individual firm/unit is observed only once. Estimation of inefficiency in these models require distributional assumptions (unless one uses COLS and makes the assumption that there is no noise). Schmidt and Sickles (1984) mentioned three problems with the cross-sectional models that are used to measure inefficiency. First, the ML method used to estimate parameters and the inefficiency estimates using the JLMS formula depend on distributional assumptions for the noise and the inefficiency components. Second, the technical inefficiency component has to be independent of the regressor(s) (at least in the single equation models) – an assumption that is unlikely to be true if firms maximize profit and inefficiency is known to the firm (see Mundlak [1961]). Third, the JLMS estimator is not consistent, in the sense that the conditional mean or mode of $u(v - u)$ never approaches u as the number of firms (cross-sectional units) approaches infinity.

If panel data are available, that is, each unit is observed at several different points of time, some of these rigidities/limitations can be removed. However, to overcome some of these limitations, the panel models make some other assumptions, some of which may or may not be realistic. In this chapter, we review the panel models that are used in the efficiency literature.

A key advantage of panel data is that it enables the modeler to take into account some heterogeneity that may exist beyond what is possible to control using a cross-sectional approach. This can be achieved by introducing an "individual (unobservable) effect," say, α_i, that is time-invariant and individual-specific, and not interacted with other variables.

Having information on units over time also enables one to examine whether inefficiency has been persistent over time or whether the inefficiency of units is time-varying. Indeed, there may be a component of inefficiency that has been persistent over time and another that varies over time. Related to this, and a key question that needs to be considered with regard to the time-invariant individual effects, is whether the individual effects represent (persistent) inefficiency, or whether the effects are independent of the inefficiency and capture (persistent) unobserved heterogeneity. A second question related to this is whether the individual effects are fixed parameters or are realizations of a random variable.

Comparing the productivity of countries, for example, and recognizing country heterogeneity (something that a panel dataset enables us to do), we can examine whether there is evidence of economic growth convergence, that is, whether countries move toward the world production frontier. This setting is examined in some of the empirical examples in this chapter.

Alternatively, in a regulated industry, it may be of interest to examine a number of questions that can only be considered in a panel data setting. For example, due to the regulatory incentives of the regime and the cost reduction assumptions applied by the regulator in setting allowances, have companies in the industry converged to the industry frontier or has their relative inefficiencies remain unchanged? What has been the rate of this change in performance and has it been related to any of the changes introduced by the regulator? Furthermore, have the incentives been strong enough for the best performing companies to strive to continually improve and, thus, has the rate of frontier shift been significant? Similarly, a regulator may use these techniques to examine historic rates of frontier shift and catchup in order to set cost reduction targets for the next period.

Again, at the firm level, one might be interested in the impact of financing constraints on firms' level of capital investment. That is, do financing constraints affect the level of investments and, in particular, is the degree of financing constraint smaller for larger firms? One might be interested to examine whether the effects of financing constraints changed over time, especially, say, during a financial crisis. It is this setting that is examined in some of the later empirical examples in this chapter.

Before discussing the panel models, it is worth mentioning that one can simply pool the panel data and treat it as cross-sectional data (as we did in some of the examples in earlier chapters). That is, data on the same unit observed in different points in time are treated as separate units. Both the inefficiency and the noise components can either be assumed to be independently and identically distributed or they can be heteroscedastic. Temporal variations can be captured by including either a time trend variable or time dummies in the list of regressors. These models can be estimated using the techniques discussed under cross-sectional models. However, this is clearly not the best way to take advantage of a panel dataset since multiple observations of an individual over time may reveal important information about the individuals. One such important information is the time-invariant and individual-specific characteristics of the producers. In this chapter, we introduce stochastic frontier models for panel data that take into account the time-invariant and individual-specific effects. An important feature of these panel data models is modeling the temporal behavior of inefficiency.

In the rest of the chapter, we classify the models in terms of the assumptions made on the temporal behavior of inefficiency. Section 10.2 introduces models that assume the inefficiency effects to be time-invariant and individual-specific. Various estimation methods are available for this type of model, depending on whether the inefficiency effects are assumed to be fixed or random, and whether distributional assumptions on the inefficiency and noise components are made. Section 10.3 allows inefficiency to be individual-specific but time-varying (i.e., the inefficiency of each cross-sectional unit evolves along a specific path which can be either the same for all units or different for different cross-sectional units). Section 10.4 introduces models which separate the inefficiency effects from the unobserved individual effects (i.e., inefficiency is separated from unobserved firm-specific effects, either fixed or random, by making appropriate assumptions). Finally, Section 10.5 introduced models that separate persistent inefficiency and time-varying inefficiency from the unobservable individual effects.

10.2 Time-Invariant Technical Inefficiency (Distribution-Free) Models

We first consider the case in which the inefficiency is assumed to be individual-specific and time-invariant. In this case, the unobservable individual effects of the panel data model is the base from where inefficiency is measured. The model may be written as

$$\begin{aligned} y_{it} &= f(\boldsymbol{x}_{it}; \boldsymbol{\beta}) + \epsilon_{it}, \\ \epsilon_{it} &= v_{it} - u_i, \qquad u_i \geq 0, i = 1, \ldots, N; t = 1, \ldots, T \end{aligned} \tag{10.1}$$

where $f(\boldsymbol{x}_{it}; \boldsymbol{\beta})$ is a linear function of the variables in the vector $\boldsymbol{x}_{it}$, and $u_i \geq 0$ is the time-invariant technical inefficiency of individual i. This model utilizes the panel feature of the data via u_i, which is specific to an individual and does not change over time.

The model can be estimated assuming either u_i is a fixed parameter (the fixed-effects model) or a random variable (the random-effects model). None of these approaches require distributional assumptions on u_i and are, thus, labeled as distribution-free approaches. These models are discussed in detail in Schmidt and Sickles (1984). Note that the model in (10.1) is the same as the one-way error component model widely discussed in the panel data literature,[1] except that individual effects are made one-sided. The idea is to make a simple transformation and interpret the transformed individual effects as time-invariant inefficiency.

One restriction of the fixed- and random-effects models is that the model does not allow for the inefficiency and individual heterogeneity to be separated. Recently development in the literature has proposed models that allow both effects to be separated and existed. Examples include the true fixed-effect model and the true random-effect model to be discussed in Section 10.4.

10.2.1 The Fixed-Effects Model (Schmidt and Sickles [1984])

For ease of disposition, we assume $f(\cdot)$ is linear in $\boldsymbol{x}_{it}$ (e.g., the log of input quantities in a Cobb-Douglas production function model). The fixed-effects model can then be written as

$$y_{it} = \beta_0 + \boldsymbol{x}_{it}'\boldsymbol{\beta} + v_{it} - u_i \tag{10.2}$$

$$= (\beta_0 - u_i) + \boldsymbol{x}_{it}'\boldsymbol{\beta} + v_{it}$$

$$= \alpha_i + \boldsymbol{x}_{it}'\boldsymbol{\beta} + v_{it} \tag{10.3}$$

where $\alpha_i \equiv \beta_0 - u_i$. In this model, u_i and thus α_i, $i = 1, \ldots, N$ are assumed to be fixed parameters that are to be estimated along with the parameter vector $\boldsymbol{\beta}$.

The model in (10.3) looks similar to a standard fixed-effects (FE) panel data model. Schmidt and Sickles (1984) showed that we can apply standard FE panel data estimation methods (for example, the within estimator) to estimate the model where α_i are treated as fixed and unobserved individual effects. The standard FE panel methods yield consistent estimates of $\boldsymbol{\beta}$, but $\hat{\alpha}_i$ is a biased estimator of u_i because $u_i > 0$ by construction. Nevertheless, after $\hat{\alpha}_i$ is obtained a simple transformation can be applied to recover $\hat{u}_i \geq 0$ which is consistent as $T \to \infty$.

An important implication of the assumption that u_i is fixed is that it is allowed to be freely correlated with $\boldsymbol{x}_{it}$ in the model. This may be a desirable property for empirical applications

[1] See, for example, Baltagi (2008), Hsiao (2003), among others.

in which inefficiency is believed to be correlated with the inputs used (Mundlak [1961]). A disadvantage of the FE approach, by contrast, is that no other time-invariant variables, such as gender, race, and region, can be included in $\boldsymbol{x}_{it}$ because doing so entails perfect multicollinearity between the α_i and the time-invariant regressors.

This model may be estimated using OLS after including individual dummies as regressors for α_i. This technique is often referred to as the least square dummy variable (LSDV) method. The coefficients of the dummies are the estimates of α_i. Notice that, since there is one FE parameter for each cross-sectional unit (individual, firm, etc.), the number of dummies to be included in the model is equal to the number of cross-sectional units in the data (when no intercept model is chosen). For a panel dataset with many cross-sectional units, estimation might be an issue because it requires inverting an $(N+K) \times (N+K)$ matrix where N is the number of cross-sectional units and K is the number of regressors (x_{it} variables).

This difficulty can be easily overcome by transforming the model before estimation to get rid of α_i. The transformation can be carried out either using a first-difference transformation or using a within transformation. For example, the within transformation subtracts cross-sectional means of the data from each cross section (e.g., replacing y_{it} by $y_{it} - \bar{y}_{i\cdot}$ and x_{it} by $x_{it} - \bar{x}_{i\cdot}$, where $\bar{y}_{i\cdot} = (1/T)\sum_t y_{it}$), thereby eliminating α_i. The resulting model can then be easily estimated by OLS (which requires inversion of a $K \times K$ matrix). The values of $\hat{\alpha}_i$ are recovered from the mean of the residuals for each cross-sectional unit. The transformed models yield consistent estimates of $\boldsymbol{\beta}$ for either T or $N \to \infty$. Consistency of $\hat{\alpha}_i$, however, requires $T \to \infty$.

Once the $\hat{\alpha}_i$ are available, the following transformation is used to obtain estimated value of $\hat{u}_i$ (Schmidt and Sickles [1984]):

$$\hat{u}_i = \max_i\{\hat{\alpha}_i\} - \hat{\alpha}_i \geq 0, \quad i = 1, \ldots, N. \tag{10.4}$$

This formulation implicity assumes that the most efficient unit in the sample is 100 percent efficient. In other words, estimated inefficiency in the fixed-effects model is relative to the best unit in the sample. If one is interested in estimating firm-specific efficiency, it can be obtained from

$$\widehat{TE}_i = \exp(-\hat{u}_i), \quad i = 1, \ldots, N. \tag{10.5}$$

Example

The dataset we use in the initial set of empirical examples in this chapter is from the World Bank STARS database and the examples follow Kumbhakar and Wang (2005). The data provide information on production related variables for eighty-two countries (represented by the variable `code`) over the period 1960–1987 (represented by the variable `yr`), providing a total of 2,296 observations. The output, `y`, and capital, `k`, variables are measures of GDP and the aggregate physical capital stock (converted into constant, end-of-period 1987 U.S. dollars), respectively; labor, `l`, is the number of individuals in the workforce between the ages of fifteen and sixty-four.

Model 1: The Fixed-Effects Model

We estimate the fixed-effects model for a Cobb-Douglas production function, using the Stata `xtreg` command with the option `fe`. This command estimates the model given in equation (10.3). Before estimating the model, we load the dataset, `panel data 1`, define the variable set in the global macro, `xvar`, and use `xtset` to define the panel.

```
. use "panel data 1"

. global xvar lnk lnl yr

. xtset code year
       panel variable:  code (strongly balanced)
        time variable:  year, 1 to 28
                delta:  1 unit

. xtreg lny $xvar, fe

Fixed-effects (within) regression               Number of obs      =      2296
Group variable: code                            Number of groups   =        82

R-sq:  within  = 0.8927                         Obs per group: min =        28
       between = 0.9651                                        avg =      28.0
       overall = 0.9477                                        max =        28

                                                F(3,2211)          =   6130.94
corr(u_i, Xb)  = 0.8646                         Prob > F           =    0.0000

------------------------------------------------------------------------------
         lny |      Coef.   Std. Err.      t    P>|t|     [95% Conf. Interval]
-------------+----------------------------------------------------------------
         lnk |   .5414924   .0122934    44.05   0.000     .5173845    .5656003
         lnl |   .0165475   .0113259     1.46   0.144    -.005663     .038758
          yr |   .0090231   .0008554    10.55   0.000     .0073456    .0107007
       _cons |   .6512252   .0390416    16.68   0.000     .5746632    .7277871
-------------+----------------------------------------------------------------
     sigma_u |  .84596616
     sigma_e |  .12349473
         rho |  .97913429   (fraction of variance due to u_i)
------------------------------------------------------------------------------
F test that all u_i=0:     F(81, 2211) =   250.09            Prob > F = 0.0000
```

The coefficient on `yr` (0.009) implies that productivity (i.e., GDP for a given level of capital and labor) has increased in real terms by 0.9 percent per annum, on average, across all countries over the period 1960–1987.

Next we estimate efficiency from the fixed-effects using equations (10.4) and (10.5). Note that after `xtreg`, the `predict` command has the following options: `xb` for the fitted values; `ue` for the combined residuals ($\alpha_i + v_{it}$); `u` for the the fixed or random effect component (α_i); and `e` for the error component (v_{it}).

```
. predict fe, u /* fixed effect */
. quietly summarize fe
. generate double u_star = r(max) - fe   /* equation (10.4) */
. generate double eff_fe = exp(-u_star) /* equation (10.5) */
. summarize eff_fe

    Variable |       Obs        Mean    Std. Dev.       Min        Max
-------------+--------------------------------------------------------
      eff_fe |      2296    .1552271    .1617664   .0217988          1
```

As illustrated, estimated average efficiency is only 15 percent. Note that, by construction, one country is 100 percent efficient and consequently efficiency estimates are sensitive to adding/dropping "outlier" countries (i.e., countries with either very high or very low values of α_i values).

10.2.2 The Random-Effects Model

Instead of assuming α_i (and thus u_i) in (10.3) as fixed parameters, it is also possible to assume that α_i is random and uncorrelated with the regressors. If the assumption of no correlation is indeed correct, then the random-effects (RE) model provides more efficient estimates than the FE model. An important advantage of assuming α_i being random is that time-invariant variables, such as gender and race, may be included in the $\boldsymbol{x}_{it}$ vector of explanatory variables without causing the perfect multicollinearity problem.

The RE model can be estimated by two different methods. One is to estimate it by the generalized least squares (GLS) technique commonly used for a standard RE panel data model. Similar to the FE estimator, the estimated RE are modified and re-interpreted to obtain estimates of inefficiency. An alternative to the GLS method is to impose distributional assumptions on the random components of the model, and estimate the parameters by the maximum likelihood (ML) method. This approach was originally proposed by Pitt and Lee (1981). Once the parameters are estimated using the ML method, the JLMS can be used to estimate firm-specific inefficiency (Kumbhakar [1987]).

Estimation Method: The GLS Estimator

Assume u_i is a random variable and let $E(u_i) = \mu$ and $u_i^* = u_i - \mu$. We rewrite the model as

$$\begin{aligned} y_{it} &= \beta_0 + \boldsymbol{x}_{it}'\boldsymbol{\beta} + v_{it} - u_i \\ &= (\beta_0 - \mu) + \boldsymbol{x}_{it}'\boldsymbol{\beta} + v_{it} - u_i^* \\ &= \alpha^* + \boldsymbol{x}_{it}'\boldsymbol{\beta} + v_{it} - u_i^*, \end{aligned} \tag{10.6}$$

where $\alpha^* \equiv \beta_0 - \mu$.

The model in (10.6) is similar to a standard RE panel data model, and the GLS estimator can be applied to obtain $\hat{\boldsymbol{\beta}}$ and $\hat{\alpha}^*$ (but not $\hat{\beta}_0$).

If we define $\hat{\epsilon}_{it} = y_{it} - \boldsymbol{x}_{it}'\hat{\boldsymbol{\beta}}$, then an estimate of $\alpha_i \equiv \beta_0 - u_i$ may be derived by the time average of $\hat{\epsilon}_{it}$ for each cross section, viz.,

$$\hat{\alpha}_i = \frac{1}{T}\sum_t (\hat{\epsilon}_{it} - \hat{\alpha}^*), \quad i = 1, \ldots, N. \tag{10.7}$$

Here, we use the implicit assumption that the time average of $\hat{v}_i$ is zero which is true as $T \to \infty$. Finally, the estimate of firm-specific inefficiency, $\hat{u}_i$, is obtained using (10.4).

An alternative approach is to take a Bayesian approach and estimate u_i^* using the best linear unbiased predictor (BLUP), which is

$$\hat{u}_i^* = -\left\{\frac{\hat{\sigma}_u^2}{\hat{\sigma}_v^2 + T\hat{\sigma}_u^2}\right\}\sum_t \hat{\epsilon}_{it}, \quad i = 1, \ldots, N. \tag{10.8}$$

Then the estimate of firm-specific inefficiency, $\hat{u}_i$, is obtained from

$$\hat{u}_i = \max_i\{\hat{u}_i^*\} - \hat{u}_i^* \geq 0, \quad i = 1, \ldots, N. \tag{10.9}$$

Example

We estimate the random-effects model. Again, we use the Stata `xtreg` command, but this time with the option `re`.

Model 2: The Random-Effects Model

```
. xtreg lny $xvar, re

Random-effects GLS regression                   Number of obs      =      2296
Group variable: code                            Number of groups   =        82

R-sq:  within  = 0.8891                         Obs per group: min =        28
       between = 0.9668                                        avg =      28.0
       overall = 0.9582                                        max =        28

                                                Wald chi2(3)       =  18264.67
corr(u_i, X)   = 0 (assumed)                    Prob > chi2        =    0.0000

------------------------------------------------------------------------------
         lny |      Coef.   Std. Err.      z    P>|z|     [95% Conf. Interval]
-------------+----------------------------------------------------------------
         lnk |    .631657   .0115583    54.65   0.000     .6090031    .6543109
         lnl |   .0601051   .0113414     5.30   0.000     .0378763    .0823339
          yr |   .0017187   .0007751     2.22   0.027     .0001995    .0032379
       _cons |      .2957    .053227     5.56   0.000      .191377    .4000231
-------------+----------------------------------------------------------------
     sigma_u |  .34709004
     sigma_e |  .12349473
         rho |  .88763135   (fraction of variance due to u_i)
------------------------------------------------------------------------------

. matrix bre = e(b)
```

The coefficient on `yr` (0.002) implies that productivity has increased in real terms by only 0.2 percent per annum, on average, across all countries over the period 1960–1987.

Next, we estimate efficiency from the overall error term, using equations (10.7) and (10.4).

```
. predict ue, ue /* overall error */
. sort code
. by code: egen ahat = mean(ue - _b[_cons]) /*  ahat, equation (10.7) */
. quietly summarize ahat
. generate double u_star = r(max) - ahat /* equation (10.4) */
. generate double eff_re = exp(-u_star)
. summarize eff_re

    Variable |       Obs        Mean    Std. Dev.       Min        Max
-------------+--------------------------------------------------------
      eff_re |      2296     .254159     .175672   .0501415          1
```

As illustrated, estimated efficiency is 25 percent, on average.

Estimation Method: Maximum Likelihood Estimator

A strong appeal for the fixed-effects and the random-effects models is that they do not require distributional assumptions in estimating inefficiency. Although the COLS model introduced in the earlier chapter for the cross-sectional data is also distribution free, the cross-sectional COLS model does not accommodate statistical error (i.e., v_i). This is not the case with the fixed- and random-effects models where both v_{it} and u_i terms are present.

Although the distribution-free assumption may be desirable, it is still possible to estimate (10.2) using MLE by imposing distributional assumptions on v_{it} and u_i, as in Pitt and Lee (1981). The likelihood function of the model is derived based on the distributional assumptions and the parameters are estimated by maximizing the log-likelihood function. Finally, inefficiency can be estimated using a variant of the JLMS approach (Kumbhakar [1987]). If one is interested in the estimates of efficiency, the Battese and Coelli (1988) formula can be used.

For the MLE, the model is written as:

$$\begin{aligned} y_{it} &= f(\boldsymbol{x}_{it};\boldsymbol{\beta}) + \epsilon_{it}, \\ \epsilon_{it} &= v_{it} - u_i, \\ v_{it} &\sim N(0,\sigma_v^2), \\ u_i &\sim N^+(\mu,\sigma_u^2). \end{aligned} \tag{10.10}$$

The likelihood function for the ith observation is (see Appendix A; Pitt and Lee [1981]; Kumbhakar and Lovell [2000], p. 103):

$$\begin{aligned} \ln L_i = &\text{constant} + \ln \Phi\left(\frac{\mu_{i*}}{\sigma_*}\right) + \frac{1}{2}\ln(\sigma_*^2) - \frac{1}{2}\left\{\frac{\sum_t \epsilon_{it}^2}{\sigma_v^2} + \left(\frac{\mu}{\sigma_u}\right)^2 - \left(\frac{\mu_{i*}}{\sigma_*}\right)^2\right\} \\ &- T\ln(\sigma_v) - \ln(\sigma_u) - \ln \Phi\left(\frac{\mu}{\sigma_u}\right), \end{aligned} \tag{10.11}$$

where

$$\mu_{i*} = \frac{\mu\sigma_v^2 - \sigma_u^2 \sum_t \epsilon_{it}}{\sigma_v^2 + T\sigma_u^2}, \tag{10.12}$$

$$\sigma_*^2 = \frac{\sigma_v^2\sigma_u^2}{\sigma_v^2 + T\sigma_u^2}. \tag{10.13}$$

The log-likelihood function of the model is obtained by summing $\ln L_i$ over i, $i = 1, \ldots, N$. The MLE of the parameters is obtained by maximizing the log-likelihood function.

After estimating the parameters of the model, inefficiency for each i can be computed from either the mean or the mode (Kumbhakar and Lovell [2000], p. 104)

$$E(u_i|\epsilon_i) = \mu_{i*} + \sigma_*\left[\frac{\phi(-\mu_{i*}/\sigma_*)}{1 - \Phi(-\mu_{i*}/\sigma_*)}\right] \tag{10.14}$$

and

$$M(u_i|\epsilon_i) = \begin{cases} \mu_{i*} & \text{if } \mu_{i*} \geq 0, \\ 0 & \text{otherwise} \end{cases} \tag{10.15}$$

which are the extended JLMS estimators of inefficiency (Kumbhakar [1987]). We may set $\mu = 0$ in the above equations for the half-normal distribution of u_i or make μ a function of exogenous variables ($\mu = z_i'\delta$) to accommodate determinants of the inefficiency. Note that both estimators of inefficiency are consistent as $T \to \infty$ (Kumbhakar [1987]).

Example

Model 3: The Time-Invariant Model

Here, we estimate the time-invariant model using the author-written command, `sfpan`. As with the earlier commands, this command involves setting up the model first and then using `ml max` command to estimate it. The use of `sfpan` also allows us to extend the model. Here, we estimate a model with a truncated normal distribution for u_i and include a variable to define the pre-truncation mean of the distribution.

The options for `sfpan` are similar to those of previous commands. `frontier($xvar)` defines the variables, `$xvar`, to be included in the deterministic part of the frontier function (here, a Cobb-Douglas production function); `dist(t)` sets the distributional assumption of technical inefficiency to be a truncated-normal; `prod` determines that it is a production model that we are estimating; `mu(iniStat)` defines the variables, `iniStat`, used to parameterize the pre-truncation mean of the distribution of u_i; `usigmas` and `vsigmas` specify the variables, if any, used to parameterize the variance of the inefficiency, u_i, and the random error, v_i, respectively; `i(code)` identifies the variable, `code`, that describes the cross-sectional identifier; and `inv` specifies that the model is time-invariant. Note that for `sfpan` to work properly, the variables parameterizing `mu` have to be time-invariant within each cross-sectional unit (such as gender).

This example estimate a growth convergence model as in Kumbhakar and Wang (2005). First, we define the variable used to parameterize the mean of the pre-truncated distribution of the inefficiency term. The variable we used is the log of the initial capital to labor ratio of each country, `lnk - lnl`, measured at the beginning of the sample period. See Kumbhakar and Wang (2005) for more explanations on the choice of variables.

```
. sort code year
. quietly by code: generate double tem1 = lnk - lnl if _n == 1 /* initial value of ln(k/l) */
. quietly by code: egen double iniStat = mean(tem1)
```

We now run the time-invariant model using `sfpan` with the `inv` option (and save the log-likelihood value for comparison with subsequent models).

```
. sfpan lny, dist(t) mu(iniStat) prod frontier($xvar) usigmas vsigmas i(code) inv
. sf_init, frontier(bre) mu(0 0) usigmas(0) vsigmas(0)
. ml max, difficult nrtol(0.001) gtol(0.001)

(iteration log omitted)

                                                  Number of obs   =       2296
                                                  Wald chi2(3)    =   18455.45
Log likelihood =  1256.8324                       Prob > chi2     =     0.0000

------------------------------------------------------------------------------
         lny |      Coef.   Std. Err.      z    P>|z|     [95% Conf. Interval]
-------------+----------------------------------------------------------------
frontier     |
         lnk |   .5635753   .0125278    44.99   0.000     .5390213    .5881293
         lnl |   .0300092   .0114073     2.63   0.009     .0076514    .0523671
          yr |   .0070958   .0008798     8.07   0.000     .0053715    .0088201
       _cons |   2.671582   .1470164    18.17   0.000     2.383435    2.959728
-------------+----------------------------------------------------------------
```

```
mu           |
     iniStat |  -.1529176    .079698    -1.92   0.055    -.3091229    .0032877
       _cons |   2.151991   .1516171    14.19   0.000     1.854827    2.449155
-------------+----------------------------------------------------------------
usigmas      |
       _cons |  -.5006528   .1778278    -2.82   0.005    -.8491889   -.1521166
-------------+----------------------------------------------------------------
vsigmas      |
       _cons |  -4.181834     .03014  -138.75   0.000    -4.240908   -4.122761
------------------------------------------------------------------------------

. scalar ll_inv = e(ll)
```

We then calculate the BC and JLMS scores using `sf_predict`.

```
. sf_predict, bc(bc_inv) jlms(jlms_inv)

. summarize bc_inv jlms_inv

    Variable |       Obs        Mean    Std. Dev.       Min        Max
-------------+--------------------------------------------------------
      bc_inv |      2296    .1665715    .1567746    .025829    .947522
    jlms_inv |      2296    2.114254    .7835891   .0541588   3.656531
```

As illustrated, efficiency is estimated to be similar to that estimated under the FE model at around 17 percent on average and inefficiency around 211 percent. Note that $\exp(-2.11) \approx$ 12 percent, which is less than the BC estimator of efficiency of 16.7 percent. This is because $\exp(E(u|\epsilon) \neq E(\exp(u|\epsilon))$ and the difference gets small when u is small.

We compare the estimated efficiencies across the three models by comparing histograms of the efficiency scores using the following code:

```
label variable eff_fe "Efficiency from fixed effects model"
histogram eff_fe, bin(100) normal `kden' xlabel(0(.1)1) saving(panel_eff_fe, replace)

label variable eff_re "Efficiency from random effects model"
histogram eff_re, bin(100) normal `kden' xlabel(0(.1)1) saving(panel_eff_re, replace)

label variable bc_inv "Efficiency from time-invariant model"
histogram bc_inv, bin(100) normal `kden' xlabel(0(.1)1)
saving(panel_eff_inv, replace)

graph combine panel_eff_fe.gph panel_eff_re.gph panel_eff_inv.gph, col(2) scale(1) xcommon ycommon
graph export panel_eff_fe_re_inv.eps, replace
```

In the resulting figure (Figure 10.1), the slightly higher estimated efficiency from the random-effects model is clear in this comparison. It is also clear that there are a couple of outliers and this could explain the low estimated efficiency and warrants further investigation (without these outliers, estimated efficiency increases by around 10 percent).

We now turn to models that relax the restrictive assumption of time-invariant technical inefficiency.

10.3 Time-Varying Technical Inefficiency Models

Models introduced in the previous section assume technical inefficiency to be individual-specific and time-invariant. That is, the inefficiency levels may be different for different individuals, but they do not change over time. In other words, these models suggest that an inefficient unit (e.g., a firm) never learns over time. This might be the case in some situations where inefficiency is, for example, associated with managerial ability and there is no

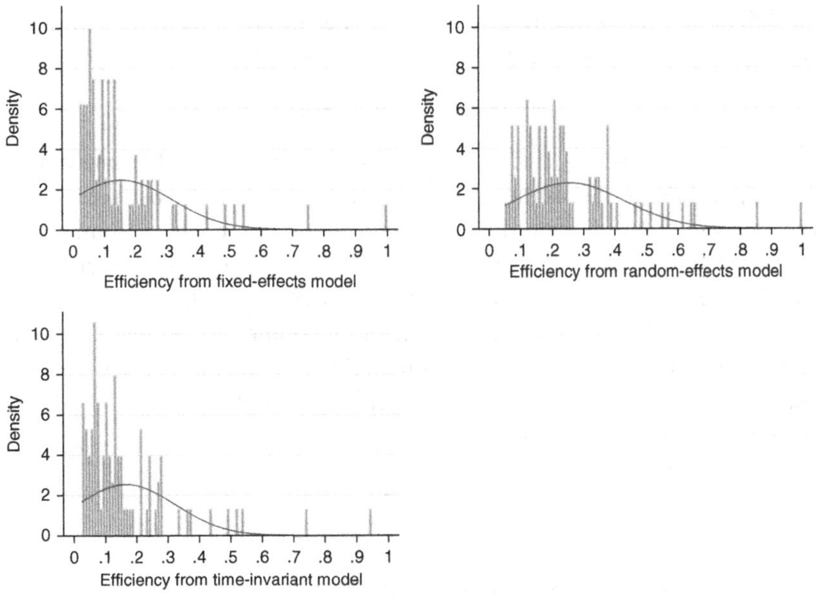

Figure 10.1. Estimated Efficiency from Models 1, 2, and 3

change in management for any of the firms during the period of the study or if the time period of the panel is particularly short. Even this is, at times, unrealistic, particularly when market competition is taken into account. To accommodate the notion of productivity and efficiency improvement, we need to consider models that allow inefficiency to change over time.

In this and the next section, we introduce models in which the inefficiency effects is time-varying. These models are more general than those introduced in the previous sections, in the sense that those earlier models can be treated as special cases of the ones introduced below. Like the time-invariant inefficiency models, we can classify the time-varying models as either fixed- or random-effects type. In the FE models the time-varying inefficiency term is non-stochastic (i.e., a parametric function of time), whereas in the RE model the inefficiency effect is composed of either a random term or a combination of a time-invariant stochastic term and a time-varying deterministic function. First, we consider the time-varying FE models.

10.3.1 Time-Varying Technical Inefficiency Models Using Distribution-Free Approaches

The Cornwell, Schmidt, and Sickles (1990) Model

Recall the Schmidt-Sickles (1984) model in (10.3):

$$y_{it} = \alpha_i + \boldsymbol{x}_{it}'\boldsymbol{\beta} + v_{it},$$

$$\text{where} \qquad \alpha_i \equiv \beta_0 - u_i,$$

and the inefficiency term (confounded in the firm-specific effect) is time-invariant. To make it time-varying, Cornwell, Schmidt, and Sickles (1990) suggest replacing α_i by α_{it} where

$$\alpha_{it} = \alpha_{0i} + \alpha_{1i}t + \alpha_{2i}t^2. \tag{10.16}$$

Note that the parameters α_{0i}, α_{1i}, and α_{2i} are firm-specific and t is the time trend variable. Hereafter, we denote the model as the CSS model. If the number of cross-sectional units (N) is not large, one can define N firm dummies and interaction of these dummies with time and time squared. These variables along with the regressors (i.e., the x variables) are then used in the OLS regression. Because all the firm-dummies are used, the intercept term in the regression has to be suppressed to avoid the exact multicollinearity problem. The coefficients associated with the firm dummies and their interactions are the estimates of α_{0i}, α_{1i}, and α_{2i}. These estimated coefficients can be used to obtain estimates of α_{it}.

More generally, if we represent the model as

$$y_{it} = \alpha_{0i} + \boldsymbol{x}_{it}'\boldsymbol{\beta} + v_{it}', \tag{10.17}$$

$$\text{where} \qquad v_{it}' \equiv v_{it} + \alpha_{1i}t + \alpha_{2i}t^2,$$

then the form of the model looks like a standard panel data model. Similar to the model of Schmidt and Sickles (1984), we may apply a within estimator on (10.17) to obtain consistent estimates of $\hat{\boldsymbol{\beta}}$, and then the estimated residuals of the model ($\hat{\epsilon}_{it} \equiv y_{it} - \boldsymbol{x}_{it}'\hat{\boldsymbol{\beta}}$). These residuals are then regressed on a constant, a time trend, and the square of the time trend for *each i*. The fitted values from these regressions provide estimates of α_{it} in (10.16). Finally, $\hat{u}_{it}$ is obtained by

$$\hat{u}_{it} = \hat{\alpha}_t - \hat{\alpha}_{it} \quad \text{and} \quad \hat{\alpha}_t = \max_j(\hat{\alpha}_{jt}). \tag{10.18}$$

That is, for each t we define the maximum and calculate efficiency relative to the best firm in that year. Because the maximum of $\hat{\alpha}_{jt}$ is likely to change over time, the same firm may not be efficient in every year. In other words, efficiency in this framework is relative to the best firm in the sample *in a given year* and this may be represented by different firms in different years. Alternatively, if one defines the maximum over all i and t, then efficiency is relative to the best firm in the sample (defined over all time periods).

The estimation procedure outlined above is easy to implement. It mainly relies on the standard panel data fixed- or random-effects estimators and OLS regression. It should be noted that as t appears in the inefficiency function, it cannot appear as a regressor in $\boldsymbol{x}_{it}$ to capture technical change (a shift in the production/cost function, $f(x)$). In other words, the above model cannot separate inefficiency from technical change.

Example

Model 4: The Cornwell, Schmidt, and Sickles (1990) Model

In the first step, we regress the dependent variable, `lny`, on all the frontier variables, `$xvar`, firm dummies, and their interactions with time and time squared and then we obtain the fitted values.

```
. forvalues i = 1(1)82 {
  2.        generate year_`i' = year*firmdum`i'
  3.        generate year2_`i' = year2*firmdum`i'
  4. }
. drop firmdum1 year_1 year2_1
```

```
. regress lny lnk lnl  firmdum* year_* year2_*

      Source |       SS       df       MS              Number of obs =    2296
-------------+------------------------------           F(245,  2050) = 9650.72
       Model |  8465.76428   245  34.5541399           Prob > F      =  0.0000
    Residual |  7.33996929  2050  .003580473           R-squared     =  0.9991
-------------+------------------------------           Adj R-squared =  0.9990
       Total |  8473.10425  2295  3.69198442           Root MSE      =  .05984

------------------------------------------------------------------------------
         lny |      Coef.   Std. Err.      t    P>|t|     [95% Conf. Interval]
-------------+----------------------------------------------------------------
         lnk |   .5690968   .0228808    24.87   0.000     .5242247    .6139689
         lnl |   .3578049   .0409965     8.73   0.000     .2774058     .438204
    firmdum2 |   -.413468   .0758895    -5.45   0.000    -.5622966   -.2646395

(output omitted)

    year2_82 |  -.0007951   .0001947    -4.08   0.000    -.0011769   -.0004133
       _cons |   .0245005   .1535675     0.16   0.873    -.2766641     .325665
------------------------------------------------------------------------------

. predict fit, xb
```

In the second step, we generate estimate of α_{it} indirectly from $\hat{y}_{it} - \boldsymbol{x}'_{it}\hat{\boldsymbol{\beta}}$. This follows from the fact that one can write $\hat{y}_{it} = \hat{\alpha}_{it} + \boldsymbol{x}'_{it}\hat{\boldsymbol{\beta}}$.

```
. generate alpha = fit - _b[lnk]*lnk - _b[lnl]*lnl
```

In the final step, we use a procedure similar to Schmidt and Lin (1984) to get the inefficiency index based on the fitted values from the second step.

```
. quietly summarize alpha
. generate double u_star = r(max) - alpha
. generate double eff_css = exp(-u_star)
. summarize eff_css

    Variable |       Obs        Mean    Std. Dev.       Min        Max
-------------+--------------------------------------------------------
     eff_css |      2296     .247233    .1311512   .0473275          1
```

As illustrated, efficiency is estimated to be around 25 percent.

The Lee–Schmidt (1993) Model

The advantage of the CSS model is the flexibility in the inefficiency function. Temporal behavior of inefficiency is flexible enough to allow efficiency to increase or decrease and is different for different cross-sectional units. A problem of the CSS model is that it may be over parameterized in the specification of inefficiency. In a model with large N and small T the model will have too many parameters ($3N$ parameters in the α_{it} function alone).

A somewhat parsimonious time-varying inefficiency model was proposed by Lee and Schmidt (1993) in which u_{it} is specified as

$$u_{it} = u_i \lambda_t, \tag{10.19}$$

where λ_t, $t = 1, \ldots, T$, are parameters to be estimated. In the FE version of the model, one can view u_i as the coefficients of firm-dummies and the λ_t are the coefficients of time dummies (after imposing appropriate identification restrictions, because all the coefficients of firm and time dummies cannot be estimated due to the perfect multicollinearity problem). Although the model is quite flexible (compared to the CSS model), because no parametric function is assumed for the temporal behavior of inefficiency, the downside is that the temporal pattern of inefficiency is exactly the same for all firms (λ_t).

Although Lee and Schmidt considered both the fixed- and random-effects models, here we present their model slightly differently. The reason for this is to make the model comparable to some other time-varying efficiency models such as Kumbhakar (1990), Battese and Coelli (1992), and Kumbhakar and Wang (2005). In this vein, we assume u_i to be random and λ_t to be fixed parameters. Because λ_t are parameters (i.e., coefficients of time dummies, TD_t, after an arbitrary normalization of one coefficient being set to unity for identification purposes), the Lee–Schmidt model is much more general than the Kumbhakar (1990), Battese and Coelli (1992), and Kumbhakar and Wang (2005) models. All these models can be derived as a special case of the Lee–Schmidt model by imposing appropriate restrictions on λ_t. The downside of this model is the presence of too many parameters in λ_t, and hence it may not be suitable for large T.

The time-invariant inefficiency model can be derived as a special case from all these model. That is, if $\lambda_t = 1 \; \forall \; t$, then the model reduces to the time-invariant inefficiency model.

Once λ_t and u_i are estimated, technical inefficiency can be estimated from

$$\hat{u}_{it} = \max_i\{\hat{u}_i\hat{\lambda}_t\} - \{\hat{u}_i\hat{\lambda}_t\}. \tag{10.20}$$

10.3.2 Time-Varying Inefficiency Models with Deterministic and Stochastic Components

The time-varying models that we have considered so far model inefficiency through some parametric functions. For example, in the Lee–Schmidt model both the components of u_i and λ_t are deterministic. In fact, the model can be estimated assuming u_i is random while λ_t is a deterministic function of time (e.g., time dummies). Although Lee and Schmidt estimated this model without any distributional assumptions on u_i, we will consider these type of models with distributional assumptions on u_i. We use the following generic formulation to discuss the various models in a unifying framework, viz.,

$$\begin{aligned}
y_{it} &= f(\boldsymbol{x}_{it}; \boldsymbol{\beta}) + \epsilon_{it},\\
\epsilon_{it} &= v_{it} - u_{it},\\
u_{it} &= G(t)u_i,\\
v_{it} &\sim N(0, \sigma_v^2),\\
u_i &\sim N^+(\mu, \sigma_u^2),
\end{aligned} \tag{10.21}$$

where $G(t) > 0$ is a function of time (t).

In this model, the inefficiency (u_{it}) is not fixed for a given individual; instead, it changes over time and also across individuals. Inefficiency in this model is composed of two distinct components: one is a non-stochastic time component, $G(t)$, and the other is a stochastic individual component, u_i. It is the stochastic component, u_i, that utilizes the panel structure of the data in this model. The u_i component is individual-specific and the $G(t)$ component is time-varying and is common for all the individuals.

Given $u_i \geq 0$, $u_{it} \geq 0$ is ensured by having a nonnegative $G(t)$. We now consider some specific forms of $G(t)$ that are used in the literature. For example, the Kumbhakar (1990) model assumes

$$G(t) = \left[1 + \exp(\gamma_1 t + \gamma_2 t^2)\right]^{-1}, \tag{10.22}$$

and Lee and Schmidt (1993) model assumes

$$G(t) = \sum_t \lambda_t TD_t, \tag{10.23}$$

where λ_t are coefficients of time dummy variables, TD_t. Note that, in this model, u_{it} is not restricted to be positive because $G(t)$ is not restricted to be positive. This model has not been used much in the literature. Therefore, we do not provide either the stata code or an empirical example of this model.

Battese and Coelli (1992) model assumes

$$G(t) = \exp\left[\gamma(t - T)\right], \tag{10.24}$$

where T is the terminal period of the sample. The Kumbhakar (1990) and Battese and Coelli (1992) specifications can be directly comparable if one writes the Kumbhakar formulation as

$$G(t) = 2 \times \left[1 + \exp(\gamma_1 (t - T) + \gamma_2 (t - T)^2)\right]^{-1}. \tag{10.25}$$

Then, at the terminal point $u_{iT} = u_i$.

Finally, Kumbhakar and Wang (2005) use the following specification

$$G(t) = \exp\left[\gamma(t - \underline{t})\right], \tag{10.26}$$

where $\underline{t}$ is the beginning period of the sample. Analytically, (10.24) and (10.26) are the same, but they are interpreted differently. In the Battese and Coelli (1992) and the reformulated specification of Kumbhakar (1990), $u_i \sim N^+(\mu, \sigma_u^2)$ specifies the distribution of inefficiency at the terminal point, that is, $u_{it} = u_i$ when $t = T$. With (10.26), $u_i \sim N^+(\mu, \sigma_u^2)$ specifies the initial distribution of inefficiency. Depending on applications, one of the specifications may be preferred over the other. Note that the Kumbhakar and Wang (2005) model controlled for fixed firm effects which is not done in any of the models discussed so far.

Note that the time-invariant random-effects model can be obtained as a special case from all these models by imposing appropriate parametric restrictions. Further, these restrictions can be tested using the LR test. For example, if $\gamma = 0$, then the Kumbhakar and Wang (2005) model and the Battese and Coelli (1992) model collapse to the time-invariant RE model in (10.10). Similarly, the Lee–Schmidt (1993) model becomes a time-invariant random-effects model in (10.10) if $\lambda_t = 1 \; \forall \; t$, that is the coefficients of time dummies are all unity. Finally, the Kumbhakar (1990) model reduces to the time-invariant random-effects model in (10.10) if $\gamma_1 = \gamma_2 = 0$. Because the Kumbhakar (1990) model has two parameters in the $G(t)$ function, the temporal pattern is more flexible than those of the Battese and Coelli (1992) and the Kumbhakar and Wang (2005) models. It is worth noting that the Lee–Schmidt (1993) model is more general and all the other models in which the $G(t)$ function is parametric can be viewed as a special case of the Lee-Schmidt model.[2] In the original RE version of the Lee–Schmidt model no distributional assumption was made on u_i. However, to compare it with the Kumbhakar (1990), Battese and Coelli (1992), and Kumbhakar and Wang (2005) models we made similar assumptions on u_i.

Given the similarity of all these models we specify the log-likelihood function of each cross-sectional observation i in generic form, that is, the one in (10.21), which is (Kumbhakar and Lovell [2000], p. 111):

$$\ln L_i = \text{constant} + \ln\Phi\left(\frac{\mu_{i*}}{\sigma_*}\right) + \frac{1}{2}\ln(\sigma_*^2) - \frac{1}{2}\left\{\frac{\sum_t \epsilon_{it}^2}{\sigma_v^2} + \left(\frac{\mu}{\sigma_u}\right)^2 - \left(\frac{\mu_{i*}}{\sigma_*}\right)^2\right\} - T\ln(\sigma_v) - \ln(\sigma_u) - \ln\Phi\left(\frac{\mu}{\sigma_u}\right), \tag{10.27}$$

where

$$\mu_{i*} = \frac{\mu\sigma_v^2 - \sigma_u^2\sum_t G(t)\epsilon_{it}}{\sigma_v^2 + \sigma_u^2\sum_t G(t)^2}, \tag{10.28}$$

$$\sigma_*^2 = \frac{\sigma_v^2\sigma_u^2}{\sigma_v^2 + \sigma_u^2\sum_t G(t)^2}. \tag{10.29}$$

The log-likelihood function of the model is obtained by summing $\ln L_i$ over i, $i = 1, \ldots, N$, which is maximized to get the ML estimates of the parameters.

Once the parameter estimates are obtained, inefficiency can be predicted from either the mean or the mode (Kumbhakar and Lovell [2000], p. 111):

$$E(u_i|\epsilon_i) = \mu_{i*} + \sigma_*\left[\frac{\phi(-\mu_{i*}/\sigma_*)}{1 - \Phi(-\mu_{i*}/\sigma_*)}\right] \tag{10.30}$$

and

$$M(u_i|\epsilon_i) = \begin{cases} \mu_{i*} & \text{if } \mu_{i*} \geq 0, \\ 0 & \text{otherwise.} \end{cases} \tag{10.31}$$

Example

Now we illustrate the Kumbhakar (1990) model, the Battese and Coelli (1992) model, and the Kumbhakar and Wang (2005) model.

Model 5: The Kumbhakar (1990) Model

We present the results from the Kumbhakar (1990) model. To run this model, the command `sfpan` is appended with the option `kumbhakar` and gamma is defined with `gamma(year year2, nocons)`, where `year2` is the square of `year`, as per equation (10.22).

```
. quietly generate year2 = year^2

. sfpan  lny, dist(t) mu(iniStat) prod frontier($xvar) usigmas vsigmas ///
> gamma(year year2, nocons) i(code) kumbhakar
. sf_init, frontier(b0) mu(0 0) gamma(0 0) usigmas(0) vsigmas(0)
. sf_srch, n(4) frontier($xvar) mu(iniStat) gamma(year year2) usigmas() ///
```

[2] Cuesta (2000) considered a model in which the parameters in the $G(t)$ function is made firm-specific.

```
> vsigmas() fast
. ml max, difficult  gtol(1e-5) nrtol(1e-5)

(iteration log omitted)


                                                  Number of obs   =       2296
                                                  Wald chi2(3)    =   16057.32
Log likelihood =  1251.3737                       Prob > chi2     =     0.0000

------------------------------------------------------------------------------
         lny |      Coef.   Std. Err.      z    P>|z|     [95% Conf. Interval]
-------------+----------------------------------------------------------------
frontier     |
         lnk |   .8548155   .0079039   108.15   0.000      .839324    .8703069
         lnl |   .1119533   .0106264    10.54   0.000     .0911259    .1327806
          yr |  -.0652729   .0162274    -4.02   0.000    -.0970779   -.0334678
       _cons |   2.395566   .9131893     2.62   0.009     .6057479    4.185384
-------------+----------------------------------------------------------------
mu           |
     iniStat |   .0367902   .0477245     0.77   0.441    -.0567481    .1303284
       _cons |   2.871213   .9102817     3.15   0.002     1.087093    4.655332
-------------+----------------------------------------------------------------
gamma        |
        year |   .0403159   .0024664    16.35   0.000     .0354818      .04515
       year2 |  -.0000336   .0000758    -0.44   0.658    -.0001822     .000115
-------------+----------------------------------------------------------------
usigmas      |
       _cons |  -1.520743   .1587721    -9.58   0.000    -1.831931   -1.209556
-------------+----------------------------------------------------------------
vsigmas      |
       _cons |  -4.118436   .0300562  -137.02   0.000    -4.177345   -4.059527
------------------------------------------------------------------------------
```

The estimated coefficients are very different to the earlier models. This is often the case with panel models and is not surprising since the capital and labor variables in the current model are likely to pick up some of the omitted heterogeneity effects, which can be particularly acute in comparisons across countries. Some of the heterogeneity are captured in the alternative models by using the country dummy variables (the fixed-effects model (Model 1)). Dealing with such heterogeneity is an important consideration in panel data models. In addition, it can sometimes be difficult to get this model to converge (given the flexibility and, hence, additional complexity of the form of $G(t)$ in this model).

The coefficient on `yr` (-0.065) now implies technical regress of 6.5 percent per annum. The coefficient on `iniStat` of 0.037 implies that for every 10 percent increase in the initial country-specific capital to labor ratio inefficiency is increased by 3.7 percent (the mean of the pre-truncated distribution is related to (log of) the initial capital to labor ratio ($\mathtt{k}_{it}/\mathtt{l}_{it}$)).

A key characteristic of the models in this section, compared to the previous section, is the models' time-varying characteristic of the inefficiency index. However, as can be seen from the estimation results, γ_1 is highly significant, while γ_2 is not significant. Recall that the Kumbhakar (1990) and the Battese and Coelli (1992) model differ only in that the former has one more parameter. That additional parameter comes from the coefficient of `year2` in our data. That coefficient, however, is very small in size (−0.0000336) and insignificant (p value=0.662). This means this extra parameter is not warranted in the current dataset.

We now turn to the Battese and Coelli (1992) Time Decay Model, which has a less flexible form for $G(t)$.

Model 6: The Battese and Coelli (1992) Time Decay Model

We estimate the Battese and Coelli (1992) model. This model is the default option under the command `sfpan`, so it does not require appending, but gamma requires defining appropriately. This is achieved by defining `gamma(yearT, nocons)`, where `yearT` is the difference between the current year and the end period, as per equation (10.24).

```
. by code: egen bigT = max(year) /* the end time period of each panel */
. generate yearT = (year - bigT) /*the (t-T) variable */

. sfpan lny, dist(t) mu(iniStat) prod frontier($xvar) usigmas vsigmas ///
> gamma(yearT, nocons) i(code)
. sf_init, frontier(bf_inv) mu(0 0) gamma(0) usigmas(0) vsigmas(0)
. sf_srch, frontier($xvar) usigmas() vsigmas() n(4) gamma(yearT) mu(iniStat) fast
. ml max, difficult nrtol(0.001) gtol(0.001)

(iteration log omitted)

                                                Number of obs     =       2296
                                                Wald chi2(3)      =    4955.69
Log likelihood =  1259.9666                     Prob > chi2       =     0.0000

------------------------------------------------------------------------------
         lny |      Coef.   Std. Err.      z    P>|z|     [95% Conf. Interval]
-------------+----------------------------------------------------------------
frontier     |
         lnk |   .5806205   .0147401    39.39   0.000     .5517305    .6095105
         lnl |   .0189589   .0122978     1.54   0.123    -.0051444    .0430622
          yr |   .0040164   .0015531     2.59   0.010     .0009725    .0070603
       _cons |   2.644054   .1562832    16.92   0.000     2.337745    2.950364
-------------+----------------------------------------------------------------
mu           |
     iniStat |  -.1362478   .0773941    -1.76   0.078    -.2879375    .0154418
       _cons |   2.065482   .1581313    13.06   0.000     1.755551    2.375414
-------------+----------------------------------------------------------------
gamma        |
       yearT |   -.001283   .0005279    -2.43   0.015    -.0023176   -.0002483
-------------+----------------------------------------------------------------
usigmas      |
       _cons |  -.5683633   .1821242    -3.12   0.002    -.9253201   -.2114064
-------------+----------------------------------------------------------------
vsigmas      |
       _cons |  -4.183417    .030156  -138.73   0.000    -4.242522   -4.124312
------------------------------------------------------------------------------

. matrix bbc = e(b)
. matrix bf_bc = bbc[1,"frontier:"]
. matrix bmu_bc = bbc[1,"mu:"]
```

The estimated coefficients are similar to the earlier models. The coefficient on `iniStat`, the logarithm of the initial capital to labor ratio, is -0.136 and implies that countries with a higher initial capital labor ratio will grow at a slower rate (for a 1 percent increase in initial capital labor ratio, the growth rate will decline by 0.136 percent).

We now examine the model's time-varying characteristic of the inefficiency index. From equation (10.24), u_i specifies the terminal distribution of inefficiency because $u_{it} = u_i$ when $t = T$ (as $G(t) = exp[\gamma(t-T)] = 1$). In addition, when $\gamma < 0$, inefficiency starts far higher and the model predicts convergence in inefficiency to u_i. The coefficient on `yearT` in the gamma function (-0.0013) is statistically significant. It implies that the percentage change in inefficiency for the countries is about 0.13 percent per annum.

As a further check, if $\gamma = 0$, then the model collapses to the time-invariant random-effects model in (10.10). This restriction can be tested using the LR test.

```
. scalar ll_bc = e(ll)
. display -2*(ll_inv - ll_bc)
6.2684113

. sf_mixtable, dof(1)

critical values of the mixed chi-square distribution

                      significance level
 dof  | 0.25      0.1        0.05       0.025      0.01       0.005      0.001
----------------------------------------------------------------------------------
  1     0.455     1.642      2.705      3.841      5.412      6.635      9.500

source: Table 1, Kodde and Palm (1986, Econometrica).
```

The degree of freedom of the statistic is 1 (i.e., `dof(1)`) because only one parameter (i.e., `yearT`) is restricted in the test. This table shows that critical value of the statistic at the 1% significance level is 5.4. Given that the value of the test statistic is 6.3, the null hypothesis of time-invariant technical inefficiency is rejected and therefore the time-decay model is preferred.

We now examine the efficiency estimated from this model.

```
. sf_predict, bc(bc_bc) jlms(jlms_bc) nomarginal

Note, both jlms_bc and _jlms_bc are created. The definitions are:

              storage  display     value
variable name   type    format      label      variable label
-------------------------------------------------------------------------------------
jlms_bc         double %10.0g                  conditional E(u_i|e)
_jlms_bc        double %10.0g                  conditional E(u_it|e) = E(B_t*u_i|e)

. summarize bc_bc jlms_bc

    Variable |       Obs        Mean    Std. Dev.       Min        Max
-------------+--------------------------------------------------------
       bc_bc |      2296    .1720024    .1572584    .0254882   .9473909
     jlms_bc |      2296    2.032731    .7547296    .0542897   3.544873
```

As illustrated, efficiency is estimated to be around 17 percent on average and inefficiency around 203 percent.

We now turn to the Kumbhakar and Wang (2005) Growth Model.

Model 7: The Growth Model from Kumbhakar and Wang (2005)

The Kumbhakar and Wang (2005) model is analytically the same as the Battese and Coelli (1992) model, so the estimation approach is similar.[3] Because inefficiency in the Battese and Coelli (1992) model is $G(t) \cdot u_i = \exp[\gamma(t - T)] \cdot u_i$ which can be written as $\exp\left[\gamma(t - \underline{t})\right] \cdot m \cdot u_i$ where $m = \exp\left[\gamma(\underline{t} - T)\right] > 0$, specification of inefficiency in the

[3] Note that the Kumbhakar and Wang (2005) model was designed to control for fixed country effects, which is not captured in the present model. Without the fixed effects, there is no need to estimate these two models separately.

Battese and Coelli (1992) and Kumbhakar and Wang (2005) models differ by the constant m. In practice m becomes a scaling factor of the u_i term. Thus, the estimate of γ is unchanged but the estimate of μ and σ_u will change due to the scaling factor.

```
. by code: egen smallT = min(year)   /* the beginning time period of each panel */
. generate timeT = (year - smallT)

. sfpan  lny, dist(t) mu(iniStat) prod frontier($xvar) usigmas vsigmas ///
> gamma(timeT, nocons) i(code)
. sf_init, frontier(bf_bc) mu(0 0) gamma(0) usigmas(-0.5) vsigmas(-4)
. sf_srch, frontier($xvar) usigmas() vsigmas() n(1) gamma(year2) mu(iniStat) fast
. ml max, difficult  nrtol(0.001) gtol(0.001)

(iteration log omitted)

                                                  Number of obs    =        2296
                                                  Wald chi2(3)     =     4958.09
Log likelihood =  1259.9666                       Prob > chi2      =      0.0000

------------------------------------------------------------------------------
         lny |      Coef.   Std. Err.      z    P>|z|     [95% Conf. Interval]
-------------+----------------------------------------------------------------
frontier     |
         lnk |   .5806205   .0147332    39.41   0.000     .5517439    .6094971
         lnl |    .018959   .0122965     1.54   0.123    -.0051416    .0430597
          yr |   .0040164   .0015526     2.59   0.010     .0009733    .0070595
       _cons |   2.644051   .1562032    16.93   0.000     2.337898    2.950204
-------------+----------------------------------------------------------------
mu           |
     iniStat |  -.1410502   .0799591    -1.76   0.078    -.2977671    .0156666
       _cons |   2.138282   .1581943    13.52   0.000     1.828227    2.448337
-------------+----------------------------------------------------------------
gamma        |
       timeT |   -.001283   .0005278    -2.43   0.015    -.0023175   -.0002485
-------------+----------------------------------------------------------------
usigmas      |
       _cons |  -.4990833   .1789034    -2.79   0.005    -.8497276   -.1484391
-------------+----------------------------------------------------------------
vsigmas      |
       _cons |  -4.183417   .0301559  -138.73   0.000    -4.242521   -4.124313
------------------------------------------------------------------------------

. matrix bkw = e(b)
. matrix bf_kw = bbc[1,"frontier:"]
. matrix bmu_kw = bbc[1,"mu:"]
```

The coefficients of the model (with the exception of mu and usigma) are the same as those for the Battese and Coelli (1992) model. This is because, as mentioned earlier, u_i in these two models differ by a constant which affects the parameters in u_i. This does not affect estimates of inefficiency.

However, the Kumbhakar and Wang (2005) formulation provides a more appropriate interpretation in this context. In this model, from equation (10.26), inefficiency evolves over time according to $\exp[\gamma(t - \underline{t})]$ and u_i specifies the initial distribution of inefficiency as $G(t) = \exp[\gamma(\underline{t} - \underline{t})] = 1$ when $t = \underline{t}$. In addition, because $u_i \geq 0$, if $\gamma < 0$, as $t \to \infty$, $u_{it} \to 0$. That is, if γ is negative, then catchup (i.e., movement towards the frontier) is observed. The rate of convergence depends on the initial level of technical inefficiency, u_i, which is country-specific. Because $\gamma = \partial \ln u_{it}/\partial t$, one can interpret γ as the percentage change in inefficiency over time (i.e., the rate of convergence). That is, the model captures the notion that countries operating below the frontier move toward the world production frontier (i.e., achieve efficiency improvements) over time. This convergence hypothesis is tested by $H_0 : \gamma \leq 0$ against $H_1 : \gamma > 0$.

As can be seen from these results, $\gamma < 0$ and the countries are converging to the frontier at a rate of 1.3 percent per annum. Below we test whether $\gamma = 0$ and model collapses to the time-invariant random-effects model in (10.10) by using a likelihood ratio test.

```
. scalar ll_kw = e(ll)
. display -2*(ll_inv - ll_kw)
6.2684113

. sf_mixtable, dof(1)

critical values of the mixed chi-square distribution

                          significance level
 dof  |  0.25      0.1        0.05       0.025      0.01       0.005      0.001
---------------------------------------------------------------------------------
  1      0.455     1.642      2.705      3.841      5.412      6.635      9.500

source: Table 1, Kodde and Palm (1986, Econometrica).
```

This shows that the Kumbhakar and Wang (2005) model is preferred to the time-invariant model.

We now examine the efficiency estimated from this model:

```
. sf_predict, bc(bc_kw) jlms(jlms_kw)

Note, both jlms_kw and _jlms_kw are created. The definitions are:

              storage  display     value
variable name   type   format      label      variable label
-------------------------------------------------------------------------------------
jlms_kw         double %10.0g                 conditional E(u_i|e)
_jlms_kw        double %10.0g                 conditional E(u_it|e) = E(B_t*u_i|e)

. summarize bc_kw jlms_kw

    Variable |       Obs        Mean    Std. Dev.       Min        Max
-------------+--------------------------------------------------------
       bc_kw |      2296     .172002     .157258   .0254882   .9473889
     jlms_kw |      2296    2.104381    .7813318   .0562055   3.669823
```

As illustrated, efficiency is estimated to be around 17 percent on average and inefficiency around 210 percent.

We compare the estimated efficiencies over time across three models: the time-invariant model, the Kumbhakar and Wang (2005) model (which produces the same figure as the Battese and Coelli (1992) model), and the Kumbhakar (1990) model.

First, we calculate the lower quartile, median, and upper quartile efficiency over time for the Kumbhakar and Wang (2005) model, label the new variables and plot them in a line chart.

```
. sort year
. by year, sort: egen bc_kw_tlq = pctile(bc_kw), p(25)
. by year, sort: egen bc_kw_tmed = pctile(bc_kw), p(50)
. by year, sort: egen bc_kw_tuq = pctile(bc_kw), p(75)

. label variable bc_kw_tlq "Lower quartile"
. label variable bc_kw_tuq "Upper quartile"
. label variable bc_kw_tmed "Median"
. graph two line bc_kw_tlq bc_kw_tmed bc_kw_tuq year, ///
> title("Efficiency from Kumbhakar & Wang (2004) model", size(medium)) ///
> saving(panel_eff_kw_time, replace)
```

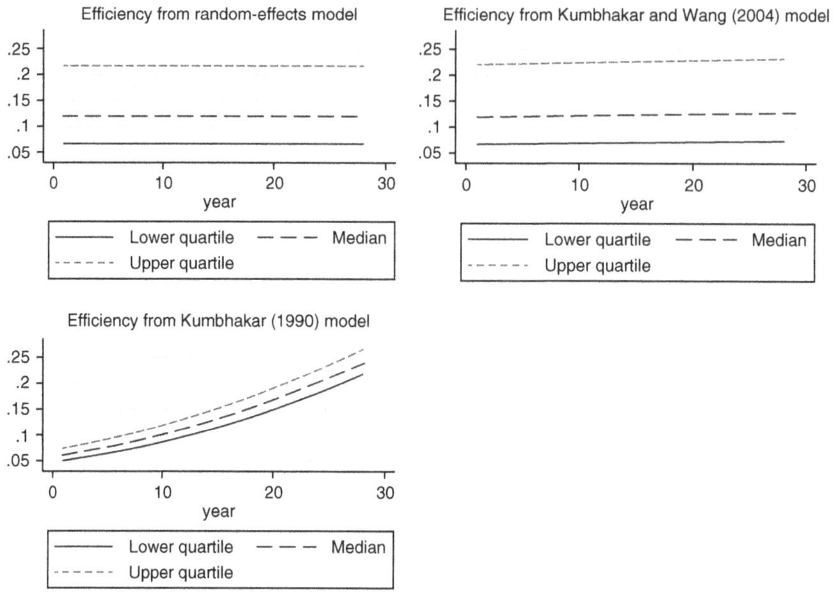

Figure 10.2. Efficiency over Time, Models 3, 5, and 7

This is repeated for the other two models and then the three charts are combined and then illustrated in Figure 10.2.

```
. graph combine  panel_eff_inv_time.gph panel_eff_kw_time.gph panel_eff_kum_time.gph, ///
> col(2) scale(1)  xcommon  ycommon
```

We now examine models that separate firm heterogeneity from inefficiency.

10.4 Models That Separate Firm Heterogeneity from Inefficiency

Recall the time-invariant inefficiency model (where inefficiency is fixed or random) discussed earlier and specified in (10.2) and (10.3):

$$y_{it} = \beta_0 + \boldsymbol{x}_{it}'\boldsymbol{\beta} + v_{it} - u_i \tag{10.2}$$

$$= \alpha_i + \boldsymbol{x}_{it}'\boldsymbol{\beta} + v_{it} \tag{10.3}$$

$$\text{where} \quad \alpha_i \equiv \beta_0 - u_i.$$

The model is a standard panel data model where α_i is the unobservable individual effect. Indeed, standard panel data fixed- and random-effects estimators are applied here to estimate the model parameters including α_i. The only difference is that we transform the estimated value of $\hat{\alpha}_i$ to obtain estimated value of u_i, $\hat{u}_i$.

A notable drawback of this approach is that individual heterogeneity cannot be distinguished from inefficiency. In other words, all the time-invariant heterogeneity is confounded into inefficiency, and therefore $\hat{u}_i$ might be picking up heterogeneity in addition to or even instead of inefficiency (Greene [2005b]).

Another potential issue of the model is the time-invariant assumption of inefficiency. If T is large, it seems implausible that the inefficiency of a firm may stay constant for an extended period of time and that a firm with persistent inefficiency would survive in the market.

So the question is: Should one view the time-invariant component as persistent inefficiency (as per Kumbhakar [1991], Kumbhakar and Heshmati [1995], Kumbhakar and Hjalmarsson [1993], [1998]) or as individual heterogeneity that captures the effects of time-invariant covariates and has nothing to do with inefficiency? If the latter case is true, then the results from the time-invariant inefficiency models are wrong. Perhaps the truth is somewhere in between. That is, part of inefficiency might be persistent. Unless it is separated from time-invariant individual effects, one has to choose either the model in which α_i represents persistent inefficiency or the model in which α_i represents an individual-specific effect (heterogeneity). Here, we will consider both specifications. In particular, we will consider models in which inefficiency is time-varying irrespective of whether the time-invariant component is treated as inefficiency or not. Thus, the models we examine here can be written as

$$y_{it} = \alpha_i + \boldsymbol{x}_{it}'\boldsymbol{\beta} + v_{it} - u_{it}. \tag{10.32}$$

Compared to a standard panel data model, (10.32) has an additional term, $-u_{it}$, representing time-varying inefficiency. If one treats α_i, $i = 1, \ldots, N$ as fixed parameters which are not part of inefficiency, then the above model becomes the "true fixed-effects" panel stochastic frontier model (Greene [2005a]). The model is labeled as "true random-effects" stochastic frontier model when α_i is treated as a random variable. Note that these specifications are not different from the models proposed by Kumbhakar and coauthors mentioned earlier. The difference is in the interpretation of the "time-invariant term."

Below, we examine the "true fixed-effects" model.

Example

The previous dataset did not include any z variables (variables explaining inefficiency). As such, we now introduce a different dataset that includes z variable(s). The new data is based on Wang and Ho (2010) and is taken from the Taiwan Economic Journal Data Bank. The sample consists of data on one hundred Taiwanese manufacturing firms (represented by the variable `id`) and covers the six-year period 2000 to 2005 (represented by the variable `time`), providing a total of six hundred observations.

The dependent variable, `y`, is $\ln(I/K)$, which is the log of the investment to capital ratio. Capital is measured at the beginning of each period and is used to normalize most of the variables in the model (in order to control for heteroscedasticity). The explanatory variables include `x1`, the log of Tobin's Q, and `x2`, the sales to capital ratio, $\ln(S/K)$. In addition, `z1` represents the cash flow to capital ratio variable (CF/K).

Model 8: True Fixed-Effects Model (Greene [2005a])

We use `sfmodel` to estimate a half-normal stochastic frontier model, using Greene's dummy variable approach (i.e., including dummies for each of the cross-sectional observations).

```
. use "panel data 2.dta"

. quietly tab id, gen(dum) /* generate firm dummies in dum1, dum2, ... */
. drop dum1   /* drop one of the dummies to avoid multicollinearity */
. global xvar x1 x2 /* save variable names in macro for easy reference */
```

```
. global dvar dum*
. global zvar z1

. quietly regress y $xvar $dvar  /* OLS regression, to get initial values */
. matrix b0 = e(b)            /* save the entire coefficient vector in a matrix */
. matrix b0a = b0[1,1..2]     /* save the first two coefficients (x1 and x2) in a matrix */

. sfmodel y, prod dist(h) frontier($xvar $dvar) usigmas($zvar) vsigmas()
. sf_init, frontier(b0) usigmas(-0.1 -0.1 ) vsigmas(-0.1)
. sf_srch, n(2) nograph fast
. ml max, diff gtol(1e-4) nrtol(1e-4)

(iteration log omitted)

                                                Number of obs   =        600
                                                Wald chi2(101)  =    5698.25
Log likelihood =  -183.8421                     Prob > chi2     =     0.0000

------------------------------------------------------------------------------
           y |      Coef.   Std. Err.      z    P>|z|     [95% Conf. Interval]
-------------+----------------------------------------------------------------
frontier     |
          x1 |   .5226104   .0144288    36.22   0.000     .4943305    .5508903
          x2 |   .6765214   .0141753    47.73   0.000     .6487384    .7043045

(dummies omitted)

       _cons |   .7758231    .135208     5.74   0.000     .5108204    1.040826
-------------+----------------------------------------------------------------
usigmas      |
          z1 |   1.658682   .2768241     5.99   0.000     1.116117    2.201247
       _cons |  -3.602955   .5241321    -6.87   0.000    -4.630235   -2.575675
-------------+----------------------------------------------------------------
vsigmas      |
       _cons |  -2.440428   .0885938   -27.55   0.000    -2.614069   -2.266788
------------------------------------------------------------------------------

. matrix b1 = e(b)
. matrix b1a = b1[1,"frontier:"]
```

The estimated coefficients on Tobin's Q and sales to capital ratio are positive and significant. The variance parameters are also significant, as are many of the dummy variables (not reported).

From the estimate of the variance parameters (`usigmas` and `vsigmas`), we can get back the original parameters using the `sf_transform` command.

```
. sf_transform

        sigma_u_sqr = exp(usigmas);
        sigma_v_sqr = exp(vsigmas).

    ---convert the parameters to original form---

    sigma_u_sqr appears to be a function of variables.
    The transformation is done only if sigma_u_sqr is constant.

variable      |      Coef.   Std. Err.       t    P>|t|      [95% Conf. Interval]
--------------+-----------------------------------------------------------------
 sigma_v_sqr  |   .0871235   .0077186    11.29   0.000      .0732359    .1036446
```

Next, we estimate efficiency.

```
. sf_predict, jlms(jlms1) bc(bc1)
. summarize  jlms1 bc1

    Variable |       Obs        Mean    Std. Dev.       Min        Max
-------------+--------------------------------------------------------
       jlms1 |       600    .1872034    .2301797   .0102787   3.559044
         bc1 |       600    .8500427    .1239143   .0297206    .989803
```

As illustrated, efficiency is estimated to be around 85 percent on average and inefficiency around 19 percent.

We now examine the "true random-effects" model.

Model 9: The True Random-Effects Model (Greene [2005a])

We use `sfpan` with the option `truerandom` to estimate a half-normal stochastic frontier model, using Greene's true random-effects approach.

```
. quietly xtreg y $xvar, re  /* RE regression, to get initial values */
. scalar ll_re = e(ll)
. matrix bre = e(b) /* save the entire coefficient vector in a matrix */

. sfpan y, prod dist(h) frontier($xvar) id(id) time(time) truerandom
. sf_init, frontier(bre) usigmas(-0.1) vsigmas(-0.1) esigmas(-0.1)
. sf_srch, frontier($xvar) usigmas() vsigmas() esigmas() n(2) fast
. ml max, diff

(iteration log omitted)
                                                  Number of obs    =       600
                                                  Wald chi2(2)     =   1296.79
Log likelihood =  138.03811                       Prob > chi2      =    0.0000

------------------------------------------------------------------------------
           y |      Coef.   Std. Err.      z    P>|z|     [95% Conf. Interval]
-------------+----------------------------------------------------------------
frontier     |
          x1 |   .5326851   .0178782    29.80   0.000     .4976444    .5677258
          x2 |   .6749392   .0289126    23.34   0.000     .6182715    .7316068
       _cons |   .6055592   .0834885     7.25   0.000     .4419247    .7691936
-------------+----------------------------------------------------------------
usigmas      |
       _cons |  -1.180022   .2753858    -4.28   0.000    -1.719768   -.6402755
-------------+----------------------------------------------------------------
vsigmas      |
       _cons |  -2.735726   .4318925    -6.33   0.000     -3.58222   -1.889232
-------------+----------------------------------------------------------------
esigmas      |
       _cons |  -1.862261   .1622865   -11.48   0.000    -2.180337   -1.544185
------------------------------------------------------------------------------
```

From the estimate of the variance parameters (`usigmas` and `vsigmas`), we can get back the original parameters using the `sf_transform` command.

```
. sf_transform

    sigma_u_sqr = exp(usigmas);
    sigma_v_sqr = exp(vsigmas).
    sigma_e_sqr = exp(esigmas).

  ---convert the parameters to original form---

variable     |      Coef.   Std. Err.      t    P>|t|     [95% Conf. Interval]
-------------+----------------------------------------------------------------
 sigma_u_sqr |    .307272   .0846184     3.63   0.000     .1791077    .5271472
 sigma_v_sqr |   .0648469   .0280069     2.32   0.021     .0278139    .1511878
 sigma_e_sqr |   .1553211   .0252065     6.16   0.000     .1130035    .2134857
```

Next, we estimate efficiency.

```
. sf_predict, bc(bc_tre)
. summarize bc_tre

    Variable |       Obs        Mean    Std. Dev.       Min        Max
-------------+--------------------------------------------------------
      bc_tre |       600    .5799537    .2419028   .0613922   .9501817
```

As illustrated, efficiency is estimated to be around 58 percent on average.

Estimation of the model in (10.32) is not easy. When α_i, $i = 1, \ldots, N$, are assumed to be fixed, the model encounters the incidental parameters problem (Neyman and Scott [1948]). The incidental parameters problem arises when the number of parameters to be estimated increases with the number of cross sections in the data, which is the case with the α_i in (10.32). In this situation, consistency of the parameter estimates is not guaranteed even if $N \to \infty$ because the number of α_i increases with N. Therefore, the usual asymptotic results may not apply.

In addition to the statistical problem, another technical issue in estimating (10.32) is: Given that α_i, $i = 1, \ldots, N$, are fixed parameters, the number of parameters to be estimated can be prohibitively large for a large N.

For a standard linear panel data model (i.e., one that does not have $-u_{it}$ in (10.32)), the literature has developed estimation methods to deal with this problem. The methods involve transforming the model so that α_i is removed before estimation. Without α_i in the transformed model, the incidental parameters problem no longer exists and the number of parameters to be estimated is not large. Methods of transformation include conditioning the model on α_i's sufficient statistic[4] to obtain the conditional MLE, and the within-transformation model or the first-difference transformation model to construct the marginal MLE (see, for example, Cornwell and Schmidt [1992]).

These standard methods, however, are usually not applicable to (10.32). For the conditional MLE, Greene (2005b) found that there is no sufficient statistic of α_i in a panel stochastic frontier model. For the marginal MLE, the resulting model after the within or first-difference transformation usually does not have a closed form likelihood function, if one uses the standard procedure.[5]

Greene (2005b) proposed a tentative solution. He assumed u_{it} to follow a simple i.i.d. half-normal distribution, that is, $u_{it} \sim N^+(0, \sigma_u^2)$, and suggested including N dummy variables in the model for α_i, $i = 1, \ldots, N$ and then estimating the model by MLE without any transformation. He found that the incidental parameters problem does not cause significant bias to the model parameters when T is large. The problem of having to estimate more than N parameters is dealt with by employing an advanced numerical algorithm.

There are some recent development on this issue. Chen et al. (2014) proposed a solution to the problem when firm-effects are fixed. Following a theorem in Dominguez-Molina et al. (2004), they showed that the likelihood function of the within transformed and the first-difference model have closed form expressions. The same theorem in Dominguez-Molina et al. (2004) is used in Colombi et al. (2014) to derive the log-likelihood function when the firm-effects are random. They also used a persistent inefficiency component in addition to the time-varying component. Given the complex estimation issues, we do not providing any examples of these models.

Using a different approach, Wang and Ho (2010) solve the problem in Greene (2005a) by proposing a class of stochastic frontier model in which the within and first-difference transformation on the model can be carried out and yet a closed-form likelihood function is still obtained using the standard practice used in the literature. The main advantage of such

[4] A sufficient statistic contains all the information needed to compute any estimate of the parameter.

[5] Colombi et al. (2011) showed that the likelihood function has a closed form expression. But this involves knowledge of a closed skew-normal distribution – something that has not been very well known in stochastic frontier models until recently. See, also Chen et al. (2014).

a model is that because the α_is are dropped from the estimation equation, the incidental parameters problem are avoided entirely. Therefore, consistency of the estimates is obtained for either $N \to \infty$ or $T \to \infty$, which is a valuable property for many empirical applications. The elimination of α_is also implies that the number of parameters to be estimated is not too large. The Wang and Ho (2010) model is:

$$\begin{aligned} y_{it} &= \alpha_i + \boldsymbol{x}_{it}'\boldsymbol{\beta} + \varepsilon_{it}, \\ \varepsilon_{it} &= v_{it} - u_{it}, \\ v_{it} &\sim N(0, \sigma_v^2), \\ u_{it} &= h_{it} u_i^*, \\ h_{it} &= f(\boldsymbol{z}_{it}'\boldsymbol{\delta}), \\ u_i^* &\sim N^+(\mu, \sigma_u^2), \qquad i = 1, \ldots, N, \quad t = 1, \ldots, T. \end{aligned} \tag{10.33}$$

The key feature that allows the model transformation to be applied is the multiplicative form of inefficiency effects, u_{it}, in which the individual-specific effects, u_i, appear in multiplicative form with the individual- and time-specific effects, h_{it}. As u_i^* does not change with time, the within and the first-difference transformations leave this stochastic term intact. Wang and Ho (2010) show that the within-transformed and the first-differenced models are algebraically identical. We therefore present only the first-differenced model here.

First, we define the following notation: $\Delta w_{it} = w_{it} - w_{it-1}$, and the stacked vector of Δw_{it} for a given i and $t = 2, \ldots, T$ is denoted as $\Delta \tilde{w}_i = (\Delta w_{i2}, \Delta w_{i3}, \ldots, \Delta w_{iT})'$. With these notations, the log-likelihood function for the ith cross-sectional unit is (see Wang and Ho [2010], p. 288):

$$\begin{aligned} \ln L_i^D =& -\frac{1}{2}(T-1)\ln(2\pi) - \frac{1}{2}\ln(T) - \frac{1}{2}(T-1)\ln(\sigma_v^2) - \frac{1}{2}\Delta\tilde{\varepsilon}_i'\Sigma^{-1}\Delta\tilde{\varepsilon}_i \\ &+ \frac{1}{2}\left(\frac{\mu_*^2}{\sigma_*^2} - \frac{\mu^2}{\sigma_u^2}\right) + \ln\left(\sigma_*\Phi\left(\frac{\mu_*}{\sigma_*}\right)\right) - \ln\left(\sigma_u\Phi\left(\frac{\mu}{\sigma_u}\right)\right), \end{aligned} \tag{10.34}$$

where

$$\mu_{*i} = \frac{\mu/\sigma_u^2 - \Delta\tilde{\varepsilon}_i'\Sigma^{-1}\Delta\tilde{h}_i}{\Delta\tilde{h}_i'\Sigma^{-1}\Delta\tilde{h}_i + 1/\sigma_u^2}, \tag{10.35}$$

$$\sigma_{*i}^2 = \frac{1}{\Delta\tilde{h}_i'\Sigma^{-1}\Delta\tilde{h}_i + 1/\sigma_u^2}, \tag{10.36}$$

$$\Delta\tilde{\varepsilon}_i = \Delta\tilde{y}_i - \Delta\tilde{\boldsymbol{x}}_i\boldsymbol{\beta}, \tag{10.37}$$

and the $(T-1) \times (T-1)$ variance-covariance matrix Σ of $\Delta\tilde{v}_i = (\Delta v_{i2}, \Delta v_{i3}, \ldots, \Delta v_{iT})'$ is

$$\Sigma = \begin{bmatrix} 2\sigma_v^2 & -\sigma_v^2 & 0 & \cdots & 0 \\ -\sigma_v^2 & 2\sigma_v^2 & -\sigma_v^2 & \cdots & 0 \\ 0 & \ddots & \ddots & \ddots & \vdots \\ \vdots & \ddots & \ddots & \ddots & -\sigma_v^2 \\ 0 & 0 & \cdots & -\sigma_v^2 & 2\sigma_v^2 \end{bmatrix}. \tag{10.38}$$

The matrix has $2\sigma_v^2$ on the diagonal and $-\sigma_v^2$ on the off-diagonals. The marginal log-likelihood function of the model is obtained by summing the above function over

$i = 1, \ldots, N$. The model parameters are estimated by numerically maximizing the marginal log-likelihood function of the model.

After the model parameters are estimated, the observation-specific inefficiency index is computed from

$$E(u_{it}|\Delta\tilde{\varepsilon}_i) = h_{it}\left[\mu_{*i} + \sigma_{*i}\left\{\frac{\phi(\mu_{*i}/\sigma_{*i})}{\Phi(\mu_{*i}/\sigma_{*i})}\right\}\right] \tag{10.39}$$

evaluated at $\Delta\tilde{\varepsilon}_i = \Delta\hat{\tilde{\varepsilon}}_i$.

Example

Model 10: The Wang and Ho (2010) Model

Below we estimate the Wang and Ho (2010) model using the author-written command, `sf_fixeff`. The syntax is similar to previous stochastic frontier models. The option `zvar($zvar)` is required as part of this model and cannot be left blank.

```
. sf_fixeff y, production dist(h) frontier($xvar) zvar($zvar) id(id) ///
> time(time) vsigmas usigmas
. sf_init, frontier(b0a) zvar(0.1) vsigmas(-0.1) usigmas(-0.1)
. sf_srch, frontier(x1 x2) zvar(z1 ) n(1) nograph fast
. ml max, diff

(iteration log omitted)

                                                  Number of obs   =        600
                                                  Wald chi2(2)    =    3223.03
Log likelihood = -182.58806                       Prob > chi2     =     0.0000

------------------------------------------------------------------------------
        _y_M |      Coef.   Std. Err.      z    P>|z|     [95% Conf. Interval]
-------------+----------------------------------------------------------------
frontier     |
       _x1_M |   .5244044   .0149866    34.99   0.000     .4950313    .5537775
       _x2_M |    .684083   .0148099    46.19   0.000      .655056    .7131099
-------------+----------------------------------------------------------------
hleq         |
          z1 |   .5317585   .1254704     4.24   0.000      .285841     .777676
-------------+----------------------------------------------------------------
vsigmas      |
       _cons |  -2.227779   .0678884   -32.82   0.000    -2.360837    -2.09472
-------------+----------------------------------------------------------------
usigmas      |
       _cons |   -1.87254   .6366893    -2.94   0.003    -3.120428   -.6246518
------------------------------------------------------------------------------
```

From the estimates of the variance parameters (`vsigmas` and `usigmas`), we can get back the original parameters using the `sf_transform` command.

```
. sf_transform

        sigma_u_sqr = exp(usigmas);
        sigma_v_sqr = exp(vsigmas).

    ---convert the parameters to original form---

variable     |      Coef.   Std. Err.      t    P>|t|     [95% Conf. Interval]
-------------+----------------------------------------------------------------
 sigma_u_sqr |   .1537327     .09788     1.57   0.116     .0441383    .5354478
 sigma_v_sqr |   .1077676   .0073162    14.73   0.000     .0943412    .1231048
```

Next, we estimate efficiency.

```
. sf_predict, jlms(jlms_who) bc(bc_who)
. summarize jlms_who bc_who

    Variable |       Obs        Mean    Std. Dev.       Min        Max
-------------+--------------------------------------------------------
    jlms_who |       600    .3599123    .3143756   .0263061   3.993955
      bc_who |       600    .7362391    .1514462   .0201173   .9742609
```

Mean estimated efficiency is found to be around 74 percent and mean inefficiency is around 36 percent.

The average estimated inefficiencies (across firms) from Models 8, 9, and 10 are plotted over time here:

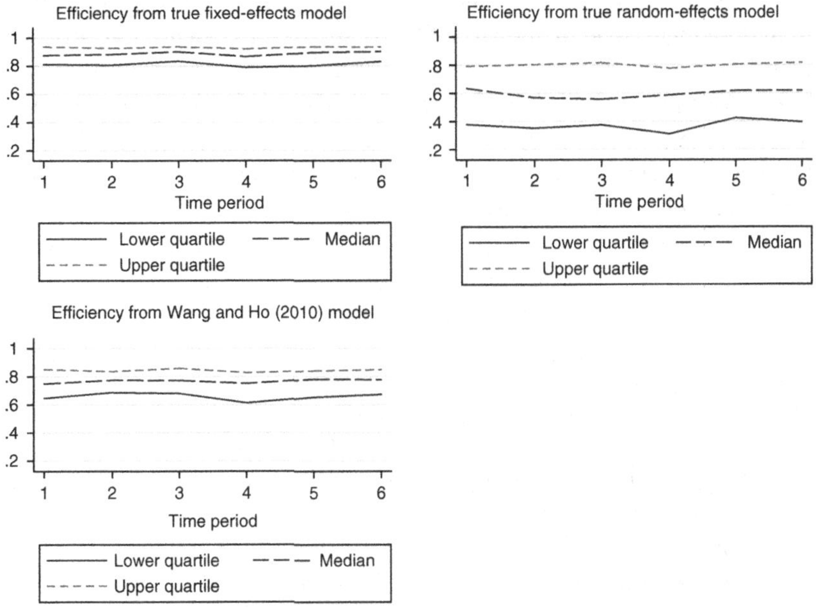

Figure 10.3. Estimated Efficiency over Time from Models 8, 9, and 10

So far, in this section, we have discussed two types of time-varying panel data models. In the first group of models inefficiency is a product of a time-varying function of a time trend. These models are further generalized to accommodate firm heterogeneity in the intercept. The advantage of this specification of inefficiency is that the likelihood function is easy to derive. The assumption of time-invariant inefficiency can be tested from these models. The second class of models examined controlled for firm-effects and allowed inefficiency to be time-varying (either i.i.d. over time and across firms or some kind of dependence on covariates via the mean and/or the variance of the random inefficiency term). Unfortunately, these two classes of models are not nested and, therefore, the data cannot help one to choose which formulation is appropriate.

However, both classes of models discussed in this section view firm effects (fixed or random) as something different from inefficiency. That is, inefficiency in these models is always time-varying and can either be i.i.d. or a function of exogenous variables. Thus, these models fail to capture persistent inefficiency, which is hidden within firm effects. Consequently, these models are misspecified and tend to produce a downward bias in the estimate of overall inefficiency, especially if persistent inefficiency exists.

We now consider models that separate persistent and time-varying inefficiency.

10.5 Models That Separate Persistent and Time-Varying Inefficiency

Although some of the models discussed earlier can separate firm-heterogeneity from time-varying inefficiency (which is either modeled as the product of a time-invariant random variable and a deterministic function of covariates or distributed i.i.d. across firms and over time), none of these models consider persistent technical inefficiency. Identifying the magnitude of persistent inefficiency is important, especially in short panels, because it reflects the effects of inputs like management (Mundlak [1961]) as well as other unobserved inputs which vary across firms but not over time. Thus, unless there is a change in something that affects the management style of individual firms such as a change in government policy toward the industry, a change in firm-ownership, and so on, it is very unlikely that the persistent inefficiency component will change. By contrast, the residual component of inefficiency might change over time without any change in the operation of the firm. Therefore, the distinction between the persistent and residual components of inefficiency is important because they have different policy implications.

We consider the model

$$\begin{aligned} y_{it} &= \beta_0 + \boldsymbol{x}_{it}'\boldsymbol{\beta} + \epsilon_{it}, \\ \epsilon_{it} &= v_{it} - u_{it}, \\ u_{it} &= u_i + \tau_{it} \end{aligned} \tag{10.40}$$

The error term, ϵ_{it}, is decomposed as $\epsilon_{it} = v_{it} - u_{it}$ where u_{it} is technical inefficiency and v_{it} is statistical noise. The technical inefficiency part is further decomposed as $u_{it} = u_i + \tau_{it}$ where u_i is the persistent component (for example, time-invariant management effect) and τ_{it} is the residual (time-varying) component of technical inefficiency, both of which are nonnegative. The former is only firm-specific, while the latter is both firm- and time-specific. Such a decomposition is desirable from a policy point of view because the persistent component is unlikely to change over time without any change in government policy or ownership of the firm, whereas the residual component changes both across firms and over time. The size of overall inefficiency, as well as the components, are important to know because they convey different types of information. Thus, for example, if the residual inefficiency component for a firm is relatively large in a particular year then it may be argued that inefficiency is caused by something which is unlikely to be repeated in the next year. By contrast, if the persistent inefficiency component is large for a firm, then it is expected to operate with a relatively high level of inefficiency over time, unless some changes in policy and/or management take place. Thus, a high value of u_i is of more concern from a long-term point of view because of its persistent nature.

The advantage of the present specification is that one can test the presence of the persistent nature of technical inefficiency without imposing any parametric form of time-dependence. By including time in the $\boldsymbol{x}_{it}$ vector, we separate exogenous technical change from technical inefficiency.

To estimate the model we rewrite (10.40) as

$$\begin{aligned} & y_{it} = \alpha_i + \boldsymbol{x}_{it}'\boldsymbol{\beta} + \omega_{it}, \\ \text{where} \quad & \alpha_i \equiv \beta_0 - u_i - E(\tau_{it}) \quad \text{and} \quad \omega_{it} = v_{it} - (\tau_{it} - E(\tau_{it})). \end{aligned} \tag{10.41}$$

The error components, ω_{it}, have zero mean and constant variance. Thus, the model in (10.41) fits perfectly into the standard panel data model with firm-specific effects (one-way error component model), and can be estimated either by the least-squares dummy variable approach (when the firm-effects, α_i, are treated as fixed) or by the generalized least-squares (GLS) method (when the firm-effects are assumed to be random, and a further transformation is made to make α_i a zero-mean random variable).

10.5.1 The Fixed-Effects Model

We use a multistep procedure to estimate the model. In Step 1, we estimate (10.41) using standard fixed-effects panel data model to obtain consistent estimates of $\boldsymbol{\beta}$. In Step 2, we estimate persistent technical inefficiency, u_i. In Step 3, we estimate β_0 and the parameters associated with the random components, v_{it} and τ_{it}. Finally, in Step 4, the time-varying (residual) component of inefficiency, τ_{it}, is estimated.

Step 1: The standard within transformation can be performed on (10.41) to remove α_i before estimation. Because both the components of ω_{it} are zero mean and constant variance random variables, the within transformed ω_{it} will generate a random variable that has zero mean and constant variance. So one can use OLS on the within transformed version of (10.41) and obtain consistent estimates of $\boldsymbol{\beta}$.

Step 2: Given the estimate of $\boldsymbol{\beta}$, say $\hat{\boldsymbol{\beta}}$, from Step 1, we obtain pseudo residuals $r_{it} = y_{it} - \boldsymbol{x}'_{it}\hat{\boldsymbol{\beta}}$, which contain $\alpha_i^* + \omega_{it}$. Using these, first, we estimate α_i^* from the mean of r_{it} for each i. Then, we can estimate u_i from $\max_i \hat{\alpha}_i - \hat{\alpha}_i^* = \max_i\{\bar{r}_i\} - \bar{r}_i$ where $\bar{r}_i$ is the mean (over time) of r_{it} for firm i. Note that the intercept, β_0, and effects of ω_{it} are washed away in taking the mean of r by firm. This formula gives an estimate of u_i relative to the best firm in the sample.

Step 3: After obtaining estimates of $\boldsymbol{\beta}$ and u_i, we calculate residuals e_{it} as $\eta_{it} = y_{it} - \boldsymbol{x}'_{it}\hat{\boldsymbol{\beta}} + \hat{u}_i$, which contains $\beta_0 + v_{it} - \tau_{it}$. At this stage, we make the following additional assumptions on v_{it} and τ_{it}: (i) $v_{it} \sim$ i.i.d. $N(0, \sigma_v^2)$, (ii) $\tau_{it} \sim$ i.i.d. $N^+(0, \sigma_\tau^2)$ truncated at zero from below (half-normal). The SF technique is then used (treating e_{it} as the dependent variable which is i.i.d.) to estimate β_0 and the parameters associated with v_{it} and τ_{it}.

Step 4: In step 4, we use the JLMS technique to estimate τ_{it} for each observation.

Note that no distributional assumptions are used in the first two steps. Distributional assumptions are used to estimate residual inefficiency.

10.5.2 The Random-Effects Model

If u_i is assumed to be random, we rewrite (10.41) as

$$\begin{aligned} y_{it} &= \beta_0^* + \boldsymbol{x}'_{it}\boldsymbol{\beta} - u_i^* + \omega_{it}, \\ \text{where} \quad \beta_0^* &\equiv \beta_0 - E(u_i) - E(\tau_{it}),\ u_i^* = u_i - E(u_i) \quad \text{and} \\ \omega_{it} &= v_{it} - (\tau_{it} - E(\tau_{it})), \end{aligned} \tag{10.42}$$

so that the error components, u_i^* and ω_{it}, are zero mean and constant variance random variables. Thus, the model in (10.42) fits into the standard one-way error component panel model that can be estimated using GLS. That is, in **Step 1** the GLS is used to estimate $\boldsymbol{\beta}$ and

β_0^*. In **Step 2**, the pseudo residuals $\tilde{r}_{it} = y_{it} - \boldsymbol{x}_{it}'\hat{\boldsymbol{\beta}} - \beta_0^*$ can be used to estimate u_i^*. The best linear unbiased predictor (BLUP) of u_i^* is

$$\tilde{u}_i^* = -\left\{\frac{\hat{\sigma}_u^2}{\hat{\sigma}_\omega^2 + T\hat{\sigma}_u^2}\right\}\sum_t \tilde{r}_{it}, \quad i = 1, \ldots, N, \tag{10.43}$$

where σ_u^2 and σ_ω^2 are the variances of u_i^* and ω_{it}. Once u_i^* is estimated, we can get an estimate of u_i from $u_i = \max_i\{u_i^*\} - u_i^*$. **Step 3** and **Step 4** are the same as those under the fixed-effects model. As such, we do not repeat these steps here.

Example

Model 11: The Kumbhakar and Heshmati (1995) Model

We estimate the model in Kumbhakar and Heshmati (1995), which corresponds to the fixed-effects model discussed earlier. This involves four steps discussed under the fixed-effects model. In the first step, a fixed-effects panel model is estimated.

```
. xtreg y $xvar, fe

Fixed-effects (within) regression               Number of obs      =       600
Group variable: id                              Number of groups   =       100

R-sq:  within  = 0.8086                         Obs per group: min =         6
       between = 0.5468                                        avg =       6.0
       overall = 0.7090                                        max =         6

                                                F(2,498)           =   1052.08
corr(u_i, Xb)  = 0.1016                         Prob > F           =    0.0000

------------------------------------------------------------------------------
           y |      Coef.   Std. Err.      t    P>|t|     [95% Conf. Interval]
-------------+----------------------------------------------------------------
          x1 |   .5261768   .0185683    28.34   0.000     .4896949    .5626587
          x2 |   .6747711   .0180752    37.33   0.000     .6392582    .7102841
       _cons |   .1706229   .0196376     8.69   0.000     .1320402    .2092056
-------------+----------------------------------------------------------------
     sigma_u |  .44912147
     sigma_e |  .42149449
         rho |  .53170077   (fraction of variance due to u_i)
------------------------------------------------------------------------------
F test that all u_i=0:     F(99, 498) =     6.70             Prob > F = 0.0000
```

The second step involves estimating persistent efficiency using the estimated fixed effect from the model above, as given by `predict` with the option u. This gives an estimate of u_i^*. We can then estimate u_i from $\max_i \hat{u}_i^* - \hat{u}_i^*$, or the efficiency from $\exp(-u_i) = \exp(\hat{u}_i^* - \max_i \hat{u}_i^*)$.

```
. predict e_u, u /* fixed effect */
. egen maxu = max(e_u)
. generate KH_TE = exp(e_u - maxu)
. summarize KH_TE

    Variable |       Obs        Mean    Std. Dev.       Min        Max
-------------+--------------------------------------------------------
       KH_TE |       600     .464747    .1971401   .0978678          1
```

In the third step, the stochastic frontier technique is used (treating e_{it} as the dependent variable which is i.i.d.) with just a constant on the right-hand side to estimate β_0 and the parameters associated with v_{it} and τ_{it}. A constant is needed to force `sfmodel` to run, and we use `nocons` to instruct Stata not to (automatically) append another constant.

```
. generate onee=1 /* constant */
. predict error,e /* the error component  */
. sfmodel error, dist(h) prod frontier(onee, nocons) usigmas() vsigmas()
. ml max, difficult gradient gtol(0.001) nrtol(0.001)

(iteration log omitted)

                                                  Number of obs    =        600
                                                  Wald chi2(1)     =      78.99
Log likelihood =  -268.7395                       Prob > chi2      =     0.0000

------------------------------------------------------------------------------
       error |      Coef.   Std. Err.      z    P>|z|     [95% Conf. Interval]
-------------+----------------------------------------------------------------
frontier     |
        onee |   .3291111   .0370306     8.89   0.000     .2565324    .4016898
-------------+----------------------------------------------------------------
usigmas      |
       _cons |  -1.756525   .2137388    -8.22   0.000    -2.175446   -1.337605
-------------+----------------------------------------------------------------
vsigmas      |
       _cons |  -2.487395   .1474151   -16.87   0.000    -2.776323   -2.198467
------------------------------------------------------------------------------
```

The fourth step involves estimating the residual technical efficiency. We use the JLMS technique to estimate τ_{it} for each observation. We also calculate the overall efficiency from the persistent and residual efficiency.

```
. sf_predict, jlms(tau_mean) bc(TE_R)

. generate OTE = TE_R*KH_TE
. summarize TE_R KH_TE OTE

    Variable |       Obs        Mean    Std. Dev.       Min        Max
-------------+--------------------------------------------------------
        TE_R |       600    .7406228    .1057117   .1174499   .9385711
       KH_TE |       600     .464747    .1971401   .0978678          1
         OTE |       600    .3445488    .1547352   .0206341   .8786938
```

As illustrated in this table, persistent efficiency is estimated to be 46 percent on average, residual efficiency 74 percent, and total efficiency 34 percent. Note that because the firm-effects are treated as persistent inefficiency, overall efficiency is quite low. Although part of the firm-effects might be due to time-invariant regressors (observed or unobserved), the Kumbhakar-Heshmati formulation does not recognize this.

The average (across firms) of these efficiency measures is plotted over time in Figure 10.4.

The procedure to estimate a random effects model is the same, except that the fixed-effects option in step 1 is replaced by the random-effects option. The results from this model are reported here:

```
. summarize TE_R KH_TE_P OTE

    Variable |       Obs        Mean    Std. Dev.       Min        Max
-------------+--------------------------------------------------------
        TE_R |       600    .7194619    .1220949   .0826049   .9336899
     KH_TE_P |       600    .5177271    .1852775   .1410462          1
         OTE |       600    .3765382    .1574199   .0190012   .8960249
```

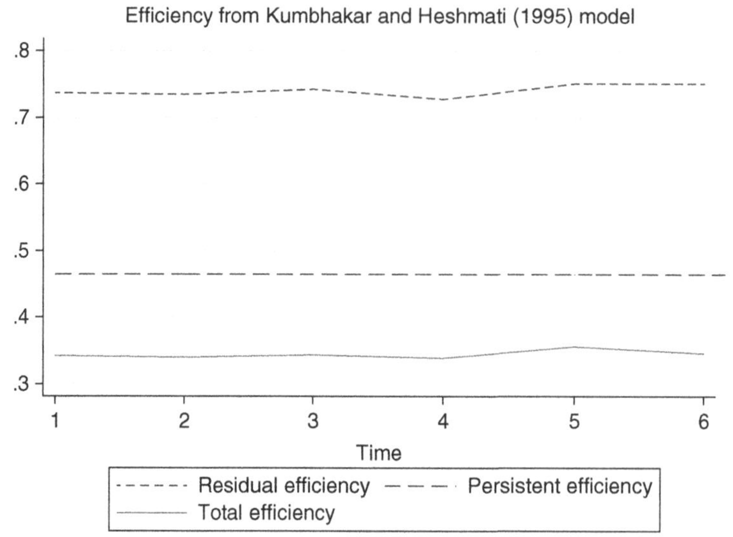

Figure 10.4. Estimated Average Efficiency over Time from Model 11

As illustrated in this table, persistent efficiency is estimated to be 51 percent on average, residual efficiency 72 percent, and total efficiency 38 percent.

10.6 Models That Separate Firm Effects, Persistent Inefficiency and Time-Varying Inefficiency

The model in Section 10.5 views firm effects (fixed or random) as long-term (persistent) inefficiency, with an added second component to capture time-varying technical inefficiency. As such, this model confounds firm effects (that are not part of inefficiency) with persistent inefficiency. Consequently, the model is mis-specified and is likely to produce an upward bias in inefficiency by treating firm-effects as inefficiency. The previous models in Section 10.4 view firm effects (fixed or random) as something other than inefficiency. Thus, these models fail to capture persistent inefficiency, which is confounded within firm effects. Consequently, these models are also misspecified and tend to produce a downward bias in the estimate of overall inefficiency.

Because the assumptions made in the previous models (including those in Section 10.4 and Section 10.5) are not fully satisfactory, we introduce in this final section a model by Kumbhakar, Lien, and Hardaker (2014) and Colombi et al. (2014) that overcomes some of the limitations of the earlier models. In this model the error term is split into four components to take into account different factors affecting output, given the inputs. The first component captures firms' latent heterogeneity (Greene [2005a], [2005b]), which has to be disentangled from the inefficiency effects; the second component captures short-run (time-varying) inefficiency. The third component captures persistent or time-invariant inefficiency as in Kumbhakar and Hjalmarsson (1993, 1995), Kumbhakar and Heshmati (1995), while the last component captures random shocks.

This model is specified as:

$$y_{it} = a_0 + f(x_{it}; \beta) + \mu_i + v_{it} - \eta_i - u_{it} \tag{10.44}$$

This model has four components two of which, $\eta_i > 0$ and $u_{it} > 0$, are inefficiency and the other two are firm effects and noise, μ_i and v_{it}, respectively. These components appeared in other models in various combinations but not all at the same time in one model.

This new model improves upon the previous models in several ways. First, although some of the time-varying inefficiency models presented above can accommodate firm effects, these models fail to take into account the possible presence of some factors that might have permanent (i.e., time-invariant) effects on a firm's inefficiency. Here we call them persistent/time-invariant components of inefficiency. Second, SF models allowing time-varying inefficiency assume that a firm's inefficiency at time t is independent of its previous level inefficiency. It is more sensible to assume that a firm may eliminate part of its inefficiency by removing some of the short-run rigidities, while some other sources of inefficiency might stay with the firm over time. The former is captured by the time-varying component, η_i, and the latter by the time-varying component, u_{it}. Finally, many panel SF models do consider persistent/time-invariant inefficiency effects, but do not take into account the effect of unobserved firm heterogeneity on output. By doing so, these models confound persistent/time-invariant inefficiency with firm effects (heterogeneity). Models proposed by Greene (2005a, 2005b), Kumbhakar and Wang (2005), Wang and Ho (2010), and Chen et al. (2014) decompose the error term in the production function into three components: a producer-specific time-varying inefficiency term; a producer-specific random- or fixed-effects capturing latent heterogeneity; and a producer- and time-specific random error term. However, these models consider any producer-specific, time-invariant component as unobserved heterogeneity. Thus, although firm heterogeneity is now accounted for, it comes at the cost of ignoring long-term (persistent) inefficiency. In other words, long-run inefficiency is again confounded with latent heterogeneity.

Estimation of the model in (10.44) can be undertaken in a single stage ML method based on distributional assumptions on the four components (Colombi et al. [2011]). Here, we consider a simpler multistep procedure. For this, we rewrite the model in (10.44) as

$$y_{it} = \alpha_0^* + f(x_{it};\beta) + \alpha_i + \varepsilon_{it}, \qquad (10.45)$$

where $\alpha_0^* = \alpha_0 - E(\eta_i) - E(u_{it})$; $\alpha_i = \mu - \eta_i + E(\eta_i)$; and $\varepsilon_{it} = v_{it} - u_{it} + E(u_{it})$. With this specification α_i and ε_{it} have zero mean and constant variance. This model can be estimated in three steps.

Step 1: Since (10.45) is the familiar panel data model, in the first step the standard random-effect panel regression is used to estimate $\hat{\beta}$. This procedure also gives predicted values of α_i and ε_{it}, which we denote by $\hat{\alpha}_i$ and $\hat{\varepsilon}_{it}$.

Step 2: In the second step, the time-varying technical inefficiency, u_{it}, is estimated. For this we use the predicted values of ε_{it} from Step 1. As

$$\varepsilon_{it} = v_{it} - u_{it} + E(u_{it}), \qquad (10.46)$$

by assuming v_{it} is i.i.d. $N(0,\sigma_v^2)$ and u_{it} is $N^+(0,\sigma_u^2)$, which means $E(u_{it}) = (\sqrt{2/\pi}\,\sigma_u)$, and ignoring the difference between the true and predicted values of ε_{it} (which is the standard practice in any two- or multistep procedure), we can estimate (10.46) using the standard SF technique. This procedure gives prediction of the time-varying residual technical inefficiency components, $\hat{u}_{it}$ (i.e., Jondrow et al. [1982]) or residual technical efficiency (i.e., Battese and Coelli [1988]), $\exp(-u_{it}|\varepsilon_{it})$.

Step 3: In the final step we can estimate η_i following a similar procedure as in Step 2. For this we use the best linear predictor of α_i from step 1. As

$$\alpha_i = \mu_i - \eta_i + E(\eta_i), \tag{10.47}$$

by assuming μ_i is i.i.d. $N(0, \sigma_\mu^2)$, η_i is i.i.d. $N^+(0, \sigma_\eta^2)$, which in turn means $E(\eta_i) = \sqrt{2/\pi}\,\sigma_\eta$, we can estimate (10.47) using the standard normal–half-normal SF model cross-sectionally and obtain estimates of the persistent technical inefficiency components, η_i, using the Jondrow et al. (1982) procedure. Persistent technical efficiency can then be estimated from PTE $= \exp(-\eta_i)$. The overall technical efficiency, OTE, is then obtained from the product of PTE and RTE, that is, $OTE = PTE \times RTE$.

It is possible to extend this model (in steps 2 and 3) to include nonzero mean of persistent and time-varying inefficiency and also to account for heteroscedasticity in either or both. This model is illustrated here:

Example

Model 12: The Kumbhakar, Lien, and Hardaker (2014) Model

In this example, we follow the approach in Kumbhakar, Lien, and Hardaker (2014). The first step involves estimating a fixed- or random-effects panel model (here, we estimate a random-effects model).

```
. xtreg y $xvar, re

Random-effects GLS regression                   Number of obs      =       600
Group variable: id                              Number of groups   =       100

R-sq:  within  = 0.8086                         Obs per group: min =         6
       between = 0.5478                                        avg =       6.0
       overall = 0.7094                                        max =         6

                                                Wald chi2(2)       =   2197.78
corr(u_i, X)   = 0 (assumed)                    Prob > chi2        =    0.0000

------------------------------------------------------------------------------
           y |      Coef.   Std. Err.      z    P>|z|     [95% Conf. Interval]
-------------+----------------------------------------------------------------
          x1 |   .5363332   .0182329    29.42   0.000     .5005975    .5720689
          x2 |   .6774347   .0179135    37.82   0.000     .6423248    .7125445
       _cons |   .1654945   .0448421     3.69   0.000     .0776055    .2533834
-------------+----------------------------------------------------------------
     sigma_u |  .40140187
     sigma_e |  .42149449
         rho |   .4755976   (fraction of variance due to u_i)
------------------------------------------------------------------------------
```

We then save the error component and the (random) effect for use in subsequent steps (we also test their skewness).

In the second step, we estimate residual inefficiency, u_{it} (i.e., time-varying technical inefficiency). This is achieved by running a stochastic frontier model on the predicted error component. As with Model 11, a constant is needed to force `sfmodel` to run, and we use `nocons` to instruct Stata not to append another constant.

```
. sfmodel error, dist(h) prod frontier(onee, nocons) usigmas() vsigmas()
. ml max, difficult gradient gtol(0.001) nrtol(0.001)

(iteration log omitted)

                                                  Number of obs   =        600
                                                  Wald chi2(1)    =     116.22
Log likelihood =  -274.1884                       Prob > chi2     =     0.0000

------------------------------------------------------------------------------
       error |      Coef.   Std. Err.      z    P>|z|     [95% Conf. Interval]
-------------+----------------------------------------------------------------
frontier     |
        onee |   .3642523    .033788    10.78   0.000      .298029    .4304755
-------------+----------------------------------------------------------------
usigmas      |
       _cons |  -1.551269   .1752633    -8.85   0.000    -1.894779   -1.207759
-------------+----------------------------------------------------------------
vsigmas      |
       _cons |  -2.616847   .1564185   -16.73   0.000    -2.923422   -2.310273
------------------------------------------------------------------------------

. sf_predict, bc(TE_R_klh)
```

In the third step, we estimate persistent efficiency. Again, we use `sfmodel` with a constant to force `sfmodel` to run.

```
. sfmodel muf, dist(h) prod frontier(onee, nocons) usigmas() vsigmas()
. ml max, difficult gradient gtol(0.001) nrtol(0.001


(iteration log omitted)

                                                  Number of obs   =        600
                                                  Wald chi2(1)    =      92.77
Log likelihood = -256.26988                       Prob > chi2     =     0.0000

------------------------------------------------------------------------------
         muf |      Coef.   Std. Err.      z    P>|z|     [95% Conf. Interval]
-------------+----------------------------------------------------------------
frontier     |
        onee |   .3610324   .0374829     9.63   0.000     .2875673    .4344976
-------------+----------------------------------------------------------------
usigmas      |
       _cons |   -1.58349   .1969817    -8.04   0.000    -1.969567   -1.197413
-------------+----------------------------------------------------------------
vsigmas      |
       _cons |    -2.7073   .1850215   -14.63   0.000    -3.069936   -2.344665
------------------------------------------------------------------------------

. sf_predict, bc(TE_P_klh) jlms(tau_mean)
```

A likelihood-ratio test of $\sigma_u = 0$ confirms σ_u to be highly significant.

```
. scalar ll_muf = e(ll)
. regress muf onee, noconst
. scalar ll_muf_ols = e(ll)
. display -2*(ll_muf_ols - ll_muf)
-17.463436

. sf_mixtable, dof(1)

critical values of the mixed chi-square distribution
```

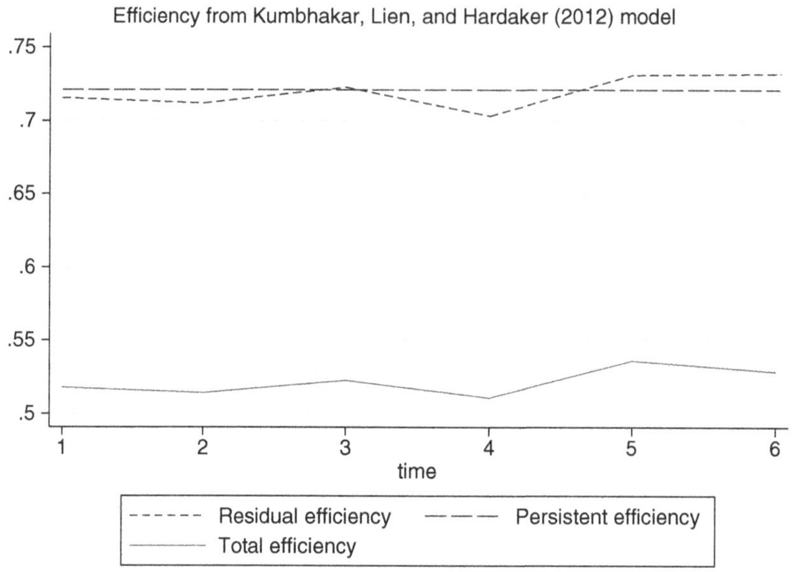

Figure 10.5. Efficiency over Time, Model 12

```
                           significance level
dof  |  0.25      0.1       0.05       0.025      0.01       0.005      0.001
---------------------------------------------------------------------------
 1      0.455     1.642     2.705      3.841      5.412      6.635      9.500

source: Table 1, Kodde and Palm (1986, Econometrica).
```

Finally, we calculate overall technical efficiency.

```
. generate OTE_klh = TE_R_klh * TE_P_klh
. summarize TE_R_klh TE_P_klh OTE_klh

    Variable |       Obs        Mean    Std. Dev.       Min        Max
-------------+--------------------------------------------------------
    TE_R_klh |       600    .7194619    .1220949   .0826049   .9336899
    TE_P_klh |       600    .7211131    .1255843   .3078475   .9010456
     OTE_klh |       600     .521729    .1336095   .0367781   .8073593
```

As illustrated in this table, persistent efficiency is estimated to be 72 percent on average, residual efficiency 72 percent, and overall efficiency 52 percent. The average (across firms) of these efficiency measures is plotted over time in Figure 10.5.

Note that persistent efficiency is now 72 percent (not 46 percent as predicted by the Kumbhakar-Heshmati formulation, residual efficiency is 72 percent (which was 74 percent in Kumbhakar-Heshmati formulation), and the overall efficiency is 52 percent (much higher than 34 percent predicted by the Kumbhakar-Heshmati formulation). In contrast, the overall efficiency is lower compared to true fixed-effects model (85%). As mentioned earlier, failure to separate firm-effects from persistent inefficiency in the true fixed-effects model is likely to produce biased estimates of overall efficiency.

11

Productivity and Profitability Decomposition

11.1 Introduction

In this chapter, we focus on the examination of changes in productivity and profitability over time and decomposing them into their constituent parts. Such analysis can help to examine the impact of policy or management decisions on efficiency and whether certain approaches are better than others at improving efficiency. For instance, such analysis can examine whether the introduction of competition, the privatization of state enterprises, the removal of trade barriers, and the introduction of regulation or deregulation have resulted in efficiency improvements or, indeed, whether evidence suggests that changes are likely to lead to future efficiency improvement.

For specific industries or individual firms, one can untangle what has driven improvement in efficiency. For example, if we were to examine efficiency in agricultural production, we could examine how efficiency has changed over time and how different farms have performed over time. We could then examine if the change in productivity for a particular farm has been driven by the farm improving its relative efficiency, by scale improvement, or by general technological improvement. Extending the analysis to an examination of profitability, one can untangle what has driven the improvement in profitability. That is, one can examine whether the increase in profitability in a particular farm was driven by efficiency improvements, or whether it was driven by other factors, such as an increase in the price of produce sold, a reduction in input prices or by the farm increasing its markup. Indeed, we use farming as a way of illustrating the approaches introduced throughout this chapter. In particular, Philippine rice farms are examined in the initial set of examples, and subsequent examples examine dairy farms in Norway.

Such questions can be important from a policy perspective, in terms of whether consumers are getting value for money through companies improving their efficiency and passing such savings on to consumers or whether companies are considered to be making excessive profits. But it can also be looked at from a forward looking perspective. For example, in many regulatory regimes across the world, regulators often set regulated companies an allowed revenue level over a fixed future period. In order to determine an appropriate allowance, regulators need to assess what a reasonable, efficient cost level should be going forward and often assess what can be achieved through catching up to best practice and what can be achieved through frontier shift. By examining recent historic trends and what has driven these, regulators can set companies reasonable expectations for future improvements. Indeed, understanding what has driven past performance may be critical if a regulator is to avoid setting overly challenging or overly lenient targets. For example, if historically the majority of a company's efficiency improvements have come from technical efficiency improvements such that it is now close to the efficiency frontier, going forward its ability to further reduce costs will be more limited as they will be predominantly focused on improvements in technology (technical change).

11.2 Productivity, Technical Efficiency, and Profitability

We start our discussion on productivity and profitability assuming that the underlying technology is the same whether we are talking about firms, regions, or countries. Although this is not realistic, the assumption of homogeneous technology is universally used. For example, in international trade theory it is assumed that technologies are the same for all the countries. In growth theory, it is assumed that countries share the same technology. Unlike other products there is no market where technologies are sold. In theoretical discussions it is implicitly assumed that technology or technologies are freely available. Homogeneous technology is not essential for our discussion of productivity and profitability in this chapter. However, to fix ideas for the discussion, we will follow the other chapters and start with the assumption that technology is homogeneous and also assume that all the producers are technically efficient. Both of these assumptions are relaxed later.

Sometimes productivity and efficiency are used interchangeably in the sense that, if a firm A is more productive than another firm B, firm A is also regarded as more efficient. This is not always true, however. Although closely related, these are two fundamentally different concepts. The difference between these two concepts can be easily illustrated using a single input, single output production technology that is common to two firms. This is illustrated in Figure 11.1.

If firm A (B) produces output level y_A (y_B) using input level x_A (x_B) then both firms are technically efficient. However, their productivity are not the same. For a single input and a single output technology, productivity is measured by the ratio of y to x (i.e., the average product, AP, of x) using the actual data. Viewed this way, the productivity measurement does not require any econometric estimation. It is clear, from Figure 11.1, that firm A is more productive than firm B (or alternatively, that the productivity of firm A is higher than that

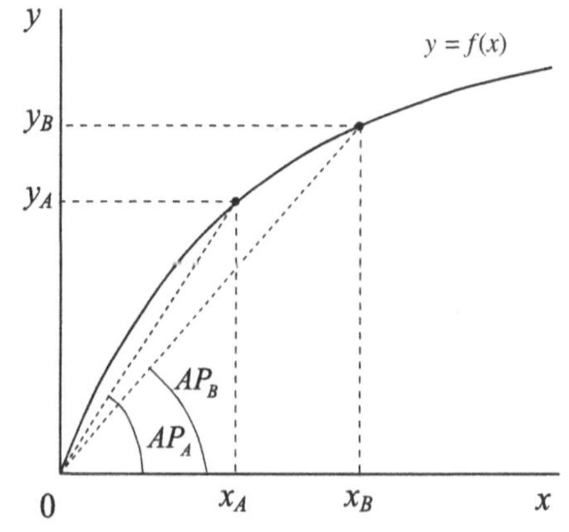

Figure 11.1. Productivity and Efficiency

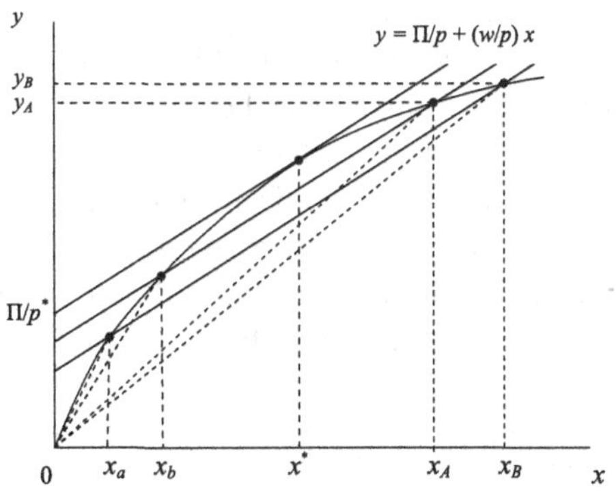

Figure 11.2. Profit Maximization

of B) because $AP_A > AP_B$. Thus, firm A is more productive, although it is not more efficient than firm B. It is clear that if the production function is concave (i.e., exhibits decreasing returns to scale), then productivity declines as more and more of the input is used unless there is a shift in the technology.

So, the question is whether the use of more inputs, or increasing the size of the firm, which is associated with declining productivity, is "bad" in some sense. Put differently, can one say that firm B (a bigger size firm) is not as "good" as firm A? This requires a definition of "good" and "bad." We use profit as the criterion of defining "good" and "bad" meaning that higher profit is "good" and lower profit is "bad."

If firms maximize profit, then the optimal use of x is given by the point of tangency between the straight line obtained by rewriting profit as $y = \pi/p + (w/p)x$ and the production function, $y = f(x)$, where w and p are input and output prices, respectively. If we denote this optimal x by x^*, then the rule is: Any firm using an input quantity less than x^* (e.g., x_a and x_b in Figure 11.2) could increase its profit by increasing the use of x, although it will reduce its productivity. That is, high productivity is associated with low profitability. On the other hand, if $x > x^*$ for both firms (e.g., x_A and x_B in Figure 11.2), then the one that is more productive is also more profitable. This can easily be seen from the vertical intercepts in Figure 11.2.

Thus, lower (higher) productivity does not necessarily mean lower (higher) profit, although we often associate high productivity with high profitability. That is, in a cross country comparison, if one says that the (labor) productivity of the United States is higher than the United Kingdom, it does not mean that the producers in the United States are more profitable than those in the United Kingdom, if they share the same technology and prices are the same.

Algebraically, we can show this by expressing differences in profit $\frac{\pi}{p}|_A - \frac{\pi}{p}|_B$ as

$$\begin{aligned} \frac{\pi}{p}|_A - \frac{\pi}{p}|_B &= x_A\left\{\frac{y}{x}|_A\right\} - x_B\left\{\frac{y}{x}|_B\right\} - (w/p)(x_A - x_B) \\ &= (x_A - x_B)(AP_A - (w/p)) + x_B(AP_A - AP_B) \end{aligned} \tag{11.1}$$

If firm A is more productive than firm B (i.e., $AP_A > AP_B$), then the second term is positive. Since the production function is concave $AP_A > AP_B \Rightarrow x_A < x_B$. However, $AP_A \gtreqless (w/p)$. Thus, the sign on the first term is indeterminate, although $x_A - x_B < 0$. The same conclusion is reached if firm B is more productive than firm A. Based on this, one can conclude that high productivity does not necessarily mean high profitability.

Now, assume that all firms in the industry use the same technology (which is the standard assumption in most studies), but they face different prices (i.e., w and p are not the same for all firms). It can easily be shown, both algebraically and graphically, that the conventional belief that high productive countries/regions/firms are more profitable is not true when firm behavior (i.e., profit maximization) is added to the technology. To show this we start with a more general case and assume that the technology as well as the prices are different. We express the difference in profits as

$$\begin{aligned}\pi_A - \pi_B &= (p_A.y_A - w_A.x_A) - (p_B.y_B - w_B.x_B)\\ &= x_A(p_A.AP_A - w_A) - x_B(p_B.AP_B - w_b)\\ &= p_A.x_A(AP_A - AP_B) + (AP_B.p_A - w_A)(x_A - x_B) + AP_B.x_B(p_A - p_B)\\ &\quad - x_B(w_A - w_B).\end{aligned} \tag{11.2}$$

Note that, if AP_A and AP_B are calculated from two different production technologies, then it is possible to have $AP_A > AP_B$ even if $x_A \lesseqqgtr x_B$. It is clear from the above expression that, even if $AP_A > AP_B$ and $x_A < x_B$, it does not guarantee that $\pi_A > \pi_B$ without knowing the sign and magnitude on the other terms. However, if the productivity difference is large (and positive) it can outweigh other negative effects and can make the profit difference positive.

It is possible to show that $AP_A > AP_B \Rightarrow \pi_A - \pi_B > 0$ if one assumes that technologies are different but prices are the same. For example, consider the extreme case when $AP_A > AP_B$ but $x_A = x_B$. This is possible because the technologies are different. In this case, all the terms except the first one drops out and, therefore, if $AP_A > AP_B$, $\pi_A - \pi_B > 0$. Thus, if country/region/firm A has a superior technology than country/region/firm B (in the sense that for all levels of x output for A is higher than B), then it is possible (see Figure 11.3) for A to be more productive and, at the same time, more profitable. Note that we assumed w and p to be the same for both countries/regions/firms in Figure 11.3, however, this assumption is not necessary for the conclusion to hold.

One can think of two other cases in which higher productivity means higher profit. First, the production function is concave but the technology is defined for $x > a$ where $a > 0$ is the minimum amount of x required to produce positive output. Second, the production

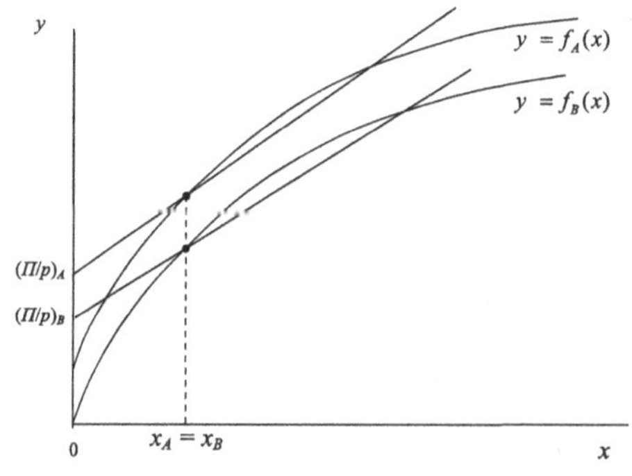

Figure 11.3. Profit Maximization with Different Technologies

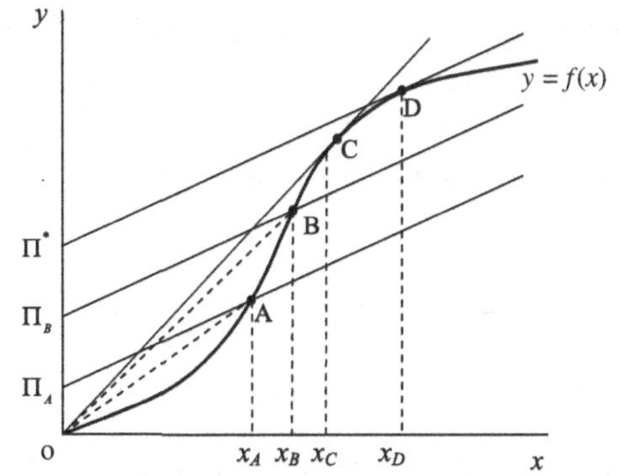

Figure 11.4. Production Function When the Minimum x Is Positive

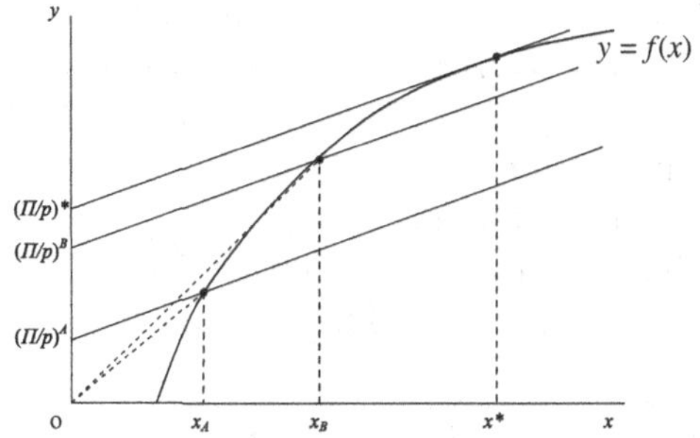

Figure 11.5. Production Function Is Nonconcave

function is not concave. In both cases, as the amount of x increases AP will increase first, then it will fall after reaching a maximum. Thus, if the amount of x used is less than the optimal x, where profit is maximized, profit will increase so long as AP increases as x increases.

The first case is shown in Figure 11.4.

To understand Figure 11.4, consider x values less than x^* and draw parallel lines through points associated with $x < x^*$, to show that profit for $x < x^*$ is less, i.e., $\frac{\pi}{p}|_x < \frac{\pi}{p}|_{x^*}$ for $x < x^*$.

For the second case, the type of nonconcave production function that we need is what is usually discussed in undergraduate microeconomics textbooks. Textbooks start with production functions that exhibit increasing returns to scale (convex) followed by constant and finally decreasing returns to scale (concave) technology. Translated into AP it means that AP increases first, then reaches the maximum, and then starts declining. This is similar to the previous case and therefore, if the amount of x used is less than the optimal x where profit is maximized, profit will increase so long as AP increases with an increase in x. This is shown in Figure 11.5.

Our discussion, so far, has assumed that firms are fully efficient. If firms are technically inefficient, then the comparison of productivity and profitability becomes more complex. If a firm is technically inefficient, then its productivity can be improved by eliminating inefficiency. This is true irrespective of how inefficiency is measured (i.e., input or output oriented). It is also true that eliminating inefficiency will increase profitability (assuming that it is costless to eliminate inefficiency), given that prices are unchanged. The difficult part is to compare productivity and profitability of two firms that are technically inefficient.

First, we examine productivity. If we write the production function as $y = f(x)e^{-u}$, then $\frac{y}{x} = \frac{f(x)}{x}e^{-u}$. Thus, the productivity difference between firm A and B, $AP_A - AP_B = \frac{y}{x}|_A - \frac{y}{x}|_B$ can be expressed as

$$\begin{aligned} AP_A - AP_B &= \left\{\frac{f(x)}{x}|_A \times e^{-u}|_A\right\} - \left\{\frac{f(x)}{x}|_B \times e^{-u}|_B\right\} \\ &= \left\{(AP_A^0 - AP_B^0)\right\} e^{-u}|_A + AP_B^0 \left\{(e^{-u}|_A - e^{-u}|_B)\right\}, \end{aligned} \tag{11.3}$$

the first term of which reflects the productivity differences at the frontier weighted by technical efficiency of firm A at the frontier and the second term is the technical efficiency differential weighted by the productivity of firm B at the frontier. Note that AP_A^0 and AP_B^0 are productivity measures for firms A and B at the frontier. Thus, even if firm A is more efficient than firm B (i.e., $e^{-u}|_A > e^{-u}|_B$ meaning that the second term is positive) we cannot say that it is also more productive (i.e. $AP_A - AP_B > 0$) because $(AP_A^0 - AP_B^0)$ can be negative. If $AP_A^0 > AP_B^0$ and firm A happens to be also more efficient, i.e., $(e^{-u}|_A > e^{-u}|_B)$, then it will be more productive than firm B. Conversely, if firm A is more productive than firm B it does not mean that firm A is also more efficient.

To examine the profitability of firms A and B we consider the following algebraic expression, instead of graphical analysis for the difference in profit, $\frac{\pi}{p}|_A - \frac{\pi}{p}|_B$, which can be rewritten as

$$\begin{aligned} \frac{\pi}{p}|_A - \frac{\pi}{p}|_B &= x_A\left\{\frac{y}{x}|_A\right\} - x_B\left\{\frac{y}{x}|_B\right\} - (w/p)(x_A - x_B) \\ &= (x_A - x_B)(AP_A - (w/p)) + x_B(AP_A - AP_B). \end{aligned} \tag{11.4}$$

Even if $AP_A > AP_B$ and $x_A > x_B$ (which is possible because of inefficiency), firm A cannot be more profitable unless $AP_A > (w/p)$. If a firm is maximizing profit ($MP = w/p$) and the production function is concave (which implies $AP > MP$), then $AP > w/P$. In general, we conclude that high productivity does not necessarily mean high profitability irrespective of whether the firms are efficient or not, unless firms are maximizing profit and there is no allocative inefficiency (which is defined as $MP \neq w/p$).

One can repeat this analysis allowing technology and prices to be different. We leave this for the reader.

So far, we used a physical measure of productivity. If the output and input are in value terms, that is, output is the value of output (revenue, R) and input is the cost of input (C), then productivity, in value terms, can be defined as $AV = R/C$, where AV can be viewed as returns to outlay. So, the question now is whether higher productivity, in value terms, means higher profitability (i.e., higher rate of return). To examine this, in terms of our two firm example, we can express the difference in profit, $\pi_A - \pi_B$, in terms of productivity differences, viz.,

$$\begin{aligned} \pi_A - \pi_B &= (R_A - C_A) - (R_B - C_B) = C_A(AV_A - 1) - C_B(AV_B - 1) \\ &= C_A(AV_A - AV_B) + (C_A - C_B)(AV_B - 1). \end{aligned} \tag{11.5}$$

Thus, even if firm A is more productive (in terms of returns to the outlay) than firm B (i.e., $AV_A - AV_B > 0$), it is not guaranteed that firm A will be more profitable (i.e., $\pi_A - \pi_B > 0$).

It is also possible to generalize the analysis to accommodate (i) single output but multiple inputs and (ii) multiple inputs and multiple output technologies. In the single output but multiple inputs case, it is important to aggregate the inputs, either in terms of costs (of inputs), or to define an input aggregator function. In the multiple inputs and multiple outputs case, it is important to either aggregate the inputs, in terms of cost, and aggregate the outputs, in terms of revenue, or to define input and output aggregator functions. These aggregator functions can be viewed as input and output indices. These indices are used in the context of the multifactor productivity (total factor productivity) decomposition discussed later.

When we move from single to multiple inputs we lose the notion of productivity as AP because now one can define AP for each input. These APs are called partial factor productivity measures. Because we do not get a single number, like y/x, it is not straightforward to compare two firms in terms of their partial factor productivity indexes. This is because it is very unlikely to have a situation where the partial factor productivity of each input for firm A will be higher than those for firm B. This problem can be avoided by defining an aggregate input X as the cost of all the inputs, i.e., $X = \sum_j w_j x_j = C$, and define productivity as if there is one input, X. Using this procedure, productivity can be defined as $y/X = y/C \equiv 1/AC$. Thus, the inverse of average cost (AC) can be used as a single measure of productivity. AC might be an appropriate measure when the objective is to minimize the cost to produce a given level of output.

Note that if the productivity of firm A, in terms of AP, is more than that of firm B (assuming a single-input, single-output technology), it does not mean that the same relationship holds in terms of AC, unless input prices are the same. That is, even if y/X for firm A is greater, it does not mean that its AC is lower. Higher input price might result in lower productivity in terms of AC.

Moving further along this line we can define a single measure of productivity as the ratio of total revenue R from all outputs and C when a multiple input, multiple output technology is used. Thus, a firm's productivity is its (gross) rate of return on outlay (R/C). The firm with a higher rate of return is deemed to be the more productive. As shown earlier, even with this definition of productivity, high productivity might not mean high profitability.

11.3 Productivity and Profitability Decomposition

While comparing productivity and profit in the preceding section, we used two firms A and B. Instead of two firms, if the comparison is for the same firm between two time periods, the difference in productivity and profit becomes changes in productivity and profit. In this section our focus is on productivity change and we relate it to efficiency and profit. The main objective is to derive components of changes in profit and productivity. In doing so we allow the firm to be technically inefficient. We will focus on whether an increase in productivity is a "good" thing for a firm in terms of profit maximizing behavior.

In a single input and single output case, productivity change is simply the difference in the rates of changes in y and x ($\dot{y}$ and $\dot{x}$), that is, $\dot{y} - \dot{x}$, where a "dot" over a variable indicates its rate of change. Even in this simple case, it is not very intuitive, for example, what a positive productivity change (productivity growth) means for an individual firm, and, for that matter, if a firm/region/country has a higher productivity growth, whether it is better (i.e., more desirable) from the point of view of profitability. To address this, we first examine the production function approach.

11.3.1 Total Factor Productivity Decomposition: The Production Function Approach

The measurement of total factor productivity (TFP) growth and its decomposition has been the subject of investigations in many empirical studies on industrial productivity (see, for example, Jorgenson [1995]). These studies have followed several well-known directions. The various approaches used in the literature have been classified by Diewert (1981) into: parametric estimation of production and cost functions, nonparametric indices, exact index numbers, and nonparametric methods using linear programming. In the nonparametric approach, the Divisia index has been widely used as a convenient measure of TFP growth over time and space. This is because of the fact that computation of the Divisia index does not require any econometric estimation. However, if one wants to decompose TFP growth into its sources such as technical change, returns to scale and efficiency changes, econometric estimation of the underlying technology is essential. We start with a production function approach.

We consider a single-output production function, which, with panel data and output-oriented technical inefficiency, is written as

$$y_{it} = f(x_{it}, t)\exp(-u_{it}), \tag{11.6}$$

where y_{it} is the output of the ith firm ($i = 1, \ldots, N$) in period t ($t = 1, \ldots, T$), $f(\cdot)$ is the production technology, x_{it} is a vector of J inputs, t is the time trend variable, and $u_{it} \geq 0$ is output-oriented technical inefficiency.

Productivity change, when there are multiple inputs, is measured by, what is popularly known as, TFP change and is defined as[1]

$$\dot{TFP} = \dot{y} - \sum_j S_j^a \dot{x}_j, \tag{11.7}$$

where $S_j^a = w_j x_j / C^a$ and $C^a = \sum_j w_j x_j$, with w_j being the price of input x_j. Differentiating (11.6) totally and using the definition of TFP change in (11.7), we get

$$\begin{aligned}
\dot{TFP} &= TC - \frac{\partial u}{\partial t} + \sum_j \left\{ \frac{f_j x_j}{f} - S_j^a \right\} \dot{x}_j \\
&= (RTS - 1)\sum_j \lambda_j \dot{x}_j + TC + TEC + \sum_j \{\lambda_j - S_j^a\}\dot{x}_j,
\end{aligned} \tag{11.8}$$

where $TC = \frac{\partial \ln f(.)}{\partial t}$, $TEC = -\frac{\partial u}{\partial t}$, $RTS = \sum_j \frac{\partial \ln y}{\partial \ln x_j} = \sum_j \frac{\partial \ln f(.)}{\partial \ln x_j} = \sum_j f_j(.) x_j / f(.) \equiv \sum_j \varepsilon_j$ is the measure of returns to scale[2] and ε_j are input elasticities defined at the production frontier, $f(x, t)$. Finally, $\lambda_j = \{f_j x_j / \sum_k f_k x_k\} = \varepsilon_j / RTS$ when f_j is the marginal product of input x_j.

[1] Subscripts i and t are omitted to avoid notational clutter.

[2] In deriving the expression for RTS it is assumed that inefficiency affects, u_{it}, are not functions of inputs.

The relationship in (11.8) decomposes TFP change into:

- scale components, $(RTS - 1)\sum_j \lambda_j \dot{x}_j$;
- technical change (TC), $\frac{\partial \ln f(.)}{\partial t}$;
- technical efficiency change (TEC), $-\frac{\partial u}{\partial t}$;
- allocative component, $\sum_j \{\lambda_j - S_j^a\}\dot{x}_j$, which capture either deviations of input prices from the value of their marginal products in the allocation of inputs, that is, $w_j \neq pf_j$, or departures of the marginal rate of technical substitution from the ratio of input prices $(f_j/f_k \neq w_j/w_k)$.

If technical inefficiency is time-invariant (i.e., $-\frac{\partial u}{\partial t} = 0$), the decomposition in (11.8) shows that TEC does not affect TFP change. Under the assumption of CRS, the TFP change formula in (11.8) is identical to the one derived in Nishimizu and Page (1982), viz.,

$$T\dot{F}P = TC - \frac{\partial u}{\partial t} + \sum_j \{\varepsilon_j - S_j^a\}\dot{x}_j. \tag{11.9}$$

As argued before, the concept of TFP change is not quite intuitive (especially from a micro perspective) because, even if TFP change for a firm is positive, it is not clear whether its profitability is increasing over time or not. To make the concept more intuitive, we examine the change in profit as a percentage of total cost as opposed to profit because actual profit is often negative. If profit is negative but the change in profit is positive (i.e., things are getting better), then the percentage change in profit will be negative and there is no way to separate this from the case in which change in profit is negative (i.e., things are getting worse) but actual profit is positive. This problem can be avoided by expressing profit change as a percentage of cost or revenue.

After total differentiation of the profit $\pi = py - w \cdot x$ and dividing both sides by C, we get

$$\frac{1}{C}\frac{d\pi}{dt} = \frac{py}{C}\{\dot{p} + \dot{y}\} - \{\sum_j S_j^a \dot{w}_j + \sum_j S_j^a \dot{x}_j\}. \tag{11.10}$$

Using the expression for TFP change in (11.7) we can express (11.10) as

$$\frac{1}{C}\frac{d\pi}{dt} = \frac{R}{C}\dot{p} + \{\frac{R}{C} - 1\}\dot{y} - \sum_j S_j^a \dot{w}_j + T\dot{F}P. \tag{11.11}$$

This gives three additional components for profitability change and these are related to output and output price changes, as well as changes in input prices. The decomposition formula in (11.11) can, alternatively, be written as

$$\begin{aligned}\frac{1}{C}\frac{d\pi}{dt} &= \dot{y}(\frac{R}{C} - 1) + (RTS - 1)\sum_j \lambda_j \dot{x}_j + TC + TEC \\ &+ \frac{R}{C}\dot{p} - \sum_j S_j \dot{w}_j + \sum (\lambda_j - S_j^a)\dot{x}_j.\end{aligned} \tag{11.12}$$

The components of profitability change in (11.12) are:

- the output growth rate component, $\dot{y}(\frac{R}{C} - 1)$, which will increase profitability if the output growth rate is positive and profit is positive;
- scale component, $(RTS - 1)\sum_j \lambda_j \dot{x}_j$, which will increase profitability if $RTS > 1$ and the aggregate input growth rate $(\sum_j \lambda_j \dot{x}_j)$ is positive;

- the TC component, $\frac{\partial \ln f(.)}{\partial t}$, which will affect profitability positively if there is technical progress;
- the TEC component, $-\frac{\partial u}{\partial t}$, which will affect profit positively if technical efficiency improves over time;
- the output price change component, $\frac{R}{C}\dot{p}$, which will affect profit positively if output price increases over time;
- the input price change component, which will affect profit positively if the aggregate input price change ($\sum_j S_j \dot{w}_j$) is negative;
- the allocative component, $\sum(\lambda_j - S_j^a)\dot{x}_j$, which will affect profit positively if allocation of inputs improves over time.

An alternative to TFP change is to simply focus on rate of change of output and examine how much of it is driven by (i) rate of changes in inputs, (ii) changes in technology, and (iii) changes in efficiency. This is a step back from the TFP change, but it might be easier to explain and is, perhaps, more intuitive. If we start from (11.6) and differentiate it totally with respect to t, we get $\dot{y} = \sum_j \epsilon_j \dot{x}_j + TC + TEC$. This shows that output growth is driven by input growth ($\sum_j \epsilon_j \dot{x}_j$), TC and TEC. Note that the part driven by input changes can be linked to returns to scale because $\sum_j \epsilon_j \dot{x}_j = RTS \sum_j \lambda_j \dot{x}_j + \sum_j \lambda_j \dot{x}_j$.

We examine this approach first, in the following example, before examining the TFP change approach.

Example

This example uses data on Philippine rice farms. We use four inputs: `l` (labor, in person days), `k` (area cultivated, in hectares), `f` (fertilizer used, in kg of active ingredients), and `m` (other materials used; an index based on seed, insecticides, herbicides, animals, and tractors used during land preparation). A time variable, `t`, is also considered in the model. Output, `y`, is the quantity of freshly threshed rice (in tonnes). We add `l` in front of the variable name to indicate the logarithm level of the variable. For instance, `lk` is the log of capital. This is a panel dataset (the farmer identification is provided in `farmtag`), but we estimate it as pooled cross section.

We do not introduce any new commands in these examples. The only new element is the subsequent calculations to estimate rate of change of output, TFP change, profitability change and their respective components, after estimating the models. As such, we focus, primarily, on explaining the postestimation calculations in the following examples.

Model 1: Output Growth Approach

We begin by estimating a Cobb-Douglas production function.

```
. global xvar_cd ll lk lf lm t
. regress ly $xvar_cd

      Source |       SS       df       MS              Number of obs =     344
-------------+------------------------------           F(  5,   338) =  415.54
       Model |  226.650035     5  45.3300069           Prob > F      =  0.0000
    Residual |  36.8715166   338  .109087327           R-squared     =  0.8601
-------------+------------------------------           Adj R-squared =  0.8580
       Total |  263.521551   343  .768284406           Root MSE      =  .33028
```

```
------------------------------------------------------------------------------
          ly |      Coef.   Std. Err.      t    P>|t|     [95% Conf. Interval]
-------------+----------------------------------------------------------------
          ll |   .3937272   .0666311     5.91   0.000     .2626633    .5247912
          lk |   .3258236   .0646837     5.04   0.000     .1985904    .4530568
          lf |   .2681355   .0415334     6.46   0.000     .1864389     .349832
          lm |   .0093745   .0212492     0.44   0.659    -.0324227    .0511718
           t |   .0090105   .0083812     1.08   0.283    -.0074754    .0254964
       _cons |  -1.718961     .25162    -6.83   0.000    -2.213899   -1.224023
------------------------------------------------------------------------------

. matrix b0 = e(b)

. sfmodel ly, prod dist(h) frontier($xvar_cd) usigmas(t) vsigmas()
. sf_init, frontier(b0) usigmas(0 0) vsigmas(0)
. ml max, difficult gtol(1e-5) nrtol(1e-5)

(iteration log omitted)

                                                  Number of obs   =        344
                                                  Wald chi2(5)    =    2393.40
Log likelihood = -81.608608                       Prob > chi2     =     0.0000

------------------------------------------------------------------------------
          ly |      Coef.   Std. Err.      z    P>|z|     [95% Conf. Interval]
-------------+----------------------------------------------------------------
frontier     |
          ll |   .3453447   .0631893     5.47   0.000     .2214959    .4691935
          lk |   .3277085   .0609055     5.38   0.000      .208336    .4470811
          lf |   .2560365   .0349676     7.32   0.000     .1875014    .3245716
          lm |   .0257792    .018782     1.37   0.170    -.0110328    .0625911
           t |   .0187282   .0082775     2.26   0.024     .0025047    .0349517
       _cons |  -1.188983   .2593305    -4.58   0.000    -1.697261   -.6807042
-------------+----------------------------------------------------------------
usigmas      |
           t |   .0667334    .043556     1.53   0.125    -.0186347    .1521015
       _cons |  -1.813351   .2486658    -7.29   0.000    -2.300726   -1.325975
-------------+----------------------------------------------------------------
vsigmas      |
       _cons |  -3.782811   .2574219   -14.69   0.000    -4.287348   -3.278273
------------------------------------------------------------------------------

. sf_predict, bc(bc_cd) jlms(jlms_cd) marginal

The following is the marginal effect on unconditional E(u).

The average marginal effect of t on uncond E(u) is .01253046 (see t_M).

The following is the marginal effect on uncond V(u).

The average marginal effect of t on uncond V(u) is .00540331 (see t_V).
```

Next, we compute output growth and its components: technical change, input-driven growth, and efficiency change

```
. sort fmercode
. by fmercode: generate dot_y = (y-y[_n-1])/(.5*(y+y[_n-1]))
(43 missing values generated)

. generate TC = _b[t] if farmtag ~= 1
(43 missing values generated)

. generate input_driven_growth = _b[ll]*dot_l + _b[lk]*dot_k + _b[lf]*dot_f + _b[lm]*dot_m
(43 missing values generated)

. generate TEC = t_M if farmtag ~= 1
(43 missing values generated)
```

Summing technical change, input-driven growth, and efficiency change gives the explained output change.

```
. generate expl_output_change = TC + input_driven_growth +TEC
(43 missing values generated)

. generate unexpl_output_change = dot_y - expl_output_change
(43 missing values generated)

. summarize dot_y  TC input_driven_growth TEC expl_output_change unexpl_output_change

    Variable |       Obs        Mean    Std. Dev.       Min        Max
-------------+--------------------------------------------------------
       dot_y |       301    .0206575    .4138526  -1.686957   1.094017
          TC |       301    .0187282           0   .0187282   .0187282
input_driv~h |       301   -.0085464    .2227392  -1.337619   .7135305
         TEC |       301    .0127324    .0008507    .011494   .0140416
expl_outpu~e |       301    .0229142    .2227265  -1.305755   .7453938
-------------+--------------------------------------------------------
unexpl_out~e |       301   -.0022567    .3563205  -1.018947   1.150445
```

This demonstrates, that output growth, of around 2.1 percent, has been driven by technical progress, of 1.9 percent, as well as technical efficiency change, of 1.3 percent, offset by a 0.9 percent reduction in inputs.

We now examine the TFP change approach.

Model 2: OLS Production Function

First, we run an OLS regression using a translog functional form. For the notations, `lk2` is the square of `lk` multiplied by $\frac{1}{2}$, `tt` is also the square of `t` multiplied by $\frac{1}{2}$, and `lklf` is the product of `lk` and `lf`. Other variables are similarly defined.

```
. use rice.dta, replace

. global xvar_prod ll lk lf lm ll2 lk2 lf2 lm2 lllk lllf lllm lklf lklm ///
> lflm t tt tll tlk tlf tlm

. regress ly $xvar_prod

      Source |       SS       df       MS              Number of obs =     344
-------------+------------------------------           F( 20,   323) =  112.52
       Model |  230.445492    20  11.5222746           Prob > F      =  0.0000
    Residual |  33.0760592   323   .10240266           R-squared     =  0.8745
-------------+------------------------------           Adj R-squared =  0.8667
       Total |  263.521551   343  .768284406           Root MSE      =     .32

------------------------------------------------------------------------------
          ly |      Coef.   Std. Err.      t    P>|t|     [95% Conf. Interval]
-------------+----------------------------------------------------------------
          ll |   3.941985   .9439771     4.18   0.000     2.084866    5.799105
          lk |  -2.502061   1.034796    -2.42   0.016    -4.537852   -.4662692
          lf |   1.169408   .5912926     1.98   0.049     .0061368    2.332679
          lm |  -.2279761   .3251042    -0.70   0.484    -.8675653     .411613
         ll2 |  -.7148922   .3110148    -2.30   0.022    -1.326763   -.1030216
         lk2 |  -.4316089   .3193024    -1.35   0.177    -1.059784    .1965661
         lf2 |   .0585541   .1029839     0.57   0.570    -.1440498    .2611579
         lm2 |   .0180417   .0463785     0.39   0.698    -.0732003    .1092837
        lllk |   .6402475   .2372383     2.70   0.007     .1735201    1.106975
        lllf |  -.2446499   .1482602    -1.65   0.100    -.5363275    .0470278
        lllm |   .0541818   .0767844     0.71   0.481    -.0968788    .2052425
        lklf |   .0911146   .1559011     0.58   0.559    -.2155952    .3978244
        lklm |  -.0272037   .0817303    -0.33   0.739    -.1879945    .1335872
        lflm |   -.007587   .0419918    -0.18   0.857     -.090199     .075025
```

```
          t |   .0234492    .1234279     0.19   0.849    -.2193748    .2662733
         tt |   .0098551    .0088699     1.11   0.267    -.0075949    .0273052
        tll |   .0292619     .030996     0.94   0.346    -.0317175    .0902414
        tlk |   .0061607    .0310184     0.20   0.843     -.054863    .0671843
        tlf |  -.0379764    .0207196    -1.83   0.068    -.0787388    .0027861
        tlm |  -.0016961    .0115746    -0.15   0.884    -.0244672    .0210751
      _cons |  -10.23977    1.861767    -5.50   0.000    -13.90249   -6.577047
------------------------------------------------------------------------------

. matrix b1 = e(b)
```

We then compute the cost shares and the growth rates of the inputs and their prices (as well as an indicator variable for subsequent use).

```
. generate S1 = (wl*labor)/tc
. generate S2 = (wk*area)/tc
. generate S3 = (wf*npk)/tc
. generate S4 = (wm*other)/tc

. by fmercode: generate dot_l = (labor-labor[_n-1])/(.5*(labor+labor[_n-1]))
. by fmercode: generate dot_k = (area-area[_n-1])/(.5*(area+area[_n-1]))
. by fmercode: generate dot_f = (npk-npk[_n-1])/(.5*(npk+npk[_n-1]))
. by fmercode: generate dot_m = (other-other[_n-1])/(.5*(other+other[_n-1]))

. by fmercode: generate dot_wl = (wl-wl[_n-1])/(.5*(wl+wl[_n-1]))
. by fmercode: generate dot_wk = (wk-wk[_n-1])/(.5*(wk+wk[_n-1]))
. by fmercode: generate dot_wf = (wf-wf[_n-1])/(.5*(wf+wf[_n-1]))
. by fmercode: generate dot_wm = (wm-wm[_n-1])/(.5*(wm+wm[_n-1]))

. by fmercode: generate dot_w =  S1*dot_wl + S2*dot_wk + S3*dot_wf + S4*dot_wm

. sort fmercode year
. egen farmtag = tag(fmercode)
```

We now compute TFP and its components, using equation (11.8), without technical efficiency change (TEC). First, we compute the scale component, which itself is composed of several elements. We then compute returns to scale, $RTS = \sum_j \varepsilon_j$, where $\varepsilon_j = \frac{\partial \ln f(.)}{\partial \ln x_j}$.

```
. generate eta_l = _b[ll] + _b[ll2]*ll + _b[lllk]*lk + _b[lllf]*lf + _b[lllm]*lm + _b[tll]*t
. generate eta_k = _b[lk] + _b[lk2]*lk + _b[lllk]*ll + _b[lklf]*lf + _b[lklm]*lm + _b[tlk]*t
. generate eta_f = _b[lf] + _b[lf2]*lf + _b[lllf]*ll + _b[lklf]*lk + _b[lflm]*lm + _b[tlf]*t
. generate eta_m = _b[lm] + _b[lm2]*lm + _b[lllm]*ll + _b[lklm]*lk + _b[lflm]*lf + _b[tlm]*t

. generate RTS = eta_l + eta_k + eta_f + eta_m
```

The following provides $\lambda_j = \varepsilon_j / RTS$:

```
. generate lambda_l = eta_l / RTS
. generate lambda_k = eta_k / RTS
. generate lambda_f = eta_f / RTS
. generate lambda_m = eta_m / RTS
```

The scale component, $(RTS - 1) \sum_j \lambda_j \dot{x}_j$, is then given by

```
. generate sum_lambda_dotx = (lambda_l)*dot_l + (lambda_k)*dot_k  + (lambda_f)*dot_f ///
> + (lambda_m)*dot_m

. generate scale = (RTS - 1) * sum_lambda_dotx
```

We now compute technical change or frontier shift, $TC = \frac{\partial \ln f(.)}{\partial t}$. Note that we ignore the first year in its computation for consistency with the other calculated components, which also do not include the first year given the use of lagged terms. This is done by using the "`if farmtag ~= 1`" statement in the following code.

```
. generate TC =  _b[t] + _b[tt]*t + _b[tll]*ll + _b[tlk]*lk + _b[tlf]*lf  + _b[tlm]*lm ///
> if farmtag ~= 1
```

We next compute the allocative component, $\sum_j \{\lambda_j - S_j^a\}\dot{x}_j$.

```
. generate allocative  = (lambda_l - S1)*dot_l + (lambda_k - S2)*dot_k  ///
> + (lambda_f - S3)*dot_f + (lambda_m - S4)*dot_m
```

There is no estimated inefficiency in this model, and, thus, no technical efficiency change component, so we have now computed all the necessary components to calculate TFP growth. We compute TFP as the sum of these components (see equation (11.8), without the technical efficiency change component).

```
. generate TFP = scale + TC + allocative

. summarize scale TC allocative TFP

    Variable |       Obs        Mean    Std. Dev.       Min        Max
-------------+--------------------------------------------------------
       scale |       301   -.0073368    .0491582  -.5539713   .3062518
          TC |       301    .0133175    .0248081   -.045981   .0937182
  allocative |       301   -.0315634     .155058  -1.509872   .4192818
         TFP |       301   -.0255826    .1657012  -1.167479   .4461955
```

Overall, although there has been some technical progress (TC is positive), it appears as though TFP has been declining, driven, primarily, by a negative allocative component.

We now introduce inefficiency into the model.

Model 3: Half-Normal Stochastic Production Frontier Model

We introduce technical inefficiency in the model using a half-normal stochastic frontier model with a time trend in the σ_u^2 term.

```
. sfmodel ly, prod dist(h) frontier($xvar_prod) usigmas(t) vsigmas()
. sf_init, frontier(b1) usigmas(0 0) vsigmas(0)
. ml max, difficult  gtol(1e-5) nrtol(1e-5)

(iteration log omitted)

  Number of obs    =          344
                                                  Wald chi2(20)    =    2833.70
Log likelihood = -67.428384                       Prob > chi2      =     0.0000

------------------------------------------------------------------------------
          ly |      Coef.   Std. Err.      z    P>|z|     [95% Conf. Interval]
-------------+----------------------------------------------------------------
frontier     |
          ll |   2.882543   .7352215     3.92   0.000     1.441536    4.323551
          lk |   -2.60575   .8937778    -2.92   0.004    -4.357523   -.8539782
          lf |   1.133138   .5981362     1.89   0.058    -.0391877    2.305463
          lo |   .0916537   .2917517     0.31   0.753    -.4801691    .6634765
         ll2 |  -.4876412   .2640281    -1.85   0.065    -1.005127    .0298445
         lk2 |  -.6286541   .2814786    -2.23   0.026    -1.180342   -.0769663
         lf2 |   .0086094    .091095     0.09   0.925    -.1699334    .1871523
         lo2 |   .0209883   .0406645     0.52   0.606    -.0587126    .1006892
        lllk |   .6000871   .1779498     3.37   0.001      .251312    .9488622
        lllf |  -.1699433   .1495637    -1.14   0.256    -.4630828    .1231962
```

```
        lllo |  -.0072964   .0674437    -0.11   0.914    -.1394835    .1248908
        lklf |   .1124761   .1511115     0.74   0.457     -.183697    .4086491
        lklo |    .039595   .0758925     0.52   0.602    -.1091516    .1883417
        lflo |   -.028495    .036417    -0.78   0.434     -.099871    .0428811
           t |   .0092059   .1053537     0.09   0.930    -.1972836    .2156953
          tt |   .0151033   .0078265     1.93   0.054    -.0002364     .030443
         tll |   .0198269   .0272709     0.73   0.467    -.0336231     .073277
         tlk |  -.0005062    .026416    -0.02   0.985    -.0522807    .0512682
         tlf |  -.0318502   .0182437    -1.75   0.081    -.0676072    .0039067
         tlo |   .0018944   .0103569     0.18   0.855    -.0184047    .0221935
       _cons |  -8.110231    1.61929    -5.01   0.000    -11.28398   -4.936481
-------------+----------------------------------------------------------------
usigmas      |
           t |   .0659044   .0454667     1.45   0.147    -.0232087    .1550176
       _cons |  -1.895363   .2579022    -7.35   0.000    -2.400842   -1.389884
-------------+----------------------------------------------------------------
vsigmas      |
       _cons |  -3.858443    .269995   -14.29   0.000    -4.387623   -3.329262
------------------------------------------------------------------------------

. sf_predict, bc(bc2_h) jlms(jlms2_h) marginal

The following is the marginal effect on unconditional E(u).

The average marginal effect of t on uncond E(u) is .01185464 (see t_M).

The following is the marginal effect on uncond V(u).

The average marginal effect of t on uncond V(u) is .00489631 (see t_V).
```

We now compute TFP and its components, using equation (11.8). First, we compute the scale component, $(RTS - 1)\sum_j \lambda_j \dot{x}_j$, where $RTS = \sum_j \varepsilon_j$, $\lambda_j = \varepsilon_j / RTS$ and $\varepsilon_j = \frac{\partial \ln f(.)}{\partial \ln x_j}$, using the same code as we used for Model 2.

```
. generate eta_l = _b[ll] + _b[ll2]*ll + _b[lllk]*lk + _b[lllf]*lf + _b[lllm]*lm + _b[tll]*t
. generate eta_k = _b[lk] + _b[lk2]*lk + _b[lllk]*ll + _b[lklf]*lf + _b[lklm]*lm + _b[tlk]*t
. generate eta_f = _b[lf] + _b[lf2]*lf + _b[lllf]*ll + _b[lklf]*lk + _b[lflm]*lm + _b[tlf]*t
. generate eta_m = _b[lm] + _b[lm2]*lm + _b[lllm]*ll + _b[lklm]*lk + _b[lflm]*lf + _b[tlm]*t

. generate RTS = eta_l + eta_k + eta_f + eta_m

. generate lambda_l = eta_l / RTS
. generate lambda_k = eta_k / RTS
. generate lambda_f = eta_f / RTS
. generate lambda_m = eta_m / RTS

. generate sum_lambda_dotx = (lambda_l)*dot_l + (lambda_k)*dot_k  + (lambda_f)*dot_f ///
> + (lambda_m)*dot_m

. generate scale = (RTS - 1) * sum_lambda_dotx
```

Again, using the same code as we used for Model 2, we also compute technical change or frontier shift, $\frac{\partial \ln f(.)}{\partial t}$, and the allocative component, $\sum_j \{\lambda_j - S_j^a\}\dot{x}_j$.

```
. generate TC =  _b[t] + _b[tt]*t + _b[tll]*ll + _b[tlk]*lk + _b[tlf]*lf + _b[tlm]*lm ///
> if farmtag ~= 1

. generate allocative  = (lambda_l - S1)*dot_l + (lambda_k - S2)*dot_k  ///
> + (lambda_f - S3)*dot_f + (lambda_m - S4)*dot_m
```

We next compute the additional component in this model, i.e. the technical efficiency change component, $-\frac{\partial u}{\partial t}$. The marginal of $E(u)$ is given by the values of the marginal effect of t on

$E(u)$. With the `marginal` option used in `sf_predict`, the program saves the marginal effect of t on $E(u)$ as `t_M`.

```
. generate TEC =  t_M if farmtag ~= 1
```

Finally, we can now compute TFP as the sum of these components (see equation (11.8)).

```
. generate TFP = scale + TC + TEC + allocative

. summarize scale TC TEC allocative TFP

    Variable |       Obs        Mean    Std. Dev.       Min        Max
-------------+--------------------------------------------------------
       scale |       301   -.0007015    .0215016  -.1514312   .1506687
          TC |       301    .0251492    .0335054  -.0491073   .0996801
         TEC |       301    .0120434    .0007946   .0108861    .013266
  allocative |       301   -.0287965    .1316219  -1.104978   .4279563
         TFP |       301    .0076946    .1303307  -.9584957   .4249167
```

Having introduced inefficiency into the model, it now appears as though TFP has been slightly increasing, driven, primarily, by positive technical change and technical efficiency change more than offsetting the negative price effect.

These components are plotted in Figure 11.6.

At this point we could also extend this to provide a decomposition of profitability change using equation (11.12); however, given the similarity of the additional components we will leave this for the example using the cost function approach, which we turn to next.

11.3.2 Productivity Decomposition: The Cost Function Approach

With the explicit cost minimization behavioral assumptions, the technology is often specified by the dual the cost function $C = C(w, y, t)e^{\eta}$ where $\eta \geq 0$ is input-oriented technical inefficiency. Differentiating it totally gives:

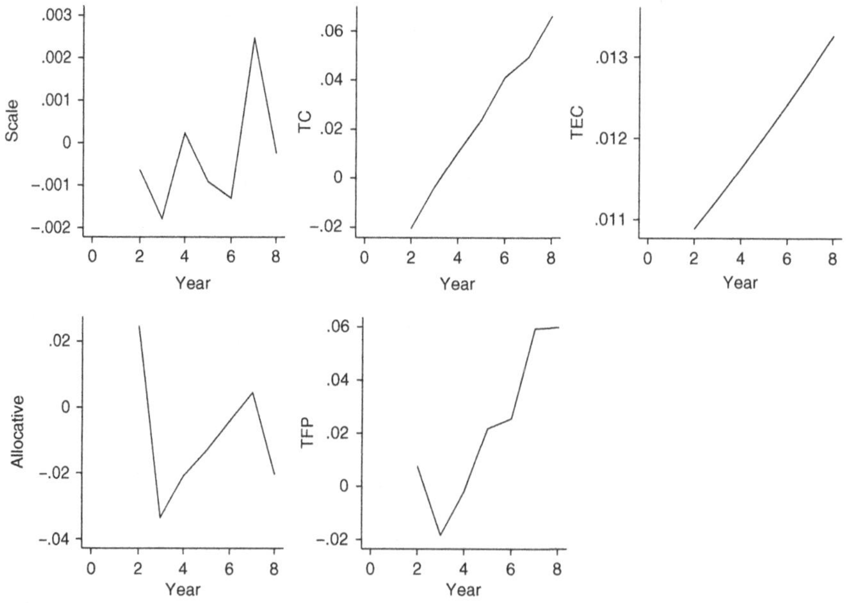

Figure 11.6. TFP Decomposition Using a Production Function

$$\dot{C}^a = \sum_j \frac{\partial \ln C}{\partial \ln w_j}\dot{w}_j + \frac{\partial \ln C}{\partial \ln y}\dot{y} + \frac{\partial \ln C}{\partial t} + \frac{\partial \eta}{\partial t}$$
$$= \sum S_j^a \dot{w}_j + \frac{1}{RTS}\dot{y} - TC - TEC, \tag{11.13}$$

where $\frac{1}{RTS} = \frac{\partial \ln C}{\partial \ln y}$, $TC = -\frac{\partial \ln C}{\partial t}$, $TEC = -\frac{\partial \eta}{\partial t}$, and using Shepherd's lemma: $\frac{\partial \ln C}{\partial \ln w_j} = \frac{w_j}{C}x_j = S_j^a$.

Differentiating $C^a = w'x$ gives

$$\dot{C}^a = \sum_j S_j^a(\dot{w}_j + \dot{x}_j). \tag{11.14}$$

Equating (11.13) and (11.14) gives

$$\dot{TFP} = \dot{y} - \sum_j S_j^a \dot{x}_j = \dot{y}(1 - RTS^{-1}) + TC + TEC, \tag{11.15}$$

which is used to compute the components of TFP growth after estimating the cost function. The components in (11.15) are:

- scale, $\dot{y}(1 - RTS^{-1})$;
- TC, $-\frac{\partial \ln C}{\partial t}$;
- TEC, $-\frac{\partial \eta}{\partial t}$.

We can use (11.15) to express profitability change in (11.11) as

$$\frac{1}{C}\frac{d\pi}{dt} = \frac{R}{C}\dot{p} + \frac{R}{C}\dot{y} - \sum_j S_j^a \dot{w}_j + \dot{TFP}, \tag{11.16}$$

where $\dot{TFP}$ in (11.16) is given in (11.15). Note that if one uses data to compute $\dot{TFP}$ (known as the Divisia index: $\dot{y} - \sum S_j^a \dot{x}_j$), then there is nothing to estimate in (11.16): Every component can be directly computed from the data. In doing so, one cannot get components such as RTS, TC, and TEC. To do so, we rewrite (11.16) using (11.15) as:

$$\frac{1}{C}\frac{d\pi}{dt} = \frac{R}{C}\dot{p} + (\frac{R}{C} - 1)\dot{y} - \sum_j S_j^a \dot{w}_j + \dot{y}(1 - \frac{1}{RTS}) + TC + TEC. \tag{11.17}$$

The components in (11.17) are:

- output price change, $\frac{R}{C}\dot{p}$;
- output change, $(\frac{R}{C} - 1)\dot{y}$;
- input price change, $-\sum_j S_j^a \dot{w}_j$;
- scale, $\dot{y}(1 - \frac{1}{RTS})$;
- TC, $-\frac{\partial \ln C}{\partial t}$;
- TEC, $-\frac{\partial \eta}{\partial t}$.

Note that in (11.17), RTS (and, hence, the scale component), TC, and TEC are estimated from a cost function (not directly from the data), while the other components (output price change, ouput change and input price change) can be computed directly from the data.

If there are quasi-fixed inputs Z, then the variable cost function can be written as $C(y, w, z, t)e^{\eta}$ and the $\dot{TFP}$ formula in (11.15) will have a $\dot{Z}$ component, where

$$\dot{Z} = -\sum_{q} \frac{\partial \ln C}{\partial \ln Z_q} \dot{Z}_q,$$

and, in (11.17), we will have an extra term $\dot{Z}$, which cannot be directly obtained from data. That is, this component can be computed using the estimated cost function and data on Z_q.

Example

This example again uses data on Philippine rice farms, but instead uses a cost function approach. We use the prices and quantities of the inputs to construct total cost (`tc`). The price of land (i.e., the rental price) is used as the numeraire (to impose linear homogeneity constraints). To impose linear homogeneity (in input prices), we normalize input prices and total cost by `wk`. We denote normalized input prices as `lwjD` = log(`wj`/`wk`), j=`l`,f,m; normalized cost `ltcD` =log(`tc`/`wk`); `ly` =log(`y`); and `lylwjD`=`ly`*`lwjD`, j= `l`, `f`, `m`.

Model 4: OLS Cost Function

First, we run an OLS regression using a translog functional form.

```
. global xvar ly ly2 lwlD lwfD lwmD lwlD2 lwfD2 lwmD2 lwlfD lwlmD lwfmD ///
. lylwlD lylwfD lylwmD t tt tly tlwlD tlwfD tlwmD

. regress ltcD $xvar

      Source |       SS       df       MS              Number of obs =     344
-------------+------------------------------           F( 20,    323) =  303.58
       Model |  246.080115    20  12.3040058           Prob > F      =  0.0000
    Residual |  13.0909236   323  .040529175           R-squared     =  0.9495
-------------+------------------------------           Adj R-squared =  0.9464
       Total |  259.171039   343  .755600696           Root MSE      =  .20132

------------------------------------------------------------------------------
        ltcD |      Coef.   Std. Err.      t    P>|t|     [95% Conf. Interval]
-------------+----------------------------------------------------------------
          ly |   .9053708   .1136954     7.96   0.000     .6816938    1.129048
         ly2 |   .0581959   .0296829     1.96   0.051    -.0002004    .1165921
        lwlD |   1.497606   .2359315     6.35   0.000      1.03345    1.961763
        lwfD |  -.0469061   .2917939    -0.16   0.872    -.6209627    .5271505
        lwmD |   .1933562    .126048     1.53   0.126    -.0546225    .4413348
       lwlD2 |   .0269912   .1021402     0.26   0.792    -.1739529    .2279353
       lwfD2 |  -.2971075   .1046145    -2.84   0.005    -.5029194   -.0912956
       lwmD2 |  -.0342542   .0374908    -0.91   0.362    -.1080111    .0395027
       lwlfD |   .1867871   .0836233     2.23   0.026     .0222719    .3513023
       lwlmD |  -.0232073   .0390378    -0.59   0.553    -.1000078    .0535933
       lwfmD |   .0756403    .045541     1.66   0.098     -.013954    .1652347
      lylwlD |  -.0733812   .0393733    -1.86   0.063    -.1508416    .0040793
      lylwfD |   .0656624   .0400449     1.64   0.102    -.0131194    .1444441
      lylwmD |  -.0016971   .0184437    -0.09   0.927    -.0379822    .0345879
           t |  -.0091644   .0485848    -0.19   0.851    -.1047471    .0864183
          tt |    .008154   .0063199     1.29   0.198    -.0042793    .0205874
         tly |   .0053297    .006923     0.77   0.442     -.00829     .0189495
       tlwlD |  -.0129893   .0182213    -0.71   0.476    -.0488368    .0228581
       tlwfD |   .0065446   .0173686     0.38   0.707    -.0276253    .0407144
       tlwmD |   .0021294   .0086114     0.25   0.805    -.0148121    .0190708
       _cons |   5.657004    .527502    10.72   0.000     4.619231    6.694777
------------------------------------------------------------------------------

. matrix b3 = e(b)
```

Before proceeding, we compute the growth rate of output (if this has not already been calculated) and price.

```
. by fmercode: generate dot_y = (y-y[_n-1])/(.5*(y+y[_n-1]))
. by fmercode: generate dot_price = (price-price[_n-1])/(.5*(price+price[_n-1]))
```

We now use the estimated parameters from the OLS model to compute TFP and its components, using equation (11.15). We compute the scale component, $\dot{y}(1 - RTS^{-1})$, where $\frac{1}{RTS} = \frac{\partial \ln C}{\partial \ln y}$.

```
. generate inv_RTS =_b[ly] + _b[ly2]*ly + _b[lylwlD]*lwlD + _b[lylwfD]*lwfD ///
> + _b[lylwmD]*lwmD +_b[tly]*t

. generate scale = (1-inv_RTS)*dot_y
```

We then compute technical change or frontier shift, $-\frac{\partial \ln C}{\partial t}$.

```
. generate TC = - _b[t] - _b[tt]*t - _b[tly]*ly - _b[tlwlD]*lwlD - _b[tlwfD]*lwfD ///
> - _b[tlwmD]*lwmD
```

There is no technical efficiency change in this model, so we can go straight to computing TFP as the sum of these components (see equation (11.15), without technical efficiency change).

```
. generate TFP = scale + TC

. summarize scale TC TFP

    Variable |       Obs        Mean    Std. Dev.       Min        Max
-------------+--------------------------------------------------------
       scale |       301   -.0052503    .0404602  -.4707492   .0966097
          TC |       301    -.045864    .0182219  -.0797331   .0021033
         TFP |       301   -.0511143    .0438856  -.5070245   .0475513
```

Overall, it appears as though TFP has been declining, driven, primarily, due to technical regress.

We now introduce inefficiency into the model.

Model 5: Half-Normal Stochastic Cost Frontier Model

We introduce inefficiency into the model using a half-normal stochastic frontier model with a time trend in the σ_u^2 term.

```
. sfmodel ltcD, cost dist(h) frontier($xvar) usigmas(t) vsigmas()
. sf_init, frontier(b3) usigmas(0 0) vsigmas(0)
. ml max, difficult gtol(1e-5) nrtol(1e-5)

(iteration log omitted)

                                                  Number of obs   =        344
                                                  Wald chi2(20)   =    6426.85
Log likelihood =  76.323711                       Prob > chi2     =     0.0000

------------------------------------------------------------------------------
        ltcD |      Coef.   Std. Err.      z    P>|z|     [95% Conf. Interval]
-------------+----------------------------------------------------------------
frontier     |
          ly |   .9123888   .1105191     8.26   0.000     .6957753    1.129002
         ly2 |   .0601157    .028627     2.10   0.036     .0040078    .1162236
        lwlD |   1.501748   .2272659     6.61   0.000     1.056315    1.947181
```

```
        lwfD |  -.0482556    .280243    -0.17   0.863    -.5975219    .5010106
        lwmD |   .1988521   .1207181     1.65   0.100     -.037751    .4354552
       lwlD2 |   .0236079   .0975968     0.24   0.809    -.1676783     .214894
       lwfD2 |  -.2981554   .1000147    -2.98   0.003    -.4941806   -.1021301
       lwmD2 |   -.033892   .0360626    -0.94   0.347    -.1045735    .0367895
       lwlfD |   .1898241   .0799377     2.37   0.018      .033149    .3464992
       lwlmD |  -.0230675   .0372183    -0.62   0.535     -.096014    .0498789
       lwfmD |   .0757554    .043752     1.73   0.083    -.0099969    .1615078
      lylwlD |  -.0657151   .0379708    -1.73   0.084    -.1401365    .0087062
      lylwfD |   .0606447   .0385155     1.57   0.115    -.0148443    .1361337
      lylwmD |  -.0018066   .0176491    -0.10   0.918    -.0363981    .0327849
           t |   .0588873   .0599537     0.98   0.326    -.0586199    .1763945
          tt |  -.0030291   .0076016    -0.40   0.690    -.0179281    .0118698
         tly |   .0044898   .0067731     0.66   0.507    -.0087852    .0177648
       tlwlD |   -.012386   .0178619    -0.69   0.488    -.0473947    .0226227
       tlwfD |   .0071161   .0170714     0.42   0.677    -.0263432    .0405755
       tlwmD |   .0017316   .0083786     0.21   0.836    -.0146901    .0181534
       _cons |   5.486559    .515563    10.64   0.000     4.476074    6.497044
-------------+----------------------------------------------------------------
usigmas      |
           t |  -2.777637   1.651996    -1.68   0.093    -6.015489    .4602148
       _cons |  -.9110648   1.601773    -0.57   0.570    -4.050481    2.228352
-------------+----------------------------------------------------------------
vsigmas      |
       _cons |  -3.305961   .0803336   -41.15   0.000    -3.463412    -3.14851
------------------------------------------------------------------------------

. sf_predict, bc(bc4_h) jlms (jlms4_h) marginal

The following is the marginal effect on unconditional E(u).

The average marginal effect of t on uncond E(u) is -.02917908 (see t_M).

The following is the marginal effect on uncond V(u).

The average marginal effect of t on uncond V(u) is -.00336393 (see t_V).
```

We next compute TFP and its components, using equation (11.15). We compute the scale component, $\dot{y}(1 - RTS^{-1})$, where $\frac{1}{RTS} = \frac{\partial \ln C}{\partial \ln y}$, using the same code as we used for Model 4.

```
. generate inv_RTS = _b[ly] + _b[ly2]*ly + _b[lylwlD]*lwlD + _b[lylwfD]*lwfD ///
> + _b[lylwmD]*lwmD +_b[tly]*t

. generate scale = (1-inv_RTS)*dot_y
```

Again, using the same code as we used for Model 4, we now compute technical change or frontier shift, $-\frac{\partial \ln C}{\partial t}$.

```
. generate TC = - _b[t] - _b[tt]*t - _b[tly]*ly - _b[tlwlD]*lwlD - _b[tlwfD]*lwfD ///
> - _b[tlwmD]*lwmD
```

We next compute the additional component in this model, i.e., the technical efficiency change component, $\frac{\partial \eta}{\partial t}$. The marginal of $E(u)$ is given by the values of marginal effect of t on $E(u)$. With the "marginal" option, the program saves the marginal effect of t on E(u) as t_M.

```
. generate TEC = - t_M
```

Finally, we can compute TFP as the sum of these components (see equation (11.15)).

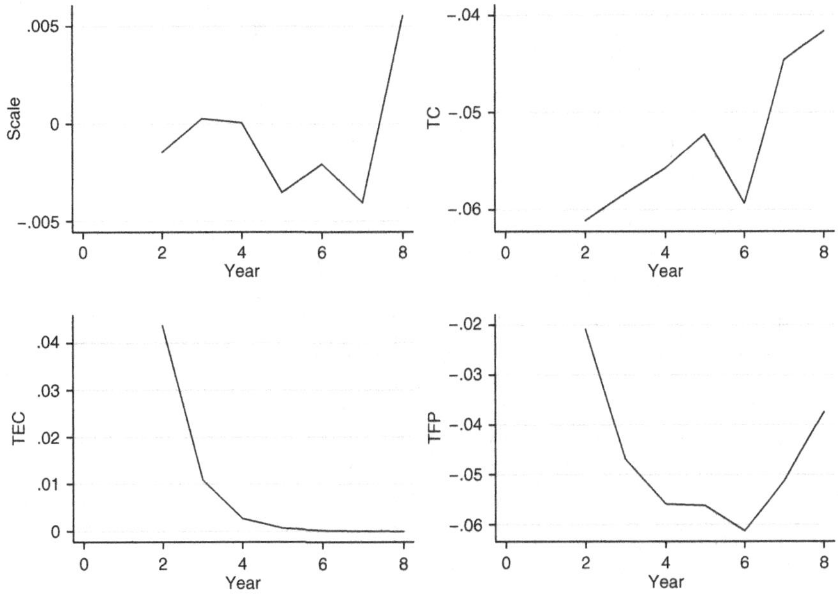

Figure 11.7. TFP Components from a Cost Function

```
. generate TFP = scale + TC + TEC

. summarize scale TC TEC TFP

    Variable |       Obs        Mean    Std. Dev.       Min        Max
-------------+--------------------------------------------------------
       scale |       301   -.0052826    .0399111  -.4708333   .0949043
          TC |       301   -.0529625    .0086931   -.070725  -.0154009
         TEC |       301    .0083155    .0149143   .0000105   .0436956
         TFP |       301   -.0499297    .0409086  -.4862237   .0652839
```

Overall, it appears as though TFP has been declining, driven, primarily, by the frontier regressing, while there has been some improvement in technical efficiency.

These components are plotted in Figure 11.7.

We now compute profitability change and its components, using equation (11.17). First, we compute the output price change component, $\frac{R}{C}\dot{p}$.

```
. generate output_p_change = rev / tc * dot_price
```

Then, we compute the output change component, $(\frac{R}{C} - 1)\dot{y}$.

```
. generate output_change = (rev / tc - 1) * dot_y
```

Finally, we compute the input price change, $\sum_j S_j^a \dot{w}_j$, which is subtracted when computing the profitability change (which we had previously calculated on page 291).

```
. generate input_p_change = dot_w
```

These additional components can then be added to TFP to provide a decomposition of profitability change.

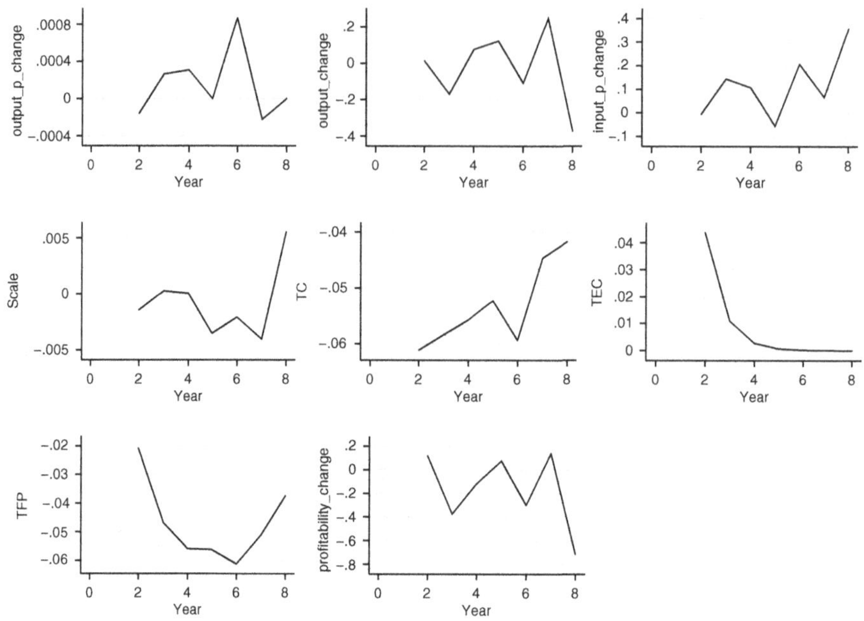

Figure 11.8. Profitability Change Decomposition Using a Cost Function

```
. generate profitability_change = output_p_change + output_change - input_p_change + TFP

. summarize output_p_change output_change input_p_change  TFP profitability_change

    Variable |       Obs        Mean    Std. Dev.       Min        Max
-------------+--------------------------------------------------------
output_p_c~e |       301    .0001512    .0003455  -.0002664   .0009911
output_cha~e |       301   -.0205805    .4131142  -1.091699   1.686025
input_p_ch~e |       301    .1381229    .2949107  -.7190061   1.121998
         TFP |       301   -.0499297    .0409086  -.4862237   .0652839
profitabil~e |       301   -.2084819    .6336066   -2.27936   1.296494
```

The results indicate that profitability is declining, driven by the declining TFP noted earlier, but also by input price increases and, to a lesser extent, by reductions in output.

These components are plotted in Figure 11.8.

11.3.3 Multiple Outputs

If the technology produces multiple outputs, TFP growth is defined as

$$\dot{TFP} = \sum_m R_m \dot{y}_m - \sum_j S_j^a \dot{x}_j, \tag{11.18}$$

where $R_m = \frac{p_m y_m}{R}$, $R - \sum_m p_m y_m$ (total revenue), $S_j^a = \frac{w_j x_j}{C}$, $C = \sum_j w_j x_j$ (total cost). The multiple output technology can be specified in terms of a cost function, $C(y, w, t)e^{\eta}$, where y is a vector of outputs. It is shown in Denny et al. (1981) and Kumbhakar and Lozano-Vivas (2005) that[3]

$$\dot{TFP} = TC + TEC + [(1 - RTS^{-1})\dot{y}_c] + [\dot{y}_p - \dot{y}_c], \tag{11.19}$$

where $\dot{y}_c = RTS\left\{\sum_m \frac{\partial \ln C}{\partial \ln y_m}\dot{y}_m\right\}$, $RTS^{-1} = \sum_m \frac{\partial \ln C}{\partial \ln y_m}$, $\dot{y}_p = \sum_m R_m \dot{y}_m$.

[3] TEC is not a component in these papers because they did not consider inefficiency.

We start with the definition of profit and define profitability change (i.e., the change in profit as a percentage of total cost, C),

$$\begin{aligned}
\pi &= \sum_m p_m y_m - \sum_j w_j x_j,\\
\frac{d\pi}{dt} &= \sum_m p_m \frac{\partial y_m}{\partial t} + \sum_m y_m \frac{\partial p_m}{\partial t} - \sum_j w_j \frac{\partial x_j}{\partial t} - \sum_j x_j \frac{\partial w_j}{\partial t}\\
&= \sum_m p_m y_m \frac{\partial ln y_m}{\partial t} + \sum_m p_m y_m \frac{\partial \ln p_m}{\partial t} - \sum_j w_j x_j \frac{\partial \ln x_j}{\partial t} - \sum_j w_j x_j \frac{\partial \ln w_j}{\partial t}\\
&= R[\sum_m R_m \dot{y}_m + \sum R_m \dot{p}_m] - C[\sum_j S_j^a \dot{x}_j + \sum_j S_j^a \dot{w}_j],
\end{aligned}$$

where $\dot{y}_m = \frac{\partial \ln y_m}{\partial t}$, etc. Thus

$$\frac{1}{C}\frac{d\pi}{dt} = \frac{R}{C}[\sum_m R_m \dot{y}_m + \sum_m R_m \dot{p}_m] - [\sum_j S_j^a \dot{x}_j + \sum_j S_j^a \dot{w}_j]. \tag{11.20}$$

From (11.18) and (11.19), we get

$$-\sum_j S_j^a \dot{x}_j = TC + TEC + [(1 - \sum_m \frac{\partial \ln C}{\partial \ln y_m})]\dot{y}_c + (\dot{y}_p - \dot{y}_c) - \sum_m R_m \dot{y}_m.$$

Inserting this in (11.20) gives

$$\begin{aligned}
\frac{1}{C}\frac{d\pi}{dt} &= \frac{R}{C}[\sum_m R_m \dot{y}_m + \sum_m R_m \dot{p}_m] - \sum_j S_j^a \dot{w}_j + TC + TEC + [(1 - \sum_m \frac{\partial \ln C}{\partial \ln y_m})]\dot{y}_c\\
&\quad + (\dot{y}_p - \dot{y}_c) - \sum R_m \dot{y}_m,\\
\Rightarrow \frac{1}{C}\frac{d\pi}{dt} &= (\frac{R}{C} - 1)\dot{y}_p + \frac{R}{C}\dot{p} - \dot{w} + TC + TEC + (1 - RTS^{-1})\dot{y}_c + (\dot{y}_p - \dot{y}_c),
\end{aligned} \tag{11.21}$$

where $\dot{p} = \sum_m R_m \dot{p}_m$, $\dot{w} = \sum S_j^a \dot{w}_j$.

Equation (11.21) is of primary interest because it decomposes the change in profit as a percent of total cost in to several components. Profitability is measured as a percentage of total cost and not as a percentage of profit because profit can be negative and this will create problems in interpretation (see page 287).

Following Kumbhakar et al. (2009), we can give an interpretation of each component in (11.21):

- $\dot{y}_p(\frac{R}{C} - 1)$ is the output growth component;
- $\dot{p}\frac{R}{C}$ is the output price change component;
- $\dot{w}$ is the input price change component;
- TC is the technical change component;
- TEC is the technical efficiency change component;
- $(1 - RTS^{-1})\dot{y}_c$ is the RTS, or scale, component;
- $\dot{y}_p - \dot{y}_c$ is the markup component.

Some of the components can be computed simply from the data, while others require econometric estimation. For example, the TC, TEC, scale, and markup components require econometric estimation.

This decomposition (that is, the parts that require econometric estimation) is based on a cost function. Estimation of cost function requires input price data with enough variability. In the absence of such data, one can use the input distance function (IDF), that is,

$$-\ln x_1 = \ln D_I(\tilde{x}, y, t) - \eta,$$

where $\tilde{x} = x_2/x_1, \ldots, x_j/x_1$.

Following Karagiannis et al. (2004) and Kumbhakar et al. (2013), we get the following:

$$-\frac{\partial \ln C}{\partial t} = TC = -\frac{\partial \ln D_I}{\partial t},$$
$$\frac{\partial \ln C}{\partial \ln y_m} = -\frac{\partial \ln D_I}{\partial \ln y_m},$$

which are used in the definition of $\dot{y}_c$, RTS, and TC.

Thus, in order to compute profitability change and its components, we need to

(i) estimate the IDF with multiple outputs;
(ii) use the estimated IDF and data, to compute $\frac{\partial \ln D_I}{\partial t}$ and $\frac{\partial \ln D_I}{\partial y_m}$ and to estimate the components in (11.21).

Example

This example examines the data on Philippine rice farms, using an input distance function approach with one output. This is followed by another example of an input distance function with multiple outputs.

Model 6: Half-Normal Stochastic Input Distance Frontier Function Model

For brevity, we ignore the OLS approach and include inefficiency in the model using a half-normal stochastic frontier model with a time trend in the σ_u^2 term. Details of the variable construction are also omitted but are quite obvious.

The translog covariates are first saved in `xlist1` and then a half-normal stochastic input distance frontier model estimated.

```
. global xlist1 ly ly2  lyltk lyltf lyltm tilde_k tilde_f tilde_m ///
>          ltkltk ltkltf ltkltm ltfltf ltfltm ltmltm  ///
>          t tt tly ltkt ltft ltmt

. sfmodel llneg, prod dist(h) frontier($xlist1) usigmas(t) vsigmas()
. ml max, difficult  gtol(1e-5) nrtol(1e-5)

(iteration log omitted)

                                                  Number of obs   =        344
                                                  Wald chi2(20)   =    2400.54
Log likelihood = -50.593473                       Prob > chi2     =     0.0000

------------------------------------------------------------------------------
       llneg |      Coef.   Std. Err.      z    P>|z|     [95% Conf. Interval]
-------------+----------------------------------------------------------------
frontier     |
          ly |   .1009495   .2836374     0.36   0.722    -.4549696    .6568685
         ly2 |  -.0621411   .0342651    -1.81   0.070    -.1292993    .0050172
```

```
      lyltk |   .2206879   .0725099     3.04   0.002     .0785711    .3628048
      lyltf |  -.0549552   .0494339    -1.11   0.266    -.1518438    .0419334
      lyltm |  -.0060194   .0225158    -0.27   0.789    -.0501494    .0381107
    tilde_k |  -.8299761   .8883745    -0.93   0.350    -2.571158    .9112059
    tilde_f |    .150571   .5692987     0.26   0.791    -.9652339    1.266376
    tilde_m |  -.0556655    .275466    -0.20   0.840     -.595569     .484238
     ltkltk |  -.2201423   .2477852    -0.89   0.374    -.7057923    .2655077
     ltkltf |   -.055111   .1441354    -0.38   0.702    -.3376113    .2273893
     ltkltm |  -.0317216   .0705395    -0.45   0.653    -.1699765    .1065334
     ltfltf |   .1053298   .0989902     1.06   0.287    -.0886875     .299347
     ltfltm |  -.0302425   .0377092    -0.80   0.423    -.1041512    .0436662
     ltmltm |    .073325   .0400798     1.83   0.067      -.00523    .1518799
          t |   .0636429   .1020881     0.62   0.533     -.136446    .2637319
         tt |   .0140566   .0077029     1.82   0.068    -.0010408     .029154
        tly |  -.0008592   .0086938    -0.10   0.921    -.0178987    .0161804
       ltkt |   .0230729   .0252563     0.91   0.361    -.0264286    .0725744
       ltft |  -.0344541   .0181168    -1.90   0.057    -.0699624    .0010543
       ltmt |  -.0043033   .0100494    -0.43   0.668    -.0239997    .0153931
      _cons |   -4.53129   1.597408    -2.84   0.005    -7.662152   -1.400427
------------+----------------------------------------------------------------
usigmas     |
          t |   .0506642   .0722813     0.70   0.483    -.0910046     .192333
      _cons |  -2.351194    .423053    -5.56   0.000    -3.180363   -1.522026
------------+----------------------------------------------------------------
vsigmas     |
      _cons |  -3.294592   .2250796   -14.64   0.000     -3.73574   -2.853444
-----------------------------------------------------------------------------

. sf_predict, bc(bc5_h) jlms(jlms5_h) marginal

The following is the marginal effect on unconditional E(u).

The average marginal effect of t on uncond E(u) is .00700317 (see t_M).

The following is the marginal effect on uncond V(u).

The average marginal effect of t on uncond V(u) is .00221763 (see t_V).
```

Next, we compute TFP and its components, using equation (11.19), and the profitability change components, using equation (11.21). First, we compute technical efficiency change, $-\frac{\partial \eta}{\partial t}$, and technical change (or frontier shift), $-\frac{\partial \ln D_I}{\partial t}$.

```
. generate TEC =  t_M if farmtag ~= 1
. generate TC = _b[t] + _b[tt]*t + _b[tly]*ly + _b[ltkt]*tilde_k ///
> + _b[ltft]*tilde_f + _b[ltmt]*tilde_m if farmtag ~= 1
```

We compute the scale component, $(1 - RTS^{-1})\dot{y}$.

```
. generate neg_inv_RTS = _b[ly] + _b[ly2]*ly + _b[lyltk]*tilde_k ///
> + _b[lyltf]*tilde_f + _b[lyltm]*tilde_m
. generate RTS = -1 / (neg_inv_RTS) if farmtag ~= 1
. generate scale = (1- 1/RTS)* dot_y
```

The remaining components – output growth component ($\dot{y}(\frac{R}{C} - 1)$), output price change component ($\dot{p}\frac{R}{C}$) and the input price change component ($\dot{w}$) – were all computed for Model 5, so they do not need to be recomputed. Thus, finally, we can compute TFP and profitability change, using equation (11.19) and equation (11.21).

```
. generate TFP = TC + scale - TEC
. generate Profit_ch = output_change + output_p_change - input_p_change + TC + scale - TEC
. summarize output_change output_p_change input_p_change  ///
>           TC scale TFP Profit_ch RTS TEC
```

Variable	Obs	Mean	Std. Dev.	Min	Max
output_cha~e	301	-.0205805	.4131142	-1.091699	1.686025
output_p_c~e	301	.0001512	.0003455	-.0002664	.0009911
input_p_ch~e	301	.1381229	.2949107	-.7190061	1.121998
TC	301	.0279396	.0297486	-.0406522	.1011909
scale	301	-.0056129	.0830247	-.7615104	.2591363
TFP	301	.0152372	.0865215	-.6931423	.3247904
Profit_ch	301	-.1433151	.5901634	-2.150909	1.273495
RTS	301	1.146902	.1381401	.9409777	2.110729
TEC	301	.0070896	.0003597	.0065623	.0076396

Overall, TFP growth is positive, driven by the technical change component. Profitability change is negative, with increases in input prices and reductions in output offsetting the TFP improvement.

The components of TFP and profitability change (their mean, 25th, and 75th percentiles) are plotted in Figure 11.9.

We used three approaches, viz., a production function, cost function, and input distance function, to illustrate how to estimate TFP growth components as well as decompose profitability. The results are not always consistent. There are several points to explain these differences. First, the production and IDF approaches are primal in which no explicit behavioral assumptions are made. In a production function approach inputs are assumed exogenous, whereas the opposite is true in an IDF. The cost function approach makes use of cost minimization behavioral assumption explicitly in treating inputs as endogenous. Furthermore, TC in a cost function is not the same TC in a production function. The former is related to cost diminution over time, ceteris paribus, whereas, in a production function, it is related to output increase over time, ceteris paribus. Similarly, output-oriented technical inefficiency, u, in the production function is not the same as input-oriented technical inefficiency, η, in the cost and input distance functions. The differences in results will also

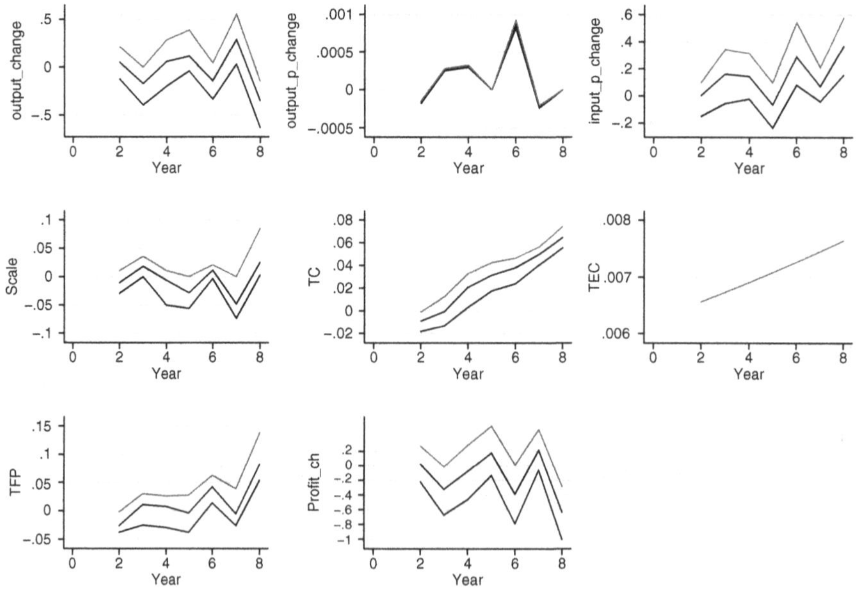

Figure 11.9. Profitability Change Decomposition Using an Input Distance Function

depend on the data and it is not possible to say which way the results will move when one uses different approaches.

We now provide a multiple output example using the input distance function approach. However, for this, we need to introduce a new dataset.

Example

This example uses data on dairy farms in Norway. Although the data covers the period 1999–2006, the panel data is unbalanced, but has at least three observations per farm. The four output variables are: `Y1` (milk sold, in 1,000 liters), `Y2` (meat, in 1,000 Norwegian Krone, or NOK), `Y3` (support payments, in 1,000 NOK), and `Y4` (other outputs, in 1,000 NOK). The respective output prices are: `P1` (milk, in NOK/liters), `P2` (meat, in a cattle index), `P3` (support payments, in a CP index), and `P4` (other outputs, again as an index). Prices are deflated to 2006 levels using the consumer price index or CPI.

Input quantities include: `X1` (land, in decare, where 1 decare (daa) is 0.1 hectares), `X2` (labor, in 1,000 hours), `X3` (purchased feed, in 1,000 NOK), and `X4` (other variable costs, in 1,000 NOK). The respective input prices are: `W1` (Land, in NOK/daa), `W2` (Labor, in NOK/hours), `W3` (purchased feed, in a feed index), and `W4` (other variable costs, in a variable cost index).

Model 7: Half-Normal Stochastic Input Distance Frontier Model, with Multiple Outputs

First, we estimate the multiple output distance function, using a half-normal stochastic frontier model with a time trend in the σ_u^2 term. (Details of the variable construction are omitted.)

```
. use norway.dta

. sfmodel lx1neg, prod dist(h) frontier($xlist1) usigmas(t) vsigmas()
. ml max, difficult  gtol(1e-5) nrtol(1e-5)

(iteration log omitted)


                                                  Number of obs   =       2727
                                                  Wald chi2(65)   =   61346.39
Log likelihood =  2836.1284                       Prob > chi2     =     0.0000

------------------------------------------------------------------------------
      lx1neg |      Coef.   Std. Err.      z    P>|z|     [95% Conf. Interval]
-------------+----------------------------------------------------------------
frontier     |
         ly1 |  -.3556625   .2401114    -1.48   0.139    -.8262723    .1149473
         ly2 |   .1469725   .1550927     0.95   0.343    -.1570037    .4509486
         ly3 |  -1.087778    .519113    -2.10   0.036    -2.105221   -.0703351
         ly4 |  -.1387953   .0487934    -2.84   0.004    -.2344286   -.0431621
      ly1ly1 |  -.3801724   .0374651   -10.15   0.000    -.4536026   -.3067421
      ly1ly2 |   .1016183   .0206524     4.92   0.000     .0611403    .1420963
      ly1ly3 |   .1148822   .0578832     1.98   0.047     .0014333    .2283311
      ly1ly4 |  -.0010264   .0060191    -0.17   0.865    -.0128235    .0107708
      ly2ly2 |  -.1156928   .0099584   -11.62   0.000    -.1352109   -.0961748
      ly2ly3 |  -.0896752    .038761    -2.31   0.021    -.1656453   -.0137051
      ly2ly4 |  -.0060623   .0039127    -1.55   0.121     -.013731    .0016064
      ly3ly3 |   .2680804   .1333207     2.01   0.044     .0067766    .5293841
      ly3ly4 |   .0244072   .0120283     2.03   0.042     .0008322    .0479822
      ly4ly4 |  -.0040185   .0010827    -3.71   0.000    -.0061406   -.0018965
     ly1ltx2 |  -.1359409   .0301334    -4.51   0.000    -.1950012   -.0768805
```

```
     ly1ltx3 |   .0559299   .0222295     2.52   0.012      .0123609     .099499
     ly1ltx4 |  -.0469156   .0329776    -1.42   0.155     -.1115505    .0177194
     ly1ltx5 |   .0177447   .0316332     0.56   0.575     -.0442552    .0797445
     ly1ltx6 |  -.0092568   .0168777    -0.55   0.583     -.0423364    .0238229
     ly2ltx2 |  -.0695944   .0182321    -3.82   0.000     -.1053287   -.0338602
     ly2ltx3 |   .0288079   .0172881     1.67   0.096     -.0050762    .0626919
     ly2ltx4 |  -.0769208   .0195585    -3.93   0.000     -.1152549   -.0385868
     ly2ltx5 |   .0505192   .0226526     2.23   0.026      .0061209    .0949175
     ly2ltx6 |  -.0000171   .0114352    -0.00   0.999     -.0224297    .0223954
     ly3ltx2 |   .2936641   .0584808     5.02   0.000      .1790439    .4082843
     ly3ltx3 |  -.1039928   .0444309    -2.34   0.019     -.1910758   -.0169097
     ly3ltx4 |    .184706   .0672329     2.75   0.006      .0529319    .3164801
     ly3ltx5 |  -.0548343   .0653173    -0.84   0.401     -.1828539    .0731854
     ly3ltx6 |   .0050591   .0348671     0.15   0.885     -.0632791    .0733974
     ly4ltx2 |  -.0000448   .0056857    -0.01   0.994     -.0111885    .0110989
     ly4ltx3 |   .0013985   .0048347     0.29   0.772     -.0080773    .0108743
     ly4ltx4 |   .0022504    .006472     0.35   0.728     -.0104345    .0149353
     ly4ltx5 |  -.0103281    .006245    -1.65   0.098     -.0225681     .001912
     ly4ltx6 |   .0136271   .0030932     4.41   0.000      .0075644    .0196897
    tilde_x2 |  -.7076905   .2411882    -2.93   0.003     -1.180411   -.2349704
    tilde_x3 |   .3607351   .1981518     1.82   0.069     -.0276353    .7491055
    tilde_x4 |  -.6370359   .2653293    -2.40   0.016     -1.157072       -.117
    tilde_x5 |    .906829   .2668504     3.40   0.001      .3838118    1.429846
    tilde_x6 |   .0161474   .1329883     0.12   0.903     -.2445049    .2767997
    ltx2ltx2 |  -.0356825   .0383941    -0.93   0.353     -.1109336    .0395686
    ltx2ltx3 |  -.0123848   .0230711    -0.54   0.591     -.0576035    .0328338
    ltx2ltx4 |  -.0576628   .0316196    -1.82   0.068      -.119636    .0043105
    ltx2ltx5 |   .1662355   .0329094     5.05   0.000      .1017342    .2307369
    ltx2ltx6 |  -.0167297   .0156328    -1.07   0.285     -.0473694    .0139099
    ltx3ltx3 |   .0968439    .010245     9.45   0.000      .0767641    .1169238
    ltx3ltx4 |   .0141393   .0219378     0.64   0.519     -.0288579    .0571365
    ltx3ltx5 |  -.1045537   .0273448    -3.82   0.000     -.1581486   -.0509589
    ltx3ltx6 |   .0243549   .0133377     1.83   0.068     -.0017865    .0504964
    ltx4ltx4 |   .0301442   .0478404     0.63   0.529     -.0636212    .1239097
    ltx4ltx5 |   .0023714   .0343656     0.07   0.945      -.064984    .0697268
    ltx4ltx6 |   .0121205   .0171809     0.71   0.481     -.0215535    .0457945
    ltx5ltx5 |   -.053818   .0460643    -1.17   0.243     -.1441024    .0364663
    ltx5ltx6 |   .0213027   .0185883     1.15   0.252     -.0151296    .0577351
    ltx6ltx6 |  -.0277914   .0128513    -2.16   0.031     -.0529795   -.0026033
           t |  -.0237513   .0287057    -0.83   0.408     -.0800135    .0325108
          t2 |  -.0028948   .0006977    -4.15   0.000     -.0042623   -.0015274
        ly1t |   .0120228   .0033684     3.57   0.000      .0054209    .0186247
        ly2t |   .0032405   .0023564     1.38   0.169     -.0013778    .0078589
        ly3t |   -.000476   .0069587    -0.07   0.945     -.0141148    .0131629
        ly4t |   .0021957   .0006619     3.32   0.001      .0008984     .003493
       ltx2t |   .0090157   .0034831     2.59   0.010       .002189    .0158423
       ltx3t |  -.0035689    .002633    -1.36   0.175     -.0087295    .0015916
       ltx4t |   .0071146   .0037988     1.87   0.061     -.0003308    .0145601
       ltx5t |   .0006549   .0040188     0.16   0.871     -.0072217    .0085315
       ltx6t |  -.0021476   .0018943    -1.13   0.257     -.0058603     .001565
       _cons |     .31695   1.128875     0.28   0.779     -1.895605    2.529505
-------------+----------------------------------------------------------------
usigmas      |
           t |   -.078155   .0367107    -2.13   0.033     -.1501067   -.0062033
       _cons |  -4.644374   .2141923   -21.68   0.000     -5.064184   -4.224565
-------------+----------------------------------------------------------------
vsigmas      |
       _cons |  -5.305629   .0878199   -60.41   0.000     -5.477753   -5.133505
------------------------------------------------------------------------------

. sf_predict, bc(bc_h) jlms(jlms_h) marginal
. summarize bc_h jlms_h

(2 missing values generated)
```

```
The following is the marginal effect on unconditional E(u).

The average marginal effect of t on uncond E(u) is -.00252711 (see t_M).

The following is the marginal effect on uncond V(u).

The average marginal effect of t on uncond V(u) is -.00018832 (see t_V).

. summarize bc_h jlms_h

    Variable |       Obs        Mean    Std. Dev.       Min        Max
-------------+--------------------------------------------------------
        bc_h |      2727    .9385461    .0272894   .7636475   .9837496
      jlms_h |      2727    .0646278    .0300266   .0165011    .271104
```

Next, we compute TFP and its components, using equation (11.19), and the profitability change components, using equation (11.21). We compute technical efficiency change, $-\frac{\partial \eta}{\partial t}$, and technical change (or frontier shift), $-\frac{\partial \ln D_I}{\partial t}$.

```
. generate TEC =  t_M if farmtag ~= 1

. generate TC = _b[t]+_b[t2]*t+_b[ly1t]*ly1+_b[ly2t]*ly2+_b[ly3t]*ly3+_b[ly4t]*ly4 ///
>              +_b[ltx2t]*tilde_x2+_b[ltx3t]*tilde_x3+_b[ltx4t]*tilde_x4 ///
>              +_b[ltx5t]*tilde_x5+_b[ltx6t]*tilde_x6
```

We compute the scale component, $(1 - RTS^{-1})\dot{y}_c$.

```
. generate lambda_y1 = _b[ly1]+_b[ly1ly1]*ly1+_b[ly1ly2]*ly2+_b[ly1ly3]*ly3+_b[ly1ly4]*ly4  ///
>                     +_b[ly1ltx2]*tilde_x2+_b[ly1ltx3]*tilde_x3+_b[ly1ltx4]*tilde_x4 ///
>                     +_b[ly1ltx5]*tilde_x5+_b[ly1ltx6]*tilde_x6+_b[ly1t]*t

. generate lambda_y2 = _b[ly2]+_b[ly1ly2]*ly1+_b[ly2ly2]*ly2+_b[ly2ly3]*ly3+_b[ly2ly4]*ly4 ///
>                     +_b[ly2ltx2]*tilde_x2+_b[ly2ltx3]*tilde_x3+_b[ly2ltx4]*tilde_x4 ///
>                     +_b[ly2ltx5]*tilde_x5+_b[ly2ltx6]*tilde_x6+_b[ly2t]*t

. generate lambda_y3 = _b[ly3]+_b[ly1ly3]*ly1+_b[ly2ly3]*ly2+_b[ly3ly3]*ly3+_b[ly3ly4]*ly4 ///
>                     +_b[ly3ltx2]*tilde_x2+_b[ly3ltx3]*tilde_x3+_b[ly3ltx4]*tilde_x4 ///
>                     +_b[ly3ltx5]*tilde_x5+_b[ly3ltx6]*tilde_x6+_b[ly3t]*t

. generate lambda_y4 = _b[ly4]+_b[ly1ly4]*ly1+_b[ly2ly4]*ly2+_b[ly3ly4]*ly3+_b[ly4ly4]*ly4 ///
>                     +_b[ly4ltx2]*tilde_x2+_b[ly4ltx3]*tilde_x3+_b[ly4ltx4]*tilde_x4 ///
>                     +_b[ly4ltx5]*tilde_x5+_b[ly4ltx6]*tilde_x6+_b[ly4t]*t

. generate neg_inv_RTS = -1 / (lambda_y1 + lambda_y2 + lambda_y3 + lambda_y4)

. generate RTSmin = 1/neg_inv_RTS


. generate dot_Y_C = neg_inv_RTS * (lambda_y1*dot_y1_m + lambda_y2*dot_y2_m + ///
>                    lambda_y3*dot_y3_m + lambda_y4*dot_y4_m)

. generate scale = (1-RTSmin)* dot_Y_C
```

We then compute the remaining components; the output growth component, $\dot{y}_p(\frac{R}{C} - 1)$; the output price change component, $\dot{p}\frac{R}{C}$; the input price change component, $\dot{w}$; and the mark-up component, $\dot{y}_p - \dot{y}_c$. These are computed using the following lines, respectively.

```
. generate OutGrow_comp = dot_y_p*((R/C)-1)
. generate OutPric_comp = dot_p_m*(R/C)
. generate InpPric_comp = dot_w
. generate Mark_Up = dot_y_p - dot_Y_C
```

We now compute TFP change using equation (11.19).

```
. generate TFP = TC_comp + scale + Mark_Up - TEC

    Variable |       Obs        Mean    Std. Dev.       Min        Max
-------------+--------------------------------------------------------
          TC |      2727   -.0008848    .0095819  -.0436691   .0272306
       scale |      2726     .003444    .0273354  -.3784304   .2705076
     Mark_Up |      2726    .0377816    .3532008  -2.226283   2.420222
         TEC |      2269   -.0024761    .0002171  -.0028276  -.0021509
         TFP |      2267    .0437259    .1768882  -1.099932   1.372668
```

Finally, we compute profitability change using equation (11.21).

```
. generate Profit_ch = OutGrow_comp + OutPric_comp - InpPric_comp + ///
>                     TC + scale + Mark_Up - TEC

. summarize OutGrow_comp OutPric_comp InpPric_comp  ///
>           TC scale Mark_Up TEC Profit_ch

    Variable |       Obs        Mean    Std. Dev.       Min        Max
-------------+--------------------------------------------------------
OutGrow_comp |      2727   -.0027205     .048431  -.3097256   .6219394
OutPric_comp |      2728    .0008422    .0337498  -.2319495   .7807856
InpPric_comp |      2728    .0038548    .0445525  -.2306547   .2361573
          TC |      2727   -.0008848    .0095819  -.0436691   .0272306
       scale |      2726     .003444    .0273354  -.3784304   .2705076
-------------+--------------------------------------------------------
     Mark_Up |      2726    .0377816    .3532008  -2.226283   2.420222
         TEC |      2269   -.0024761    .0002171  -.0028276  -.0021509
   Profit_ch |      2267       .0215    .1669728  -.8847447   1.449186
```

These components are plotted in Figure 11.10.

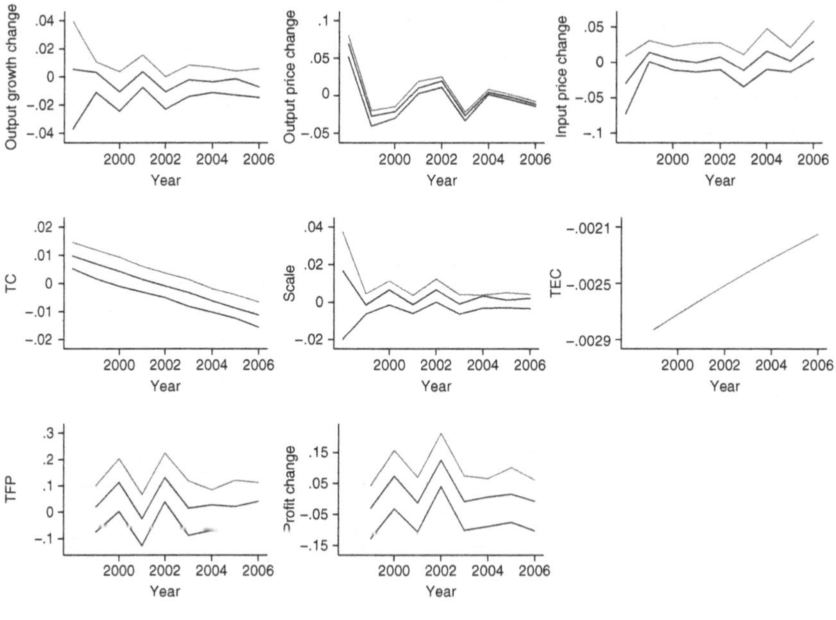

Figure 11.10. Profitability Change Decomposition Using an Input Distance Function

PART VI

LOOKING AHEAD

12

Looking Ahead

In this book, we have examined how to estimate productive efficiency using Stochastic Frontier Analysis. We have provided a basic understanding of the theoretical underpinnings and a practical understanding of how to estimate production, profit, and cost efficiency.

We have, in our time as academics and practitioners, seen a significant increase in the theoretical models and practical applications in this field. However, despite these developments, it is still the case that important policy, strategic, regulatory, and operational decisions are based on approaches that do not take into account all these developments and improvements.

As such, as we set out at the beginning of this book, our two main goals in writing this book were to extend the everyday application of Stochastic Frontier Analysis beyond the expert practitioner or academic and to ensure that the latest theoretical models can be implemented by as many practitioners in the area as possible. Utlimately, we hope that this will improve the decisions made in these situations, by improving the evidence base used to make such decsions. We hope to have achieved this by making it relatively easy for the reader to carry out the complex computations necessary to both estimate and interpret these models.

Through the course of the chapters, we have examined a number of different settings, including dairy farming, rice farming, electricity generation, airlines, mining, manufacturing, and economy-wide production. There are clearly countless settings in which the tools set out in this book can be applied. We hope we have inspired the reader to go away and apply these tools to their own datasets and uncover insights that had previously remained hidden within those dataset. At the very least, we hope to have informed policy makers, regulators, government advisors, companies, and the like on what tools are available and what insights can be uncovered by using them, such that they commission such analysis to be undertaken to help them in making their cirtical decions.

Despite the broad range of models that we have covered in this book, there are many advanced and interesting topics that we have not covered. Some of these topics are briefly set out in the rest of this chapter.

12.1 Latent Class Models

When heterogeneous technologies are present for different groups of firms, say, estimates of production technology and inefficiency can be misleading if one assumes a homogeneous technology for all firms. A simple way to handle this heterogeneity in technology is to incorporate a priori information in order to split the sample of firms into some ad hoc homogeneous groups and estimate the technology and inefficiency for each group separately. The main feature of this appoach is that the firms are first classified into several groups based on some a priori sample separation information, such as the type of ownership of the firms and the location (e.g., country) of the firms. Once such classification has been made, separate analyses are then carried out for each group. Inefficiency is then estimated relative to the group-specific frontier, and the difference in technology frontiers across groups are viewed as the technology gap (for example, see O'Donnell, Rao, and Battese [2008]; Casu et al. [2013]).

This procedure is not efficient in the sense that (i) the classification might be inappropriate, and (ii) the information contained in one group is not used to estimate the technology (production or cost) frontier of firms that belong to other groups. In most of the empirical applications, this intergroup information may be quite important because firms belonging to different groups often come from the same industry such that, although their technologies may be different, they share some common features.

As such, an alternative apprach may be warranted. The latent class model (LCM) permits us to exploit the information contained in the data more efficiently, with the advantage that the LCM can easily incorporate technological heterogeneity. In the standard finite mixture model, the proportion of firms (or observations) in a group is assumed to be fixed (and a parameter to be estimated), see, for example, Beard et al. (1991, 1997) and Caudill (2003). The approach assumes that firms in the sample use multiple technologies and the probability of a firm using a particular technology can be explained by some covariates and these may vary over time. The LCM approach can also be extended to accommodate the simultaneous existence of multiple technologies in which firms are not necessarily fully efficient. A few studies have combined the stochastic frontier approach with the latent class structure in order to estimate a mixture of frontier functions (Tsionas [2000]). In particular, Caudill (2003) introduces an expectation-maximization (EM) algorithm to estimate a mixture of two stochastic cost frontiers in the presence of no sample separation information. Orea and Kumbhakar (2004) and Greene (2005b) use the standard procedure to obtain the maximum likelihood estimator in which the (prior) probability of adopting a particular technology is assumed to depend on firm characteristics. Based on the estimated (posterior) probability, the sample of firms is classified into several groups. It is also possible to find the optimal number of groups/classes that the data support. Inefficiency can then be estimated as the probability weighted average of inefficiency relative to each technology. See Beard, Caudill, and Gropper (1991); Orea and Kumbhakar (2004); El-Gamal and Inanoglu (2005); and Greene (2005b) for the development of latent class stochastic frontier models. See also applications by Barros (2009, 2013); Bos et al. (2010a, 2010b); Koetter and Poghosyan (2009); and Poghosyan and Kumbhakar (2010).

12.2 Zero-Inefficiency SF Models

Traditional stochastic frontier models impose inefficient behavior on *all* firms in the sample of interest. If the data under investigation represent a mixture of both fully efficient and inefficient firms then "off-the-shelf" frontier models are statistically inadequate. Kumbhakar et al. (2013) introduce a zero-inefficiency stochastic frontier model which can accommodate the presence of both efficient and inefficient firms in the sample. They add a parameter p, which is the probability that a firm is fully efficient. This model is estimated by MLE and provides estimates of the fraction of firms that are fully efficient and the distribution of inefficiency for the inefficient firms. See also Rho and Schmidt (2013) and Grassetti (2011) for a similar approach.

12.3 Selectivity in SF Models

In the LCM approach, producers are allowed to use different technologies. But the choice/selection of technologies is not modeled. Kumbhakar et al. (2009), Greene (2010), and Bravo-Ureta et al. (2012) proposed an internally consistent method of incorporating "sample selection" in a stochastic frontier framework. The sample selection SF model assumes that the unobserved characteristics in the selection equation are correlated with the noise in the stochastic frontier model. This can be viewed as a significant improvement of Heckman's (1979) self-selection specification for the linear regression model. These models use both the selection and outcome equations and estimate them jointly using MLE.

12.4 Modeling Good and Bad Outputs That Separate Technical Efficiency from Environmental Efficiency

Production of intended/good outputs, in many cases, also generates some unintended/bad outputs. Pollution is a common example of a bad output. Because this is an unintended outcome, modeling production processes using standard tools might not be appropriate. If there is inefficiency in the production process, one has to deal with two important modeling issues: how to model technical and environmental efficiency and whether they can be separated. A production process is said to be environmentally inefficient when the production of pollutants can be reduced without reducing the production of good outputs, given the technology and the input vector. In general, if a firm is fully efficient technically, a decrease in the bad output is only possible if the production of the good output is also reduced. This property is not automatically satisfied in a model where the same technology is used to produce good and bad outputs jointly.

Given that the production of bad outputs increases with good outputs,[1] it is often argued that the monotonic relationship between good and bad outputs is similar to the relationship between inputs and good outputs. Färe et al. (2005) criticized the idea of treating bad outputs as inputs. They argued that the treatment of bad outputs as inputs with strong disposability properties (Lee et al. [2002] or Hailu and Veeman [2001]) would yield an unbounded output set which is not physically possible if traditional inputs are a given. Good and bad outputs should satisfy the weak disposability condition. This is an important consideration and implies that bad outputs cannot be treated as inputs.

Fernández, Koop, and Steel (2002) separate the production of good outputs (Y) from the production of bad outputs (Z) and use the stochastic frontier model for each technology. By doing so they separate technical efficiency from environmental efficiency. Forsund (2009) and Murty, Russell, and Levkoff (2012) also advocated separating the technology for the

[1] That is, if more good outputs are produced, then more bad outputs are automatically produced because of their by-product nature.

production of bad outputs (material balance) from the technology of producing good outputs.

Kumbhakar and Tsionas (2013) followed this idea and considered a modeling approach in which the technology for the production of good outputs is specified in terms of a standard transformation function with input-oriented technical inefficiency. Because bad outputs are viewed as by-products of good outputs, technology for the production of bad outputs is naturally separated from the technology for good outputs. This allows them to estimate technical and environmental efficiencies, defined in terms of the technologies for the production of good and bad outputs, respectively.

12.5 Two-Tier SF Models

Polachek and Yoon (1987) introduced a three component error structure with two one-sided terms, one positive and one negative, in order to capture imperfections on both sides of a transaction (the 2TSF model). They originally applied their model to the labor market in order to estimate the earnings equation, where the two one-sided error terms were interpreted as representing the quantitative impact of informational deficiencies of employers and of workers separately, leading the former to pay more than workers' reservation wages, and the latter to work for less than maximum wages acceptable by employers. Kumbhakar and Parmeter (2009) used the model to measure the effects of wage bargaining in a framework of productivity uncertainty. Kumbhakar and Parmeter (2010) presented a 2TSF generalized hedonic price model with an application to the housing market. Ferona and Tsionas (2012) applied the model to assess the extent of underbidding and overbidding behavior, using data from timber auctions. See also Papadopoulos (2014).

12.6 SF Models with Copula Functions (To Introduce Correlation between the Noise and Inefficiency Terms)

The previous discussion has maintained the assumption that production shocks and inefficiency are independent. This allowed us to easily recover $f(\varepsilon) = f(v)f(u)$. The independence of v and u is ubiquitous in the frontier literature. This undoubtedly stems from the ease with which likelihood functions can be constructed. Recently, Smith (2008) has challenged the orthogonality assumption. As an example, consider farmers whose input decisions today are, in part, based on seasonal fluctuations which affect production. Given that agricultural data is aggregated at a monthly, quarterly or even yearly level, we might expect that, if farmers misjudge shocks, then they could, in turn, make poor input decisions. In this setting, it is most likely that u and v are correlated. For system frontier estimation using copula functions see Lai and Huang (2013) and Amsler et al. (2014).

12.7 Nonparametric and Semiparametric SF Models

In many real world applications, the production units might be using different technologies (in a parametric sense) which can be captured by LCM. This can be further extended by assuming a purely nonparametric technology. Fan, Li, and Weersink (1996) introduced an approach that was nonparametric with respect to the production function and parametric with respect to the error components. Horrace and Parmeter (2011) introduced an approach that was parametric with respect to production function and semiparametric with respect to the error components.

Kumbhakar et al. (2007) proposed a model that is almost fully nonparametric. Kumbhakar and Tsionas (2008) applied this model. See also Martins-Filho and Yao (2014). Recent work on convex nonparametric least squares (CNLS) by Kuosmanen (2008), Kuosmanen and Johnson (2010), and Kuosmanen and Kortelainen (2012) have attempted to integrate DEA and SFA into a unified framework of productivity analysis.

Parmeter et al. (2014) develop a model that allows for nonparametric estimation of the production technology. This approach exploits the additive separability of the conditional mean of inefficiency and the technology. Similar to the work of Fan, Li, and Weersink (1996), they propose kernel methods that eliminate the need for parametric assumptions on the production technology.

Sun and Kumbhakar (2013) propose a semiparametric smooth-coefficient stochastic production frontier model in which all the coefficients are expressed as some unknown functions of environmental variables (Z). The inefficiency term is multiplicatively decomposed into a scaling function of the environmental factors and a standard truncated normal random variable. They not only consider the impact of Z variables on the technical inefficiency part but also introduce the Z variables into the frontier part in a semiparametric fashion. Specifically, in a production framework, the intercept and slope coefficients are expressed as unknown functions of the Z variables. This allows the environmental factors to shift the frontier non-neutrally.

12.8 Testing Distribution Assumptions

The parametric approach of a stochastic frontier model estimation requires imposing distributional assumptions on the two random variables, v and u, of the model. The computation of the inefficiency index is also based on the distribution assumptions. Consequently, if the distributional assumptions are incorrect, the MLEs of the model parameters are likely to be inconsistent and the inefficiency index biased. However, in many of the empirical applications of stochastic frontier models, the distribution assumptions are assumed rather than tested.

Some tests regarding the model's error distribution have been proposed in the literature, including the tests by Schmidt and Lin (1984) and Coelli (1995) that we have introduced in the book. The Schmidt-Lin test is supposed to be a preestimation test to see if the data exhibits the desired skewness needed for a stochastic frontier analysis. The test, however, does not discriminate among different distribution assumptions on v and u. Coelli's likelihood ratio test is to examine the existence of u in the model. The test is not on the particular distribution assumption of u, and it takes the distribution of v as given.

Both of these tests would only detect the presence of u but not test the distribution assumption of it. Both of them also take the distribution of v as given without testing it. Kopp and Mullahy (1990) go a step further by testing the distribution assumption of u. The GMM test proposed by the authors is applicable only to models where u is an one-parameter distribution. The test maintains v to be symmetric without testing.

Lee (1983) may be the first one to directly test the distribution assumptions of both v and u. Based on Rao's score test principle, the test is proposed only for the normal–half-normal and the normal-truncated normal models. Wang et al. (2014) suggest the use of Pearson's chi-squared test and the Kolmogorov–Smirnov test for checking the distributions of v and u of a SF model. A limitation of the test is that it requires simulating the quantiles of the composed error distribution even when the composed error PDF has a closed form. Chen and Wang (2012) propose a centered-residuals-based method of moments test, which can be easily and flexibly applied to models with various distribution assumptions on v and u. The u is not limited to one-parameter distributions and no simulation on quantiles is required.

All of these tests assume u to be homoscedastic which is often not the case in today's empirical applications. Su et al. (2014) show that the simulated integrated conditional moment test of Bierens and Wang (2012) can be extended to stochastic frontier models as a general specification test. One of the applications that is particularly appealing is the test on the distributional assumptions of v and u when u is heteroscedastic.

APPENDIX

Appendix A

Deriving the Likelihood Functions of Single Equation Frontier Models

In this appendix, we show how to derive the likelihood functions of the single equation frontier models introduced in Part II of the book. More specifically, the derivations are pertinent to the likelihood functions of the half-normal model (3.22), the truncated-normal model (3.47), the scaling-property model (3.68), and, to some extent, the exponential model (3.87). First, we derive the likelihood function for the case of a truncated-normal model, and then we discuss how the derivations can be straightforwardly modified for the other models.

Following Section 3.4.4, a cross-sectional truncated-normal stochastic frontier model is (subscripts i are omitted)

$$\ln y = \boldsymbol{x}'\boldsymbol{\beta} + \epsilon, \tag{A.1}$$

$$\epsilon = v - u, \tag{A.2}$$

$$u \sim N^{+}(\mu, \sigma_u^2), \tag{A.3}$$

$$v \sim N(0, \sigma_v^2), \tag{A.4}$$

$$u \text{ and } v \text{ are independent.} \tag{A.5}$$

We know

$$f(v) = \frac{1}{\sqrt{2\pi}\sigma_v} \exp\left(-\frac{v^2}{2\sigma_v^2}\right), \tag{A.6}$$

$$f(u) = \frac{1}{\sqrt{2\pi}\sigma_u\left[1 - \Phi\left(-\frac{\mu}{\sigma_u}\right)\right]} \exp\left[-\frac{1}{2}\left(\frac{u-\mu}{\sigma_u}\right)^2\right] \tag{A.7}$$

$$= \frac{1}{\sqrt{2\pi}\sigma_u \Phi\left(\frac{\mu}{\sigma_u}\right)} \exp\left[-\frac{1}{2}\left(\frac{u-\mu}{\sigma_u}\right)^2\right]. \tag{A.8}$$

Given the independence assumption,

$$f(v, u) = f(v) \cdot f(u) = \frac{1}{2\pi\sigma_v\sigma_u\Phi\left(\frac{\mu}{\sigma_u}\right)} \exp\left\{-\frac{1}{2}\left[\frac{v^2}{\sigma_v^2} + \left(\frac{u-\mu}{\sigma_u}\right)^2\right]\right\}. \tag{A.9}$$

Therefore,

$$f(\epsilon + u, u) = \frac{1}{2\pi \sigma_v \sigma_u \Phi\left(\frac{\mu}{\sigma_u}\right)} \exp\left\{-\frac{1}{2}\left[\left(\frac{\epsilon + u}{\sigma_v}\right)^2 + \left(\frac{u - \mu}{\sigma_u}\right)^2\right]\right\}. \tag{A.10}$$

The expression can be simplified. Note that

$$\begin{aligned}
\left(\frac{\epsilon + u}{\sigma_v}\right)^2 + \left(\frac{u - \mu}{\sigma_u}\right)^2 &= \frac{\epsilon^2 + 2u\epsilon + u^2}{\sigma_v^2} + \frac{u^2 - 2u\mu + \mu^2}{\sigma_u^2} \\
&= u^2\left(\frac{1}{\sigma_v^2} + \frac{1}{\sigma_u^2}\right) - 2u\left(\frac{\mu}{\sigma_u^2} - \frac{\epsilon}{\sigma_v^2}\right) + \left(\frac{\epsilon^2}{\sigma_v^2} + \frac{\mu^2}{\sigma_u^2}\right) \\
&= \frac{\sigma_v^2 + \sigma_u^2}{\sigma_v^2 \sigma_u^2}\left[u^2 - 2u\left(\frac{\mu\sigma_v^2 - \epsilon\sigma_u^2}{\sigma_v^2 + \sigma_u^2}\right)\right] + \left(\frac{\epsilon^2}{\sigma_v^2} + \frac{\mu^2}{\sigma_u^2}\right). \qquad \text{(A.11)}
\end{aligned}$$

Now, define

$$\mu_* = \frac{\mu\sigma_v^2 - \epsilon\sigma_u^2}{\sigma_v^2 + \sigma_u^2}, \tag{A.12}$$

$$\sigma_*^2 = \frac{\sigma_v^2 \sigma_u^2}{\sigma_v^2 + \sigma_u^2}. \tag{A.13}$$

So, (A.11) becomes

$$\frac{1}{\sigma_*^2}\left(u^2 - 2u\mu_* + \mu_*^2\right) - \frac{\mu_*^2}{\sigma_*^2} + \frac{\epsilon^2}{\sigma_v^2} + \frac{\mu^2}{\sigma_u^2} = \left(\frac{u - \mu_*}{\sigma_*}\right)^2 + \frac{(\epsilon + \mu)^2}{\sigma_v^2 + \sigma_u^2}. \tag{A.14}$$

Therefore, the function of $f(\epsilon + u, u)$ in (A.10) is simplified to

$$f(\epsilon + u, u) = \frac{1}{2\pi \sigma_v \sigma_u \Phi\left(\frac{\mu}{\sigma_u}\right)} \exp\left\{-\frac{1}{2}\left[\left(\frac{u - \mu_*}{\sigma_*}\right)^2 + \frac{(\epsilon + \mu)^2}{\sigma_v^2 + \sigma_u^2}\right]\right\}. \tag{A.15}$$

Thus, the density of $f(\epsilon)$ is

$$\begin{aligned}
f(\epsilon) &= \int_0^\infty f(\epsilon + u, u)du \qquad \text{(A.16)} \\
&= \int_0^\infty \frac{1}{2\pi \sigma_v \sigma_u \Phi\left(\frac{\mu}{\sigma_u}\right)} \exp\left[-\frac{1}{2}\left(\frac{u - \mu_*}{\sigma_*}\right)^2\right] \exp\left[-\frac{1}{2}\frac{(\epsilon + \mu)^2}{\sigma_v^2 + \sigma_u^2}\right] du \qquad \text{(A.17)} \\
&= \frac{1}{\sqrt{2\pi}\sigma_v \sigma_u \Phi\left(\frac{\mu}{\sigma_u}\right)} \exp\left[-\frac{1}{2}\frac{(\epsilon + \mu)^2}{\sigma_v^2 + \sigma_u^2}\right] \int_0^\infty \frac{1}{\sqrt{2\pi}} \exp\left[-\frac{1}{2}\left(\frac{u - \mu_*}{\sigma_*}\right)^2\right] du. \qquad \text{(A.18)}
\end{aligned}$$

Let

$$\tilde{u} = \frac{u - \mu_*}{\sigma_*}. \tag{A.19}$$

Then

$$\tilde{u} \in \left[-\frac{\mu_*}{\sigma_*}, \infty\right), d\tilde{u} = \frac{du}{\sigma_*}. \tag{A.20}$$

Thus, we have

$$f(\epsilon) = \int_0^\infty \frac{1}{\sqrt{2\pi}} \exp\left[-\frac{1}{2}\left(\frac{u-\mu_*}{\sigma_*}\right)^2\right] du = \int_{-\frac{\mu_*}{\sigma_*}}^\infty \frac{1}{\sqrt{2\pi}} \exp\left(-\frac{1}{2}\tilde{u}^2\right)\sigma_* d\tilde{u} = \sigma_* \Phi\left(\frac{\mu_*}{\sigma_*}\right), \tag{A.21}$$

and, therefore,

$$f(\epsilon) = \frac{1}{\sqrt{2\pi}\sigma_v\sigma_u\Phi\left(\frac{\mu}{\sigma_u}\right)} \exp\left[-\frac{1}{2}\frac{(\epsilon+\mu)^2}{\sigma_v^2+\sigma_u^2}\right]\sigma_*\Phi\left(\frac{\mu_*}{\sigma_*}\right) \tag{A.22}$$

$$= \frac{1}{\sqrt{2\pi}\sqrt{\sigma_v^2+\sigma_u^2}\left[\frac{\Phi\left(\frac{\mu}{\sigma_u}\right)}{\Phi\left(\frac{\mu_*}{\sigma_*}\right)}\right]} \exp\left[-\frac{1}{2}\frac{(\epsilon+\mu)^2}{\sigma_v^2+\sigma_u^2}\right] \tag{A.23}$$

$$= \frac{\phi\left(\frac{\epsilon+\mu}{\sqrt{\sigma_v^2+\sigma_u^2}}\right)}{\sqrt{\sigma_v^2+\sigma_u^2}\left[\frac{\Phi\left(\frac{\mu}{\sigma_u}\right)}{\Phi\left(\frac{\mu_*}{\sigma_*}\right)}\right]}. \tag{A.24}$$

Now, taking logs of the above equation, we obtain the log-likelihood function observation i for the truncated-normal model, which is the same as (3.47):

$$L_i = -\frac{1}{2}\ln(\sigma_v^2+\sigma_u^2) + \ln\phi\left(\frac{\mu+\epsilon}{\sqrt{\sigma_v^2+\sigma_u^2}}\right) + \ln\Phi\left(\frac{\mu_*}{\sigma_*}\right) - \ln\Phi\left(\frac{\mu}{\sigma_u}\right). \tag{A.25}$$

For the case of the half-normal model of Section 3.4.3, which assumes $u \sim N^+(0, \sigma_u^2)$, the derivation is essentially the same except that we set $\mu = 0$ in all the equations.

For the scaling-property model of Section 3.4.5, the distribution of u is (see also (3.65)):

$$u \sim \exp(\mathbf{z}'\boldsymbol{\delta}) \cdot N^+(\tau, \sigma_u^2) \tag{A.26}$$

$$= N^+(\tau \cdot \exp(\mathbf{z}'\boldsymbol{\delta}), \sigma_u^2 \exp(2\mathbf{z}'\boldsymbol{\delta})) \tag{A.27}$$

$$\equiv N^+(\breve{\mu}, \breve{\sigma}^2). \tag{A.28}$$

Therefore, to derive the likelihood function, we only need to substitute μ by $\breve{\mu}$ and σ_u by $\breve{\sigma}$ in all the equations.

For the case of the exponential model of Section 3.4.6, the derivation is different but nevertheless similar. We sketch the derivation here. If $u \geq 0$ has an exponential distribution,

$$f(u) = \frac{1}{\eta}\exp\left(-\frac{u}{\eta}\right), \qquad \text{for } \eta > 0. \tag{A.29}$$

The joint distribution of u and ϵ is

$$f(\epsilon+u, u) = \frac{1}{\sqrt{2\pi}\eta\sigma_v}\exp\left\{-\left[\frac{(\epsilon+u)^2}{2\sigma_v^2} + \frac{u}{\eta}\right]\right\}$$

$$= \frac{1}{\sqrt{2\pi}\eta\sigma_v}\exp\left\{-\frac{1}{2\sigma_v^2}\left[u + \left(\epsilon + \frac{\sigma_v^2}{\eta}\right)\right]^2 + \frac{\epsilon}{\eta} + \frac{\sigma_v^2}{2\eta^2}\right\}. \tag{A.30}$$

Then, the density function of ϵ can be derived as

$$\begin{aligned} f(\epsilon) &= \int_0^{\infty} f(\epsilon + u, u) du \\ &= \int_0^{\infty} \frac{1}{\sqrt{2\pi}\eta\sigma_v} \exp\left\{-\frac{1}{2\sigma_v}\left[u + \left(\epsilon + \frac{\sigma_v^2}{\eta}\right)\right]^2\right\} \exp\left(\frac{\epsilon}{\eta} + \frac{\sigma_v^2}{2\eta^2}\right) du \\ &= \frac{1}{\eta} \exp\left(\frac{\epsilon}{\eta} + \frac{\sigma_v^2}{2\eta^2}\right) \Phi\left(-\frac{\epsilon}{\sigma_v} - \frac{\sigma_v}{\eta}\right). \end{aligned} \tag{A.31}$$

Taking logs on this function, we then obtain the log-likelihood function shown in (3.87).

Appendix B

Deriving the Efficiency Estimates

In this appendix, we derive the inefficiency index $E(u_i|\epsilon_i)$ of Jondrow et al. (1982), and the technical efficiency index $E(\exp(-u_i)|\epsilon_i)$ of Battese and Coelli (1988). Again, we give detailed derivations assuming u has a truncated-normal distribution. Derivations for models with a half-normal distribution, a truncated normal distribution with scaling property, and an exponential distribution are sketched at the end of this appendix.

For the truncated-normal model, the density function of $u|\epsilon$ is given by the density of the joint distribution of u and ϵ given by (A.10) over the density of ϵ given by (A.24). The result is

$$f(u|\epsilon) = \frac{1}{\sqrt{2\pi}\sigma_*\Phi\left(\frac{\mu_*}{\sigma_*}\right)} \exp\left[-\frac{1}{2}\left(\frac{u-\mu_*}{\sigma_*}\right)^2\right], \tag{B.1}$$

where μ_* and σ_* are defined in (A.12) and (A.13), respectively. Then,

$$E(u|\epsilon) = \int_0^\infty u \cdot f(u|\epsilon)du = \int_0^\infty \frac{u}{\sqrt{2\pi}\sigma_*\Phi\left(\frac{\mu_*}{\sigma_*}\right)} \exp\left[-\frac{1}{2}\left(\frac{u-\mu_*}{\sigma_*}\right)^2\right]du. \tag{B.2}$$

Let

$$w = \frac{u-\mu_*}{\sigma_*}, \quad \text{then w} \in \left[-\frac{\mu_*}{\sigma_*}, \infty\right), \quad dw = \frac{du}{\sigma_*}.$$

Then

$$\begin{aligned} E(u|\epsilon) &= \int_{-\frac{\mu_*}{\sigma_*}}^\infty \frac{\mu_* + w\sigma_*}{\sqrt{2\pi}\Phi\left(\frac{\mu_*}{\sigma_*}\right)} \exp\left(-\frac{1}{2}w^2\right)dw \\ &= \frac{\mu_*}{\Phi\left(\frac{\mu_*}{\sigma_*}\right)} \int_{-\frac{\mu_*}{\sigma_*}}^\infty \frac{1}{\sqrt{2\pi}} \exp\left(-\frac{1}{2}w^2\right)dw + \frac{\sigma_*}{\Phi\left(\frac{\mu_*}{\sigma_*}\right)} \int_{-\frac{\mu_*}{\sigma_*}}^\infty \frac{w}{\sqrt{2\pi}} \exp\left(-\frac{1}{2}w^2\right)dw \\ &= \mu_* + \frac{\sigma_*}{\Phi\left(\frac{\mu_*}{\sigma_*}\right)} \cdot \frac{1}{\sqrt{2\pi}} \exp\left[-\frac{1}{2}\left(\frac{\mu_*}{\sigma_*}\right)^2\right] = \mu_* + \frac{\phi\left(\frac{\mu_*}{\sigma_*}\right)}{\Phi\left(\frac{\mu_*}{\sigma_*}\right)}\sigma_*. \end{aligned} \tag{B.3}$$

Now, for $E(\exp(-u)|\epsilon)$,

$$E\left(\exp(-u)|\epsilon\right) = \int_0^\infty \exp(-u)f\left(u|\epsilon\right)du$$

$$= \int_0^\infty \frac{1}{\sqrt{2\pi}\sigma_*\Phi\left(\frac{\mu_*}{\sigma_*}\right)} \exp\left[-\frac{1}{2}\left(\frac{u-\mu_*}{\sigma_*}\right)^2 - u\right]du \tag{B.4}$$

$$= \frac{1}{\sigma_*\Phi\left(\frac{\mu_*}{\sigma_*}\right)} \int_0^\infty \frac{1}{\sqrt{2\pi}} \exp\left[-\frac{1}{2}\left(\frac{u-\mu_*}{\sigma_*}\right)^2 - u\right]du. \tag{B.5}$$

Note that

$$-\frac{1}{2}\left(\frac{u-\mu_*}{\sigma_*}\right)^2 - u = \frac{u^2 - 2\left(\mu_* - \sigma_*^2\right)u + \mu_*^2}{-2\sigma_*^2} = \frac{\left[u - \left(\mu_* - \sigma_*^2\right)\right]^2 + \sigma_*^2\left(2\mu_* - \sigma_*^2\right)}{-2\sigma_*^2}$$
$$= -\frac{\left[u - \left(\mu_* - \sigma_*^2\right)\right]^2}{2\sigma_*^2} - \frac{1}{2}\left(2\mu_* - \sigma_*^2\right), \tag{B.6}$$

therefore, the formula is simplified to

$$E\left(\exp(-u)|\epsilon\right) = \frac{1}{\sigma_*\Phi\left(\frac{\mu_*}{\sigma_*}\right)} \int_0^\infty \frac{1}{\sqrt{2\pi}} \exp\left\{-\frac{\left[u - \left(\mu_* - \sigma_*^2\right)\right]^2}{2\sigma_*^2} - \frac{1}{2}\left(2\mu_* - \sigma_*^2\right)\right\}du \tag{B.7}$$

$$= \frac{\exp\left[-\frac{1}{2}\left(2\mu_* - \sigma_*^2\right)\right]}{\sigma_*\Phi\left(\frac{\mu_*}{\sigma_*}\right)} \int_0^\infty \frac{1}{\sqrt{2\pi}} \exp\left\{-\frac{1}{2}\left[\frac{u - \left(\mu_* - \sigma_*^2\right)}{\sigma_*}\right]^2\right\}du. \tag{B.8}$$

Let

$$z = \frac{u - \left(\mu_* - \sigma_*^2\right)}{\sigma_*}, \quad \text{then } z \in \left[-\frac{\mu_*}{\sigma_*} + \sigma_*, \infty\right), \quad dz = \frac{du}{\sigma_*}.$$

Finally,

$$E\left(\exp(-u)|\epsilon\right) = \frac{\exp\left[-\frac{1}{2}\left(2\mu_* - \sigma_*^2\right)\right]}{\sigma_*\Phi\left(\frac{\mu_*}{\sigma_*}\right)} \int_{-\frac{\mu_*}{\sigma_*}+\sigma_*}^\infty \frac{1}{\sqrt{2\pi}}\sigma_* \exp\left\{-\frac{1}{2}z^2\right\}dz$$

$$= \exp\left(-\mu_* + \frac{1}{2}\sigma_*^2\right)\frac{\Phi\left(\frac{\mu_*}{\sigma_*} - \sigma_*\right)}{\Phi\left(\frac{\mu_*}{\sigma_*}\right)}. \tag{B.9}$$

To derive the estimates for models with the half-normal distribution, we only need to substitute $\mu = 0$ into the equations. For the truncated-normal model with scaling property, we have shown in (A.26) to (A.28) that the distribution is a reparameterization of a standard truncated-normal distribution. Therefore, we derive the estimates by substituting μ by $\check{\mu}$ and σ by $\check{\sigma}$, where $\check{\mu}$ and $\check{\sigma}$ are shown in (A.26) to (A.28).

To derive the estimates for an exponential distribution model, we need to know the distribution of $u|\epsilon$, where u has an exponential distribution. The density, $f(u|\epsilon)$, is obtained by dividing the joint density of u and ϵ in (A.30) by the density of ϵ in (A.31). After simplifications, the result is

$$f(u|\epsilon) = \frac{1}{\sqrt{2\pi}\sigma_v \Phi\left(\frac{\mu_*}{\sigma_v}\right)} \exp\left[-\frac{1}{2}\left(\frac{u-\mu_*}{\sigma_v}\right)^2\right], \tag{B.10}$$

where

$$\mu_* = -\left(\frac{\epsilon\eta + \sigma_v^2}{\eta}\right) = -\left(\epsilon + \frac{\sigma_v^2}{\eta}\right). \tag{B.11}$$

Note the similarity between (B.10) and (B.1): The differences are in the definitions of μ_* and σ_*. Because of this similarity, we can derive the efficiency estimates for the exponential distribution following exactly the same steps outlined in this appendix, except that different definitions of μ_* and the σ_* are used in the derivation. As a result, the formulas of $E(u|\epsilon)$ and $E(\exp(-u)|\epsilon)$ for the exponential distribution model are similar to that of (B.3) and (B.9), respectively, with the only differences being how μ_* and σ_* are defined.

Appendix C

Deriving Confidence Intervals

In this appendix, we derive the confidence intervals for $E(u|\epsilon)$, and then we use the result to derive the confidence intervals for $E(\exp(-u)|\epsilon)$. We assume u has a truncated-normal distribution. We explain at the end of this appendix of how the confidence intervals may be derived for models with different distributions.

From (B.1), it is clear that the $u|\epsilon$ has a truncated-normal distribution:

$$u|\epsilon \sim N^+(\mu_*, \sigma_*^2), \tag{C.1}$$

where μ_* and σ_*^2 are defined in (A.12) and (A.13), respectively. Therefore, the $(1-\alpha)100\%$ confidence interval for $E(u|\epsilon)$ is

$$\mu_* + Z_L\sigma_* \ \leq \ E(u|\epsilon) \ \leq \ \mu_* + Z_U\sigma_*, \tag{C.2}$$

where $Z \sim N(0, 1)$, and

$$\Pr(Z \geq Z_L) = \left(1 - \frac{\alpha}{2}\right)\left[1 - \Phi\left(-\frac{\mu_*}{\sigma_*}\right)\right], \tag{C.3}$$

$$\Pr(Z \geq Z_U) = \frac{\alpha}{2}\left[1 - \Phi\left(-\frac{\mu_*}{\sigma_*}\right)\right]. \tag{C.4}$$

The values of Z_L and Z_U can be obtained as follows.

$$\Phi(Z_L) = 1 - \left(1 - \frac{\alpha}{2}\right)\left[1 - \Phi\left(-\frac{\mu_*}{\sigma_*}\right)\right], \tag{C.5}$$

$$\Longrightarrow Z_L = \Phi^{-1}\left\{1 - \left(1 - \frac{\alpha}{2}\right)\left[1 - \Phi\left(-\frac{\mu_*}{\sigma_*}\right)\right]\right\}; \tag{C.6}$$

$$\Phi(Z_U) = 1 - \frac{\alpha}{2}\left[1 - \Phi\left(-\frac{\mu_*}{\sigma_*}\right)\right], \tag{C.7}$$

$$\Longrightarrow Z_U = \Phi^{-1}\left\{1 - \frac{\alpha}{2}\left[1 - \Phi\left(-\frac{\mu_*}{\sigma_*}\right)\right]\right\}. \tag{C.8}$$

Now, denote the lower and the upper bounds of the confidence interval of $E(u|\epsilon)$ in (C.2) as follows:

$$L_i = \mu_* + Z_L\sigma_*, \tag{C.9}$$

$$U_i = \mu_* + Z_U\sigma_*. \tag{C.10}$$

Thus, the $(1-\alpha)100\%$ confidence interval for $E(\exp(-u)|\epsilon)$ is

$$\exp(-U_i) \leq E(\exp(-u)|\epsilon) \leq \exp(-L_i). \tag{C.11}$$

The results followed because of the monotonicity of $\exp(-u_i)$ as a function of u_i.

The confidence intervals for the half-normal model, the truncated-normal model with scaling property, and the exponential model can be derived by modifying the above equations slightly, mainly on the different definitions of μ_* and σ_* for the different models. We have shown how to do the modifications in Appendix A and B, and the changes to be made are similar here.

Appendix D

Bootstrapping Standard Errors of Marginal Effects on Inefficiency

This appendix shows an example of how to bootstrap standard errors of variables' marginal effects on inefficiency. The example follows the model discussed on page 81.

Recall the model we considered is estimated by the following commands.

```
. use milk
. global xvar llabor lfeed lcattle lland
. sfmodel ly, prod dist(t) frontier($xvar) mu(comp) usigmas(comp) vsigmas()
. sf_srch, n(1) frontier($xvar) mu(comp) usigmas(comp)
. ml max, difficult gtol(1e-5) nrtol(1e-5)
```

The marginal effects of comp on the inefficiency is calculated here:

```
. sf_predict, bc(bc_w) marginal

The following is the marginal effect on unconditional E(u) from FOC.

The mean marginal effect of comp on uncond E(u) is -.03604191 (see comp_M).

The following is the marginal effect on uncond V(u) from FOC.

The mean marginal effect of comp on uncond V(u) is -.0064839 (see comp_V).
```

Now, we bootstrap the standard errors of the statistics −.03604191 and −.0064839; that is, the mean marginal effect of comp on both $E(u)$ and $V(u)$. This is undertaken using the program below.

Before the illustration, we discuss an important issue. One of the difficulties in bootstrapping statistics from an ML model is what to do with a replication for which the numerical maximization fails. The approach, which we recommend, is to record and examine the problematic bootstrap sample and try to understand and fix the problem. The problem may be solved, for example, by using a different set of initial values. This procedure, however, requires more elaborate codes and user interaction with the program.

The following program, however, takes an easier route for demonstration purposes. It simply discards the samples that fail to converge. In order to make it work, the program has to aim at a number of replications which is larger than the desired (user specified) number in order to make room for the error samples. By default, the program aims at bootstrapping five times as many as the specified samples, but an algorithm is added so that the program stops when the desired (user specified) number of *useable* (i.e., no estimation error) bootstrap samples is reached.

```
. use dairy
. * parameters
. global nofrep = 1000 /*  the number of replications */
. global savedata demo_boot2 /* the saved filename */
. set seed 1234    /* random seed; this is important for the purpose of reproducibility */
. scalar itlimit = 30 /* The iteration limit in the ML estimation; */
                   /* should be sufficient, but not overly large. */
                   /* Should test run a few replications and see what is */
                   /* the appropriate number.*/
. global xvar llabor lfeed lcattle lland
.   * Estimate the model and record the results to be used as initial values in the bootstrapping
. sfmodel ly, prod dist(t) frontier($xvar) mu(comp) usigmas(comp) vsigmas()
. sf_srch, n(1) frontier($xvar) mu(comp) usigmas(comp) nograph fast
. ml max, difficult gtol(1e-5) nrtol(1e-5)
. matrix b0 = e(b)
. matrix bf = b0[1, "frontier:"]
. matrix bm = b0[1, "mu:"]
. matrix bu = b0[1, "usigmas:"]
. matrix bv = b0[1, "vsigmas:"]
.   * define the bootstrap program
. scalar nc = 0
. scalar done = 0
. scalar error_run = 0
. capture program drop bootpgm
. program define bootpgm, rclass
  1.
. if done == 0
  2.
.   * define the maximization problem
. local itlimit = scalar(itlimit) /* take the scalar to a local */
  3.
. sfmodel ly, prod dist(t) frontier($xvar) mu(comp) usigmas(comp) vsigmas()
  4. sf_init, frontier(bf) mu(bm) usigmas(bu) vsigmas(bv)
  5. capture ml max, difficult gtol(1e-5) nrtol(1e-5) iterate(`itlimit')
  6.
.   * error checking
. if ( e(rc) ~= 0) | (e(ic)==`itlimit')    /* means the convergence is */
  7.    scalar error_run = error_run + 1     /* problematic; discard this result */
  8.    exit                                 /* immediately exit the current sample, */
  9.                                        /* and move on to the next one. */
 10.
.   * calculating the desired statistics
. tempvar bcvar
 11.
. quietly sf_predict, bc(`bcvar') marginal /* calcualte the inefficiency measure and the */
 12.                                       /* marginal effects   */
. quietly summarize comp_M, meanonly /* get the summary statistic of comp's marginal effect */
 13. return scalar mM = r(mean)    /* on the inefficiency's mean */
 14.
. quietly summarize comp_V, meanonly /* repeat the same thing comp's marginal effect on the */
 15. return scalar mV = r(mean)    /* inefficiency's variance */
 16.
. scalar nc = nc + 1
 17.
. if scalar(nc) == $nofrep + 1  /* When the desired number of replications is reached, */
 18.  scalar done = 1            /*  calculation shall stop. */
 19.
 20.
.
 21.
. end
```

```
. local nofrun = 5*$nofrep /* Give it a larger number of runs to allow for aborted cases */
                           /* of unsuccessful ML estimation. */
                           /* The program would stop if the desired numbers of */
                           /* replications are reached. */

. global nofrun = `nofrun'

. capture program drop disp_msg
. program define disp_msg
  1. di " "
  2. di in yel "*************************************************************************"
  3. di in yel " The program is bootstraping with " in gre "$nofrun " in yel "bootstrap samples,"
  4. di in yel " which is 5 times as many as your specified number of bootstrap samples."
  5. di in yel " The program will stop, nevertheless, when the number of your specified"
  6. di in yel " number of bootstrap samples, which is " in gre "$nofrep" in yel", is reached."
  7. di in yellow "*************************************************************************"
  8. di " "
  9. end

. disp_msg

. bootstrap "bootpgm" B_comp_M=r(mM) B_comp_V = r(mV), reps(`nofrun') ///
>                                   double saving($savedata) replace
```

The following is the printout from the last few lines of the program.

```
. disp_msg

**********************************************************************
 The program is bootstraping with 5000 bootstrap samples,
 which is 5 times as many as your specified number of bootstrap samples.
 The program will stop, nevertheless, when the number of your specified
 number of bootstrap samples, which is 1000, is reached.
**********************************************************************

. bootstrap "bootpgm" B_comp_M=r(mM) B_comp_V = r(mV), reps(`nofrun') ///
>                                   double saving($savedata) replace

command:       bootpgm
statistics:    B_comp_M   = r(mM)
               B_comp_V   = r(mV)

Bootstrap statistics                          Number of obs    =       196
                                              Replications     =      5000

------------------------------------------------------------------------------
Variable     |  Reps  Observed      Bias  Std. Err. [95% Conf. Interval]
-------------+----------------------------------------------------------------
    B_comp_M |  1000 -.0360419 -.0049772  .0130549     -.06166  -.0104238   (N)
             |                                       -.0706245  -.0194365   (P)
             |                                       -.0582686  -.0151667  (BC)
    B_comp_V |  1000 -.0064839 -.0004528  .0035988    -.013546   .0005782   (N)
             |                                       -.0157074  -.0014413   (P)
             |                                       -.0156892  -.0014207  (BC)
------------------------------------------------------------------------------
Note:  N   = normal
       P   = percentile
       BC  = bias-corrected
```

The standard error of the marginal effect of comp on the mean inefficiency is 0.0131, and on the variance of the inefficiency is 0.0036.

Appendix E

Software and Estimation Commands

E.1 Download and Install the User-Written Programs

We provide Stata programs written by authors of the book to estimate most of the models discussed in the book. The programs are Stata ado-files. Once they are installed, the estimation commands, as shown in the book, will become available.

The ado-files can be downloaded from https://sites.google.com/site/sfbook2014/. After the download, save them to one of Stata's ado-file paths. The ado-file paths are directories in your computer where Stata will automatically search for estimation commands. Thus, programs saved in one of those directories will become available to Stata. To see the full list of available ado-file paths in your computer, enter

```
. adopath
```

A safe place to install the ado-files is the "personal" directory shown in the list. To check whether the files are installed correctly, enter

```
. sfbook
```

in Stata command window after the installation. A congratulation message will appear if the ado-files are installed correctly. Otherwise, you will see

```
. unrecognized command:  sfbook
```

and that means that the ado-files are not saved in the correct directory.

Important: There is a version control issue that may cause problems to users of newer versions of Stata starting from Stata 11. Please see the section of Version Control Issue on https://sites.google.com/site/sfbook2014/ for how to get around the problem and other information update.

E.2 Download the Empirical Data and the Do-Files

The dataset and the Stata do-files used as empirical examples in the book can also be downloaded from https://sites.google.com/site/sfbook2014/.

E.3 Cross-Sectional Models and Basic Utilities

E.3.1 sfmodel

```
sfmodel depvar [if] [in],  distribution(halfnormal | truncated | exponential)
                           production | cost
                           frontier(varlist_f [, noconstant])
                           vsigmas([varlist_v [, noconstant]])
```

```
[ mu( [varlist_m [, noconstant]]) etas( [varlist_e [, noconstant]])
  usigmas( [varlist_u [, noconstant]])
  scaling hscale(varlist_h) tau cu robust cluster(varname)
  technique( nr | dfp | bfgs | bhhh) show ]
```

Description

The command `sfmodel` sets up the log-likelihood function for a cross-sectional stochastic frontier model introduced in Section 3.4. The command does *not* carry out the estimation which is done through `ml max`. After `sfmodel` and before `ml max`, users have the option of using `sf_init` to provide initial values and `sf_srch` to refine initial values. After the model is estimated by `ml max`, users then have the option of using `sf_transform` to obtain variance parameters in the original form, and `sf_predict` to obtain the inefficiency index of Jondrow et al. (1982) and the efficiency index of Battese and Coelli (1988).

The following is a representative model when the technical inefficiency (u_i) is assumed to have a half-normal or a truncated-normal distribution.

$$\ln y_i = \boldsymbol{x}_i\boldsymbol{\beta} + v_i - u_i, \tag{E.1}$$

$$u_i \sim N^+(\mu, \sigma_u^2), \tag{E.2}$$

$$v_i \sim N(0, \sigma_v^2). \tag{E.3}$$

The following parameterizations are considered.

$$\mu = \boldsymbol{z}_i'\boldsymbol{\delta}, \qquad \sigma_u^2 = \exp(\boldsymbol{z}_{ui}'\boldsymbol{w}), \qquad \sigma_v^2 = \exp(\boldsymbol{z}_{vi}'\boldsymbol{\theta}). \tag{E.4}$$

The command specifies the dependent and independent variables of the frontier function, selects the distribution assumption of u for the model, and optionally specifies the exogenous determinants of inefficiency.

Options

distribution(halfnormal | truncated | exponential) indicates the distribution assumption of the technical inefficiency term (u_i). The choices are `halfnormal` for the model of half-normal distribution, `truncated` for the truncated-normal distribution model and the scaling-property model, and `exponential` for exponential distribution model.

production|cost indicates whether the model is a production-type model (production) or a cost-type model (cost).

frontier(*varlist$_f$* [, *noconstant*]) specifies variables to be included in the deterministic part of the frontier function; i.e., the $\boldsymbol{x}_i$ in (E.1).

Note that, according to Stata's convention, only *non-constant* variables should be specified in a variable list of a regression. By default, a constant (of 1) will be automatically appended to the specified variable list by Stata.

There are three different possibilities in specifying the variable list of *varlist$_f$*. (i) Leave it blank (e.g., `frontier()`), in which case the function will contain only a constant (automatically appended by Stata). (ii) Specify a list of existing variables (e.g., `frontier(x1 x2)`). Then the function will contain those specified plus a constant. (iii) Specify a list of existing variables and ask Stata not to automatically include the constant (e.g., `frontier(x1 x2, noconstant)`). Then the function will contain only the specified variables, and no constant will be appended to the list by Stata.

mu([*varlist*$_m$[, *noconstant*]]) is used only when u_i is assumed to have a truncated-normal distribution. It specifies variables used to parameterize the pre-truncation mean of the distribution of u_i, i.e., the $\boldsymbol{z}_i$ in places such as (E.4). If `mu()` is specified without argument, the pre-truncation mean is a constant. If variables are specified in the argument, such as `mu(z1 z2)`, then the pre-truncation mean is a function of these variables plus a constant, which is automatically appended by Stata.

etas([*varlist*$_e$[, *noconstant*]]) is used only when u_i is assumed to have an exponential distribution where the density function is $f(u) = (1/\eta)\exp((-1/\eta)u)$, $u \geq 0$. Note that it parameterizes η^2 (which is the variance of u), not η (which is the mean): $\eta^2 = \exp(\boldsymbol{z}_i'\boldsymbol{w})$. This is emphasized by the last letter 's' (for *square*) of this syntax. If `etas()` is specified without argument, then η^2 is assumed to be a constant.

hscale(*varlist*$_h$) is used only for the scaling property model of Wang and Schmidt (2002). The technical inefficiency term of the model is specified as follows.

$$\begin{aligned} u_i &\sim h(\boldsymbol{z}_{ui}, \boldsymbol{\delta}) \cdot N^+(\tau, \sigma^2) \\ &\equiv \exp(\boldsymbol{z}_{ui}'\boldsymbol{\delta}) \cdot N^+(\tau, \exp(c_u)). \end{aligned} \tag{E.5}$$

Thus, this option specifies the variables in the scaling function; that is, the $\boldsymbol{z}_{ui}$ in (E.5). Since the scaling function of (E.5) needs to be specified as a function of a set of variables, the empty string (`hscale()`) is not allowed. Also, because the function does not have a constant by construction, the `noconstant` option is not allowed.

tau is used only for the scaling property model of Wang and Schmidt (2002). It indicates the τ parameter in (E.5).

cu is used only for the scaling property model of Wang and Schmidt (2002). It indicates the c_u parameter in (E.5).

usigmas([*varlist*$_u$ [, *noconstant*]]) specifies $\boldsymbol{z}_{ui}$ to parameterize σ_u^2 (see (E.4)). Note that it parameterizes the σ_u^2 (the variance), not σ_u (the standard deviation). This is emphasized by the last letter 's' (for *square*) of this syntax. If `usigmas()` is specified without argument, a constant variance of u_i is assumed. In this case, the parameter being estimated is the C_u as in $\sigma_u^2 = \exp(C_u)$, and `sf_transform` can be used to recover $\hat{\sigma}_u^2$ after estimation.

vsigmas([*varlist*$_v$ [, *noconstant*]]) specifies $\boldsymbol{z}_{vi}$ to parameterize σ_v^2 (see (E.4)). Note that it parameterizes the σ_v^2 (the variance), not σ_v (the standard deviation). This is emphasized by the last letter 's' (for *square*) of this syntax. If `usigmas()` is specified without argument, a constant variance of v_i is assumed. In this case, the parameter being estimated is the C_v as in $\sigma_v^2 = \exp(C_v)$, and `sf_transform` can be used to recover $\hat{\sigma}_v^2$ after the estimation.

robust reports robust variance estimates. `robust` is a native Stata option; to get more information on this option type `help robust`.

cluster(*varname*) specifies the name of a variable that contains identifiers for the primary sampling unit. `cluster` is a native Stata option; to get more information on this option type `help cluster`.

technique(nr | dfp | bfgs | bhhh) specifies the algorithm used to maximize the log-likelihood function. The default is *nr* which is a modified Newton-Raphson algorithm. The `dfp`, `bfgs`, and `bhhh` are the algorithms by Davidon-Fletcher-Powell, Berndt-Hall-Hall-Hausman, and Broyden-Fletcher-Goldfarb-Shanno, respectively. `technique` is a native Stata option; to get more information on this option type `help technique`.

show prints the likelihood function set up by `sfmodel` in Stata's `ml model` syntax. It is mainly used for debugging purposes. It might also be useful if, for example, the user wants to supply initial values using Stata's `ml init` in lieu of `sf_init` and needs to know the order of the equations and variables in the likelihood function.

Note

Users are reminded that to estimate the model of Wang (2002), the variable list specified in `mu()` and `usigmas()` should be identical, including the order of the variables.

E.3.2 sf_init

```
sf_init,   [ frontier(numlist) inputs(numlist) linear(numlist) mu(numlist)
             usigmas(numlist) vsigmas(numlist) esigmas(numlist)
             etas(numlist) hscale(numlist) tau(numlist) cu(numlist)
             share1(numlist) share2(numlist) share3(numlist) share4(numlist)
             gamma(numlist) sigmauv(numlist) s11(numlist) s22(numlist) s33(numlist)
             s44(numlist) s21(numlist) s31(numlist) s32(numlist) s41(numlist)
             s42(numlist) s43(numlist) m1(numlist) m2(numlist) m3(numlist)
             m4(numlist) m5(numlist) zvar(numlist) show ]
```

Description

The `sf_init` command is used to supply initial values for the model parameters to be estimated by the maximum likelihood method. It is used after setting up the model's likelihood function by `sfmodel`, `sfsystem`, `sfsystem_profitshares`, `sfpan`, `sf_fixeff`, and `sfprim`. This is an optional command. Stata will pick an arbitrary set of initial values to begin the maximization process if no initial values are given by the user. However, since stochastic frontier models are numerically difficult, *good* initial values can be important for achieving convergence in the estimation.

The `sf_init` is essentially a wrapper of the native Stata command `ml init`. Unlike `ml init`, users using `sf_init` do not need to worry about the order of the equations (`frontier()`, `mu()`, etc.) used in the model; `sf_init` will sort it out for you. For example, users can put `vsigmas(`*numlist*`)` before `frontier(`*numlist*`)` or vice versa. Experienced users may specify the `show` option in `sfmodel` to see the order of the equations/variables, and use `ml init` to provide initial values directly. See [R] `ml` for information on `ml init`.

It is important to note that if the user uses `sf_init` (or, for that matter, `ml init` as well), then a *complete* set of initial values for the model needs to be supplied. This means initial values for each of variables (including the constants) in each of the equations. That is, users cannot specify only a subset of initial values.

Options

The options, `frontier(`*numlist*`)`, `mu(`*numlist*`)`, etc., correspond to the equations used in the various models of `sfmodel`, `sfsystem`, `sfsystem_profitshares`, `sfpan`, `sf_fixeff`, and `sfprim`. These specify a list of numbers or a $1 \times k$ matrix of numerical values where k is the number of parameters in the equation including a constant (intercept).

The `show` option, which is mainly used for debugging purposes, prints the initial value vector set up by `sf_init` in Stata's `ml init` syntax.

Example

Consider the function `frontier()` set up by `sfmodel` and suppose that, in the `sfmodel` command line, you specify `frontier(x1 x2)`. This implies that the deterministic part of the frontier equation contains two variables, $x1$ and $x2$, and a constant. (The constant is automatically appended to the equation by Stata unless `noconstant` is also specified). The corresponding initial values in `sf_init` would be specified as, for example, `frontier(0.1 0.2 0.5)`. In this example, 0.1 and 0.2 are the initial values of $x1$ and $x2$, respectively, and the value 0.5 (the *last* value in the list) is the initial value of the constant of the deterministic frontier function. The above rule applies to almost all the equations, except for the `hscale()` and `zvar()` functions, and the `frontier()` function set up by `sf_fixeff`. For these functions, there is no constant term by construction. So, for instance, if in the `sf_fixeff` command line you specify `frontier(x1 x2)`, then in the `sf_init` line you would specify something like `frontier(0.1 0.2)`. That is, no initial value for the *additional constant* is provided since no constant is added to the equation.

E.3.3 sf_srch

```
sf_srch, n(numeric) [ frontier(varlist) inputs(varlist) linear(varlist) mu(varlist)
         usigmas(varlist) vsigmas(varlist) esigmas(varlist)
         etas(varlist) hscale(varlist) tau cu
         share1(varlist) share2(varlist) share3(varlist) share4(varlist)
         gamma(varlist) sigmauv(varlist) zvar(varlist)
         nograph fast ]
```

Description

The `sf_srch` command is used in a ML estimation of a stochastic frontier model. It searches for better initial values for the variables' parameters specified in the functions. This is an optional command. The `sf_srch` is essentially a wrapper of Stata's native command `ml plot`, which graphs the likelihood profile against values of a specified parameter (while holding other parameters unchanged) and then replaces the parameter's initial value by the one that yields the highest likelihood value on the plot. The command is useful for fine-tuning the initial value of the specified parameter, while holding the other parameter values unchanged. For more information see [R] `ml`.

If `sf_init` is used to provide initial values before issuing `sf_srch`, `sf_srch` will perform the search using those initial values as starting points. Otherwise, the search starts at the initial values chosen by the internal algorithm of Stata. By default, all the constants in the equations (such as the constants in functions of `frontier`, `mu`, etc. and the `tau`, `cu`, `s11`, `s12` parameters, etc.) will be searched, and users only need to specify the non-constant variables.

Unlike `sf_init`, users do not need to specify a complete set of variables with `sf_srch`. That is, users can choose to perform the search on only a subset of variables from all or part of the equations.

Options

n(*numeric*) specifies the number of times the search is to be performed on the specified parameters. For example, `n(1)` will do the search once for each of the specified variables, and `n(2)` will allow the search to cycle through the variables once again. There is no upper limit on the number, but it has to be an integer and greater than 0.

frontier([*varlist*]), **inputs**([*varlist*]), . . ., **zvars**([*varlist*]) specifies the variables in the equations for which the search for better initial values is to be performed.

nograph asks Stata to perform the search silently without showing the graphs of the likelihood function profile in a graph window. Although the graphs are sometimes informative, they are unnecessary most of the time.

fast asks Stata to draw graphs of variables' likelihood profiles using a more basic formatting style, which is faster than the default.

Note that the `nograph` option does not cut the search time as much as `fast` would do. The `nograph` option only suppresses graph renderings in the screen.

E.3.4 sf_transform

```
sf_transform
```

Description

The `sf_transform` command is issued after a stochastic frontier model is estimated in order to obtain the variance parameters in their original form. For instance, consider the statistical error random variable $v_i \sim N(0, \sigma_v^2)$ where $\sigma_v^2 > 0$ is the variance parameter. Instead of directly estimating σ_v^2 in the maximum likelihood estimation, we parameterize it as

$$\sigma_v^2 = \exp(C_v), \tag{E.6}$$

and estimate $C_v \lesseqqgtr 0$ as an unconstrained parameter. The `sf_transform` then uses the result to report $\hat{\sigma}_v^2 = \exp(\hat{C}_v)$.

E.3.5 sf_predict

```
sf_predict [if] [in], bc(newvarname1) jlms(newvarname2) [ ci(#) marginal ]
```

Description

This command is issued after a stochastic frontier model is estimated using the author-written commands in this book (`sfmodel`, `sfpan`, and `sf_fixeff`). It computes the observation-specific efficiency index of Battese and Coelli (1988) (`bc`) and/or Jondrow et al. (1982) (`jlms`), and the confidence intervals of these index (`ci`). Except for models with systems of equations (`sfsystem`, `sfsystem_profitshares`, and `sfprim`), the addition of the option `marginal` results in the marginal effects of the exogenous determinants on the mean and the variance of inefficiency u_i (Wang [2002]) also being calculated. If marginal effects are requested, the sample mean of the marginal effects will be printed on Stata's result window, and the observation-specific marginal effects will be saved in the dataset.

Options

bc(*newvarname*$_1$) calculates the technical efficiency index $E(\exp(-u_i)|\epsilon_i)$, where ϵ_i is the composed error of the model, of Battese and Coelli (1988), and saves the observation-specific values in the variable *newnvarname*$_1$.

jlms(*newvarname*$_2$) calculates the inefficiency index $E(u_i|\epsilon_i)$, where ϵ_i is the composed error of the model, of Jondrow et al. (1982), and saves the observation-specific values in the variable *newvarname*$_2$.

ci(#) calculates, for each observation, the lower and upper bounds of the confidence intervals of the efficiency score specified by either `bc(`*newvarname*$_1$`)`, or `jlms(`*newvarname*$_2$`)`, or both. The number (#) indicates the coverage of the confidence interval. For example, ci(95) indicates that the lower and upper bounds of a 95% confidence intervals are to be calculated. Values of the bounds are saved in new variables, with the names being *newvarname*$_1$`_#L` and *newvarname*$_1$`_#U`, or *newvarname*$_2$`_#L` and *newvarname*$_2$`_#U`, respectively, in the case of `bc` and `jlms`.

For example, if `bc(r1)` and `ci(95)` are specified, then three variables will be created. One is `r1` created per the option `bc(r1)`, which takes values of the point estimates of $E(\exp(-u_i)|\epsilon_i)$ of each observation. The other two are `r1_95L` and `r1_95U`. The former contains values of the lower bound of the 95% confidence interval of `r1` and the latter contains values of the upper bound of the 95% confidence interval of `r1` for each observation. If `jlms(k2)` is also specified, then, in addition to the variable `k2`, two other variables are created that contains values of the lower and upper bounds of the associated confidence interval: `k2_95L` and `k2_95U`.

marginal calculates the marginal effects of the exogenous determinants on inefficiency. The marginal effects are observation-specific, and those values are saved in the variables *variable*_M and *variable*_V for the marginal effects on the mean and the variance, respectively, of the inefficiency, where *variable* is the variable name of the exogenous determinant. In addition, the sample mean of the variable's marginal effects will be printed in Stata's results window.

For example, if `mu(z1)` is specified in `sfmodel` for a truncated normal model and `marginal` is specified in `sf_predict`, then variables z1_M and z1_V are created, taking values of the marginal effects of z1 on the mean and the variance, respectively, of expected inefficiency ($E(u_i)$). The sample means of z1_M and z1_V are also printed in Stata's results window.

Currently, the marginal effects are not available for models with systems of equations (`sfsystem`, `sfsystem_profitshares`, and `sfprim`).

E.3.6 sf_mixtable

`sf_mixtable, dof(`*numeric*`)`

Description

The command `sf_mixtable` tabulates critical values of a mixed Chi-square distribution at different significance levels with the degree of freedom specified in `dof()`. The values are taken from Table 1 of Kodde and Palm (1986). This table is useful for hypothesis testing using LR tests.

Options

dof(*numeric***)** specifies the degrees of freedom of the test statistic, which is usually the number of restrictions in the test. The degrees of freedom is restricted to values between 1 and 40 (inclusive).

E.4 System Models

E.4.1 sfsystem

```
sfsystem depvar  [if] [in], distribution(halfnormal | truncated)
                 frontier(varlist_f [, noconstant]) corr(no|partial|full)
                 constraints(numbers) share1(depvar_s1 = varlist_s)
                 [share2(depvar_s2 = varlist_s) share3(depvar_s3 = varlist_s)
                  share4(depvar_s4 = varlist_s) mu([varlist [, noconstant]])
                  cost gamma sigmauv usigmas s11 s22 s33 s44 s21 s31
                  s32 s41 s42 s43 show]
```

Description

The command `sfsystem` sets up the log-likelihood function for a cost system model introduced in Chapter 6. The command specifies the dependent and independent variables of the frontier function, the distribution assumption of the inefficiency term, and the correlation assumption of the error terms of the main and the share equations.

Options

distribution(halfnormal | truncated) indicates the distribution assumption of the inefficiency term (u_i). The possible choices are `halfnormal` for the model of half-normal distribution, `truncated` for the truncated-normal distribution model.

frontier(*varlist*$_f$ **[,** ***noconstant*****])** specifies variables to be included in the deterministic part of the frontier function.

corr(no|partial|full) specifies the error terms' correlation assumption: `no` indicates no correlation and all the equations are independent, `partial` indicates correlations among the share equations, and `full` allows correlations between the cost function and all the share equations.

constraints(*numbers***)** specifies constraint equations.

share1(*depvar*$_{s1}$ = *varlist*$_s$) to **share4**(*depvar*$_{s4}$ = *varlist*$_s$) specifies the first to the fourth share equations, where *depvar*$_{si}$ is the ith input variable, $i = 1, \ldots, 4$, and *varlist*$_s$ is the list of input prices and output variables.

Note that at least one share equation needs to be specified. The specified number of share equations should be continuous. For instance, specifying `share1` and `share3` but skipping `share2` is not permissible.

mu([*varlist*$_m$[, *noconstant*]]) is used only when u_i is assumed to have a truncated-normal distribution. It specifies the variables used to parameterize the pre-truncation mean of the distribution of the inefficiency term. If `mu()` is specified without argument, the the pre-truncation mean is a constant. See the equivalent entry in `sfmodel` for more information.

cost indicates that it is a cost system model.

gamma, sigmauv, usigmas are unconstrained parameters in the following parameterization equations:

$$\frac{1}{1+\exp(\texttt{gamma})} = \frac{\sigma_u^2}{\sigma_u^2+\sigma_v^2}, \tag{E.7}$$

$$\exp(\texttt{sigmauv}) = \sqrt{\sigma_v^2+\sigma_u^2}, \tag{E.8}$$

$$\exp(\texttt{usigmas}) = \sigma_u^2. \tag{E.9}$$

Note that `gamma, sigmauv, usigmas` are optional, although we feel that specifying them helps to remind users about the parameters used in the estimation. After the model is estimated, we can recover the estimates of σ_v^2 and σ_u^2 by issuing the `sf_transform` command.

s11 to **s43** specify the elements of the symmetric variance-covariance matrix (up to 4×4) between the (correlated) equations. The numeric index denotes the matrix subscript. With `corr(no)`, only the diagonal elements are estimated. Specifying the elements is optional; the appropriate variance-covariance matrix will be estimated regardless.

show prints the likelihood function set up by `sfsystem` in Stata's `ml model` syntax. It is mainly used for debugging purposes. It might also be useful if, for example, the user wants to supply initial values using Stata's `ml init` in lieu of `sf_init` and needs to know the order of the equations and variables in the likelihood function.

E.4.2 showini

`showini,` [`covmat(`*matrix*`) sigmaus(`*numeric*`) sigmavs(`*numeric*`)`]

Description

The command `showini` is a utility for `sfsystem` which helps to obtain the initial values for the elements of the variance-covariance matrix. The initial values thus obtained can be fed into the maximum likelihood estimation of the model via `sf_init`. See Chapter 6 for examples.

Options

covmat(*matrix*) specifies the variance covariance matrix. `sfsystem` estimates the variance-covariance matrix using the Cholesky decomposition, and so initial values of the elements of the matrix need to be in the form *after* the matrix underwent Cholesky decomposition. For instance, if the user has prior knowledge that the 2×2 variance covariance matrix is

$$\begin{pmatrix} 1 & -0.5 \\ -0.5 & 2 \end{pmatrix}, \tag{E.10}$$

then the corresponding initial values for elements of the decomposed matrix may be obtained by

```
showini, cov(1, -0.5 \ -0.5, 2)
```

which returns

```
. s11ini = 0
. s22ini = .27980789
. s21ini = -.5
```

These initial values are also saved in the return macros (such as r(s11ini), etc.). Note that the initial values of the diagonal elements are log-transformed. It is informative to show how these values relate to the original matrix.

```
. matrix chol = (exp(0), 0 \ -0.5, exp(0.27980789))
. matrix aa = chol*chol'
. matrix list aa

symmetric aa[2,2]
       r1   r2
r1      1
r2    -.5    2
```

sigmaus(*numeric*) and **sigmavs(*numeric*)** specify the values of σ_u^2 and σ_v^2, respectively. Given the values, `showini` will return the corresponding values of `gamma` and `sigmauv` (described above), which can be used as initial values for model estimation. For instance, if prior information indicates that $\sigma_u^2 = 2$ and $\sigma_v^2 = 1$, then

```
. showini, sigmaus(2) sigmavs(1)
```

returns

```
gammaini = -.69314718
sigmauvini = .54930614
```

and the values are saved in `r(gammaini)` and `r(sigmauvini)`, respectively.

E.4.3 sfsysem_profitshares

```
sfsystem_profitshares [if] [in],  distribution(halfnormal | truncated)
                                  output(varlist_y) yprice(varlist_yp)
                                  inputs(varlist_x) prices(varlist_p)
                                  [usigmas([varlist_u [, noconstant]])
                                  mu([varlist_m [, noconstant]])
                                  classical noask show]
```

Description

The command `sfsystem_profitshares` estimates the profit frontier model using the profit share equations introduced in Chapter 7. More specifically, it sets up the log-likelihood function of (7.18). The required inputs include the output and input variables and the corresponding prices, and the distribution assumption of the inefficiency term. With the `classical` option, it estimates the system without the inefficiency term.

Note that the model assumes that the underlying production has a translog technology. Similar to `sfsystem`, users only need to supply a list of individual input variables, and the full list of regressors (including the square and cross-product terms) for the translog specification will be automatically generated by the program.

The command does *not* carry out the estimation. This is done through `ml max`. After `sfsyste_profitshares` and before `ml max`, users have the option of using `sf_init` to provide initial values and `sf_srch` to refine initial values. After the model is estimated by `ml max`, users then have the options of using `sf_transform` to obtain variance parameters in the original form, and `sf_predict` to obtain the inefficiency index of Jondrow et al. (1982) and the efficiency index of Battese and Coelli (1988).

Options

distribution(halfnormal | truncated) indicates the distribution assumption of the inefficiency term (u_i). The possible choices are `halfnormal`, for the half-normal distribution model, and `truncated`, for the truncated-normal distribution model.

output(*varlist*$_y$) specifies the *logarithm* of the output variable.

yprice(*varlist*$_{yp}$) specifies the *logarithm* of the output price variable.

inputs(*varlist*$_x$) specifies a $1 \times m$ vector of variable inputs and (if applicable) quasi-fixed inputs in *logarithms*. The names of the quasi-fixed inputs must follow the names of the variable inputs. Also, the order of the variable inputs need to follow the same order of the variable inputs' prices listed in `prices()`.

prices(*varlist*$_p$) specifies a $1 \times n$ vector of price variables (in *logarithms*) for the variable inputs. The order in which the prices are listed should correspond to the order of the variable inputs listed in `inputs()`. If $m > n$, then the first n inputs listed in `inputs()` are taken as variable inputs, with the rest being quasi-fixed inputs.

Note: The program uses information of the supplied output, output prices, inputs, and input prices to construct profit shares which are variables used in the model.

mu([*varlist*$_m$[, *noconstant*]]) is used only when u_i is assumed to have a truncated-normal distribution. It specifies variables used to parameterize the pretruncation mean of the distribution of the inefficiency term. If `mu()` is specified without argument, the pre-truncation mean is a constant. See the equivalent entry in `sfmodel` for more information.

usigmas([*varlist*$_u$ [, *noconstant*]]) specifies the pretruncation variance of the inefficiency term. See the equivalent entry in `sfmodel` for more information.

classical assumes that there is no inefficiency in the model, which effectively drops the inefficiency term from the model estimation. Results of this model can serve as initial values for the full model with technical inefficiency.

noask suppresses the confirmation prompt during the estimation process.

show prints the likelihood function set up by `sfsystem_profitshares` in Stata's `ml model` syntax. It is mainly used for debugging purposes. It might also be useful if, for example, the user wants to supply initial values using Stata's `ml init` in lieu of `sf_init` and needs to know the order of the equations and the variables in the likelihood function.

E.5 Panel Data Models

E.5.1 sfpan

```
sfpan y [if] [in],  distribution(half | truncated) production|cost
                    frontier(varlist_f [, noconstant]) i(id)
                    usigmas(varlist_u [, noconstant]) vsigmas(varlist_v [, noconstant])
                    [invariant kumbhakar truerandom
                     gamma(varlist_t, noconstant) mu([varlist_m [, noconstant]])
                     robust cluster(varname)
                     technique(nr | dfp | bfgs) show]
```

Description

The command `sfpan` sets up the log-likelihood function of panel frontier models introduced in Chapter 10. It allows users to choose between the time-decay model of Battese and Coelli (1992), the time-invariant model (`invariant`), the Kumbhakar (1990) model (`kumbhakar`), the growth convergence model of Kumbhakar and Wang (2005), and the true random-effects model (`truerandom`).

The command does *not* carry out the estimation. This is done through `ml max`. After `sfpan` and before `ml max`, users have the option of using `sf_init` to provide initial values and `sf_srch` to refine the initial values. After the model is estimated by `ml max`, users then have the option of using `sf_transform` to obtain the variance parameters in the original form, and `sf_predict` to obtain the inefficiency index of Jondrow et al. (1982) and the efficiency index of Battese and Coelli (1988).

Consider the following panel data model.

$$y_{it} = f(\boldsymbol{x}_{it}; \boldsymbol{\beta}) + \epsilon_{it}, \tag{E.11}$$

$$\epsilon_{it} = v_{it} - u_i, \tag{E.12}$$

$$v_{it} \sim N(0, \sigma_v^2), \tag{E.13}$$

$$u_i \sim N^+(\mu, \sigma_u^2). \tag{E.14}$$

The inefficiency (u_i) of the model is time-invariant, which is estimated with the `invariant` option. Alternatively, we may replace (E.12) by the following:

$$\epsilon_{it} = v_{it} - u_{it}, \tag{E.15}$$

$$u_{it} = G(t) u_i, \quad G(t) > 0. \tag{E.16}$$

Different specifications on $G(t)$ lead to different models. For example, the Kumbhakar (1990) model (`kumbhakar`), where $G(t) = \left[1 + \exp(\gamma_1 t + \gamma_2 t^2)\right]^{-1}$ (see the example on page 256); the Battese and Coelli (1992) time-decay model, where $G(t) = \exp[\gamma(t - T)]$ (see the example on page 258); and the growth convergence model of Kumbhakar and Wang (2005), where $G(t) = \exp[\gamma(t - \underline{t})]$ and $\underline{t}$ is the beginning period of the sample (see the example on page 259).

A different, but related, model is

$$y_{it} = \alpha_i + \boldsymbol{x}_{it}'\boldsymbol{\beta} + v_{it} - u_{it}, \tag{E.17}$$

where α_i is individual-specific and time-invariant heterogeneity and $u_{it} > 0$ is inefficiency. The *true fixed-effect model* assumes α_i to be fixed parameters to be estimated; the model can be estimated by `sf_fixeff` (see the example on page 268). The *true random-effect model* assumes α_i to be a random variable, and the current command `sfpan` with the `truerandom` option is able to estimate such a model (see the example on page 265).

Options

distribution(halfnormal | truncated) indicates the distribution assumption on the inefficiency term. The possible choices are `halfnormal` for the model of half-normal distribution and `truncated` for the truncated-normal distribution mode.

production|cost indicates whether the model is a production-type model (production) or a cost-type model (cost).

frontier(*varlist*$_f$ [, *noconstant*) specifies *nonconstant* variables to be included in the deterministic part of the frontier function.

i(*id*) specifies the name of a variable that contains identifiers for each panel.

usigmas([*varlist*$_u$ [, *noconstant*]]) specifies the pretruncation variance of the inefficiency term. See the equivalent entry in `sfmodel` for more information.

vsigmas([*varlist*$_v$ [, *noconstant*]]) specifies the variance of the statistical error random variable. See the equivalent entry of `sfmodel` for more explanation.

invariant indicates that the inefficiency term is time invariant, that is, u_i.

kumbhakar indicates the Kumbhakar (1990) model.

truerandom indicates the true random-effect model of Greene (2005a).

gamma(*varlist*$_t$, *noconstant*) specifies the time variable in the G_t function. Note that the `noconstant` option is necessary.

mu([*varlist*$_m$ [, *noconstant*]]) is used only when u_i is assumed to have a truncated-normal distribution. It specifies variables used to parameterize the pretruncation mean of the distribution of the inefficiency term. If `mu()` is specified without argument, the pre-truncation mean is a constant. See the equivalent entry in `sfmodel` for more information.

robust reports robust variance estimates. `robust` is a native Stata option; to get more information on this option type `help robust`.

cluster(*varname*) specifies the name of a variable that contains identifiers for the primary sampling unit. `cluster` is a native Stata option; to get more information on this option type `help cluster`.

technique(nr | dfp | bfgs) specifies the algorithm used to maximize the log-likelihood function. The default is *nr*, which is a modified Newton-Raphson algorithm. The `dfp` and `bfgs` are the algorithms by Davidon-Fletcher-Powell and Broyden-Fletcher-Goldfarb-Shanno, respectively. `technique` is a native Stata option; to get more information on this option type `help technique`.

show prints the likelihood function set up by `sfpan` in Stata's `ml model` syntax. It is mainly for debugging purposes. It might also be useful if, for example, the user wants to supply initial values using Stata's `ml init` in lieu of `sf_init` and needs to know the order of equations and variables in the likelihood function.

E.5.2 sf_fixeff

`sf_fixeff` *depvar* `[if] [in],` `distribution(halfnormal | truncated)` `production | cost` `frontier(`*varlist$_f$*`)` `zvar(`*varlist$_z$*`)` `id(`*varname*`)` `time(`*varname*`)` `[mu usigmas vsigmas show]`

Description

The command `sf_fixeff` sets up the log-likelihood function for a true fixed-effect panel stochastic frontier model of Wang and Ho (2010) introduced in Section 10.4 (in particular, page 266). The command specifies the dependent and independent variables of the frontier function, the exogenous determinants of inefficiency, and selects the distribution assumption of u^* of the model. It handles balanced and unbalanced panels automatically.

The estimation is carried out using `ml max`. After `sf_fixeff` and before `ml max`, users have the option of using `sf_init` to provide initial values and `sf_srch` to refine initial values. After the model is estimated by `ml max`, users then have the option of using `sf_transform` to obtain the variance parameters in the original form, and `sf_predict` to obtain the inefficiency index of Jondrow et al. (1982) and the efficiency index of Battese and Coelli (1988).

Consider a fixed-effects panel stochastic frontier model with the following specifications (Wang and Ho [2010]):

$$y_{it} = \alpha_i + \boldsymbol{x}_{it}\boldsymbol{\beta} + \varepsilon_{it}, \tag{E.18}$$

$$\varepsilon_{it} = v_{it} - u_{it}, \tag{E.19}$$

$$v_{it} \sim N(0, \sigma_v^2), \tag{E.20}$$

$$u_{it} = h_{it} \cdot u_i^*, \tag{E.21}$$

$$h_{it} = f(\boldsymbol{z}_{it}\boldsymbol{\delta}), \tag{E.22}$$

$$u_i^* \sim N^+(\mu, \sigma_u^2), \tag{E.23}$$

$$\sigma_v^2 = \exp(C_v), \tag{E.24}$$

$$\sigma_u^2 = \exp(C_u), \qquad i = 1, \ldots, N, \quad t = 1, \ldots, T. \tag{E.25}$$

In this setup, α_i is individual i's fixed unobservable effect, and other variables are defined as usual.

Wang and Ho (2010) show that the within-transformed and the first-differenced versions of the model are algebraically the same. The command `sf_fixeff` uses only the within-transformation method. Users do not need to transform the variables prior to using the command; the program will automatically do this. The command will create a list of within-transformed variables after estimation.

Options

distribution(halfnormal | truncated **)** indicates the distribution assumption of u_i^*. The possible choices are `halfnormal` for the model of half-normal distribution and `truncated` for the truncated-normal distribution mode. If `halfnormal` is chosen, $\mu = 0$ in (E.23).

production | cost indicates whether the model is a production-type model (production) or a cost-type model (cost).

frontier(*varlist*$_f$**)** specifies variables to be included in the frontier function, that is, $\boldsymbol{x}_{it}$ in (E.18). It cannot be empty.

Note that the individual-specific and the time-invariant variables, such as gender and regional dummies, cannot be specified. Unlike most other equation specifications, a constant *will not be* automatically added to the equation.

Note also that users should not within-transform (i.e., subtract the variable's cross-sectional mean) the variables specified here. The transformation will be undertaken automatically by the program.

zvar(*varlist*$_z$**)** specifies variables to be included in the scaling function, that is, $\boldsymbol{z}_{it}$ in (E.22). It cannot be empty.

Similar to the `frontier()`, variables included here should not be within-transformed. A constant will *not* be automatically added to this equation.

id(*varname***)** specifies the name of the variable that contains identifiers for each panel.

time(*varname***)** specifies the time variable.

mu is used only when u_i^* is assumed to have a truncated-normal distribution. It indicates the μ parameter in (E.23).

vsigmas indicates the C_v parameter in (E.24). It is a constant. After the estimation, `sf_transform` can be used to obtain $\hat{\sigma}_v^2$.

usigmas indicates the C_u parameter in (E.25). It is a constant. After the estimation, `sf_transform` can be used to obtain $\hat{\sigma}_u^2$.

show prints the likelihood function set up by `sf_fixeff` in Stata's `ml model` syntax. It is mainly used for debugging purposes. It might also be useful if, for example, the user wants to supply initial values using Stata's `ml init` in lieu of `sf_init` and needs to know the order of the equations and the variables in the likelihood function.

E.6 Primal Models

E.6.1 sfprim

```
sfprim output [if] [in],   inputs(varlist) prices(varlist)
                           distribution( halfnormal | truncated)
                           profit | cost
                           cd | translog
```

```
[yprice(varlist) linear(varlist)
 mu([varlist_m [, noconstant]])
 usigmas([varlist_u [, noconstant]])
 vsigmas([varlist_v [, noconstant]])
 syserror noask mltrick]
```

Description

The command `sfprim` sets up the log-likelihood function for the primal cost or primal profit models of Kumbhakar and Wang (2006) which is introduced in Chapters 8 and 9. It specifies the quantity and price variables of the inputs and output, the exogenous determinants of inefficiency, the functional form of the production function (Cobb-Douglas or translog), and selects the distribution assumption of inefficiency of the model. An important feature of the command is that, given a vector of production inputs, the correct regression variables will be automatically generated for the estimation regardless of the specified functional form. In other words, in the case of a translog production function, the square and cross-product terms will be generated by the program.

The estimation is carried out using `ml max`. After `sfprim` and before `ml max`, users have the option of using `sf_init` to provide initial values and `sf_srch` to refine initial values. After the model is estimated by `ml max`, users then have the option of using `sf_transform` to obtain the variance parameters in the original form, and `sf_predict` to obtain the inefficiency index of Jondrow et al. (1982) and the efficiency index of Battese and Coelli (1988).

Options

inputs(*varlist*) specifies a $1 \times m$ vector of variable inputs and (if applicable) quasi-fixed inputs in logarithms. Names of the quasi-fixed inputs must follow the names of the variable inputs. Also, the order of the variable inputs need to follow the same order of the variable inputs' prices listed in `prices()`.

Note that, regardless of whether `cd` or `translog` is specified, the vector of inputs should only contain the individual input variables and not the square and cross-product terms of the inputs. The program will generate those terms (in the case of `translog`) automatically.

prices(*varlist*) specifies a $1 \times n$ vector of price variables (in logarithms) for the variable inputs. The order in which the prices are listed should correspond to the order of the variable inputs listed in `inputs()`. If $m > n$, then the first n inputs listed in `inputs()` are taken as variable inputs, with the rest being quasi-fixed inputs.

distribution(halfnormal | truncated) indicates the distribution assumption of the inefficiency term. The possible choices are `halfnormal` for the model of half-normal distribution and `truncated` for the truncated-normal distribution mode.

profit | cost indicates whether it is a profit or a cost primal model.

cd | translog indicates the functional form of the production function.

yprice(*varlist*) specifies the output price variable. This is required for a profit primal model (`profit`).

linear(*varlist*) specifies a vector of variables that should be included in the frontier function in addition to the input variables. Variables specified here will not have interaction terms with other variables, even if the production is translog (`translog`).

mu([$varlist_m$ [, <u>nocon</u>*stant*]]) is used only when u_i is assumed to have a truncated-normal distribution. It specifies variables used to parameterize the pretruncation mean of the distribution of the inefficiency term. If `mu()` is specified without argument, then the pre-truncation mean is a constant. See the equivalent entry in `sfmodel` for more information.

usigmas([$varlist_u$ [, <u>nocon</u>*stant*]]) specifies the variance of the inefficiency random variable before truncation. See the equivalent entry of `sfmodel` for more explanation.

vsigmas([$varlist_v$ [, <u>nocon</u>*stant*]]) specifies the variance of the statistical error random variable. See the equivalent entry of `sfmodel` for more explanation.

syserror indicates that there is systematic error in the input allocation decision. Essentially, with `syserror` the mean of the random variables (representing allocative errors) is set to a constant which is to be estimated. Without `syserror`, the mean of the random variables is assumed to be 0 (i.e., no systematic error).

noask suppresses the confirmation prompt during the estimation process.

mltrick is a numerical trick for the maximum likelihood estimation. This is rarely used. Users may attempt to use it only when encountering convergence problems.

E.6.2 sf_cst_compare

`sf_cst_compare,` `jlms(`*varname*`)` `error(tech | alloc | both)` `cd`

Description

This command is used following an estimation of a primal cost model (`sfprim, cost cd`) to calculate the impact of technical and/or allocative inefficiency on cost. It works only when the production is Cobb-Douglas (the `cd` option). The effect of inefficiency is shown as the ratio of excess cost to minimum cost (i.e., the cost without both technical and allocative inefficiency).

Options

jlms(*varname*) identifies the variable of JLMS technical inefficiency estimated from the primal model.

error(tech | alloc | both) indicates the type of inefficiency to be investigated. If `error(tech)` is specified, the command computes the ratio of excess cost due to technical inefficiency to the minimum cost. Similarly, `error(alloc)` computes the effect of allocative inefficiency, and `error(both)` computes the effect of both technical and allocative inefficiency.

cd indicates that the production function used in `sfprim` is Cobb-Douglas. This option is required to reaffirm that only models with Cobb-Douglas functions are supported by this command.

E.6.3 sf_pft_compare

`sf_pft_compare,  jlms(`*varname*`) error(tech | alloc | both)`

Description

This command is used following an estimation of a primal profit model (`sfprim, profit`) to calculate the impact of technical and/or allocative inefficiency on profit. Unlike the similar command `sf_cst_compare`, the command `sf_pft_compare` works regardless of whether the production function specified in `sfprim` is Cobb-Douglas or translog, and the program will automatically identify the correct type of function without user input. The effect of the inefficiency is shown as the ratio of profit loss to optimal profit (i.e., the profit without both technical and allocative inefficiency).

Options

jlms(*varname*) identifies the variable of JLMS technical inefficiency estimated from the primal model.

error(tech | alloc | both) indicates the type of inefficiency to be investigated. If `error(tech)` is specified, the command computes the ratio of profit loss due to technical inefficiency to the optimal profit. Similarly, `error(alloc)` computes the effect of allocative inefficiency, and `error(both)` computes the effect of both technical and allocative inefficiency.

Bibliography

Aigner, D., Lovell, C. A. K., and Schmidt, P. (1977), "Formulation and Estimation of Stochastic Frontier Production Function Models," *Journal of Econometrics*, **6**, 21–37.

Allen, R. G. D. (1938), *Mathematical Analysis for Economists*, London: Macmillan.

Andrew, J., and Timo, K. (2011), "One-Stage Estimation of the Effects of Operational Conditions and Practices on Productive Performance: Asymptotically Normal and Efficient, Root-N Consistent Stonezd Method," *Journal of Productivity Analysis*, **36**, 219–30.

Azzalini, A. (1985), "A Class of Distributions Which Includes the Normal Ones," *Scandinavian Journal of Statistics*, **12**, 171–8.

Amsler, C., Prokhorov, A., and Schmidt, P. (2014), "Using Copulas to Model Time Dependence in Stochastic Frontier Models," *Econometric Reviews*, **33**, 497–522.

Baltagi, B. H. (2008), *Econometric Analysis of Panel Data*, Chichester, UK; Hoboken, NJ: John Wiley.

Bandyopadhyay, D., and Das, A. (2006), "On Measures of Technical Inefficiency and Production Uncertainty in Stochastic Frontier Production Model with Correlated Error Components," *Journal of Productivity Analysis*, **26**, 165–80.

Barros, C. P. (2009), "The Measurement of Efficiency of UK Airports, Using a Stochastic Latent Class Frontier Model," *Transport Reviews*, **29**, 479–98.

Barros, C. P., De Menezes, A. G., and Vieira, J. C. (2013), "Measurement of Hospital Efficiency, Using a Latent Class Stochastic Frontier Model," *Applied Economics*, **45**, 47–54.

Battese, G. E. and Coelli, T. J. (1988), "Prediction of Firm-Level Technical Efficiencies with a Generalized Frontier Production Function and Panel Data," *Journal of Econometrics*, **38**, 387–99.

Battese, G. E., and Coelli, T. J. (1992), "Frontier Production Functions, Technical Efficiency and Panel Data: With Application to Paddy Farmers in India," *Journal of Productivity Analysis*, **3**, 153–69.

Battese, G. E., and Coelli, T. J. (1995), "A Model for Technical Inefficiency Effects in a Stochastic Frontier Production Function for Panel Data," *Empirical Economics*, **20**, 325–32.

Battese, G. E., and Corra, G. S. (1977), "Estimation of a Production Frontier Model: With Application to the Pastoral Zone of Eastern Australia," *Australian Journal of Agricultural and Resource Economics*, **21**, 169–79.

Battese, G. E., Rao, D. S. P., and O'Donnell, C. J. (2004), "A Metafrontier Production Function for Estimation of Technical Efficiencies and Technology Gaps for Firms Operating under Different Technologies," *Journal of Productivity Analysis*, **21**, 91–103.

Beard, T., Caudill, S., and Gropper, D. (1991), "Finite Mixture Estimation of Multiproduct Cost Functions," *Review of Economics and Statistics*, **73**, 654–64.

Beard, T., Caudill, S., and Gropper, D. (1997), "The Diffusion of Production Processes in the U.S. Banking Industry: A Finite Mixture Approach," *Journal of Banking & Finance*, **21**, 721–40.

Bera, A. K., and Sharma, S. C. (1999), "Estimating Production Uncertainty in Stochastic Frontier Production Function Models," *Journal of Productivity Analysis*, **12**, 187–210.

Berger, A. N., and Humphrey, D. B. (1991), "The Dominance of Inefficiencies over Scale and Product Mix Economies in Banking," *Journal of Monetary Economics*, **28**, 117–48.

Bhaumik, S. K., Das, P. K., and Kumbhakar S. C. (2012), "A stochastic frontier approach to modelling financial constraints in firms: An application to India," *Journal of Banking & Finance*, **36(5)**, 1311–19.

Bierens, H. J., and Wang, L. (2012), "Integrated Conditional Moment Tests for Parametric Conditional Distributions," *Econometric Theory* **28**, 328–62.

Bos, J. W. B., Economidou, C., and Koetter, M. (2010a), "Technology Clubs, R&D and Growth Patterns: Evidence from Eu Manufacturing," *European Economic Review*, **54**, 60–79.

Bos, J. W. B., Economidou, C., Koetter, M., and Kolari, J. W. (2010b), "Do All Countries Grow Alike?," *Journal of Development Economics*, **91**, 113–27.

Bravo-Ureta, B. E., Greene, W. H., and Solís, D. (2012), "Technical Efficiency Analysis Correcting for Biases from Observed and Unobserved Variables: An Application to a Natural Resource Management Project," *Empirical Economics*, **43**, 55–72.

Casu, B., Ferrari, A., and Zhao, T. (2013), "Regulatory Reform and Productivity Change in Indian Banking," *Review of Economics and Statistics*, **95(3)**, 1066–77.

Caudill, S. B., and Ford, J. M. (1993), "Biases in Frontier Estimation Due to Heteroscedasticity," *Economics Letters*, **41**, 17–20.

Caudill, S. B., Ford, J. M. and Gropper, D. M. (1995), "Frontier Estimation and Firm-Specific Inefficiency Measures in the Presence of Heteroscedasticity," *Journal of Business & Economic Statistics*, **13**, 105–11.

Caudill, S. B. (2003), "Estimating a Mixture of Stochastic Frontier Regression Models via the Em Algorithm: A Multiproduct Cost Function Application," *Empirical Economics*, **28**, 581–98.

Chambers, R. G. (1988), *Applied Production Analysis: A Dual Approach*, New York: Cambridge University Press.

Chen, Y.-Y., Schmidt, P., and Wang, H.-J. (2014), "Consistent Estimation of the Fixed Effects Stochastic Frontier Model," *Journal of Econometrics*, **18(2)**, 65–76.

Chen, Y.-T., and Wang, H.-J. (2012), "Centered-Residuals-Based Moment Tests for Stochastic Frontier Models," *Econometric Reviews*, **31**, 625–53.

Christensen, L. R., and Greene, W. H. (1976), "Economies of Scale in U.S. Electric Power Generation," *Journal of Political Economy*, **84**, 655–76.

Christensen, L. R., Jorgenson, D. W., and Lau, L. J. (1971), "Conjugate Duality and Transcendental Logarithmic Function," *Econometrica*, **39**, 255–6.

Coelli, T. (1995), "Estimators and Hypothesis Tests for a Stochastic Frontier Function: A Monte Carlo Analysis," *Journal of Productivity Analysis*, **6**, 247–68.

Colombi, R., Martini, G., and Vittadini, G. (2011), "A Stochastic Frontier Model with Short-Run and Long-Run Inefficiency Random Effects." Department of Economics and Technology Management, University of Bergamo, *Working Paper Series*.

Colombi, R., Kumbhakar, S. C., Martini, G. and Vittadini, G. (2014), "Closed-Skew Normality in Stochastic Frontiers with Individual Effects and Long/Short-Run Efficiency," *Journal of Productivity Analysis*, **42(2)**, 123–36.

Cornwell, C., and Schmidt, P. (1992), "Models for Which the MLE and the Conditional MLE Coincide," *Empirical Economics*, **17**, 67–75.

Cornwell, C., Schmidt, P., and Sickles, R. C. (1990), "Production Frontiers with Cross-Sectional and Time-Series Variation in Efficiency Levels," *Journal of Econometrics*, **46**, 185–200.

Cuesta, R. A. (2000), "A Production Model with Firm-Specific Temporal Variation in Technical Inefficiency: With Application to Spanish Dairy Farms," *Journal of Productivity Analysis*, **13**, 139–52.

Cuesta, R. A., and Zofio, J. L. (2005), "Hyperbolic Efficiency and Parametric Distance Functions: With Application to Spanish Savings Banks," *Journal of Productivity Analysis*, **24**, 31–48.

D'Agostino, R. B., and Pearson, E. S. (1973), "Tests for Departure from Normality. Empirical Results for the Distributions of $B2$ and $\sqrt{B1}$," *Biometrika*, **60**, 613–22.

D'Agostino, R. B., Belanger, A., and D'Agostino, R. B., Jr. (1990), "A Suggestion for Using Powerful and Informative Tests of Normality," *The American Statistician*, **44**, 316–21.

Denny, M., Fuss, M., Everson, C., and Waverman, L. (1981), "Estimating the Effects of Diffusion of Technological Innovations in Telecommunications: The Production Structure of Bell Canada," *The Canadian Journal of Economics*, **14**, 24–43.

Denny, M., Fuss, M., and May, J. D. (1981), "Intertemporal Changes in Regional Productivity in Canadian Manufacturing," *The Canadian Journal of Economics*, **14**, 390–408.

Diewert, W. E. (1974), "Functional Forms for Revenue and Factor Requirements Functions," *International Economic Review*, **15**, 119–30.

Diewert, W. E. (1981), "The Theory of Total Factor Productivity Measurement in Regulated Industries," in T. G. Cowing and R. Stevenson (Eds.), New York: Academic Press, 17–44.

Diewert, W. E., and Wales, T. J. (1987), "Flexible Functional Forms and Global Curvature Conditions," *Econometrica*, **55**, 43–68.

Dominguez-Molina, J. A., Gonzalez-Farìas, G., and Ramos-Quiroga, R. (2004), *Skew-Elliptical Distribution and Application: A Journey Beyond Normality*. Boca Raton, FL: Chapman & Hall/CRC.

El-Gamal, M. A., and Inanoglu, H. (2005), "Inefficiency and Heterogeneity in Turkish Banking: 1990–2000," *Journal of Applied Econometrics*, **20**, 641–64.

Fan, Y., Li, Q., and Weersink, A. (1996), "Semiparametric Estimation of Stochastic Production Frontier Models," *Journal of Business & Economic Statistics*, **14**, 460–8.

Färe, R., Grosskopf, S., and Lee, W.-F. (1995), "Productivity in Taiwanese Manufucturing Industries," *Applied Economics*, **27**, 259–65.

Färe, R., Grosskopf, S., Noh, D.-W., and Weber, W. (2005), "Characteristics of a Polluting Technology: Theory and Practice," *Journal of Econometrics*, **126**, 469–92.

Farrell, M. J. (1957), "The Measurement of Productive Efficiency," *Journal of the Royal Statistical Society. Series A (General)*, **120**, 253–90.

Fernandez, C., Koop, G., and Steel, M. F. J. (2002), "Multiple-Output Production with Undesirable Outputs: An Application to Nitrogen Surplus in Agriculture," *Journal of the American Statistical Association*, **97**, 432–42.

Ferona, A., and Tsionas, E. G. (2012), "Measurement of Excess Bidding in Auctions," *Economics Letters*, **116**, 377–80.

Forsund, F. R., and Hjalmarsson, L. (1987), *Analyses of Industrial Structure: A Putty Clay Approach*. Stockholm: Almqvist & Wiksell.

Forsund, F. R., Hjalmarsson, L., and Summa, T. (1996), "The Interplay Between Micro-Frontier and Sectoral Short-Run Production Functions," *The Scandinavian Journal of Economics*, **98**, 365–86.

Forsund, F. R. (2009), "Good Modelling of Bad Outputs: Pollution and Multiple-Output Production," *International Review of Environmental and Resource Economics*, **3**, 1–38.

Fuss, M., and McFadden, D. (1978), *Production Economics: A Dual Approach to Theory and Applications Volume I: The Theory of Production*, Amsterdam: North-Holland.

Grassetti, L. (2011), "A note on transformed likelihood approach in linear dynamic panel models," *Statistical Methods & Applications*, **20(2)**, 221–240.

Greene, W. H. (1980), "On the estimation of a flexible frontier production model," *Journal of Econometrics*, **13(1)**, 101–15.

Greene, W. H. (2003), "Simulated Likelihood Estimation of the Normal-Gamma Stochastic Frontier Function," *Journal of Productivity Analysis*, **19**, 179–90.

Greene, W. H. (2004), "Distinguishing Between Heterogeneity and Inefficiency: Stochastic Frontier Analysis of the World Health Organization Panel Data on National Care Systems," *Health Economics*, **13**, 959–980.

Greene, W. H. (2005a), "Fixed and Random Effects in Stochastic Frontier Models," *Journal of Productivity Analysis*, **23**, 7–32.

Greene, W. H. (2005b), "Reconsidering Heterogeneity in Panel Data Estimators of the Stochastic Frontier Model," *Journal of Econometrics*, **126**, 269–303.

Greene, W. H. (2010), "A Stochastic Frontier Model with Correction for Sample Selection," *Journal of Productivity Analysis*, **34**, 15–24.

Guermat, C., and Hadri, K. (1999), "Heteroscedasticity in Stochastic Frontier Models: A Monte Carlo Analysis." Department of Economics, Exeter University, *Discussion Papers 9914*.

Hadri, K. (1999), "Estimation of a Doubly Heteroscedastic Stochastic Frontier Cost Function," *Journal of Business & Economic Statistics*, **17**, 359–63.

Hailu, A., and Veeman, T. S. (2001), "Non-Parametric Productivity Analysis with Undesirable Outputs: An Application to the Canadian Pulp and Paper Industry," *American Journal of Agricultural Economics*, **83(3)**, 605–16.

Halter, A. N., Carter, H. O., and Hocking, J. G. (1957), "A Note on the Transcendental Production Function $y = cx_1^{a1} e^{b1x1} x_2^{a2} e^{b2x2}$," *Journal of Farm Economics*, **39(4)**, 966–74.

Heckman, J., and Navarro-Lozano, S. (2004), "Using Matching, Instrumental Variables, and Control Functions to Estimate Economic Choice Models," *Review of Economics and Statistics*, **86**, 30–57.

Heckman, J. (1979), "Sample Selection Bias as a Specification Error," *Econometrica*, **47**, 153–61.

Hoch, I. (1958), "Simultaneous Equation Bias in the Context of the Cobb-Douglas Production Function," *Econometrica*, **26**, 566–78.

Hoch, I. (1962), "Estimation of Production Function Parameters Combining Time-Series and Cross-Section Data," *Econometrica*, **30**, 34–53.

Horrace, W. C., and Parmeter, C. F. (2011), "Semiparametric Deconvolution with Unknown Error Variance," *Journal of Productivity Analysis*, **35**, 129–41.

Horrace, W. C., and Schmidt, P. (1996), "Confidence Statements for Efficiency Estimates from Stochastic Frontier Models," *Journal of Productivity Analysis*, **7**, 257–82.

Hsiao, C. (2003), *Analysis of Panel Data*, Cambridge University Press.

Huang, C., and Liu, J.-T. (1994), "Estimation of a Non-Neutral Stochastic Frontier Production Function," *Journal of Productivity Analysis*, **5**, 171–80.

Johnson, N. L., Kotz, K., and Balakrishnan, N. (1995), *Continuous Univariate Distributions*, Vol. 2, New York: John Wiley & Sons.

Jondrow, J., Lovell, C. A. K., Materov, I. S., and Schmidt, P. (1982), "On the Estimation of Technical Inefficiency in the Stochastic Frontier Production Function Model," *Journal of Econometrics*, **19**, 233–8.

Jorgenson, D. (1995), *Postwar Us Economic Growth*. Cambridge: MIT Press.

Karagiannis, G., Midmore, P., and Tzouvelekas, V. (2004), "Parametric Decomposition of Output Growth Using a Stochastic Input Distance Function," *American Journal of Agricultural Economics*, **86**, 1044–57.

Kodde, D. A., and Palm, F. C. (1986), "Wald Criteria for Jointly Testing Equality and Inequality Restrictions," *Econometrica*, **54**, 1243–8.

Kopp, R. J., and Mullahy, J. (1990). "Moment-Based Estimation and Testing of Stochastic Frontier Models," *Journal of Econometrics* **46**, 165–83.

Koenker, R., and Bassett, G., Jr. (1982), "Robust Tests for Heteroscedasticity Based on Regression Quantiles," *Econometrica*, **50**, 43–61.

Koetter, M., and Poghosyan, T. (2009), "The Identification of Technology Regimes in Banking: Implications for the Market Power-Fragility Nexus," *Journal of Banking & Finance*, **33**, 1413–22.

Kumbhakar, S. C. (1987), "The Specification of Technical and Allocative Inefficiency in Stochastic Production and Profit Frontiers," *Journal of Econometrics*, **34**, 335–48.

Kumbhakar, S. C. (1988), "On the Estimation of Technical and Allocative Inefficiency Using Stochastic Frontier Functions: The Case of U.S. Class 1 Railroads," *International Economic Review*, **29**, 727–43.

Kumbhakar, S. C. (1990), "Production Frontiers, Panel Data, and Time-Varying Technical Inefficiency," *Journal of Econometrics*, **46**, 201–11.

Kumbhakar, S. C. (1991), "The Measurement and Decomposition of Cost-Inefficiency: The Translog Cost System," *Oxford Economic Papers*, **43**, 667–83.

Kumbhakar, S. C. (1992), "Allocative Distortions, Technical Progress, and Input Demand in U.S. Airlines: 1970–1984," *International Economic Review*, **33**, 723–37.

Kumbhakar, S. C. (2001), "Estimation of Profit Functions When Profit Is Not Maximum," *American Journal of Agricultural Economics*, **83**, 1–19.

Kumbhakar, S. C. (2002), "Productivity Measurement: A Profit Function Approach," *Applied Economics Letters*, **9**, 331–4.

Kumbhakar, S. C. (2012), "Specification and Estimation of Primal Production Models," *European Journal of Operational Research*, **217**, 509–18.

Kumbhakar, S. C., and Bokusheva, R. (2009), "Modelling Farm Production Decisions under an Expenditure Constraint," *European Review of Agricultural Economics*, **36**, 343–67.

Kumbhakar, S. C., Ghosh, S., and Mcguckin, J. T. (1991), "A Generalized Production Frontier Approach for Estimating Determinants of Inefficiency in U.S. Dairy Farms," *Journal of Business & Economic Statistics*, **9**, 279–86.

Kumbhakar, S. C., and Heshmati, A. (1995), "Efficiency Measurement in Swedish Dairy Farms: An Application of Rotating Panel Data, 1976–88," *American Journal of Agricultural Economics*, **77**, 660–74.

Kumbhakar, S. C., and Hjalmarsson, L. (1993), "Technical Efficiency and Technical Progress in Swedish Dairy Farms," Fried H., Schmidt S. and Lovell, C. A. K. (Eds.), *The Measurement of Productive Efficiency: Techniques and Applications*. Oxford University Press.

Kumbhakar, S. C., and Hjalmarsson, L. (1995a), "Decomposing Technical Change with Panel Data: An Application to the Public Sector," *The Scandinavian Journal of Economics*, **97**, 309–23.

Kumbhakar, S. C., and Hjalmarsson, L. (1995b), "Labour-Use Efficiency in Swedish Social Insurance Offices," *Journal of Applied Econometrics*, **10**, 33–47.

Kumbhakar, S. C., Hjalmarsson, L., and Heshmati, A. (1996), "DEA, DFA, and SFA: A Comparison," *Journal of Productivity Analysis*, **7**, 303–27.

Kumbhakar, S. C., and Hjalmarsson, L. (1998), "Relative Performance of Public and Private Ownership under Yardstick Competition: Electricity Retail Distribution," *European Economic Review*, **42**, 97–122.

Kumbhakar, S. C., and Lien, G. (2009), "Productivity and Profitability Decomposition: A Parametric Distance Function Approach," *Food Economics – Acta Agricult Scand C*, **6**, 143–55.

Kumbhakar, S. C., Lien, G., and Hardaker, J. B. (2014), "Technical Efficiency in Competing Panel Data Models: A Study of Norwegian Grain Farming," *Journal of Productivity Analysis*, **41(2)**, 321–37.

Kumbhakar, S. C. and Lovell, C. A. K. (2000), *Stochastic Frontier Analysis*. Cambridge: Cambridge University Press.

Kumbhakar, S. C., and Lozano-Vivas, A. (2005), "Deregulation and Productivity: The Case of Spanish Banks," *Journal of Regulatory Economics*, **27**, 331–51.

Kumbhakar, S. C., and Parmeter, C. F. (2009), "The Effects of Match Uncertainty and Bargaining on Labor Market Outcomes: Evidence from Firm and Worker Specific Estimates," *Journal of Productivity Analysis*, **31**, 1–14.

Kumbhakar, S. C., and Parmeter, C. F. (2010), "Estimation of Hedonic Price Functions with Incomplete Information," *Empirical Economics*, **39**, 1–25.

Kumbhakar, S. C., Parmeter, C. F., and Tsionas, E. G. (2013), "A Zero Inefficiency Stochastic Frontier Model," *Journal of Econometrics*, **172**, 66–76.

Kumbhakar, S. C., Park, B. U., Simar, L., and Tsionas, E. G. (2007), "Nonparametric Stochastic Frontiers: A Local Maximum Likelihood Approach," *Journal of Econometrics*, **137**, 1–27.

Kumbhakar, S. C., and Tsionas, E. G. (2005), "Measuring Technical and Allocative Inefficiency in the Translog Cost System: A Bayesian Approach," *Journal of Econometrics*, **126**, 355–84.

Kumbhakar, S. C., and Tsionas, E. G. (2006), "Estimation of Stochastic Frontier Production Functions with Input-Oriented Technical Efficiency," *Journal of Econometrics*, **133**, 71–96.

Kumbhakar, S. C., and Tsionas, E. G. (2008), "Estimation of Input-Oriented Technical Efficiency Using a Nonhomogeneous Stochastic Production Frontier Model," *Agricultural Economics*, **38**, 99–108.

Kumbhakar, S. C., and Tsionas, E. G. (2008), "Scale and Efficiency Measurement Using a Semiparametric Stochastic Frontier Model: Evidence from the U.S. Commercial Banks," *Empirical Economics*, **34**, 585–602.

Kumbhakar, S. C., and Tsionas, E. G. (2013), "The Good, the Bad and the Ugly: A System Approach to Good Modeling of Bad Outputs," Working Paper.

Kumbhakar, S. C., Tsionas, E., and Sipiläinen, T. (2009), "Joint Estimation of Technology Choice and Technical Efficiency: An Application to Organic and Conventional Dairy Farming," *Journal of Productivity Analysis*, **31**, 151–61.

Kumbhakar, S. C., and Wang, D. (2007), "Economic Reforms, Efficiency and Productivity in Chinese Banking," *Journal of Regulatory Economics*, **32**, 105–29.

Kumbhakar, S. C., and Wang, H.-J. (2005), "Estimation of Growth Convergence Using a Stochastic Production Frontier Approach," *Economics Letters*, **88**, 300–5.

Kumbhakar, S. C., and Wang, H.-J. (2006), "Estimation of Technical and Allocative Inefficiency: A Primal System Approach," *Journal of Econometrics*, **134**, 419–40.

Kumbhakar, S. C., Wang, H.-J., and Horncastle, A. (2010), "Estimation of Technical Inefficiency in Production Frontier Models Using Cross-Sectional Data," *Indian Economic Review*, **45**, 7–77.

Kuosmanen, T. (2008), "Representation Theorem for Convex Nonparametric Least Squares," *Econometrics Journal*, **11**, 308–25.

Kuosmanen, T. and Johnson A. L. (2010), "Data Envelopment Analysis as Nonparametric Least-Squares Regression," *Operations Research*, **58(1)**, 149–60.

Kuosmanen, T., and Kortelainen, M. (2012), "Stochastic Non-Smooth Envelopment of Data: Semi-Parametric Frontier Estimation Subject to Shape Constraints," *Journal of Productivity Analysis*, **38**, 11–28.

Lau, L. J. (1978), "Applications of Profit Functions," in M. Fuss and D. L. Mcfadden (eds), *Production Economics: A Dual Approach to Theory and Applications Volume I: The Theory of Production*. North-Holland: Elsevier.

Lai, H.-P., and Huang, C. (2013), "Maximum Likelihood Estimation of Seemingly Unrelated Stochastic Frontier Regressions," *Journal of Productivity Analysis*, **40**, 1–14.

Lee, L. F. (1983). "A Test for Distributional Assumptions for the Stochastic Frontier Functions," *Journal of Econometrics*, **22**, 245–67.

Lee, J.D., Park, J. B., and Kim, T. Y. (2002), "Estimation of the shadow prices of pollutants with production/environment inefficiency taken into account: a nonparametric directional distance function approach," *Journal of Environmental Management*, **64(4)**, 365–75.

Lee, H., and Chambers, R. G. (1986), "Expenditure Constraints and Profit Maximization in U.S. Agriculture," *American Journal of Agricultural Economics*, **68**, 857–65.

Lee, Y., and Schmidt, P. (1993), "A Production Frontier Model with Flexible Temporal Variation in Technical Efficiency," in H. Fried, K. Lovell and S. Schmidt (Eds.), *The Measurement of Productive Efficiency*. Oxford: Oxford University Press.

Luca, G. (2011), "A Note on Transformed Likelihood Approach in Linear Dynamic Panel Models," *Statistical Methods and Applications*, **20**, 221–40.

Martins-Filho, C., and Yao, F. (2014), "Semiparametric Stochastic Frontier Estimation via Profile Likelihood," *Econometric Reviews* (forthcoming).

Meeusen, W., and van den Broeck, J. (1977), "Efficiency Estimation from Cobb-Douglas Production Functions with Composed Error," *International Economic Review*, **18**, 435–44.

Mundlak, Y. (1961), "Aggregation over Time in Distributed Lag Models," *International Economic Review*, **2**, 154–63.

Mundlak, Y., and Hoch, I. (1965), "Consequences of Alternative Specifications in Estimation of Cobb-Douglas Production Functions," *Econometrica*, **33**, 814–28.

Murty, S., Russell, R., and Levkoff, S. B. (2012), "On Modeling Pollution-Generating Technologies," *Journal of Environmental Economics and Management*, **64**, 117–35.

Neyman, J., and Scott, E. L. (1948), "Consistent Estimates Based on Partially Consistent Observations," *Econometrica*, **16**, 1–32.

Nishimizu, M., and Page, J. M., Jr. (1982), "Total Factor Productivity Growth, Technological Progress and Technical Efficiency Change: Dimensions of Productivity Change in Yugoslavia, 1965–78," *The Economic Journal*, **92**, 920–36.

O'Donnell, C. J., Rao, D. S. P., and Battese, G. E. (2008), "Metafrontier Frameworks for the Study of Firm-Level Efficiencies and Technology Ratios," *Empirical Economics*, **34**, 231–55.

Orea, L., and Kumbhakar, S. C. (2004), "Efficiency Measurement Using a Latent Class Stochastic Frontier Model," *Empirical Economics*, **29**, 169–83.

Papadopoulos, A. (2014), "The Half-Normal Specification for the Two-Tier Stochastic Frontier Model," *Journal of Productivity Analysis* (forthcoming).

Parmeter, C. F., Wang, H-J., and Kumbhakar, S. C. (2014), "Nonparametric Estimation of the Determinants of Inefficiency." Unpublished manuscript.

Pitt, M. M., and Lee, L.-F. (1981), "The Measurement and Sources of Technical Inefficiency in the Indonesian Weaving Industry," *Journal of Development Economics*, **9**, 43–64.

Poghosyan, T., and Kumbhakar, S. C. (2010), "Heterogeneity of Technological Regimes and Banking Efficiency in Former Socialist Economies," *Journal of Productivity Analysis*, **33**, 19–31.

Polachek, S. W., and Yoon, B. J. (1987), "A Two-Tiered Earnings Frontier Estimation of Employer and Employee Information in the Labor Market," *The Review of Economics and Statistics*, **69**, 296–302.

Powell, A. A., and Gruen, F. H. G. (1968), "The Constant Elasticity of Transformation Production Frontier and Linear Supply System," *International Economic Review*, **9**, 315–28.

Reifschneider, D., and Stevenson, R. (1991), "Systematic Departures from the Frontier: A Framework for the Analysis of Firm Inefficiency," *International Economic Review*, **32**, 715–23.

Rho, S., and Schmidt, P. (2013), "Are All Firms Inefficient?" *Journal of Productivity Analysis* (forthcoming).

Ryan, D. L., and Wales, T. J. (2000), "Imposing Local Concavity in the Translog and Generalized Leontief Cost Functions," *Economics Letters*, **67**, 253–60.

Schmidt, P., and Lovell, C. A. K. (1979), "Estimating technical and allocative inefficiency relative to stochastic production and cost frontiers," *Journal of Econometrics*, **9(3)**, 343–66.

Schmidt, P., and Lovell, C. A. K. (1980), "Estimating stochastic production and cost frontiers when technical and allocative inefficiency are correlated," *Journal of Econometrics*, **13(1)**, 83–100.

Schmidt, P., and Lin, T.-F. (1984), "Simple Tests of Alternative Specifications in Stochastic Frontier Models," *Journal of Econometrics*, **24**, 349–61.

Schmidt, P., and Sickles, R. C. (1984), "Production Frontiers and Panel Data," *Journal of Business & Economic Statistics*, **2**, 367–74.

Shephard, R. W. (1953), *Cost and Production Functions*, Princeton, NJ: Princeton University Press.

Shephard, R. W. (1974), "Semi-Homogeneous Production Functions and Scaling of Production," in W. Eichhorn, R. Henn, O. Opitz, and R. Shephard (Eds.), *Production Theory*. Springer Berlin-Heidelberg.

Simar, L., and Wilson, P. (2007), "Estimation and Inference in Two-Stage, Semi-Parametric Models of Production Processes," *Journal of Econometrics*, **136**, 31–64.

Smith, R. J. (2008), "The Econometrics Journal of the Royal Economic Society," *Econometrics Journal*, **11**, i–iii.

Stevenson, R. E. (1980), "Likelihood Functions for Generalized Stochastic Frontier Estimation," *Journal of Econometrics*, **13**, 57–66.

Su, H. W., Chen, Y.-T., and Wang, H.-J. (2014), "Testing Distribution Assumptions on the Composed Error of Stochastic Frontier Models." Unpublished manuscript.

Sun, K., and Kumbhakar, S. C. (2013), "Semiparametric Smooth-Coefficient Stochastic Frontier Model," *Economics Letters*, **120**, 305–9.

Terrell, D. (1996), "Incorporating Monotonicity and Concavity Conditions in Flexible Functional Forms," *Journal of Applied Econometrics*, **11**, 179–94.

Tsionas, G. E. (2000), "Likelihood Analysis of Random Effect Stochastic Frontier Models with Panel Data," *European Research Studies Journal*, **3(3–4)**, 35–42.

Varian, H. R. (2009), *Microeconomic Analysis*, W. W. Norton & Company.

Wang, H.-J. (2002), "Heteroscedasticity and Non-Monotonic Efficiency Effects of a Stochastic Frontier Model," *Journal of Productivity Analysis*, **18**, 241–53.

Wang, H.-J. (2003), "A Stochastic Frontier Analysis of Financing Constraints on Investment: The Case of Financial Liberalization in Taiwan," *Journal of Business & Economic Statistics*, **21**, 406–19.

Wang, H.-J., Chang, C.-C., and Chen, P.-C. (2008), "The Cost Effects of Government-Subsidised Credit: Evidence from Farmers' Credit Unions in Taiwan," *Journal of Agricultural Economics*, **59**, 132–49.

Wang, H.-J., and Ho, C.-W. (2010), "Estimating Fixed-Effect Panel Stochastic Frontier Models by Model Transformation," *Journal of Econometrics*, **157**, 286–96.

Wang, H.-J., and Schmidt, P. (2002), "One-Step and Two-Step Estimation of the Effects of Exogenous Variables on Technical Efficiency Levels," *Journal of Productivity Analysis*, **18**, 129–44.

Wang, W. S., Amsler, C., and Schmidt, P. (2011). "Goodness of Fit Tests in Stochastic Frontier Models," *Journal of Productivity Analysis*, **35**, 95–118.

Winsten, C. (1957), "Discussion on Mr. Farrell's Paper," *Journal of the Royal Statistical Society. Series A (General)*, **120**, 282–4.

Zellner, A., and Revankar, N. S. (1969), "Generalized Production Functions," *The Review of Economic Studies*, **36**, 241–50.

Index

Printed in the United States
By Bookmasters